SAP PRESS e-books

Financial Accounting in SAP® ERP: Business User Guide

SAP PRESS

David Burns

Financial Accounting in SAP® ERP: Business User Guide

Rheinwerk Publishing

Editor Megan Fuerst
Acquisitions Editor Emily Nicholls
Copyeditor Julie McNamee
Cover Design Graham Geary
Photo Credit iStockphoto.com: 186819094/© wsfurlan, 665997388/© stevecoleimages; Shutterstock.com: 706471024/© Allexxandar
Layout Design Vera Brauner
Production Hannah Lane
Typesetting III-Satz, Husby (Germany)
Printed and bound in the United States of America, on paper from sustainable sources

ISBN 978-1-4932-1678-9

2nd edition 2018

Library of Congress Cataloging-in-Publication Data
Names: Burns, David, (Financial accounting specialist), author.
Title: Financial accounting in SAP ERP : business user guide / David Burns.
Other titles: Financial accounting in SAP
Description: 2nd edition. | Bonn ; Boston : Rheinwerk Publishing, [2018] | Includes index.
Identifiers: LCCN 2017057250 (print) | LCCN 2017059057 (ebook) | ISBN 9781493216796 (ebook) | ISBN 9781493216789 (alk. paper)
Subjects: LCSH: SAP ERP. | Accounting--Computer programs. | Accounting--Data processing.
Classification: LCC HF5679 (ebook) | LCC HF5679 .B837 2018 (print) | DDC 657.0285/53--dc23
LC record available at https://lccn.loc.gov/2017057250

Contents at a Glance

Dear Reader,

Bookkeeping is not my strong suit. Day-to-day transactions for my household of one usually end with a receipt, which often gets crammed into my back pocket and reappears fresh from the laundry. Of course, businesses with substantially higher cash flow need better oversight and tighter control of their financial accounting processes. From the G/L, to customer and vendor accounts, to a company's assets, to all the banks involved, financial accounting is as complex as it is critical for your business.

Luckily, David Burns is the finance whiz you need to successfully navigate your myriad financials tasks and transactions and keep your books in order. A reader-attested authority in SAP FI, David writes with you, dear reader, in mind, and has delivered the updates you need to ensure your business' financial accounting workflows are equal to today's challenges. I can certainly say I've learned a great deal from editing this new edition, although my biggest takeaway may be relief that I only need to worry about balancing my checkbook.

What did you think about *Financial Accounting in SAP ERP: Business User Guide*? Your comments and suggestions are the most useful tools to help us make our books the best they can be. Please feel free to contact me and share any praise or criticism you may have.

Thank you for purchasing a book from SAP PRESS!

Megan Fuerst
Editor, SAP PRESS

meganf@rheinwerk-publishing.com
www.sap-press.com
Rheinwerk Publishing · Boston, MA

Contents

Chapter 1
Introduction to Financial Accounting

In this chapter, we cover some basic terms and concepts that make up the organizational structure of Financial Accounting in SAP ERP. Specifically, we cover the definition and assignment of business units, as represented in the SAP enterprise structure.

Financial Accounting (FI) in SAP ERP consists of several essential system accounting functions: General Ledger (G/L), Accounts Receivable (AR), Accounts Payable (AP), banking, financial reporting, and fixed assets (FI Asset Accounting, FI-AA). To achieve a full understanding of FI, first you need to grasp the concept of the system enterprise structure. In SAP, the *enterprise structure* is the definition of specific organizational units that together represent your company's business units and divisions.

Enterprise structures are the building blocks upon which additional configuration hinges. They also represent the relationships between the organizational units in your company and enable integration and the exchange of data.

For most SAP users, much of their time in SAP is spent creating transactions and running reports. Behind the scenes, an enterprise structure enables the execution of transactions and reports while facilitating information flow between SAP modules. The enterprise structure is the backbone of your SAP system design. When an SAP system is originally configured for use in FI, the enterprise structure is defined first. Getting this structure right is critical to the remainder of the system setup and configuration.

Regardless of your company's size, industry, or geography, you must define an enterprise structure. When an SAP system is configured, your company structure is reflected in organizational units defined in modules for accounting, logistics, human resources, and more. The assignment of these organizational units to one another is what links the modules together at an enterprise level.

As a practical guide to FI, the content in this book primarily focuses on business scenarios and transactions. However, by giving you an understanding of enterprise structures, this chapter empowers you with a better overall understanding of FI and the necessary building blocks that influence specific parts of your business processes.

Let's start our discussion by talking about company, company code, and other FI enterprise structures in the next section.

1.1 Defining the Organizational Structure

The organizational structure of your company (i.e., business units and divisions) is defined in the SAP Customizing Implementation Guide (IMG). The organizational structures as a whole make up your enterprise structure in SAP. IMG activities are considered configuration, and although we don't intend to teach you how to configure the enterprise structure here, it's important for you to have an understanding of the underlying structure of FI.

Moreover, when creating a financial transaction, it's important for you to be aware of the setup of the enterprise structure to ensure transactions are posted properly. You also need to know when and how financial transactions impact business processes and other areas within the company.

To access the IMG, enter "SPRO" in the **Command** field (as shown in Figure 1.1) and press Enter.

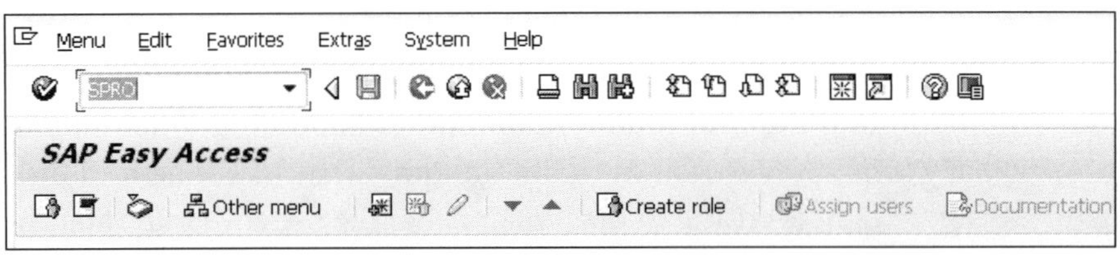

Figure 1.1 Entering "SPRO" in the Command Field

In the **Customizing: Execute Project** screen that appears (Figure 1.2), click on the **SAP Reference IMG** button. The **Display IMG** screen appears (Figure 1.3).

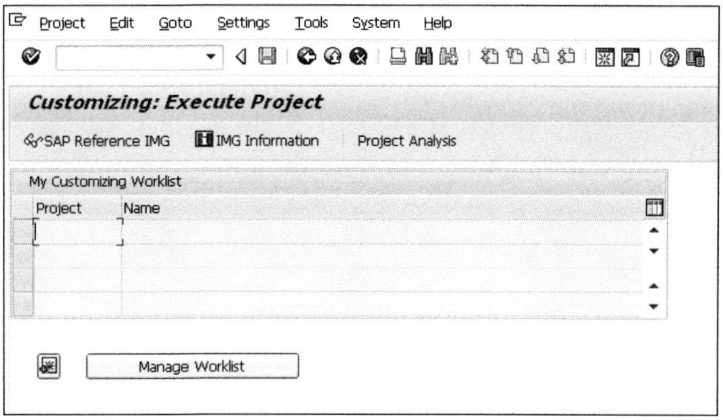

Figure 1.2 Customizing: Execute Project Screen (Transaction SPRO)

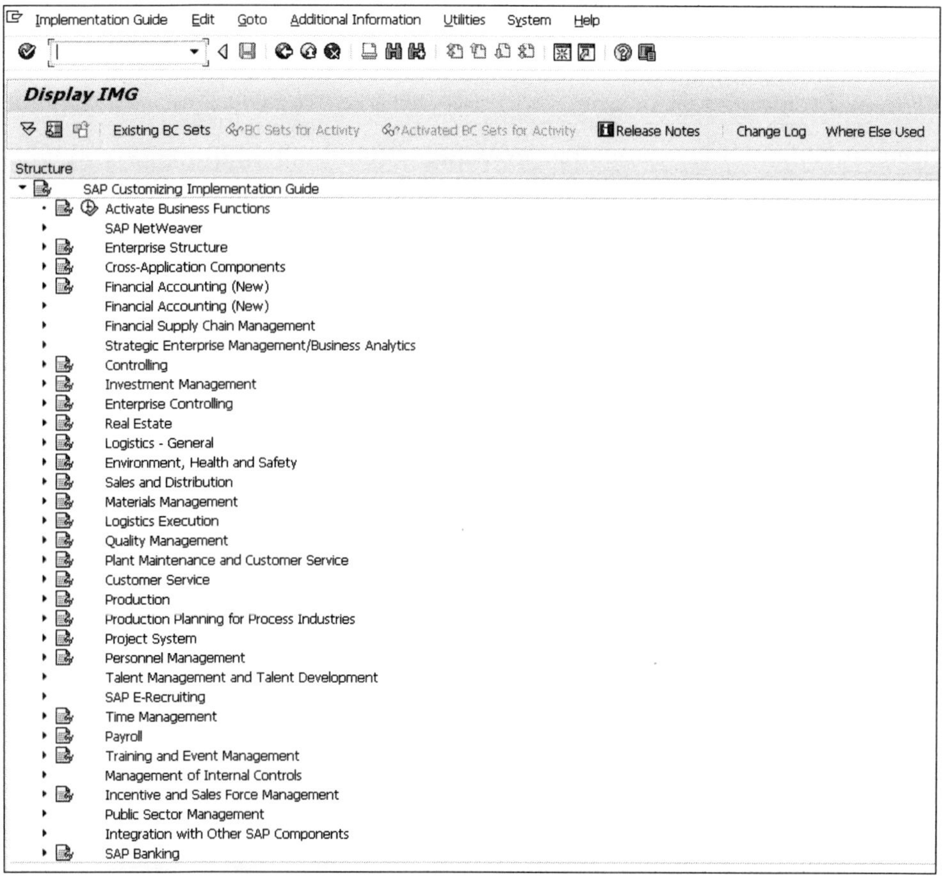

Figure 1.3 Display IMG Screen

To define the enterprise structure for FI, follow the IMG menu path, **Enterprise Structure • Definition • Financial Accounting**, as shown in Figure 1.4.

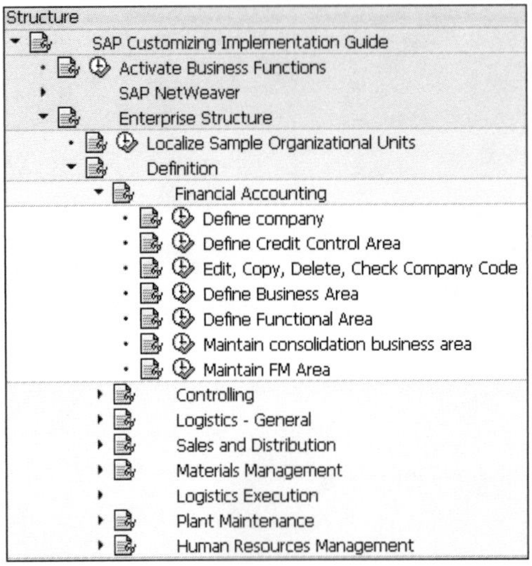

Figure 1.4 IMG Define Enterprise Structure Menu Path for FI

The IMG menu path shown in Figure 1.4 points to where you create FI enterprise structures. These enterprise structures include company, credit control area, company code, business area and consolidation business area, functional area, financial management area, segment, and profit center. All of these structures are discussed in the sections that follow.

1.1.1 Company

According to SAP, a *company* is an organizational unit in accounting that represents a business organization according to the requirements of commercial law in a particular country. Consolidation functions in FI are based on companies. One or more company codes can be assigned to a company. It's important to note that all company codes assigned to a company must use the same operational chart of accounts and fiscal year, but the currencies used can be different.

Figure 1.5 shows an example of a company defined in the IMG. The six-character **Company** field contains the company ID. In its entirety, the company definition consists of the company ID, company name, and detailed information such as address, country, language, and currency.

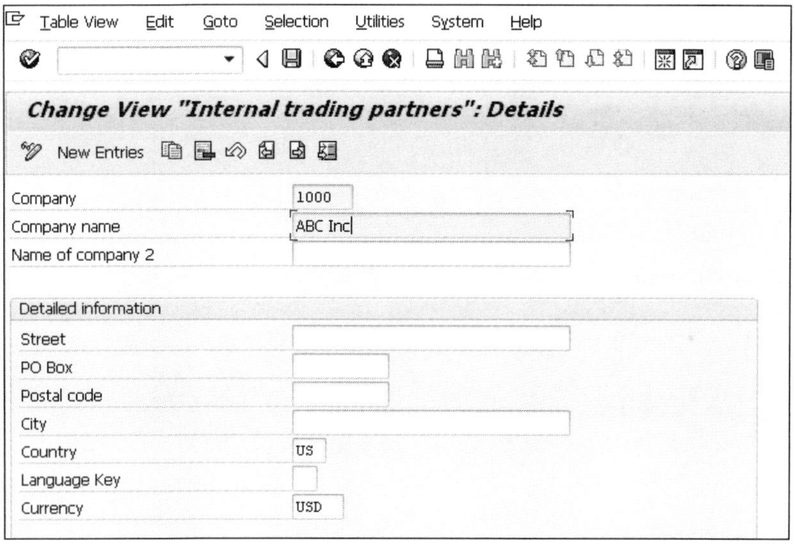

Figure 1.5 Display Company

1.1.2 Company Code

Typically, a *company code* is a legally independent company. The company code may also represent a legally dependent operating unit based abroad if there are external reporting requirements for the operating unit. You must define at least one company code to use FI because the company code is the central organizational unit for financial transactions and is necessary to configure business processes and to create master data. According to SAP, you should create a company code according to tax law, commercial law, and other financial accounting criteria.

All financial postings require a company code specification. It serves as a central link to many posting functions, including field status control, posting periods, workflows, G/L accounts, and many additional processing parameters. The company code also serves as a link to other SAP modules to enable FI integration with Sales and Distribution (SD), Materials Management (MM), Controlling (CO), Funds Management (FM), and more.

Figure 1.6 shows an example of a company code. **Company Code** is a four-character field. Within a company code, you can set many essential specifications, including a chart of accounts, fiscal year variant, posting period variant, and workflow variant. The company code is a fundamental enterprise structure in FI, with numerous

Accounting organization settings and **Processing parameters** linked to it that influence and control financial postings.

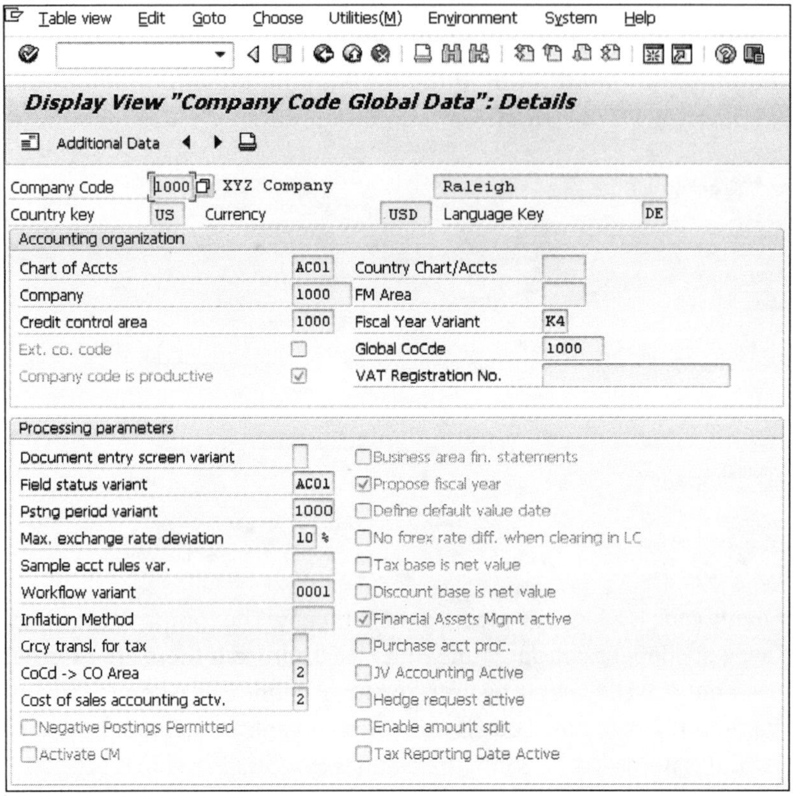

Figure 1.6 Example Company Code

Note that while the IMG node **Edit, Copy, Delete, Check Company Code** (refer to Figure 1.4) is used to create your company code initially, the functional characteristics of the company code aren't specified until FI is configured. These settings are made using Transaction OBY6.

1.1.3 Credit Control Area

The *credit control area* is an FI organizational unit that specifies and checks a credit limit for customers. The credit control area is where customer credit is given and monitored. A credit control area can be assigned to more than one company code, but each company code can only be assigned to one credit control area.

Figure 1.7 shows an example of a credit control area defined in the IMG. **Cred.Contr.Area** is a four-character field within which a credit limit is specified based on a risk category and/or group. In addition, the **Update** field specifies when value checks take place for sales orders, deliveries, and billing documents.

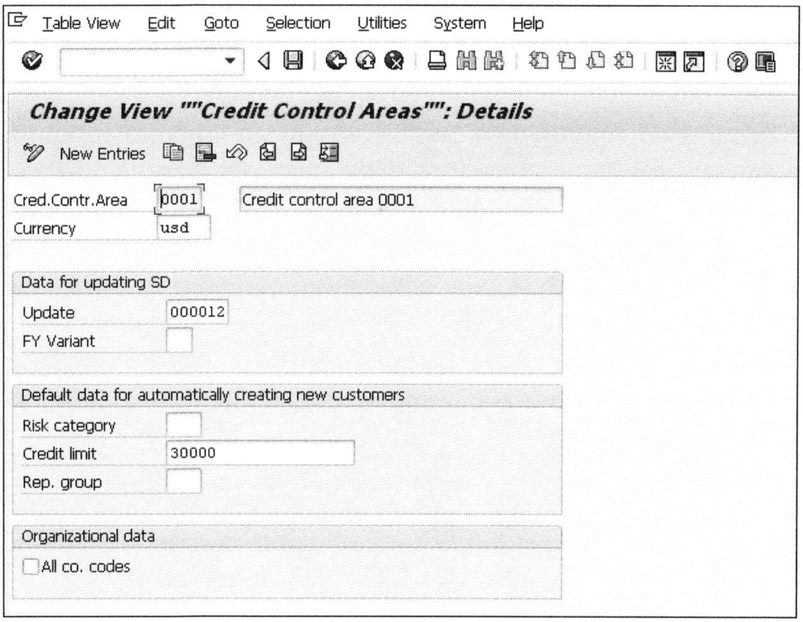

Figure 1.7 Example Credit Control Area

The **Cred.Contr.Area** field is also referred to as the *credit control key*.

A simple approach to the credit control area is to create one area for each company code, which is referred to as the *decentralized credit management* approach. In other words, credit is awarded and monitored based on a singular relationship between the credit control area and the company code, sales organization, and currency.

When you have the same customer created in multiple company codes, you have a unique challenge because the credit management for each customer is determined by the credit control area assigned to the company code. Yet, if a customer is created in multiple company codes, and each company code is assigned to the same credit control area, then the cross-company customers are managed by the same credit management settings in a common credit control area. This is referred to as the *central credit management* approach, in which customer credit management across company codes is combined.

As a final note on credit control areas, it's possible for a company code to have a different local currency from the one specified in the credit control area. In this case, the system converts receivable amounts (e.g., open sales orders, deliveries, and bills) into the currency of the credit control area. Credit limits and monitoring are done in the credit control area currency.

1.1.4 Segment

A *segment* is a division of a company with significant enough expenses, revenues, and operating results (according to accounting rules) to warrant separate financial statements for external reporting. According to accounting principles in US GAAP and IFRS, companies must perform *segment reporting*; that is, a complete balance sheet at the segment level. The segment dimension was introduced by SAP in the new G/L (see Appendix A) to fulfill this requirement.

You can enter a segment in the master record of a profit center, and then the segment is derived from the assigned profit center during posting. You can also enter a segment manually in FI transactions.

Figure 1.8 shows an example of a segment defined in the IMG. **Segment** is a 10-character field with a 50-character **Description** field. A segment has no other fields, parameters, or control settings.

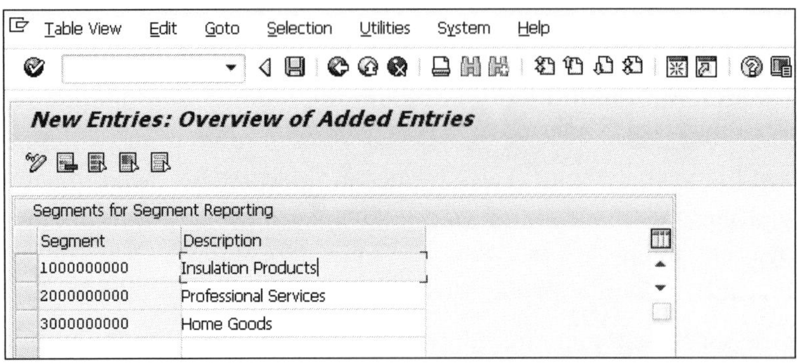

Figure 1.8 Example Segment

Throughout this book, the segment characteristic is presented and discussed numerous times. It's an important concept for financial managers and accountants to understand.

1.1.5 Profit Center

A *profit center* is a management-oriented organizational unit used for internal control purposes. Dividing your company into profit centers allows you to analyze areas of responsibility and delegate responsibility to decentralized units. Before you can create a profit center in SAP, you must create a controlling area and a standard hierarchy.

Figure 1.9 shows an example profit center. **Profit Center** is a 10-character field. Notice that in the **General Data** area of the screen, a **Profit Center** is assigned to a **Controlling Area**.

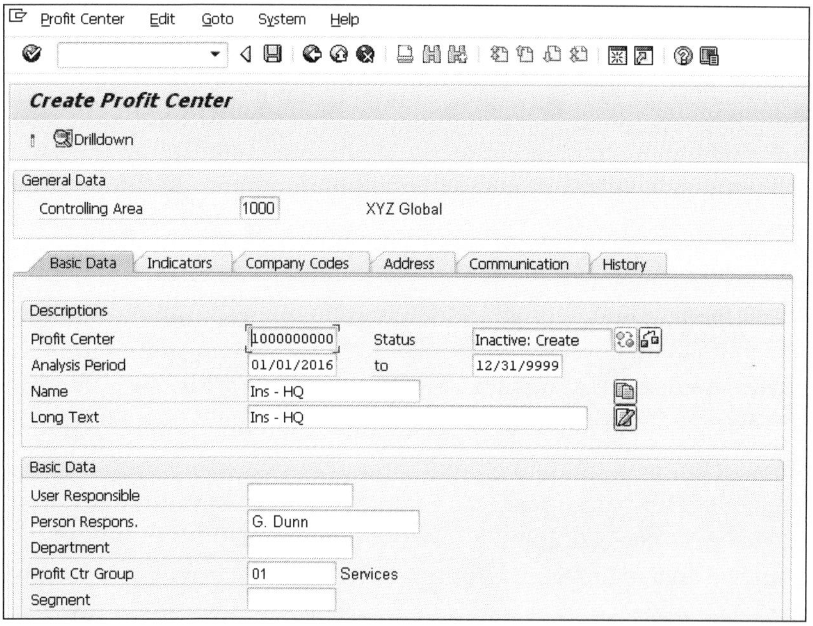

Figure 1.9 Example Profit Center

> **Note**
>
> Covering the profit center tabs— **Basic Data, Indicators, Company Codes, Address, Communication**, and **History**—in detail is beyond the scope of this book. However, you should become familiar with these tabs and settings if you use Profit Center Accounting (PCA).

It's important to know that profit centers were integrated into FI with the new G/L. For more information, see Appendix A.

1.1.6 Business Area

A *business area* is an optional FI organizational unit. It defines organizational units within accounting that represent separate areas of operations or responsibilities. Financial statements can be created by business area for internal purposes. For the most part, companies have transitioned away from the use of business areas with the introduction of segments and the new G/L.

Figure 1.10 shows an example of a business area. **Business Area** is a 4-character field with a 30-character **Description** field. A business area has no other fields, parameters, or control settings.

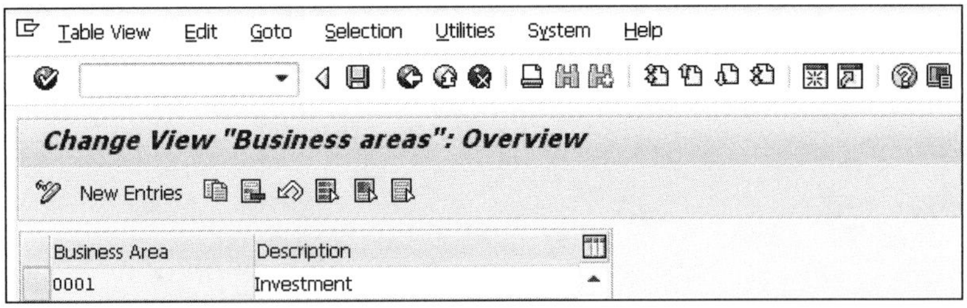

Figure 1.10 Example Business Area

Before moving on, let's discuss the distinction among business areas, segments, and profit centers to clear up any confusion about when and how to use each object.

Today, SAP defines a business area as a separate area of responsibility or operations. However, in the past, it was also referred to as a separate segment of the business. With the introduction of new G/L and the segment dimension, segment—not business area—should be used to fulfill accounting requirements for segment reporting.

Profit centers, on the other hand, are management-oriented organizational units used for internal controlling purposes.

On a final point, the **Maintain consolidation business area** node shown previously in Figure 1.4 allows you to create consolidation business areas to represent central business segments. Because of the variability in the use of business areas, this topic isn't addressed in this section. Moreover, with the introduction of the segment dimension, the applicability of business areas and consolidated business areas is in flux.

1.1.7 Functional Area

A *functional area* is an organizational unit in FI that classifies expenses according to function. It was originally designed for use in cost-of-sales accounting. SAP lists possible functional classifications as administration, sales, marketing, production, and research and development. In traditional applications, functional areas can be used to create profit and loss (P&L) statements using cost-of-sales accounting. Since its original creation, the functional area has also been used in FM for government accounting, in which it represents government functions, such as public safety.

Figure 1.11 shows an example of a functional area. **Functional Area** is a 16-character field with a 25-character **Functional area text** field.

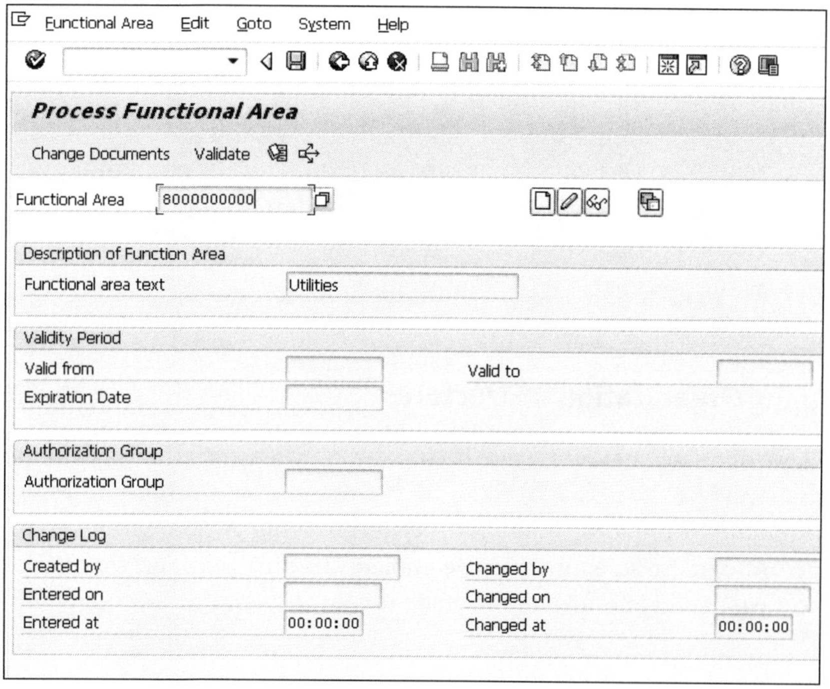

Figure 1.11 Example Functional Area

1.1.8 Financial Management Area

The *financial management area* is an organizational unit in FI that structures the business organization from the perspective of Cash Budget Management and FM. The system derives the financial management area from the company code when you assign the company code to a financial management area. Several company codes can be assigned to a financial management area.

Figure 1.12 shows an example of a financial management area defined in the IMG. **FM Area** is a 4-character field with a 25-character description (**FM area text**) and a currency assigned (**FM area currency**).

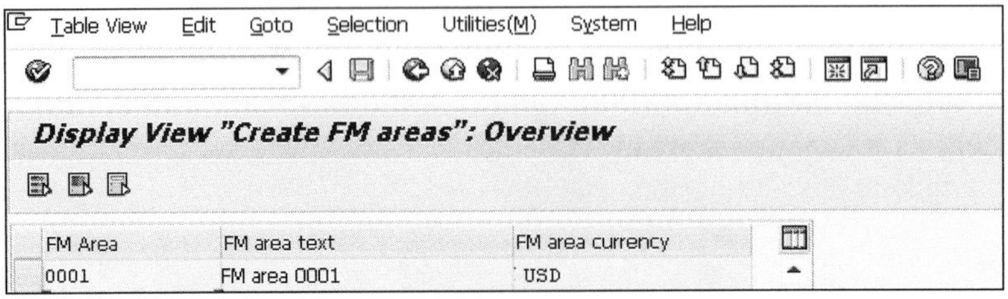

Figure 1.12 Example Financial Management Area

Now that we've discussed the definition of enterprise structures in FI, let's move on to discuss the assignment of specific structures to one another—much like putting together the pieces of a puzzle. Organizational structures are linked in the IMG to establish relationships and enable system integration.

1.2 Assigning Organizational Structures

In Section 1.1, we discussed defining organizational structures in FI; that is, defining the enterprise structure. The next step after defining these structures is to assign them to one another by building references between the organizational units that you've defined. After these assignments are complete, the organizational framework is, for the most part, complete, active, and ready for data integration between modules.

To assign organizational structures for your company (i.e., business units and divisions), you'll use the IMG. To access the IMG, enter "SPRO" in the **Command** field (as shown in Figure 1.13) and press Enter.

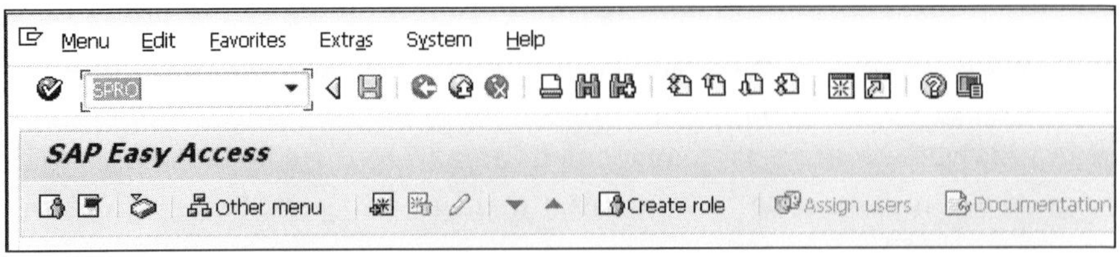

Figure 1.13 Entering "SPRO" in the Command Field

When the **Customizing: Execute Project** screen appears (Figure 1.14), click on the **SAP Reference IMG** button. The **Display IMG** screen appears (Figure 1.15).

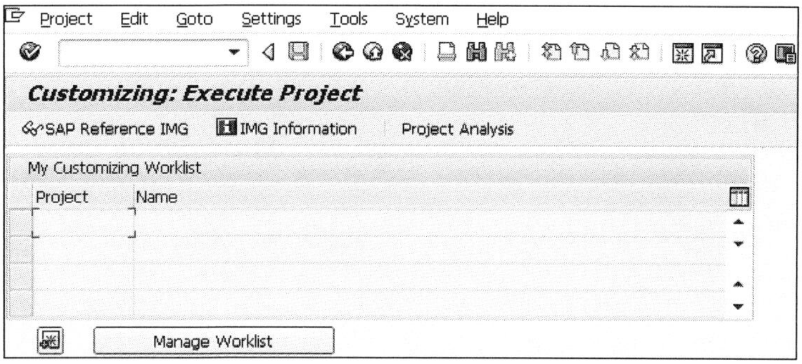

Figure 1.14 Customizing: Execute Project Screen (Transaction SPRO)

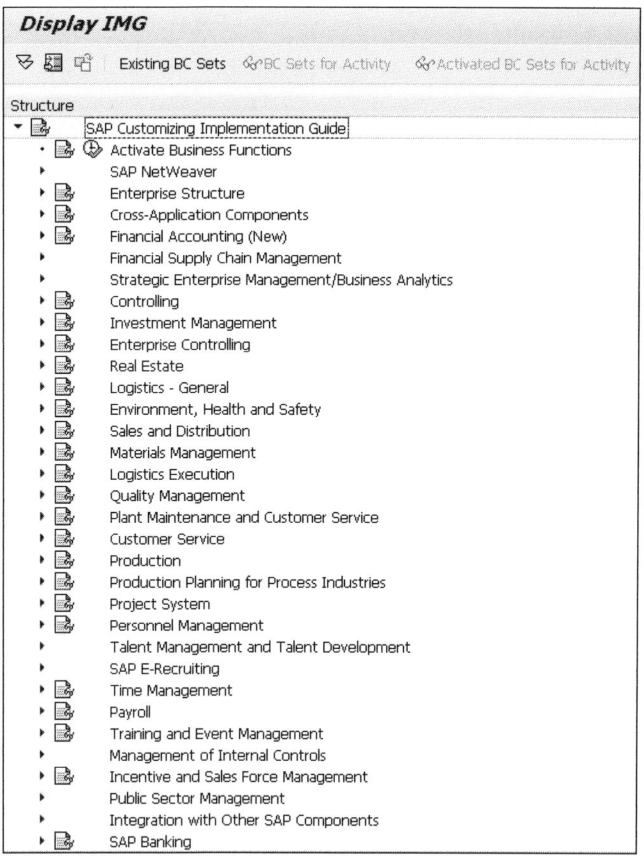

Figure 1.15 Display IMG Screen

To assign the enterprise structure for FI, follow IMG menu path, **Enterprise Structure • Assignment • Financial Accounting**, as shown in Figure 1.16.

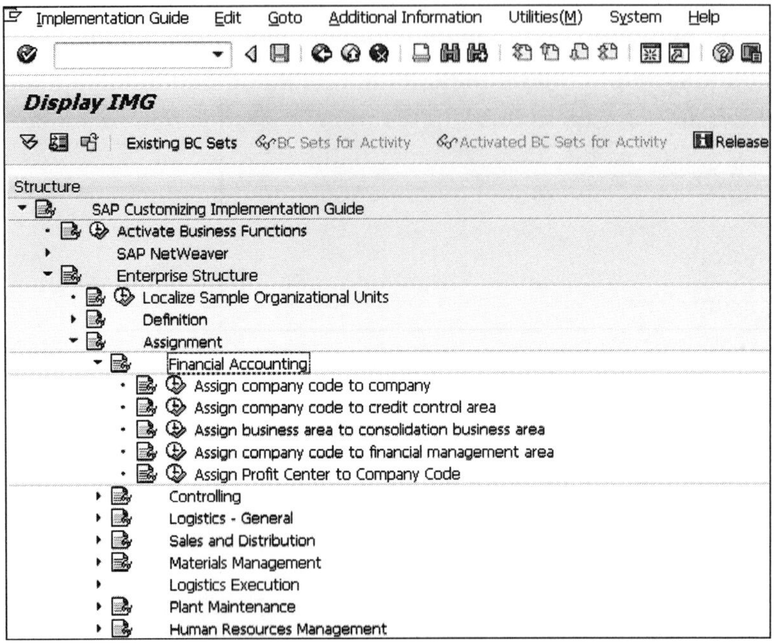

Figure 1.16 IMG Assign Enterprise Structure Menu Path for FI

This menu path points to where you assign FI enterprise structures, which we'll discuss in the sections that follow.

1.2.1 Company Code to Company

Assigning a company code to a company establishes a relationship between these objects. Consolidation functions in FI are built on the company object. A company can be composed of one or more company codes.

When assigning organizational units, it's important to know that they have dependencies and limitations. In the case of assigning a company code to a company, all company codes assigned to the same company must use the same operational chart of accounts and fiscal year.

Figure 1.17 shows an example of a company code assignment (**CoCd**) to a company.

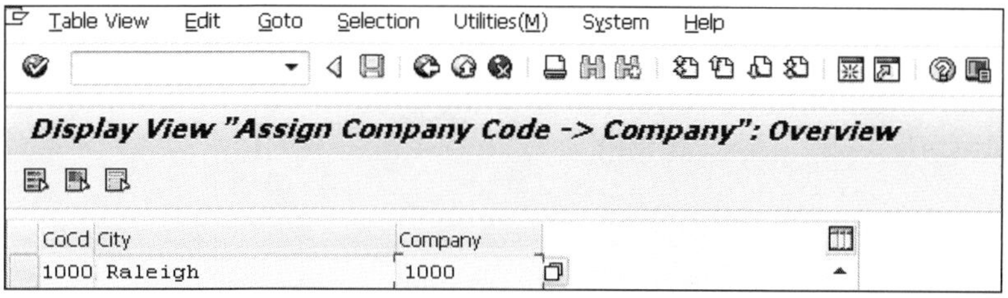

Figure 1.17 Example Assignment of Company Code to Company

1.2.2 Company Code to Credit Control Area

Assigning a company code to a credit control area enables you to specify and check a credit limit for customers. A credit control area can include one or more company codes, but it's not possible to assign a company code to more than one credit control area. Figure 1.18 shows an example of a company code assignment to a credit control area (**CCAr**).

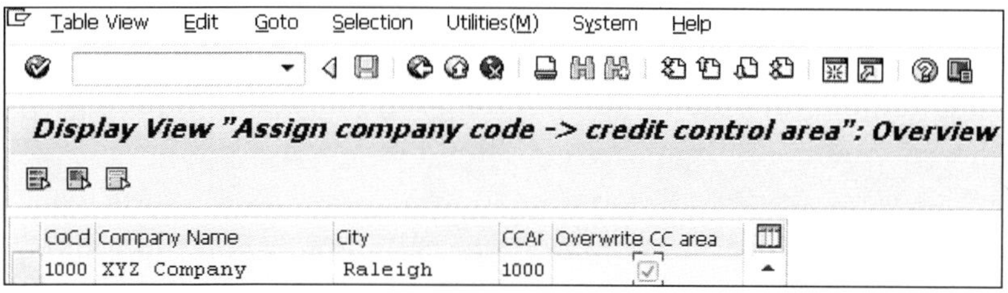

Figure 1.18 Example Assignment of Company Code to Credit Control Area

If the **Overwrite CC area** checkbox is checked, you can overwrite the credit control area defaulted from the company code while posting a financial transaction. This capability only exists during document creation; it doesn't work when changing a document.

1.2.3 Company Code to Financial Management Area

In this activity, you assign each company code that is relevant to Cash Budget Management or FM to a financial management area. You can assign multiple company codes to a financial management area, but you can't assign a single company code to multiple financial management areas.

Figure 1.19 shows an example of company code assignment to a financial management area.

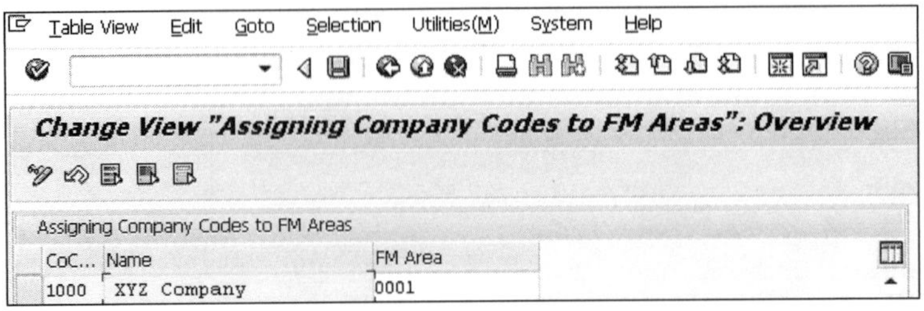

Figure 1.19 Example Assignment of Company Code to Financial Management Area

In making enterprise structure assignments, you must be aware of irreversible links. When assigning a company code to a financial management area, the assignment is irreversible after Cash Budget Management or FM is active or after actual data has been posted. Posting actual data includes posting commitment items to any of the G/L accounts in a company code.

1.2.4 Profit Centers to Company Code

In this activity, you assign one or more profit centers to a company code. If no assignment is made, the system will assign the profit center to all company codes in the controlling area by default.

Figure 1.20 shows an example of profit centers assigned to a company code. As you can see, assignment options are based on the profit center **Standard hierarchy** or **Profit center grp**. From this screen, you can also enter a range of company codes or a single value. An assignment is made by checking the box next to a profit center.

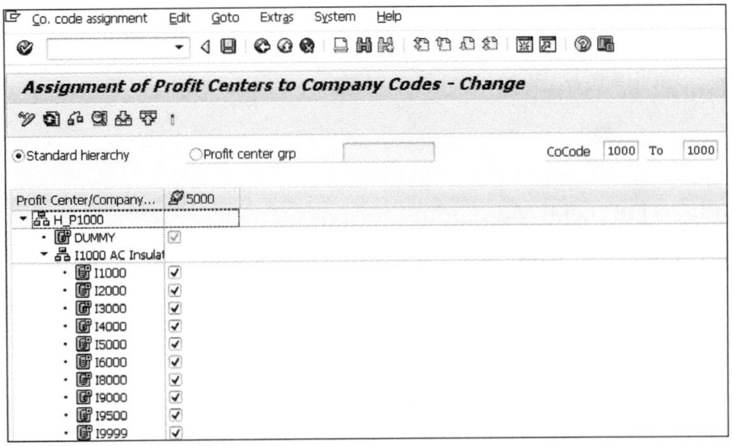

Figure 1.20 Example Assignment of Profit Centers to Company Code

Now that we've looked at enterprise structure assignments within FI, let's discuss some relationships between FI and organizational structures in other modules.

1.3 Making Cross-Modular Assignments

In Section 1.1 and Section 1.2, we discussed the definition of enterprise structures in FI and the assignment of these structures to one another within FI. In this section, we broaden our reach by discussing the links between FI enterprise structures and organizational structures in other modules. We use several specific assignments as examples to demonstrate the enablement of integration and data flows.

The assignments discussed in this section don't include a complete list of the assignments available for enterprise objects in FI. Rather, we limit our discussion to some of the more common assignments used to enable integration of FI, Sales and Distribution (SD), Controlling (CO), and Human Capital Management (HCM).

1.3.1 Company Code to Controlling Area

The assignment of a company code to a controlling area is the link that integrates the FI and CO modules. The controlling area is an organizational unit for cost accounting purposes that is assigned to one or more company codes. The relationship can be one to one, but, more often than not, it's one to many (one controlling area to many company codes) to enable cost accounting across company codes. This one-to-many relationship between a controlling area and company codes is a common practice. Internal management reporting is usually a global function. While corporate controllers usually exist at the local level, a chief or global controller is centrally responsible for controlling functions overall for an enterprise. Therefore, management accounting data needs to be integrated and available across company codes.

To assign a company code to a controlling area, access the IMG by entering "SPRO" in the **Command** field (as shown in Figure 1.21) and pressing [Enter].

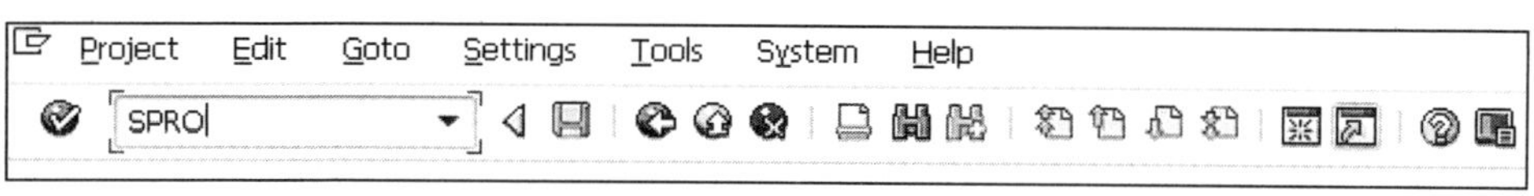

Figure 1.21 Entering "SPRO" in the Command Field

The **Customizing: Execute Project** screen appears (Figure 1.22).

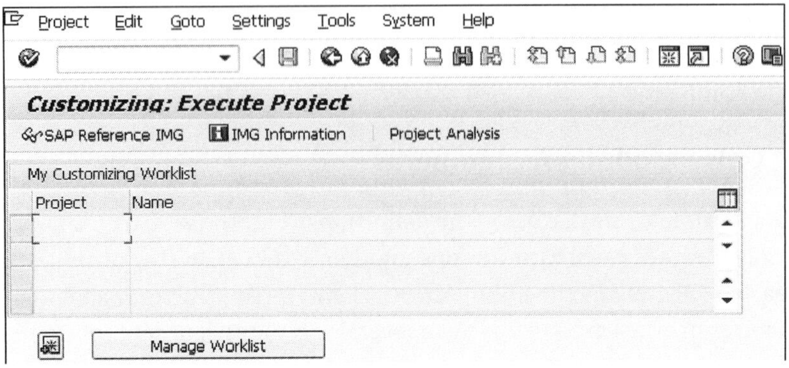

Figure 1.22 Customizing: Execute Project Screen (Transaction SPRO)

Click on the **SAP Reference IMG** button, and the **Display IMG** screen appears (Figure 1.23).

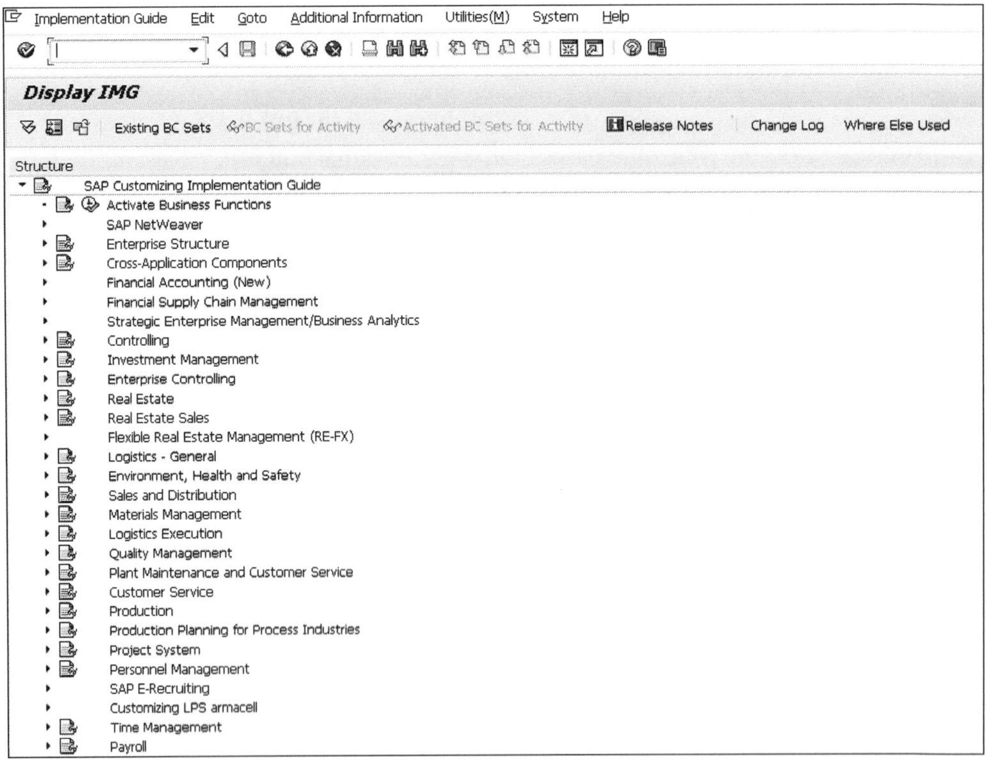

Figure 1.23 Display IMG Screen

To assign the enterprise structures for CO, follow IMG menu path, **Enterprise Structure • Assignment • Controlling**, as shown in Figure 1.24. This menu path points to where you assign company codes to controlling areas. Figure 1.25 shows an example assignment of company code to controlling area.

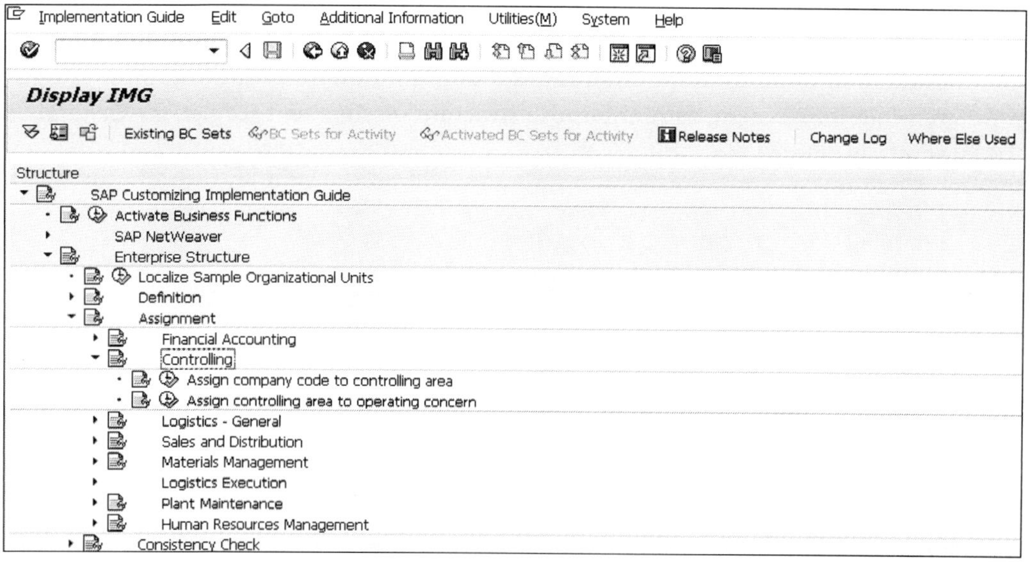

Figure 1.24 IMG Assign Enterprise Structure Menu Path for CO

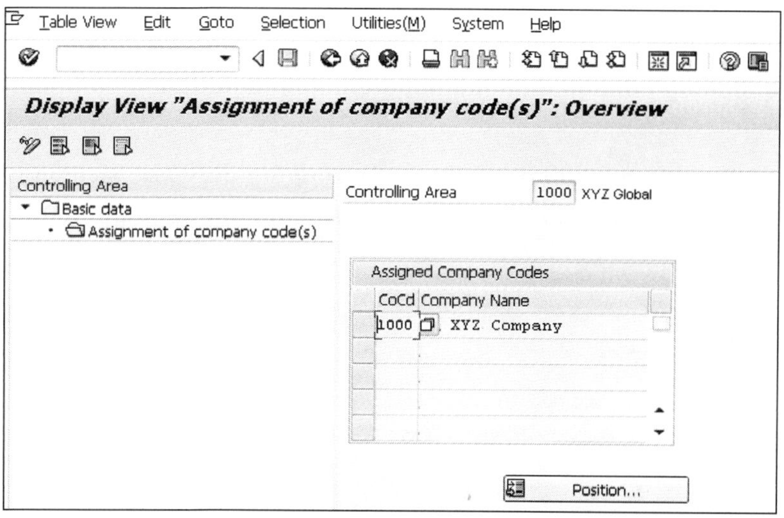

Figure 1.25 Example Assignment of Company Code to Controlling Area

1.3.2 Plants to Company Code

A *plant* is an enterprise structure in SAP logistics that represents a physical location where materials are produced or goods or services are provided. The plant can also be described as an organizational unit in logistics that divides an enterprise according to key logistical functions, such as production, procurement, maintenance, and materials planning. Typically, a plant should only be assigned to a company code in the same country—but exceptions do exist. To assign the enterprise structures for logistics, follow IMG menu path, **Enterprise Structure • Assignment • Logistics – General**, as shown in Figure 1.26.

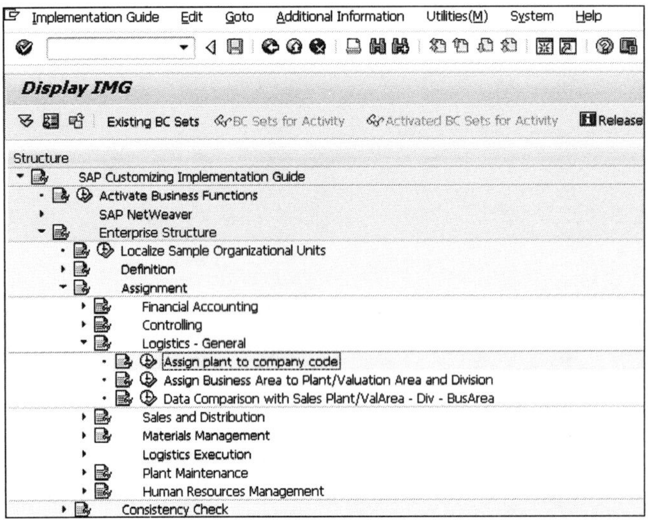

Figure 1.26 IMG Assign Enterprise Structure Menu Path for Plant to Company Code

This IMG menu path points to where you assign plants to company codes. Figure 1.27 shows an example assignment of plant to company code.

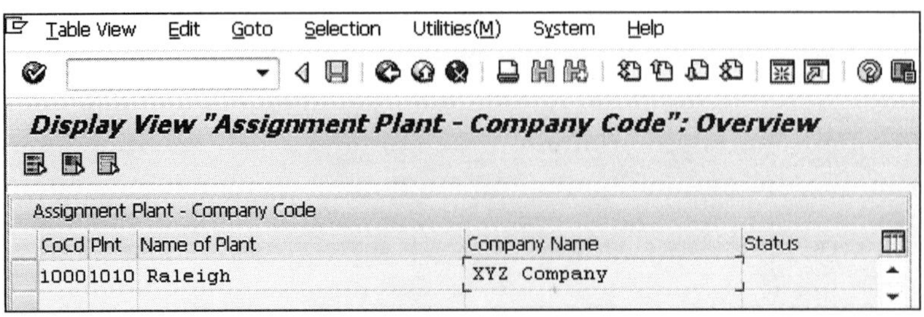

Figure 1.27 Example Assignment of Plant to Company Code

1.3.3 Sales Organization to Company Code

A *sales organization* is an organizational unit in the SD module responsible for the sale and distribution of goods and services. A sales organization can only be linked to one company code. This linkage is the key integration between the FI and SD modules. To assign the enterprise structure for SD, follow IMG menu path, **Enterprise Structure • Assignment • Sales and Distribution**, as shown in Figure 1.28.

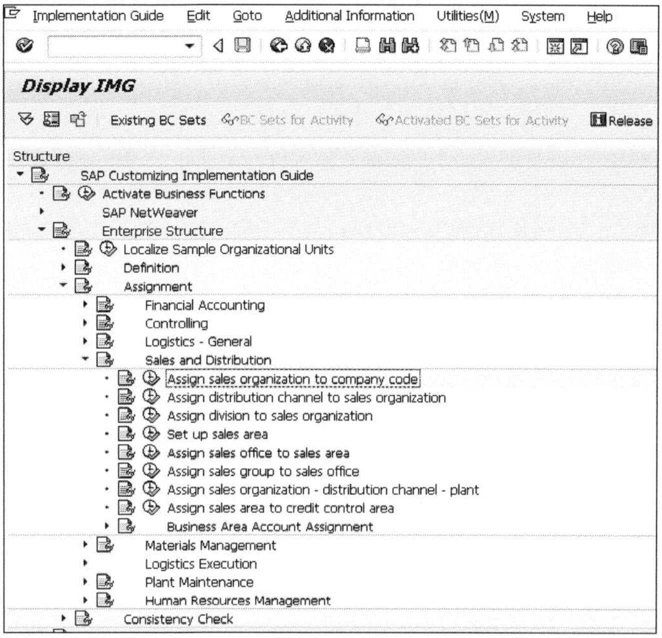

Figure 1.28 IMG Assign Enterprise Structure Menu Path for Sales Organization to Company Code

This IMG menu path points to where you assign sales organizations to company codes. Figure 1.29 shows an example assignment of sales organization to company code.

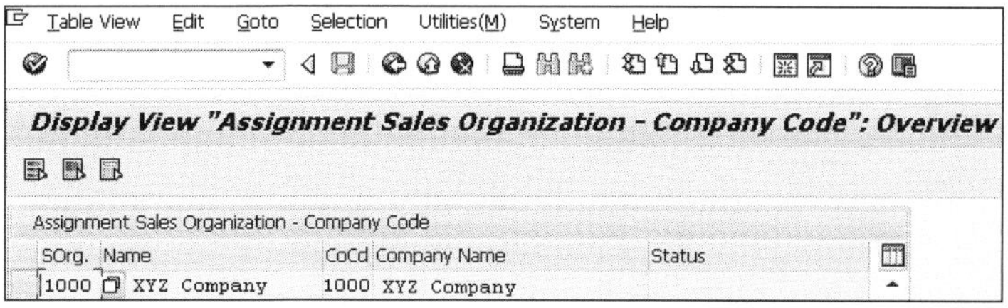

Figure 1.29 Example Assignment of Sales Organization to Company Code

1.3.4 Purchasing Organization to Company Code

The purchasing organization is an enterprise structure in the Materials Management (MM) module. A *purchasing organization* is an organizational unit responsible for purchasing activities, such as purchasing requisitions and purchase orders.

If corporate purchasing is centralized, the assignment of purchasing organization to company code may be a one-to-many relationship, but it can also be a one-to-one relationship if purchasing is a company code-specific function. A purchasing organization can also exist without being assigned to a company code. Because each plant must be assigned to a company code, the company code can be derived from the plant during a procurement transaction. To assign the enterprise structure for MM, follow IMG menu path, **Enterprise Structure • Assignment • Materials Management**, as shown in Figure 1.30. This menu path points to where you assign purchasing organizations to company codes. Figure 1.31 shows an example assignment of purchasing organization to company code.

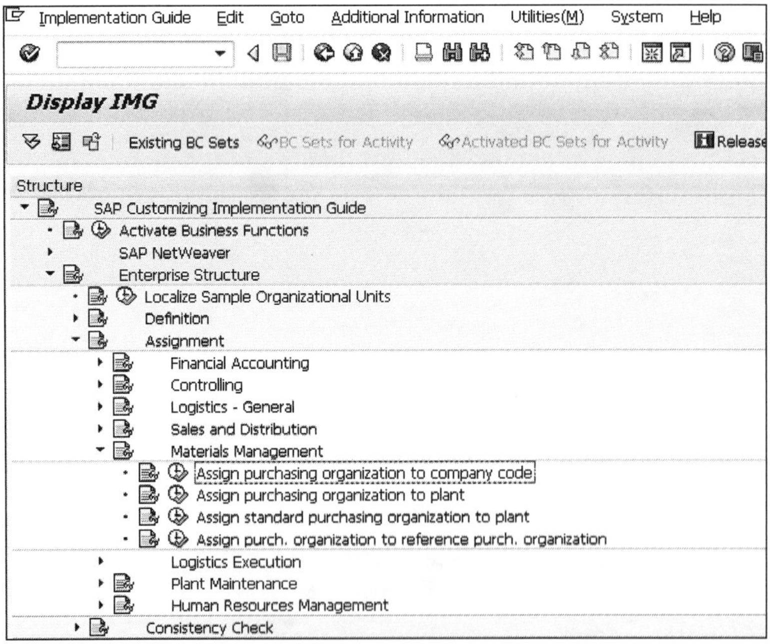

Figure 1.30 IMG Assign Enterprise Structure Menu Path for Purchasing Organization to Company Code

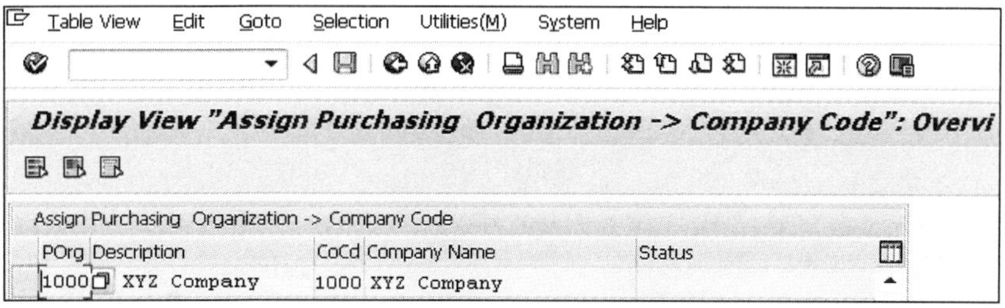

Figure 1.31 Example Assignment of Purchasing Organization to Company Code

1.3.5 Personnel Area to Company Code

A *personnel area* is an organizational unit in the HR module that represents a specific area of the enterprise according to aspects of personnel, time management, and payroll. A personnel area is assigned to one company code.

To assign the enterprise structure for HCM, follow IMG menu path, **Enterprise Structure • Assignment • Human Resources Management**, as shown in Figure 1.32.

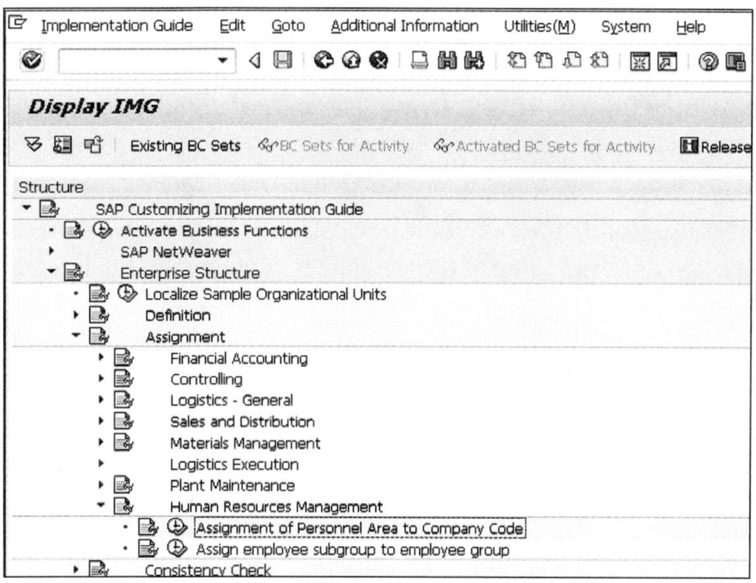

Figure 1.32 IMG Assign Enterprise Structure Menu Path for Personnel Area to Company Code

This menu path points to where you assign personnel areas to company codes. Figure 1.33 shows an example assignment of personnel area to company code.

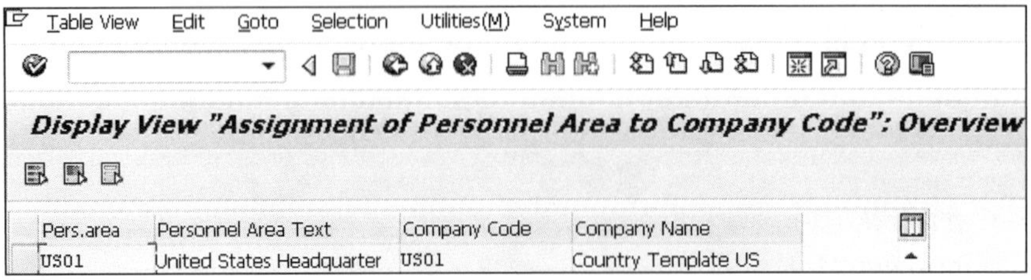

Figure 1.33 Example Assignment of Personnel Area to Company Code

1.4 Summary

This chapter laid the foundation for learning in the remainder of the book by detailing the essential elements of defining and assigning an enterprise structure. Although the remainder of this book presents specific FI business processes and transactions, you'll be better prepared to comprehend the material, having learned about the underlying structure of your organization, as represented in SAP.

Each module in SAP has its own enterprise structures. In FI, these structures include company, company code, credit control area, segment, business area, consolidation business area, functional area, profit center, and financial management area. After these enterprise structures are defined and activated in the IMG, many of them are assigned to other structures, as appropriate, to accurately reflect your company's business units and divisions. These assignments provide the basis for FI integration.

Modules outside of FI also require the definition and assignment of enterprise structures. In this chapter, we reviewed some of these modules, touching on the integration between FI and other non-FI modules, including SD, Logistics, MM, CO, and HCM. We discussed assigning company codes to controlling areas, plants, sales organizations, purchasing organizations, and personnel areas.

Defining enterprise structures and their relationships, inside and outside of FI, is important to your understanding of financial integration and data flows within your SAP system. These structures provide constraints and capabilities for posting financial transactions and reporting. Becoming aware of your own enterprise structure is an important first step in broadening your understanding of FI.

Now that you understand enterprise structures, we'll move on to discuss FI master data in the next chapter. Understanding master data is important and relevant to business processes, particularly understanding how specific master data settings influence transactions.

Chapter 2
Financial Accounting Master Data

In this chapter, we introduce Financial Accounting master data, including an overview of General Ledger accounts, vendor accounts, customer accounts, banks, and fixed assets. We also discuss business partners, which are replacing vendor and customer master data in SAP S/4HANA.

SAP defines *master data* as data that remains unchanged over a long period of time and contains information that is needed again and again in the same way. In Financial Accounting (FI), primary master data includes General Ledger (G/L) accounts, vendor accounts, customer accounts, banks, and fixed assets. Each type of master data is important in its own way to specific business processes. In this chapter, we'll cover these individual pieces of master data at a high level and then describe their structure and relevance to business processes in detail.

Before delving in, let's take a few minutes to understand the concept of master data more fully. Master data plays an essential role in all SAP business processes. It's defined as data that remains unchanged over a long period of time because it's required to fulfill business requirements and to execute transactions. G/L accounts, for example, are used to record financial entries. In addition, G/L accounts are required to produce financial statements. Over time, additional G/L accounts may be added, merged, or blocked, but the basic structure of your G/L accounts, as reflected in the chart of accounts, remains relatively static throughout a given fiscal year. In addition, within G/L accounts, specific settings indicate when and how a G/L account is used.

Another important point of master data is that, although the data is created individually in separate modules, it can be referenced and used across modules. For example, a fixed asset master record is created in FI Asset Accounting (FI-AA) but can be specified in purchase orders and FI transactions.

Now that you understand the basic concept of SAP master data, let's explore specific FI master data structures in the sections that follow.

2.1 General Ledger Accounts

General Ledger (G/L) accounts are considered fundamental master data in FI because they are essential to capturing accounting details and financial reporting. They are used for recording financial transactions and tracking account balances to fulfill external financial reporting requirements, legal or otherwise. In SAP, G/L accounts are assigned to a chart of accounts; they are used in all accounting transactions and are entered either manually or derived through *account determination*, a procedure which uses predetermined G/L accounts.

Before getting into the specifics of the G/L account master data structure, it's important that you understand the value of a clean, well-organized *chart of accounts*. The chart of accounts is simply a complete collection of the G/L accounts in your system. In SAP, a chart of accounts is defined and assigned to a company code.

When FI is first set up, one of the most important steps is to determine the structure for your chart of accounts. Over the decades, various approaches have been used. Generally, a simple structure is best to easily understand and maintain your chart of accounts and the G/L accounts in it. You also want a structure that provides a solid basis for financial reporting. Table 2.1 is an example of a G/L account structure commonly used today.

Account Type	Beginning Number Range	Ending Number Range
Assets	100000	199999
Liabilities	200000	299999
Equity	300000	399999
Expenses	500000	599999
Revenues	600000	699999

Table 2.1 Sample Chart of Accounts

The good news is that in addition to distinguishing G/L accounts by number range, SAP enables you to designate each as balance sheet or profit and loss (P&L) accounts, to subdivide G/L accounts further into account groups, and to make individual settings within each G/L account for added control.

Now that you have a better understanding of the overall structure and importance of G/L accounts, let's look at the specific elements of its structure. The G/L account itself is made up of two distinct parts: general data and company code data.

In the remainder of this section, we'll describe the details in the general data and company code data portions of a G/L master record. But first, let's take a closer look at the chart of accounts.

2.1.1 Chart of Accounts

In the previous section, we described the chart of accounts at a high level. It's an important concept, so here we will go into greater detail. SAP defines a *chart of accounts* as a classification scheme consisting of a group of G/L accounts that provides a framework for recording values to ensure an orderly rendering of accounting data. If you think that's a mouthful, you're not alone. Put more simply, a chart of accounts is a collection of G/L accounts used in a company code to record financial transactions and balances. Therefore, all the G/L accounts that a company code needs are contained in the chart of accounts. It's always important to keep in mind that financial reporting is based on G/L account transaction details and balances.

In SAP, there are three different chart of account types:

- **Operative chart of accounts**
  This type is used for your day-to-day operations and accounting entries.
- **Country chart of accounts**
  This type is used to meet a country's specific legal and tax requirements.
- **Group chart of accounts**
  This type is used for consolidation purposes.

Let's discuss each of these chart of account types in more detail, starting with the operative chart of accounts. The operative chart of accounts is also referred to as the *operating chart of accounts*. It's assigned to a company code using Transaction OBY6 and is used in the daily recording of accounting entries. In addition, both the FI and Controlling (CO) modules use this chart of accounts. For the CO module, this means that the operative chart of accounts contains the expense and revenue accounts that are also cost and revenue elements in CO.

If the operative chart of accounts doesn't meet country-specific legal and tax reporting requirements, then a country chart of accounts can be used. In other words, the country chart of accounts is the G/L account structure prescribed under national regulations. The assignment of a country chart of accounts to a company code is optional from a system configuration perspective. Like the operative chart of accounts, the country chart of accounts is assigned to a company code using Transaction OBY6. The need for a country-specific chart of accounts is typical in multinational companies, which commonly have a separate company code for each country.

Finally, the optional group chart of accounts contains the G/L accounts that are used by the entire enterprise for group reporting.

Now that you have an understanding of the chart of accounts, let's move on to discuss the specific parts of a G/L account master record. Bear in mind as you read through the remainder of this chapter and book that references to "chart of accounts" refers to the operative chart of accounts, unless otherwise specified.

2.1.2 General Ledger: General Data

G/L accounts are created and maintained in the application menu path, **Accounting • Financial Accounting • General Ledger • Master Records • G/L Accounts**, as shown in Figure 2.1.

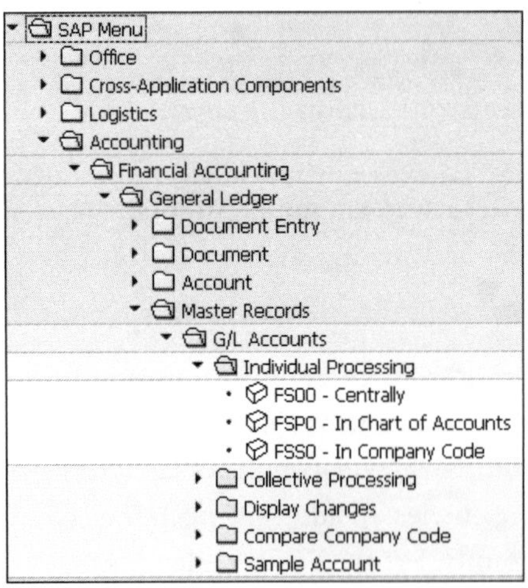

Figure 2.1 Application Menu Path for G/L Accounts

G/L accounts can be managed individually or collectively. G/L accounts must be created with basic data relevant to a chart of accounts using Transaction FSP0. After the basic data is created, it's reused to create the same G/L account in multiple company codes using Transaction FSSO. The basic data of a G/L account isn't specific to a company code; it's specific only to a chart of accounts.

Figure 2.2 shows an example G/L account screen displayed using Transaction FSPO and containing the following three tabs: **Type/Description**, **Key word/translation**, and **Information.**

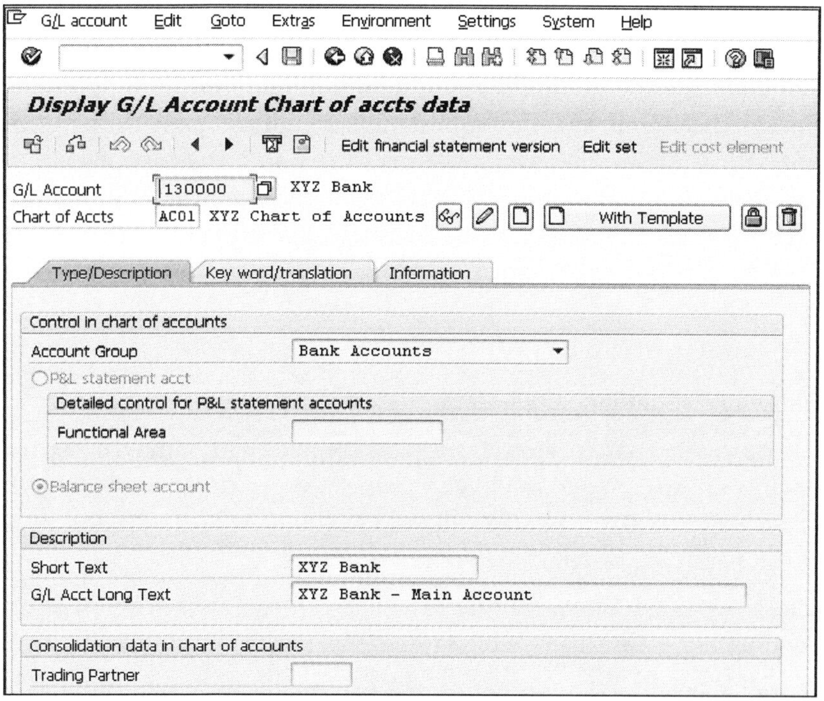

Figure 2.2 G/L Account: General Data

The **Type/Description** tab contains the **Control in chart of accounts** area, which is where the most important settings are made. The **Account Group** dropdown lets you choose and assign an account group, which determines the permitted G/L account number interval and specifies G/L master data fields as required, optional, or suppressed.

In the **Control in chart of accounts** area, you also designate each G/L account as a **P&L statement acct** or a **Balance sheet account**. Your account groups should be aligned as P&L or balance sheet accounts, so there is no chance of incorrectly assigning G/L account types to the wrong number range.

In the **Description** area of the master record, you specify G/L account **Short Text** and long text (**G/L Acct Long Text**).

The **Key word/translation** tab allows you to designate keywords for the account in the chart of accounts and to designate the language in which to display, enter, and print text.

The **Information** tab displays when the account was created and by whom, and it provides access to change documents.

As mentioned earlier in this section, after basic data for a G/L account is created, it can be used for multiple company codes. For example, if your company has two SAP company codes that use the same operative chart of accounts, the basic data only needs to be created once. However, each company code will each have its own set of company code data for each G/L account created using Transaction FSSO. This allows you to have two different settings in the company codes for the same G/L account that allows for slight differences in how the account in used.

2.1.3 General Ledger: Company Code Data

Company code data in the master record is the most complex part of the G/L master data. Without it, a company code can't post financial transactions with the G/L account. This section of the G/L master record must be completed using Transaction FSSO for each company code assigned to the chart of accounts.

Figure 2.3 shows an example G/L company code data screen, containing the following three tabs: **Control Data**, **Create/bank/interest**, and **Information**.

The **Control Data** tab includes the **Account control in company code** area with fields that determine account settings for currency, exchange rates, taxes, and reconciliation account types (i.e., assets, customers, and vendors). The **Alternative account no.** field allows you to designate an account number for a country chart of accounts.

In the **Account Management in Company Code** area, you set G/L accounts as open item managed or not. Selecting the **Open item management** checkbox turns on the open item managed function. Open item management is relevant to any business process in which a G/L line item needs to be cleared via a subsequent step (e.g., bank reconciliation).

Open item management is an important concept that is relevant to many processes, including bank reconciliation, goods receipt/invoice receipt (GR/IR), accounts payable, and accounts receivable. The basic concept is that an accounting entry posted to a G/L account is expected to be offset (i.e., cleared) in the future and net to zero in the account balance. Each accounting entry in a G/L clearing account has a status of **Open** or **Cleared**.

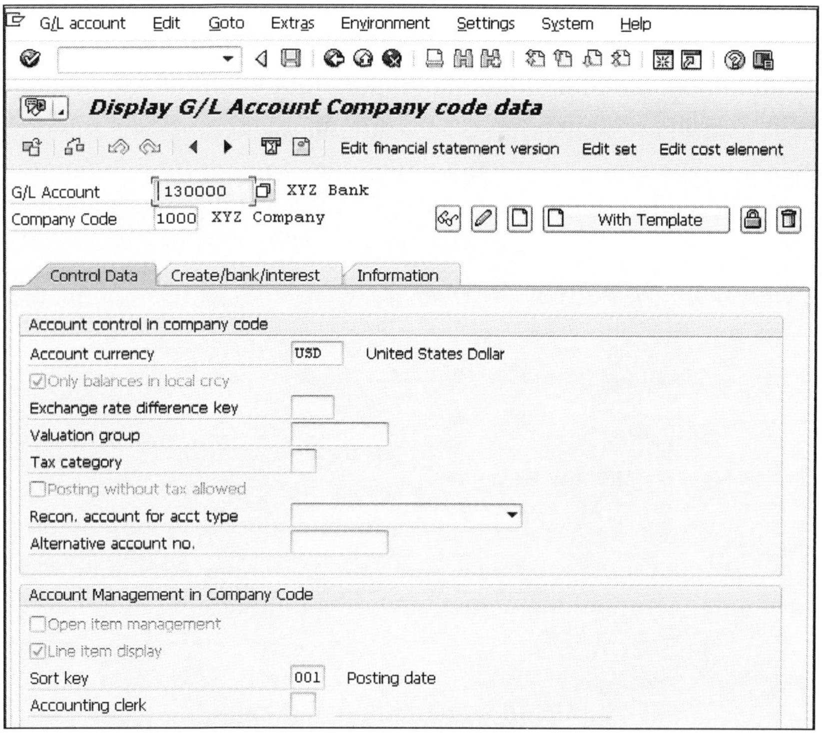

Figure 2.3 G/L Account: Control Data

Another important concept in G/L account master data is line item display. If you want to display individual line items in an account, you must set the **Line item display** flag. Doing so permits you to see individual line items that make up the G/L account balance. Be careful not to set the indicator unless it makes sense. For example, seeing individual line items in most P&L accounts is important. However, for reconciliation accounts (e.g., accounts payable), it's not because the line item detail is available via subledgers (e.g., vendor accounts).

The last field we'll cover on this screen is **Sort key**, which provides the layout rule for the **Allocation** field in the document line item, which is significant for bank and other specific accounts.

Figure 2.4 shows the **Create/bank/interest** screen, which includes the **Control of document creation in company code** area. These field control settings are used during document creation. The **Field status group** determines the screen layout for document entry and specifies document line item fields that are optional, required, or suppressed. If checked, the **Post automatically only** option indicates that the account can only be posted to through account determination and therefore can't be manually entered in a transaction. If checked, the **Supplement auto. postings** option allows the account to be used for automatic system-generated line items (e.g., bank charges).

The **Bank/financial details in company code** area is relevant to cash management. These settings are made for bank accounts and accounts relevant to cash position and liquidity forecasting.

The **Interest calculation information in company code** area is relevant to G/L accounts that use automatic interest calculation.

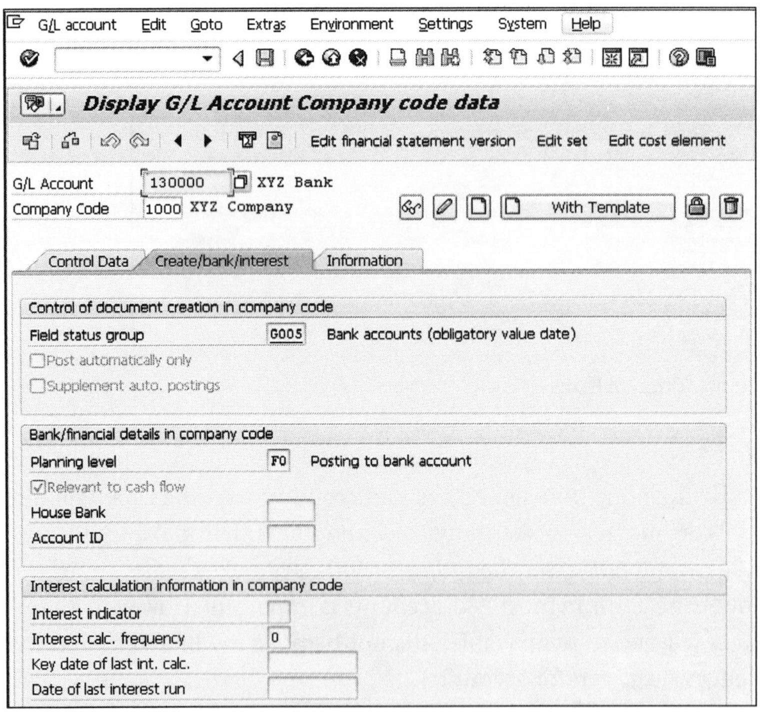

Figure 2.4 G/L Account: Create/Bank/Interest

The **Information** tab displays who created the account and when, and it provides access to change documents.

Now that you've learned about G/L account master data, we'll discuss vendor account master data. Vendor master data provides our first exposure into the subledger concept in SAP.

2.2 Vendor Accounts

Vendors are your suppliers of goods and services. Vendor master records contain all the pertinent data needed to place orders, post invoices, and issue payments. Each individual vendor master record is considered a subledger. The subledger concept means that individual vendor transaction details are maintained within the vendor master record itself. Collectively, the balances of all vendor master records roll up into a single G/L account known as an *accounts payable reconciliation account*.

Vendor master records are created and maintained in the application menu path, **Accounting • Financial Accounting • Accounts Payable • Master Records**, as shown in Figure 2.5.

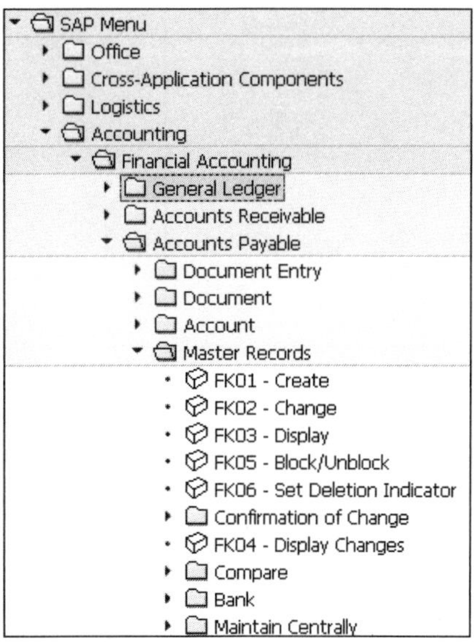

Figure 2.5 Application Menu Path for Vendor Master Records

Vendor master data is made up of three distinct parts: general data, company code data, and purchasing organization data. Because the focus of this book is FI, we won't go into detail on purchasing organization data, which is created and maintained in the Materials Management (MM) and Purchasing modules. Instead, this section covers vendor master data as it pertains to accounts payable only. In the remainder of this section, we'll describe vendor general data and company code data.

2.2.1 Vendor General Data

Figure 2.6 shows the **Display Vendor: Initial Screen** (Transaction FK03). To see **General data**, you only need to enter a **Vendor** and check the boxes under **General data** that you want to view. When all your selections are made, press Enter or click the green checkmark.

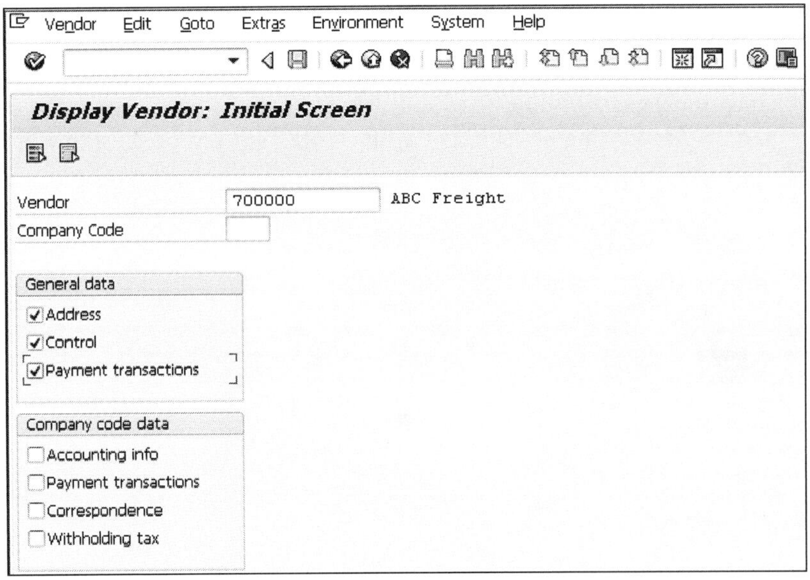

Figure 2.6 Display Vendor: Initial Screen for General Data

The **Display Vendor: Address** screen opens (Figure 2.7). You'll see the **Name** of the vendor, along with pertinent address and communication fields. In the **Search term 1/2** fields, two separate values can be entered for use when searching for vendors. The two fields are used independently of one another.

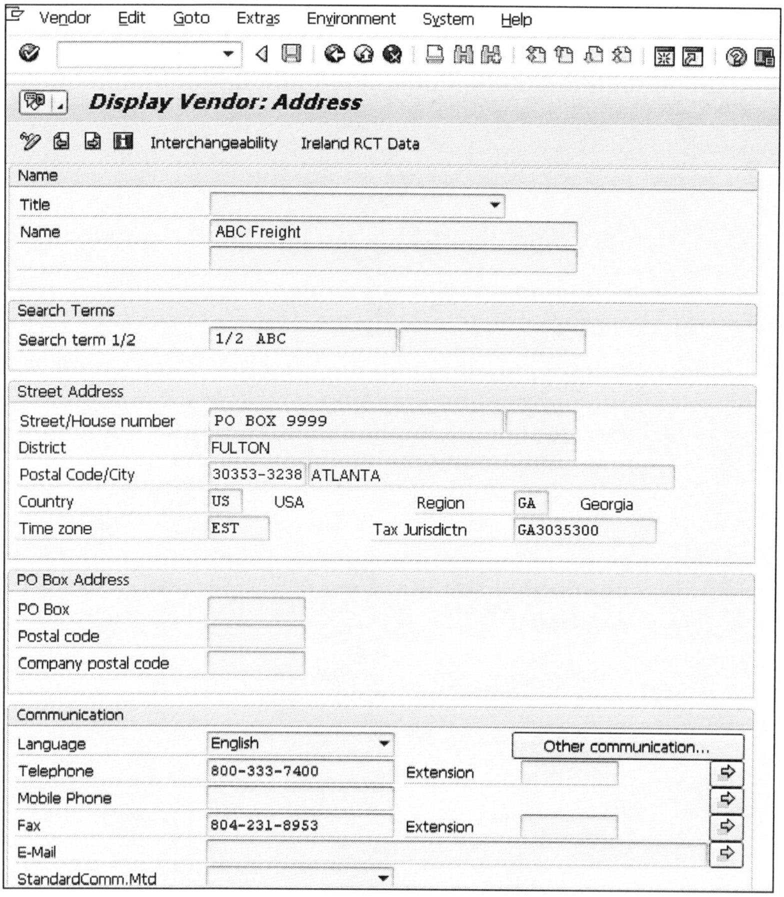

Figure 2.7 Display Vendor: Address Screen

Figure 2.8 shows the **Display Vendor: Control** screen. In the **Account control** area, grouping functions are enabled. For example, if a vendor is also a customer, you can enter the correct customer number in the **Customer** field. Doing so allows for joint management of a business partner and provides the ability to offset payables with receivables during automatic payment.

In the **Tax information** area, tax identification numbers, jurisdiction codes, and other tax-related information for the vendor is specified. If the vendor is an individual, you can enter withholding tax information at the bottom of the screen in the **Person subject to withholding tax** area.

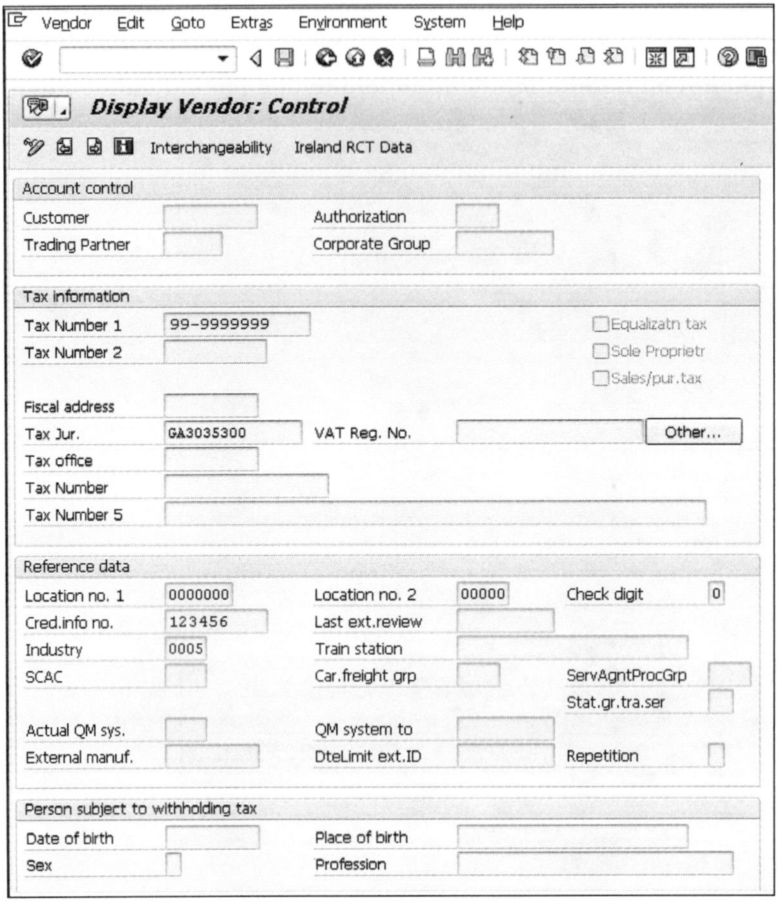

Figure 2.8 Display Vendor: Control Screen

In the **Reference data** area, you can specify external reference numbers and indicators as applicable. For example, if you report on vendors within a specific industry, you can assign a code in the **Industry** field.

Figure 2.9 shows the **Display Vendor: Payment transactions** screen. In the **Bank Details** area, you can enter a vendor's bank details.

The **Payment transactions** area largely consists of country-specific settings. However, in the **Alternate payee** field, you can enter a different vendor number if payment is to be made to a vendor different from the one to whom the payable is owed. To specify an alternate payee in the document, adjust the settings in the **Alternate payee in document** area.

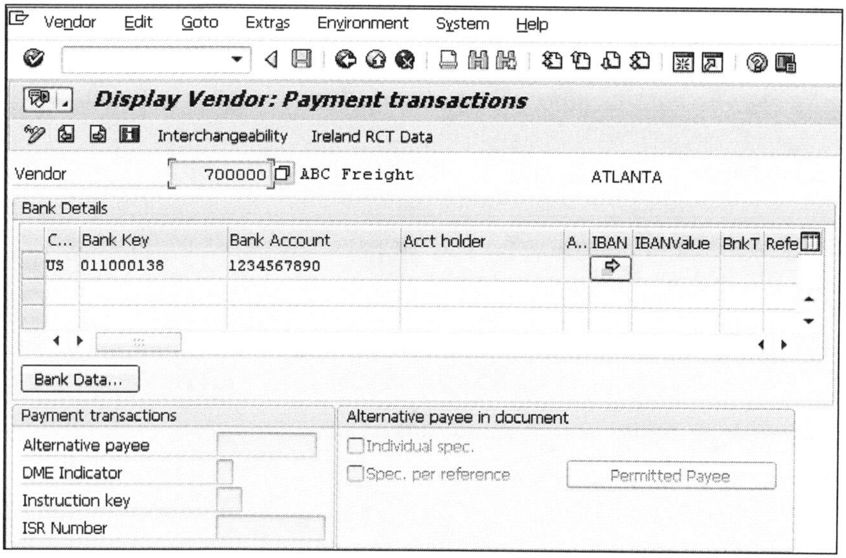

Figure 2.9 Display Vendor: Payment Transactions Screen

2.2.2 Vendor Company Code Data

Figure 2.10 shows the **Display Vendor: Initial Screen** (Transaction FK03). To display company code data, enter a **Vendor** and **Company Code**, and then check the boxes under **Company code data** that you want to view.

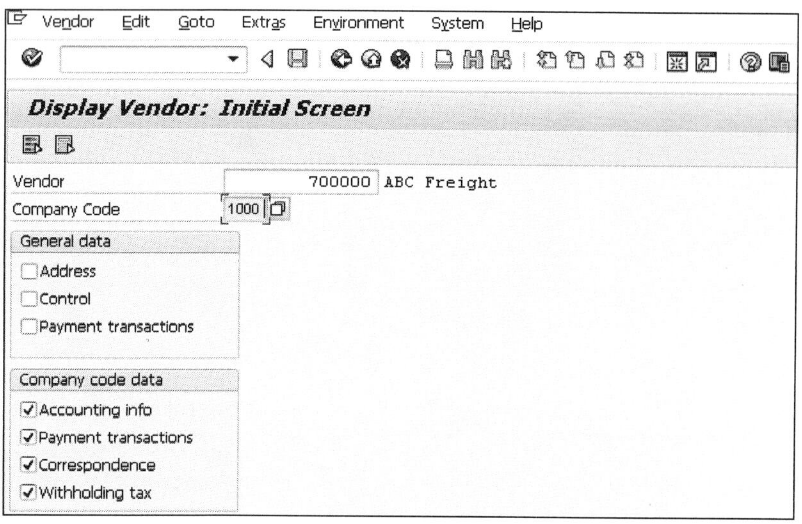

Figure 2.10 Display Vendor: Initial Screen for Company Code Data

Note that **Withholding tax** is only available when extended withholding tax is relevant. When all your selections are made, press [Enter] or click the green checkmark.

The **Display Vendor: Accounting information** screen shown in Figure 2.11 opens, corresponding to the first checkbox selected in Figure 2.11. The most important field on this screen is the **Recon. account** field in the **Accounting information** area. This field lists the reconciliation account updated in parallel to the vendor subledger account for normal postings. Special postings (e.g., down payments) post to different G/L accounts, as designated in configuration.

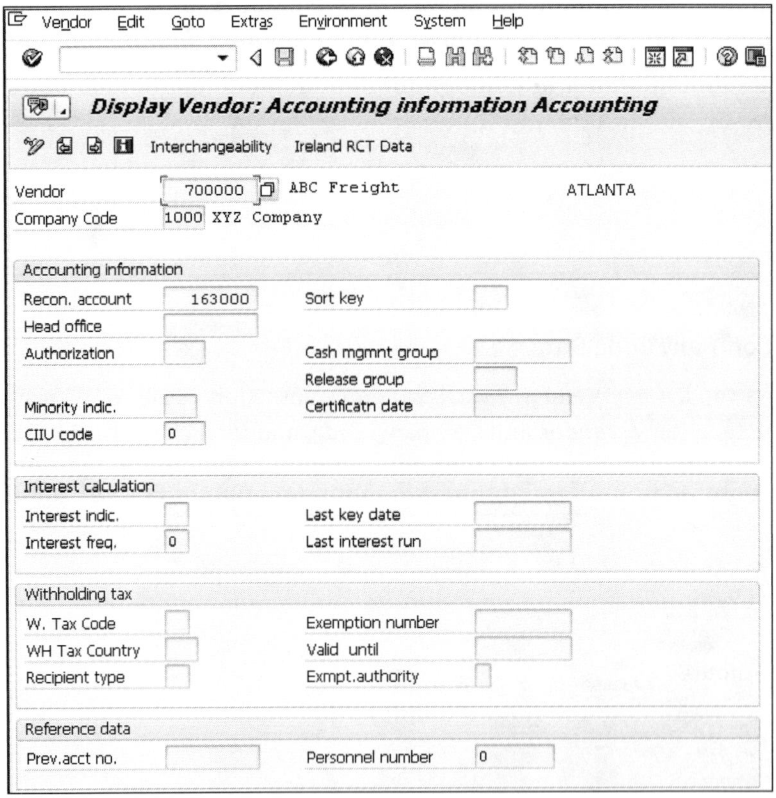

Figure 2.11 Display Vendor: Accounting Information Screen

The **Accounting information** screen of the vendor master data also contains values for interest calculations, withholding taxes, and reference data.

Click on the next page icon to open the **Display Vendor: Payment transactions** screen (Figure 2.12). This screen contains payment terms (**Payt Terms** field), which default from vendor master data into invoices during the document creation process. Also noteworthy in the **Payment Data** area are the **Tolerance group** field and the **Chk double inv.** checkbox. Tolerances affect cash discounts and allowable payment differences.

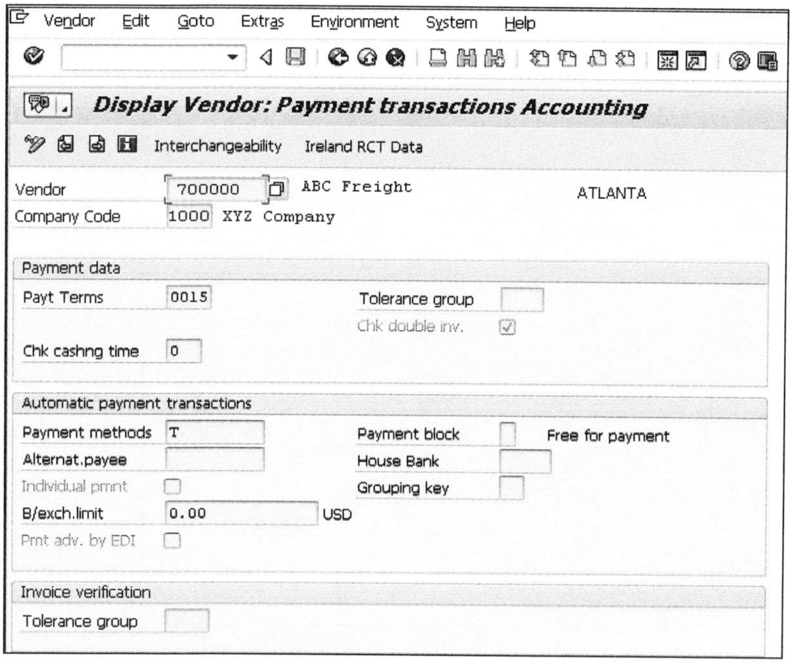

Figure 2.12 Display Vendor: Payment Transactions Screen

Selecting the **Chk double inv.** checkbox searches for duplicate invoices during document creation based on vendor, currency, company code, gross invoice amount, reference document number, and invoice date. This option provides a safeguard to avoid the risk of entering the same invoice more than once.

The **Automatic payment transactions** area contains important information relevant to the use of the automated payment program (Transaction F110). You should be familiar with these fields because they can, and often do, impact the output of your automatic payment runs.

Click on the next page icon to open the **Display Vendor: Correspondence** screen (Figure 2.13). This screen contains specifications for dunning and correspondence with a vendor.

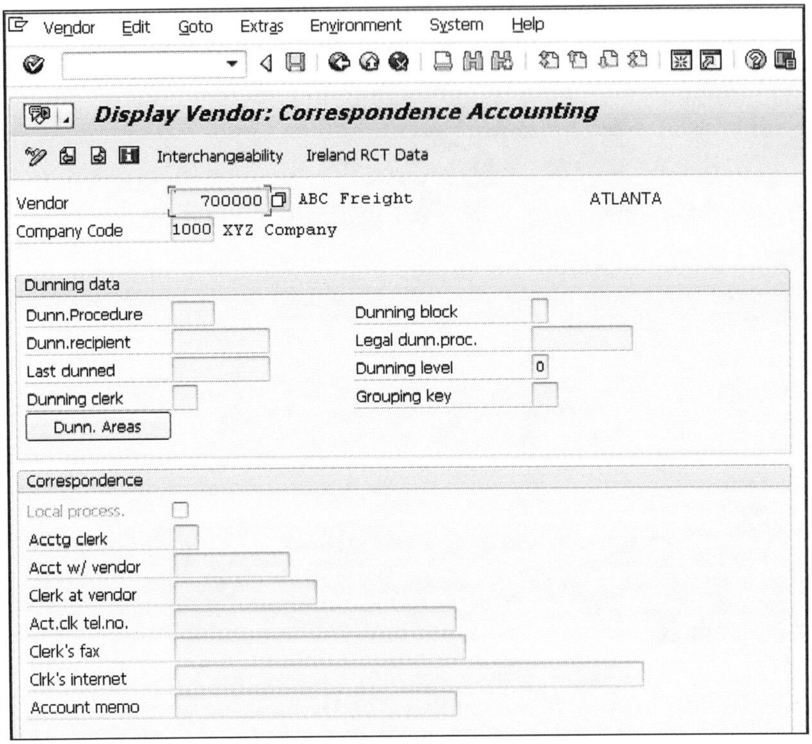

Figure 2.13 Display Vendor: Correspondence

Now that you've learned about vendor account master data, we'll discuss customer account master data. Like vendors, customers in SAP use the subledger construct, meaning that individual transaction details are managed for each individual master record separately, and their balances collectively roll up to a single G/L reconciliation account.

2.3 Customer Accounts

Customer master records contain all the pertinent data needed to receive orders, post invoices, and receive payments. Each individual customer master record is considered a subledger. The subledger concept is the same for vendor and customer accounts. For both, individual transaction details are maintained within the subledger. Collectively, the balances of all customer master records roll up into a single G/L account known as an *accounts receivable reconciliation account*.

Customer master records are created and maintained in the application menu path, **Accounting • Financial Accounting • Accounts Receivable • Master Records**, as shown in Figure 2.14.

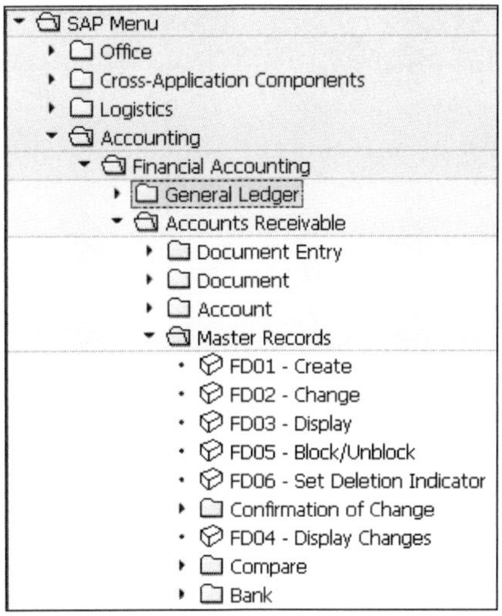

Figure 2.14 Application Menu Path for Customer Master Records

Customer master data is made up of three separate parts: general data, company code data, and sales area data. Here, we don't go into detail on the sales area data, which is created and maintained in SD. Instead, we'll discuss customer master data in relation to accounts receivable only. In the remainder of this section, we'll describe customer general data and company code data.

2.3.1 Customer General Data

Figure 2.15 shows the **Display Customer: General Data** screen (Transaction FD03). On the **Address** tab, you can see the **Name** of the customer, along with address fields. In the **Search term 1/2** fields, two separate values can be entered to search for customers. The two fields are used independently of one another.

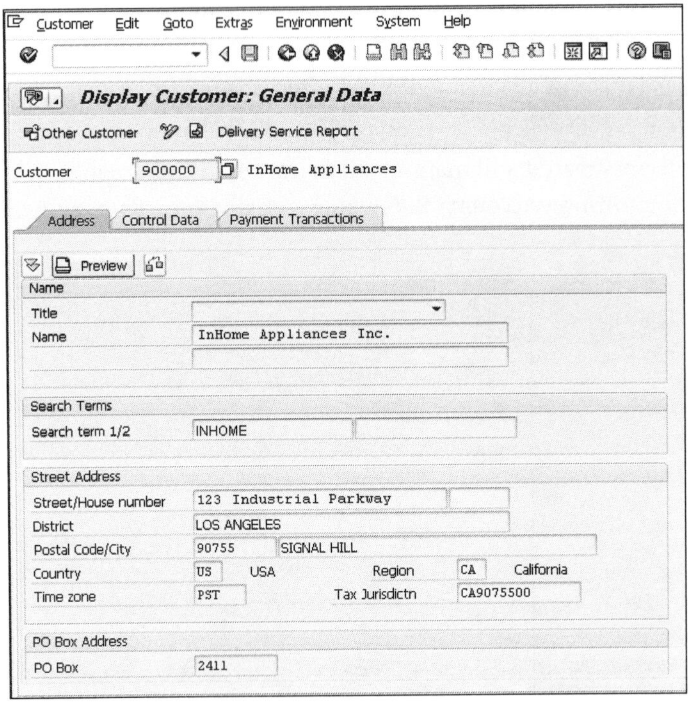

Figure 2.15 Display Customer: General Data

Click on the next page icon to open the **Control Data** tab (Figure 2.16). In the **Account control** area, grouping functions are enabled. For example, if a customer is also a vendor, you can enter the correct vendor number in the **Vendor** field. Doing so allows for joint management of a business partner and provides the ability to offset payables with receivables during automatic payment.

In **Reference data/area**, you can specify external reference numbers and indicators as applicable. For example, if you report on customers within a specific industry, you can assign a code in the **Industry** field. Finally, in the **Tax information** area, you can enter tax identification numbers, county codes, and other tax-related information for a customer.

Click on the next page icon to open the **Payment Transactions** tab (Figure 2.17). In the **Bank Details** area, enter the customer's bank details. The **Payment transactions** area of the screen provides the **Alternate payer** field, in which you can enter a different customer number if payment is to be received from a customer different from the one who owns the payable. To specify an alternative payer in the document, adjust the settings in the **Alternate payer in document** area.

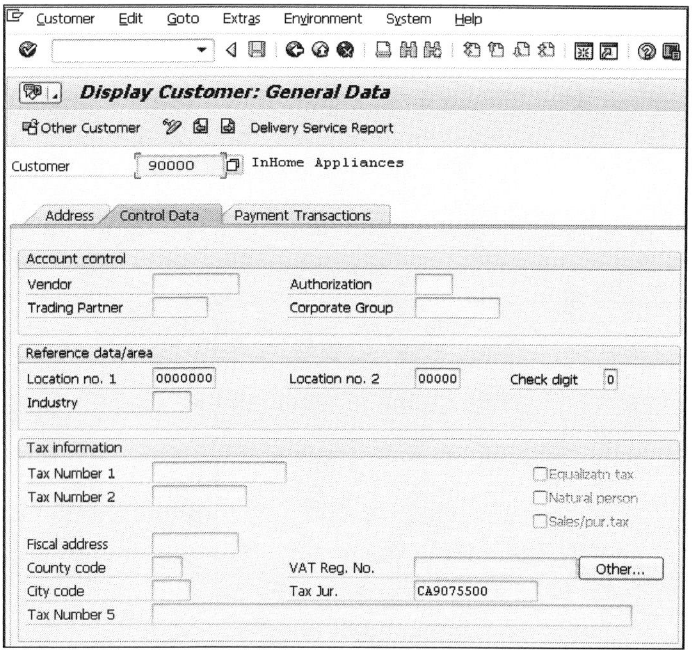

Figure 2.16 Display Customer: Control Data Tab

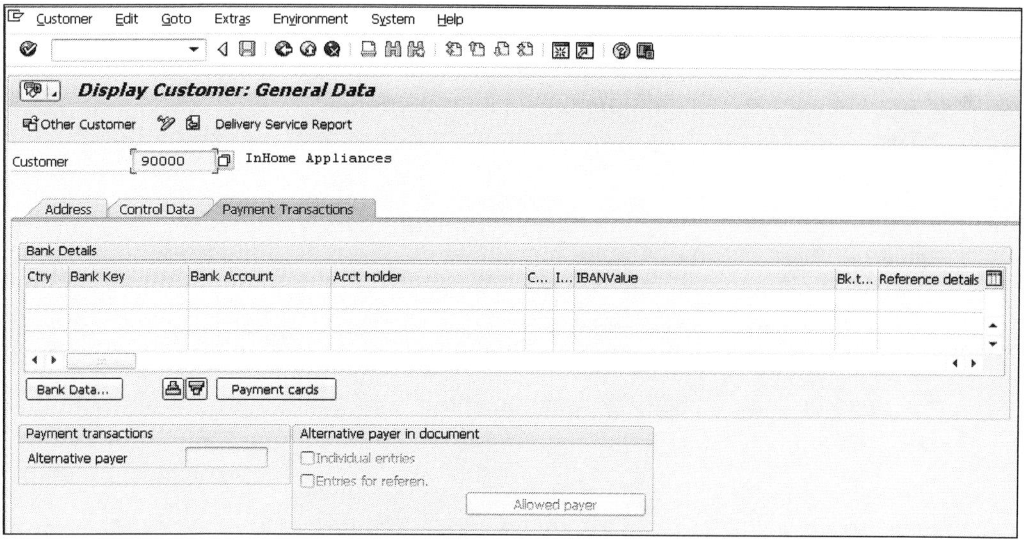

Figure 2.17 Display Customer: Payment Transactions Tab

2.3.2 Customer Company Code Data

Figure 2.18 shows the **Account Management** tab. The most important field here is **Recon. account**, which indicates the reconciliation account that is updated in parallel with the customer subledger account for normal postings. Special postings (e.g., down payments) post to different G/L accounts, as designated in configuration.

The **Account Management** tab also contains values for interest calculations, withholding taxes, and reference data.

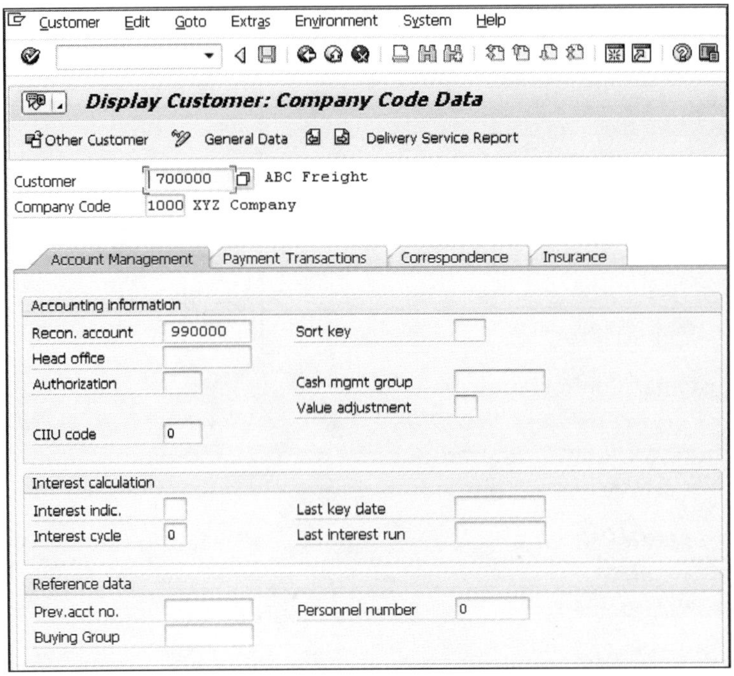

Figure 2.18 Display Customer: Account Management Tab

Next is the **Payment Transactions** tab (Figure 2.19). Most importantly, this tab contains the **Terms of payment** field, which defaults from the customer master record into invoices during document creation and is used to calculate the payment due date.

Figure 2.20 shows the **Correspondence** tab, which contains specifications for dunning and correspondence with a customer. Checkboxes in the **Payment notices to** area indicate the customer or internal department to which a payment notice is to be sent.

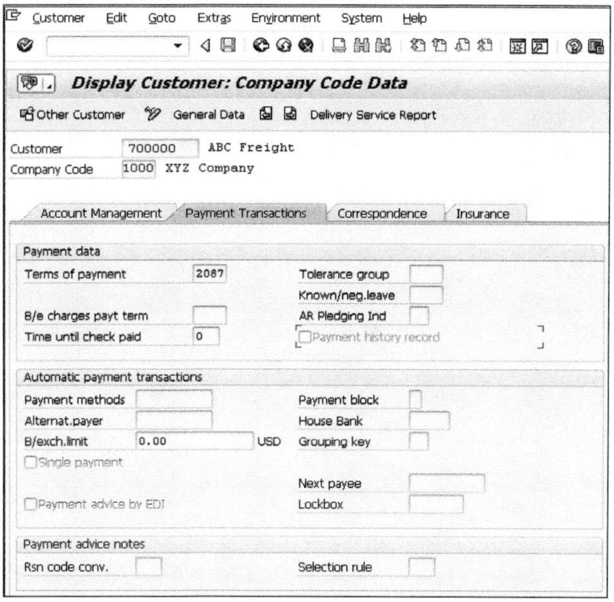

Figure 2.19 Display Customer: Payment Transactions Tab

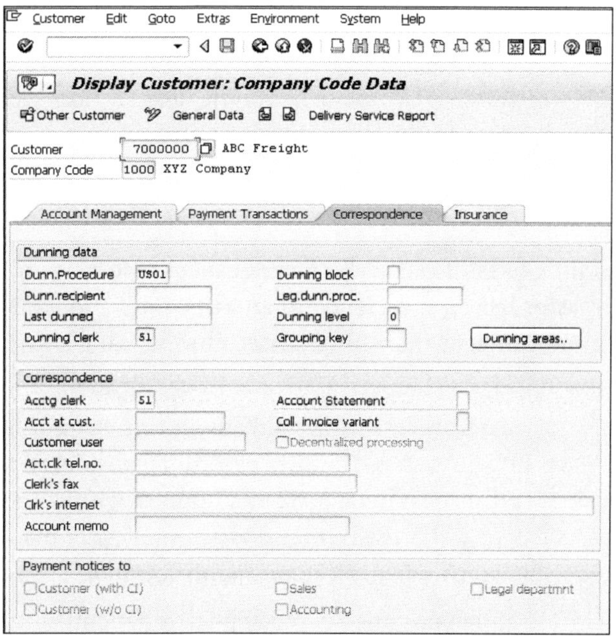

Figure 2.20 Display Customer: Correspondence Tab

The last tab in the customer master record is **Insurance**, where you can fill in the customer's insurance information (Figure 2.21).

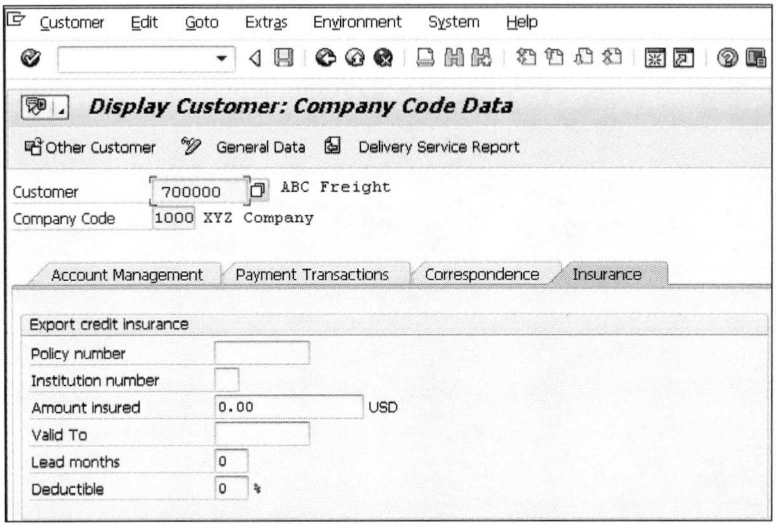

Figure 2.21 Display Customer: Insurance Tab

Now that you've learned about customer account master data, we'll discuss fixed asset master data. Like vendor and customer master data, fixed asset master records use the subledger concept in SAP, which we'll discuss further in the next section.

2.4 Fixed Assets

Fixed assets are structured according to asset classes for balance sheet reporting and depreciation. Each fixed asset master record is assigned to an asset class and company code. Asset classes determine, among other things, asset number ranges and screen layout rules.

The subledger concept that we've discussed several times already in this chapter is also applicable to fixed assets. Each individual asset master record is considered a subledger, meaning that individual transaction details are maintained within the asset master record and fixed asset ledger. Collectively, the balances of all asset master records roll up into a G/L account known as an *asset reconciliation account*.

Fixed asset master records are created and maintained in the application menu path, **Accounting • Financial Accounting • Fixed Assets • Asset**, as shown in Figure 2.22.

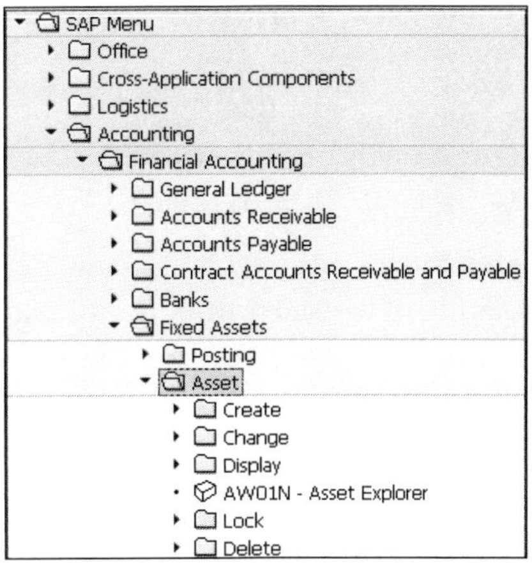

Figure 2.22 Application Menu Path for Fixed Asset Master Records

Figure 2.23 shows an example asset master record (Transaction AS03), consisting of several different tabs. In this section, we'll cover some of the important tabs and fields within the asset master record, but asset accountants should become familiar with the complete asset master record.

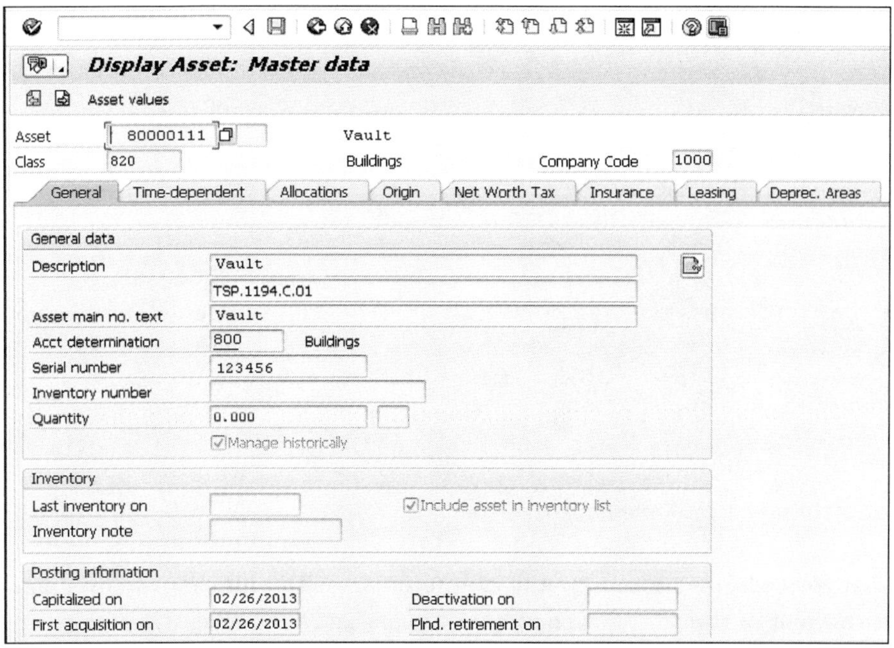

Figure 2.23 Display Asset: General Tab

In the **General data** area of the **General** tab, you'll find basic information about the asset. The **Description** and **Asset main no. text** fields describe the asset. The **Acct determination** field specifies the reconciliation account and offsetting accounts during certain business transactions. Other important fields on this screen include **Serial number**, **Inventory number**, and **Quantity**.

Click on the next page icon to open the **Time-dependent** tab (Figure 2.24), which displays an asset's association with other objects. Some of the most important links are to the **Cost Center** and **Plant**. Additional associations may be necessary depending on your business processes. For example, if you're using Plant Maintenance (PM), a maintenance order may be assigned.

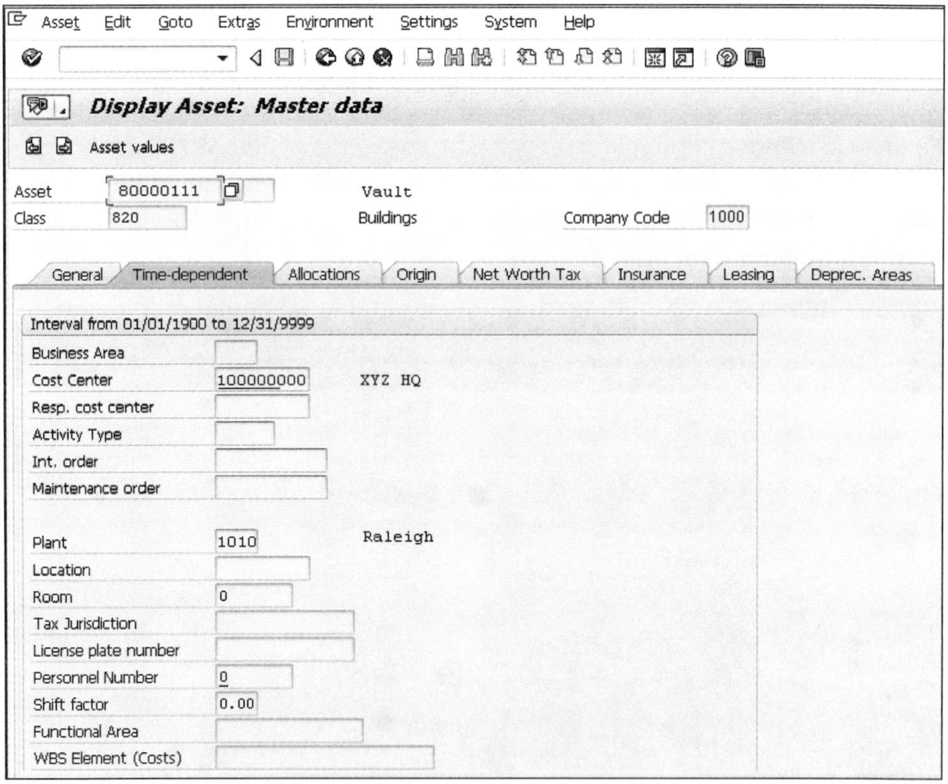

Figure 2.24 Display Asset: Time-Dependent Tab

Now that you've learned about asset master records, we'll discuss bank master data and learn about its relevance to vendors, customers, and bank-related business processes.

2.5 Banks

The two types of banks in SAP are house banks and the banks associated with customers and vendors. In this section, we'll discuss the latter category. See Chapter 15 for more details on bank master data and the specifics on setting up house banks.

Figure 2.25 shows an example bank master record. To view a bank master record using Transaction FI03, a **Bank Country** and **Bank Key** must be specified. The use of the **Bank Key** differs between countries. In the United States, the bank key is the American Bankers Association (ABA) number, commonly known as the routing transit number (RTN).

The **Address** area contains the name of the bank, address, and branch. The **Control data** area contains important information such as a **SWIFT/BIC** code, **Bank group**, and **Bank number**.

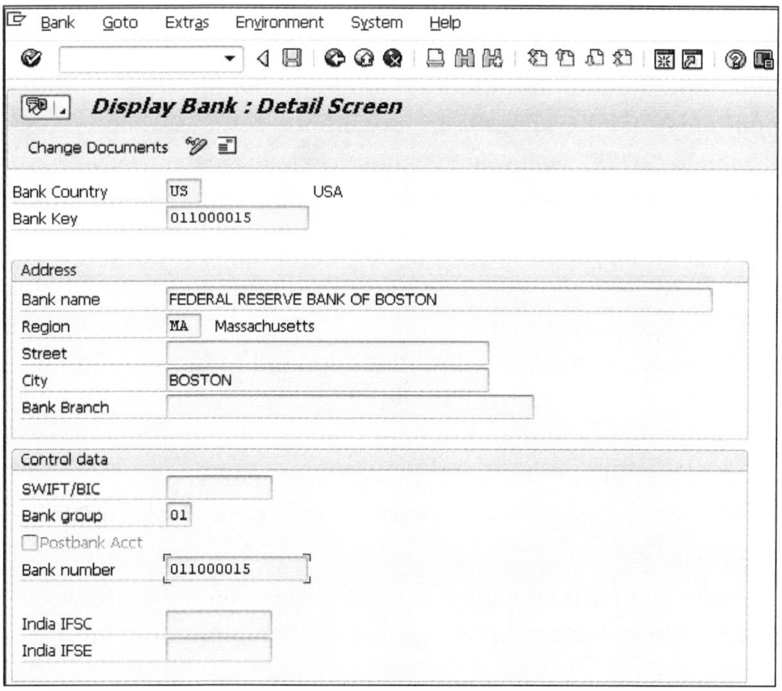

Figure 2.25 Display Bank: Detail Screen

Once created, bank master data can be assigned for use in vendor and customer master records.

This concludes our discussion of bank master data. Let's move on to discuss business partners, which are playing a greater role in the new SAP Business Suite: SAP S/4HANA.

2.6 Business Partners

The transition from SAP ERP 6.0 to SAP S/4HANA has brought with it a key change in FI master data: business partners. Converting customers and venders to business partners in SAP S/4HANA is a mandatory change that has been in the making at SAP for many years. Customer and vendor master data has always had limitations, such as the inability to house multiple address types except through the use of *partner functions*. For example, in a procurement transaction, the vendor is first the ordering address, then the supplier of goods, then the invoicing party, and finally the payee. To accomplish this, partner roles (also called partner functions) are assigned to the vendor. The Business Partner functionality was created to be a central repository of trading partner master data with greater flexibility than customers and vendors.

In SAP ERP 6.0, business partners are used in several modules, including Flexible Real-Estate Management (RE-FX), Financial Supply Chain Management (FIN-FSCM), and Treasury and Risk Management (TRM). For simplicity, this section will focus on accessing business partners through the RE-FX module.

Note

See Chapter 18 for more details on SAP S/4HANA and the major FI changes from SAP ERP 6.0.

Business partner master records are created and maintained in the application menu path, **Accounting • Flexible Real Estate Management • Master Data • Business Partner Master Data**, as shown in Figure 2.26.

Double-click on the **BP – Edit Business Partner** transaction highlighted in Figure 2.26 to open the **Maintain Business Partner** screen (Figure 2.27). Here, enter your **Business-Partner** number (one which is available in your system) and press [Enter]. For this example, **BusinessPartner 2140** was entered (Figure 2.28).

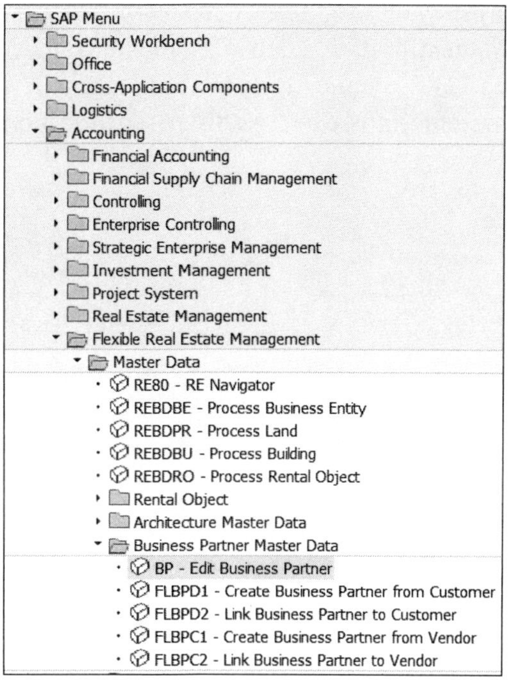

Figure 2.26 Application Menu Path for Business Partner

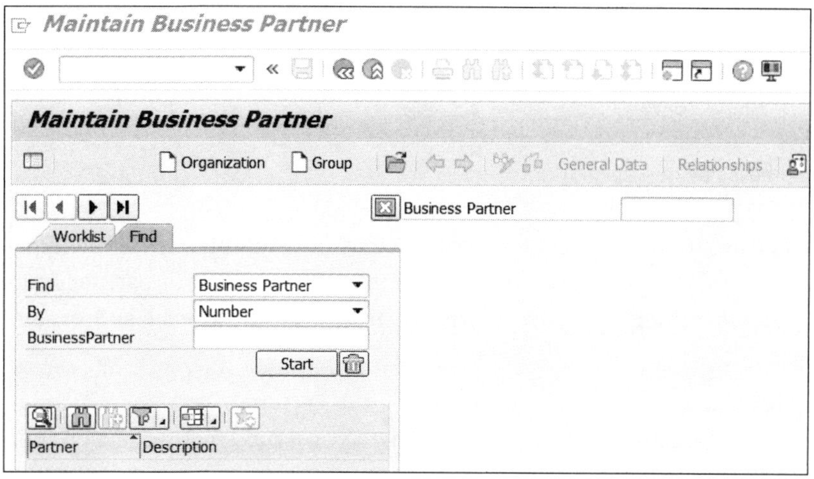

Figure 2.27 Maintain Business Partner Screen

The business partner will be displayed as shown in Figure 2.28. Notice that several tabs appear: **Address**, **Address Overview**, **Identification**, **Control**, **Payment Transactions**, **Status**, and **Technical Identification**. Let's examine these screens, noting how they compare to customer and vendor master records, which we discussed in Section 2.3 and Section 2.2, respectively.

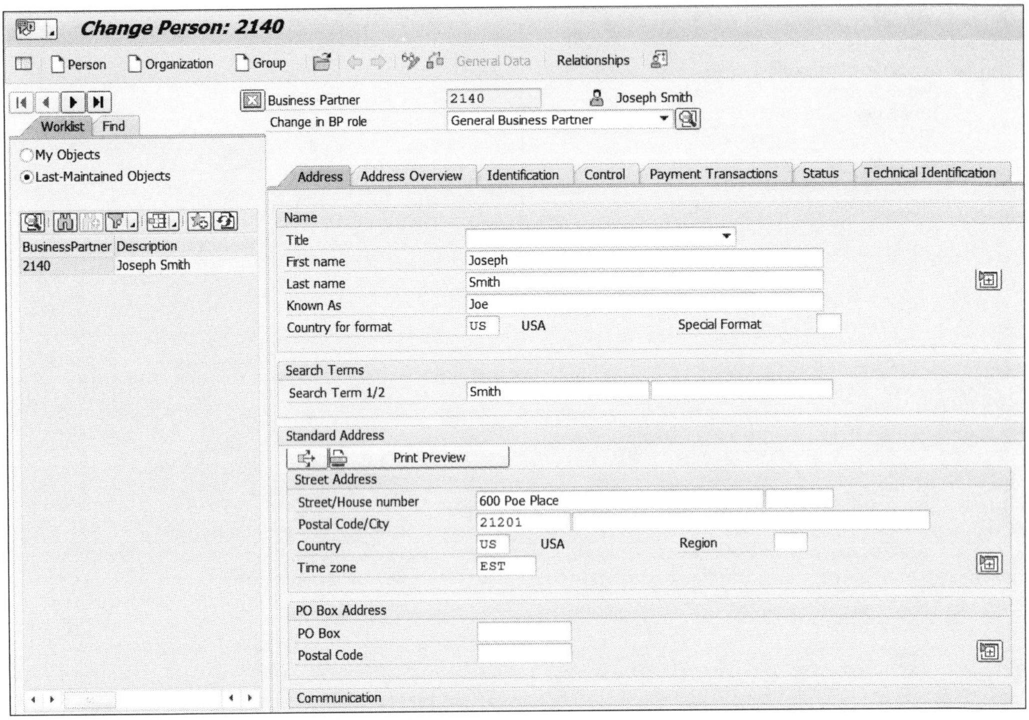

Figure 2.28 Business Partner: Display Screen

The Business Partner functionality allows you to create and maintain multiple types of addresses within the same master record, eliminating the need for partner functions. As you can see in Figure 2.29, the **Address Overview** tab shows each address and **Address Usages**.

Click on the **Identification** tab (Figure 2.30) to see the **Personal Data**, **Identification Numbers**, and **Tax Numbers** areas. This is also where you would distinguish an individual versus a corporate entity.

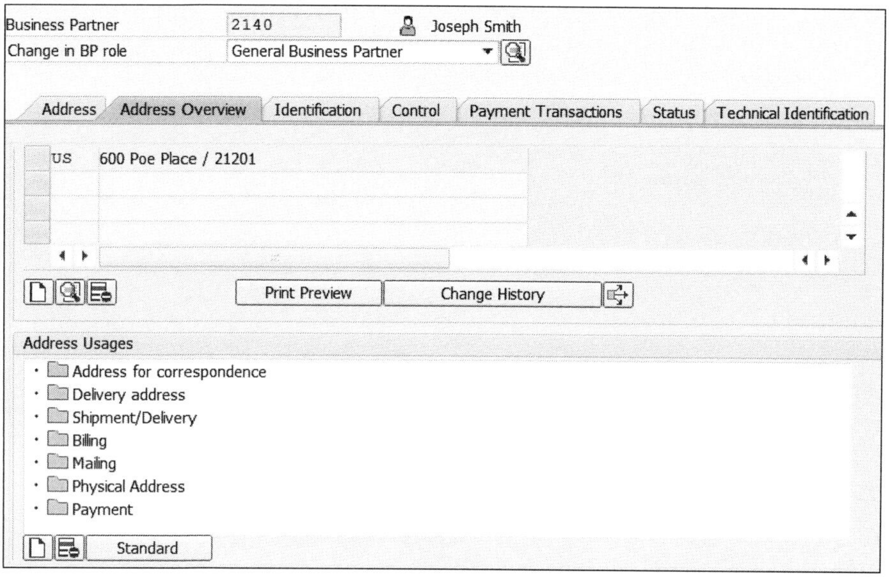

Figure 2.29 Business Partner: Address Overview Tab

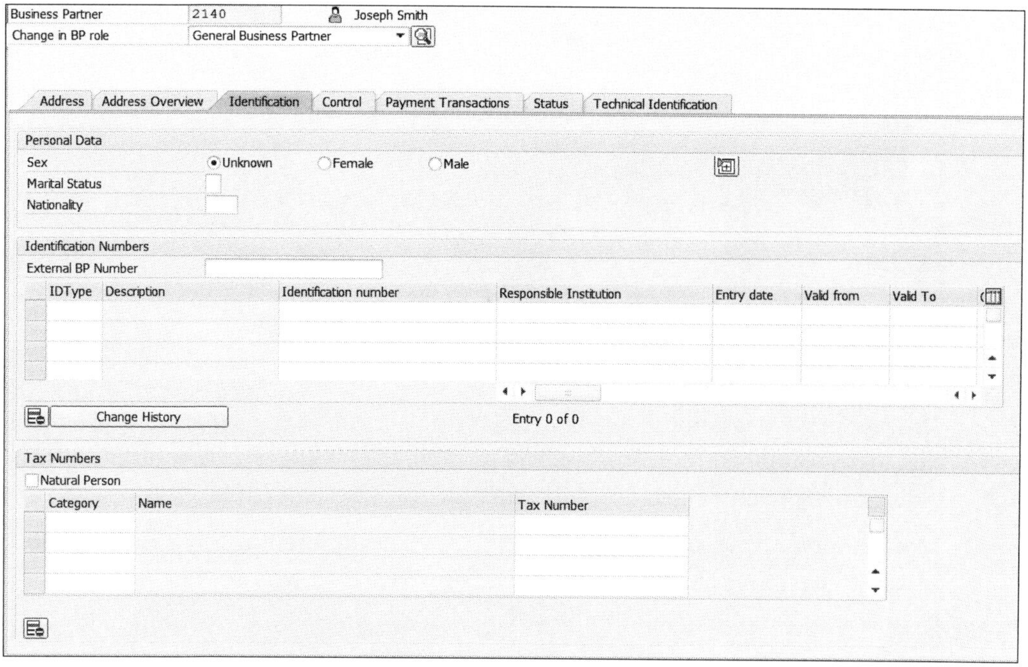

Figure 2.30 Business Partner: Identification Tab

The **Control** tab shown in Figure 2.31 provides many other features, such as an **Authorization Group** (to control access to the business partner record), correspondence, tax classifications, and more.

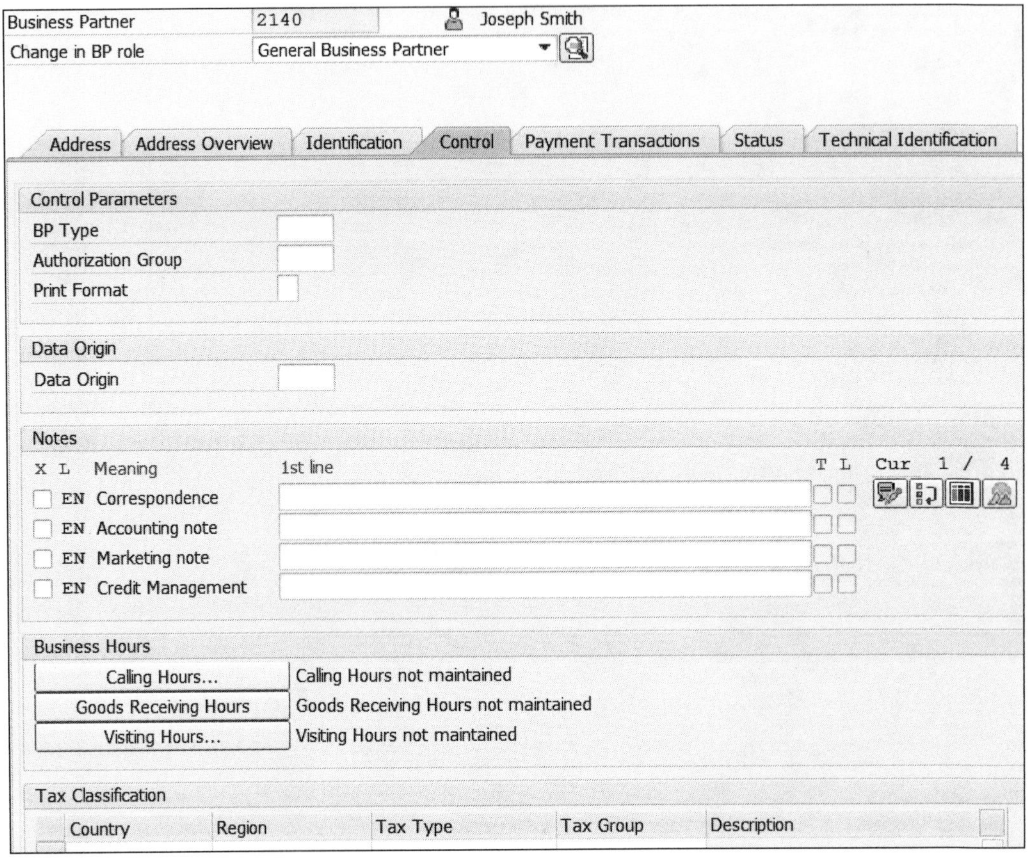

Figure 2.31 Business Partner: Control Tab

The **Payment Transactions** tab (Figure 2.32) of the business partner closely resembles that of the vendor and customer master records. The business partner differs by providing a place to enter credit card information (i.e., **Payment Cards**).

Like vendors and customers, business partners have different components. Vendors and customers have general data and company code data, whereas business partners have general data and relationships data.

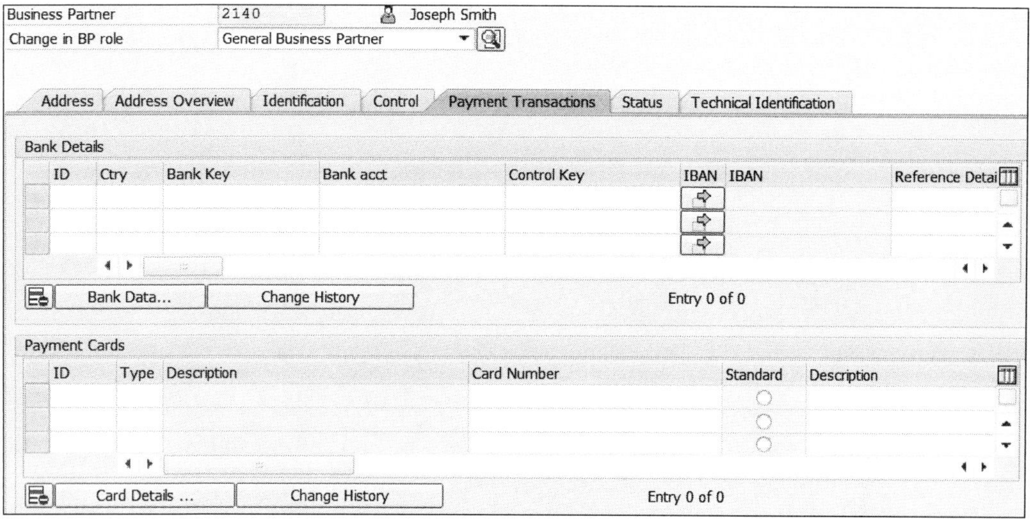

Figure 2.32 Business Partner: Payment Transactions Tab

General data is the default when you execute Transaction BP. All the tabs and data you've seen in this section are general data. Figure 2.33 shows that the **General Data** button at the top of the screen is grayed out, meaning it's currently being displayed.

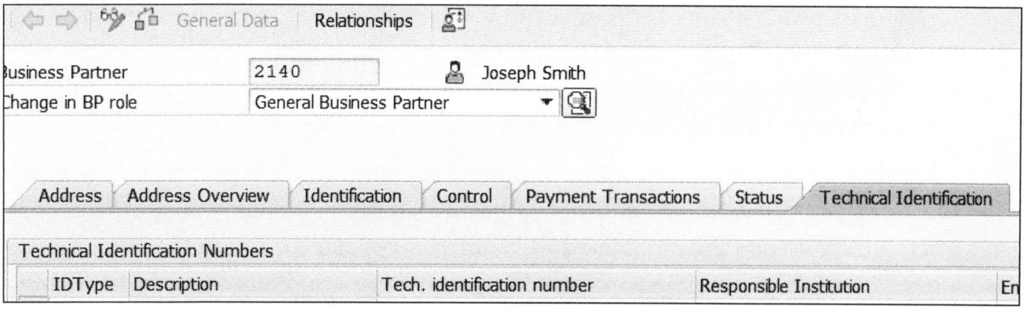

Figure 2.33 Business Partner: General Data

Figure 2.34 shows the **Relationships** button grayed out at the top of the screen, indicating that relationship data is being displayed. The flexible relationships functionality allows you to create categories of relationships and associate specific relationships to a business partner. These can be personal relationships, such as a spouse, or business-to-business relationships, philanthropic associations, and more.

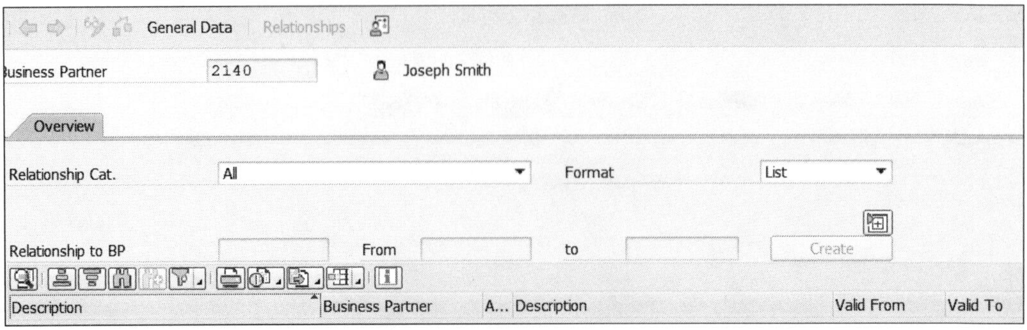

Figure 2.34 Business Partner: Relationships Data

2.7 Summary

Master data is a key element to your business processes. In this chapter, we provided an overview of FI master data to give you a foundation for the remainder of the book. In summary, master data plays an essential role in all SAP business processes. It's defined as data that remains unchanged over a long period of time and is required to fulfill business requirements and to execute transactions. As an accountant or financial manager, understanding the basic structure of FI master data is essential.

In FI, master data includes G/L accounts, vendors, customers, fixed assets, and banks. In SAP S/4HANA, business partners are replacing vendor and customer master data. Other modules have their own master data, and the cross-modular relationships between master data are important to end-to-end business processes.

G/L accounts are relevant to all accounting transactions. G/L master data is assigned to a chart of accounts and consists of basic data, general data, and company code data. G/L accounts are designated as balance sheet or P&L accounts in the master record, and the account groups should be aligned to avoid any chance of assigning the wrong account number for a specific G/L account type.

The concept of subledgers is discussed throughout this chapter. A subledger is where an individual financial transaction detail is managed in a separate ledger and then rolls up to reflect overall balances in a central set of G/L accounts. Subledgers are relevant to vendors, customers, and fixed assets.

Specific bank master data was also discussed in this chapter. In FI, there is a distinction between a house bank and bank master data. House banks, covered in Chapter 15, are configurations used by a company code to make automatic payments. Bank master data, on the other hand, is data pertaining to the bank accounts of your business partners.

In this chapter, you learned what master data is, how it's used, and the basic structures of master data in FI. In the next chapter, you'll receive your first glimpse of how master data is used in our discussion of G/L account transactions.

Chapter 3
General Ledger Transactions

3

In this chapter, we cover General Ledger (G/L) transactions in detail. These transactions consist of accounting line items without a sub-ledger entry and are created directly in the SAP General Ledger. This chapter also covers associated G/L concepts and transactions, such as credit memos, reversals, parking, and G/L document maintenance functions.

This chapter covers General Ledger (G/L) account transactions that originate in the SAP General Ledger (commonly refered to as the General Ledger [G/L]). The most common G/L transaction is the entry of a G/L accounting document using Transaction FB50. This chapter covers not only the creation of a G/L document but also associated G/L functions, such as document display, change, reverse, park, and more.

Creating a G/L accounting document is straightforward, but it's only one of many associated tasks that must be completed in the G/L module by the accounting department, including posting credit memos, making document corrections, clearing accounts, reconciling balances, and so on.

This chapter begins by covering the basics of creating a G/L accounting document. We then dive into each associated function of the G/L module.

Note

Some of the transactions covered in this chapter, such as the creation of accounting documents, are tasks you're likely to perform daily. Other transactions, such as document reverse, are executed less frequently. This chapter can be revisited repeatedly as a reference point for less frequently used transactions and can provide you with an overall refresher on the G/L module. With the full gamut of G/L capabilities provided in this chapter, you can choose the right tool for the task at hand.

3.1 Journal Vouchers

This section covers the G/L document creation process, which includes document entry, park, post, save as complete, and hold tasks. It also covers the Transaction FB50 tree display, screen variants, account assignment templates, editing options, and the post with reference task—all of which provide valuable insights to help you be more productive and organized in the G/L module.

Let's start by discussing why this section is titled "Journal Vouchers." *Journal vouchers* are accounting documents that consist of line items without a subledger entry (i.e., customer, vendor, business partner, or asset) that are created directly in the G/L module. In SAP terms, a journal voucher refers to G/L accounting documents entered via Transaction FB50.

To create a journal voucher in SAP using Transaction FB50, you must enter document header details (e.g., posting date) and at least two separate line items that net to a balance of zero. This is the balancing principal in accounting where debits and credits must be equal.

Although this is straightforward, small complications can get in the way of your ability to perform such a simple task. For example, in the middle of entering an accounting document, you might be whisked away to a meeting by your boss, or while entering a document line item, you might notice that a field you need to enter isn't on the entry screen. This section gives you the tools you need to deal with these and other challenges and provides you with the knowledge to enter G/L accounting transactions more efficiently.

3.1.1 Document Entry

To enter a G/L account document, use Transaction FB50 or application menu path, **Accounting • Financial Accounting • General Ledger • Document Entry • FB50 – Enter G/L Account Document**, as shown in Figure 3.1.

Double-click **FB50 – Enter G/L Account Document** from the menu path, or enter "FB50" in the **Command** field (as shown in Figure 3.2) and press [Enter].

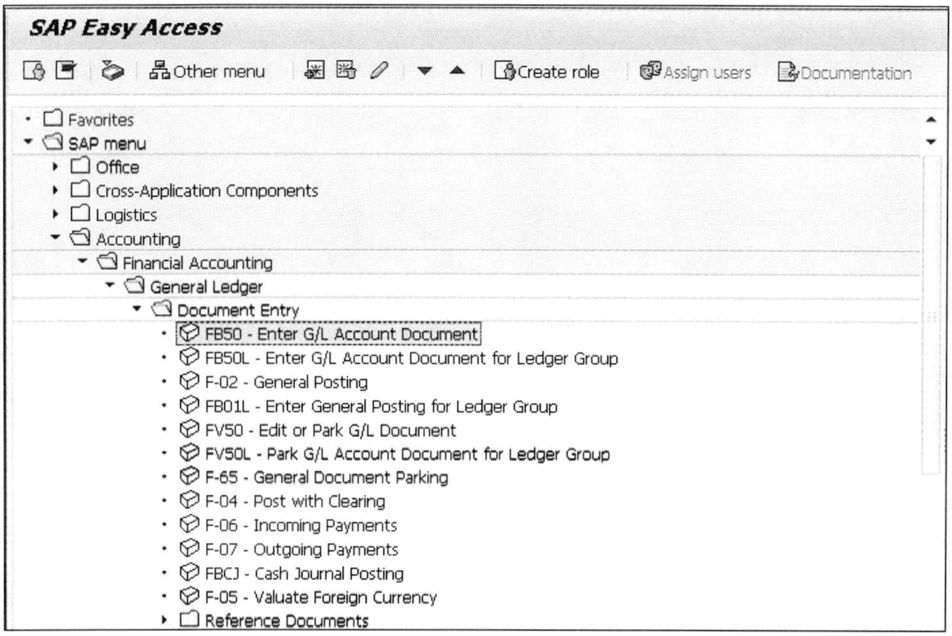

Figure 3.1 Transaction FB50 Menu Path

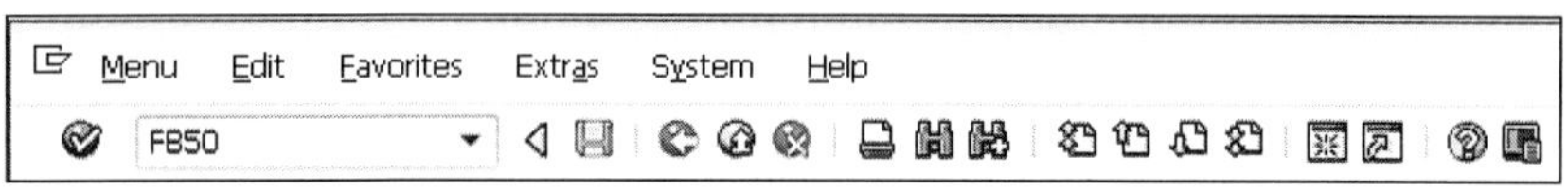

Figure 3.2 Entering "FB50" in the Command Field

The **Enter G/L Account Document** entry screen appears (Figure 3.3). The fields that appear on the header with prepopulated values may vary depending on your system configuration and editing options. In this example, the **Document Date** field was manually entered, whereas field values were defaulted for the **Currency**, **Posting Date**, **Document Type**, and **Company Code** fields. Document type configuration determines whether field entry is required in the **Reference** and **Doc.Header Text** fields. In this example, these fields aren't required for **Document Type SA**, which is the document type default for Transaction FB50.

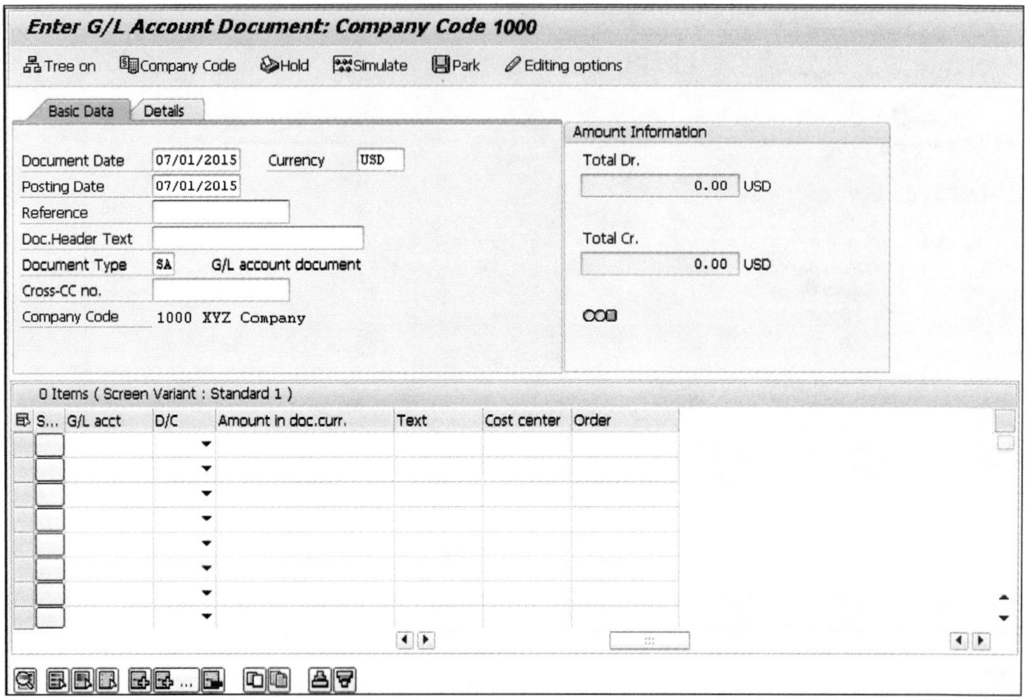

Figure 3.3 Enter G/L Account Document Screen

After entering header details, the next step is to enter at least two separate line items, as shown in Figure 3.4.

Here, the line items make up a cash movement between petty cash and a bank account. Because both G/L accounts are balance sheet accounts, only the **G/L acct**, **D/C** (debit/credit indicator), and **Amount in doc.curr.** fields require input. Additional field entry requirements may exist in your SAP system.

After entering document line items, click the **Simulate** button in the top center of the **Enter G/L Account Document** entry screen to initiate simulation of the G/L document posting logic to determine if the document can be properly posted. If the simulation is unsuccessful, an error message appears. If successful, the **Document Overview** screen appears, as shown in Figure 3.5.

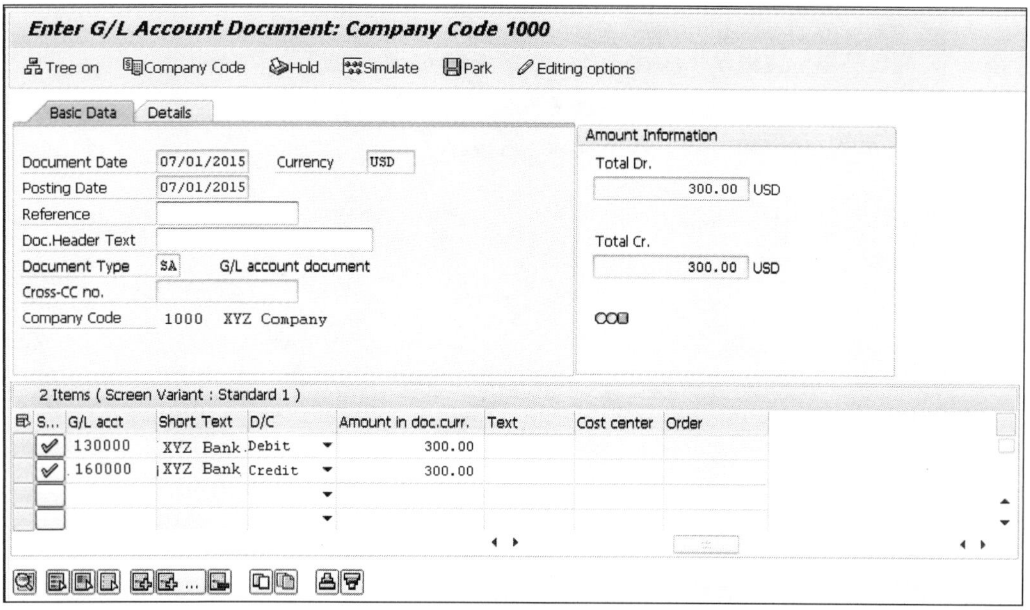

Figure 3.4 Line Items

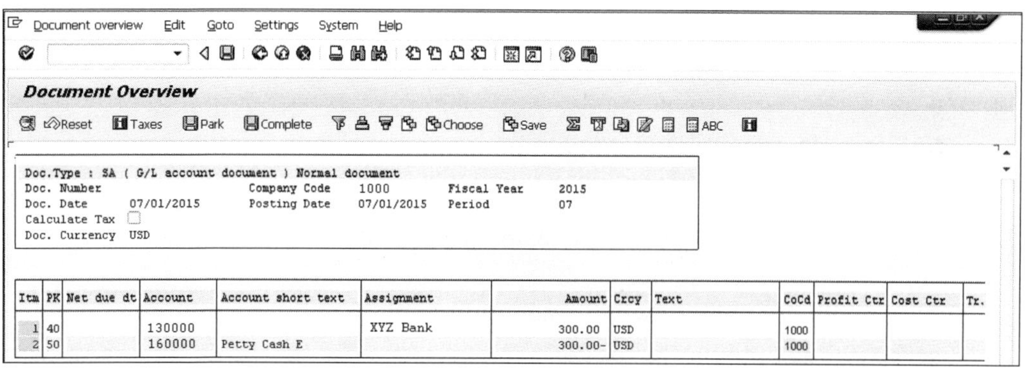

Figure 3.5 Document Overview Screen

After simulation is complete, click the **Post** button to the right of the command field in the upper-left corner of the screen to post the journal voucher, and a message will appear with the new document number, as shown at the bottom of Figure 3.6.

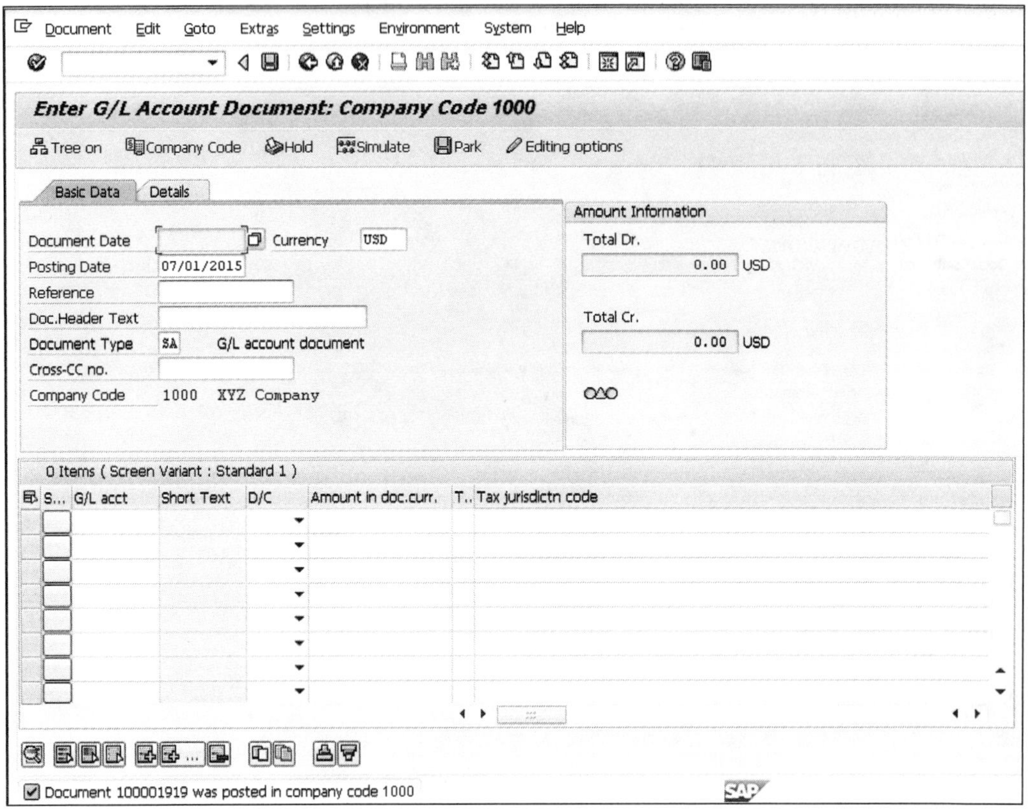

Figure 3.6 Document Posted Message

3.1.2 Post, Park, Save as Complete, and Hold

This section describes the different ways to create G/L accounting documents: post, park, save as complete, and hold. All are universal concepts in Financial Accounting (FI) and therefore aren't unique to journal vouchers and Transaction FB50. However, the discussion of their use is confined to journal vouchers in this section.

Post

Posting a journal voucher was covered in its entirety in Section 3.1.1. A posted document is a G/L document that is considered complete, produces a G/L accounting document number, and updates the G/L account balances.

After a document is posted, the only way to reverse its impact on the G/L account balance is to reverse the document. Reversing G/L documents is covered in Section 3.3.

Park

Document *parking* is a function that allows you to save a G/L document without impacting G/L account balances. This may be necessary if the document is incomplete or if further edits, data validation, or document approval is required prior to posting.

Because parked documents are considered incomplete, they can be changed or deleted. When parked, these G/L documents don't update transaction figures and G/L balances. Moreover, a parked document doesn't go through the extensive entry checks performed on posted documents. Parking only checks whether data exists.

To enter and park a G/L accounting document, use Transaction FV50 or follow application menu path, **Accounting • Financial Accounting • General Ledger • Document Entry • FV50 – Edit or Park G/L Document**, as shown in Figure 3.7.

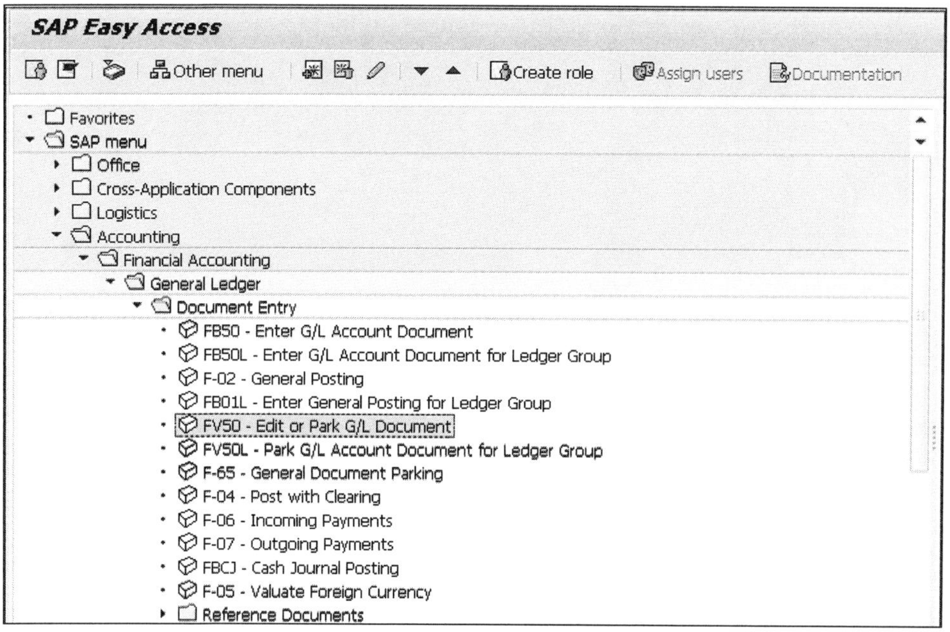

Figure 3.7 Transaction FV50 Menu Path for Park Document

Double-click **FV50 – Edit or Park G/L Document** from the menu path, or enter "FV50" in the **Command** field (as shown in Figure 3.8) and press Enter.

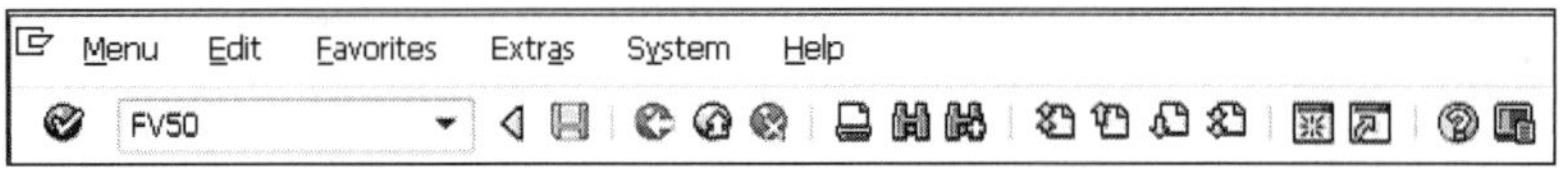

Figure 3.8 Entering "FV50" in the Command Field

The **Park G/L Account Document** entry screen opens (Figure 3.9). The fields that appear on the header with prepopulated values may vary depending on your system configuration and editing options. In this example, the **Document Date** field was manually entered, whereas field values were defaulted for the **Currency**, **Posting Date**, **Document Type**, and **Company Code** fields.

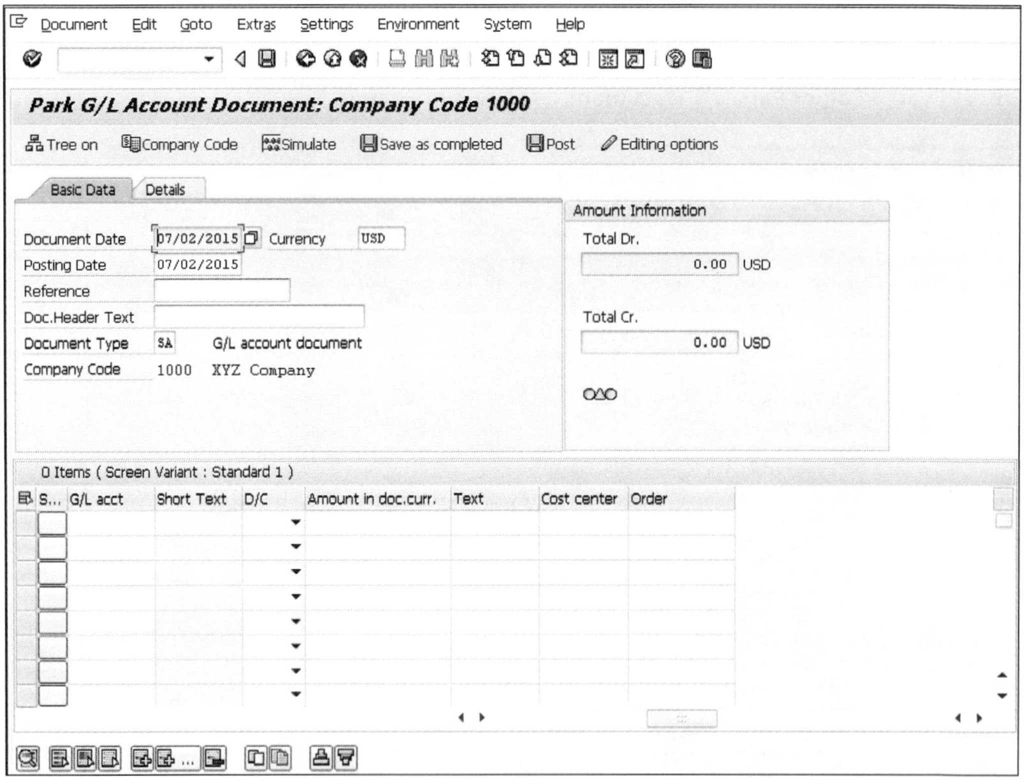

Figure 3.9 Document Park

After inputting values on the header screen, enter at least two separate line items, as shown in Figure 3.10.

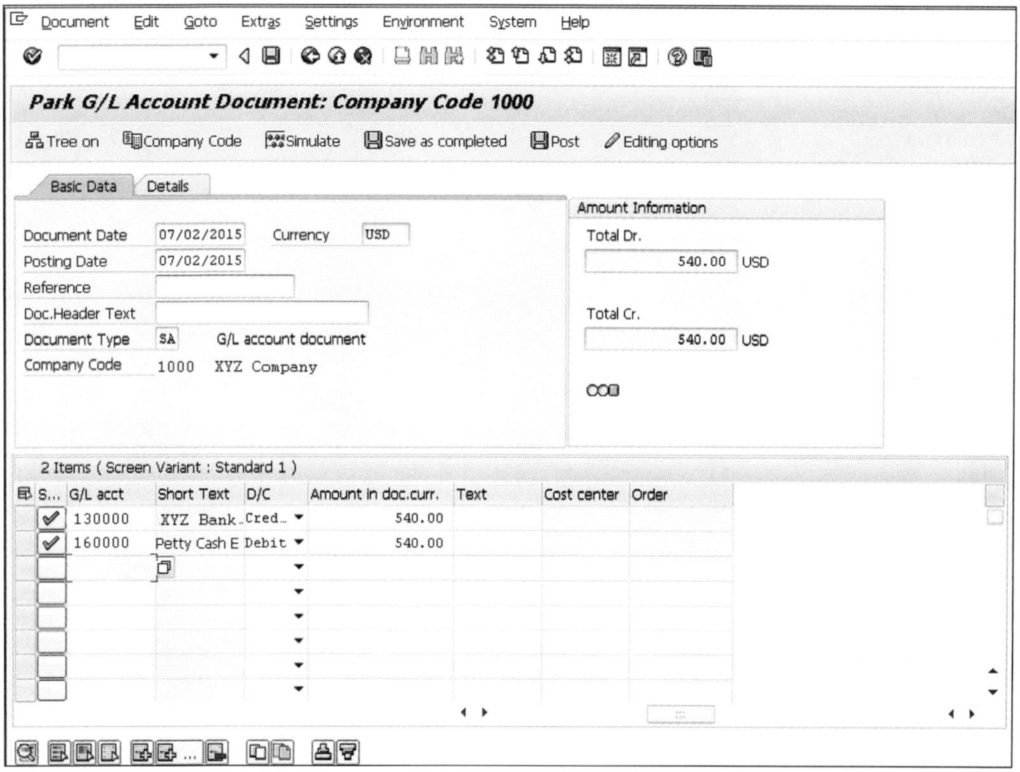

Figure 3.10 Line Items for Document Park

Next, click the **Park** button to the right of the **Command** field in the upper-left area of the screen to park the journal voucher, and a message will appear with the new parked document number, as shown at the bottom of Figure 3.11.

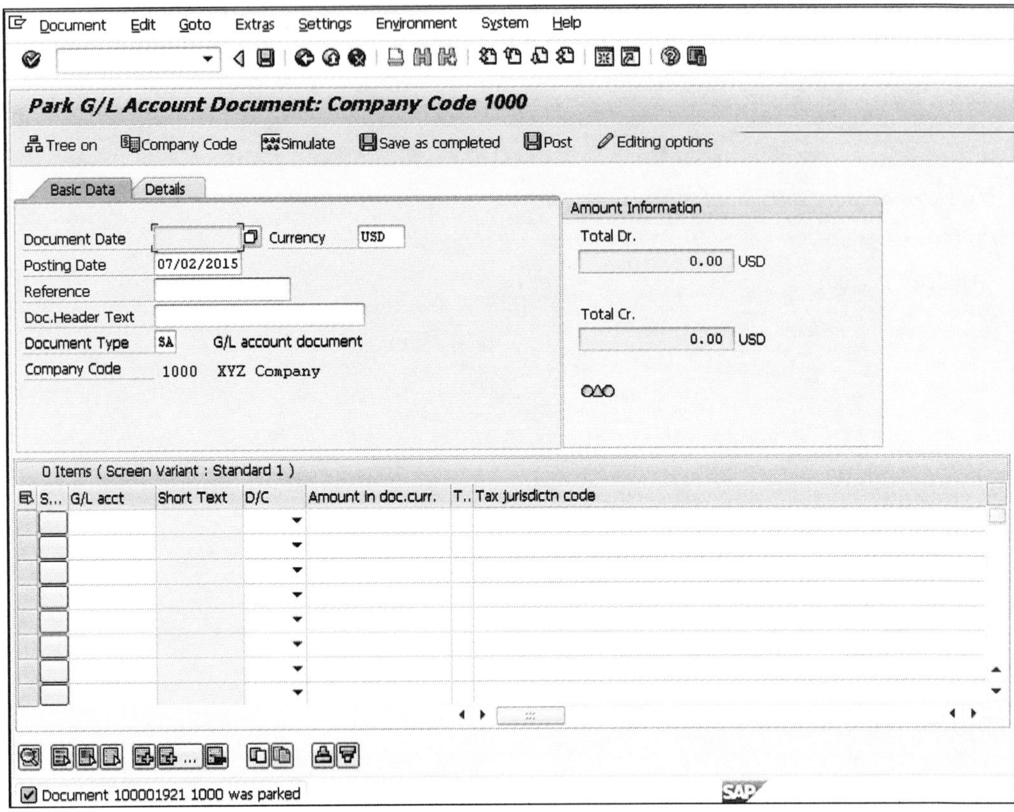

Figure 3.11 Document Parked Message

Save as Completed

The *save as completed* function is similar to document parking but with some key distinctions. When you save a document as completed, the system goes through more extensive document logic checks, just as if the document were being posted. Like parked documents, however, documents that are saved as completed can be edited and changed prior to posting.

Although the park and save as completed functions are similar, save as completed generally should be used when you're sure the document is accurate and complete and only needs final approval before being posted.

To save a G/L accounting document as completed, use Transaction FV50 or follow application menu path, **Accounting • Financial Accounting • General Ledger • Document Entry • FV50 – Edit or Park G/L Document**, as shown in Figure 3.12.

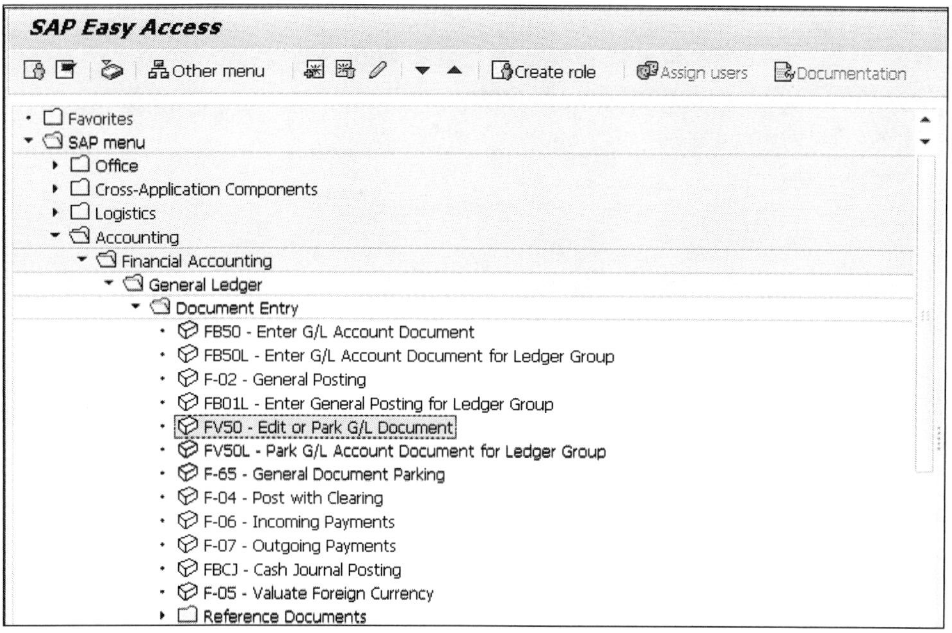

Figure 3.12 Transaction FV50 Menu Path for Save as Completed

Double-click **FV50 – Edit or Park G/L Document** from the menu path, or enter "FV50" in the **Command** field (as shown in Figure 3.13) and press [Enter].

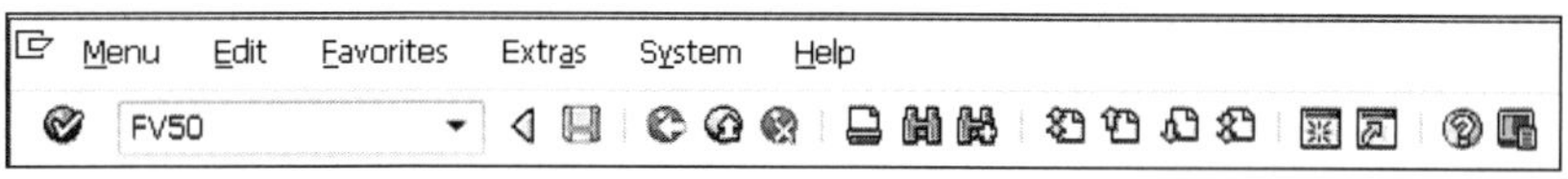

Figure 3.13 Entering "FV50" in the Command Field

The **Park G/L Account Document** entry screen opens (Figure 3.14). The fields that appear on the header with prepopulated values may vary depending on your system configuration and editing options. In this example, the **Document Date** field was manually entered, whereas field values were defaulted for the **Currency**, **Posting Date**, **Document Type**, and **Company Code** fields.

After inputting values on the **Park G/L Account Document** header screen, enter at least two separate line items, as shown in Figure 3.15.

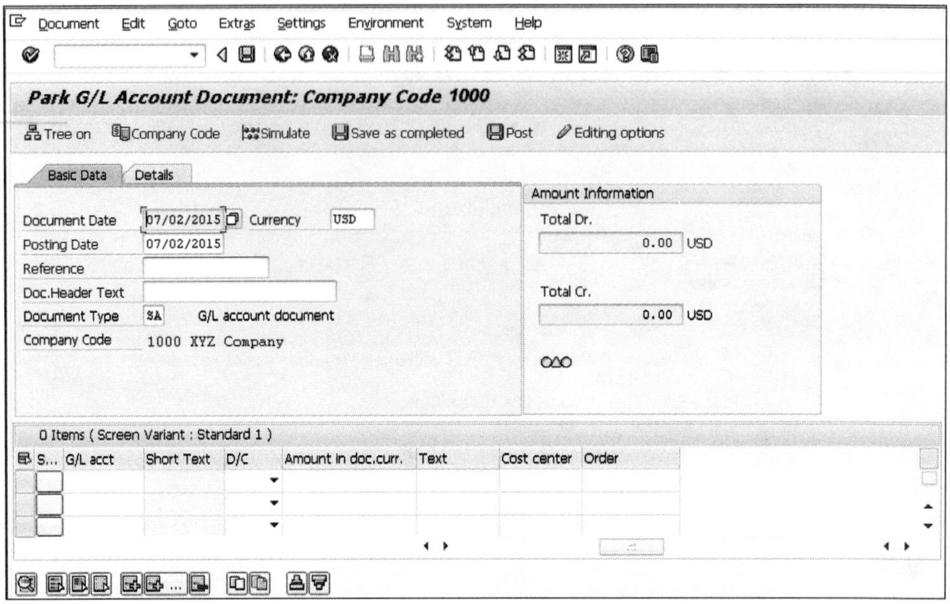

Figure 3.14 Document Save as Completed

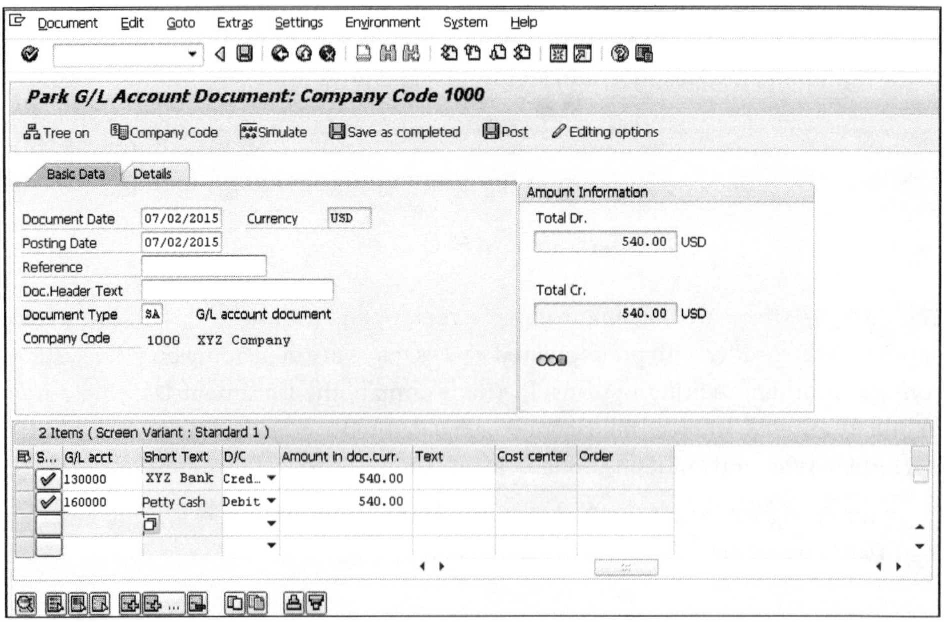

Figure 3.15 Line Items for Save as Completed Document

Now, click the **Save as completed** button at the top-center portion of the screen to save the journal voucher as completed, and a message will appear with the new document number, as shown in Figure 3.16.

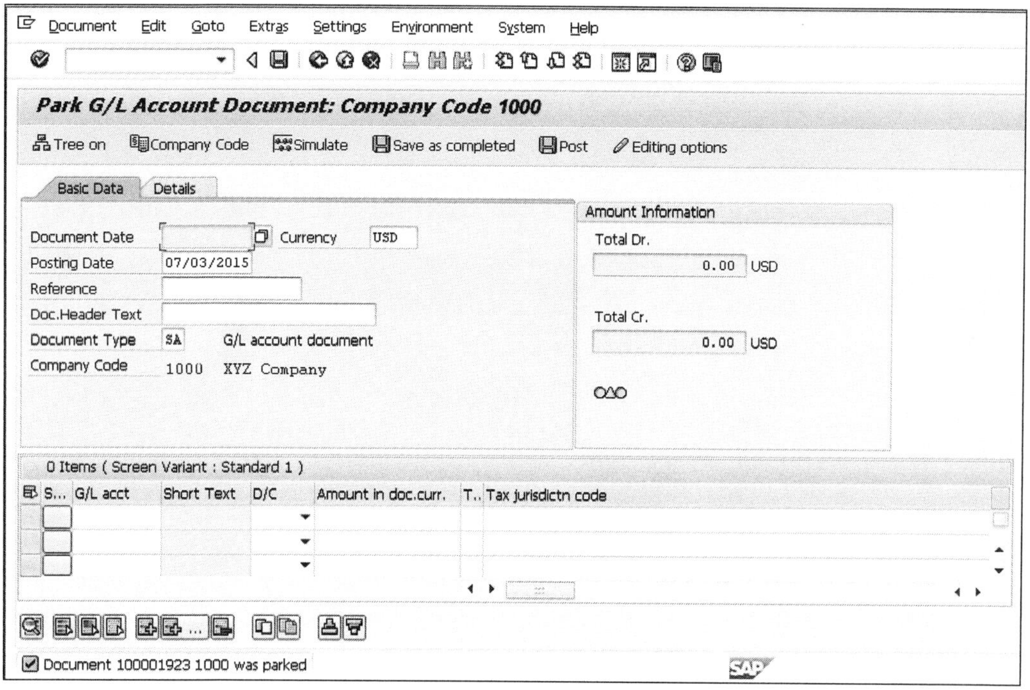

Figure 3.16 Document Parked Message for Save as Completed

Hold

Document *hold* is a function that temporarily saves your data. It's most useful when interrupted during document creation. Because held documents are temporary, they don't update G/L transactions and balances. Furthermore, in subsequent processing, they can be edited, deleted, parked, or posted. Unlike post, park, and save as completed, the hold function produces no permanent document number until the document is parked or posted.

To hold a G/L accounting document, use Transaction FB50 or application menu path, **Accounting • Financial Accounting • General Ledger • Document Entry • FB50 – Enter G/L Account Document**, as shown in Figure 3.17.

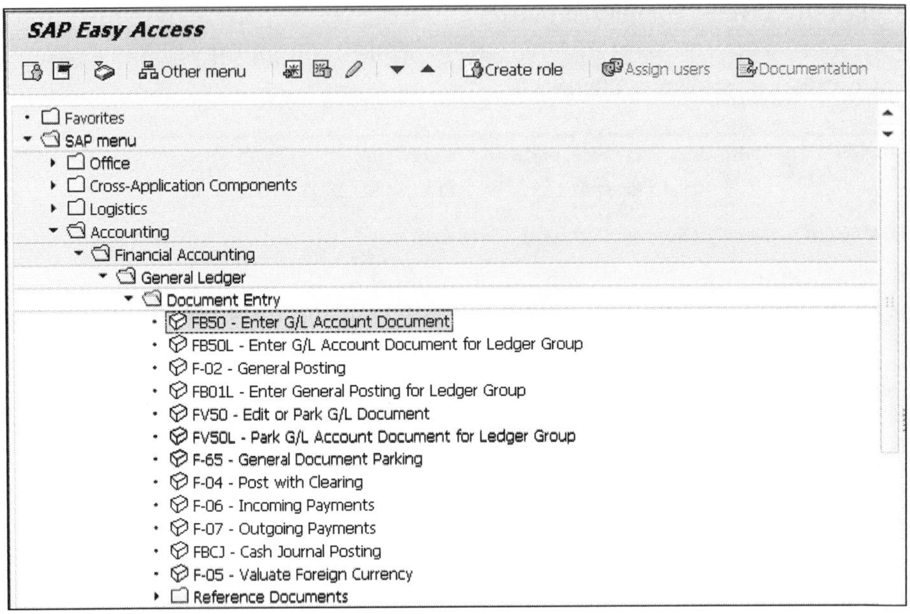

Figure 3.17 Transaction FB50 Menu Path for Document Hold

Double-click **FB50 – Enter G/L Account Document** from the menu path, or enter "FB50" in the **Command** field (as shown in Figure 3.18) and press Enter.

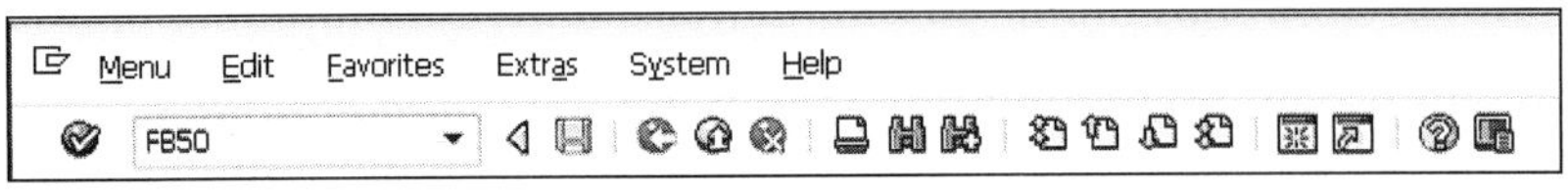

Figure 3.18 Entering "FB50" in the Command Field

You can use the hold function at any point in Transaction FB50, regardless of how much or little information has been entered because no system checks take place in holding documents.

In the example shown in Figure 3.19, the **Document Date** field has been entered, along with one complete line item. In the screen header, field values were prepopulated for the **Currency**, **Posting Date**, **Document Type**, and **Company Code** fields.

At any point, you can hold a document by pressing F5 or selecting **Document • Hold** from the menu bar, as shown in Figure 3.20.

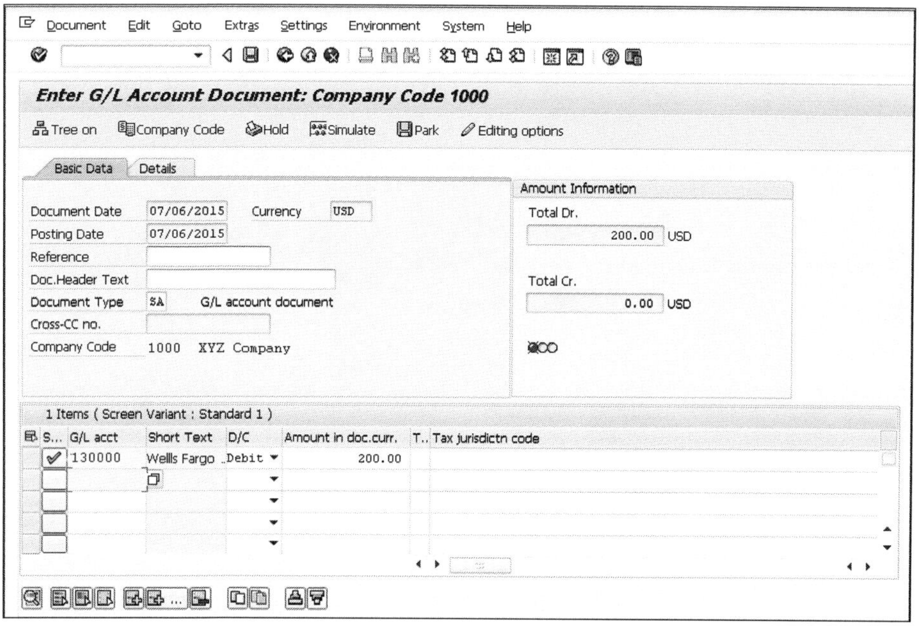

Figure 3.19 Document Hold

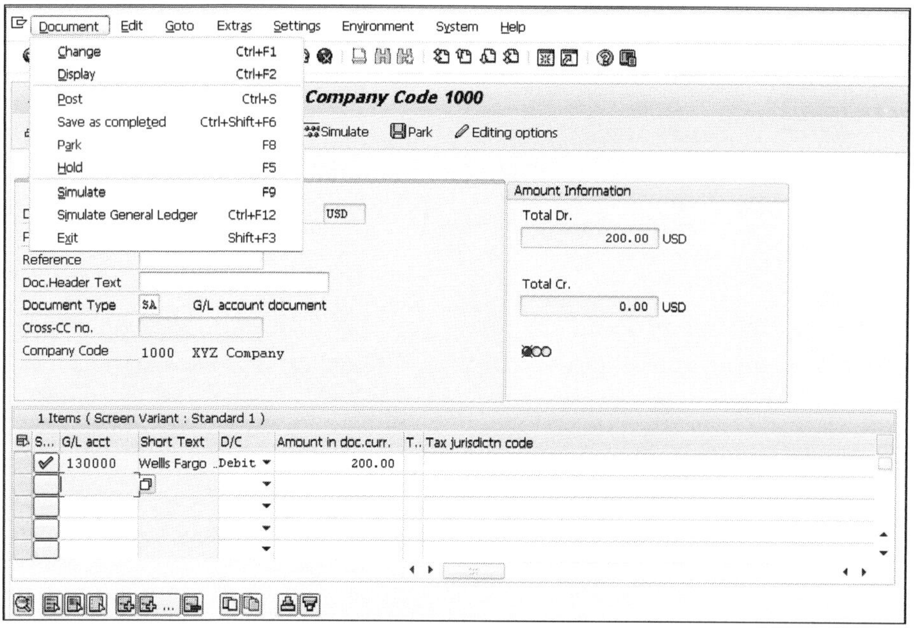

Figure 3.20 Document Hold Dropdown Menu

A **Hold Document** popup appears (Figure 3.21) and prompts you to enter a 10-character preliminary temporary document number, which can contain numbers, letters, and/or special characters. A permanent number is assigned when the document is posted, parked, or saved as complete.

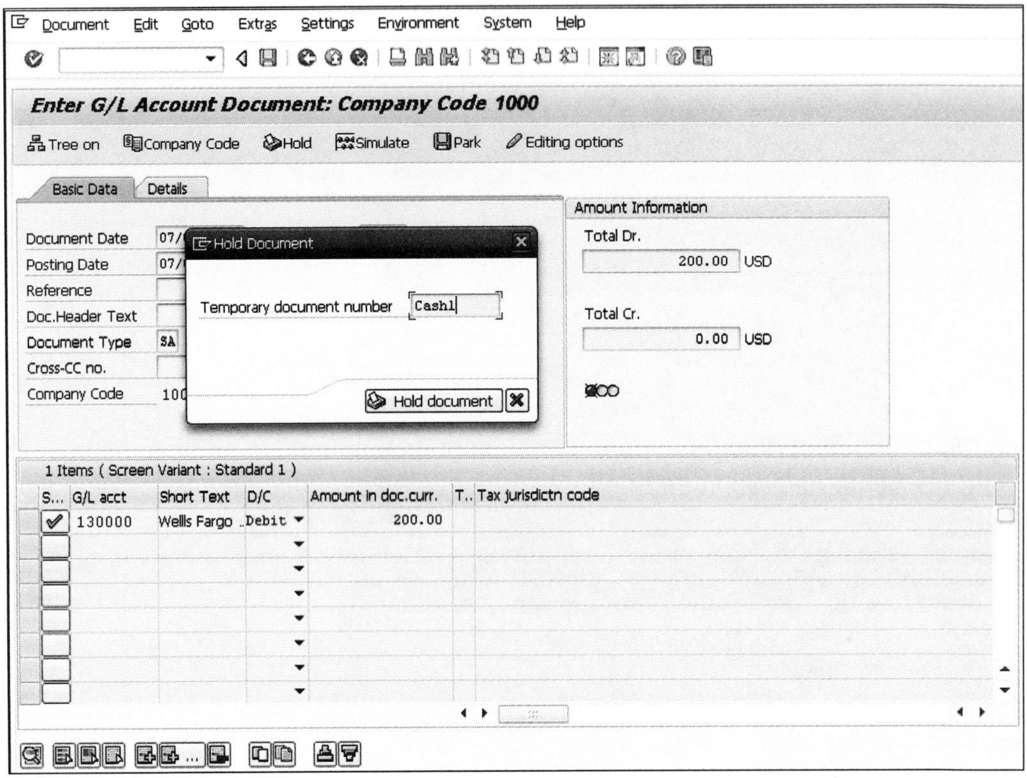

Figure 3.21 Temporary Document Number Prompt

After entering a temporary document number, press Enter, or click the **Hold document** button to create a temporary accounting document, and a message will appear with the held document number, as shown in Figure 3.22.

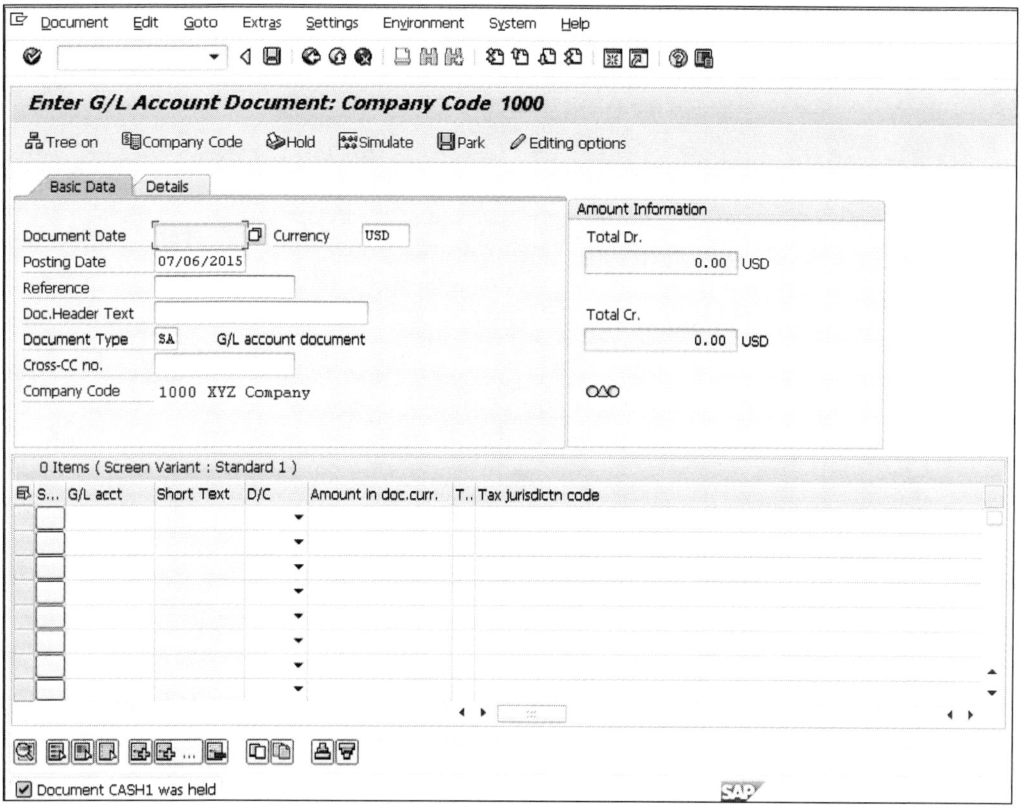

Figure 3.22 Document Held Message

3.1.3 Tree Display

The *tree display* provides an easy-to-use visual display for several functions that can also be accessed from the dropdown menu in Transaction FB50. The tree display is a universal concept, or shortcut, for accessing accounting documents and document entry tools in FI. In this section, we'll confine the discussion of the tree display to Transaction FB50 and Transaction FV50, but this capability can be used in any financial transaction in which the tree display appears.

The tree display is a toggle function, meaning that it can be turned on (i.e., made visible) or turned off (i.e., made invisible) with the click of a button or keyboard combination.

Figure 3.23 shows Transaction FB50 with the tree display on.

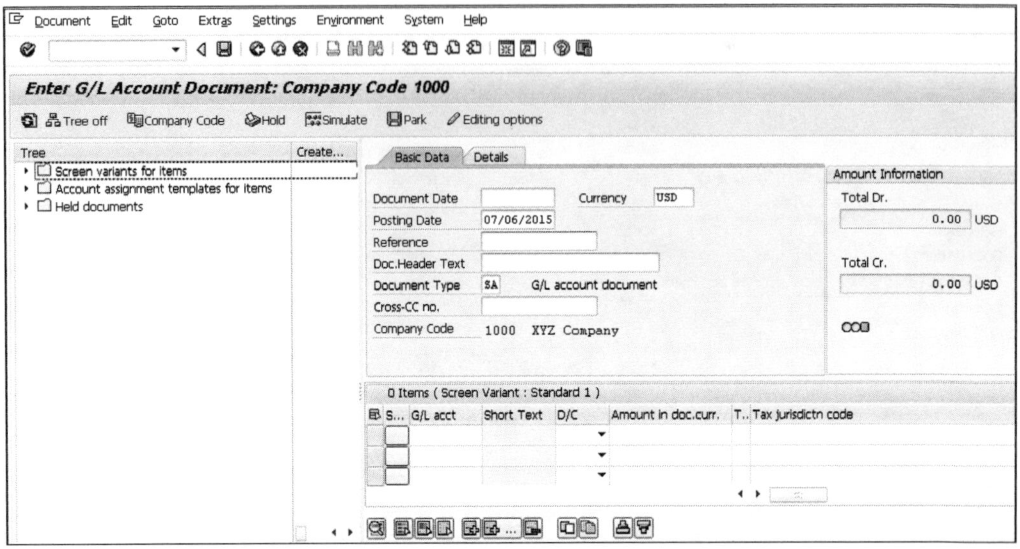

Figure 3.23 Tree Display On (Transaction FB50)

Note that the tree display panel lists folders on the left of the screen. The folders that appear in the display vary by transaction code. In Transaction FB50, you'll see the following folders:

- **Screen variants for items**
- **Account assignment templates for items**
- **Held documents**

Screen variants and account assignment templates are covered in detail in Section 3.1.4. For now, know that screen variants and account assignment templates are accessible from the tree display.

In Section 3.1.2, you learned how to hold a G/L document. Held documents can be shown in the tree display by clicking the triangle to the left of the **Held Documents** folder. This action opens the folder and displays all the held documents created by the user. Moreover, if you double-click a held document in the tree display, the details appear in the G/L document entry screen (as shown in Figure 3.24), which allows you to resume entering the document.

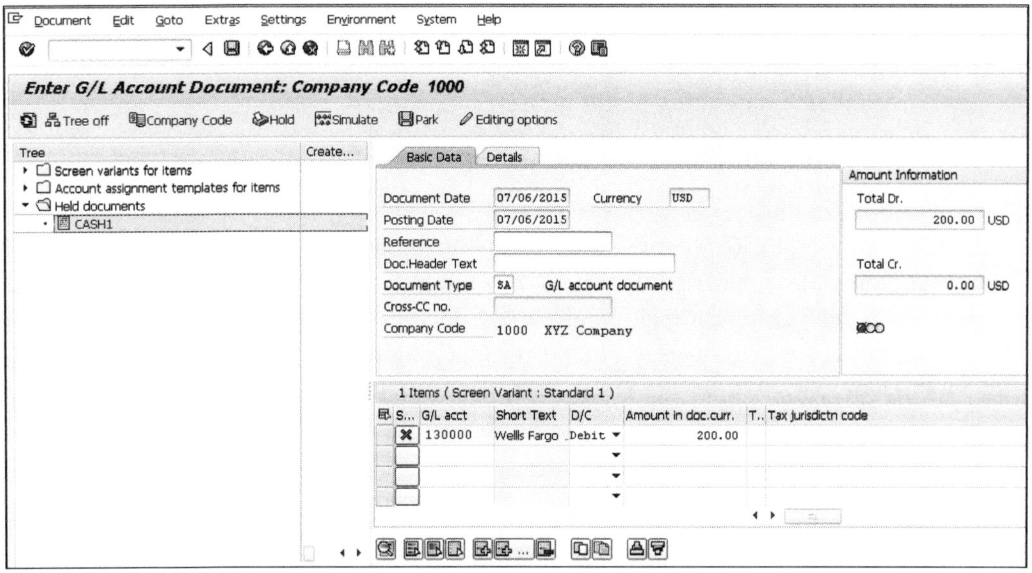

Figure 3.24 Held Document in Tree Display (Transaction FB50)

The tree display function in Transaction FV50 is the same as in Transaction FB50. It has the same toggle capability, meaning that it can be turned on (i.e., made visible) or turned off (i.e., hidden) with the click of a button or by a keyboard combination.

Figure 3.25 shows Transaction FV50 with the tree display on.

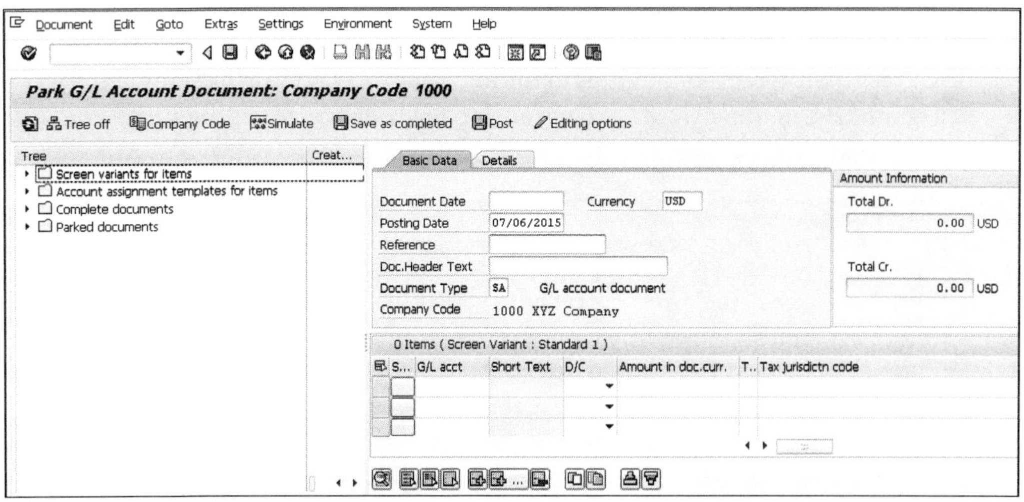

Figure 3.25 Tree Display On (Transaction FV50)

In Transaction FV50, you'll see the following folders:

- **Screen variants for items**
- **Account assignment templates for items**
- **Complete documents**
- **Parked documents**

In Transaction FV50's tree display, folders for screen variants and account assignment templates appear at the top, as they did in Transaction FB50. The display also includes folders for complete and parked documents, which didn't appear in the Transaction FB50 tree display. Finally, the folder for held documents, which appeared in Transaction FB50, doesn't appear in Transaction FV50. As you can see, the tree display default folders will vary depending on the purpose of the transaction.

3.1.4 Using Screen Variants and Account Assignment Templates

Screen variants and *account assignment templates* are tools available in FI to simplify entry of G/L documents. Although they aren't unique to Transaction FB50, in this section, we'll confine our discussion of these tools to this transaction. Note that both screen variants and account assignment templates can be accessed and maintained from the tree display in Transaction FB50 and from the dropdown menu. In this section, we'll focus on using the tree display, which is the most user-friendly and frequently used method of access.

Use of Screen Variants

A screen variant sets the columns in the line item entry portion of Transaction FB50 (Figure 3.26). In other words, it controls the fields displayed on the screen and the order in which they appear.

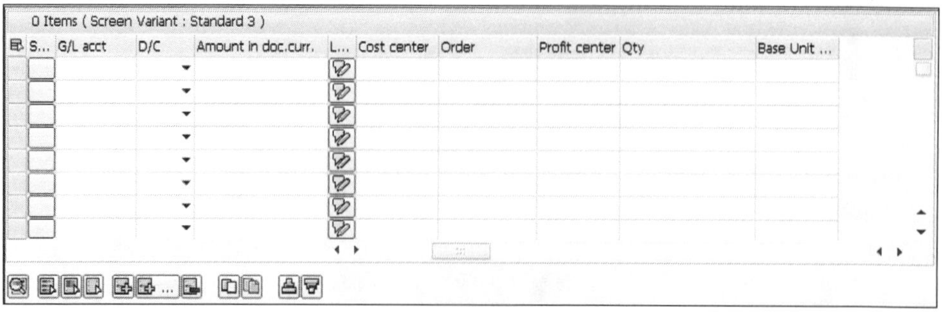

Figure 3.26 Line Entry Screen

A well-developed screen variant reduces the data entry time and the number of data entry errors. Your goal is to have only the fields you need to enter visible on the screen.

Transaction FB50 has a default screen variant assigned, which is displayed each time you execute the transaction. However, the default may not be your preferred line item entry screen, or you may prefer different screen variants depending on the type of journal voucher you're creating. Through the tree display or the dropdown menu in Transaction FB50, you can select different screen variants at any time.

Let's look at screen variants in action. Go to Transaction FB50, and make sure the tree display is on (refer to Section 3.1.3). Click the triangle next to the **Screen variants for items** folder to open a list of available variants to choose from (Figure 3.27).

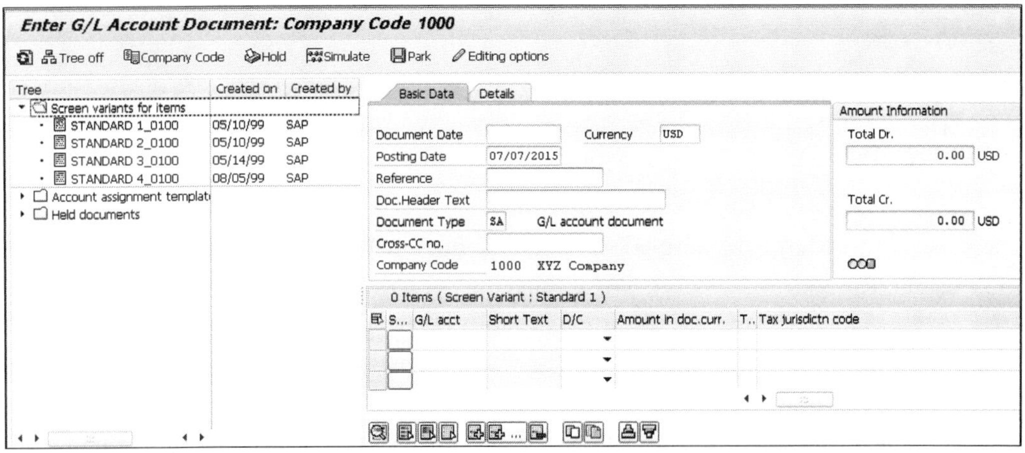

Figure 3.27 Screen Variant List

Double-click the screen variant you want to use (Figure 3.28), and the line layout at the bottom right of the screen will change.

> **Note**
>
> Discussion of the creation and maintenance of screen variants is beyond the scope of this book. It's important to note, however, that screen variants are considered *cross-client dependent*, meaning that if a screen variant change is made in one client, the change is reflected in every other client within that instance of SAP. For this reason, screen variant creation and maintenance is a function usually restricted to an SAP support team.

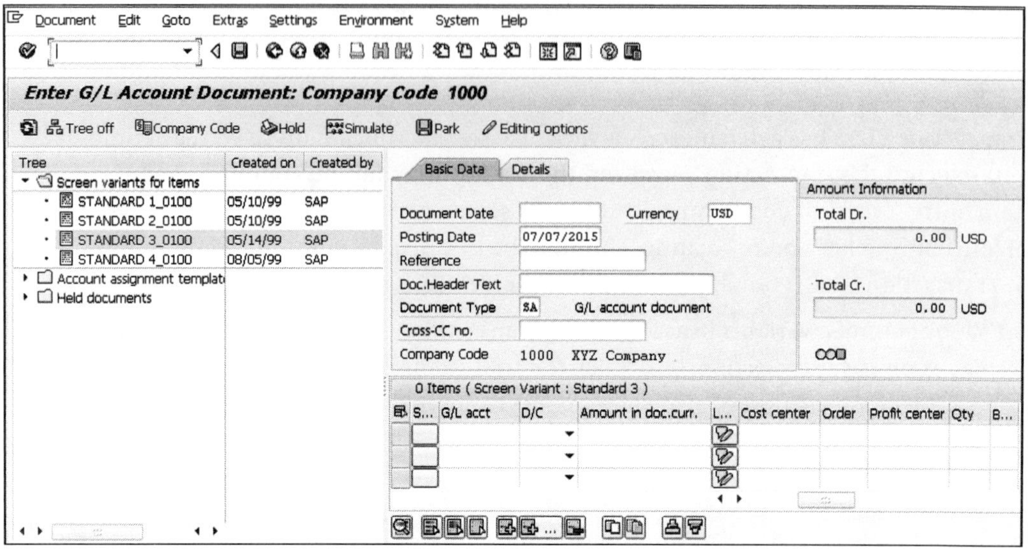

Figure 3.28 Screen Variant Selection

Use of Account Assignment Templates

Account assignment templates are line layouts in Transaction FB50 with prepopulated field values. They are useful for reducing data entry requirements for certain types of journal vouchers that are frequently created and consistent in their makeup. These templates allow you to quickly enter journal vouchers without the hassle of reentering all the necessary field values each time you create a new entry.

The next time you find yourself entering a journal voucher from scratch that you've created repeatedly in the past, consider creating an account assignment template for it. You might simplify your life by doing so, especially for journal vouchers with many line items.

Let's take a look. Go to Transaction FB50, and make sure the tree display is on (refer to Section 3.1.3). Click the triangle next to the **Account assignment template for items** folder to open a list of available templates to choose from (Figure 3.29).

Double-click the template you want to use (Figure 3.30), and the line layout in the line item entry screen will change based on the prepopulated values contained in the template. Note that you can add or edit the field values at this point.

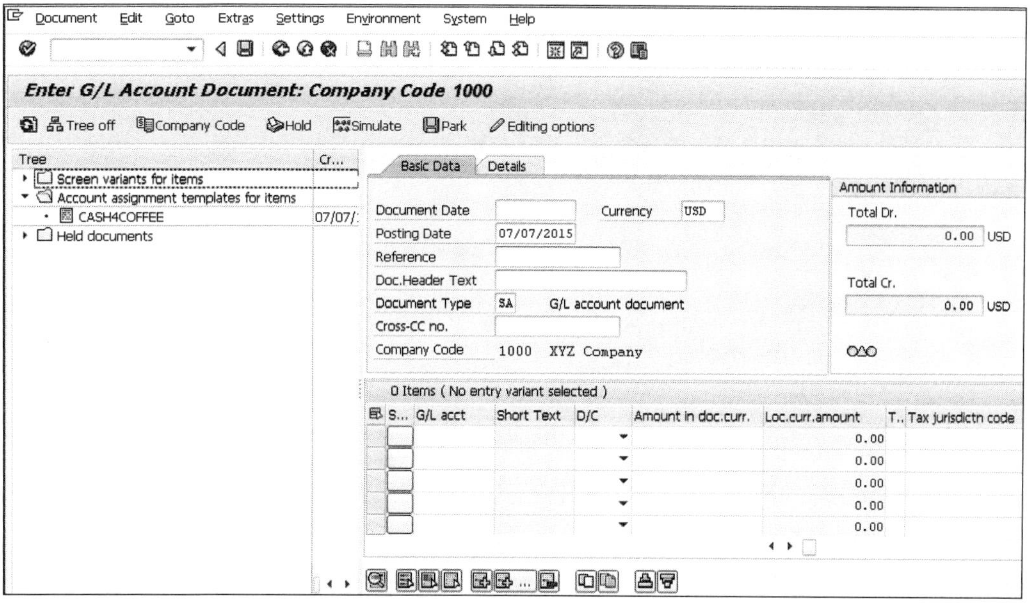

Figure 3.29 Account Assignment Templates List

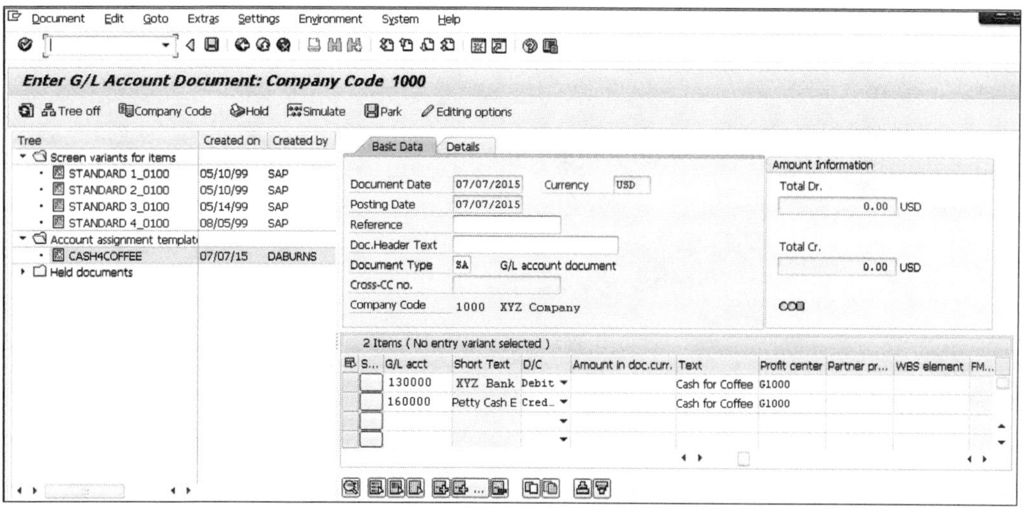

Figure 3.30 Account Assignment Template Selection

As you see in our example, account assignment template **CASH4COFFEE** contains prepopulated values for the **G/L acct**, **D/C** (debit/credit indicator), **Text**, and **Profit center** fields. With all other fields for the transaction prepopulated, you simply need to enter values in the **Amount in doc.curr.** fields to complete the document entry (Figure 3.31).

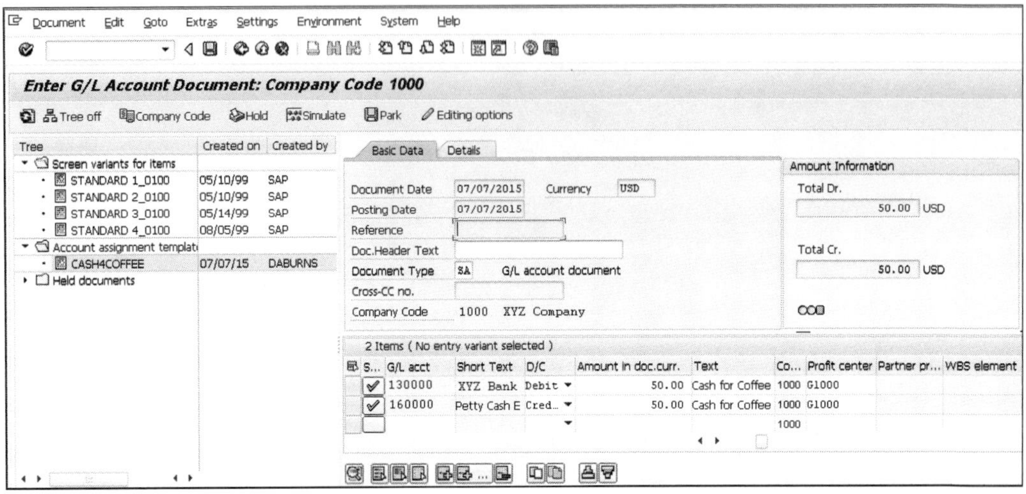

Figure 3.31 Amount Entered with Account Assignment Template

With document entry complete, you can post, park, or save this G/L journal voucher as completed (refer to Section 3.1.2). For the current example, we posted the document (Figure 3.32).

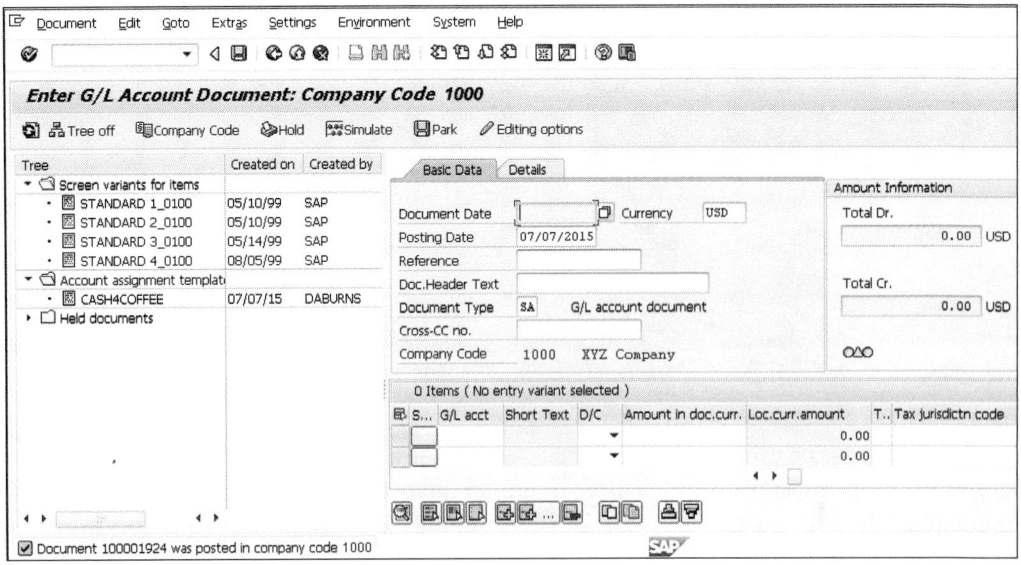

Figure 3.32 Posted Document Using Account Assignment Template

3.1.5 Controlling Document Entry with Editing Options

Controlling document entry with editing options allows you to make user-specific settings for transactions in accounting. Editing options give you some level of field control over the entry screen, what is displayed, and values that are defaulted. Some editing options determine the interpretation of certain field entry values.

Editing options are universal in FI, but discussion in this section is limited to their use in Transaction FB50. The settings you make are user-specific, not transaction-specific; therefore, after you've set an editing option in Transaction FB50, it will also apply to other accounting transactions, such as Transactions FB60 and FB70.

In this section, we'll discuss some of the most commonly used settings and provide a complete list of all editing options and their descriptions (see Table 3.1 later in this section).

To access editing options from Transaction FB50 (Figure 3.33), click the **Editing options** button in the top center of the **Enter G/L Account Document** screen, or press Shift+F4.

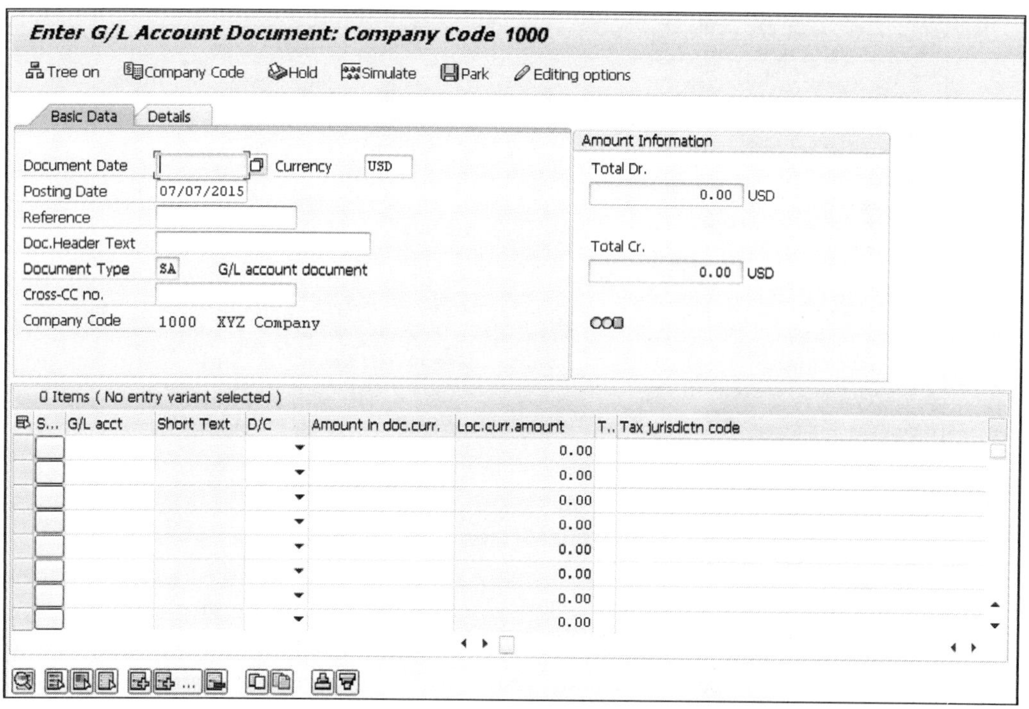

Figure 3.33 Enter G/L Account Document: Editing Options

The **Accounting Editing Options** screen opens (Figure 3.34). Editing options fall into four general categories, each with its own area of the screen:

- **General Entry Options**
- **Special options for single screen transactions**
- **Default document currency**
- **Default Company Code**

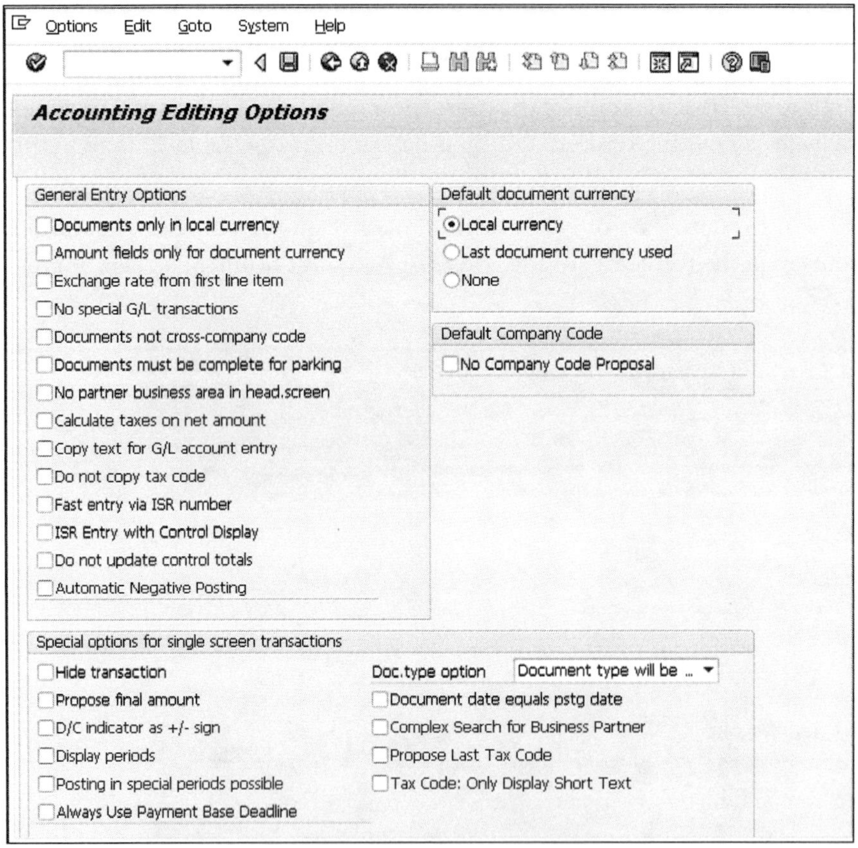

Figure 3.34 Accounting Editing Options Screen

In the upper-right corner of Figure 3.34, you can see that the **Local currency** radio button is selected in the **Default document currency** section. With this setting, the local currency of the company code to which the user is assigned will default into Transaction FB50.

For this example, we'll change **Default document currency** to **None** (Figure 3.35). This might be necessary if you process most of your accounting entries in different currencies, as may be the case if you work for a multinational company with centralized accounting functions.

After your selection is made, click the **Save** button, or press Ctrl+S.

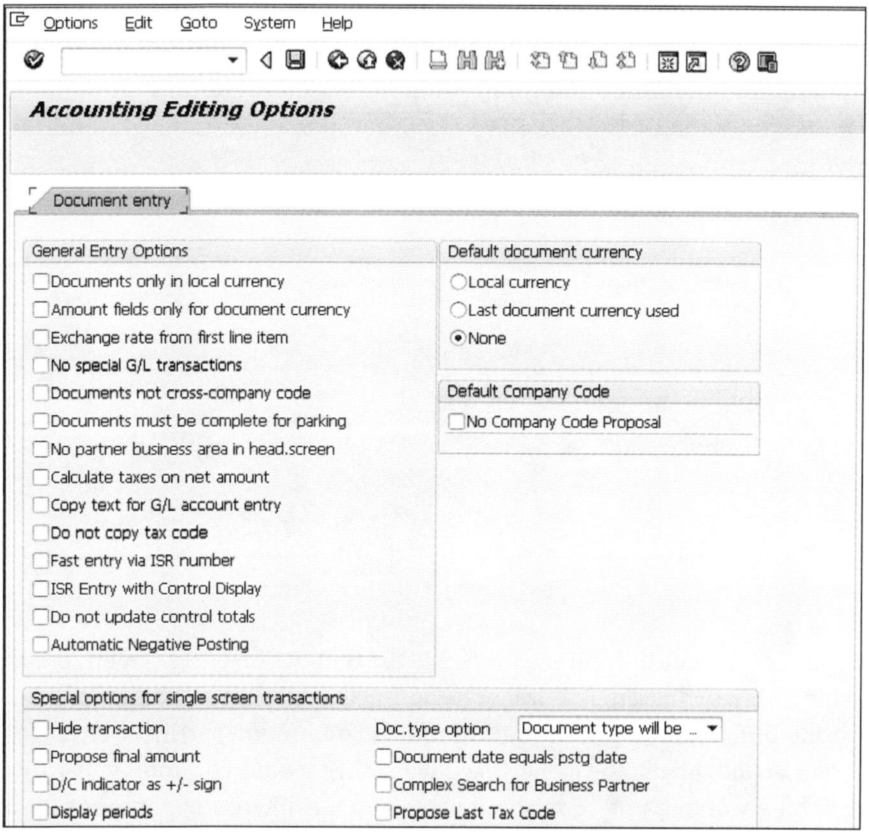

Figure 3.35 Accounting Editing Options with No Default Currency

Now, return to Transaction FB50, and you'll see that the **Currency** field in the header is blank (Figure 3.36), demonstrating that no value defaulted into the **Currency** field.

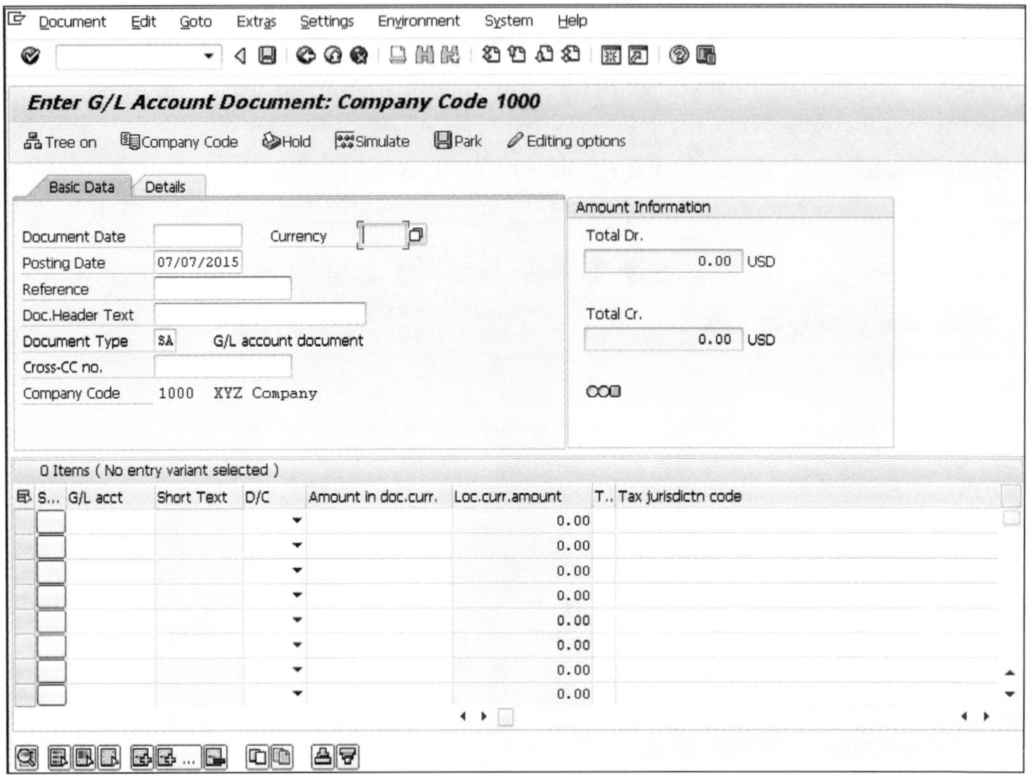

Figure 3.36 Enter G/L Account Document Screen with No Currency

Similarly, you can use editing options to change the transaction entry screen so that no company code is proposed. This might be desirable if you enter transactions frequently using different company codes. If your accounting department manages financial transactions across the globe, this is likely the case. It's common to use this setting for those working in a centralized accounting or finance department for a multinational company.

For this example, select the **No Company Code Proposal** checkbox in the **Default Company Code** area of the **Accounting Editing Options** screen (Figure 3.37). Then, click the **Save** button, or press Ctrl+S.

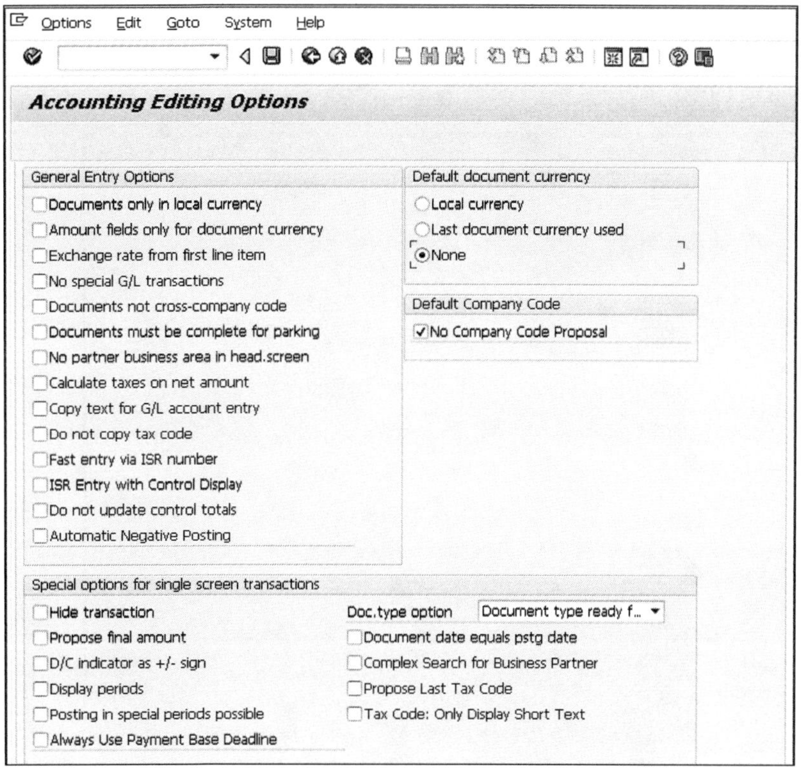

Figure 3.37 Accounting Editing Options with No Company Code Proposed

Now, return to Transaction FB50; you're immediately prompted to enter a **Company Code** (Figure 3.38).

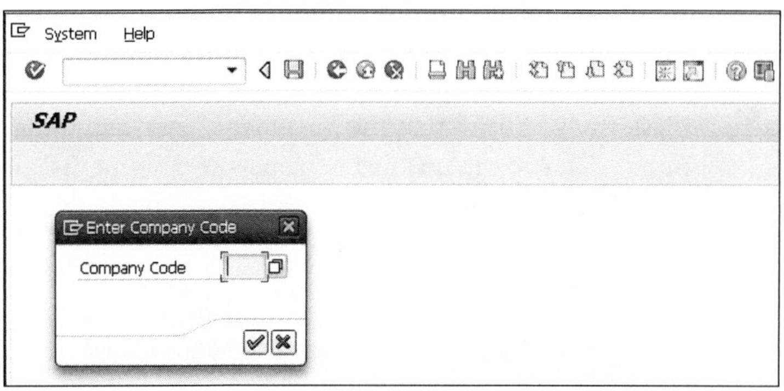

Figure 3.38 Prompt for Company Code

Another common use of editing options is to change the document type setting. For this example, change the **Doc.type Option** field to **Document type hidden** (Figure 3.39). Then, click the **Save** button, or press Ctrl+S.

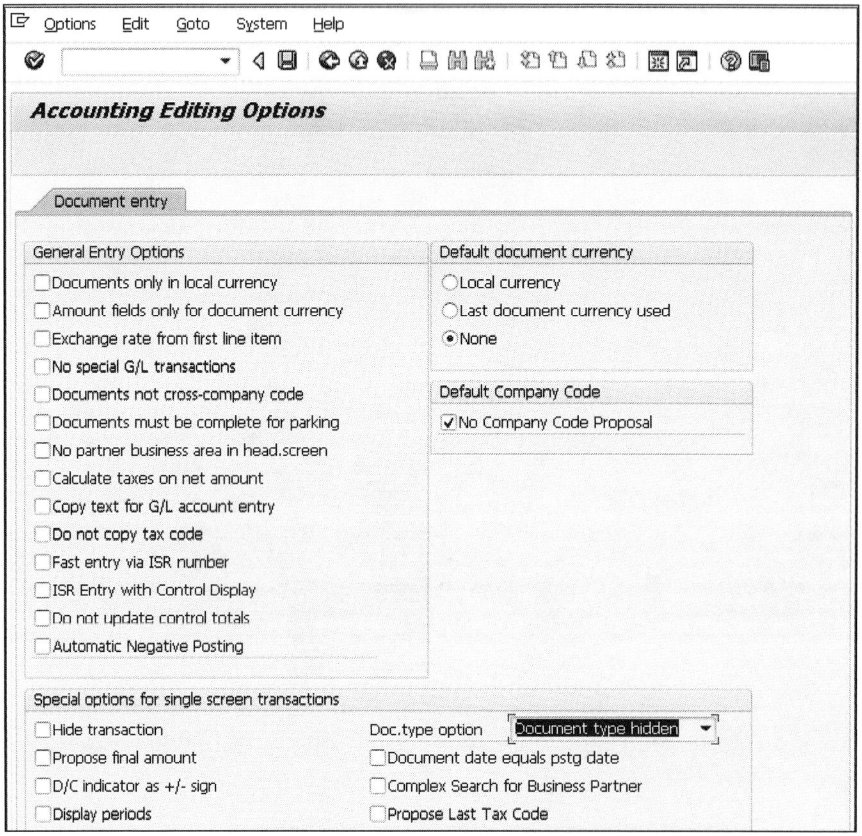

Figure 3.39 Accounting Editing Options with Hidden Document Type

Now, return to Transaction FB50, and you'll see that the **Document Type** field is hidden from view (Figure 3.40). As a result, you can no longer change the document type used in this transaction. This is a control feature, forcing users to use only one document type.

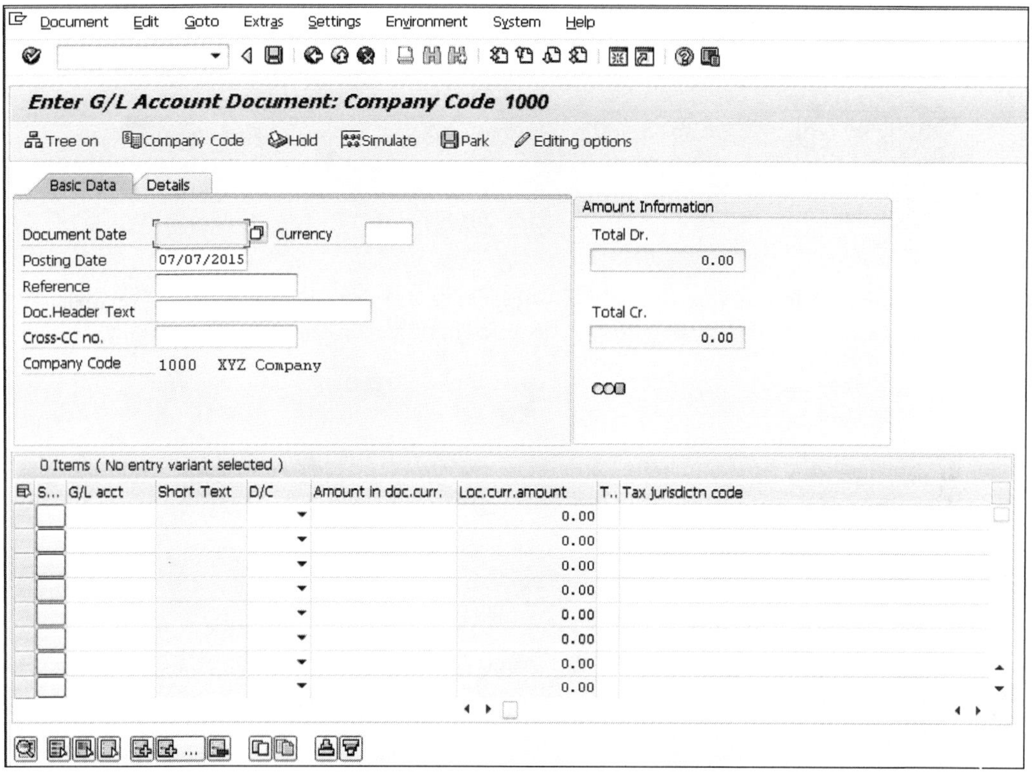

Figure 3.40 Enter G/L Account Document Screen with Hidden Document Type

The preceding examples demonstrated just a few of the editing options available to you. For a complete understanding of all the options available, see Table 3.1, which provides a complete list of editing options for controlling document entry, along with their descriptions.

Editing Option	Description
Documents only in local currency	Only allows entry of documents in local currency
Amount fields only for document currency	Only allows entry amounts in foreign currency when entering documents in foreign currency
Exchange rate from first line item	Corrects exchange rate in the document header automatically using the amounts in the first line item when posting foreign currency documents

Table 3.1 Editing Options and Descriptions

Editing Option	Description
No special G/L transactions	Prevents entry of special G/L transactions
Documents not cross-company code	Prevents entry of cross-company codes
Documents must be complete for parking	Prevents incomplete documents from being parked
No partner business area in head.screen	Prevents default partner business area from being entered in the document header
Calculate taxes on net amount	Indicates the G/L account amounts entered are net of taxes
Copy text for G/L account entry	Automatically copies text from last G/L line item to subsequent line items
Do not copy tax code	Deactivates the setting that the last tax code entered is automatically copied to G/L account line items
Fast entry via ISR number	Enables the fast entry of incoming invoices using the ISR subscriber number
ISR Entry with Control Display	Provides the ability to enter an alternative vendor number in cases in which several vendors may have the same ISR number
Do not update control totals	Prevents control totals from being updated
Automatic Negative Posting	Makes any automatically generated lines negative postings when the negative postings indicator is set for at least one manually entered line
Default document currency	▪ **Local currency**: Defaults local currency used in header currency field ▪ **Last document currency used**: Defaults last currency used in header currency field ▪ **None**: Defaults no currency in the header currency field

Table 3.1 Editing Options and Descriptions (Cont.)

Editing Option	Description
Default Company Code	Forces manual selection of the company code to be used when the **No Company Code Proposal** checkbox is selected
Hide transaction	Hides the **Transaction** field on the entry screen
Propose final amount	Proposes the final invoice amount in the customer or vendor line, after a G/L line has been entered
D/C indicator as +/- sign	Allows the entry of +/- sign with amounts, which derives the debit/credit indicator
Display periods	Enables the display of periods on the entry screen under basic data
Posting in special periods possible	Enables the period field for data input
Always use payment base deadline	Only permits payment deadline calculation based on the baseline date
Doc.type option	▪ Display document type in header ▪ Document type ready for input ▪ Display document type using short name ▪ Document type ready for input using short name ▪ Document type hidden
Document date equals pstg date	Defaults the document date from the posting date
Complex Search for Business Partner	Specifies if a complex search is possible for the number of the trading partner when entering a vendor invoice
Propose Last Tax Code	Proposes the last tax code used the next time the transaction is called
Tax Code: only display short text	Changes the tax code dropdown list in the transaction to only display the short text of the tax code

Table 3.1 Editing Options and Descriptions (Cont.)

3.1.6 Post with Reference

Post with reference is a quick and easy way to create a new G/L document by replicating all or most of the accounting data from a document that has already been posted.

It allows you to quickly create a new G/L account document based on an existing, previously posted document, with little to no additional data entry required.

In many ways, this option works much like a document copy function, except that SAP provides several flow control indicators that allow you to select specific actions in the process. For example, there is a **Do not propose amounts** flow control indicator. When this indicator is selected, you must enter document line item amounts manually. Without this indicator, you could only use the post with reference function to post a new document with the exact same amount as the reference document.

Post with reference is a universal concept in FI, but the scope of our discussion in this section is limited to its use in Transaction FB50. We'll demonstrate its use with a simple example and then provide a complete list of flow control options and their descriptions (see Table 3.2 later in this section).

Post with reference can be used when you enter a G/L accounting document via Transaction FB50 or application menu path, **Accounting • Financial Accounting • General Ledger • Document Entry • FB50 – Enter G/L Account Document** (see Figure 3.41).

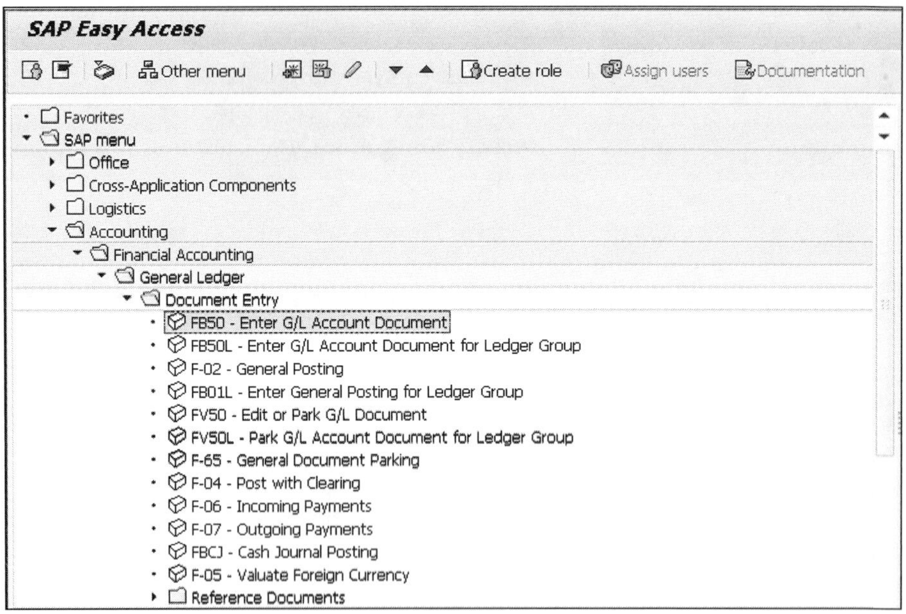

Figure 3.41 Transaction FB50 Application Menu Path

Double-click **FB50 – Enter G/L Account Document** from the menu path, or enter "FB50" in the **Command** field (as shown in Figure 3.42) and press [Enter].

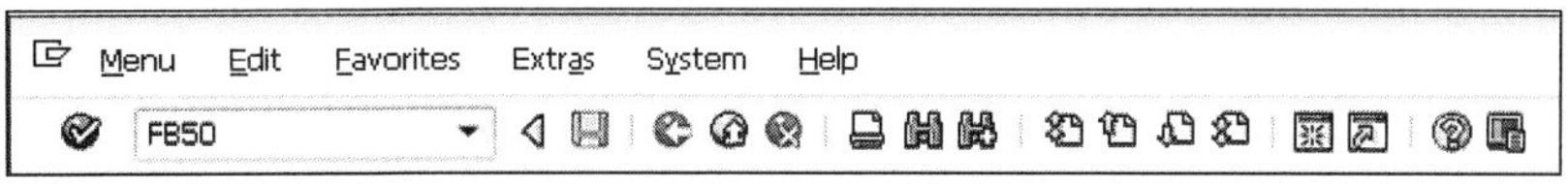

Figure 3.42 Entering "FB50" in the Command Field

From the **Enter G/L Account Document** entry screen, choose the **Goto • Post with reference** dropdown menu option or press [Shift]+[F9] (Figure 3.43).

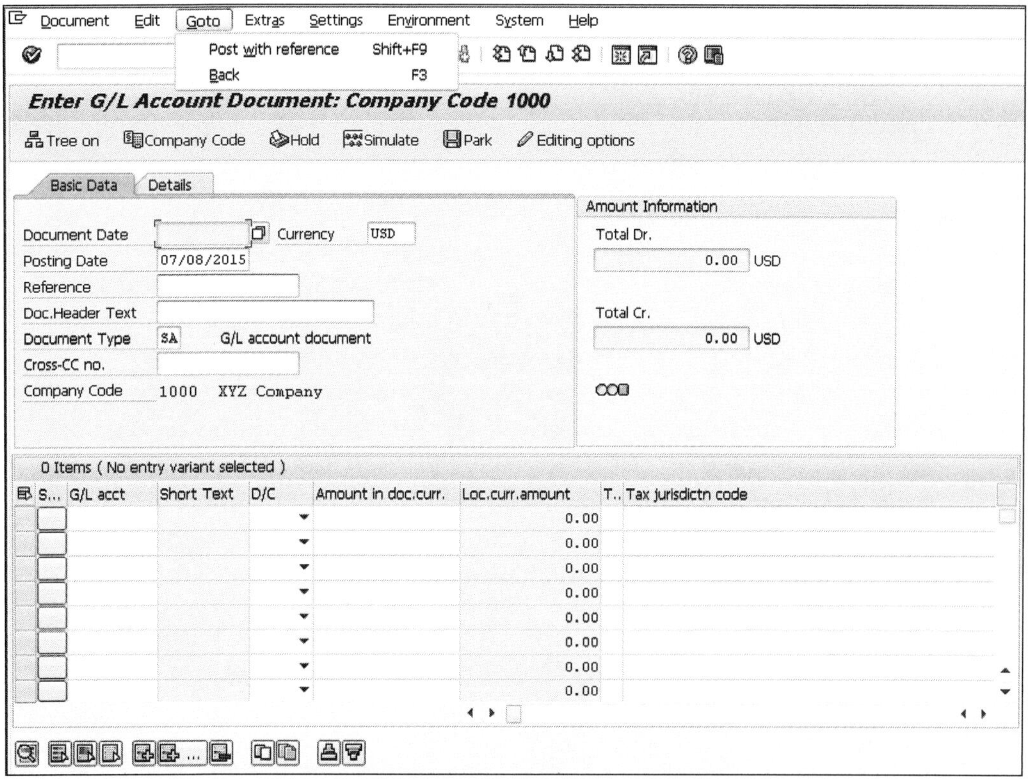

Figure 3.43 Enter G/L Account Document Screen: Post with Reference

The post with reference **Post Document: Header Data** selection screen opens (Figure 3.44). Here, complete the **Document Number**, **Company Code**, and **Fiscal Year** fields in the **Reference** area. For this example, also select the **Do not propose amounts** checkbox in the **Flow control** area.

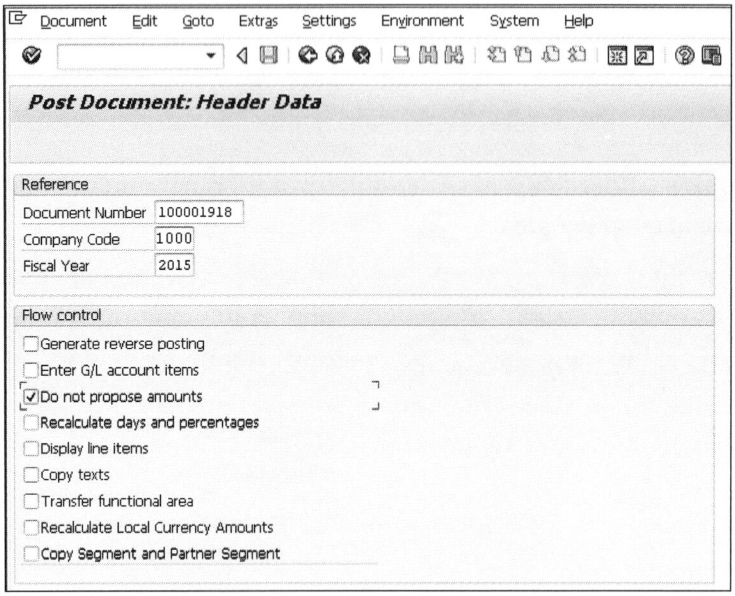

Figure 3.44 Post with Reference Header Selection Screen

After the relevant fields are populated in the **Post Document: Header Data** screen, press [Enter] to move to the first screen of the new G/L document creation process (Figure 3.45). The header data contains the field values copied from the reference document, including the **Document Date** and **Posting Date** fields from the reference transaction. At this point, you can edit many field values.

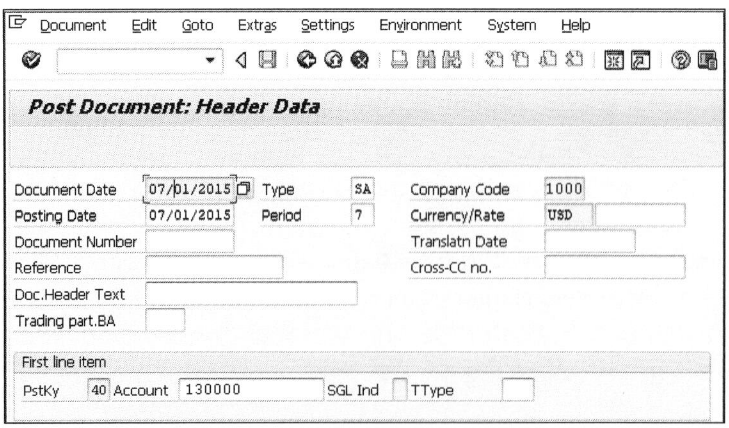

Figure 3.45 Post with Reference Header Screen

For this example, we changed both the **Document Date** and **Posting Date** fields (Figure 3.46).

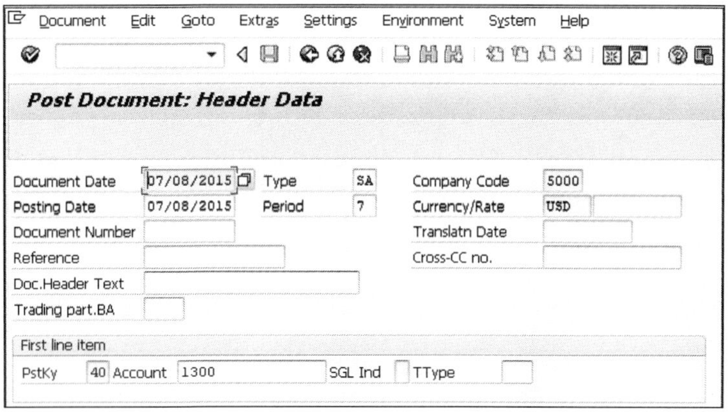

Figure 3.46 Post with Reference Header Screen: Date Change

After you've edited any header fields that you want to change, press Enter, and the **Post Document Add G/L account item** screen appears (Figure 3.47). Notice that the **Amount** field is blank because we selected the **Do not propose amounts** checkbox in **Flow Control** (refer to Figure 3.44) when we initiated the post with reference transaction.

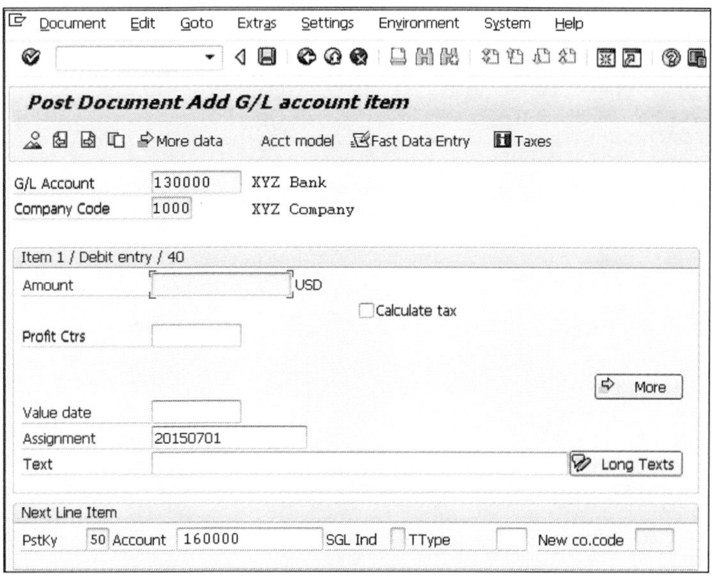

Figure 3.47 Post Document Add G/L Account Item Screen

For this example, enter "100" in the **Amount** field (Figure 3.48).

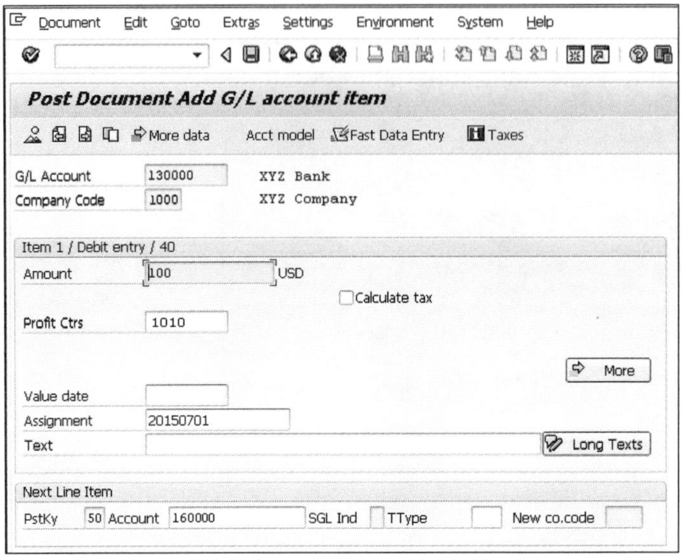

Figure 3.48 Add Amount in Line 1 Post with Reference Document

Press Enter, and a second **Post Document Add G/L account item** screen opens (Figure 3.49). You'll see that the **Amount** field is blank here as well.

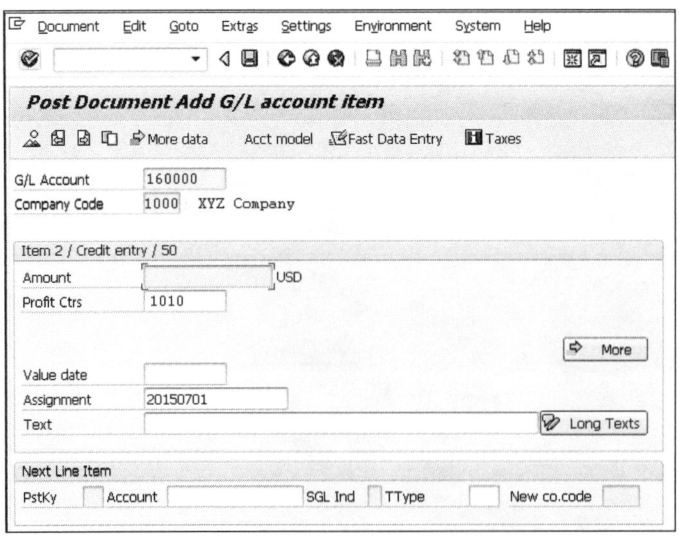

Figure 3.49 Blank Amount in Line 2 Post with Reference Document

For this example, enter "100" again in the **Amount** field (Figure 3.50).

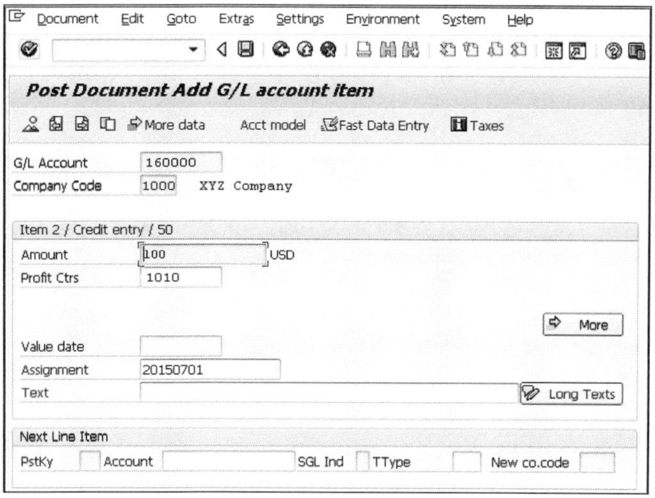

Figure 3.50 Add Amount in Line 2 Post with Reference Document

After entering G/L account line items is complete, click the **Post** button or press Ctrl+S to post the G/L document. A message pops up with the new G/L document number (Figure 3.51).

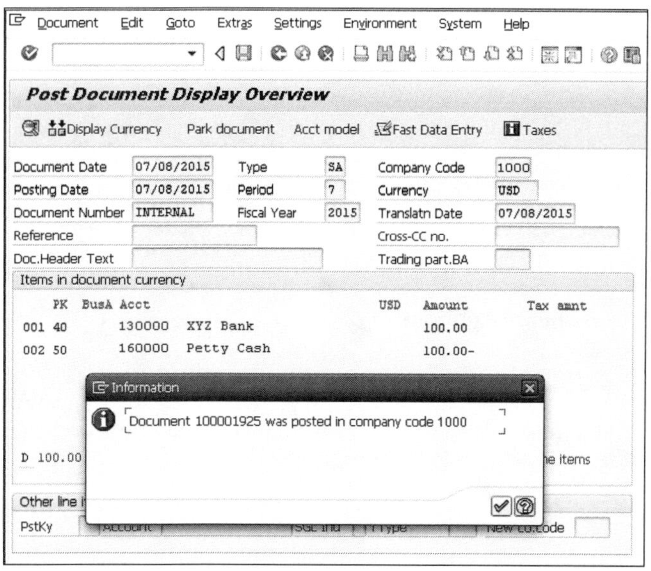

Figure 3.51 Post with Reference Document Created Message

As you can see, post with reference is a great time-saving tool, which allows you to quickly create a new G/L account document based on an existing, previously posted document with little to no data entry.

Table 3.2 provides a complete list of flow control options and their descriptions (as shown earlier in Figure 3.44).

Flow Control Checkbox	Description
Generate reverse posting	Automatically generates reverse debit/credit indicators to offset the reference document
Enter G/L account items	Transfers line items to the fast entry screen for G/L accounts so that several line items can be displayed and processed from one screen
Do not propose amounts	Requires line item amounts to be manually entered in the new document
Recalculate days and percentages	Recalculates days and percentages from payment terms
Display line items	Displays each individual line item separately so default field values can be changed if necessary
Copy texts	Copies long texts from the reference document to the new document
Transfer functional area	Transfers the reference functional area instead of re-deriving it because the functional area is normally derived
Recalculate Local Currency Amounts	Recalculates local currency amounts to account for changes in exchange rates
Copy Segment and Partner Segment	Transfers the fields instead of re-deriving their values because they are normally derived

Table 3.2 Flow Control Checkboxes and Descriptions

Post with reference allows you to copy an existing document, but note that it's an SAP best practice to allow derived field values to be re-derived with each new posting. For example, if you derive the **Segment** field from the profit center, you should allow the program to automatically re-derive the field instead of entering it manually into the transaction.

Now that we've covered post with reference and completed our tour of journal voucher transactions, let's move on to the topic of post with clearing. This is an important function in many business processes, including electronic bank statements, accounts receivable, accounts payable, and goods receipt/invoice receipt (GR/IR).

3.2 Post with Clearing

Post with clearing is a concept in FI that enables you to select and offset a G/L open item. With this transaction, you enter one select line item in a G/L accounting document and then select a G/L open item to clear. When you select an open item, the clearing program automatically produces an opposing G/L line item, netting the G/L account balance of the line items to zero.

The most notable examples of accounting business processes that perform post with clearing are posting incoming payments in accounts receivable and posting outgoing payments in accounts payable. In the G/L module, the most common example is clearing open items in bank accounts, which we'll focus on for the remainder of this section. In the G/L module, post with clearing is performed using Transaction F-04 or via application menu path, **Accounting • Financial Accounting • General Ledger • Document Entry • F-04 – Post with Clearing**, as shown in Figure 3.52.

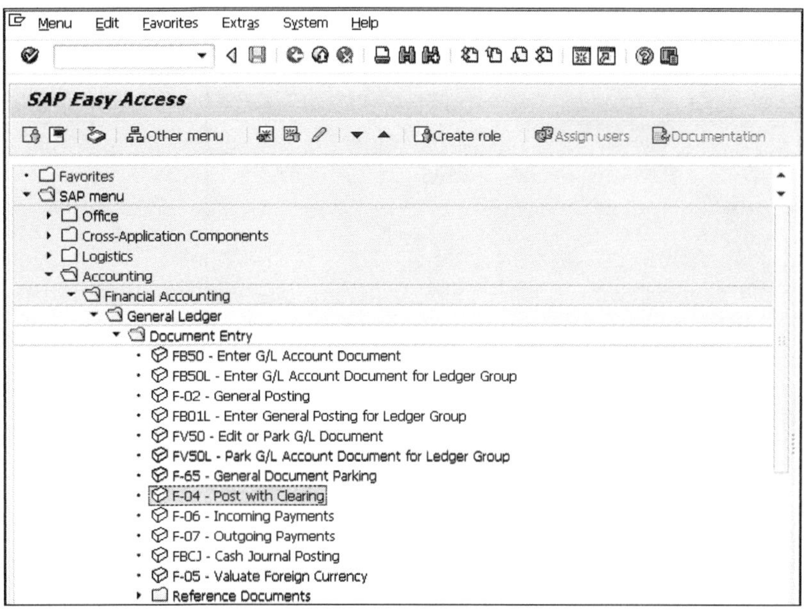

Figure 3.52 Transaction F-04 Menu Path for Post with Clearing

Double-click **F-04 – Post with Clearing** from the menu path, or enter "F-04" in the **Command** field (as shown in Figure 3.53) and press Enter.

Figure 3.53 Entering "F-04" in the Command Field

The **Post with Clearing: Header Data** screen appears (Figure 3.54). On this screen, enter a value for the **Document Date** field and any other fields that are required, but don't default a value. For this example, select **Transfer posting with clearing** in the **Transaction to be processed** area. At the bottom of the screen, you need to enter values for the **PstKy** (posting key) and **Account** fields for the first line item of the G/L document.

With your field entries complete, press Enter.

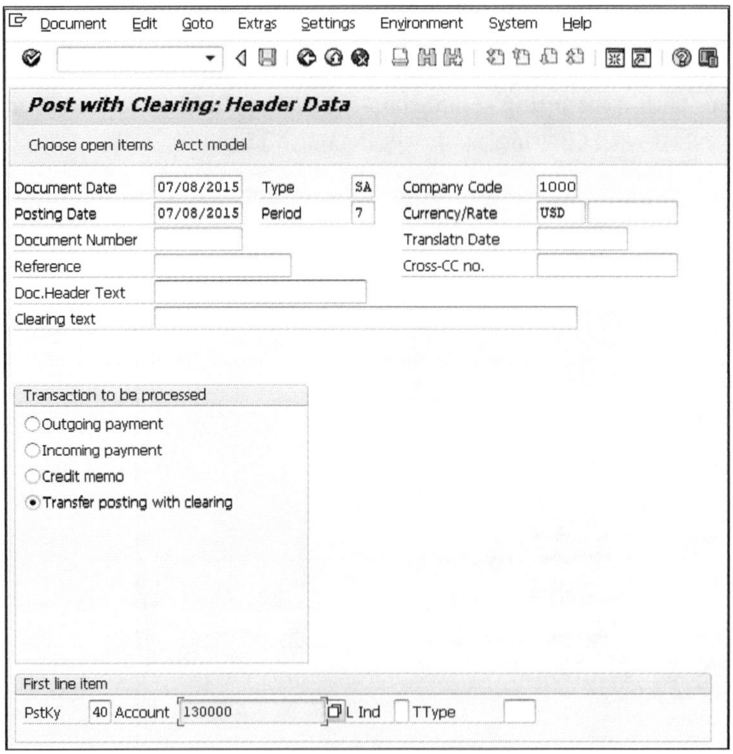

Figure 3.54 Post with Clearing: Header Data Screen

The **Post with Clearing Add G/L account item** screen opens (Figure 3.55). For this example, enter a value in the **Amount** field (we entered "4991.83" here), and click on the **Choose open items** button.

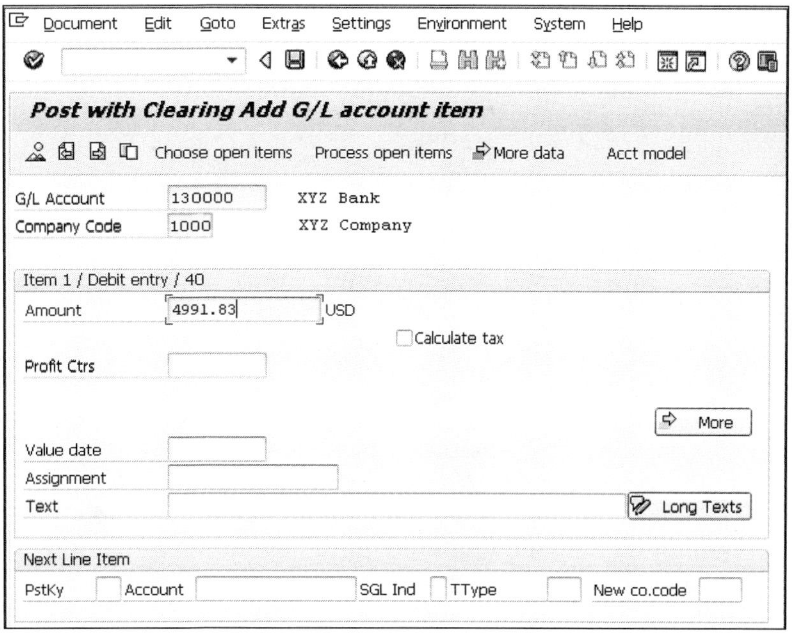

Figure 3.55 Post with Clearing Add G/L Account Item Screen

The **Post with Clearing Select open items** screen opens (Figure 3.56). In this example, values are defaulted for the **Company Code** and **Account Type** fields, and we manually entered a value into the **Account** field (here, "131100"). The **Account** field must be filled with the G/L account containing the open item to be cleared.

In the **Additional selections** area, select a field relevant to the search for open items. For this example, select the **Amount** field.

At this point, the program has all the information it needs to search for and select open items. Click on the **Process open items** button.

The **Post with Clearing Enter selection criteria** screen opens (Figure 3.57). Here, enter a dollar amount in the **From** field. Then, click the **Process open items** button.

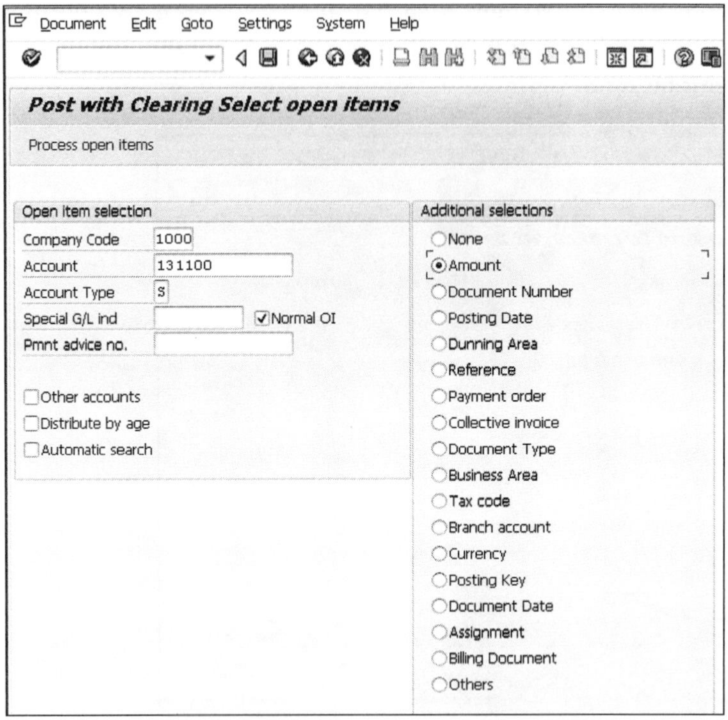

Figure 3.56 Post with Clearing Select Open Items Screen

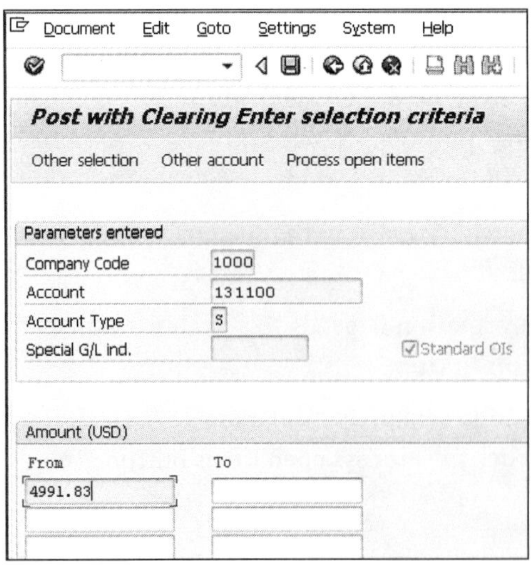

Figure 3.57 Post with Clearing Enter Selection Criteria Screen

The **Post with Clearing Process open items** screen opens with one line item selected for clearing (Figure 3.58).

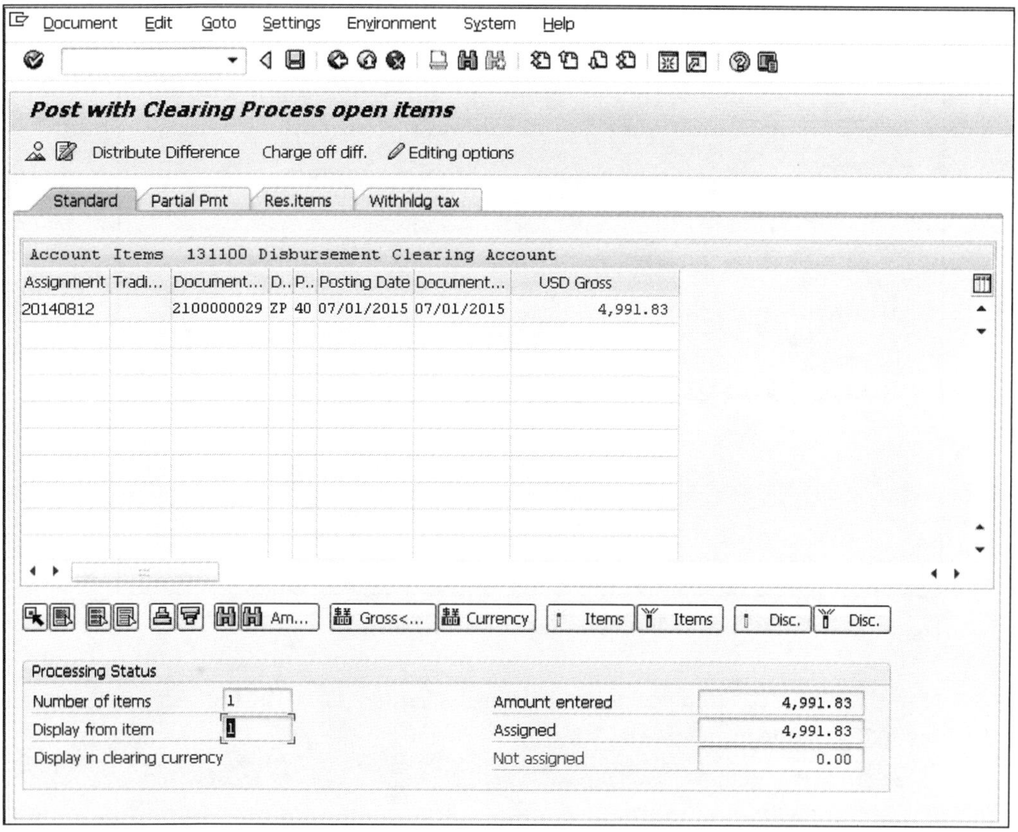

Figure 3.58 Post with Clearing Process Open Items Screen

Click the **Post** button or press Ctrl+S to post the G/L document. A message pops up with the new G/L document number (Figure 3.59).

Note that the post with clearing process, using Transaction F-04, allows you to select multiple open items to clear. In addition, if the **Amount entered** differs from the amount **Assigned** (refer to Figure 3.58), you have the option to charge off the difference or distribute the difference via pushbuttons at the top of the **Post with Clearing Process open items** screen.

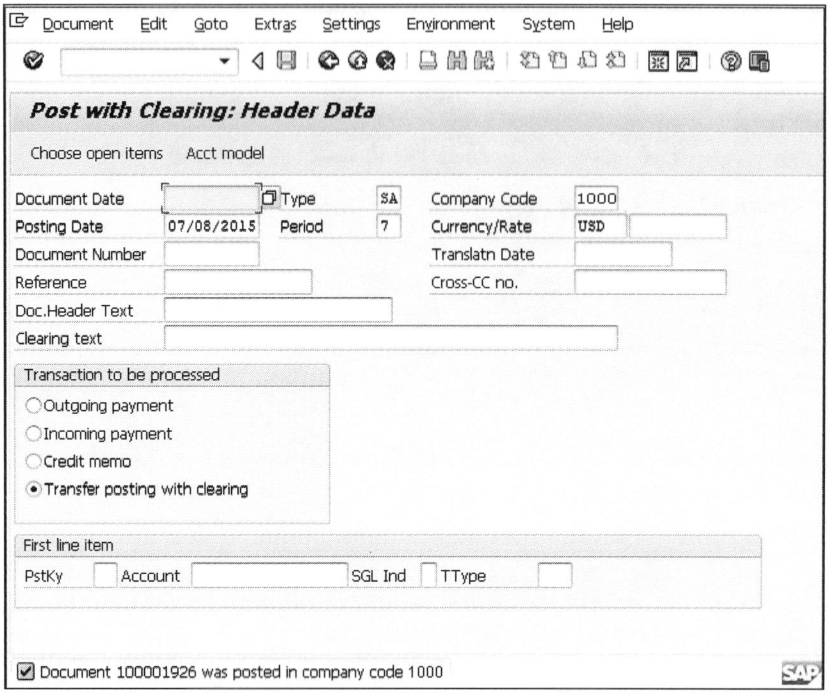

Figure 3.59 Post with Clearing Document Created Message

Now that we've covered post with clearing, let's move on to the topic of resetting and reversing G/L documents.

3.3 Resetting and Reversing Documents

Reversing documents is a common occurrence in a day in the life of an accountant. It needs to happen when some error occurred in the posting of the original document, such as when a document posts with the wrong date or, as frequently occurs, an error arose in the line of accounting.

The most important factor to know before attempting to reverse an SAP accounting document is what type of document you're using. For reversal purposes, accounting documents can be classified as either clearing or non-clearing documents.

Clearing documents are those produced through a post with clearing transaction, such as Transaction F-04 (see Section 3.2). These documents have two technical components: First, a clearing document contains complete header data and at least two completed line items with debit/credit amounts netting to zero. The second component of a clearing document is the account clearing. Through the clearing process, a G/L open item was selected and its status changed from **Open** to **Cleared** when the document was posted.

A *non-clearing accounting document* has the same attributes as a clearing document, except that it doesn't clear a G/L open item. Therefore, a non-clearing document hasn't changed the status of a G/L line item from **Open** to **Cleared**. Non-clearing documents are by far the simplest to reverse, so we'll walk through this process first.

3.3.1 Reversing a Non-Clearing Document

To reverse a single G/L accounting document, use Transaction FB08 or application menu path, **Accounting • Financial Accounting • General Ledger • Document • Reverse • FB08 – Individual Reversal**, as shown in Figure 3.60.

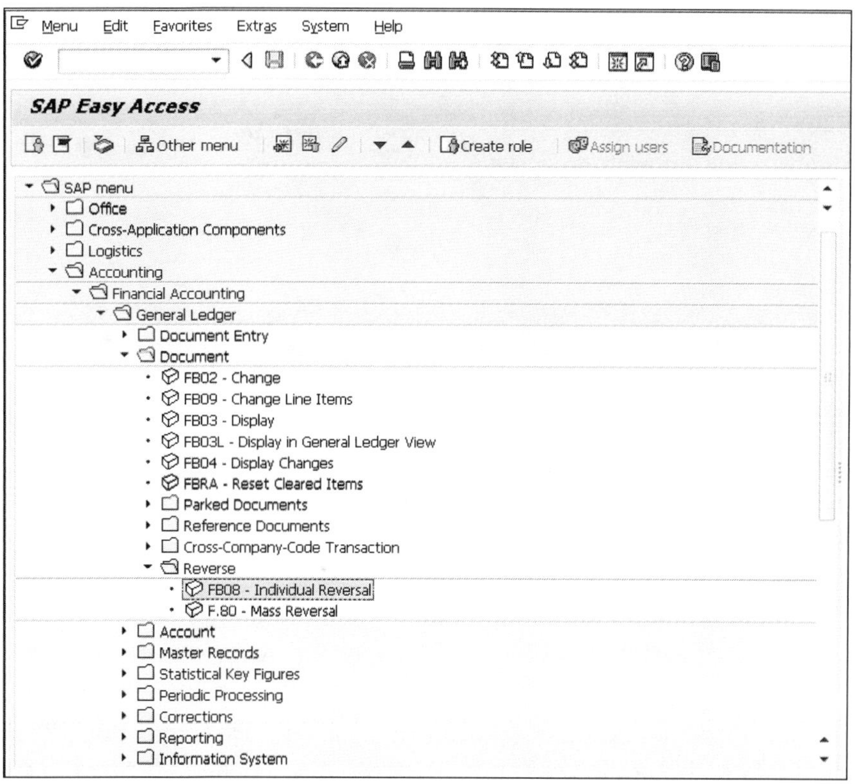

Figure 3.60 Transaction FB08 Menu Path

Double-click **FB08 – Individual Reversal** from the menu path, or enter “FB08” in the **Command** field (as shown in Figure 3.61) and press Enter.

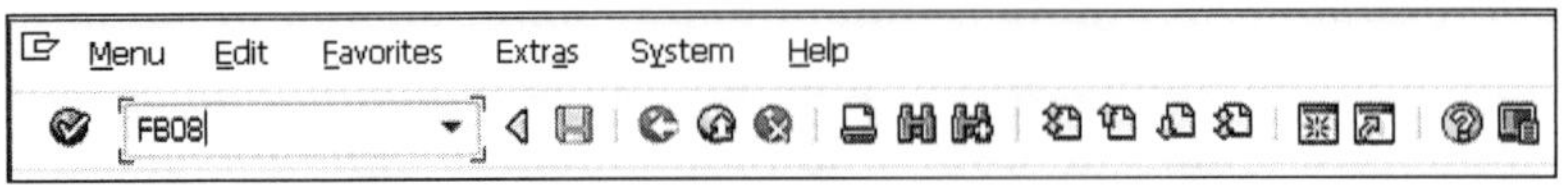

Figure 3.61 Entering “FB08” in the Command Field

The **Reverse Document: Header Data** screen appears (Figure 3.62). At a minimum, the **Document Number**, **Company Code**, **Fiscal Year**, and **Reversal Reason** fields are required.

The **Reversal Reason** field is noted in the reversed document, and it determines if an alternative posting date is allowed or if the reversal can be created from a negative posting. In this example, the **Reversal Reason** field is populated with a value of **01**, signifying that the reversal will take place in the current period.

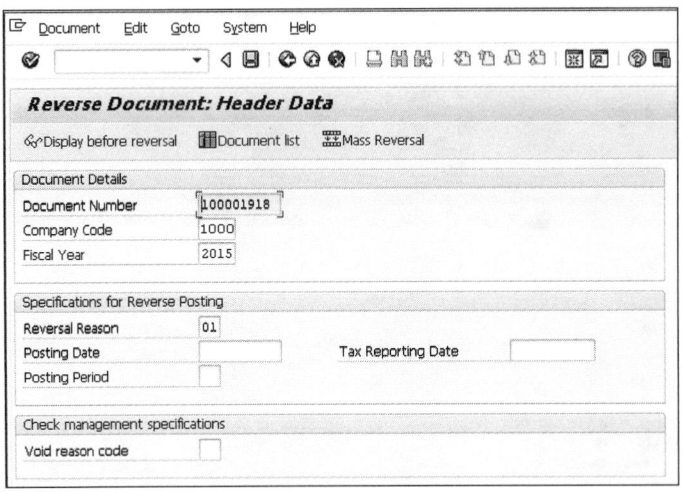

Figure 3.62 Reverse Document: Header Data Screen

When all the required fields are entered, click the **Post** icon or press Ctrl+S to post the G/L reversal document. A message pops up with the new G/L document number (Figure 3.63).

If you have more than one non-clearing document to reverse, use Transaction F.80 or application menu path, **Accounting • Financial Accounting • General Ledger • Document • Reverse • F.80 – Mass Reversal**, as shown in Figure 3.64.

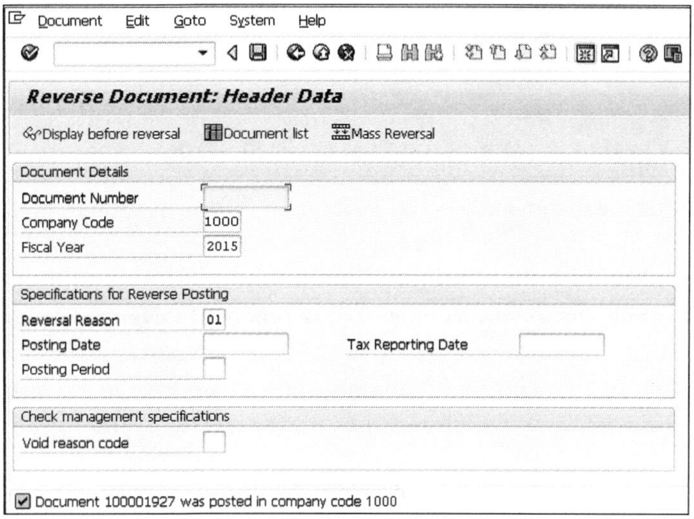

Figure 3.63 Reversal Document Created Message

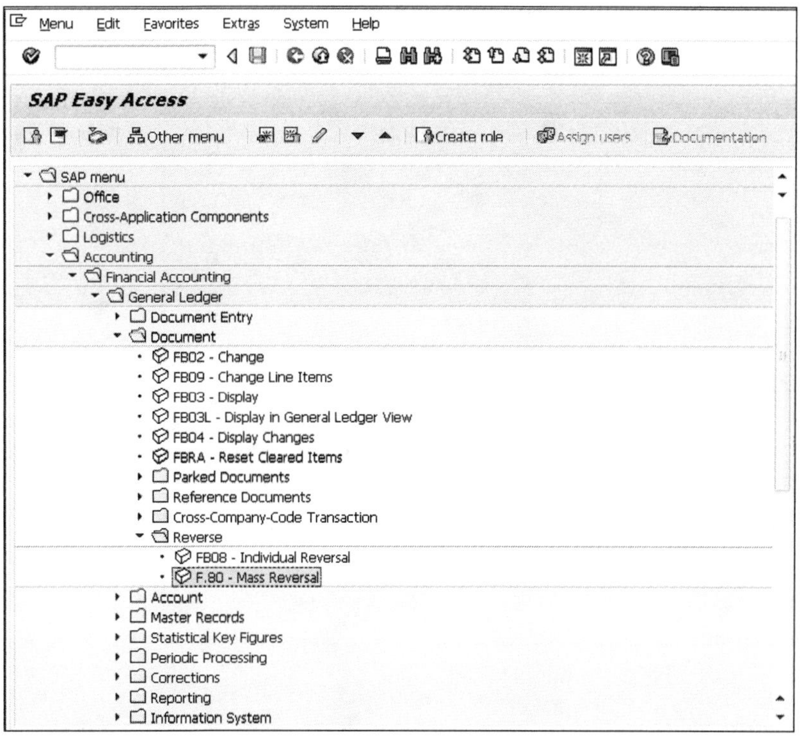

Figure 3.64 Transaction F.80 Menu Path

Double-click **F.80 – Mass Reversal** from the menu path, or enter "F.80" in the **Command** field (as shown in Figure 3.65) and press [Enter].

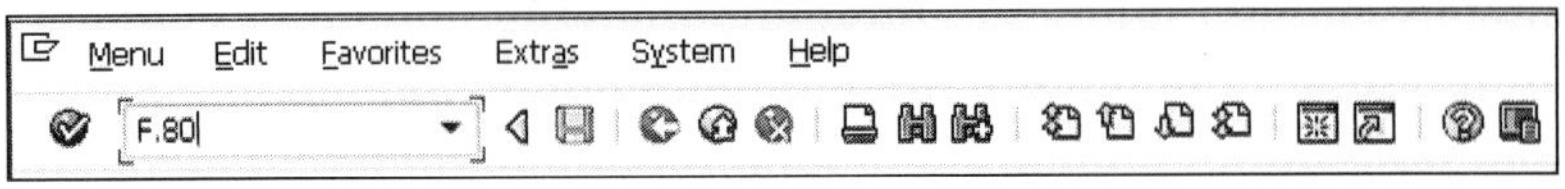

Figure 3.65 Entering "F.80" in the Command Field

The **Mass Reversal of Documents: Initial Screen** appears (Figure 3.66). As in Transaction FB08, the **Company Code**, **Document Number**, **Fiscal Year**, and **Reversal Reason** fields are required. Note that in Transaction F.80, you can enter a range of values for these fields, whereas in Transaction FB08, you can only enter a single value for each. Transaction F.80 also provides a **Ledger** field, which, in most cases, will refer to your primary ledger.

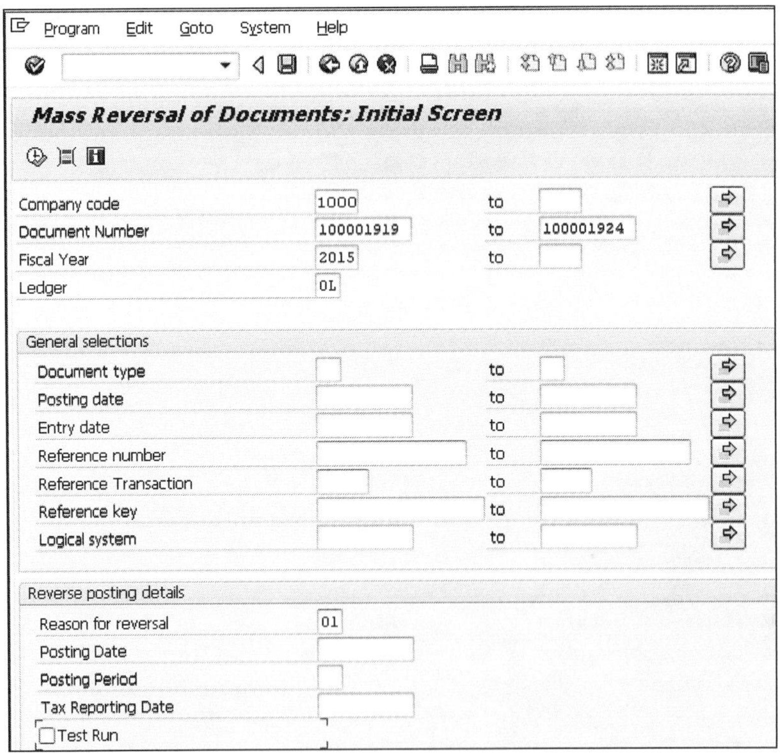

Figure 3.66 Mass Reversal of Documents Initial Screen

Transaction F.80 has some other additional features. Under **General selections**, there are several input fields that may be useful. In addition, in the **Reverse posting details** area, there is a **Test Run** checkbox. For mass reversals, it's always a good idea to run the program in test mode first. Note that you can't undo a reversal document after it has been posted.

When all the required fields are entered, click the **Execute** button or press F8 to post the G/L reversal documents.

Detailed results are provided on the **Mass Reversal of Documents** output screen (Figure 3.67).

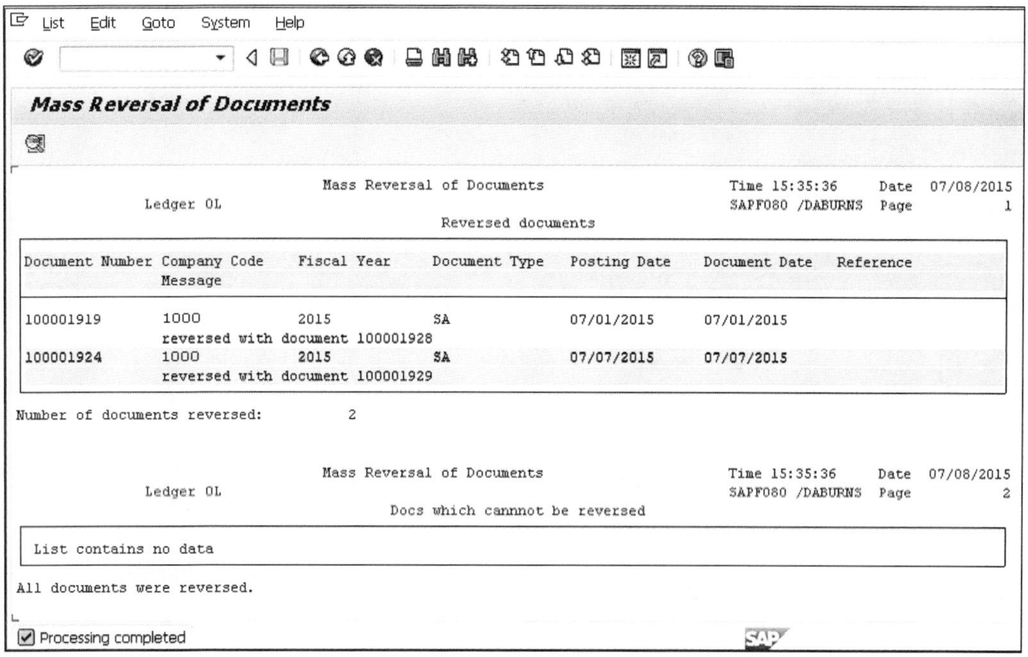

Figure 3.67 Mass Reversal of Documents Output Screen

Now that we've discussed reversing individual and multiple non-clearing documents, let's move on to the process for reversing clearing documents.

3.3.2 Reversing a Clearing Document

To reverse a G/L clearing document, use Transaction FBRA or application menu path, **Accounting • Financial Accounting • General Ledger • Document • FBRA – Reset Cleared Items**, as shown in Figure 3.68.

Double-click **FBRA – Reset Cleared Items** from the menu path, or enter "FBRA" in the **Command** field (as shown in Figure 3.69) and press Enter.

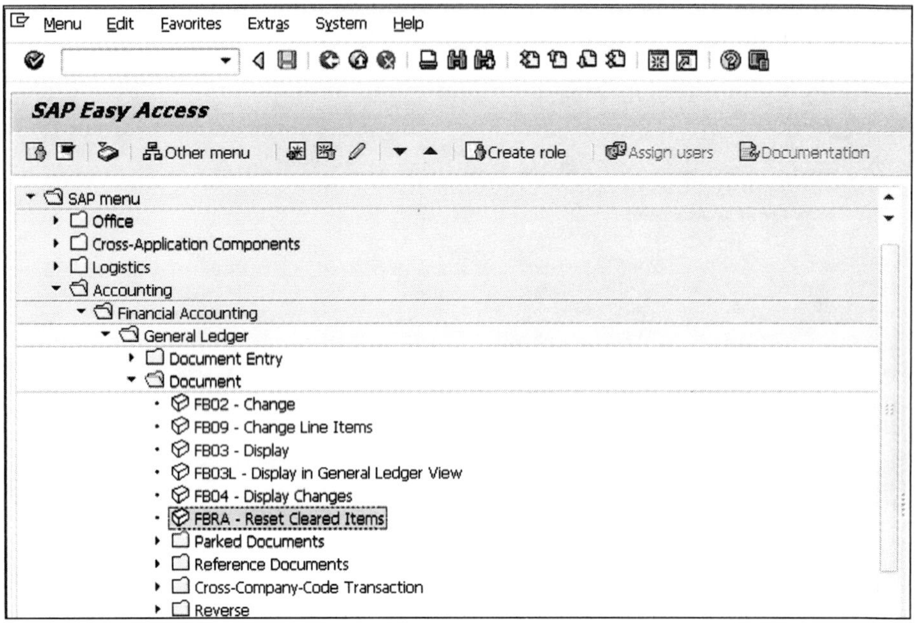

Figure 3.68 Transaction FBRA Menu Path

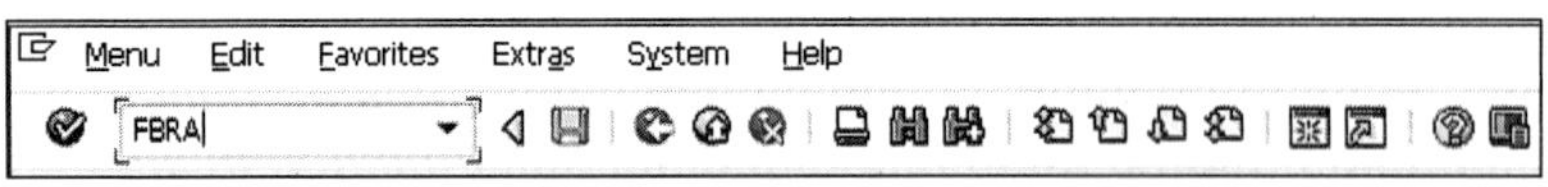

Figure 3.69 Entering "FBRA" in the Command Field

The **Reset Cleared Items** screen opens (Figure 3.70). The **Clearing Document**, **Company Code**, and **Fiscal Year** fields are all required.

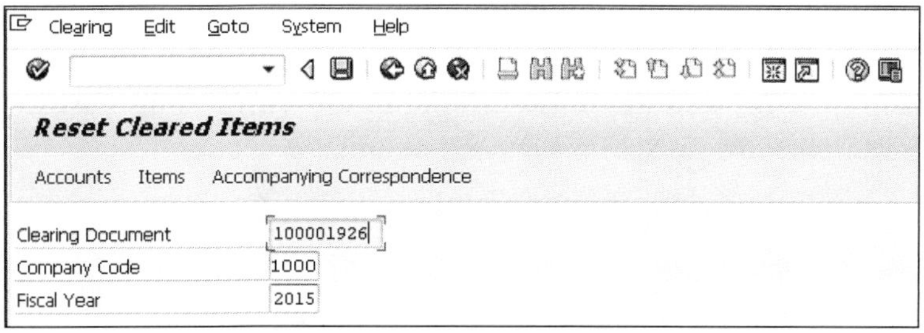

Figure 3.70 Reset Cleared Items Screen

After entering the required screen elements, click the **Reset Cleared Items** button or press Ctrl+S. This will bring up the **Reversal of clearing document** dialog box (Figure 3.71), in which you must choose one of three options: **Only resetting**, **Resetting and revers**, or **Cancel**.

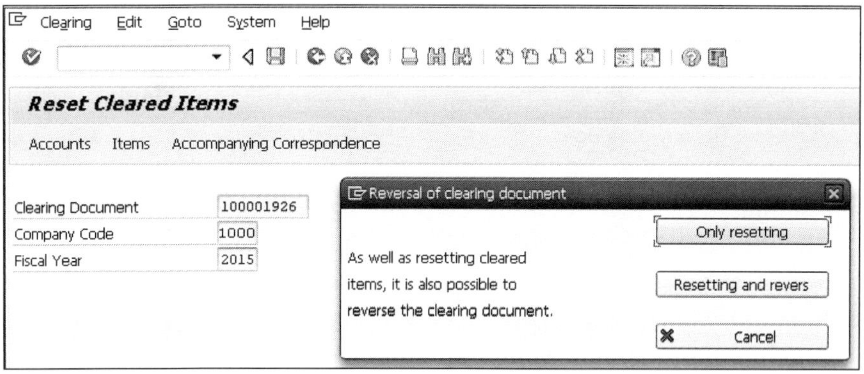

Figure 3.71 Reversal of Clearing Document Dialog Box

The **Only resetting** option doesn't reverse the clearing document. Rather, it breaks the link between a clearing document and the G/L item it cleared and changes the status of the cleared G/L item back from **Cleared** to **Open**. Only use this option when the G/L item selected for clearing was the wrong line item. The clearing document thus becomes an open item and can be reassigned to clear the correct G/L open item.

The **Resetting and revers** option not only resets the cleared item back to **Open** status but also reverses the clearing document. For this example, select the **Resetting and revers** option, and the **Reversal Data** dialog box opens (Figure 3.72).

The **Cancel** button closes the **Reversal of clearing document** dialog box without taking any further action and returns you to the **Reset Cleared Items** screen.

The **Reversal Reason** field is noted in the reversed document. It also determines if an alternative posting date is allowed or if the reversal can be created from a negative posting. In this example, the **Reversal Reason** field is populated with a value of **01**, signifying that the reversal will take place in the current period.

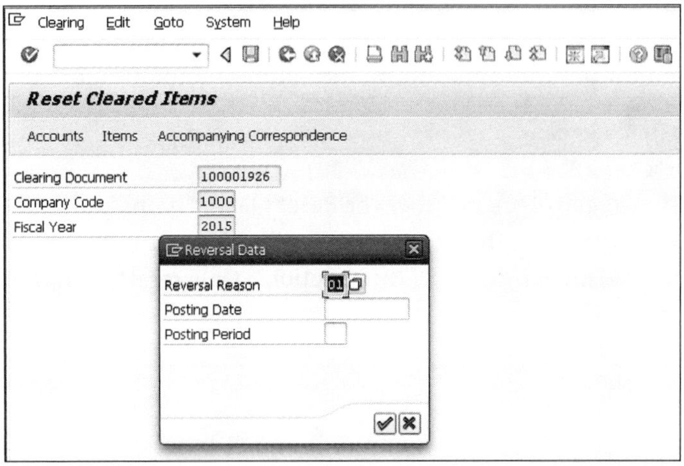

Figure 3.72 Reversal Data Dialog Box

Click the **Continue** button or press [Enter]. Two subsequent information dialog boxes appear. The first, shown in Figure 3.73, states that the clearing document was reset. The second, shown in Figure 3.74, provides the number of a new document that has been posted, which is the document that reversed the clearing document.

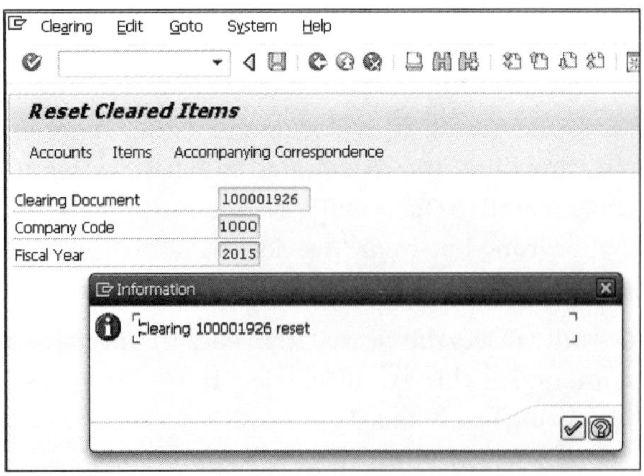

Figure 3.73 Clearing Document Reset Message

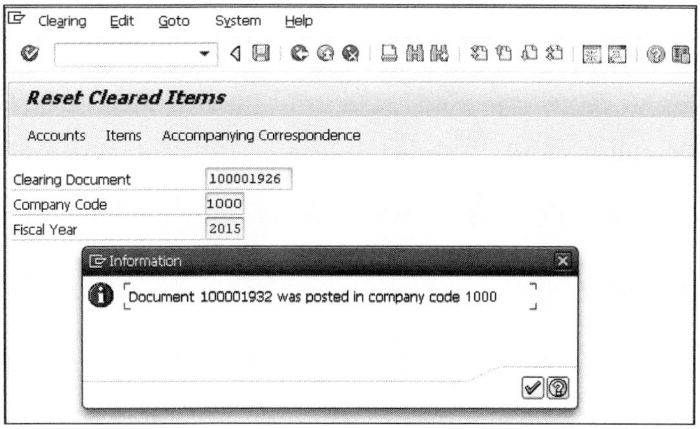

Figure 3.74 Reversal Document Posted Message

Now you know how to reverse G/L accounting documents. Next, let's look at how to change and display accounting documents.

3.4 Changing and Displaying Documents

This section covers the change and display capabilities for G/L accounting documents. Many of the concepts and transactions are applicable across FI, but the content in this chapter specifically uses accounting documents posted using Transaction FB50.

Rules for changing field values in SAP accounting documents are defined in configuration. Separate rules are defined for header and line item fields. Note, however, that SAP will never allow you to change fields considered central to the principle of orderly accounting. In other words, fields that are material to G/L account balances, posting dates, and integration can't be changed after a G/L accounting document has been posted. These include not only the **Posting Date**, **Debit/Credit Indicator**, and **Amount** fields but also update objects (i.e., cost center). If a G/L accounting document contains an incorrect value that falls into one of these categories, the document should be reversed using Transaction FB08 if it's a non-clearing document or Transaction FBRA if it's a clearing document.

To change a G/L document, use Transaction FB02 or application menu path, **Accounting • Financial Accounting • General Ledger • Document • FB02 – Change**, as shown in Figure 3.75.

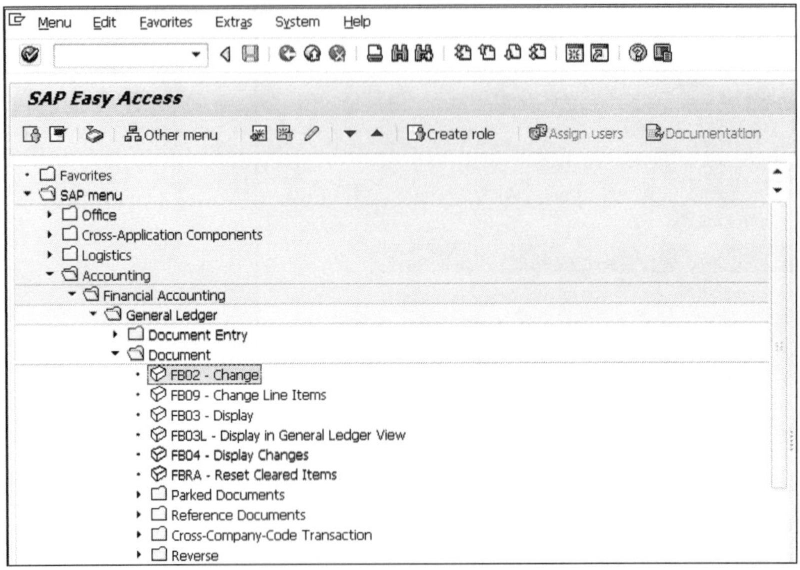

Figure 3.75 Transaction FB02 Menu Path

Double-click **FB02 – Change** from the menu path, or enter "FB02" in the **Command** field (as shown in Figure 3.76) and press Enter.

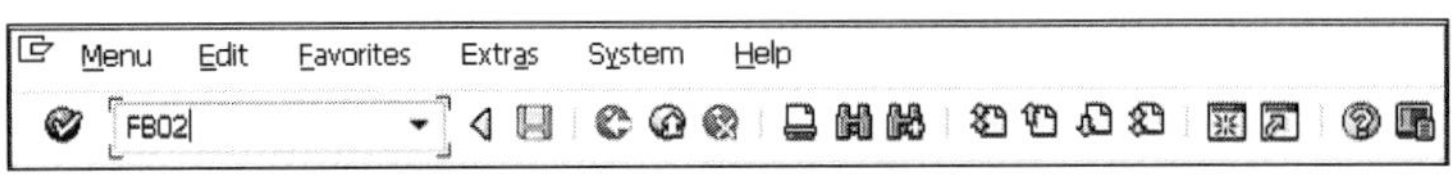

Figure 3.76 Entering "FB02" in the Command Field

The **Change Document: Initial Screen** opens (Figure 3.77). The **Document Number**, **Company Code**, and **Fiscal Year** fields are required.

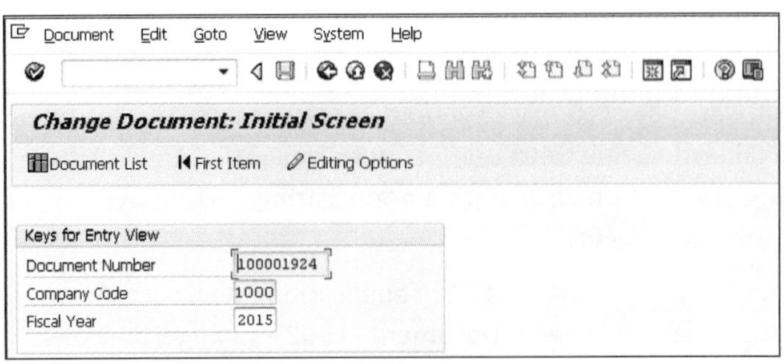

Figure 3.77 Change Document: Initial Screen

After entering all field values, press Enter. The **Change Document: Data Entry View** screen appears (Figure 3.78).

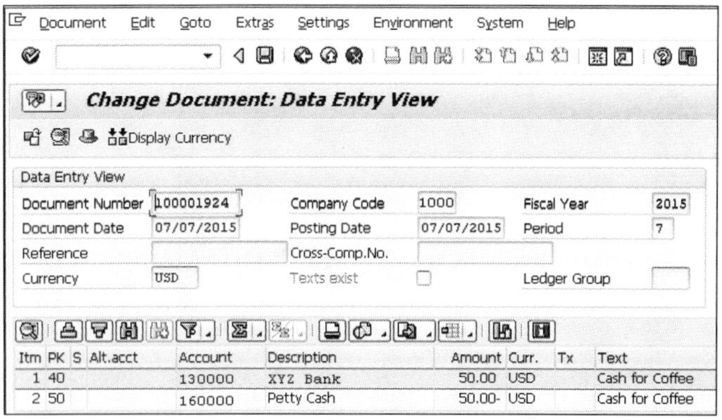

Figure 3.78 Change Document: Data Entry View Screen

To change a header field, click on the top hat icon, and the **Document Header** dialog box opens (Figure 3.79). Fields that can't be changed are grayed out (e.g., **Document Type**). Fields that can be changed are white and are ready for field values to be entered or changed (e.g., **Reference**).

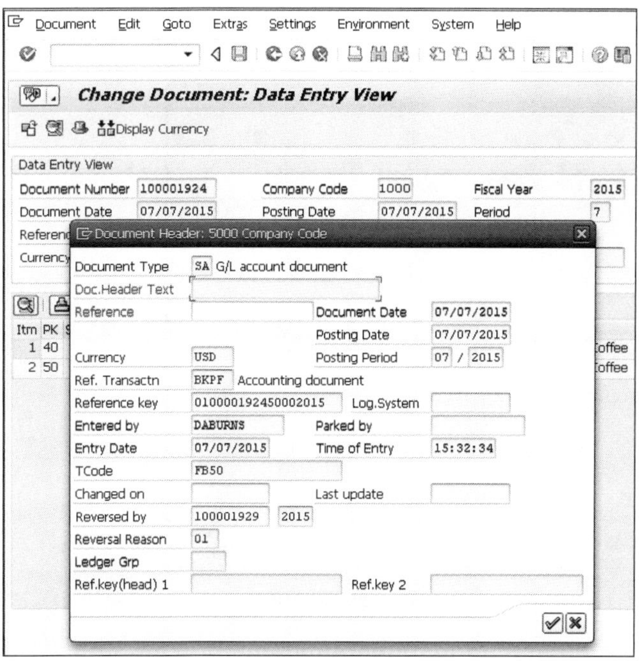

Figure 3.79 Document Header Dialog Box

From the **Change Document: Data Entry View** screen, you can change line item fields by double-clicking a line to open the **Change Document: Line Item** screen (Figure 3.80).

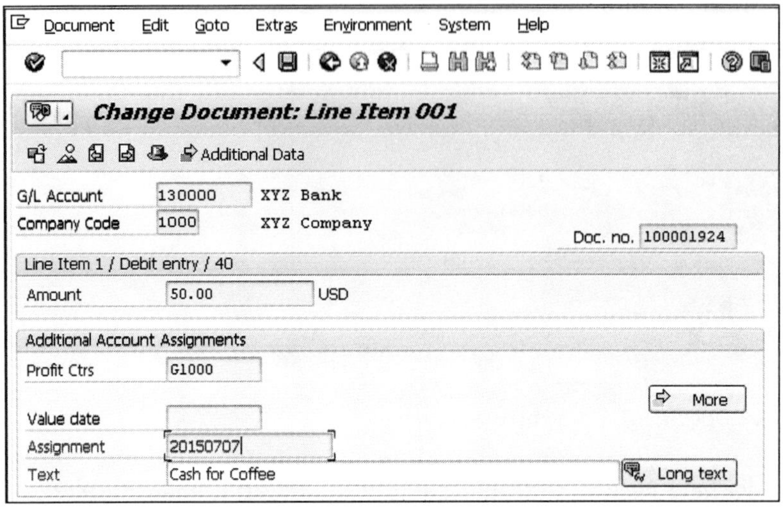

Figure 3.80 Change Document: Line Item Screen

As before, fields that can't be changed are grayed out. Those that can are white and are ready for field values to be entered or changed. For this example, change the **Text** field (Figure 3.81).

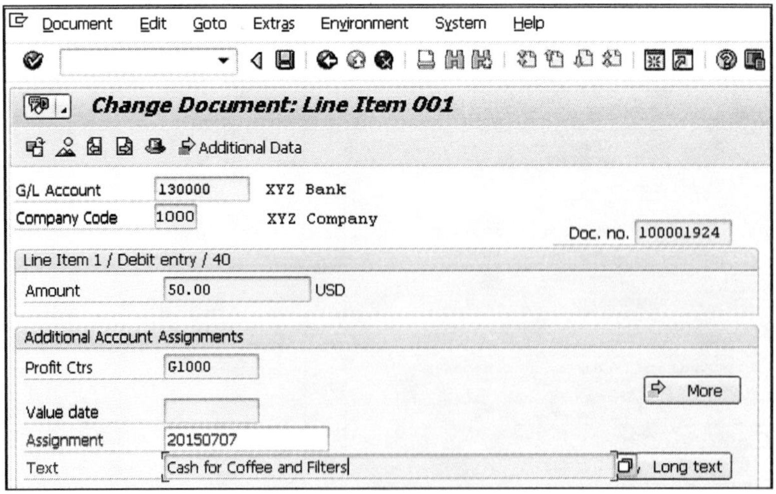

Figure 3.81 Change Document: Line Item Screen with Text Change

After changing field values, click the **Save** button or press [Ctrl]+[S]. A message will indicate that the document changes have been saved (Figure 3.82).

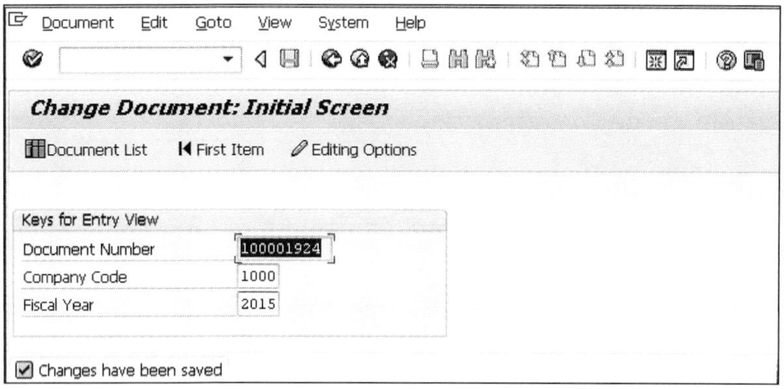

Figure 3.82 Document Changes Have Been Saved Message

To display a G/L accounting document, use Transaction FB03 or application menu path, **Accounting • Financial Accounting • General Ledger • Document • FB03 – Display**, as shown in Figure 3.83.

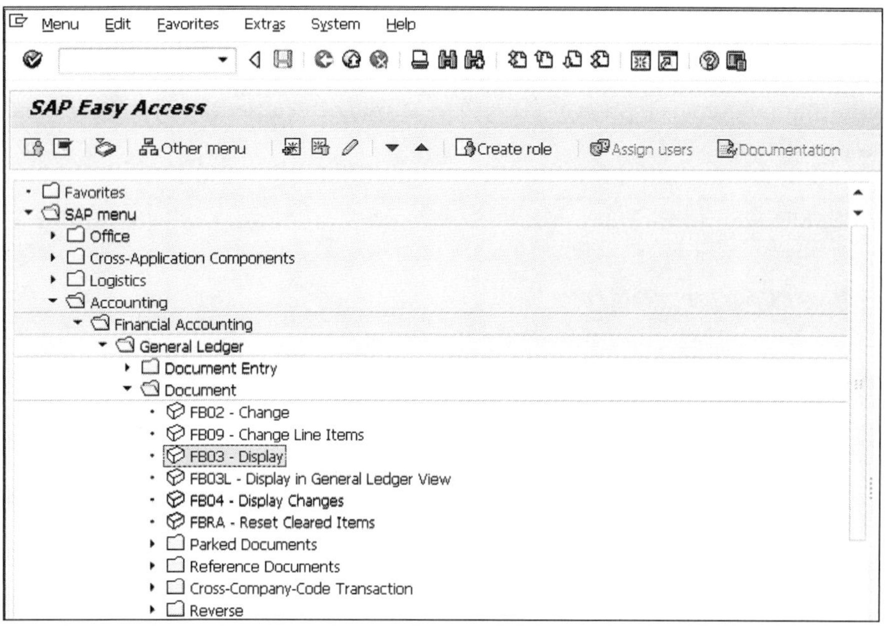

Figure 3.83 Transaction FB03 Menu Path

Double-click **FB03 – Display** from the menu path, or enter "FB03" in the **Command** field (as shown in Figure 3.84) and press [Enter].

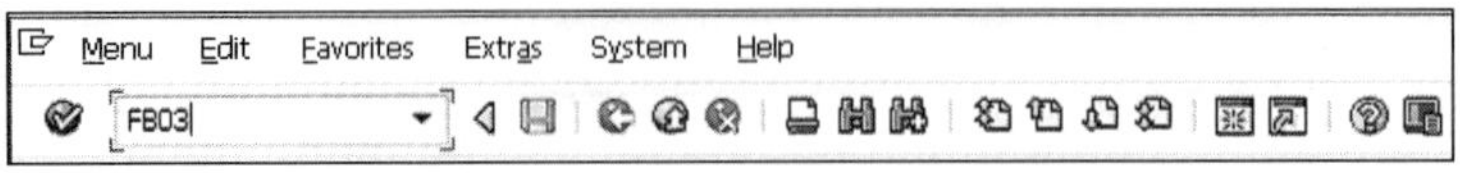

Figure 3.84 Entering "FB03" in the Command Field

The **Document Display: Initial Screen** opens (Figure 3.85). The **Document Number**, **Company Code**, and **Fiscal Year** fields are required.

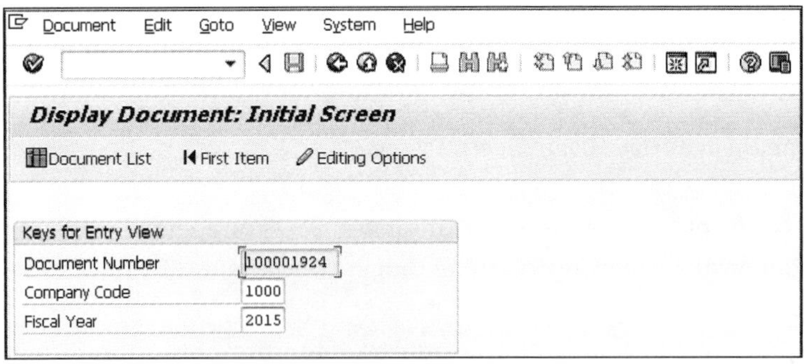

Figure 3.85 Document Display: Initial Screen

After entering field values, press [Enter]. The **Display Document: Data Entry View** screen opens (Figure 3.86).

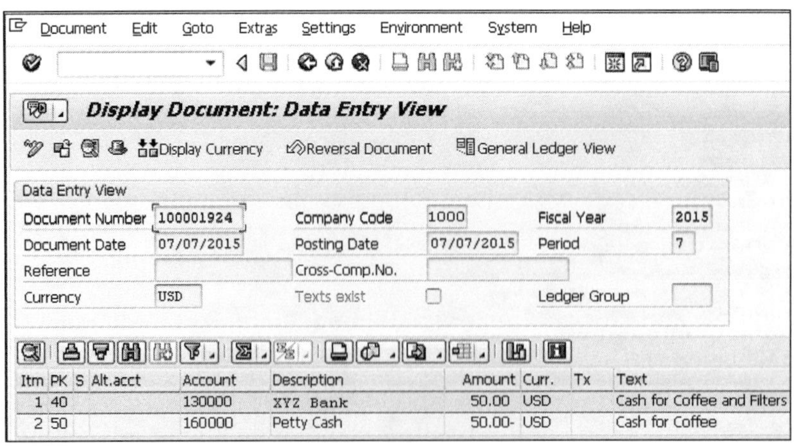

Figure 3.86 Display Document: Data Entry View Screen

From this screen, you can double-click a line to view line item details or click on the top hat icon to view header details.

Note

Any changes made to an accounting document are captured in the change log. Therefore, every change is captured, and an audit trail is provided with details on what was changed, by whom, and when.

Now that you've learned how to change and display accounting documents, let's discuss viewing associated documents using the Document Relationship Browser.

3.5 Document Relationship Browser

The *Document Relationship Browser* provides the ability to view all documents associated with an accounting document via the tree display. The Document Relationship Browser is a universal concept in FI, but our discussion in this section is limited to its application in Transaction FB50.

The Document Relationship Browser is a document tie point. By tying associated documents together in one view, it becomes simpler to understand business steps and business process flow. This browser is a useful tool for troubleshooting accounting problems. Most importantly, the Document Relationship Browser allows you to easily see follow-on documents throughout the lifecycle of a business process. It alleviates time-consuming efforts associated with manually reconciling accounts and tracking document relationships across modules.

To view the Document Relationship Browser from Transaction FB50, choose **Environment • Document Environment • Relationship Browser**, as shown in Figure 3.87.

The **Document Relationship Browser** screen opens (Figure 3.88).

From this view, you can double-click any document in the **Relationship Tree,** or you can click an item and then click the magnifying glass icon (**Details**). The Document Relationship Browser not only provides a document association view but also permits document drilldown capability.

The Document Relationship Browser is an important tool that will be discussed in a number of chapters throughout this book. In some cases, as in Materials Management (MM) and Purchasing modules, document relationships are tied together in what's called a document follow-on function. Although the terminology may change slightly from module to module, the concept is the same, which is to see all the reference documents associated with a central document in one place. These document associations are updated in real time and present a huge time savings to end users.

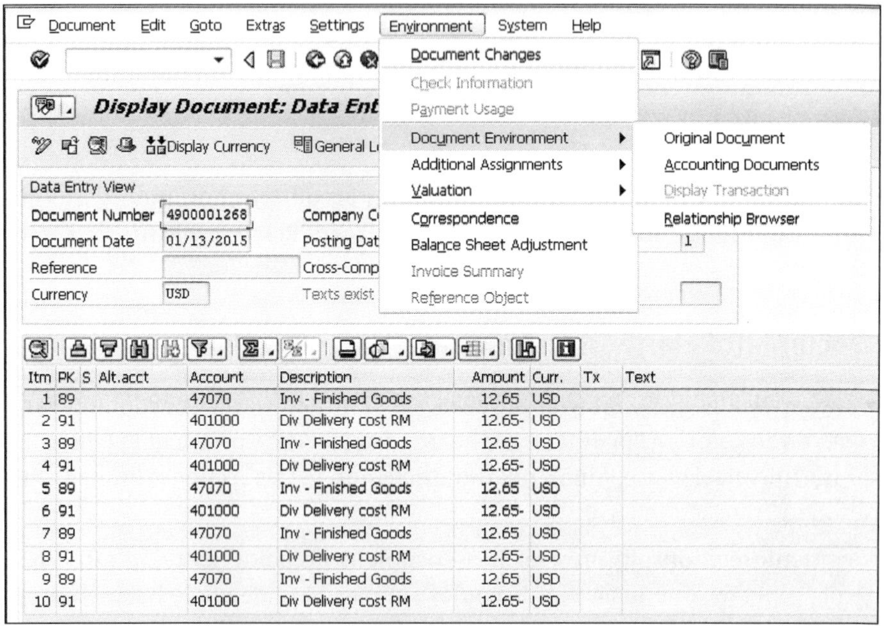

Figure 3.87 Relationship Browser Menu Path from Transaction FB50

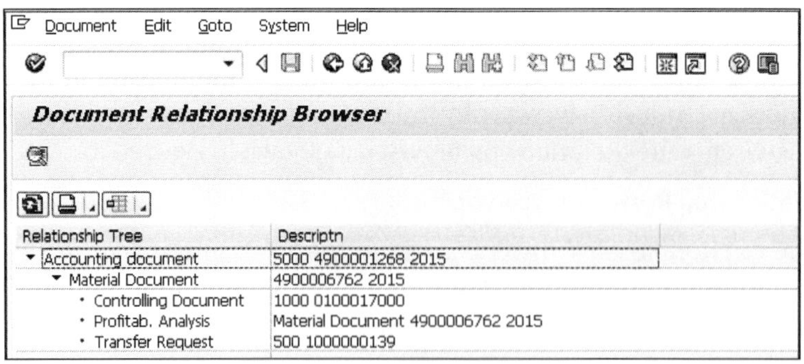

Figure 3.88 Document Relationship Browser

This concludes our discussion of the Document Relationship Browser in G/L. In the next section, we'll discuss reference documents in more detail.

3.6 Reference Documents

In addition to the other G/L functions and transactions covered previously in this chapter, SAP provides some nifty tools called *reference documents*. These include the account assignment model, recurring documents, and sample document, which we'll discuss further in the following sections. The application menu path to access them is **Accounting • Financial Accounting • General Ledger • Document Entry • Reference Documents**, as shown in Figure 3.89.

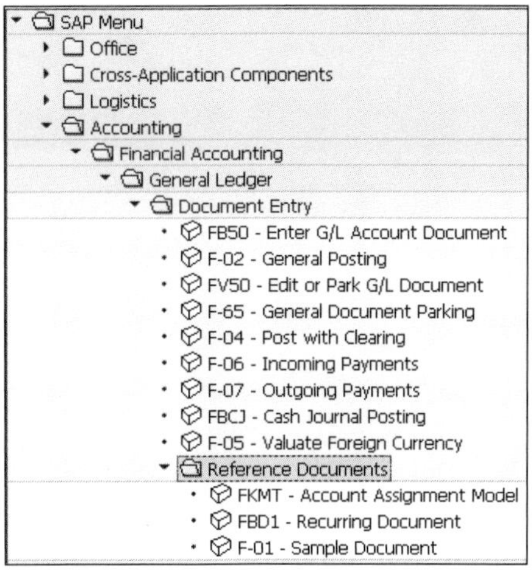

Figure 3.89 G/L Reference Documents Application Menu Path

3.6.1 Account Assignment Models

An *account assignment model* is a reference for document entry that provides default values for posting accounting transactions. It contains G/L account items that can be changed or supplemented at any time. The accounting lines entered in the account assignment model need not be complete. During document entry, the account assignment model serves as a starting reference point for the accounting transaction, but field values can be added, changed, and deleted.

To create, change, or delete an account assignment model, use Transaction FKMT. In Figure 3.90, you see an example model. The 10-character **Acct assignment model** field is used for the name of the model. In the **Attributes** area, **Currency** and **Chart of accounts** are required fields. In this example, **Sample text** was also added, but it isn't necessary.

Notice also that the **Equivalence to** checkbox is selected. This is a special feature of account assignment models. Amounts can be entered directly into account assignment models or distributed based on an equivalency entry and calculation.

With the account assignment model header information entered, press [Shift]+[F8].

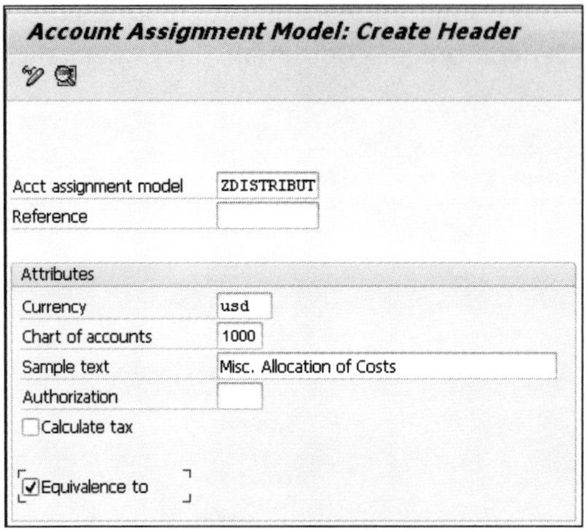

Figure 3.90 Account Assignment Model: Create Header

The **Account Assignment Model: Change Line Items** screen appears (Figure 3.91). Enter line items, and click the **Save** icon.

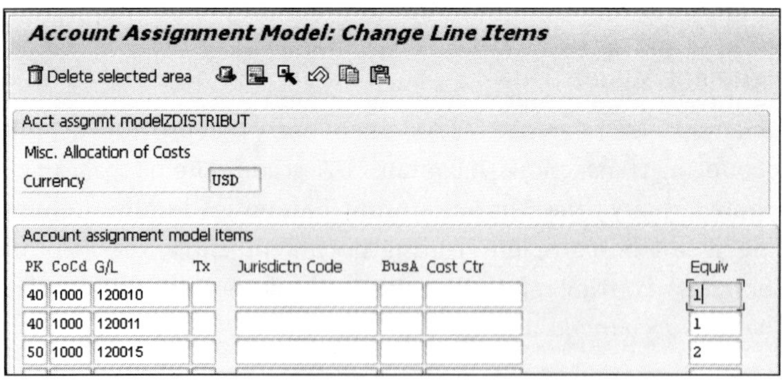

Figure 3.91 Account Assignment Model: Change Line Items

To use your account assignment model in a transaction, go to Transaction FB50. Enter a **Posting Date**, and then press [F6]. The **Display Overview** screen for Transaction FB50 appears (Figure 3.92).

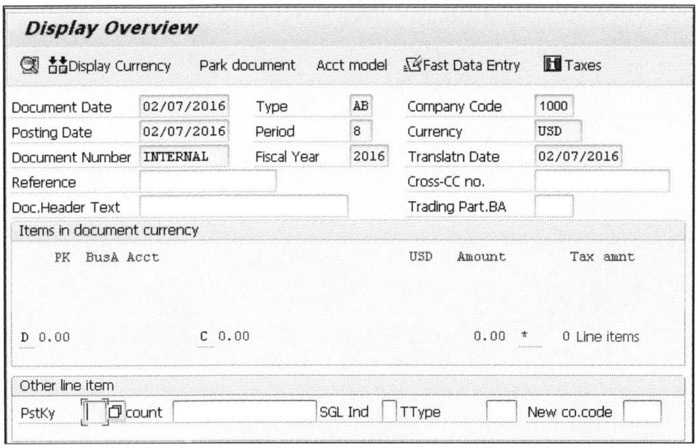

Figure 3.92 Display Overview Screen (Transaction FB50)

Press F7, and the **Select Account Assignment Model** popup appears (Figure 3.93). Enter your account assignment model, and press Enter.

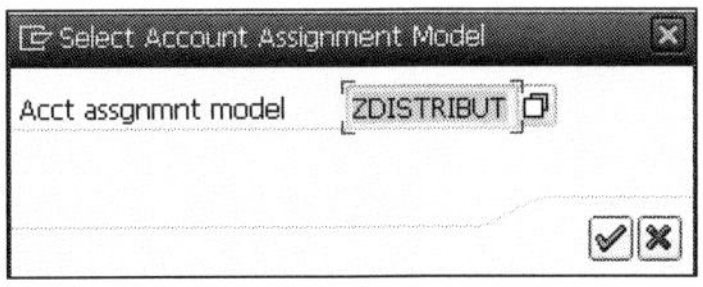

Figure 3.93 Select Account Assignment Model

The **Account Assignment Model: Entry for Posting** screen appears (Figure 3.94). Notice the fields for **Debit distribution** and **Credit distribution**. Enter amounts in each, and press Enter.

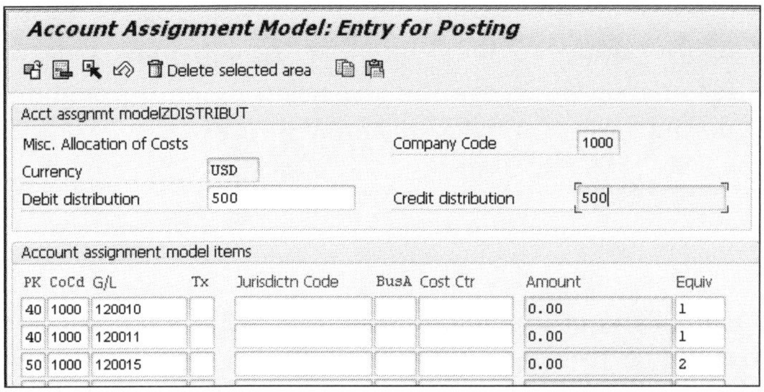

Figure 3.94 Account Assignment Model: Entry for Posting Screen

The amounts are then distributed to line items, as shown in Figure 3.95.

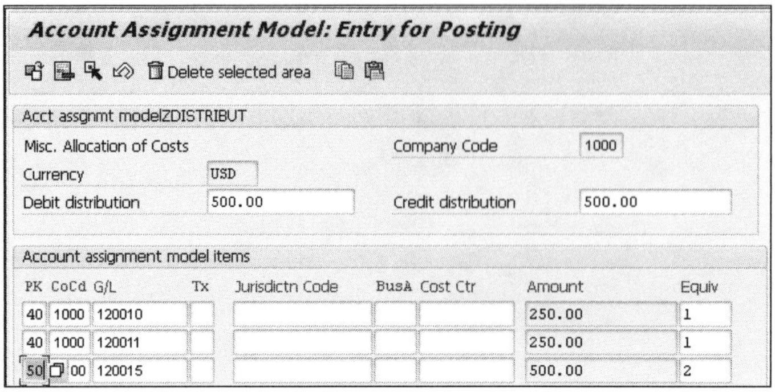

Figure 3.95 Account Assignment Model: Entry for Posting Amount Distributions

Click the **Save** icon, and a new document is posted referencing the account assignment model.

Account assignment models have been around for a long time and aren't as widely used now as in years past. Their use has largely been replaced with account assignment templates (see Section 3.1.4).

3.6.2 Recurring Documents

Recurring documents are accounting transactions that are repeated at regular intervals, usually monthly or quarterly. In other words, recurring documents are used to capture information on accounting transactions with a fixed payment date and amount, such as rent or insurance. They have a run schedule that can be configured to provide variability in the exact payment date.

Specific recurring data is entered into a recurring entry document. This document doesn't create accounting entries or update the G/L. Rather, the data in a recurring entry document is used for reference purposes for the recurring entry program, which in turn creates accounting documents when the program is executed.

To post recurring entry documents in your company codes, you must set up the X1 number range. The recurring entry original document numbers are assigned according to this number range.

To create an original recurring entry document, use Transaction FBD1. In the **Enter Recurring Entry: Header Data** screen that appears (Figure 3.96), enter a **Company Code**. The **Recurring entry run** parameters must be entered to indicate the start and end validity dates, intervals, and so on. Note here that you can enter a specific **Run date** if the accounting entry is also to be created with a specific posting date in mind. If there is some variability in the posting date, a **Run schedule** can be configured and specified.

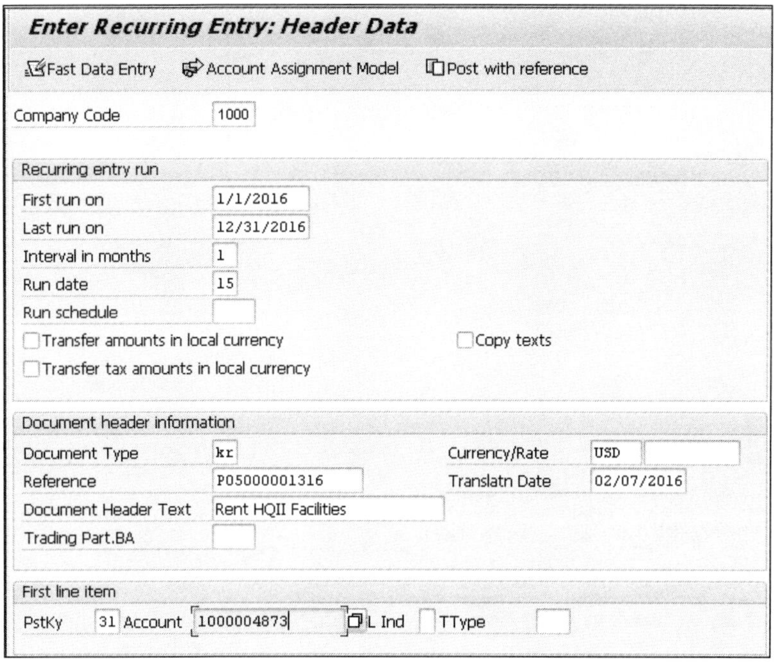

Figure 3.96 Enter Recurring Entry Header Data (Transaction FBD1)

Document header information is entered and is used and transferred to accounting documents that are created.

At the bottom of the screen, you begin to enter line items by entering a posting key (**PstKy**), **Account**, and, if applicable, a special G/L indicator (**L Ind**) or transaction type (**TType**).

With header details filled in, press [Enter]. In this example, the **Enter Recurring Entry Add Vendor Item** screen appears (Figure 3.97).

After inputting vendor line item details and a posting key and account for the second line item at the bottom of the screen, press [Enter]. The **Enter Recurring Entry Add G/L account item** screen appears (Figure 3.98). Enter an **Amount** and any other field values you require.

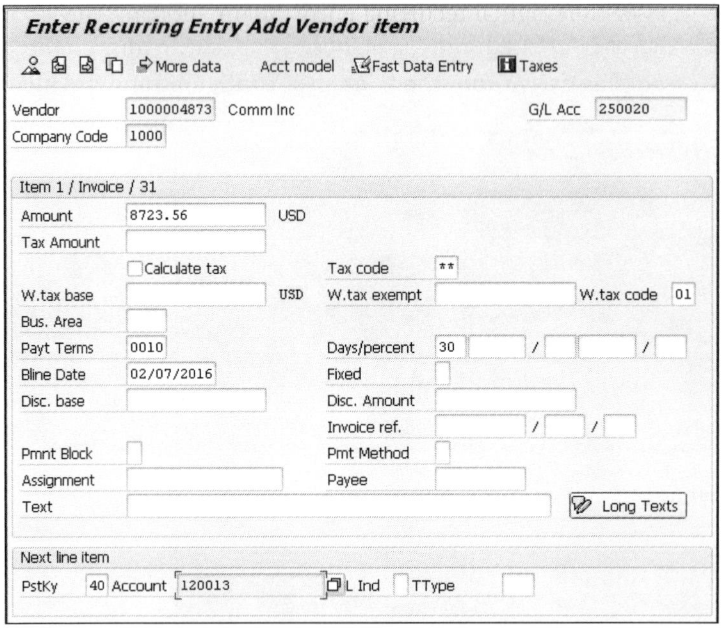

Figure 3.97 Add Vendor Line Item

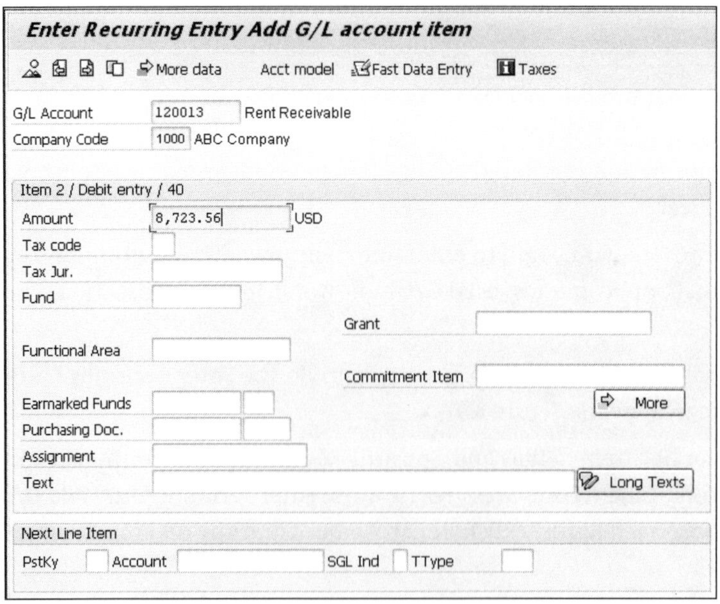

Figure 3.98 Add G/L Account Line Item

With the second line item of the original recurring entry document complete, click the **Post** icon 🖫. As shown in Figure 3.99, a message appears at the bottom of the screen saying that the document has been stored.

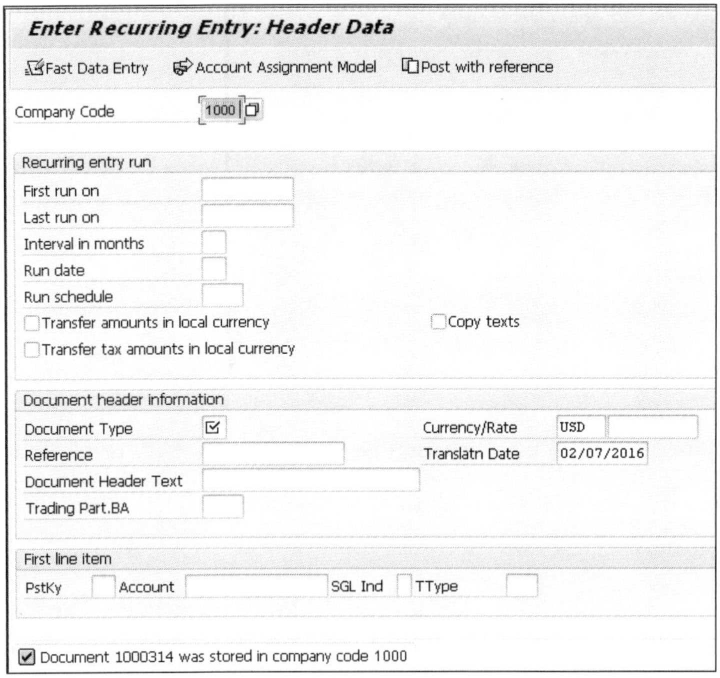

Figure 3.99 Recurring Entry Document Stored

After an original recurring entry document has been created, it can be displayed using Transaction FBD3. Figure 3.100 shows the **Display Recurring Document: Initial Screen** where you enter the **Document Number**, **Company Code**, and **Fiscal Year**. After inputting these field values, press Enter.

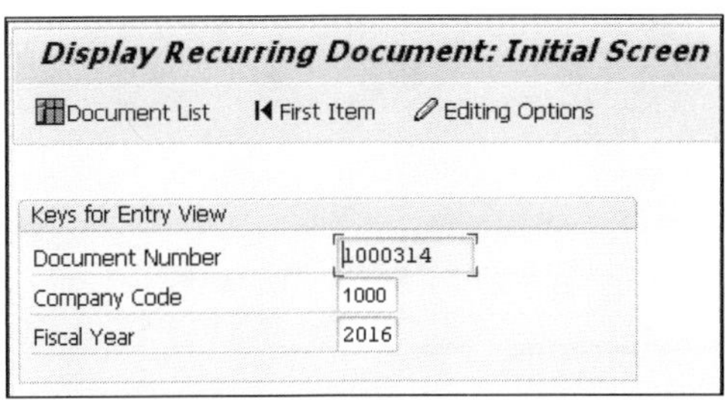

Figure 3.100 Display Recurring Document Initial Screen (Transaction FBD3)

The **Display Recurring Document: Overview** screen appears (Figure 3.101).

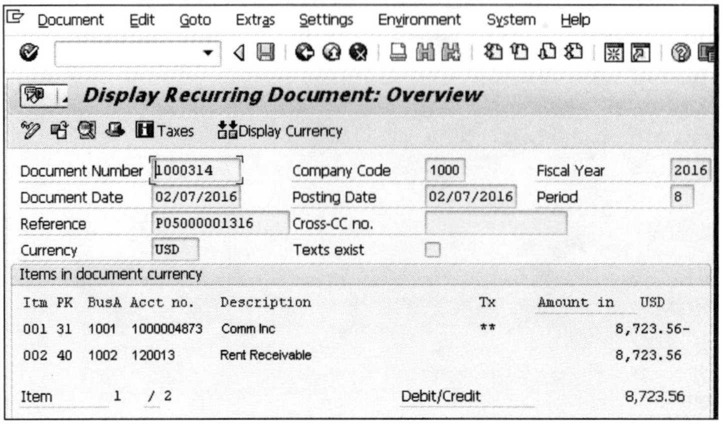

Figure 3.101 Display Recurring Document Overview Screen

To display the document header details, click on the top-hat icon (Figure 3.102) or press F5.

Figure 3.102 Display Recurring Document Header Dialog Box

Cancel out of the **Document Header** dialog box, and press F7 to display the recurring entry data of the document (Figure 3.103).

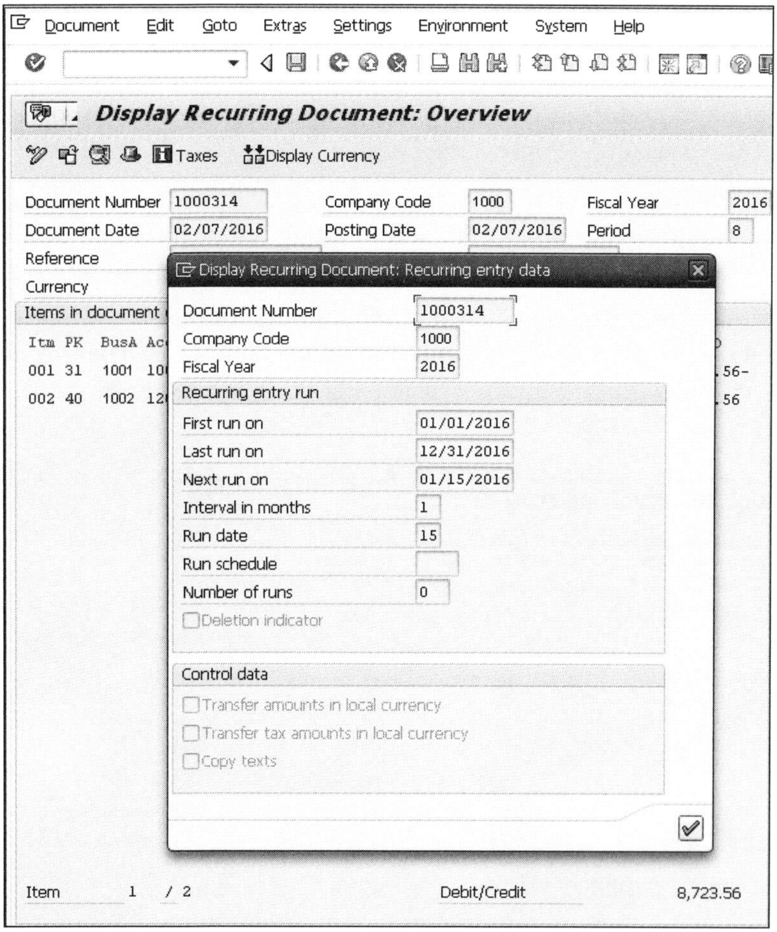

Figure 3.103 Display Recurring Entry Document Data

This concludes our discussion, for now, of recurring entry documents. In this section, we presented the creation and display of original recurring entry documents. See Chapter 16, Section 16.4, for a discussion on periodic processing and the creation of accounting documents from recurring entry documents.

3.6.3 Sample Documents

The final type of reference document discussed in this chapter is the *sample document*. A sample document is a way to create a reference document for use when posting accounting documents. To create sample documents, you must set up the X2 number range. The sample document numbers are assigned by this number range. Sample documents don't create account entries or update the G/L. Rather, the data in a sample document is used for reference purposes.

Because sample documents serve only as a data source, they present some advantages over posting with reference with a normal accounting document. Mainly, they can be changed or enhanced when creating postings.

Transaction F-01 is used to create a sample document. Figure 3.104 displays the **Enter Sample Document: Header Data** screen. Enter all the relevant fields in the header, as well as a posting key and account in the **First line item** area at the bottom of the screen. Then press [Enter].

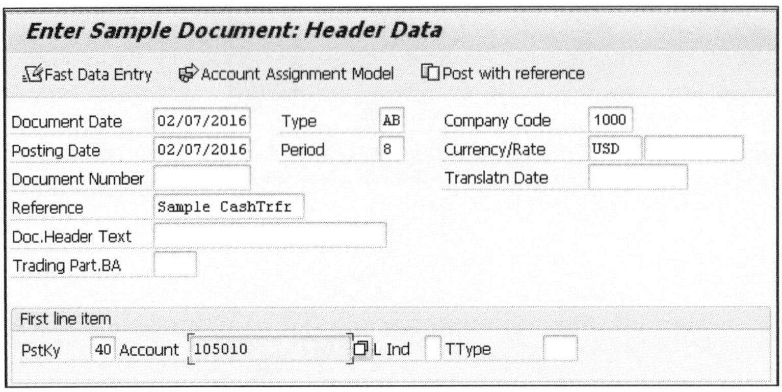

Figure 3.104 Enter Sample Document Header Data (Transaction F-01)

The **Enter Sample Document Add G/L account item** screen appears (Figure 3.105). For the first line item, be sure to enter an amount, or the line will be ignored. In addition, enter any other field values and a posting key and account in the **Next Line Item** section at the bottom of the screen before pressing [Enter].

In the next screen, you'll enter the amount and field values for the second G/L line item (Figure 3.106). After this is done, click on the **Post** icon .

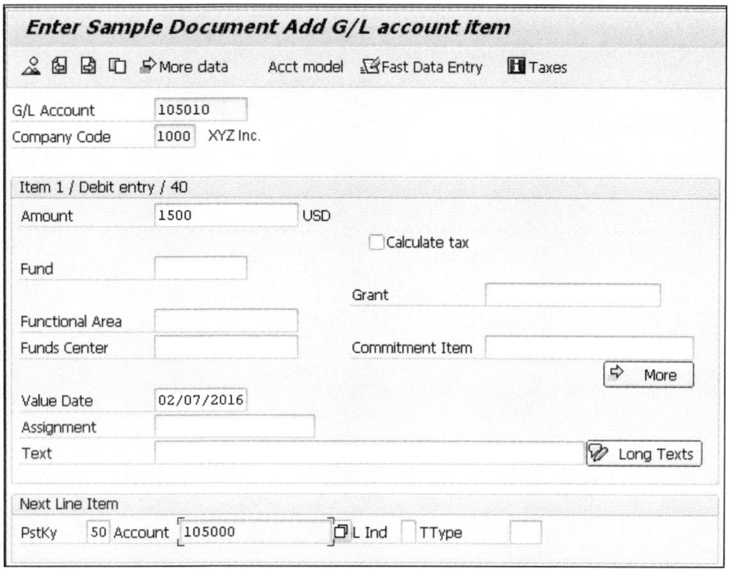

Figure 3.105 Enter Sample Document Add G/L Account Item Screen

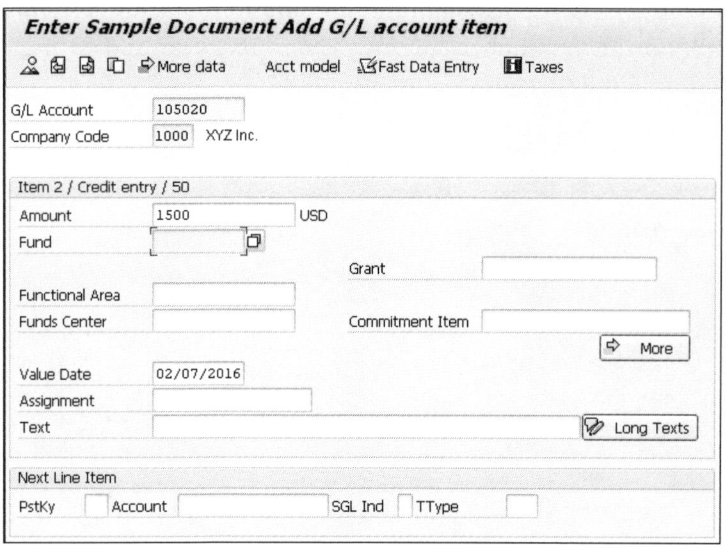

Figure 3.106 Second Enter Sample Document Add G/L Account Item

A message appears stating that the sample document number has been stored (Figure 3.107). Once again, this indicates that the document information was saved to be used for reference when creating accounting documents. However, no updates have been made to the G/L or to transaction figures and G/L balances.

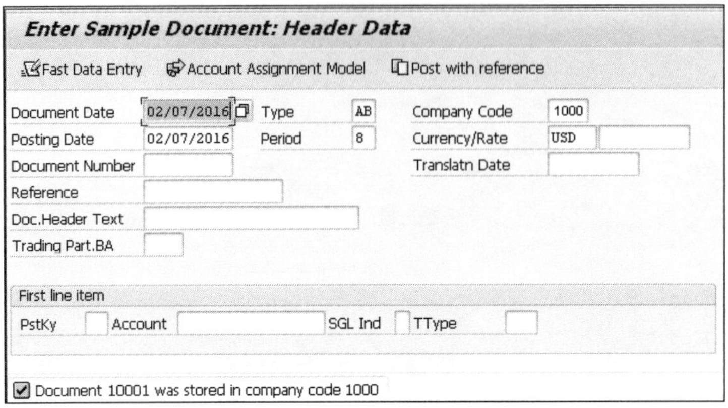

Figure 3.107 Sample Document Stored Message

To use a sample document as a reference when creating a G/L document, use Transaction FB50. Use [Shift]+[F9] to enter the transaction, or choose **Goto • Post with reference** from the menu bar. The **Post Document: Header Data** screen appears (Figure 3.108). Enter the sample document number, company code, fiscal year, and any relevant flow control indicators, and then press [Enter].

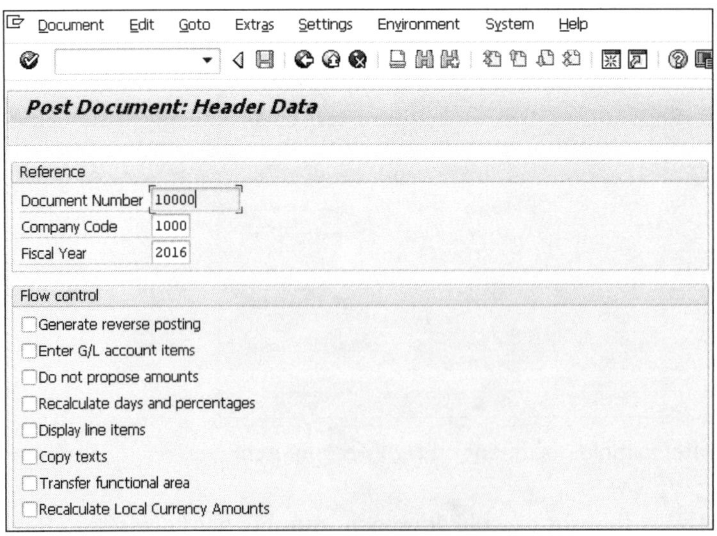

Figure 3.108 Post with Reference Sample Document (Transaction FB50)

The **Post Document: Header Data** screen appears with sample document data entered as a reference (Figure 3.109). From here, simply walk through each line item of the transaction, changing field values as you wish, and post the document when done.

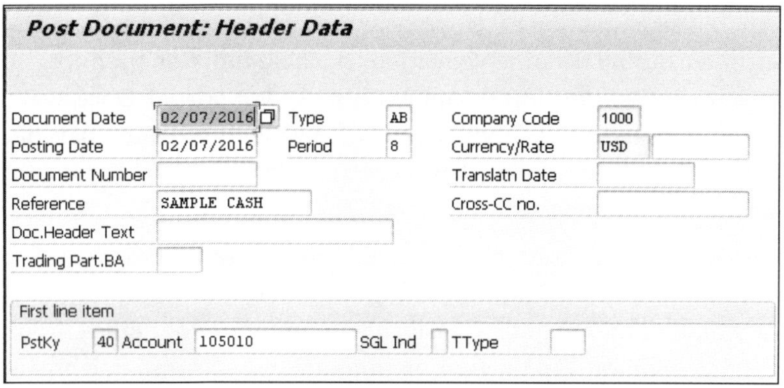

Figure 3.109 Post with Reference Sample Document Header Data

This completes our discussion of sample documents.

3.7 Summary

In this chapter, we covered G/L account transactions originating in the G/L module. The most common G/L transaction is the entry of a journal voucher using Transaction FB50. This chapter covered not only the creation of a G/L document but also associated G/L functions, such as document display, change, reverse, park, and more.

In addition, we also discussed functions associated with Transaction FB50, such as the tree display, screen variants, account assignment templates, editing options, and post with reference—all of which provide valuable insights to help you be more productive and organized in the G/L module. These are universal concepts in FI. Consider what you learned about them in this chapter as your first introduction to them. In future chapters, we'll revisit these topics and discuss them in relation to other types of transactions in FI.

In this chapter, you also learned the differences among document posting, parking, save as completed, and hold. A posted document is a G/L document that is complete, produces a G/L accounting document number, and updates the G/L account balances.

Parking a G/L document allows you to save an accounting document without impacting G/L account balances. This process may be necessary if the document is incomplete or if further edits, data validation, or document approval are required prior to posting. The save as completed function is similar to document parking, but the document undergoes more extensive document check logic, as though it was being posted. A document hold is a function to temporarily save your data. It's most useful when you're interrupted during document creation. The hold function produces no permanent document number until the document is parked or posted. Once again, these concepts aren't unique to G/L. They are also relevant to accounts payable, accounts receivable, and other accounting transactions. We'll revisit these topics for each module in which they are applicable.

Other G/L concepts discussed in this chapter include the Document Relationship Browser, account assignment templates, recurring documents, and sample documents. These all are tools to make your job easier and to improve your efficiency in creating and managing financial and accounting transactions. Account assignment templates and sample documents aren't as widely used today because other tools have evolved, but you may find some use for them.

Now that you've learned about creating and managing G/L transactions, the next chapter will teach you how to perform inquiries in the G/L module.

Chapter 4
General Ledger Account Inquiries

In Chapter 3, we covered transactions in the General Ledger (G/L) that you'll use on a daily basis. Now, in this chapter, we explore transactions and reports you can use to troubleshoot G/L account problems.

This chapter discusses the SAP General Ledger (commonly referred to as General Ledger [G/L]) account inquiry and maintenance functions that can help you research individual transactions, find account balances, display account transaction details, and run reports and queries.

G/L account inquiry and validation are essential job functions of an accounting clerk or supervisor. Often, you can use these functions to uncover data entry and other posting errors. Knowing how to perform the transactions in this chapter will provide you with essential skills needed in the day-to-day operations of an accounting department. To use a sports analogy, these transactions are the "blocking" and "tackling" of Financial Accounting (FI); that is, they are basic tasks practitioners must be able to perform quickly and routinely.

Account inquiries are important for several reasons. In particular, validation for month-end and year-end reporting must take place to ensure that accounting entries are accurate and complete. Furthermore, as a regular course of doing business, errors are found often and must be corrected. These errors could be as simple as accounting documents created with the wrong posting date, but regardless of the reason for the error, this chapter will enable you to better navigate the G/L module and analyze your accounting transactions.

Let's get started by learning how to view G/L account displays.

4.1 Account Displays

G/L account displays allow you to view individual or collective G/L account balances and transaction details (i.e., individual accounting line items). Transaction FAGLB03 is used for G/L account balances, and Transaction FAGLL03 is used for G/L account line items. In addition, from Transaction FAGLB03, you can double-click a number and drill down to the line item detail in Transaction FAGLL03. From Transaction FAGLL03, you can also double-click on a line item within a document and drill down to additional details.

The selection screens available via these transactions give you the flexibility to filter data by company code, posting date, and more. These selection options can be saved as *variants*, making them reusable. In addition, the output screen allows for further filtering, searching, sorting, and more. The output can be downloaded into various file formats (e.g., Excel), making further analysis outside SAP possible when needed.

Let's take a closer look at the G/L account displays: account balance and account line items.

4.1.1 Account Balance

The G/L account balance display shows a G/L account balance (or range of accounts) by period for the fiscal year specified. The resulting output is organized by period, debit balances, credit balances, net balances, and cumulative balances. This structure is particularly useful for reconciling G/L accounts with financial reports.

To display G/L account balances, use Transaction FAGLB03 or application menu path, **Accounting • Financial Accounting • General Ledger • Account • FAGLB03 – Display Balances (New)**, as shown in Figure 4.1.

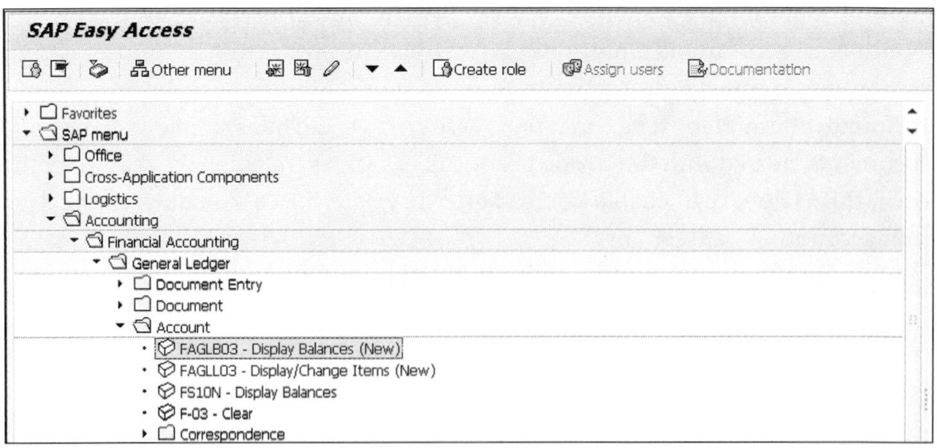

Figure 4.1 Transaction FAGLB03 Menu Path

Double-click **FAGLB03 – Display Balances (New)** from the menu path, or enter "FAGLB03" in the **Command** field (as shown in Figure 4.2) and press [Enter].

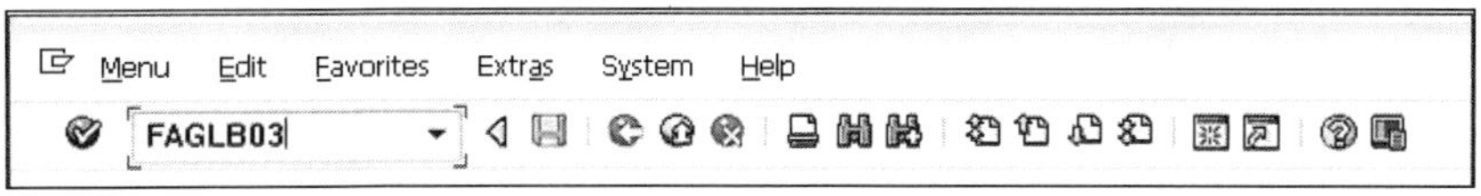

Figure 4.2 Entering "FAGLB03" in the Command Field

In the **G/L Account Balance Display** selection screen for Transaction FAGLB03, enter values in the **Account Number**, **Company Code**, and **Fiscal Year** fields. Notice that in the **Ledger** field, the leading ledger defaults into the selection screen, but you can select a nonleading ledger by clicking the **Choose Ledger** button (see Figure 4.3) and selecting the ledger of your choice.

You also can enter individual values or ranges. If you click the **Multiple Selection** icon (i.e., the yellow arrow) to the right of a field, you can enter multiple individual values or ranges, or exclude values and ranges.

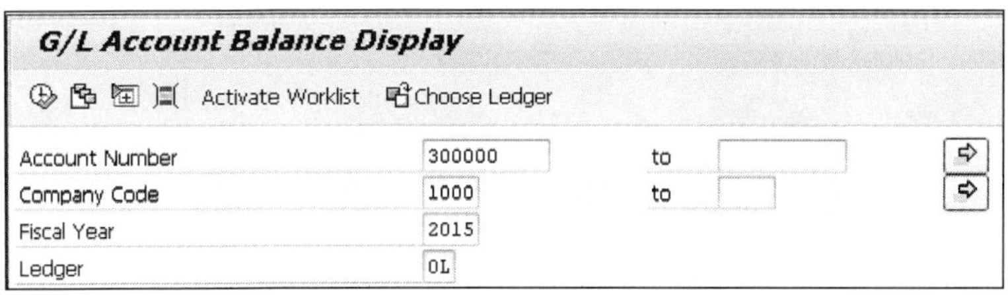

Figure 4.3 G/L Account Balance Display Selection Screen

After inputting values in the selection screen, click the **Execute** icon. The output is shown in Figure 4.4.

The resulting output is organized by period, debit balances, credit balances, net balances, and cumulative balances.

Now that you're familiar with the display of G/L account balances, let's look at G/L account line item displays. G/L line item displays are simply individual accounting lines from a financial document.

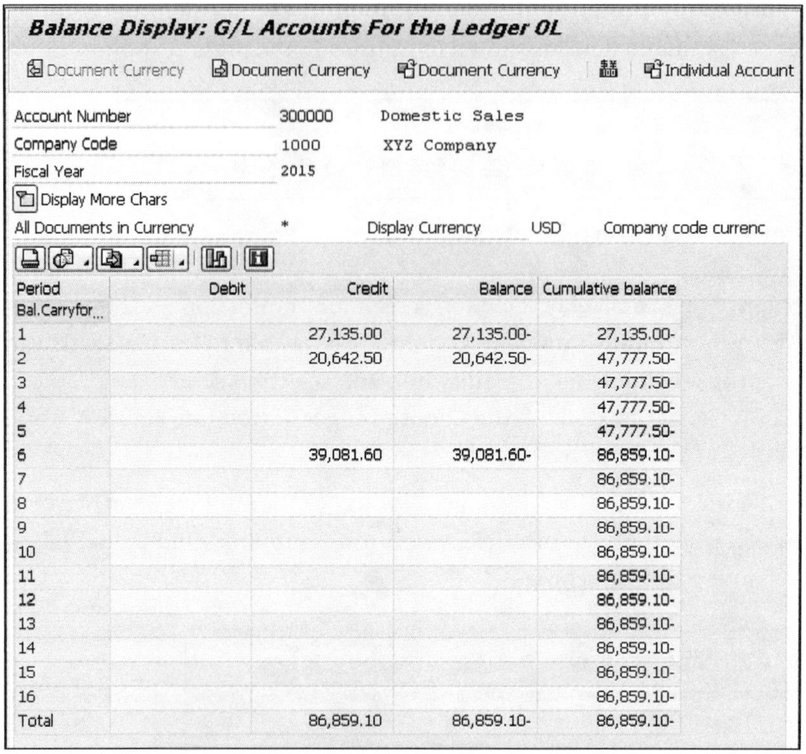

Period	Debit	Credit	Balance	Cumulative balance
Bal.Carryfor...				
1		27,135.00	27,135.00-	27,135.00-
2		20,642.50	20,642.50-	47,777.50-
3				47,777.50-
4				47,777.50-
5				47,777.50-
6		39,081.60	39,081.60-	86,859.10-
7				86,859.10-
8				86,859.10-
9				86,859.10-
10				86,859.10-
11				86,859.10-
12				86,859.10-
13				86,859.10-
14				86,859.10-
15				86,859.10-
16				86,859.10-
Total		86,859.10	86,859.10-	86,859.10-

Figure 4.4 G/L Account Balance Display Output Screen

4.1.2 Account Line Items

The *G/L account line item display* shows G/L account transaction details. Here, "details" means all the individual line item transactions that go into the G/L account balance. This transaction is particularly useful in sorting out discrepancies and suspected errors in G/L account balances.

Viewing line item displays is essential in reconciling back to account totals. The balance of a G/L account is the sum of the parts. The parts, in this instance, are individual accounting transactions. Viewing the G/L account details allows you to not only reconcile the totals but also track back to the original source of the entry. Being able to do so quickly and accurately is an important skill.

To display G/L account line items, use Transaction FAGLL03 or application menu path, **Accounting • Financial Accounting • General Ledger • Account • FAGLL03 – Display/ Change Items (New)**, as shown in Figure 4.5.

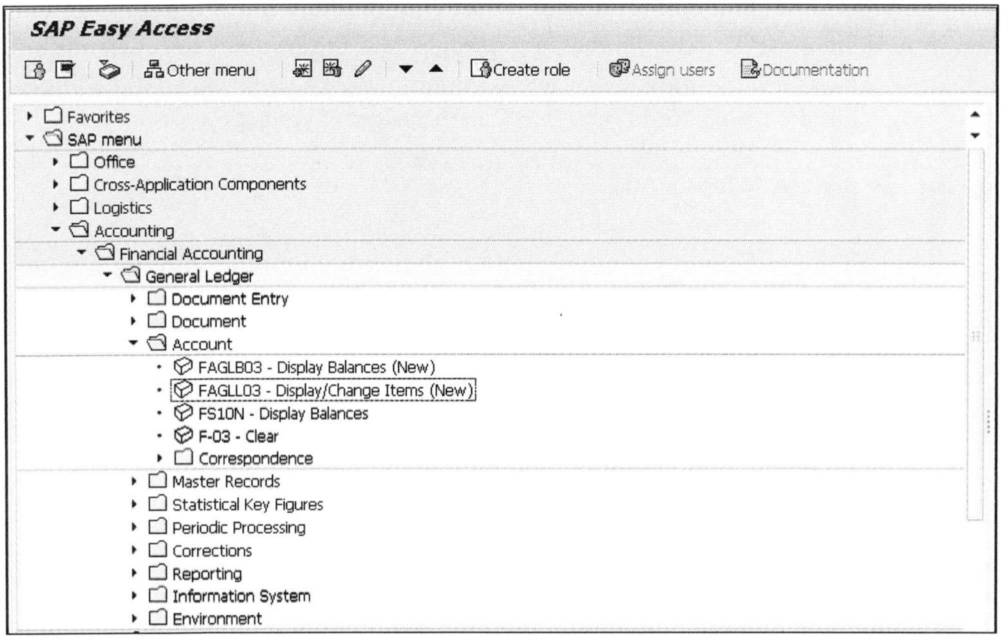

Figure 4.5 Transaction FAGLL03 Menu Path

Double-click **FAGLL03 – Display/Change Items (New)** from the menu path, or enter "FAGLL03" in the **Command** field (as shown in Figure 4.6) and press [Enter].

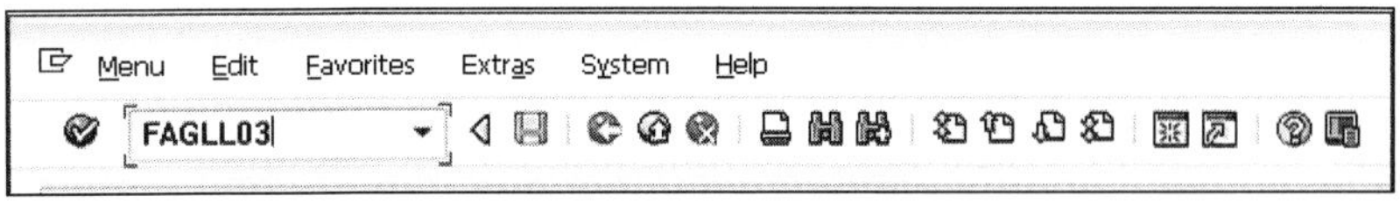

Figure 4.6 Entering "FAGLL03" in the Command Field

On the **G/L Account Line Item Display G/L View** selection screen for Transaction FAGLL03 (Figure 4.7), enter parameters for **G/L account** and **Company code** in the **G/L account selection** area, and for **Status** in the **Line Item Selection** area. The **Status** area requires you to choose one of three options:

- **Open Items**
- **Cleared Items**
- **All Items**

Each option contains date parameters, which will select relevant items without a date restriction if left blank. Notice that in the **Ledger** field, the leading ledger defaults into the selection screen, but you can select a nonleading ledger by clicking the **Choose Ledger** button (see Figure 4.7) and selecting the ledger of your choice.

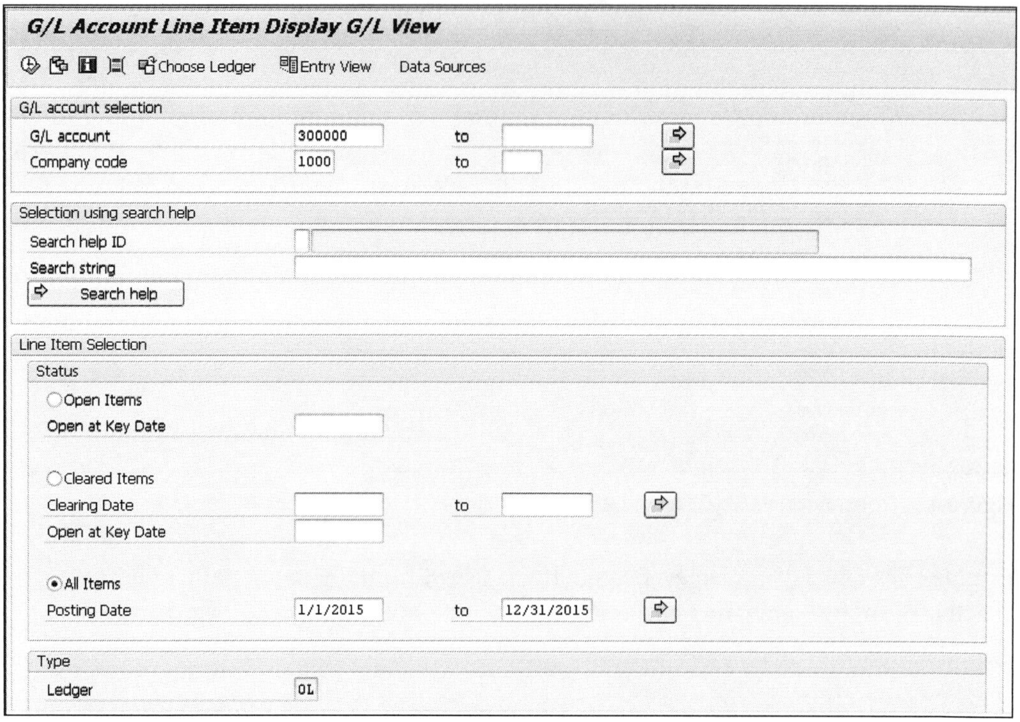

Figure 4.7 G/L Account Line Item Display G/L View Selection Screen

You can also enter individual values or ranges. If you click the **Multiple Selection** icon (i.e., the yellow arrow) to the right of a field, you can enter multiple individual values or ranges, or exclude values and ranges.

After inputting values on the selection screen, click the **Execute** icon. The output is shown in Figure 4.8.

The resulting output shows the detail of a G/L account balance. From this screen, you can sort, filter, total, and subtotal the output, and convert it to external file formats (e.g., Excel). In addition, you can create, save, and edit screen layouts.

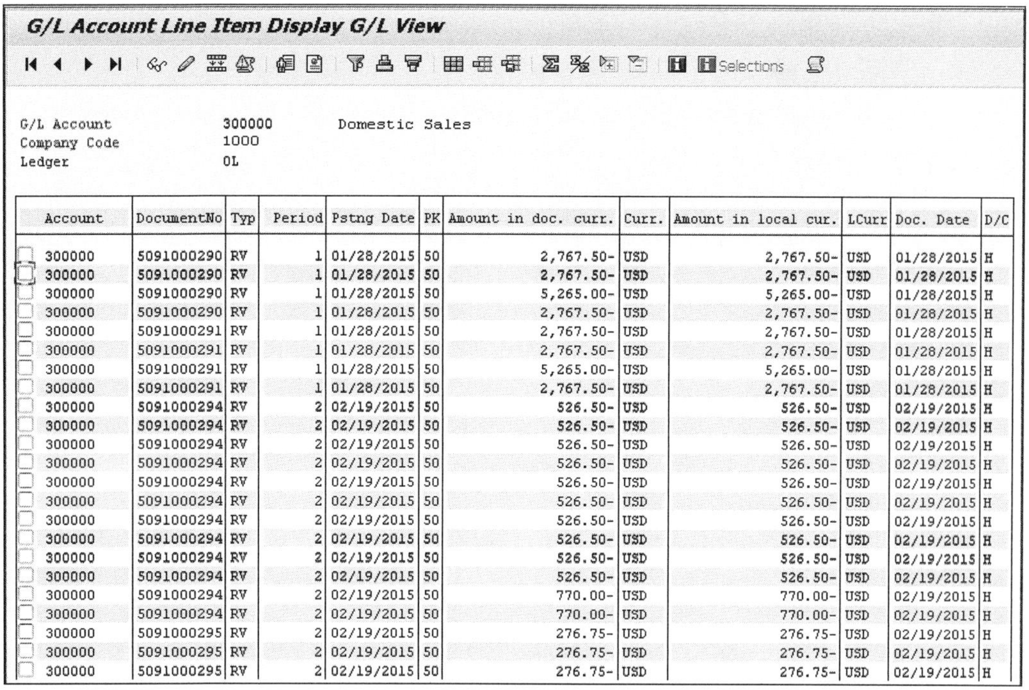

Account	DocumentNo	Typ	Period	Pstng Date	PK	Amount in doc. curr.	Curr.	Amount in local cur.	LCurr	Doc. Date	D/C
300000	5091000290	RV	1	01/28/2015	50	2,767.50-	USD	2,767.50-	USD	01/28/2015	H
300000	5091000290	RV	1	01/28/2015	50	2,767.50-	USD	2,767.50-	USD	01/28/2015	H
300000	5091000290	RV	1	01/28/2015	50	5,265.00-	USD	5,265.00-	USD	01/28/2015	H
300000	5091000290	RV	1	01/28/2015	50	2,767.50-	USD	2,767.50-	USD	01/28/2015	H
300000	5091000291	RV	1	01/28/2015	50	2,767.50-	USD	2,767.50-	USD	01/28/2015	H
300000	5091000291	RV	1	01/28/2015	50	2,767.50-	USD	2,767.50-	USD	01/28/2015	H
300000	5091000291	RV	1	01/28/2015	50	5,265.00-	USD	5,265.00-	USD	01/28/2015	H
300000	5091000291	RV	1	01/28/2015	50	2,767.50-	USD	2,767.50-	USD	01/28/2015	H
300000	5091000294	RV	2	02/19/2015	50	526.50-	USD	526.50-	USD	02/19/2015	H
300000	5091000294	RV	2	02/19/2015	50	526.50-	USD	526.50-	USD	02/19/2015	H
300000	5091000294	RV	2	02/19/2015	50	526.50-	USD	526.50-	USD	02/19/2015	H
300000	5091000294	RV	2	02/19/2015	50	526.50-	USD	526.50-	USD	02/19/2015	H
300000	5091000294	RV	2	02/19/2015	50	526.50-	USD	526.50-	USD	02/19/2015	H
300000	5091000294	RV	2	02/19/2015	50	526.50-	USD	526.50-	USD	02/19/2015	H
300000	5091000294	RV	2	02/19/2015	50	526.50-	USD	526.50-	USD	02/19/2015	H
300000	5091000294	RV	2	02/19/2015	50	526.50-	USD	526.50-	USD	02/19/2015	H
300000	5091000294	RV	2	02/19/2015	50	526.50-	USD	526.50-	USD	02/19/2015	H
300000	5091000294	RV	2	02/19/2015	50	526.50-	USD	526.50-	USD	02/19/2015	H
300000	5091000294	RV	2	02/19/2015	50	770.00-	USD	770.00-	USD	02/19/2015	H
300000	5091000294	RV	2	02/19/2015	50	770.00-	USD	770.00-	USD	02/19/2015	H
300000	5091000295	RV	2	02/19/2015	50	276.75-	USD	276.75-	USD	02/19/2015	H
300000	5091000295	RV	2	02/19/2015	50	276.75-	USD	276.75-	USD	02/19/2015	H
300000	5091000295	RV	2	02/19/2015	50	276.75-	USD	276.75-	USD	02/19/2015	H

Figure 4.8 G/L Account Line Item Display Output Screen

> **Note**
>
> Some people today do all they can to eliminate spreadsheets. In accounting and finance departments, however, spreadsheets are alive and well. In fact, it's more common today than ever before to begin with a G/L line item query, like that shown in Figure 4.8, and then filter, sort, reorder data elements, and save to a spreadsheet for further analysis. It's recommended that you do as much financial analysis as you can directly in SAP, but SAP has seamless integration with Excel to accommodate your needs.

Now that you've seen how to display G/L account balances and line item detail, let's look at a few standard SAP reports as an alternative means of obtaining this information.

4.2 Reports and Queries

In Section 4.1, Transaction FABLBO3 and Transaction FABLLO3 were discussed in detail. For validating account balances and transaction details, these transactions are beneficial particularly because they provide drilldown capability all the way to accounting documents. In addition, other tools are available to view G/L account balances and transaction detail. In this section, we'll show you where to find these alternative tools in G/L reports and how to do direct table queries.

4.2.1 Standard Reports

Standard reports are SAP delivered and are universally found in the **Information System** folder of the application menu. The most useful general-purpose G/L account balance reports can be accessed via the following application menu path: **Accounting • Financial Accounting • General Ledger • Information System • General Ledger Reports (New) • Account Balances • General** (see Figure 4.9).

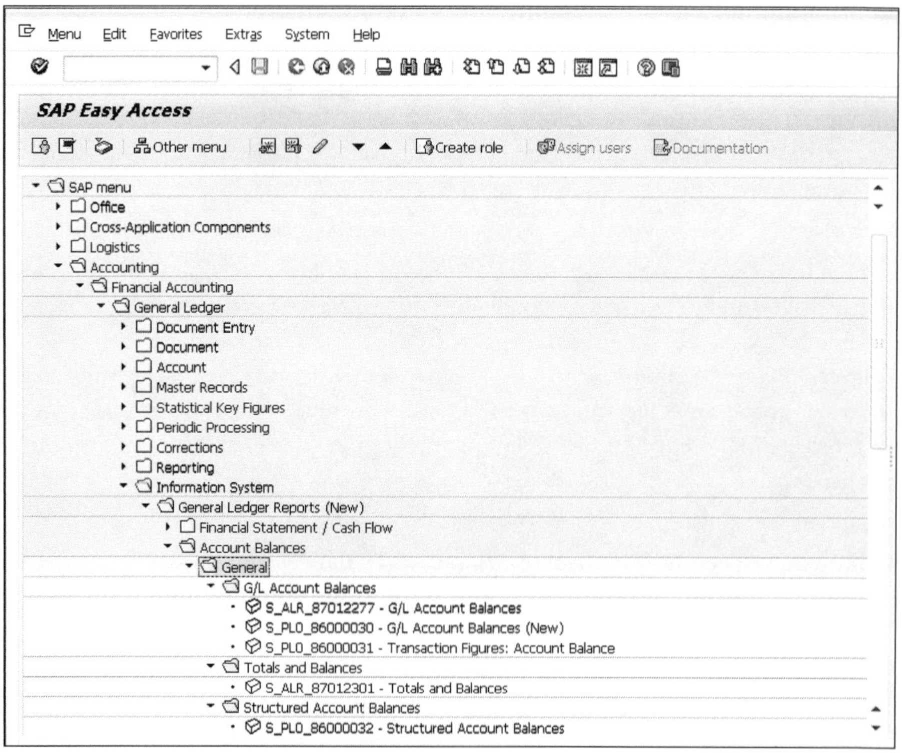

Figure 4.9 G/L Account Balances Reports

The most useful reports that aren't financial statements (i.e., general G/L account balance inquiry reports) are in the **G/L Account Balances** and **Totals and Balances** folders.

Let's look at an example. In the **G/L Account Balances** folder (Figure 4.10), you'll see report S_PLO_86000030: **S_PLO_86000030 – G/L Account Balances (New)**.

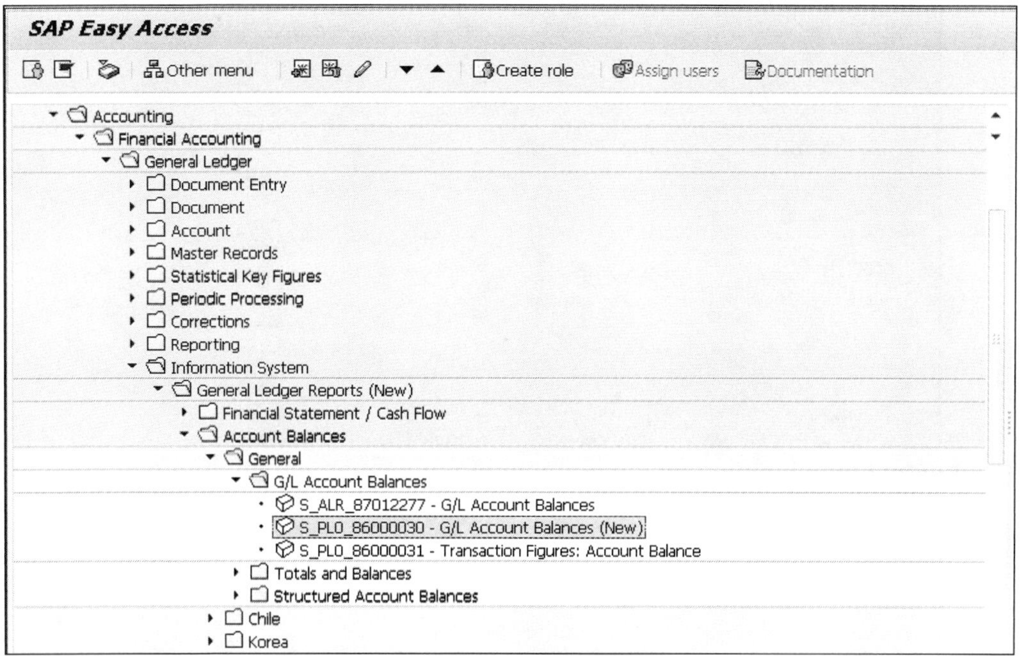

Figure 4.10 G/L Account Balances (New) Report Transaction Code

Double-click the report link to open the selection screen. The top portion (Figure 4.11) consists of **General Selections**. A powerful feature of this report is its ability to filter data upfront using a myriad of field selections. In Figure 4.11, we've added values in the **Currency Type** (i.e., **10** for company code currency), **Company Code**, **Account Number**, and **Segment** fields.

At the bottom of the selection screen, in the **Report selections** area, additional selection options are listed (Figure 4.12). Here, we've added values in the **Ledger**, **Fiscal year**, **From period**, and **To period** fields. We selected **Graphical report output** under **Output type**; avoid using the **Classic drilldown report** option, which is an outdated report view.

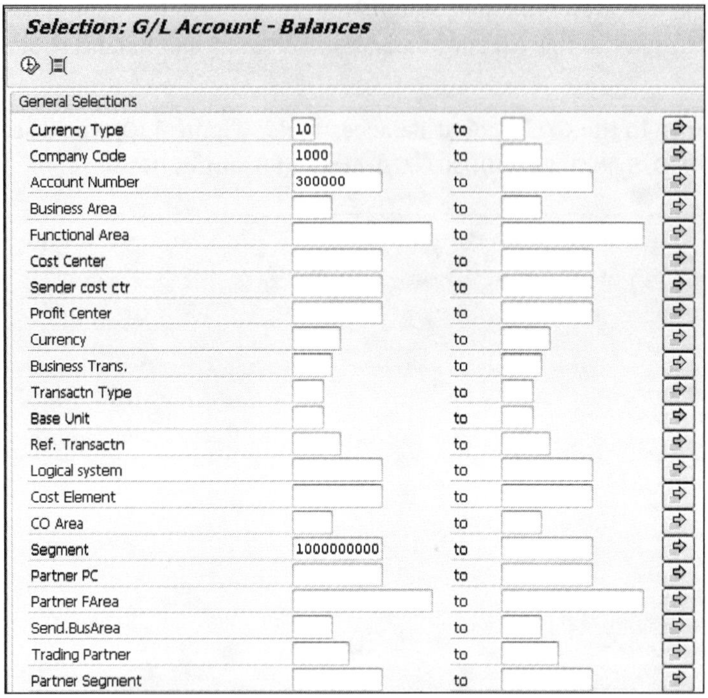

Figure 4.11 G/L Account Balances (New) Report: General Selections Screen

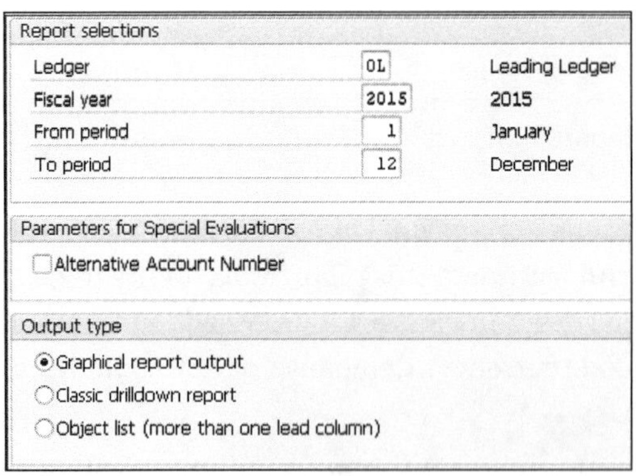

Figure 4.12 G/L Account Balances (New) Report: Additional Selections

After inputting values on the selection screen, click the **Execute** icon. The output is shown in Figure 4.13.

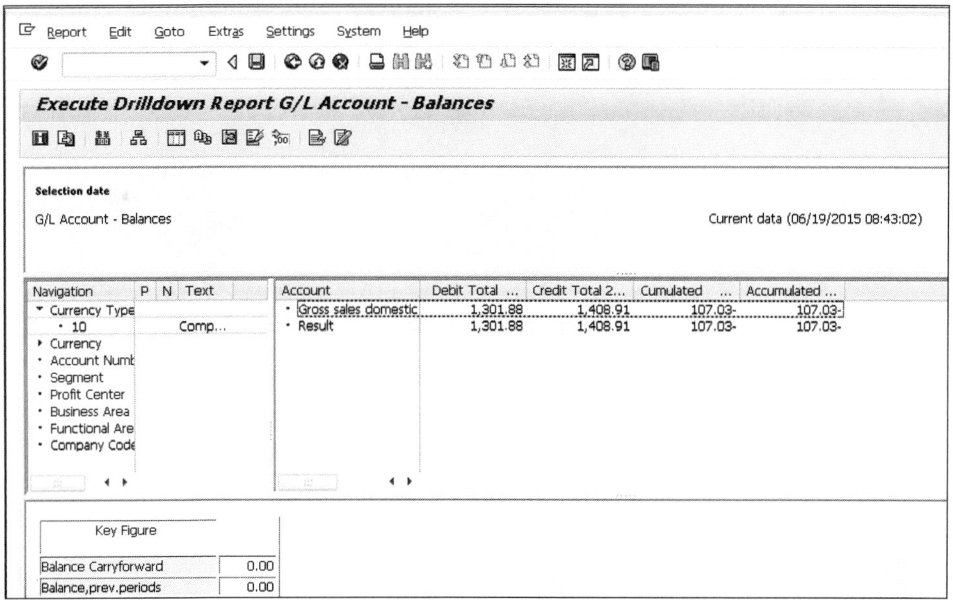

Figure 4.13 G/L Account Balances (New) Report: Output

There are pros and cons to using standard finance reports rather than Transaction FAGLB03 and Transaction FAGLL03. On the pro side, reports generally have more choices to filter data on the field selection screen, and the output screen provides a **Navigation** pane (shown in Figure 4.13), which provides built-in filtering capability.

On the con side, reports don't always have drilldown capability. This is certainly not always the case, so you should test each report you use so that you know one way or another. Moreover, reports may not provide the sorting and multidimensional filtering capabilities.

In addition to SAP standard reports, there are several methods to create custom reports and queries. These include custom ABAP reports, queries, Report Writer/Painter, and SAP Business Warehouse (SAP BW)/SAP BusinessObjects Business Intelligence (SAP BusinessObjects BI). You should check within your organization to ensure you have access to any useful custom reports and queries.

4.2.2 Direct Table Queries

Now that we've looked at the use of standard reports in G/L, let's consider how to make direct table queries to view G/L transaction details. There are two approaches to making direct table queries: Transaction SE11 and Transaction SE16. We'll cover both in the following sections.

Transaction SE11

Transaction SE11 can be accessed via the following application menu path: **Tools • ABAP Workbench • Development** (see Figure 4.14).

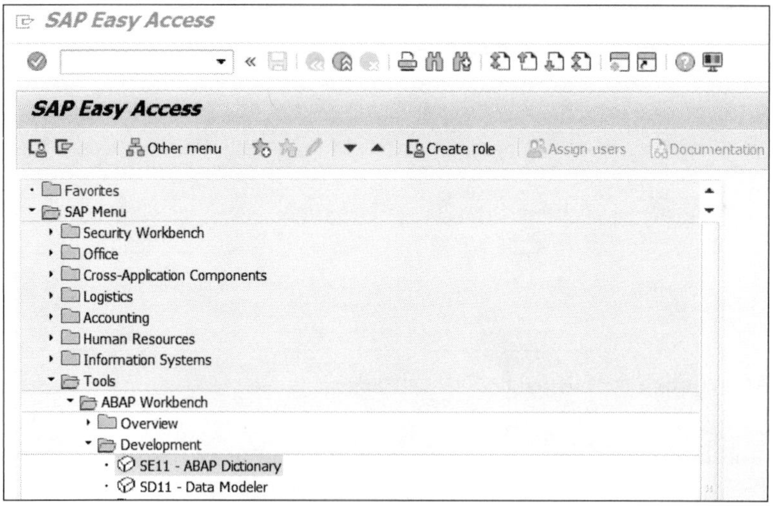

Figure 4.14 Transaction SE11 Application Menu Path

Double-click on **SE11 – ABAP Dictionary,** and the **ABAP Dictionary: Initial Screen** appears (see Figure 4.15).

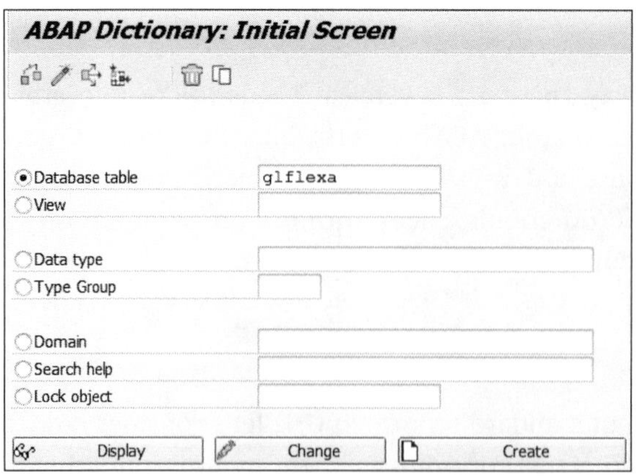

Figure 4.15 ABAP Dictionary: Initial Screen

Enter a table name in the **Database Table** field. For this example, the G/L line item table "glflexa" was entered. Press [Enter] or click the **Display** icon, and the **Dictionary: Display Table** screen appears (see Figure 4.16).

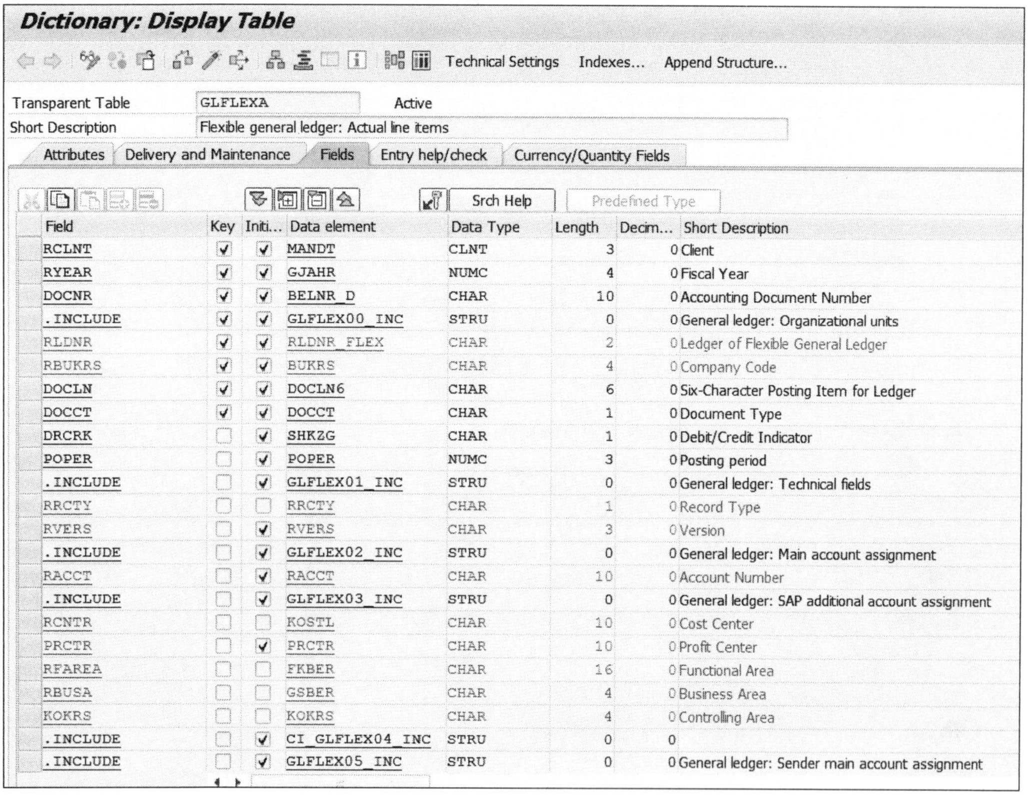

Figure 4.16 Display Table

As you can see, using Transaction SE11 allows you to view the database table before viewing its contents.

Next, click on the **Contents** icon in the toolbar as the first step toward viewing detail in the table. The **Data Browser Selection Screen** appears with the name of the table in the title bar (see Figure 4.17). Here, you can enter various field values to pare down your selection of data and find exactly what you're looking for. In this example, a value was entered for **Fiscal Year**.

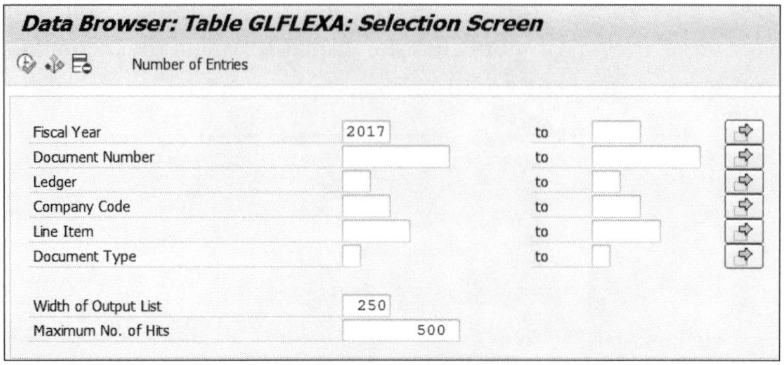

Figure 4.17 Data Browser Selection Screen

After entering field values in the selection screen, click on the **Execute** icon in the upper-left of the screen (see Figure 4.17). The G/L table entries appear (see Figure 4.18).

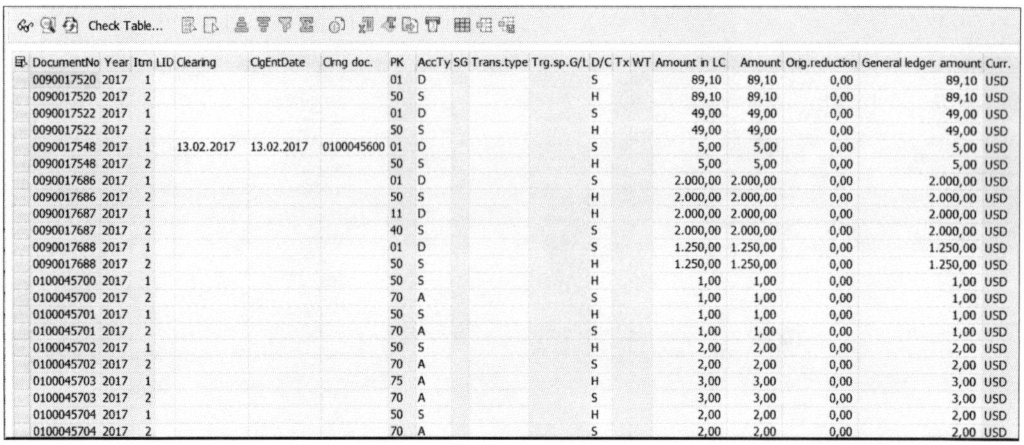

Check Table...

DocumentNo	Year	Itm	LID	Clearing	ClgEntDate	Clrng doc.	PK	AccTy	SG	Trans.type	Trg.sp.G/L	D/C	Tx	WT	Amount in LC	Amount	Orig.reduction	General ledger amount	Curr.
0090017520	2017	1					01	D				S			89,10	89,10	0,00	89,10	USD
0090017520	2017	2					50	S				H			89,10	89,10	0,00	89,10	USD
0090017522	2017	1					01	D				S			49,00	49,00	0,00	49,00	USD
0090017522	2017	2					50	S				H			49,00	49,00	0,00	49,00	USD
0090017548	2017	1		13.02.2017	13.02.2017	0100045600	01	D				S			5,00	5,00	0,00	5,00	USD
0090017548	2017	2					50	S				H			5,00	5,00	0,00	5,00	USD
0090017686	2017	1					01	D				S			2.000,00	2.000,00	0,00	2.000,00	USD
0090017686	2017	2					50	S				H			2.000,00	2.000,00	0,00	2.000,00	USD
0090017687	2017	1					11	D				H			2.000,00	2.000,00	0,00	2.000,00	USD
0090017687	2017	2					40	S				S			2.000,00	2.000,00	0,00	2.000,00	USD
0090017688	2017	1					01	D				S			1.250,00	1.250,00	0,00	1.250,00	USD
0090017688	2017	2					50	S				H			1.250,00	1.250,00	0,00	1.250,00	USD
0100045700	2017	1					50	S				H			1,00	1,00	0,00	1,00	USD
0100045700	2017	2					70	A				S			1,00	1,00	0,00	1,00	USD
0100045701	2017	1					50	S				H			1,00	1,00	0,00	1,00	USD
0100045701	2017	2					70	A				S			1,00	1,00	0,00	1,00	USD
0100045702	2017	1					50	S				H			2,00	2,00	0,00	2,00	USD
0100045702	2017	2					70	A				S			2,00	2,00	0,00	2,00	USD
0100045703	2017	1					75	A				H			3,00	3,00	0,00	3,00	USD
0100045703	2017	2					70	A				S			3,00	3,00	0,00	3,00	USD
0100045704	2017	1					50	S				H			2,00	2,00	0,00	2,00	USD
0100045704	2017	2					70	A				S			2,00	2,00	0,00	2,00	USD

Figure 4.18 G/L Table Entries

Using the toolbar at the top of Figure 4.18, you can change the layout, sort, filter, download, and more. From the G/L table line item display, you can also double-click on any row and display all the field values in G/L for a financial line item.

Transaction SE16

Another way to look at G/L data directly in tables is by using Transaction SE16, which can be accessed via the following application menu path: **Tools • ABAP Workbench • Overview • Application Hierarchy** (see Figure 4.19).

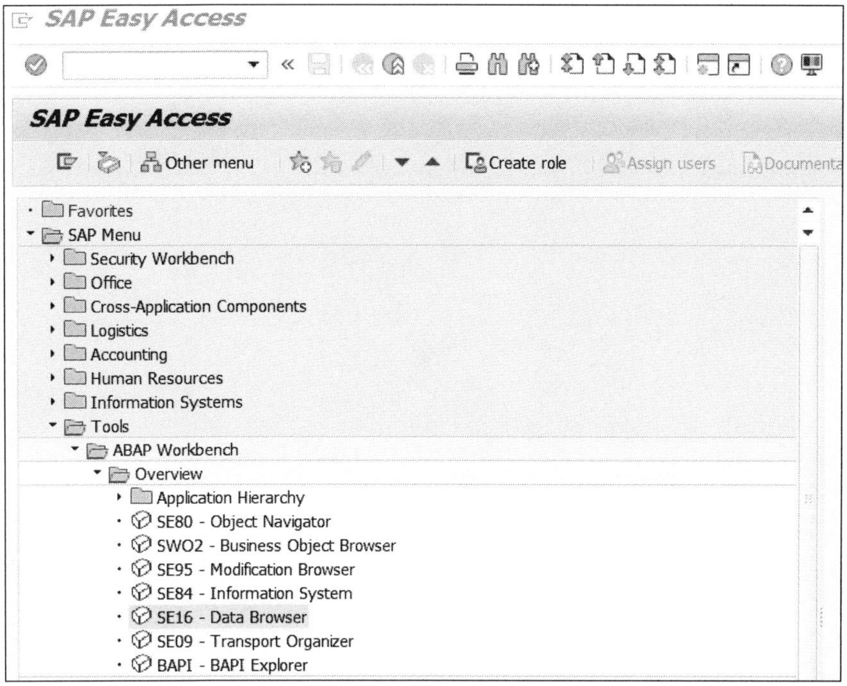

Figure 4.19 Transaction SE16 Application Menu Path

Double-click on **SE16 – Data Browser**, and the **Data Browser: Initial Screen** appears (see Figure 4.20).

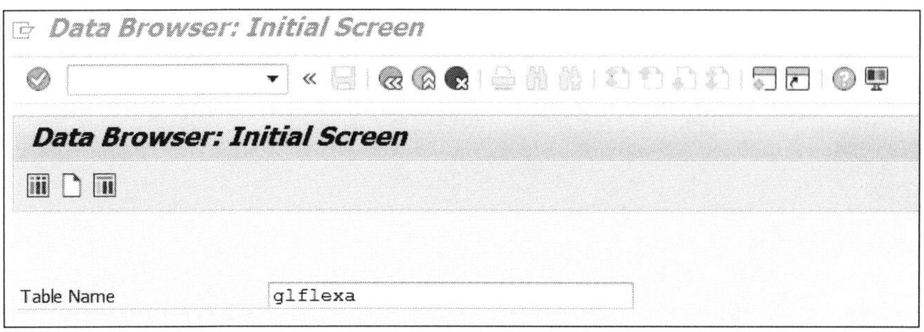

Figure 4.20 Data Browser: Initial Screen

Enter a table name (e.g., "glflexa"), and press `Enter` or click on the Contents icon. Figure 4.21 shows the table entries.

Data Browser: Table BSEG Select Entries 500

Check Table...

DocumentNo	Year	Itm	LID	Clearing	ClgEntDate	Clrng doc.	PK	AccTy	SG	Trans.type	Trg.sp.G/L	D/C	Tx	WT	Amount in LC	Amount	Orig.reduction	General ledger amount	Curr.
0090017520	2017	1					01	D				S			89,10	89,10	0,00	89,10	USD
0090017520	2017	2					50	S				H			89,10	89,10	0,00	89,10	USD
0090017522	2017	1					01	D				S			49,00	49,00	0,00	49,00	USD
0090017522	2017	2					50	S				H			49,00	49,00	0,00	49,00	USD
0090017548	2017	1		13.02.2017	13.02.2017	0100045600	01	D				S			5,00	5,00	0,00	5,00	USD
0090017548	2017	2					50	S				H			5,00	5,00	0,00	5,00	USD
0090017686	2017	1					01	D				S			2.000,00	2.000,00	0,00	2.000,00	USD
0090017686	2017	2					50	S				H			2.000,00	2.000,00	0,00	2.000,00	USD
0090017687	2017	1					11	D				H			2.000,00	2.000,00	0,00	2.000,00	USD
0090017687	2017	2					40	S				S			2.000,00	2.000,00	0,00	2.000,00	USD
0090017688	2017	1					01	D				S			1.250,00	1.250,00	0,00	1.250,00	USD
0090017688	2017	2					50	S				H			1.250,00	1.250,00	0,00	1.250,00	USD
0100045700	2017	1					50	S				H			1,00	1,00	0,00	1,00	USD
0100045700	2017	2					70	A				S			1,00	1,00	0,00	1,00	USD
0100045701	2017	1					50	S				H			1,00	1,00	0,00	1,00	USD
0100045701	2017	2					70	A				S			1,00	1,00	0,00	1,00	USD
0100045702	2017	1					50	S				H			2,00	2,00	0,00	2,00	USD
0100045702	2017	2					70	A				S			2,00	2,00	0,00	2,00	USD
0100045703	2017	1					75	A				H			3,00	3,00	0,00	3,00	USD
0100045703	2017	2					70	A				S			3,00	3,00	0,00	3,00	USD
0100045704	2017	1					50	S				H			2,00	2,00	0,00	2,00	USD
0100045704	2017	2					70	A				S			2,00	2,00	0,00	2,00	USD

Figure 4.21 G/L Table Entries via Transaction SE16

Using the toolbar at the top of Figure 4.21, you can change the layout, sort, filter, download, and more. From the G/L table line item display, you can also double-click on any row and display all the field values in G/L for that financial line item.

End users are typically not given authorization to use direct table access via Transaction SE11 because it's a transaction targeted specifically for use by developers. Transaction SE16 is more commonly authorized with restriction to specific tables. Just as a carpenter can't build a house with only one tool, so too may you need multiple tools to complete your G/L account inquiries. Use these tools to pinpoint account discrepancies in subledgers, between modules, and reports by using a variety of fields, such as company code, posting date, and other relevant selection criteria. All the relevant accounting data is easily accessible. Your job is to know how to quickly and easily get to this data using the transactions and reports we've covered.

4.3 Summary

In this chapter, we covered some of the most essential tools for G/L account inquiries. These tools include the G/L account balances transaction (Transaction FAGLB03), the G/L account line item display transaction (Transaction FAGLL03), and standard G/L reports. Use of these transactions and reports often is essential to understanding the activity posting to the G/L.

This chapter approached inquiries from two perspectives: G/L account totals (i.e., balances) and line item details. Both are important. You need account balances for numerous reasons, including financial reporting. Line item details are important to reconcile back to account totals and to manage specific account details. Being able to perform these tasks quickly and accurately is an essential skill.

In addition to covering the topics of standard G/L reports and transactions to display balances and G/L line item details, this chapter covered two ways to display financial information directly from tables. The first is using Transaction SE11, which allows you to display the table and its contents. The second way is using Transaction SE16, which takes you directly into table contents.

Now that we've completed our discussion of G/L transactions and account queries, let's explore the topic of accounts payable transactions in the next chapter.

Chapter 5
Accounts Payable Processes

In this chapter, we discuss business processes in the Accounts Payable (AP) module. The steps that make up the procurement of goods and services aren't isolated to the AP module but rather reach back into transactions in Procurement and Materials Management (MM).

Accounts Payable (AP) is the SAP module used for managing vendor accounts and issuing payments for goods and services your company procures. Specific AP transactions are covered in Chapter 6. The intent of this chapter, however, is to broaden your perspective so you learn to think of AP transactions as steps in a business process, and not as isolated business events.

Thinking in terms of business processes instead of individual transaction codes is important because it helps you grasp the bigger picture and be more effective as an accountant or financial manager working in SAP. At times, it's challenging because doing so forces you to think creatively and coordinate more closely with other departments. Yet, in the end, it's the only way to grasp the concept of real-time SAP integration. In addition, understanding end-to-end business processes is very useful in performing financial close at month-end and year-end.

There are several AP-related business processes. In this chapter, we'll focus on one core process: procure-to-pay. Using this process as the topic for discussion, you'll see the integration between Materials Management (MM) and AP in a complete procure-to-pay scenario. In addition, we'll discuss some variations of the process. Variations may exist depending regarding your industry, business practices, and SAP modules implemented.

A typical procure-to-pay business process consists of the following steps:

1. Create a purchase requisition (PR).
2. Create a purchase order (PO) or convert a PR to a PO.
3. Create an inbound delivery.

4. Post a goods receipt.
5. Perform invoice verification.
6. Issue an outgoing payment.

Let's begin our discussion with the frontend of the procure-to-pay process in the MM-Purchasing module.

5.1 Logistics

Before getting into specific procurement transactions, let's put the MM-Purchasing module into perspective. It fits within the broader category of logistics. Logistics functionality in SAP covers a broad spectrum of capabilities. Figure 5.1 shows the application menu path for **Logistics**, which includes **Materials Management**, **Sales and Distribution**, **Production**, **Plant Maintenance**, and more.

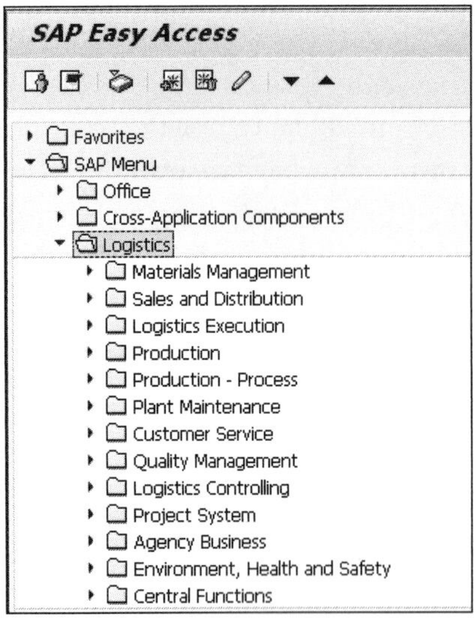

Figure 5.1 Logistics Application Menu Path

The frontend procurement transactions are in MM, which is where we'll begin our discussions, with the PR transaction.

5.1.1 Create Purchase Requisition

The first transaction in the procure-to-pay business process is the creation of a *purchase requisition* (PR). SAP defines a PR as a request or instruction to a purchasing department to procure a certain quantity of a material or a service so that it's available at a certain point in time. In other words, PRs are internal requests for purchasing actions. They aren't orders to directly procure goods or services from a specific vendor.

Most often, companies with centralized procurement use PRs, and they are particularly relevant when purchasing departments are responsible for making sourcing decisions. In some companies, PRs aren't used at all. In others, they are used only for certain types of procurements.

Even before a PR is created, the procurement process begins by identifying the need for a good or service. Several functions in SAP help you plan for these needs, particularly if you work for a manufacturing company. Some of the options for creating PRs include the following:

- Creating them automatically from Material Requirements Planning (MRP)
- Creating them automatically from SAP Advanced Planning and Optimization runs
- Creating them indirectly from modules such as Production Planning (PP), Sales and Distribution (SD), Project Maintenance (PM), and Project System (PS)
- Creating them from shopping carts in SAP Supplier Relationship Management (SAP SRM)
- Creating them manually, by an end user

5.1.2 Purchase Orders

While a PR is a purchasing request, a *purchase order* (PO) is a specific procurement action. In other words, a PO is a formal request from a purchasing organization to a specific vendor asking the vendor to supply or provide a certain quantity of goods or services. POs aren't dependent on PRs; however, if a PR is created, it can be referenced during PO creation, and the PO will adopt many details from the PR.

Figure 5.2 shows an example PO displayed using Transaction ME23N. A PO consists of three parts: header, item overview, and item details.

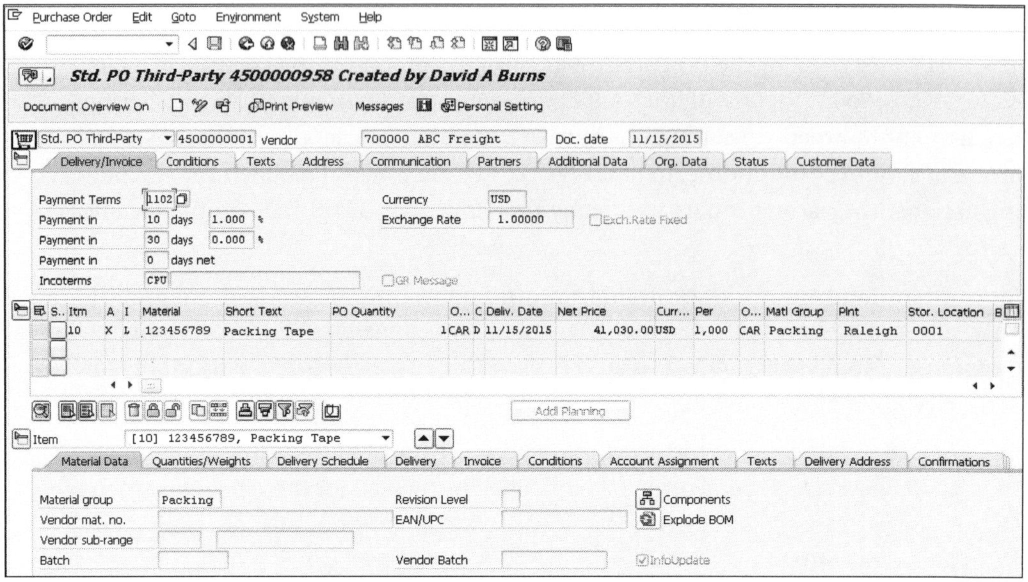

Figure 5.2 Display Purchase Order Screen

5.1.3 Inbound Delivery, Post Goods Receipt, and Invoice Receipt

After you create a PO and schedule an inbound delivery, the next step is to receive the goods and services. You can create a goods receipt using Transaction MIGO and referencing the PO. After a goods receipt exists, the PO will display a **Purchase Order History** tab in the **Item** details area of the PO (Figure 5.3) with the material document number displayed.

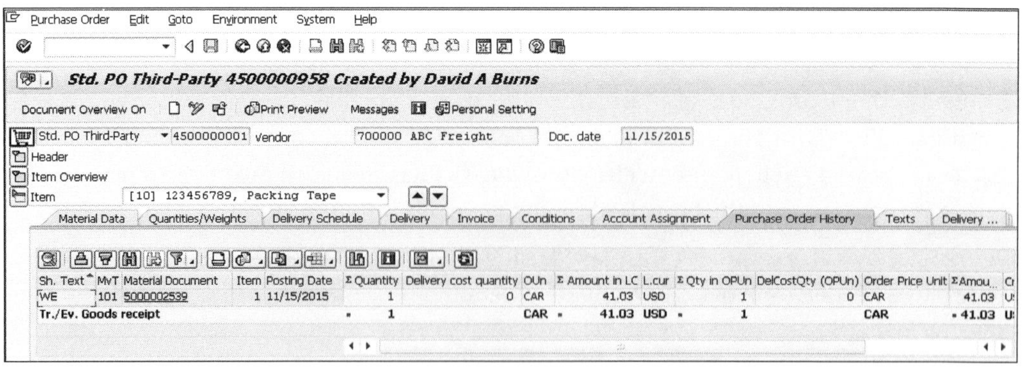

Figure 5.3 Display Purchase Order Screen with Goods Receipt

Click on the **Material Document** number to be taken directly into the material document (Figure 5.4). Note the **FI Documents** button in the center of the screen, which indicates that Financial Accounting (FI) documents were automatically created from the goods receipt transaction.

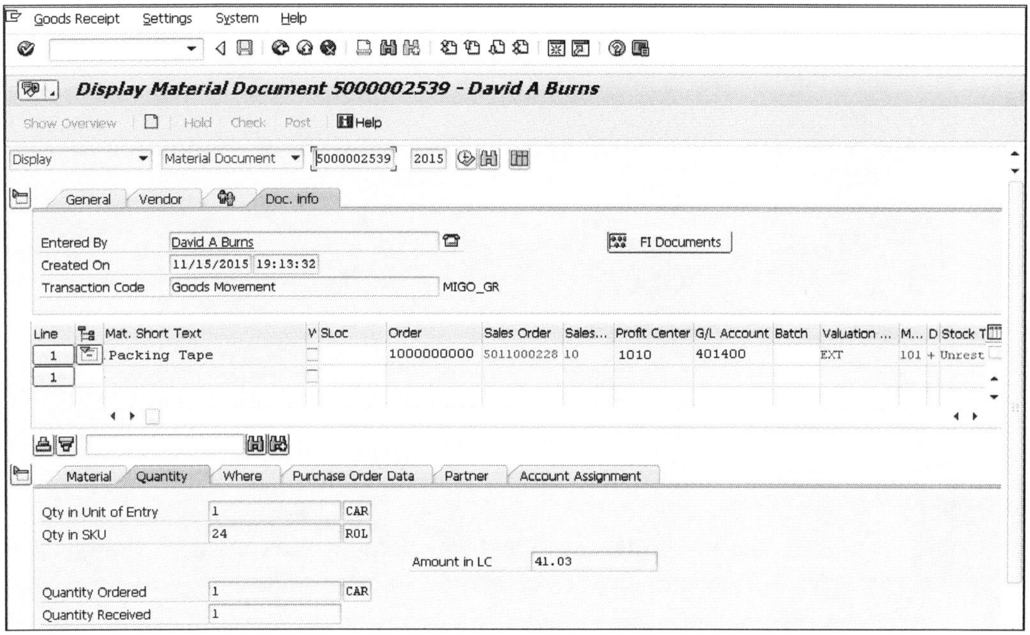

Figure 5.4 Display Goods Receipt Material Document

In this example, clicking on the **FI Documents** button opens the **List of Documents in Accounting** dialog box (Figure 5.5), which lists one accounting document and one controlling document.

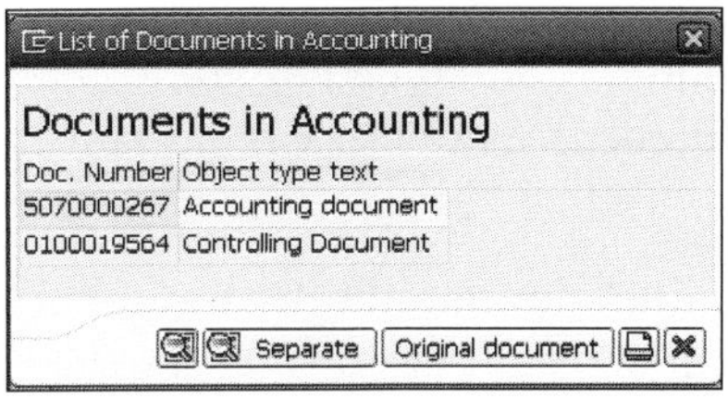

Figure 5.5 List of Documents in Accounting from Goods Receipt

Double-click on the accounting document number (**Doc. Number**) to open the financial document (Figure 5.6), which reveals that the goods receipt transaction created a goods movement to update the General Ledger (G/L). Note that the document number highlighted in Figure 5.5 is the same document number in the header of Figure 5.6.

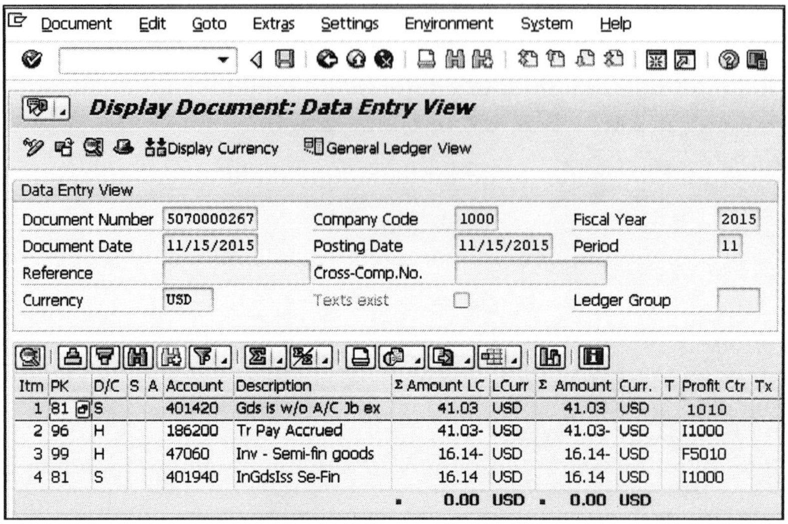

Figure 5.6 Display Accounting Document from Goods Receipt

Goods movements are configured in MM with account determination settings that specify which G/L accounts are used in G/L postings. *Account determinations* are configured settings that determine which G/L accounts to use. Account determinations are beyond the scope of this book, but it's important to obtain your company's posting models, which should lay out all the accounting entries by transaction type and their associated account determination configuration settings.

Creating an invoice receipt document typically follows the creation of the goods receipt. SAP provides configuration settings to determine if a goods receipt must precede the posting of an invoice receipt. SAP also provides functionality called Evaluated Receipt Settlement (ERS), by which invoices don't need to be posted; instead, invoices post automatically based on the PO and goods receipt. It's important to know which process your company follows.

You can create an invoice receipt document using Transaction MIRO with reference to the PO. When you create an invoice receipt, the PO will display a **Purchase Order History** tab in the **Item** details section of the PO (Figure 5.7) with the material document number displayed.

> **Note**
>
> Posting invoice receipts in MM with reference to a PO using Transaction MIRO is referred to as *Logistics Invoice Verification* (*LIV*). This differs from posting an AP invoice directly in FI using Transaction FB60 without reference to a PO.

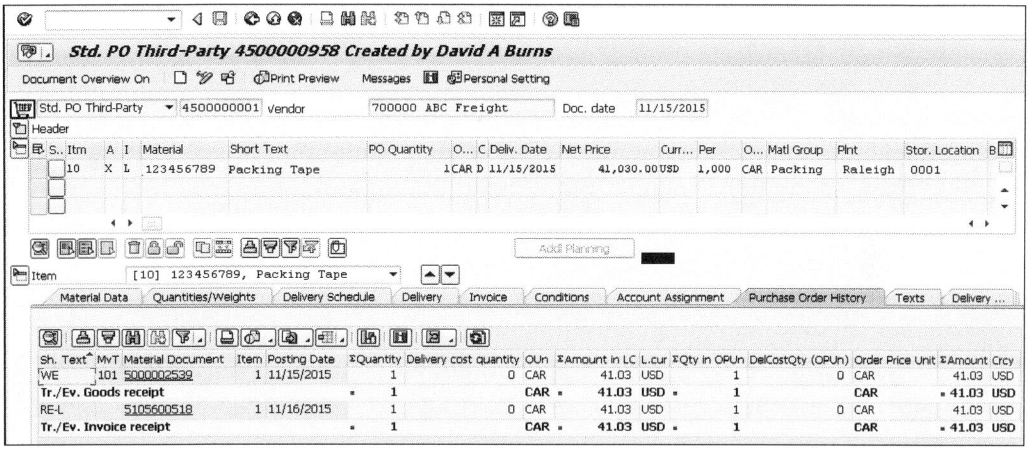

Figure 5.7 Display Purchase Order with Invoice Receipt

5.1.4 Automatic Creation of Accounting Invoice

The invoice receipt document created using Transaction MIRO creates two documents—a material document and an AP invoice—and this is where things become a little tricky. Both documents can have the same document number, which is typically the case for most SAP customers. SAP has a configuration setting that allows you to keep the MM and AP document numbers the same or allows them to be different.

Let's look at an invoice document using the example from Figure 5.7. If you click on the invoice receipt document shown in Figure 5.7, the display material invoice document will open (Figure 5.8). You know that these are the same documents because the invoice receipt document number in Figure 5.7 is the same as the document number shown in the top center of Figure 5.8.

Now, keep in mind that you have two invoice documents: a material document in MM and another in AP. The invoice shown in Figure 5.8 is the MM document; you can view the corresponding AP invoice by clicking the **Follow-On Documents** button shown in Figure 5.8. When you do so, the AP invoice opens (Figure 5.9). It's this AP invoice that triggers the open vendor payable. In other words, the AP invoice updates the G/L and vendor account with the expense and payable amounts, and this document is cleared through the payment process.

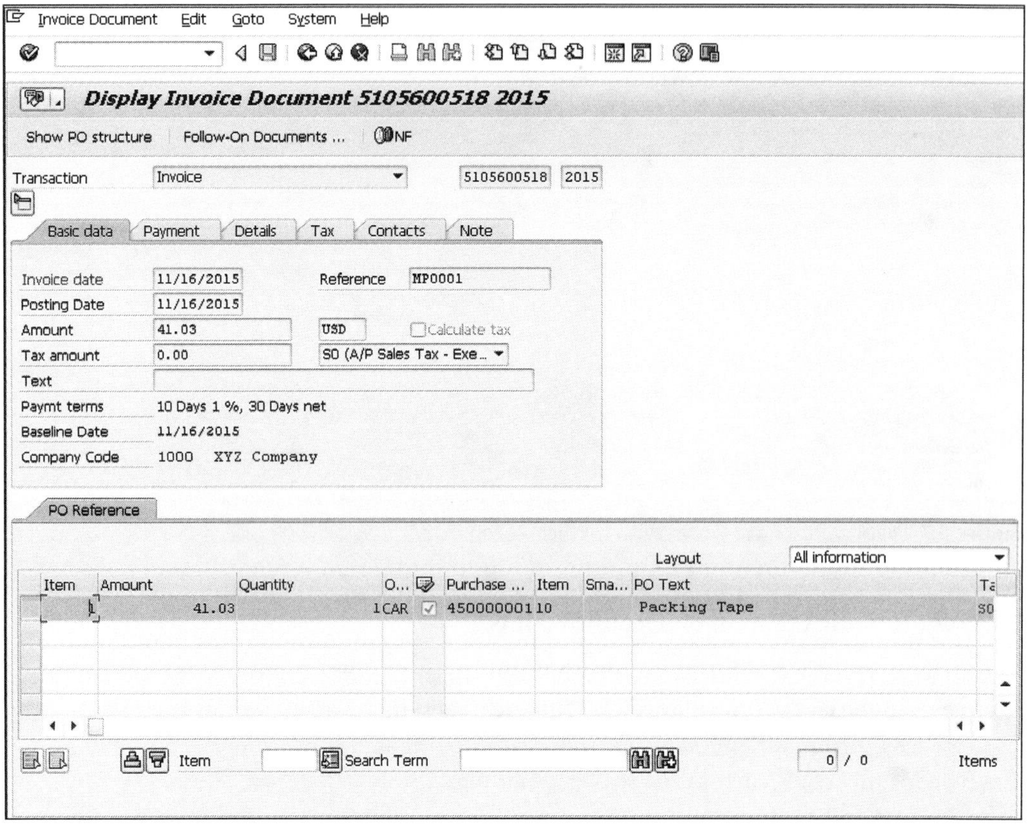

Figure 5.8 Display Material Invoice Document

Invoice receipts can be reversed in MM-LIV, but invoice receipt documents can't be changed. To change something such as payment terms, change the AP invoice directly in FI. For more complex changes, such as to a cost object, the invoice document should be reversed in MM-LIV and reposted.

Now that you've seen the procure-to-pay process all the way through to the creation of an AP invoice using MM-LIV, let's look at how to create an invoice directly in AP.

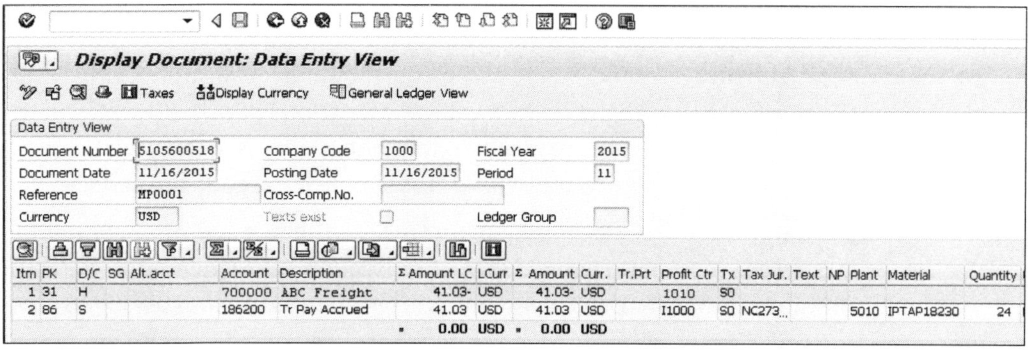

Figure 5.9 Display AP Invoice Document

5.2 Create Direct Invoices

Direct invoices often refers to AP invoices created using Transaction FB60. These are AP invoices created directly in the AP module rather than in MM.

There are a few distinguishing features of direct invoices. First, they have no corresponding material invoice number; material invoice documents are only created using Transaction MIRO in MM-LIV. A few other differences exist and are illustrated in Figure 5.10. The standard document type for direct AP invoices is KR, whereas those from MM-LIV are document type RE. The document number ranges also differ because number ranges are individually assigned to document types.

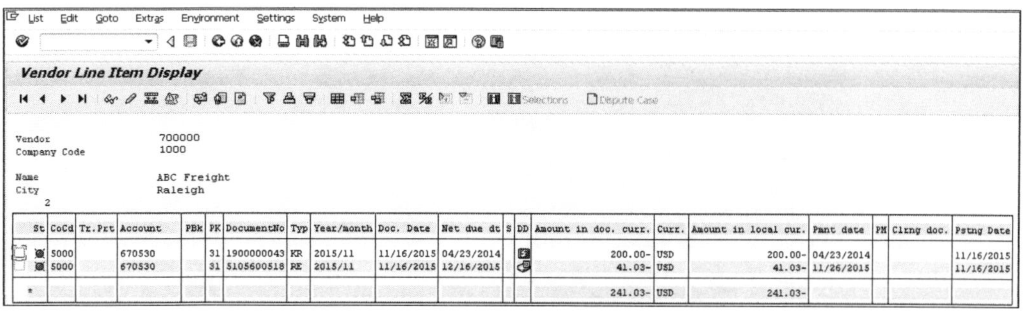

Figure 5.10 Transaction FBL1N Vendor Line Item Display Screen

For more information on direct AP invoices, see Chapter 6, Section 6.1.1.

Now that we've stepped through all the preceding steps in the procure-to-pay process, let's discuss outgoing payments.

5.3 Issue Outgoing Payments

Whether an AP invoice is created as a follow-on document from MM-LIV using Transaction MIRO or created as a direct invoice using Transaction FB60, the last step in the procure-to-pay process is to issue payment to the vendor. This is the physical transfer of money from your company to the vendor that supplied the goods or services.

There are two ways to issue outgoing payments in SAP. The first and most commonly used way is to use automatic payments via Transaction F110 (covered in detail in Chapter 7). The other way to issue payments is referred to as *manual payments*. Two transaction codes are used for manual payments: Transaction F-53 and Transaction F-58. The main difference between the two is that Transaction F-58 prints payment output forms (i.e., checks), and Transaction F-53 doesn't. Both create a payment document, which clears open AP invoices and updates the G/L. In the remainder of this section, we'll focus on Transaction F-53.

To create an outgoing payment manually in AP, follow application menu path, **Accounting • Financial Accounting • Accounts Payable • Document Entry • Outgoing Payment • F-53 – Post**, as shown in Figure 5.11.

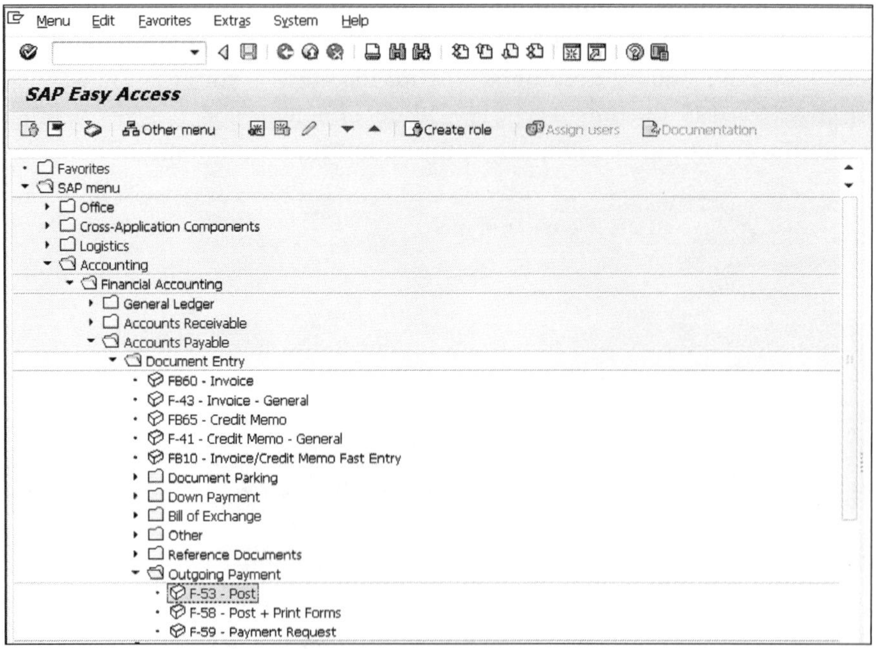

Figure 5.11 Transaction F-53 Application Menu Path

Double-click **F-53 – Post,** and the **Post Outgoing Payments: Header Data** screen opens (Figure 5.12). The fields that appear on the header with prepopulated values may vary depending on your system configuration and editing options. In this example, values defaulted into the **Posting Date**, **Period**, document **Type**, **Currency/Rate**, and **Company Code** fields, whereas we entered values into the **Document Date** and **Reference** fields.

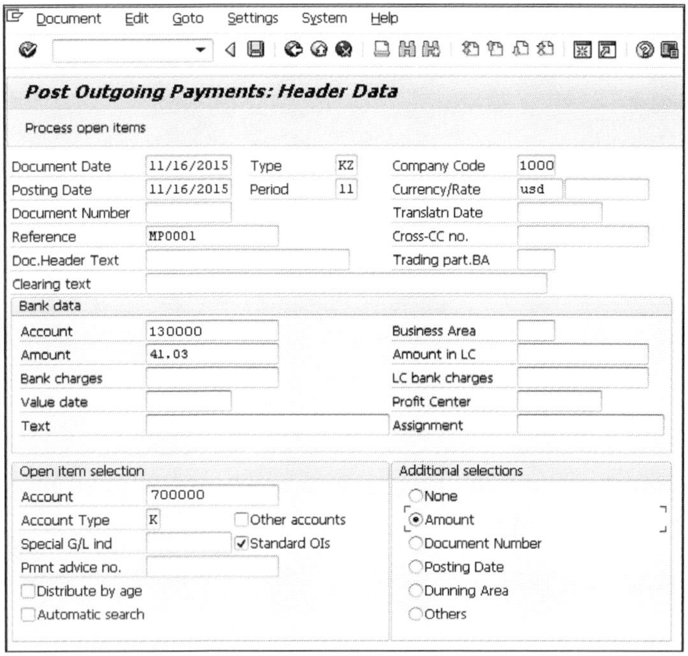

Figure 5.12 Post Outgoing Payments: Header Data

In the **Bank data** area, we entered a bank G/L account number into the **Account** field; the **Amount** field was populated with the AP invoice amount. In the **Open item selection** area, we entered the vendor number in the **Account** field, and in **Additional selections**, we selected the **Amount** radio button.

With all field values entered, click the **Process open items** button at the top-left corner of the screen.

The **Post Outgoing Payments Enter selection criteria** screen now opens (Figure 5.13). In this example, we entered the AP invoice amount in the **From** and **To** fields. When ready, click the **Process open items** button.

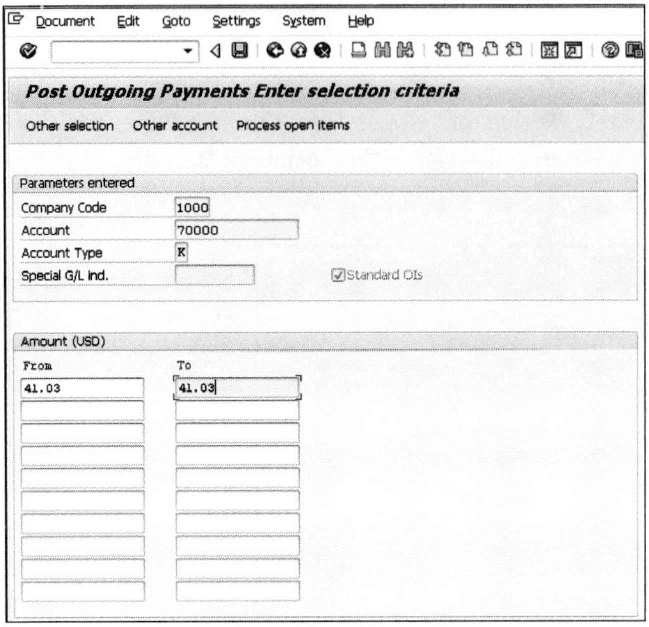

Figure 5.13 Post Outgoing Payments Selection Criteria

The **Post Outgoing Payments Process open items** screen opens (Figure 5.14). With the AP invoice selected, click the **Save** icon .

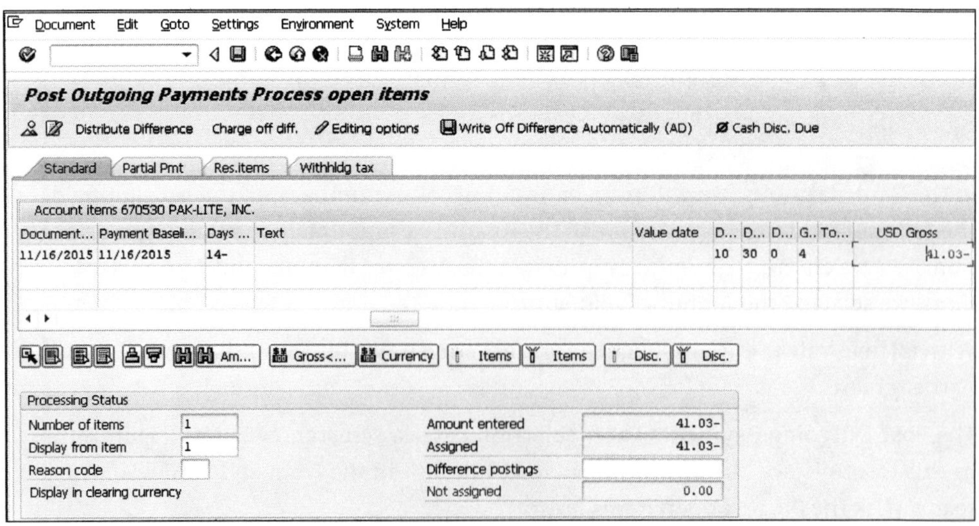

Figure 5.14 Post Ougoing Payments Process Open Items Screen

The system creates a clearing document, and the status of the invoice changes from **Open** to **Cleared**.

Now that we've discussed the procure-to-pay process, let's consider a few scenarios that require additional process steps.

5.4 Process Exceptions

Exceptions occur throughout business processes. Goods may arrive damaged and need to be returned. An invoice may contain an incorrect amount or quantity. Documents may be posted with incorrect information. In this chapter, we won't attempt to identify all the possible exceptions that can occur. Instead, the following sections will examine three transactions in FI that are frequently used to correct errors or adjust transaction details.

5.4.1 Credit Memos

Credit memos make a credit adjustment to the account of a business partner. They are applicable to both AP and Accounts Receivable (AR) and thus used for both vendor and customer account adjustments. You might create a credit memo because of a defective good, an overcharge, or another adjustment needed to a vendor or customer account. Credit memos net against amounts at the time of payment to ensure a vendor is to avoid overpayment.

There are two ways to create AP credit memos. The first is in the FI AP module using Transaction FB65 (see Chapter 6, Section 6.2). Transaction FB65 should be used for general vendor account adjustments and overcharges not specific to purchasing transactions originated in MM. When you require a credit memo for a transaction that originated in MM, the best approach is to create the credit memo via Transaction MIRO.

Figure 5.15 shows the **Transaction** dropdown box in Transaction MIRO with the **Credit memo** selection option highlighted.

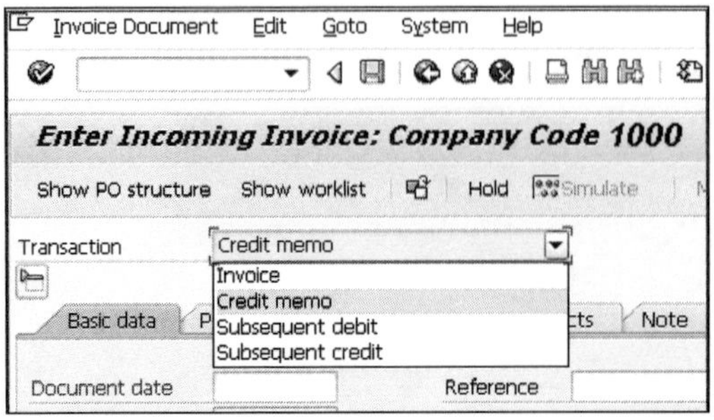

Figure 5.15 Transaction Dropdown Selection

After you've created a credit memo, the PO referenced in the credit memo displays the credit memo document number on the **Purchase Order History** tab. In the example shown in Figure 5.16, the IR line showing a quantity of **1-** is a credit memo document.

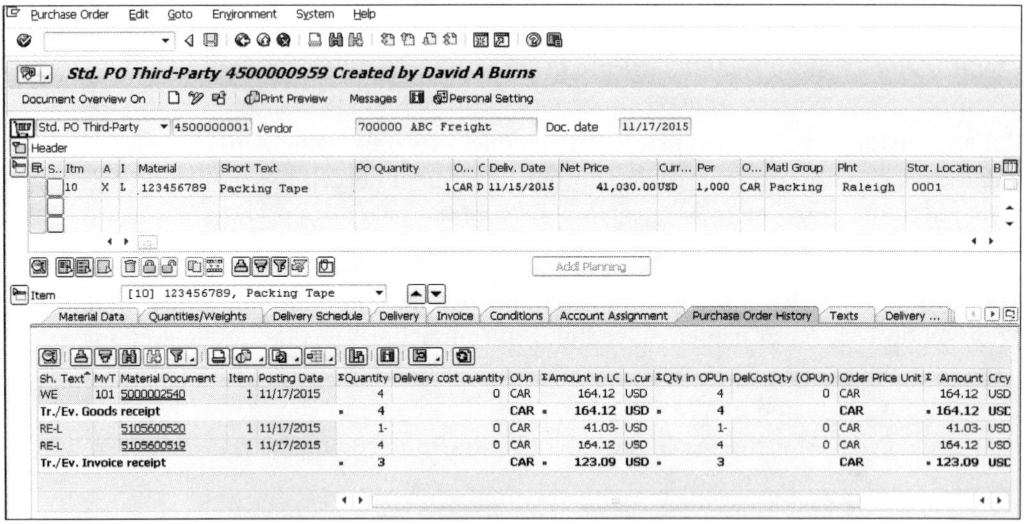

Figure 5.16 Example PO with Credit Memo

You can confirm the credit memo in the AP module via Transaction FBL1N (Figure 5.17).

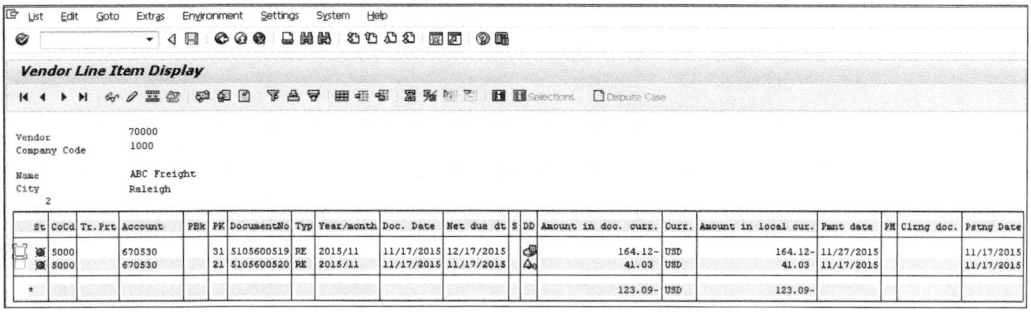

Figure 5.17 Transaction FBL1N with Credit Memo

5.4.2 Document Reversals

The need to reverse documents is universal across SAP modules. However, as you've seen throughout this chapter, not all financial documents are originated in FI. It's an SAP best practice to reverse documents using the module from which the original document was created. This is an important concept for keeping modules in sync.

In Chapter 6, Section 6.4, we discuss resetting and reversing AP documents in detail. However, for documents that originated in MM, document reversals should be completed in MM. One such transaction is Transaction ME21N, which is used to create a PO. To cancel a PO, you must unrelease it if you've implemented release strategies. Then, use Transaction ME22N (PO Change) to delete each line in the PO.

> **Note**
>
> Any change to a PO should be made by the procurement department. An AP clerk or supervisor may request that a change be made to a PO, but that individual should not make the change directly unless it's part of their job responsibilities and they have been trained. This holds true for returning goods as well, which offsets a goods receipt.

As shown in Figure 5.18, Transaction MIGO has a dropdown box from which you can select an action. Two of the dropdown selections are **Return Delivery**, which is used when products are defective or the wrong product was shipped, and **Subsequent Adjustment**, which is used when an adjustment needs to be made to quantity or price.

Figure 5.18 Executable Action Dropdown Selection

Finally, on the topic of document reversals, any AP invoice created automatically using Transaction MIRO should not be reversed in FI using Transaction FB08 or Transaction F.80. Instead, use Transaction MR8M to reverse the material invoice document, which in turn reverses the AP invoice in FI.

5.4.3 Change Posted Documents

The need to change documents is universal across SAP modules. However, as you've seen throughout this chapter, not all financial documents originate in FI. An SAP best practice is to change posted documents in the module in which they were created. This concept is important for keeping modules in sync. There is an exception to this rule, however, with the AP invoice. We'll discuss this exception toward the end of this section.

Earlier, we discussed three MM transactions. The first, Transaction ME21N, creates a PO. POs can be canceled, and their line items can be deleted and added. The transaction to change a PO is Transaction ME22N. Remember, any change to a PO should be made by the procurement department. The second MM transaction discussed is the goods receipt, Transaction MIGO. To make a subsequent adjustment to a goods receipt, see Section 5.4.2.

The last transaction is the invoice receipt, which is created using Transaction MIRO. You can't change an LIV invoice after posting it. In the case of an AP invoice, you need to make any change directly in the AP invoice in FI, which was created as a follow-on document for Transaction MIRO. The FI transaction to change the AP invoice is Transaction FB02.

One of the more common fields to change in an AP invoice is the baseline date. You may also need to change the payment terms or the payment method assigned in the document. These are simple changes that cause no reconciliation problems between AP and MM. However, if the change needed in the invoice is more complex (e.g., to a cost object), then you should reverse it using Transaction MR8M and repost.

5.5 Summary

AP is the SAP module used for managing vendor accounts and issuing payments for the goods and services your company procures. The content presented in this chapter broadened your perspective to help you think of AP as a series of steps in a business process, not as isolated transactions. Thinking in terms of business processes instead of individual transaction codes is important and makes you more effective in executing tasks, such as financial close.

In this chapter, the primary focus was the procure-to-pay business process. Using this process as the topic for discussion, you learned about fundamental integration between MM-Purchasing and AP. Integration between procurement and financials is important. A complete procure-to-pay business process isn't complete without both.

PRs and POs start the procurement process in MM-Purchasing. After goods are procured, delivery must be scheduled and the goods received, inspected, and accepted. A goods receipt document references a PO. It's in this step that the power of SAP ERP demonstrates itself in the procure-to-pay business process. Once posted, the goods receipt document is immediately displayed in PO history. Linking documents to a PO makes the management of the procure-to-pay process more streamlined and efficient.

The creation of an invoice typically follows goods receipt. In MM-LIV, this transaction is called an *invoice receipt*. The result of an invoice receipt is the creation of an MM material document, which is linked to an AP invoice. This AP invoice is referred to as a *follow-on document*.

It's an SAP best practice to change or reverse a document in the module in which it was created. Both POs and goods receipts can be changed in MM-Purchasing. By using transactions from both MM and FI, you can complete the procure-to-pay process. In this chapter, you learned about each step in the process, integration points, and the importance of when and how to reverse or change documents.

Now that you've learned about AP integration and the procure-to-pay business process, let's move on to discuss AP transactions in detail in the next chapter.

Chapter 6
Accounts Payable Transactions

In this chapter, we cover Accounts Payable (AP) transactions in detail. These include transactions such as vendor invoices and credit memos, which create vendor subledger entries.

This chapter covers Accounts Payable (AP) transactions that originate in the AP module. This may seem like a basic concept, but as you saw in Chapter 5, it's possible to create AP invoices and credit memos in Materials Management (MM) and Purchasing modules. AP processes, such as procure-to-pay, span multiple modules. That's why it's important to understand AP integration as well as AP-specific transactions.

The most common AP transaction is the entry of a vendor invoice document using Transaction FB60. This chapter covers not only the creation of an AP vendor invoice but also associated AP functions, such as document display, change, reverse, park, and more. These associated functions are also covered for General Ledger (G/L) transactions in Chapter 3 and for Accounts Receivable (AR) transactions in Chapter 10. These functions work the same in all cases, yet it's important to address them independently in each chapter to ensure you grasp their relevance to unique business scenarios.

In essence, AP exists to pay the bills. This is the tail end of the procure-to-pay business process, addressed in detail in Chapter 5. Prior to paying a vendor, an incoming invoice is created. Subsequently, the outgoing payment is issued using either the manual method (see Section 6.6) or the automated payment program (see Chapter 7).

This seemingly straightforward process of creating and paying a vendor invoice can take many twists and turns. Posting credit memos, making down payments, clearing accounts, making document corrections, and reconciling balances are just some of the additional functions that must be performed by accountants in the AP department. Vendor account maintenance and tracking is an important part of the job function.

In this chapter, we'll begin by covering the basics of creating an AP invoice before diving into each associated function of the AP module. Some of the transactions covered in this chapter are tasks you likely need to perform on a daily basis. Others, such as document reversals, are executed less frequently. This chapter can serve as a useful reference guide in the future for less frequently used transactions, and it can provide you with an overall refresher on the AP module.

6.1 Vendor Invoices

This section covers the AP invoice creation process, which includes document entry, park, post, save as complete, and hold. It also covers the Transaction FB60 tree display, screen variants, account assignment templates, editing options, and post with reference—all of which provide valuable insights to help you be more productive and organized in the AP module.

To create a vendor invoice in SAP using Transaction FB60, you must enter document header details (e.g., posting date) and at least one nonvendor line item that nets the document balance to zero. Creating a vendor invoice is a relatively simple transaction. With the vendor number, proper G/L account numbers, and lines of accounting, you can enter and post this transaction with little difficulty.

However, you need to be prepared to handle interruptions, such as a call from a business partner, that may require you to step away in the middle of entering a vendor invoice document. This section gives you the tools you need to deal with these and other challenges and provides you with the knowledge to enter AP transactions more efficiently.

6.1.1 Document Entry

To enter an AP invoice document, use Transaction FB60 or application menu path, **Accounting • Financial Accounting • Accounts Payable • Document Entry • FB60 – Invoice**, as shown in Figure 6.1.

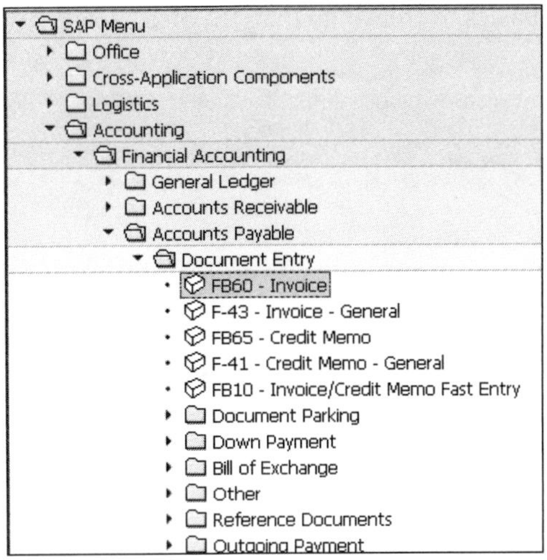

Figure 6.1 Transaction FB60 Application Menu Path

Double-click **FB60 – Invoice** from the menu path, or enter "FB60" in the **Command** field (as shown in Figure 6.2) and press [Enter].

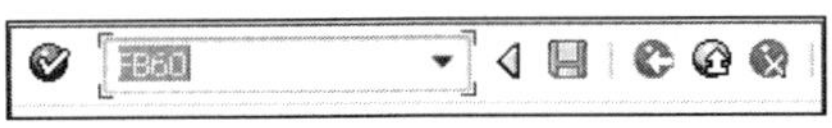

Figure 6.2 Entering "FB60" in the Command Field

The **Enter Vendor Invoice** entry screen opens (Figure 6.3). The fields that appear on the header with prepopulated values may vary depending on your system configuration and editing options. In this example, values were defaulted into the **Invoice date**, **Posting Date**, **Document Type**, **Company Code**, and currency fields. Separately, we entered values in the **Vendor**, **Reference**, and **Amount** fields.

It's a best practice to input the vendor's invoice number in the **Reference** field for quick lookup. In addition, you should make a special note of the **Invoice date** field. The invoice date is the start date for the due date calculation.

In other words, if the payment terms are net 30, then the clock starts ticking based on the date in the **Invoice date** field, not the **Posting Date** field.

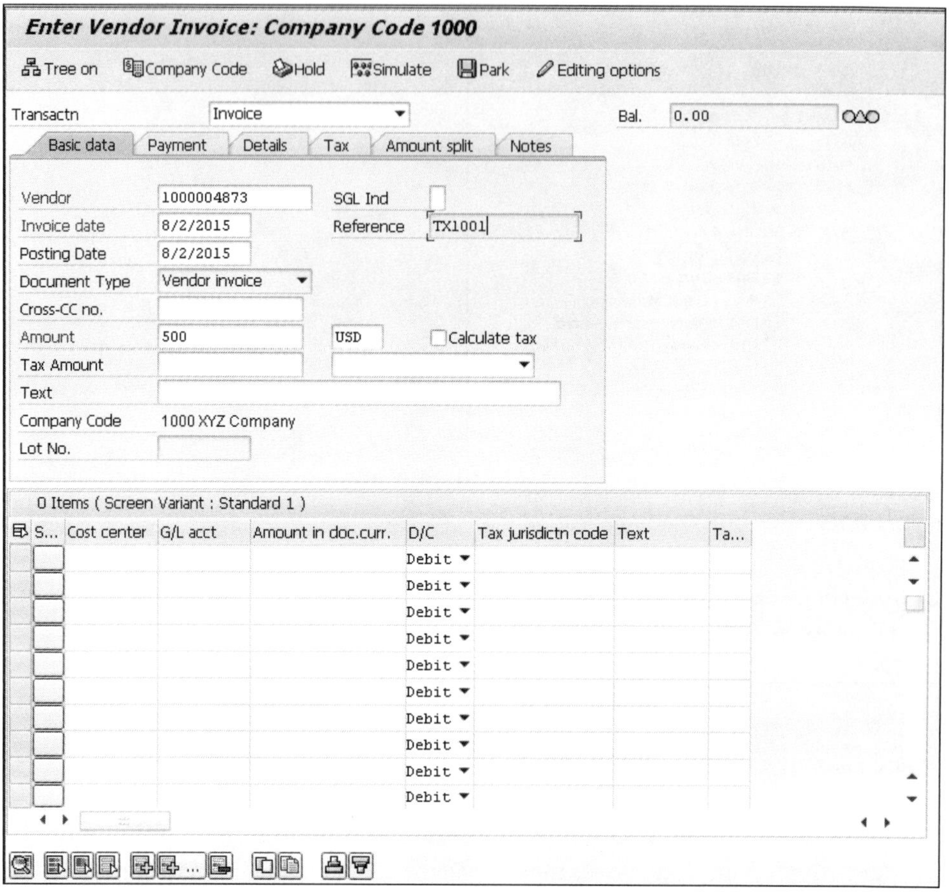

Figure 6.3 Enter Vendor Invoice Entry Screen

After entering header details, the next step is to enter at least one line item, as shown in Figure 6.4.

Here, the line item entered is a debit to an expense account. For an expense line item, you're required to enter a **G/L acct**, **D/C** (debit/credit) indicator, **Amount in doc.curr.**, and a cost object, at minimum. Here, we entered a **Cost center** as the cost object. You may also select **Internal Order** or **WBS Element**, based on your business requirements. Your SAP system may have additional field entry requirements, based on your configuration and field status settings.

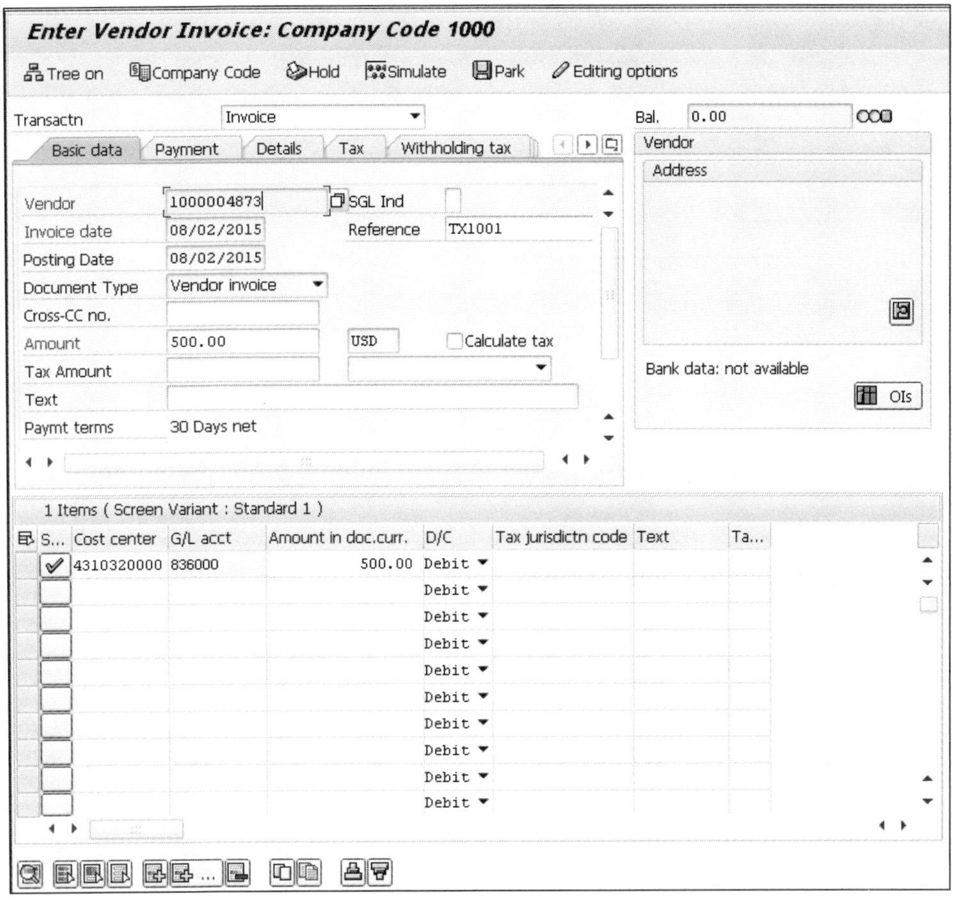

Figure 6.4 Enter Vendor Invoice: Line Item Entry

After entering your document line items, click the **Simulate** button in the top center of the entry screen. This initiates simulation of the vendor invoice posting logic to determine if the document can be properly posted. If the simulation is unsuccessful, an error message appears. If successful, the document overview screen opens, as shown in Figure 6.5.

After simulation is complete, click the **Post** icon to the right of the **Command** field in the upper-left corner of the screen to post the vendor invoice document. A message appears with the new document number, as shown in Figure 6.6.

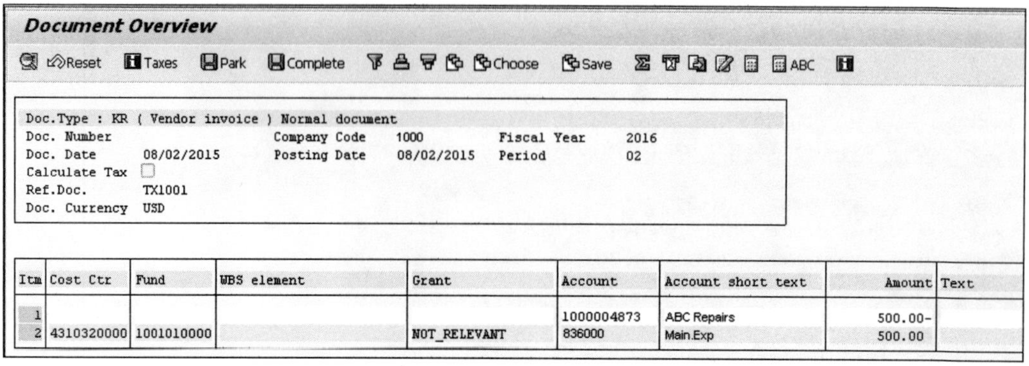

Figure 6.5 Document Overview Screen

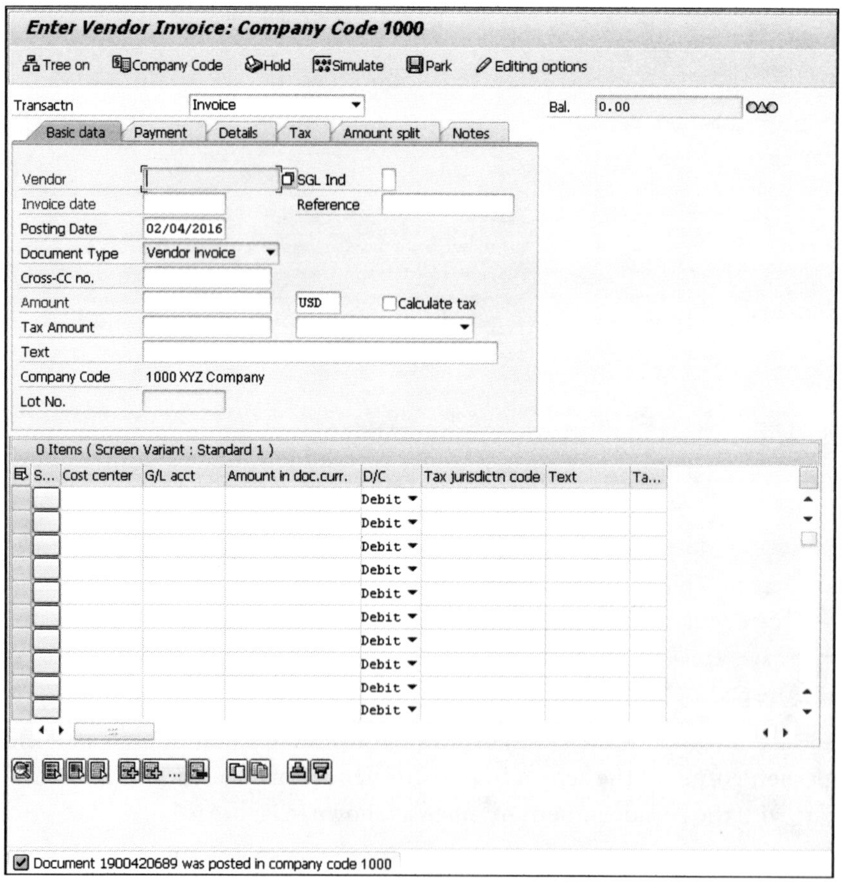

Figure 6.6 Document Posted Message

6.1.2 Post, Park, Save as Complete, and Hold

This section describes the different ways to create vendor invoice documents: post, park, save as complete, and hold. These universal concepts within Financial Accounting (FI) aren't unique to vendor invoices and Transaction FB60 (we already saw these at work in journal vouchers in Chapter 3, Section 3.1.2), but here we'll focus on their use in creating vendor invoices.

Post

Posting a vendor invoice is covered in its entirety in Section 6.1.1. A *posted document* is a vendor invoice that is considered complete, produces an accounting document number, and updates the vendor and G/L account balances.

After a document is posted, the only way to reverse its impact on the vendor and G/L account balance is to reverse the document. Reversing G/L documents is covered in Section 6.4. A vendor invoice can't be paid until it's posted.

Park

Document parking allows you to save a vendor invoice document without impacting vendor and G/L account balances. This may be necessary if the document is incomplete or if further edits, data validation, or document approvals are required prior to posting.

Because parked documents are considered incomplete, they can be changed or deleted. When parked, these vendor documents don't update transaction figures and account balances. Moreover, a parked document doesn't go through the extensive entry checks performed when documents are posted.

Another important point about parked vendor invoices is that they can't be paid, which means that the automated payment program (Transaction F110) won't select the item when the payment proposal is created (see Chapter 7 for details on running the automated payment program). Parked items also can't be paid using Transaction F-53 and Transaction F-58 (manual payments).

To park a vendor invoice document, use Transaction FV60 or application menu path, **Accounting • Financial Accounting • Accounts Payable • Document Entry • Document Parking • FV60 – Park or Edit Invoice**, as shown in Figure 6.7.

Double-click on **FV60 – Park or Edit Invoice**, or enter "FV60" in the **Command** field (as shown in Figure 6.8) and press [Enter].

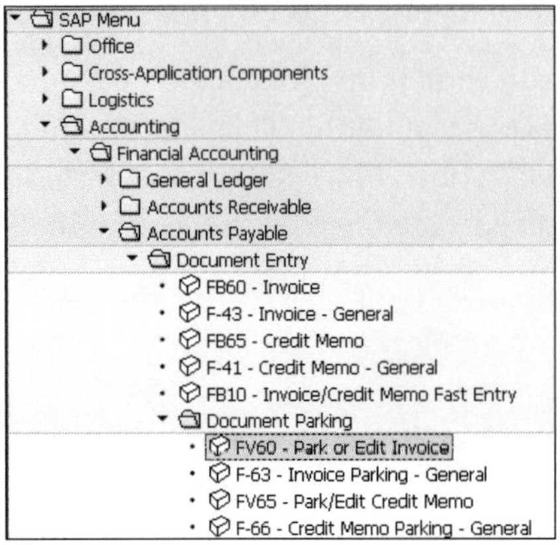

Figure 6.7 Transaction FV60 Application Menu Path for Document Park

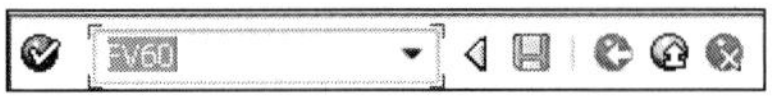

Figure 6.8 Entering "FV60" in the Command Field

The **Park Vendor Invoice** entry screen opens (Figure 6.9).

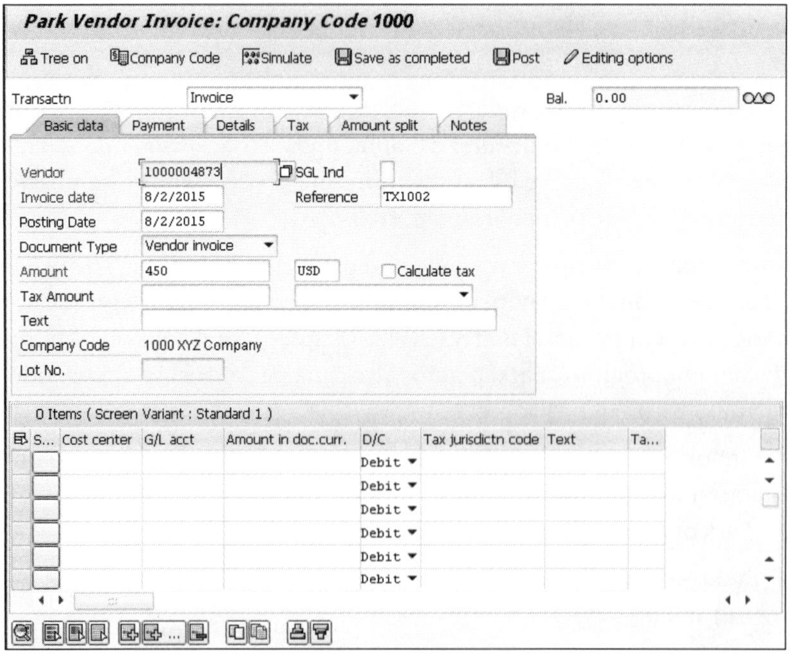

Figure 6.9 Park Vendor Invoice Screen

The fields that default values into the document header will vary depending on your system configuration and editing options. In this example, we manually entered values for the **Vendor**, **Invoice date**, **Reference**, and **Amount** fields, whereas values were defaulted for the **Posting Date**, **Document Type**, **Company Code**, and currency fields.

After inputting field values on the header screen, enter at least one line item, as shown in Figure 6.10.

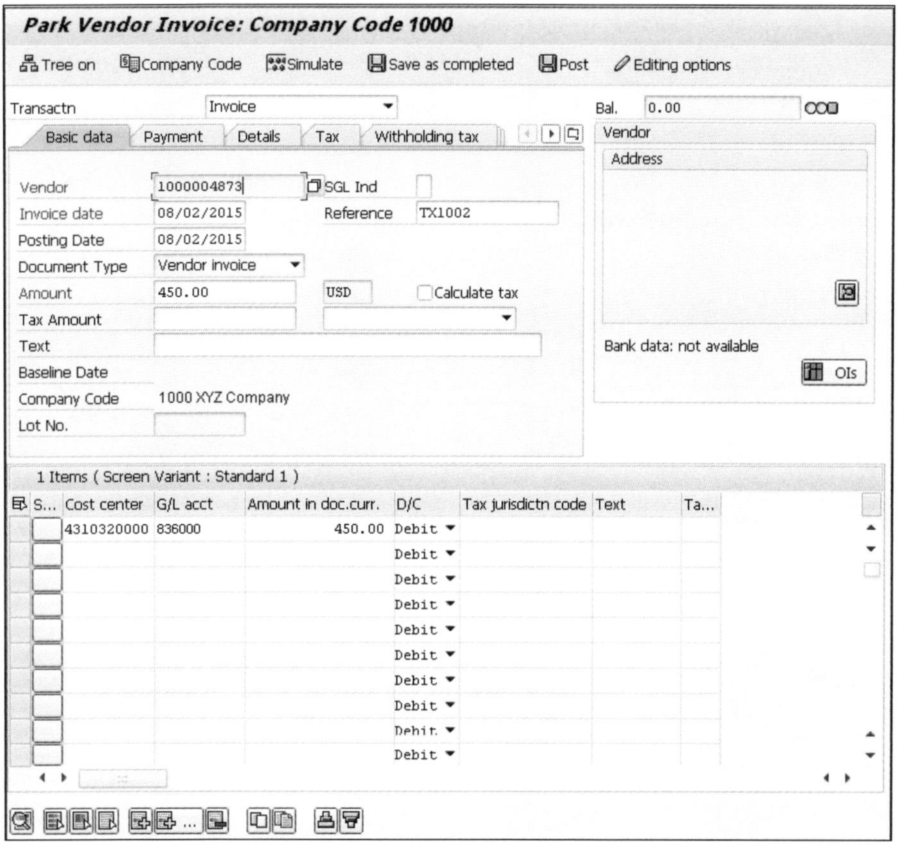

Figure 6.10 Park Vendor Invoice Entry Screen for Line Items

After the line items are entered, click the **Park** icon to the right of the **Command** field in the upper-left portion of the screen. This parks the vendor invoice, and a message appears with the new parked document number, as shown in Figure 6.11.

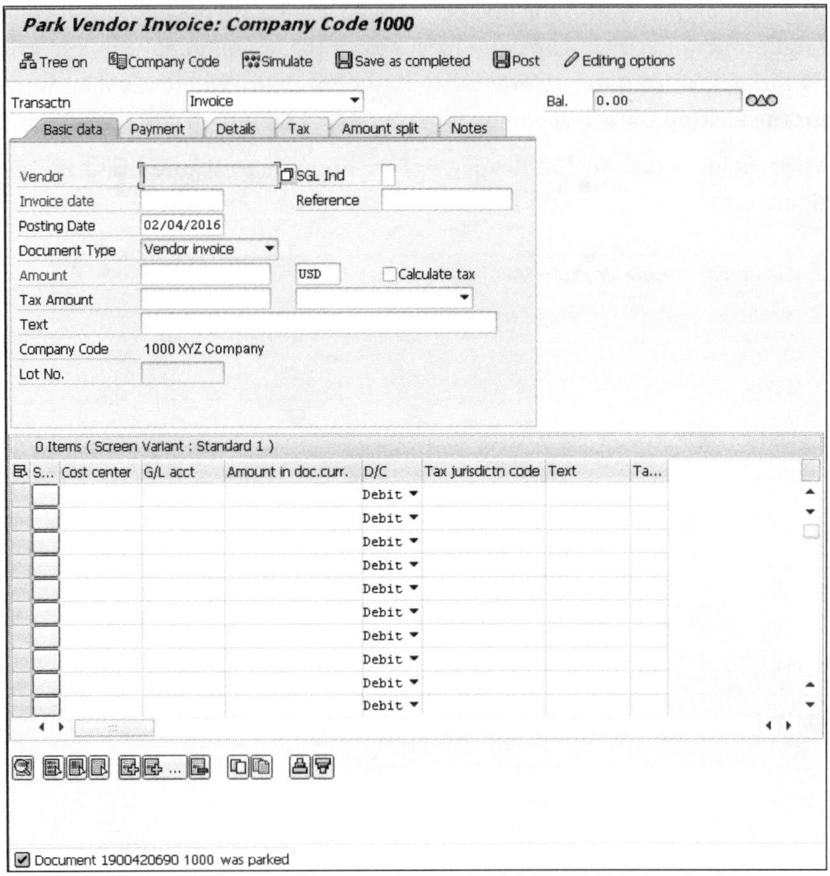

Figure 6.11 Document Parked Message

Save as Completed

The *save as completed* function is similar to document parking but with some key distinctions. When you save a document as completed, the program goes through more extensive document check logic, just as if the document were being posted. Like parked documents, however, documents that are saved as completed can be edited and changed prior to posting.

Although the park and save as completed functions are similar, the latter generally should only be used when you're sure the document is accurate and complete and only needs final approval before being posted.

> **Note**
>
> Like parked documents, documents that are saved as completed can't be paid.

To save a vendor invoice as complete, use Transaction FV60 or application menu path, **Accounting • Financial Accounting • Accounts Payable • Document Entry • Document Parking • FV60 – Park or Edit Invoice**, as shown in Figure 6.12.

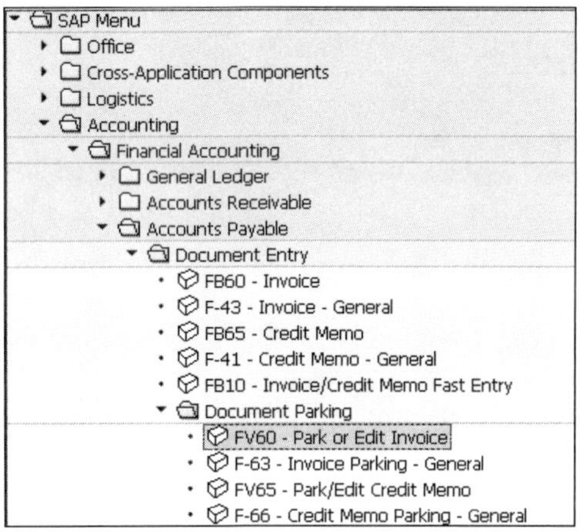

Figure 6.12 Transaction FV60 Application Menu Path for Save as Complete

Double-click **FV60 – Park or Edit Invoice** from the menu path, or enter "FV60" in the **Command** field (as shown in Figure 6.13) and press [Enter].

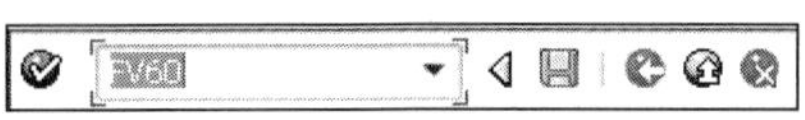

Figure 6.13 Entering "FV60" in the Command Field

The **Park Vendor Invoice** entry screen appears (Figure 6.14). The fields that appear in the header with prepopulated values may vary, depending on your system configuration and editing options. In this example, we manually entered values for the **Vendor**, **Invoice date**, **Reference**, and **Amount** fields. Values were defaulted for the **Posting Date**, **Document Type**, **Company Code**, and currency fields.

After the **Park Vendor Invoice** header screen is complete, enter at least one line item, as shown in Figure 6.15.

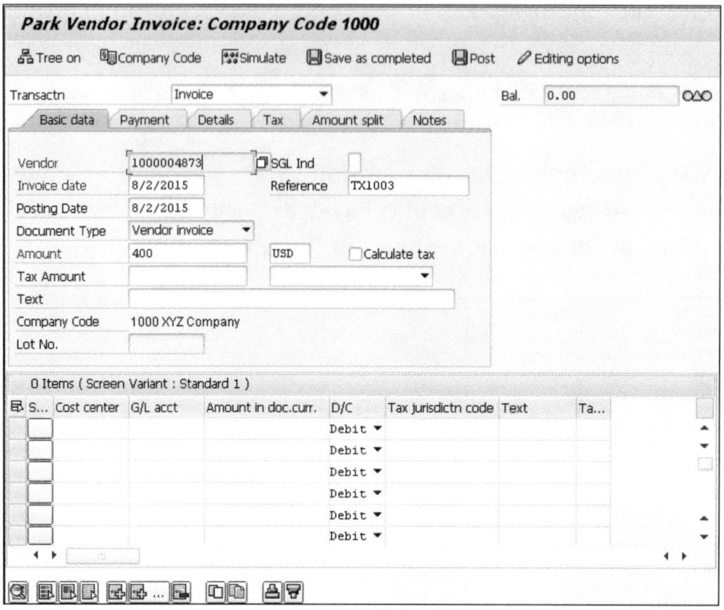

Figure 6.14 Park Vendor Invoice Entry Screen for Save as Complete

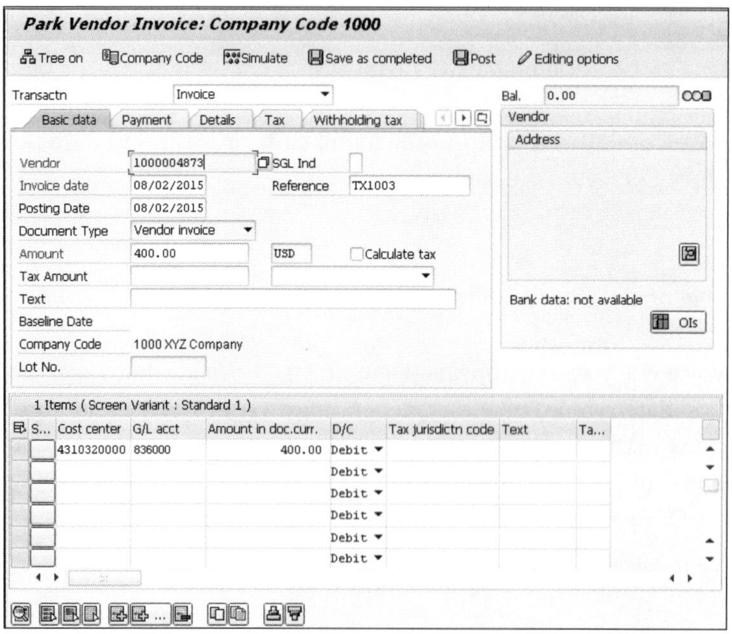

Figure 6.15 Line Item Entry Screen for Save as Complete

After entering line items, click the **Save as completed** icon in the top-center portion of the screen. This saves the vendor invoice as completed, and a message appears with the new document number, as shown in Figure 6.16.

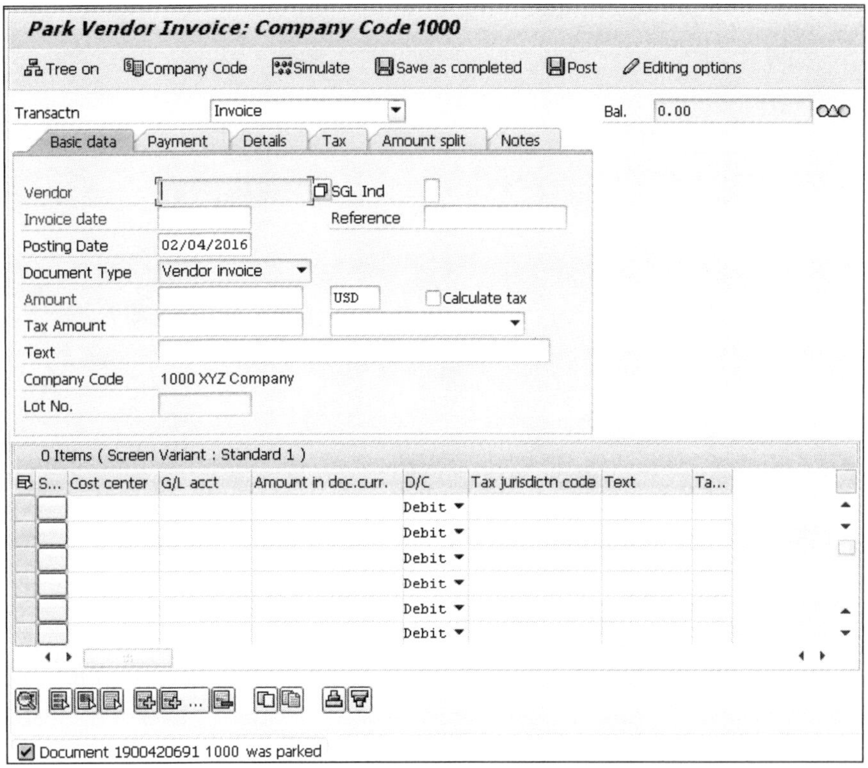

Figure 6.16 Document Created Message for Save as Completed

Hold

Document hold allows you to temporarily save your data. It's most useful when you're interrupted during document entry. Because held documents are temporary, they don't update AP and G/L transactions and balances. After holding a document, you can edit, delete, park, or post it. Unlike post, park, and save as completed, the hold function produces no permanent document number until the document is parked or posted.

To hold an AP accounting document, use Transaction FB60 or application menu path, **Accounting • Financial Accounting • Accounts Payable • Document Entry • FB60 – Invoice**, as shown in Figure 6.17.

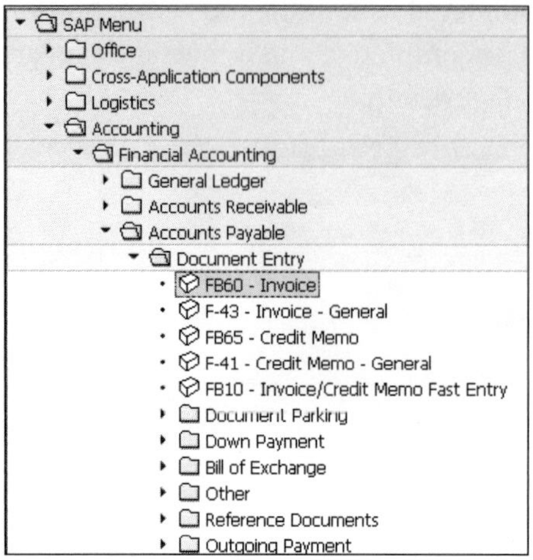

Figure 6.17 Transaction FB60 Menu Path for Document Hold

Double-click **FB60 – Invoice** from the menu path, or enter "FB60" in the **Command** field (as shown in Figure 6.18) and press [Enter].

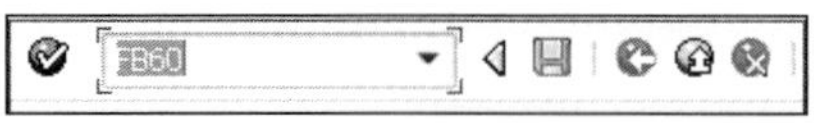

Figure 6.18 Entering "FB60" in the Command Field

You can use the hold function at any point during Transaction FB60 regardless of how much or little information you've entered because no system checks take place when you hold an AP document.

In the example shown in Figure 6.19, the **Vendor**, **Invoice date**, **Reference**, and **Amount** fields have been entered, along with one partially complete line item. In the screen header, field values were prepopulated for the **Posting Date**, **Document Type**, **Company Code**, and currency fields.

At any point, the document can be held by pressing [F5] or selecting **Document • Hold** from the dropdown menu path, as shown in Figure 6.20.

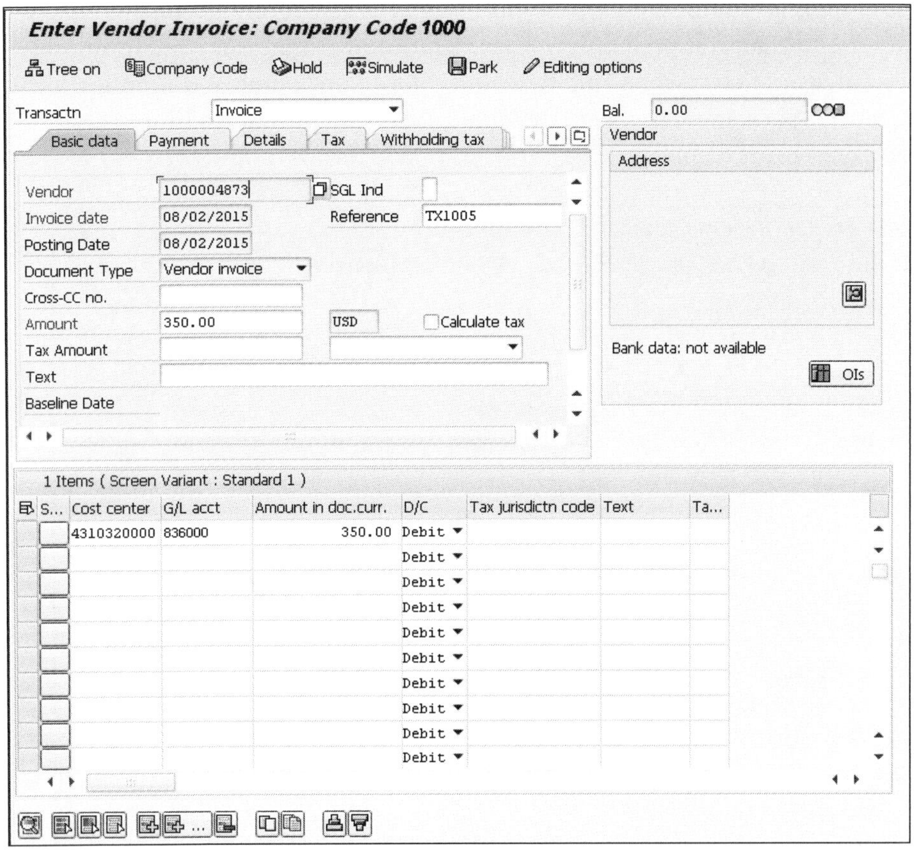

Figure 6.19 Entry Screen for Document Hold

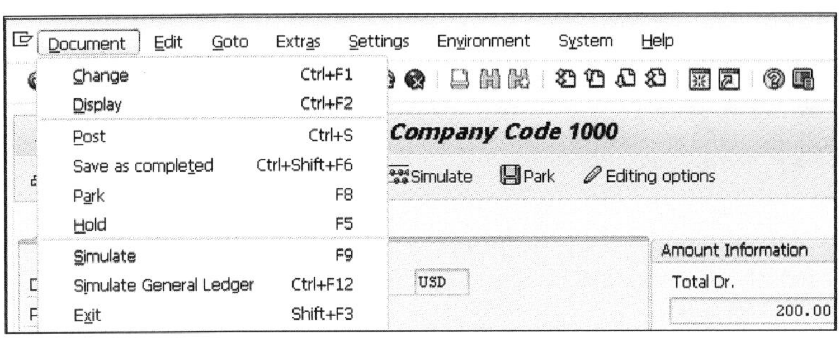

Figure 6.20 Document Hold Dropdown Menu

A dialog box (Figure 6.21) prompts you to enter a **Temporary document number**, which is a 10-character preliminary document number that can contain numbers, letters, or special characters. This temporary document number will no longer be valid when a permanent number is assigned, such as when the document is posted, parked, or saved as complete.

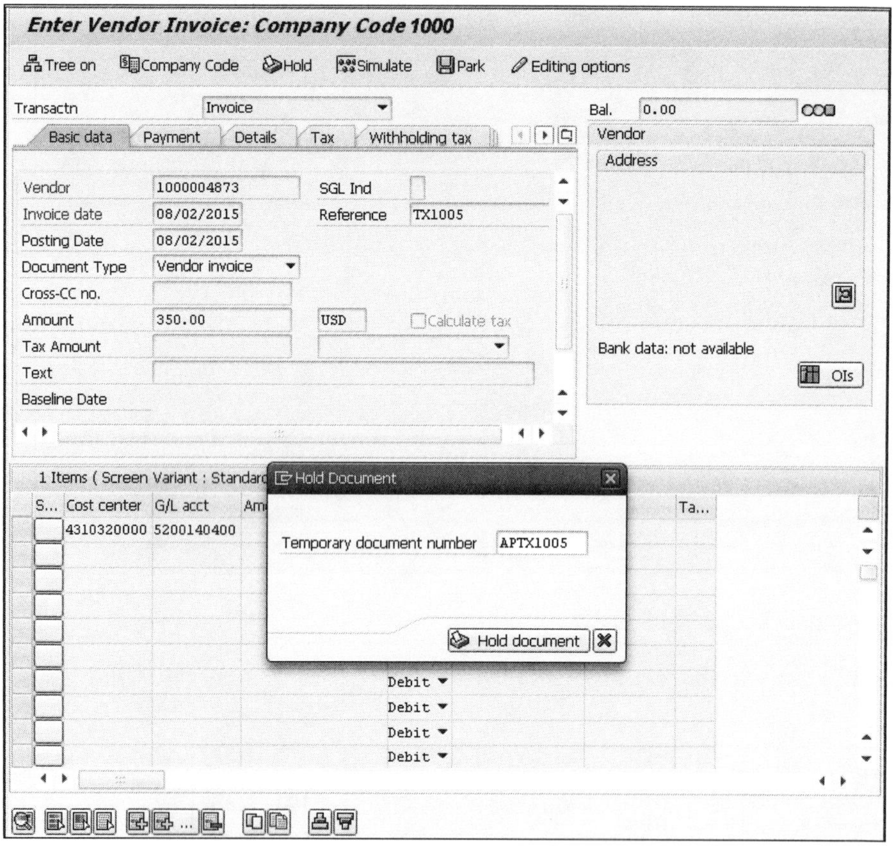

Figure 6.21 Temporary Document Number Prompt

After entering a temporary document number, press [Enter] or click the **Hold document** button. As a result, a temporary accounting document is created, and a message appears with the held document number, as shown in Figure 6.22.

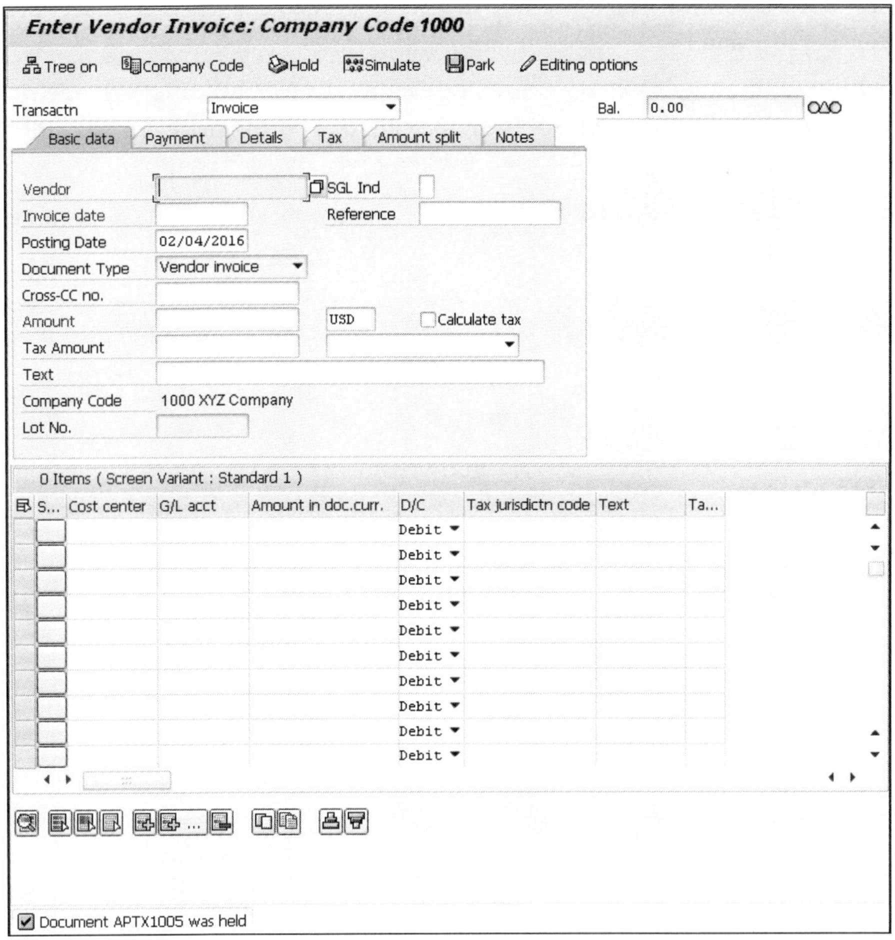

Figure 6.22 Document Held Message

6.1.3 Tree Display

The tree display provides an easy-to-use visual display for several functions that can also be accessed from the dropdown menu in Transaction FB60. The tree display is a universal concept, or shortcut, for accessing accounting documents and document entry tools in FI. In this section, we'll confine the discussion of the tree display to Transaction FB60 and Transaction FV60, but this capability can be used in any financial transaction for which the tree display is available, such as Transactions FB50, FV50, FB70, and FV70.

The tree display is a toggle function, meaning that it can be turned on (i.e., made visible) or turned off (i.e., made invisible) with the click of a button or keyboard combination.

Figure 6.23 shows Transaction FB60 with the tree display on, visible as a panel on the left side of the transaction screen.

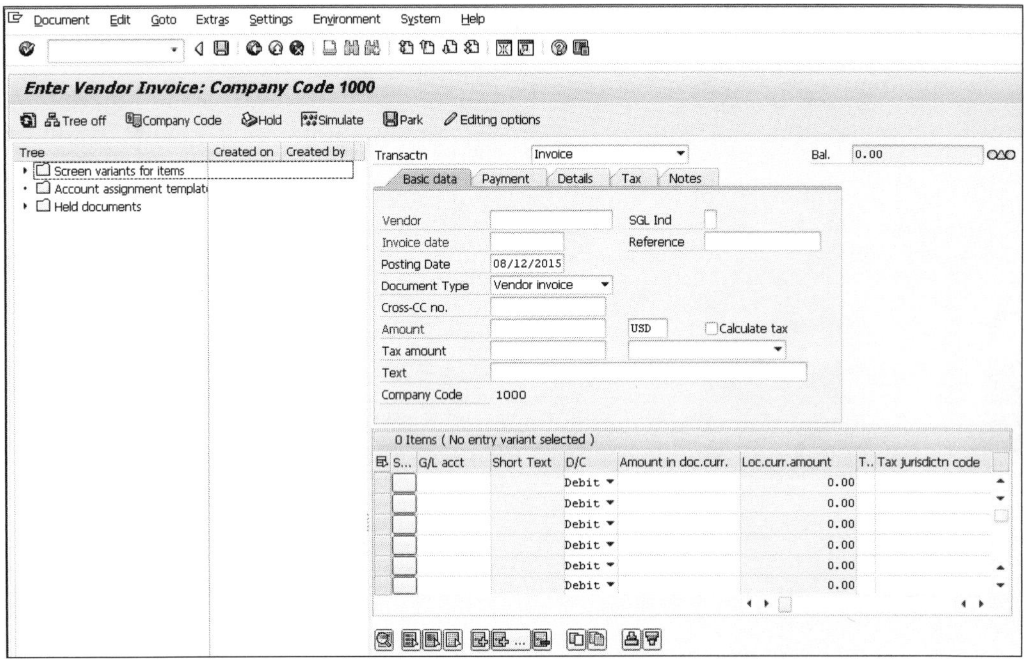

Figure 6.23 Transaction FB60 Vendor Invoice Screen with Tree Display On

Note that with the tree display on, a panel with folders is visible on the left. The folders that appear in the display vary by transaction code. In Transaction FB60, we see the following folders:

- **Screen variants for items**
- **Account assignment templates for items**
- **Held documents**

Screen variants and account assignment templates are covered in detail in Section 6.1.4.

In Section 6.1.2, you learned how to hold a vendor invoice document. Held documents can be viewed in the tree display by clicking on the triangle to the left of the **Held documents** folder. This action opens the folder and displays all the held documents created by the user.

When you double-click a held document in the tree display, its details appear in the vendor invoice document entry screen, as shown in Figure 6.24. Once displayed, held document details can be edited, parked, or posted.

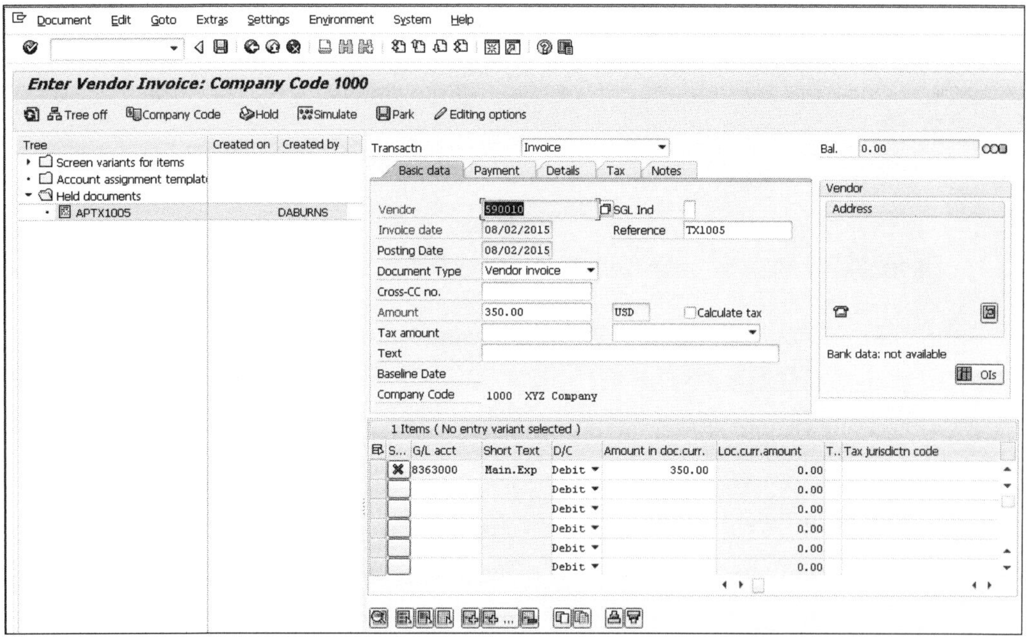

Figure 6.24 Held Document in the Tree Display

The tree display function in Transaction FV60 is the same as in Transaction FB60 and has the same toggle capability, but the folder structures in each differ slightly.

Figure 6.25 shows the tree display turned on in Transaction FV60.

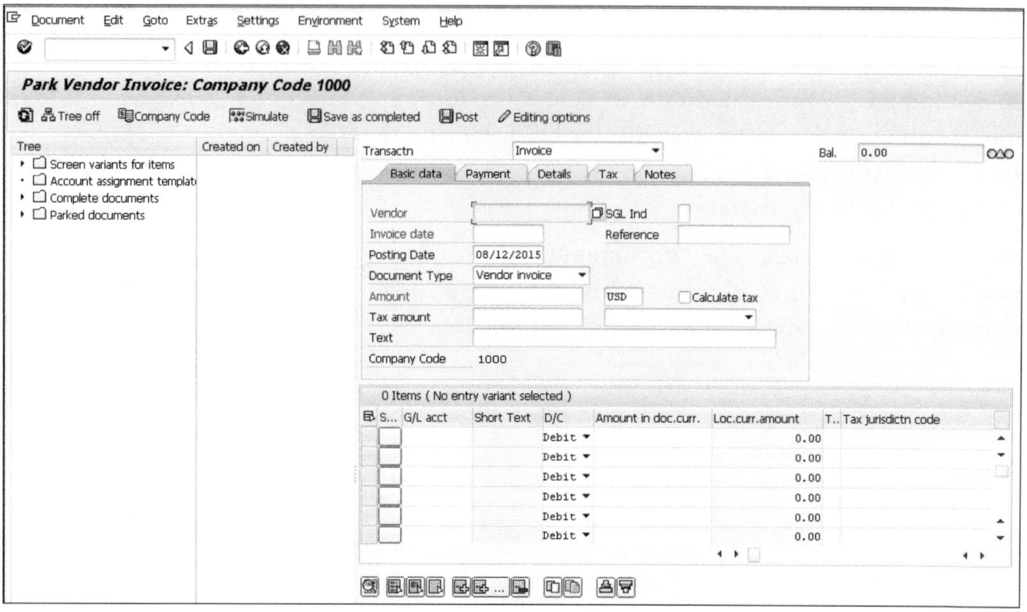

Figure 6.25 Transaction FV60 with Tree Display On

In Transaction FV60, you can see the following folders in the tree display:

- **Screen variants for items**
- **Account assignment templates for items**
- **Complete documents**
- **Parked documents**

In Transaction FV60's tree display, folders for screen variants and account assignment templates appear at the top, as they did in Transaction FB60. However, folders for complete and parked documents, which appear in Transaction FV60, aren't present in the Transaction FB60 tree display. Finally, a folder for held documents, which appeared in Transaction FB60's tree display, doesn't appear in Transaction FV60. As you can see, the tree display default folders vary by transaction.

6.1.4 Using Screen Variants and Account Assignment Templates

Screen variants and *account assignment templates* are tools available in FI that simplify the entry of vendor documents. They aren't unique to Transaction FB60, but we'll confine our discussion to this transaction in this section. Note that both screen variants and account assignment templates can be accessed and maintained from both the tree display in Transaction FB60 and the dropdown menu. In this section, we'll focus on using the tree display, which is the most user-friendly and frequently used method.

Use of Screen Variants

A screen variant sets the columns for display and entry in the line item entry portion of Transaction FB60 (Figure 6.26). In other words, it sets the fields displayed on the screen and the order in which they appear.

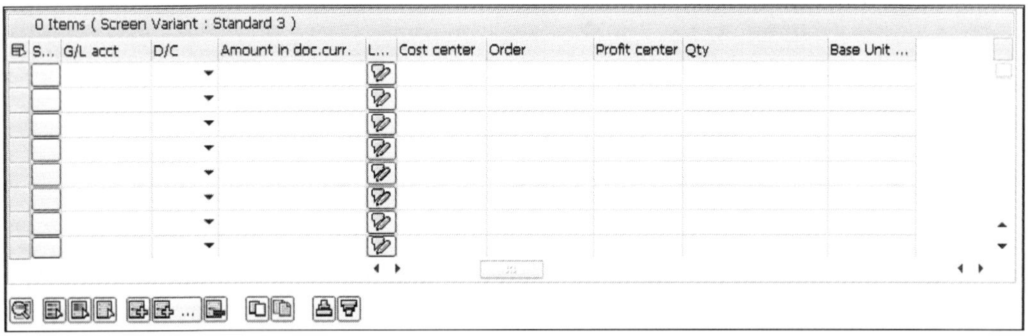

Figure 6.26 Line Entry Screen

A well-developed screen variant reduces data entry time and the number of data entry errors. In essence, your goal is to have only the fields you need to enter or display appear on the screen. Specific screen variants for AP, for instance, will have the **Cost Center**, **Internal Order**, and **WBS Element** fields prominently placed for easy data entry.

Transaction FB60 has a default screen variant assigned, which is displayed each time you execute the transaction. However, the assigned default may not be your preferred line item entry screen, and you may prefer different screen variants depending on the type of vendor invoice you're creating. In fact, it's quite common to have several screen variants for different types of vendor invoices.

The tree display and the dropdown menu in Transaction FB60 give you the ability to select different screen variants at any point in time.

Let's see screen variant selection in action. Go to Transaction FB60, and make sure the tree display is on (see Section 6.1.3). Click on the triangle next to the **Screen variants for items** folder to see a list of available variants to choose from (Figure 6.27).

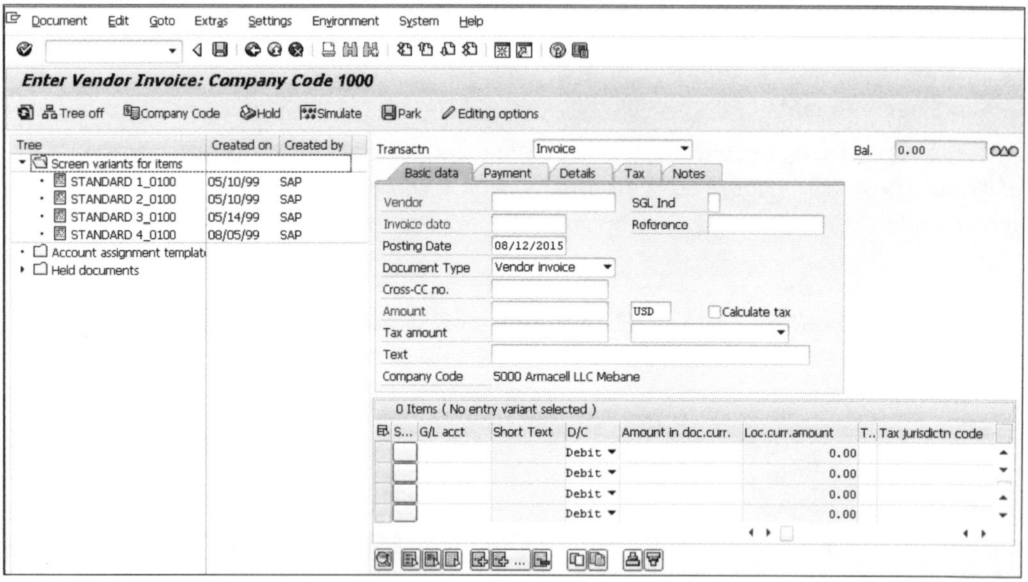

Figure 6.27 Screen Variant List

Double-click the screen variant you want to use (Figure 6.28), and the line layout in the bottom right of the screen changes accordingly.

> **Note**
>
> Screen variants are cross-client dependent, meaning that if a screen variant is created or changed in one SAP client, the change is reflected in every other client within that same SAP instance. The creation and maintenance of screen variants is beyond the scope of this book. You may not have the permissions required to create or change them because they may be restricted in SAP security profiles to an SAP support team or system administrator.

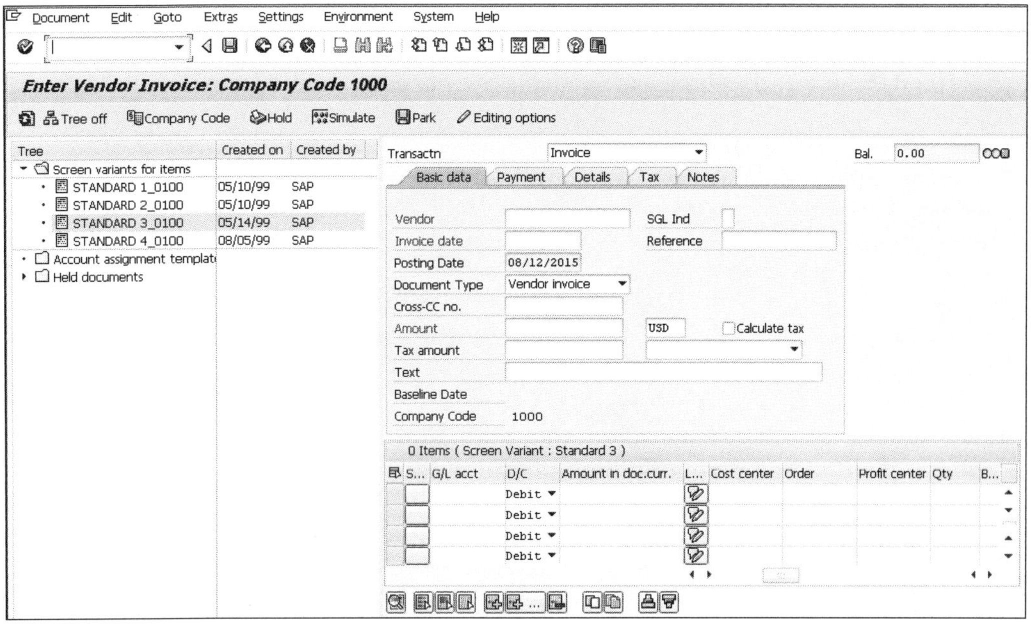

Figure 6.28 Screen Variant Selection

Use of Account Assignment Templates

Account assignment templates in Transaction FB60 are prepopulated field values in a document. These templates allow you to reduce data entry requirements for vendor invoices, which are frequent and consistent in their makeup. They allow you to expedite the creation of a vendor invoice without the hassle of reentering all the necessary field values each time you create a new document.

Account assignment templates get a lot of use in AP. Most often, they are used to prepopulate G/L accounts and cost objects that are used repetitively for certain types of invoices. They not only ease data entry but also ensure consistency.

The next time you find yourself entering a vendor invoice from scratch that you've created repeatedly in the past, consider creating an account assignment template for it. Doing so may simplify your life, especially for vendor invoices with multiple line items.

Let's take a closer look. Go to Transaction FB60, and make sure the tree display is on (see Section 6.1.3). Click on the triangle next to the **Account assignment template for items** folder to see a list of available templates to choose from (Figure 6.29).

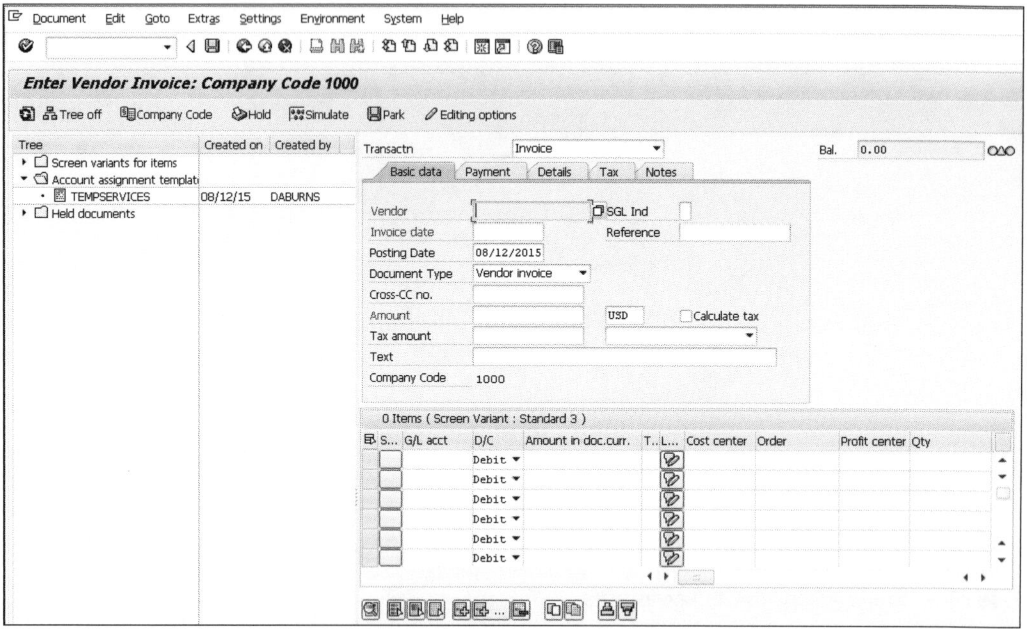

Figure 6.29 Account Assignment Template List

Double-click the template you want to use (Figure 6.30), and the line layout in the line item entry screen changes based on the prepopulated values contained in the template. Note that you can add to or edit these field values at this point.

In this example, account assignment template **TEMPSERVICES** contains prepopulated values for the **G/L acct**, **D/C** (debit/credit indicator), **Cost center**, and **Profit center** fields. In the header, we entered the **Vendor**, **Reference**, and **Invoice date** fields manually. With all the required fields populated, you simply need to enter a value in the **Amount** field to complete the document entry (Figure 6.31).

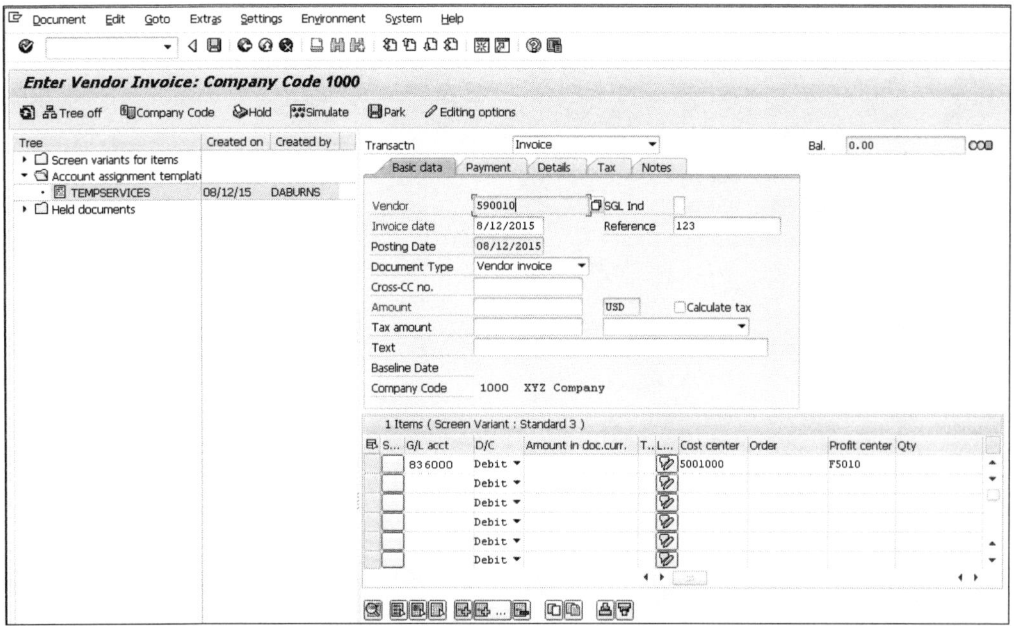

Figure 6.30 Account Assignment Template Selection

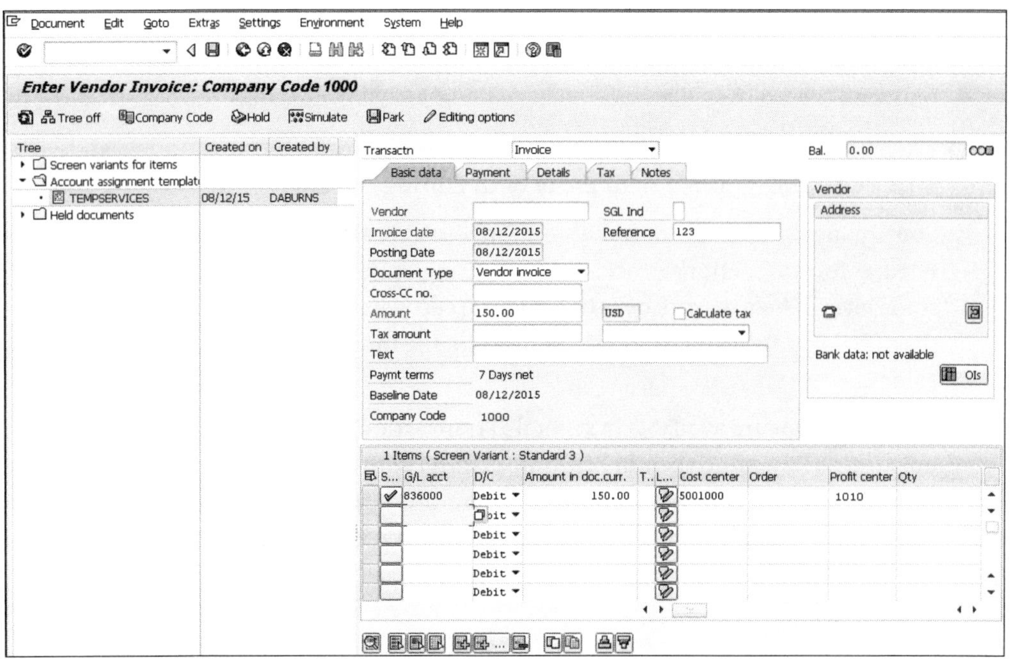

Figure 6.31 Account Assignment Template Entry Complete

With document entry complete, you can post, park, or save this vendor invoice as completed. In this example, we posted the document (Figure 6.32).

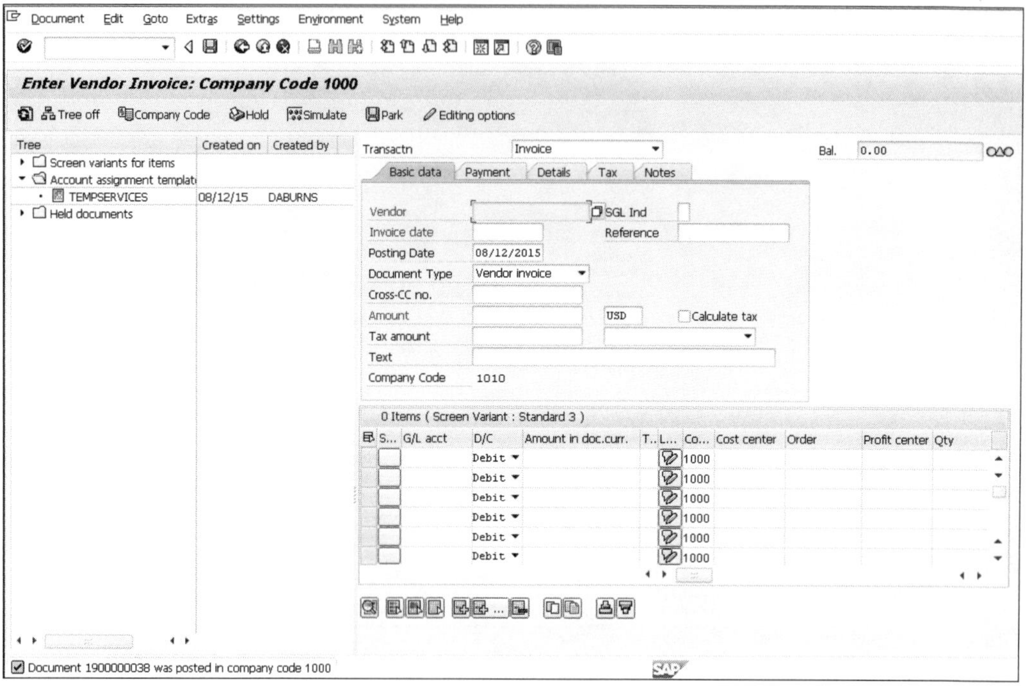

Figure 6.32 Posted Document Using the Account Assignment Template

6.1.5 Controlling Document Entry with Editing Options

Controlling document entry with editing options allows you to make user-specific settings for transactions in accounting. Editing options are useful tools that give you some level of field control over the entry screen, what fields are displayed, and values that are defaulted, which lets you determine the interpretation of certain field entry values.

Editing options are available in several FI transactions. The discussion in this section, however, is limited to their use in Transaction FB60. The editing options selected are user-specific, not transaction-specific; therefore, editing options set in Transaction FB60 will also apply to other accounting transactions, such as Transaction FB50 and Transaction FB70.

In an AP department, some of the editing options set will depend on your role. For example, if you work for a multinational corporation and your job function is to create vendor invoices for multiple company codes, you need the **Company Code** field available in Transaction FB60. If your job function is localized, and you only create vendor invoices for one company code, you don't need the **Company Code** field available for input with each transaction.

In this section, we'll demonstrate some of the most commonly used settings and then provide a complete list of all editing options and their descriptions (see Table 6.1 at the end of this section). Throughout this section, we'll also point out editing options that are of particular interest in AP.

To access editing options from Transaction FB60 (Figure 6.33), click the **Editing options** button in the top center of the **Enter Vendor Invoice** screen, or press [Shift]+[F4].

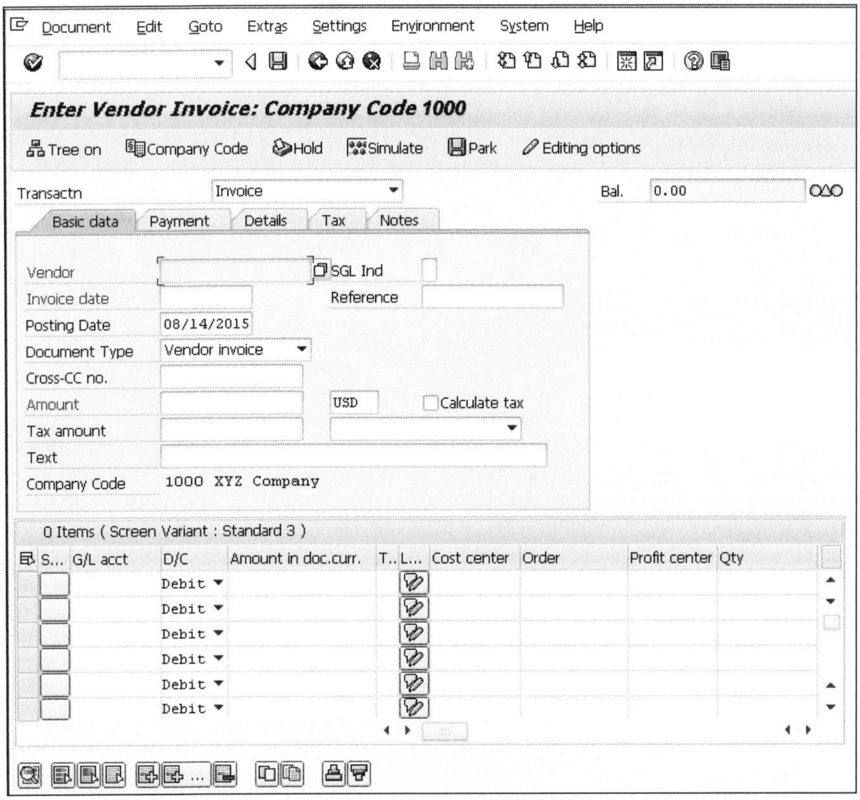

Figure 6.33 Enter Vendor Invoice Screen for Editing Options

The **Accounting Editing Options** screen opens (Figure 6.34). Editing options are divided into four general categories, each with its own area of the screen:

- **General Entry Options**
- **Special options for single screen transactions**
- **Default document currency**
- **Default Company Code**

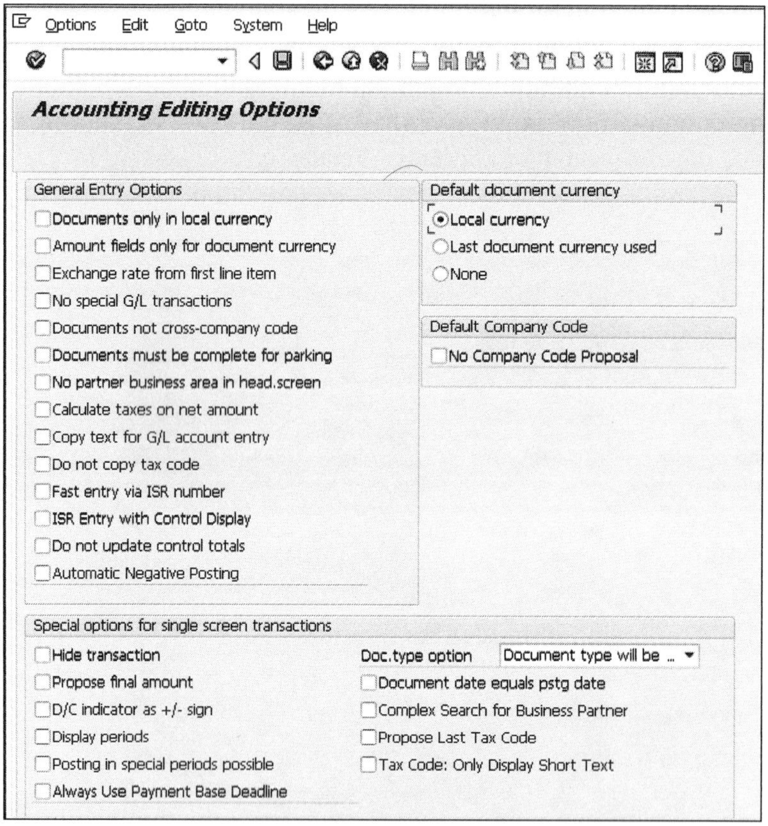

Figure 6.34 Accounting Editing Options Screen

In the **Default Document Currency** area, you can see that the **Local Currency** radio button is selected. With this setting, the local currency of the company code to which the user is assigned will default into Transaction FB60.

If you're an AP clerk or accounting supervisor creating AP transactions for multiple regions using multiple currencies, this setting may be useful. In addition, there may be times, such as period-end and year-end, when you need to make entries repeatedly in a foreign currency. Because editing options are user-specific, you can turn them on and off as needed to perform your job function.

For this example, select **None** in the **Default document currency** area (Figure 6.35), and then click the **Save** icon or press Ctrl+S.

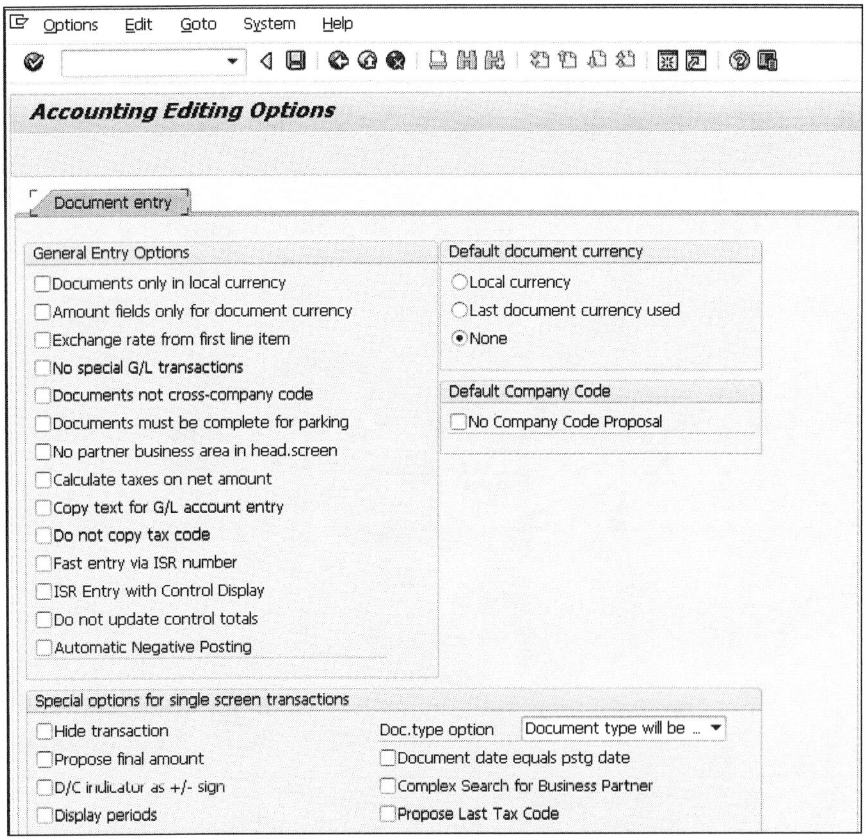

Figure 6.35 Accounting Editing Options with No Default Currency

After the editing options are saved, return to Transaction FB60 to find that the currency field next to the **Amount** field in the header is now blank (Figure 6.36), meaning that no value was defaulted into that field. As you can see, this is useful to an AP clerk who needs to select a currency different from their default currency. It's also a reminder to ensure that you enter a vendor invoice with the proper currency, instead of inadvertently posting it in your local currency.

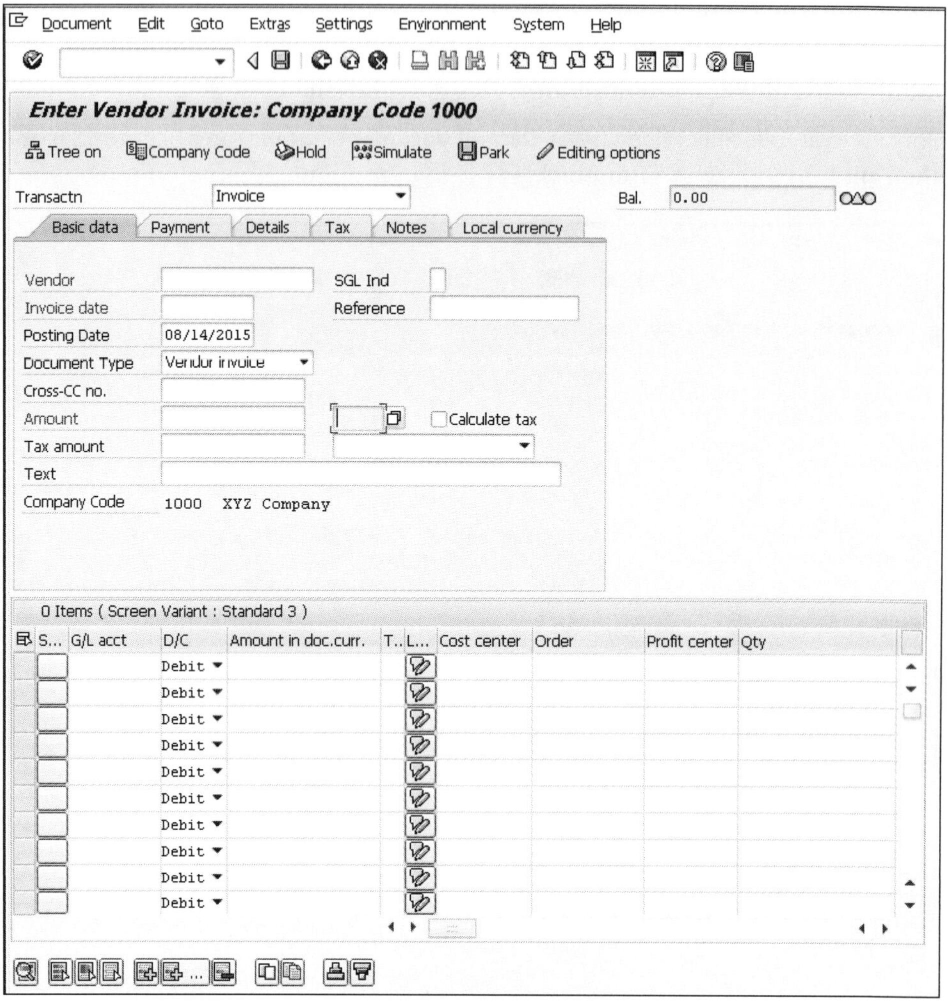

Figure 6.36 Enter Vendor Invoice Screen with No Currency

Similarly, you can use editing options to change the transaction entry screen so that no company code is proposed. For this example, select the **No Company Code Proposal** checkbox in the **Default Company Code** area of the **Accounting Editing Options** screen (Figure 6.37), and then click the **Save** icon or press Ctrl+S.

After the editing options are saved, return to Transaction FB60; you're immediately prompted to enter a **Company Code** (Figure 6.38). This is a useful feature for an AP clerk or accounting supervisor responsible for multiple regions.

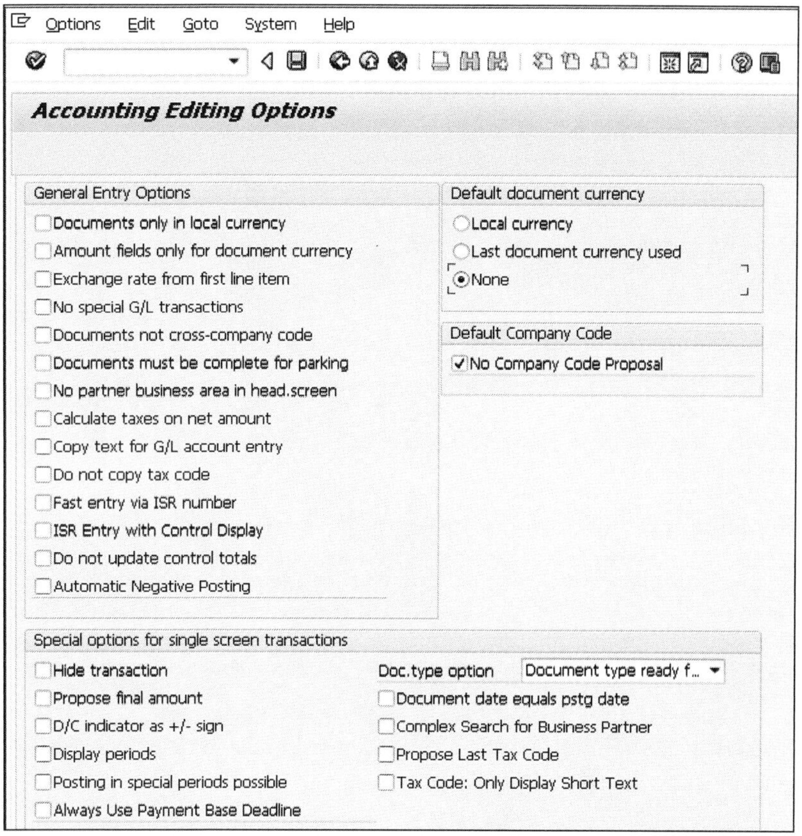

Figure 6.37 Accounting Editing Options with No Company Code Proposed

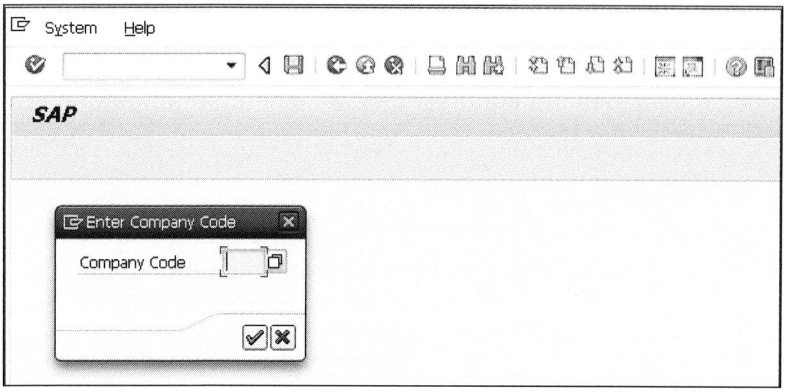

Figure 6.38 Prompt for Company Code

Another common use of editing options is to change the document type setting. For this example, change the **Doc.type option** field to **Document type hidden** (Figure 6.39), and then click the **Save** icon or press Ctrl+S.

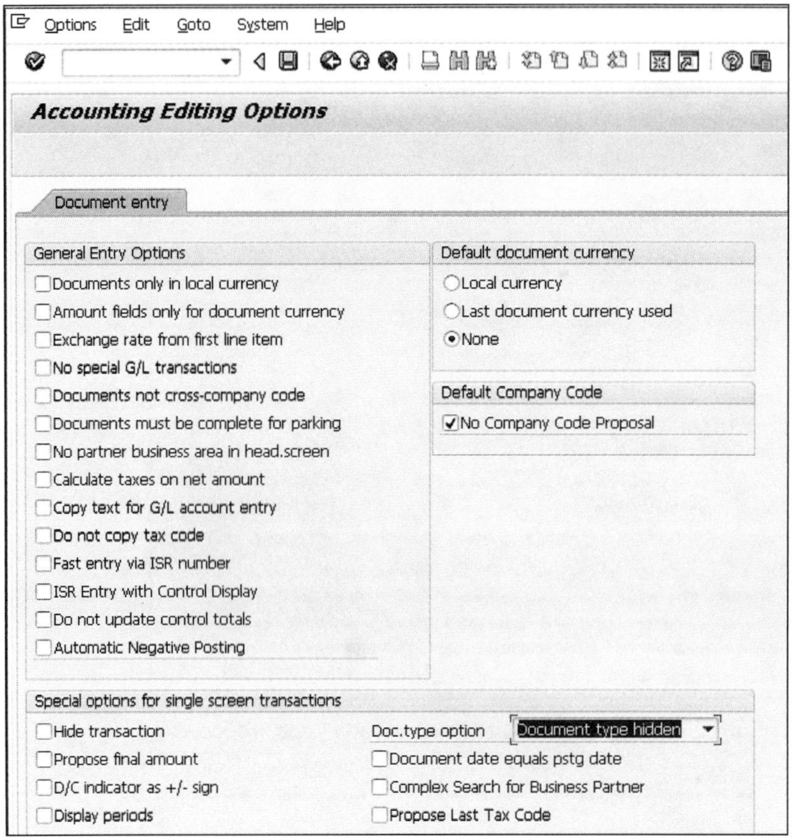

Figure 6.39 Accounting Editing Options with Hidden Document Type

After the editing options are saved, return to Transaction FB60 to see that the **Document Type** field is now hidden from view (Figure 6.40).

In AP, the applicability of this setting depends on the number of document types created for vendor invoices. The standard delivered SAP document type is KR, but you may have additional custom document types as well. Be mindful of what AP document types exist in your system (whether standard delivered by SAP or custom document types) and when to use them.

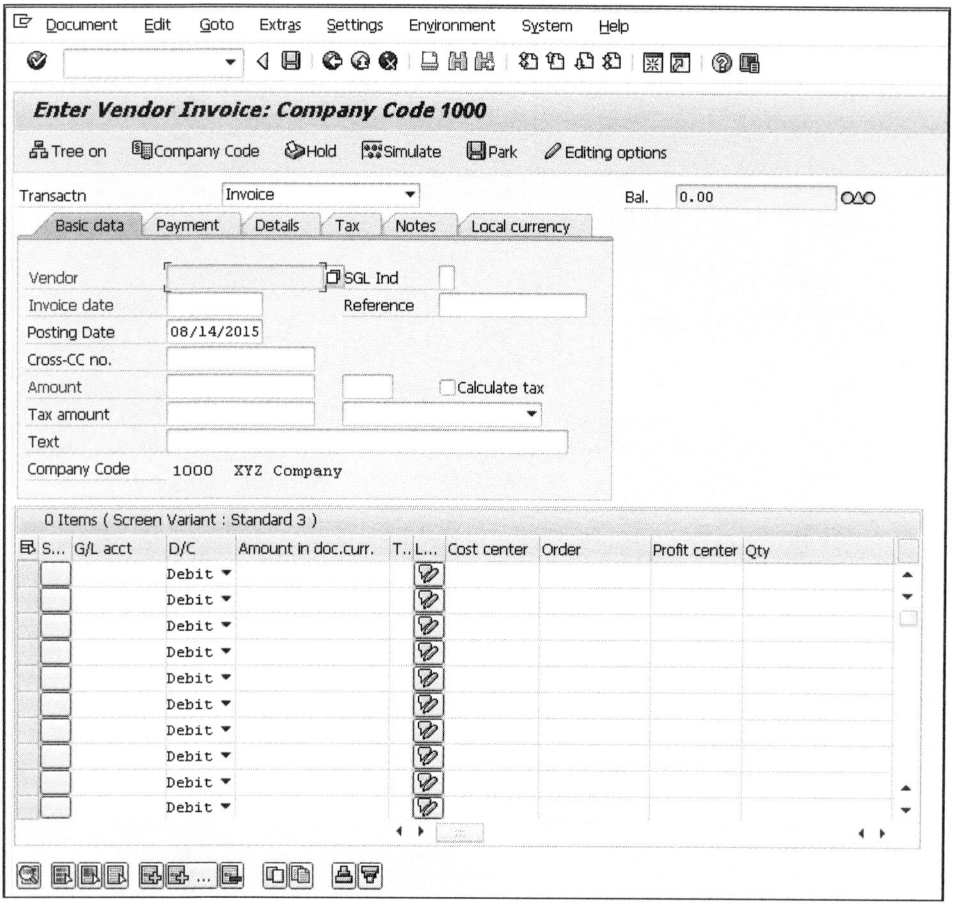

Figure 6.40 Enter G/L Account Document Screen with Hidden Document Type

Now that you've seen a few examples of changing editing options, let's take a look at the SAP descriptions for all the options available as provided in Table 6.1.

Editing Option	Description
Documents only in local currency	Only allows entry of documents in local currency
Amount fields only for document currency	Only allows entry amounts in foreign currency when entering documents in foreign currency

Table 6.1 Editing Options and Descriptions

Editing Option	Description
Exchange rate from first line item	Corrects exchange rate in the document header automatically using the amounts in the first line item when posting foreign currency documents
No special G/L transactions	Prevents entry of special G/L transactions
Documents not cross-company code	Prevents cross-company code entries
Documents must be complete for parking	Prevents incomplete documents from being parked
No partner business area in head.screen	Prevents default partner business area from being entered in the document header
Calculate taxes on net amount	Indicates the G/L account amounts entered are net of taxes
Copy text for G/L account entry	Automatically copies text from last G/L line item to subsequent line items
Do not copy tax code	Deactivates automatically copying the last tax code entered to G/L account line items
Fast entry via ISR number	Enables the fast entry of incoming invoices using the ISR subscriber number
ISR Entry with Control Display	Provides the ability to enter an alternative vendor number in cases in which several vendors may have the same ISR number
Do not update control totals	Prevents control totals from being updated
Automatic Negative Posting	Makes any automatically generated lines negative postings when the negative postings indicator is set for at least one manually entered line
Default document currency	■ **Local currency**: Defaults local currency used in header currency field ■ **Last document currency used**: Defaults last currency used in header currency field ■ **None**: Defaults no currency in the header currency field

Table 6.1 Editing Options and Descriptions (Cont.)

Editing Option	Description
Default Company Code	Forces manual selection of the company code to be used when the **No Company Code Proposal** checkbox is selected
Hide transaction	Hides the **Transaction** field on the entry screen
Propose final amount	Proposes the final invoice amount in the customer or vendor line after a G/L line has been entered
D/C indicator as +/- sign	Allows the entry of +/- sign with amounts, which derives the debit/credit indicator
Display periods	Enables the display of periods on the entry screen under basic data
Posting in special periods possible	Enables the period field for data input
Always Use Payment Base Deadline	Only permits payment deadline calculation based on the baseline date
Doc.type option	■ Displays document type in header ■ Document type ready for input ■ Display document type using short name ■ Document type ready for input using short name ■ Document type hidden
Document date equals pstg date	Defaults the document date from the posting date
Complex Search for Business Partner	Specifies when entering a vendor invoice if a complex search is possible for the number of the trading partner
Propose Last Tax Code	Proposes the last tax code used the next time the transaction is called
Tax Code: Only Display Short Text	Changes the tax code dropdown list in the transaction to only display the short text of the tax code

Table 6.1 Editing Options and Descriptions (Cont.)

As you read through Table 6.1, consider the applicability of each to your job function in AP.

6.1.6 Post with Reference

Post with reference is a quick and easy way to create a new vendor invoice by replicating all or most of the accounting data from a document that has already been posted. In many ways, it's much like a document copy function, except that SAP provides several *flow control indicators*, which allow you to select specific actions to control in the process. For example, when the **Do not propose amounts** indicator is selected, you must manually enter document line item amounts.

Post with reference is a useful feature available in several FI transactions, but the scope of our discussion in this section is limited to its use in Transaction FB60. You must be cautious while using this functionality in AP. It's often tempting to use post with reference as an easy way to replicate large documents. But if you aren't careful, it can result in posting errors. You need to make sure your posting date, reference number, amounts, and lines of accounting are all changed properly.

In this section, we'll demonstrate the use of post with reference with a simple example and then provide a complete list of flow control options and their descriptions (see Table 6.2 at the end of this section). In the example that follows, we demonstrate how to use post with reference to create a new vendor invoice document using Transaction FB60 or application menu path, **Accounting • Financial Accounting • Accounts Payable • Document Entry • FB60 – Invoice**, as shown in Figure 6.41.

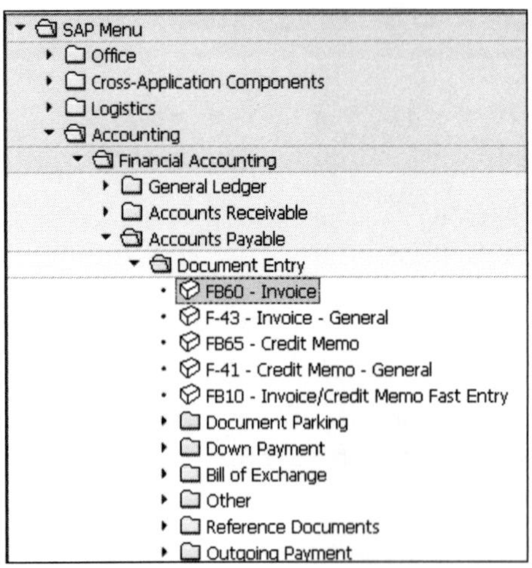

Figure 6.41 Transaction FB60 Application Menu Path for Post with Reference

Double-click **FB60 – Invoice** from the menu path, or enter "FB60" in the **Command** field (as shown in Figure 6.42) and press [Enter].

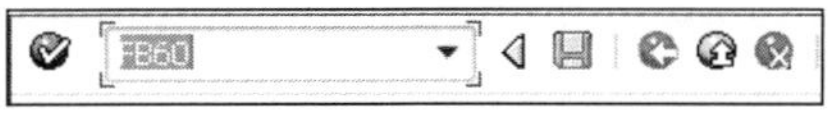

Figure 6.42 Entering "FB60" in the Command Field

From the **Enter Vendor Invoice** entry screen (Figure 6.43), initiate the post with reference function by choosing **Goto • Post with reference**, or press [Shift]+[F9].

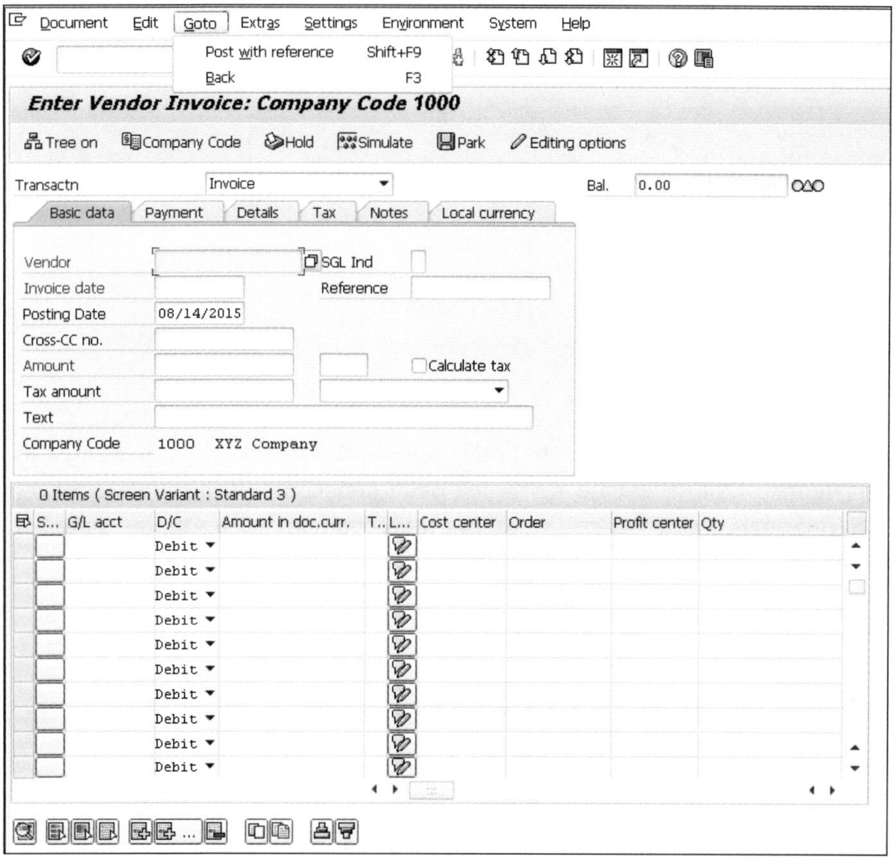

Figure 6.43 Enter Vendor Invoice Screen for Post with Reference

The post with reference **Post Document: Header Data** selection screen opens (Figure 6.44). On this screen, enter values for the **Document Number**, **Company Code**, and **Fiscal Year** fields in the **Reference** area. In this example, we selected the **Do not propose amounts** checkbox in the **Flow control** area.

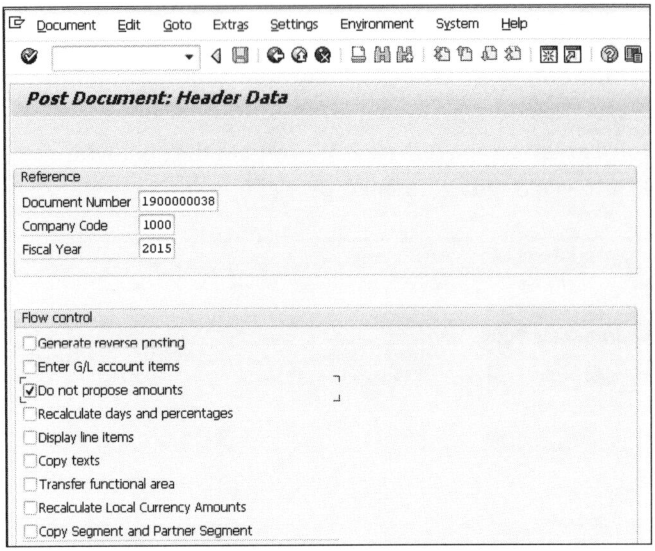

Figure 6.44 Post with Reference Header Selection Screen

After the relevant fields are populated in the **Post Document: Header Data** screen, press Enter to open the first screen of the new vendor invoice document creation process (Figure 6.45). Header data in this new document contains the field values copied from the reference document, including the **Document Date**, **Posting Date**, and **Reference** fields. Note that you can edit many field values at this point.

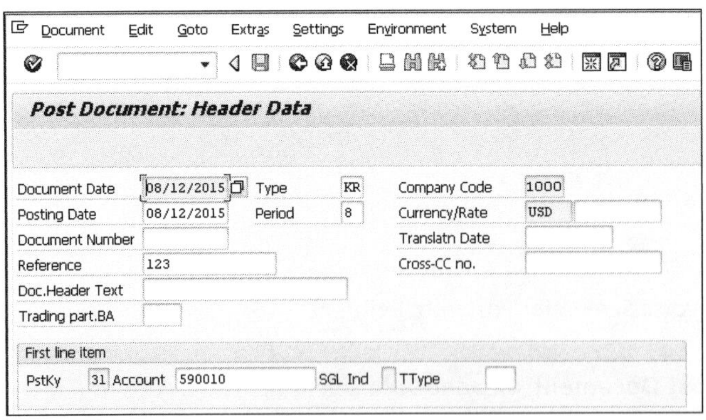

Figure 6.45 Post with Reference Header Screen

In this example, we changed the **Document Date**, **Posting Date**, and **Reference** fields (Figure 6.46).

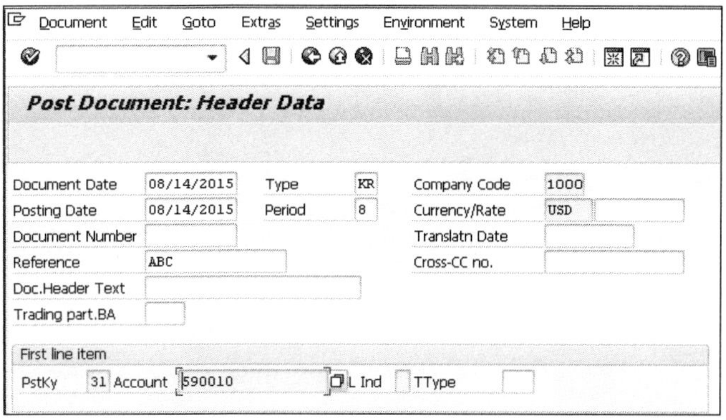

Figure 6.46 Post with Reference Header Screen with Changes

After you've changed any header fields you want to change, press Enter, and the **Post Document Add Vendor item** screen appears (Figure 6.47). Note that the **Amount** field is blank because you selected the **Do not propose amounts** indicator in **Flow control** (refer to Figure 6.44) when you initiated the post with reference transaction.

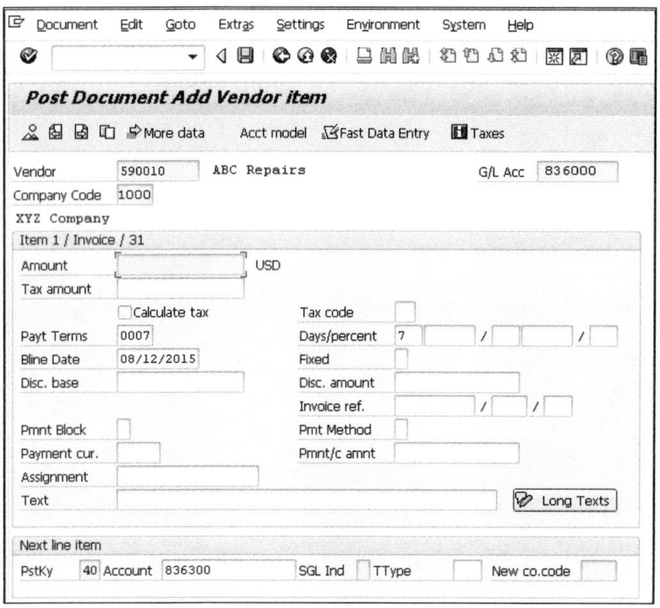

Figure 6.47 Post with Reference Add Vendor Item Screen

In this example, we entered "1000" in the **Amount** field (Figure 6.48).

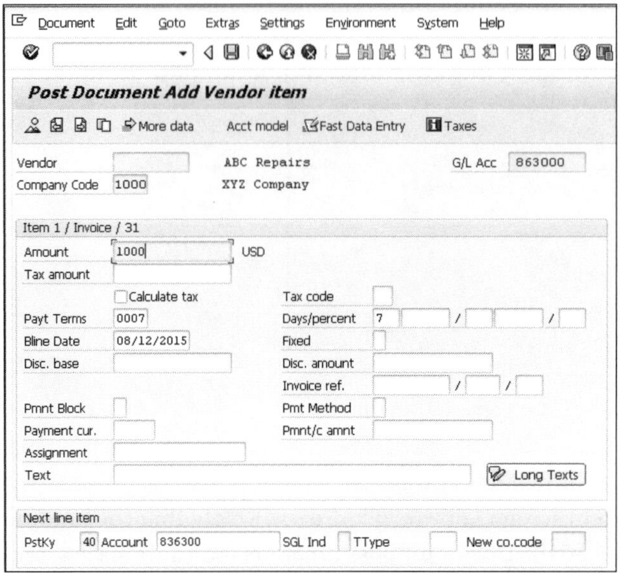

Figure 6.48 Post with Reference Add Vendor Item Screen with Amount Change

After the **Amount** field is entered, press [Enter], and a second **Post Document Add G/L account item** screen opens (Figure 6.49). Notice that the **Amount** field is blank again.

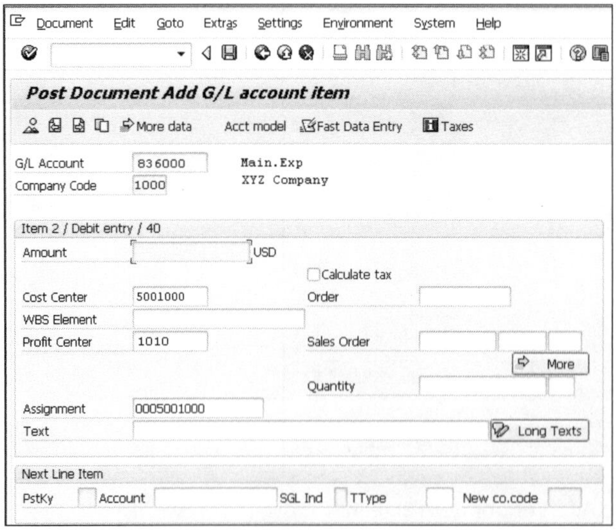

Figure 6.49 Post with Reference Add G/L Account Item Screen with Amount Blank

Again, we entered "1000" in the **Amount** field (Figure 6.50).

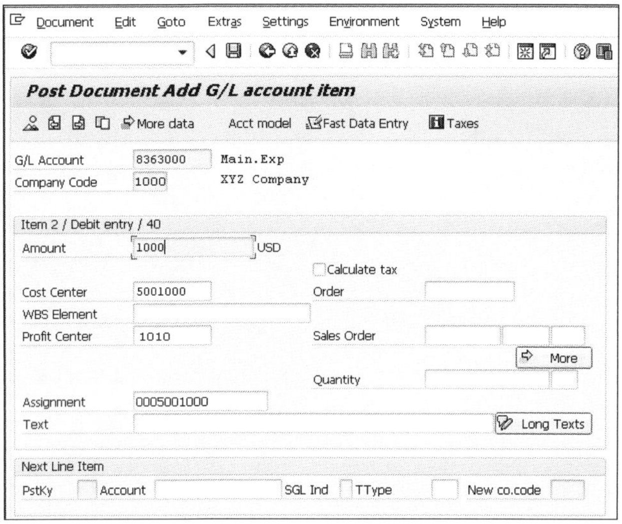

Figure 6.50 Post with Reference Add G/L Account Item Screen with Amount Change

After entering all G/L account line items, click the **Post** icon or press Ctrl+S to post the vendor invoice document (Figure 6.51). A message appears with the new vendor invoice document number.

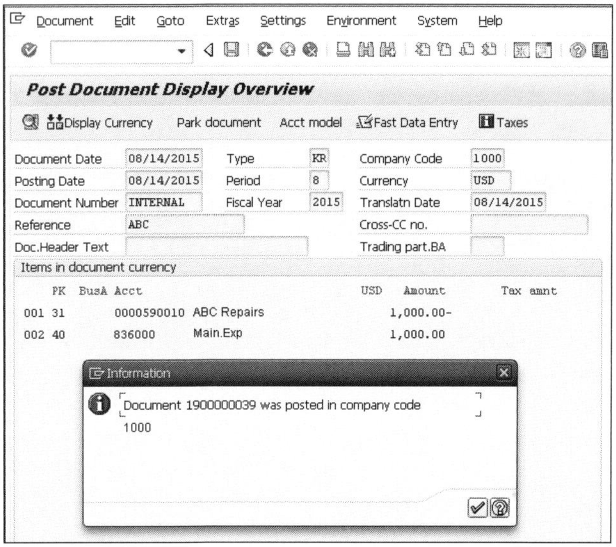

Figure 6.51 Post with Reference Document Created Message

Now that you've seen a simple example of post with reference, let's take a look at all the **Flow control** indicator options, listed in Table 6.2. As you read through them, think about their relevance to specific AP transactions, such as vendor invoices and credit memos.

Flow Control Checkbox	Description
Generate reverse posting	Automatically generates reverse debit/credit indicators to offset the reference document
Enter G/L account items	Transfers line items to the fast entry screen for G/L accounts so that several line items can be displayed and processed from one screen
Do not propose amounts	Requires line item amounts must to be manually entered in the new document
Recalculate days and percentages	Recalculates days and percentages from payment terms
Display line items	Displays each individual line item separately so that default field values can be changed if necessary
Copy texts	Copies long texts from the reference document to the new document
Transfer functional area	Transfers the reference functional area instead of re-deriving it because the functional area is normally derived
Recalculate local currency amounts	Recalculates local currency amounts to account for changes in exchange rates
Copy segment and partner segment	Transfers the fields instead of re-deriving their values because they are normally derived

Table 6.2 Flow Control Checkboxes and Descriptions

On a final note, post with reference allows you to copy an existing document, but it's an SAP best practice to allow derived field values to re-derive with each new document posting.

6.2 Credit Memos

Vendor invoices are amounts you owe to a vendor for goods or services purchased. *Credit memos*, on the other hand, are credits back to you from the vendor. A credit may be due for any number of reasons, including overpayment, damaged goods, additional discounts, and erroneously billed amounts.

Credit memos allow you to correct vendor account balances on the books and to offset outgoing payment balances. In other words, the amount paid to a vendor is the open invoice amounts due less any credit memos posted to the vendor's account.

In the AP module, you post a credit memo via Transaction FB65 or application menu path, **Accounting • Financial Accounting • Accounts Payable • Document Entry • FB65 – Credit Memo**, as shown in Figure 6.52.

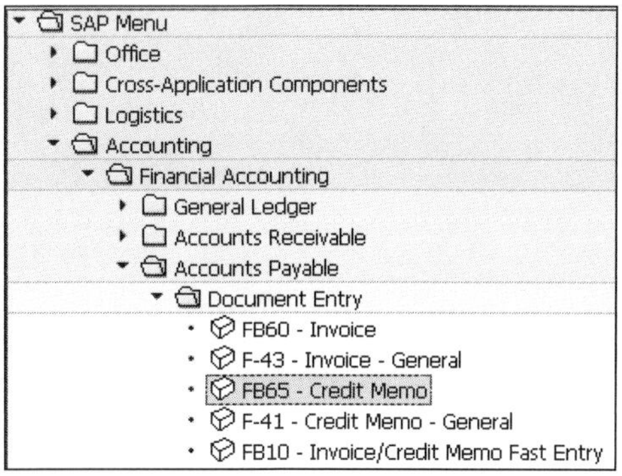

Figure 6.52 Transaction FB65 Application Menu Path

Double-click **FB65 – Credit Memo** from the menu path, or enter "FB65" in the **Command** field (as shown in Figure 6.53) and press [Enter].

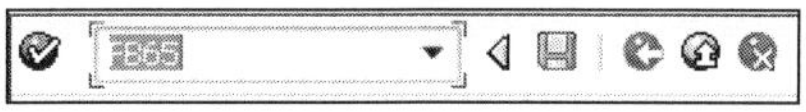

Figure 6.53 Entering "FB65" in the Command Field

The **Park Vendor Invoice** screen opens (Figure 6.54). In the document header, enter values for the **Vendor**, **Posting Date**, **Invoice date**, and **Amount,** and any other fields that are required but aren't prepopulated. In this example, values are prepopulated in the **Posting Date** and currency fields.

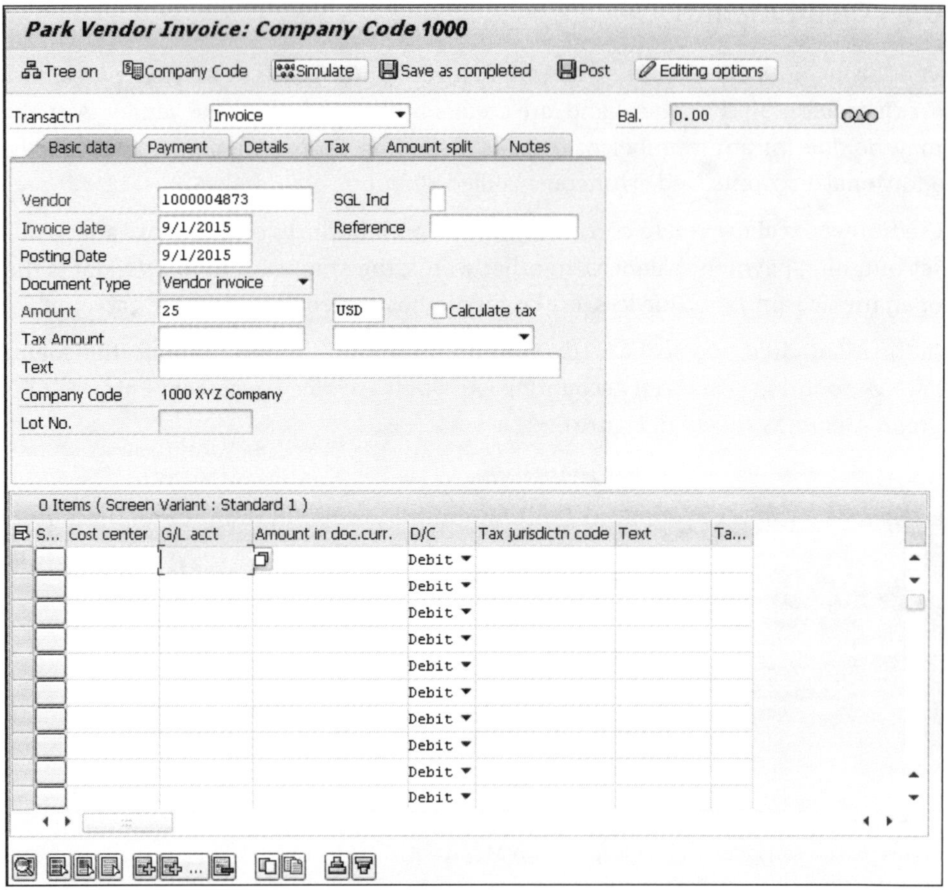

Figure 6.54 Enter Park Vendor Invoice Screen

With the header entry complete, enter at least one G/L line item (Figure 6.55). In this example, the line item is an offset (i.e., credit) to an expense account. Here, we manually entered line item values for the **G/L acct**, **D/C** (debit/credit indicator), **Amount in doc.curr.**, and **Cost center** fields.

After entering document line items, click the **Simulate** button in the top center of the **Park Vendor Invoice** screen to initiate simulation of the vendor credit memo posting logic, which will determine if the document can be properly posted. If the simulation is unsuccessful, an error message appears. If successful, the **Document Overview** screen appears, as show in Figure 6.56.

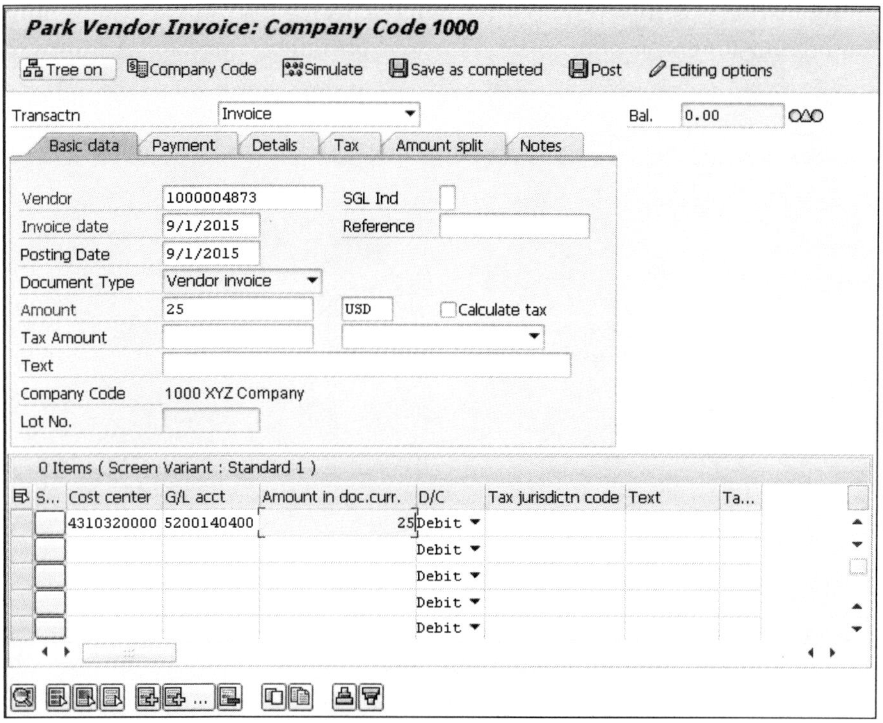

Figure 6.55 Vendor Credit Memo Line Item Entry

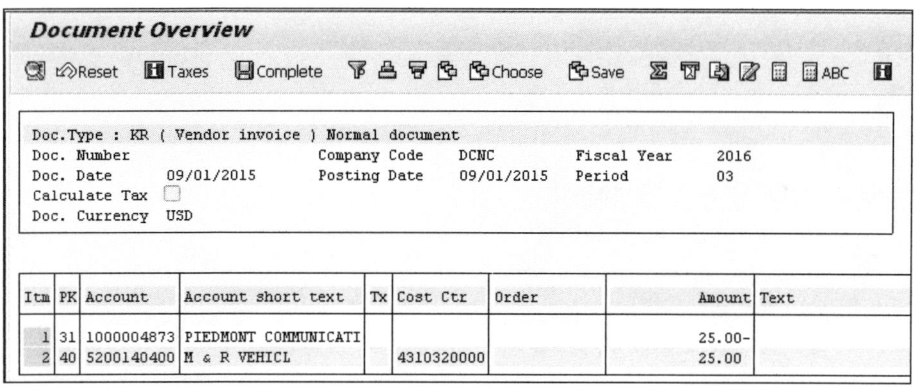

Figure 6.56 Document Overview Screen

After the simulation is complete, click the **Complete** icon. This will park the vendor credit memo, and a message appears with the new document number, as shown in Figure 6.57.

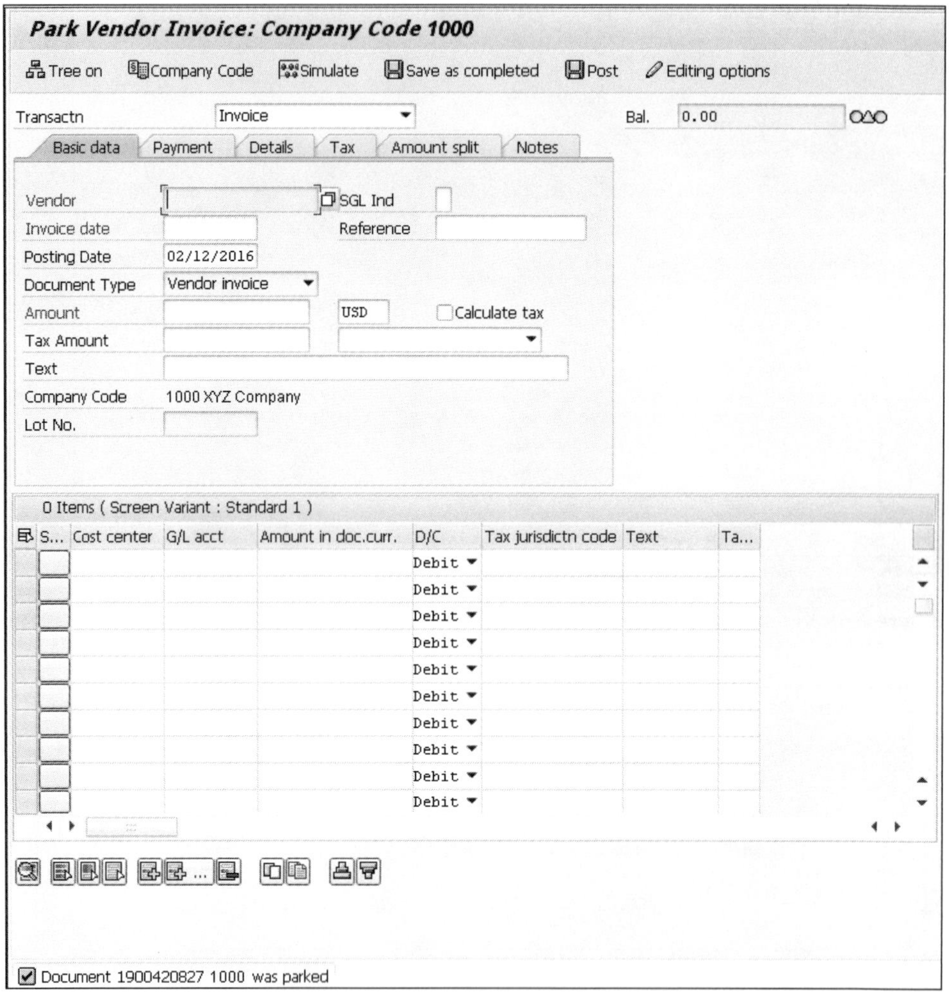

Figure 6.57 Vendor Credit Memo Parked Message

Credit memos are an important function in managing vendor accounts. Now that you've seen an example and understand the role credit memos play in AP, let's discuss the vendor down payment transaction.

6.3 Down Payments Sent

Down payments sent are prepayments to vendors in advance of receiving goods or services. A down payment may be requested by a vendor as a sign of good faith or may be required to reserve a product.

The starting point for the down payment process in AP is the *down payment request*. You enter a vendor down payment request to make a down payment automatically via the payment program. Note that down payment requests are *noted items* in FI, meaning that G/L account balances aren't updated. In other words, down payment requests aren't reflected in either the transaction figures or the balance displays. They can only be viewed in line item displays by specifying that you want to see noted items.

To enter a vendor down payment request in the AP module, use Transaction F-47 or application menu path, **Accounting • Financial Accounting • Accounts Payable • Document Entry • Down Payment • F-47 – Request**, as shown in Figure 6.58.

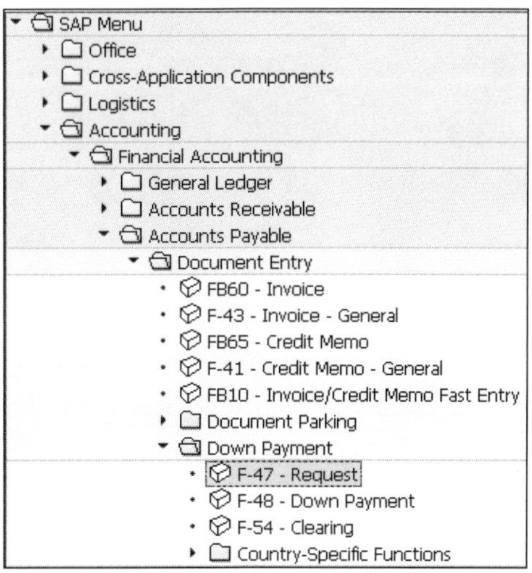

Figure 6.58 Transaction F-47 Application Menu Path

Double-click **F-47 – Request** from the menu path, or enter "F-47" in the **Command** field (as shown in Figure 6.59) and press [Enter].

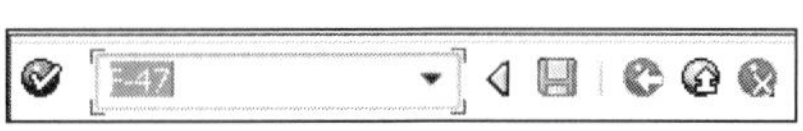

Figure 6.59 Entering "F-47" in the Command Field

The **Down Payment Request: Header Data** screen opens (Figure 6.60). In the document header, enter a value in **Document Date** and any other fields that are required, but don't prepopulate a default value. In this example, field values were defaulted for the **Posting Date**, **Type** (i.e., document type), **Period**, **Company Code**, and **Currency/Rate** fields.

In the **Vendor** area at the bottom of the screen, you must also enter an **Account** and special G/L indicator (in the **Trg.sp.G/L ind.** field).

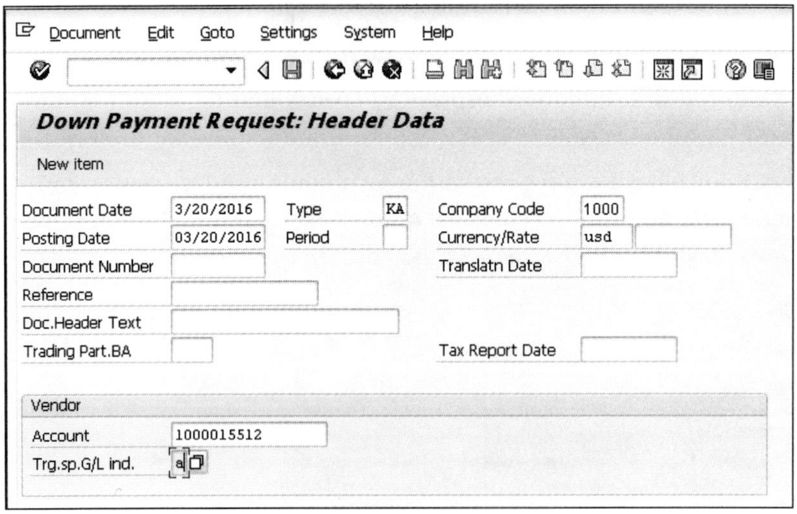

Figure 6.60 Down Payment Request: Header Data Screen

With the header data complete, click the **New item** button. The **Down Payment Request Add Vendor Item** screen opens (Figure 6.61). Here, enter values for the **Amount**, **Due on**, and any other required fields.

After entering the vendor line items, click the **Save** icon at the top of the entry screen, to the right of the **Command** field to post the vendor down payment request. A message appears with the new document number, as shown in Figure 6.62.

The down payment request is now ready to be paid to the vendor via the AP payment program (i.e., Transaction F110). See Chapter 7 for details on the automated payment program.

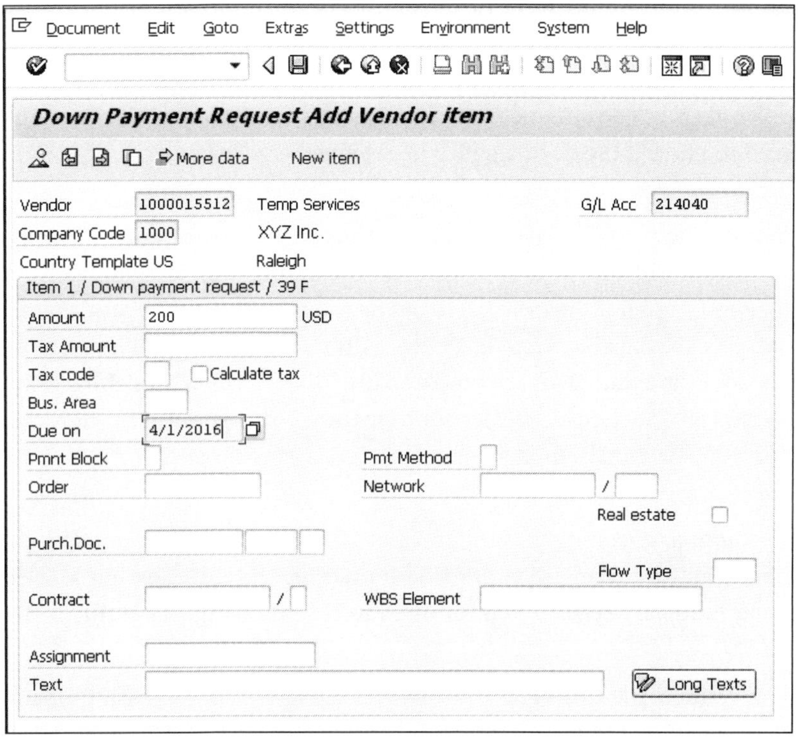

Figure 6.61 Add Vendor Item to Down Payment Request

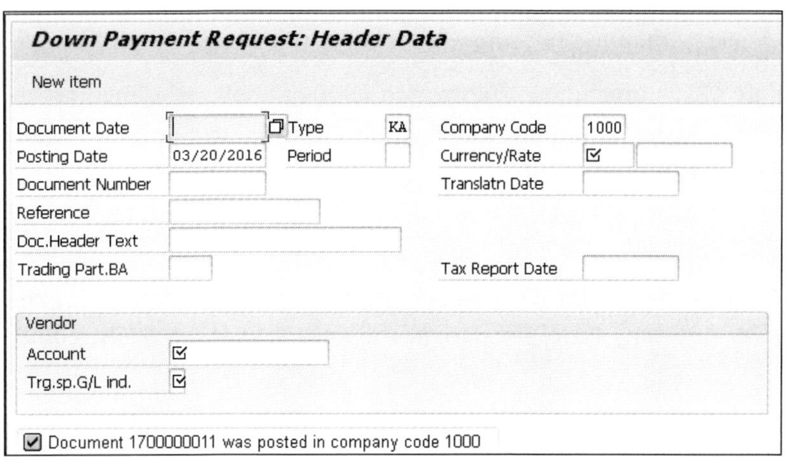

Figure 6.62 Down Payment Request Posted Message

6.4 Resetting and Reversing Documents

Before attempting to reverse an AP document, you need to know what type of document it is, for example, a vendor invoice, credit memo, or other transaction type. In addition, you need to know if the document to be reversed is a clearing document or not, and what this means.

Let's begin with a discussion of clearing versus non-clearing documents. *Clearing documents* are those produced through a post with clearing transaction, such as Transaction F-04 (see Chapter 3, Section 3.2) or Transaction F110 (i.e., the automated payment program). A clearing document has two technical components: First, it contains complete header data and at least two completed line items with debit/credit amounts netting to zero. Second is the account clearing component. Through the clearing process, a vendor open item is selected and its status changed from **Open** to **Cleared** when the clearing document is posted.

A *non-clearing accounting document* has the same attributes as a clearing document, except that it doesn't clear an open vendor line item. Therefore, in posting a non-clearing document, it doesn't select a vendor open item and change its status from **Open** to **Cleared**.

Now that you understand the difference between clearing and non-clearing documents, let's walk through some examples of document reversals. We'll begin with non-clearing documents because they are the simplest to reverse.

6.4.1 Reversing a Non-Clearing Document

To reverse a single AP document, use Transaction FB08 or application menu path, **Accounting • Financial Accounting • General Ledger • Document • Reverse • FB08 – Individual Reversal**, as shown in Figure 6.63.

Double-click **FB08 – Individual Reversal** from the menu path, or enter "FB08" in the **Command** field (as shown in Figure 6.64) and press [Enter].

The **Reverse Document: Header Data** screen opens (Figure 6.65). At a minimum, the **Document Number**, **Company Code**, **Fiscal Year**, and **Reversal Reason** fields require your input.

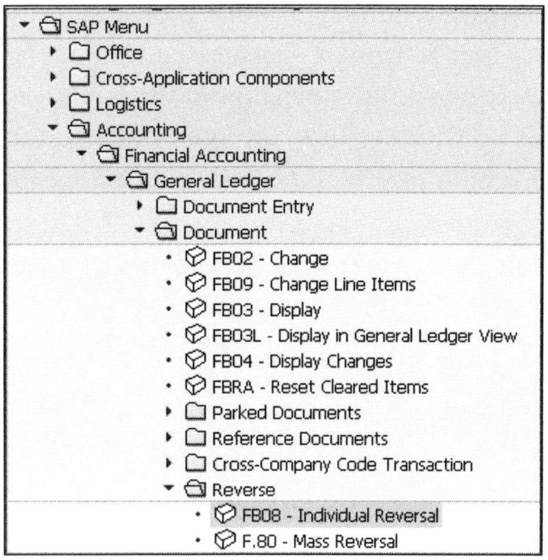

Figure 6.63 Transaction FB08 Application Menu Path

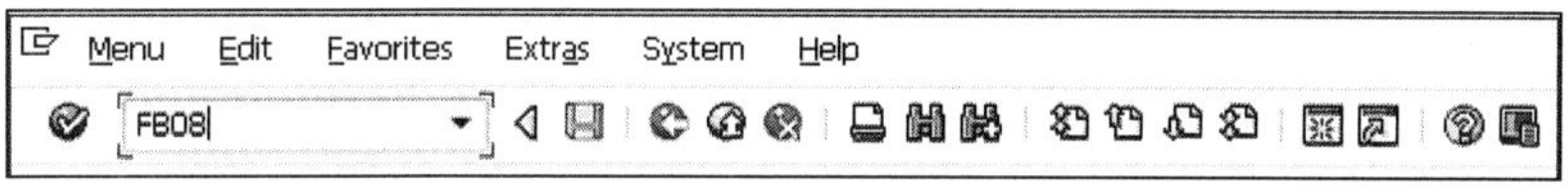

Figure 6.64 Entering "FB08" in the Command Field

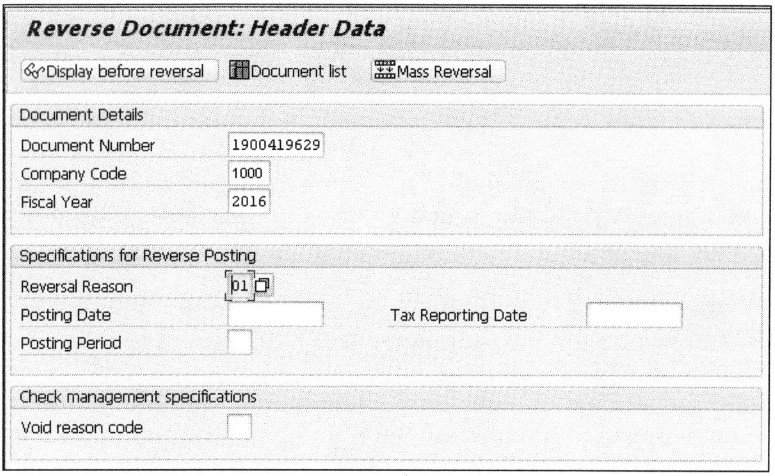

Figure 6.65 Reverse Document: Header Data Screen

The **Reversal Reason** field is noted in the reversed document. Beyond indicating why a document is reversed, the reversal reason also determines if an alternative posting date is allowed and if the reversal can be created from a negative posting. In this example, the **Reversal Reason** field is populated with a value of **01**, signifying that the reversal will take place in the current period.

When all the required fields are entered, click the **Post** icon or press Ctrl+S to post the AP reversal document. A message appears with the reverse document number (Figure 6.66).

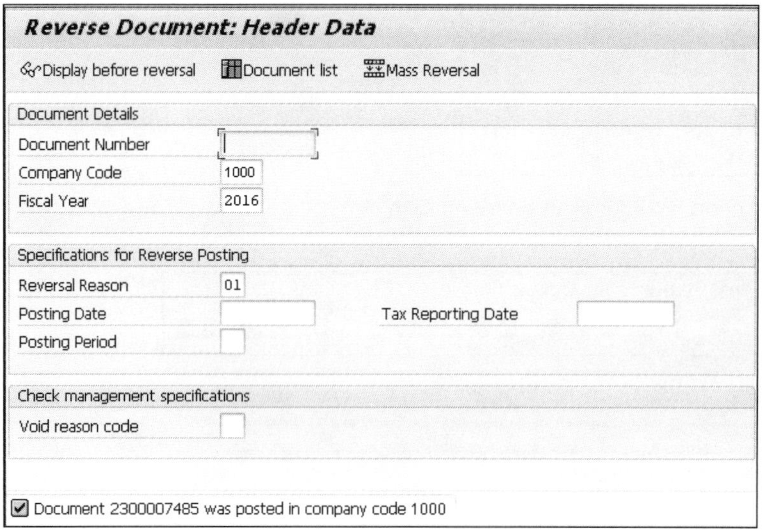

Figure 6.66 Reversal Document Created Message

Now that you know how to reverse a single non-clearing document using Transaction FB08, let's look at how you can reverse multiple non-clearing documents at the same time with a single transaction.

Mass document reversal allows you to reverse more than one non-clearing document. To do so, use Transaction F.80 or application menu path, **Accounting • Financial Accounting • General Ledger • Document • Reverse • F.80 – Mass Reversal**, as shown in Figure 6.67.

Double-click **F.80 – Mass Reversal** from the menu path, or enter "F.80" in the **Command** field (as shown in Figure 6.68) and press Enter.

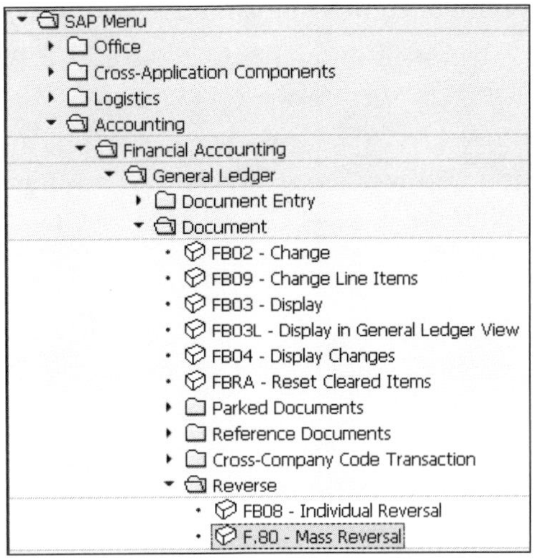

Figure 6.67 Transaction F.80 Application Menu Path

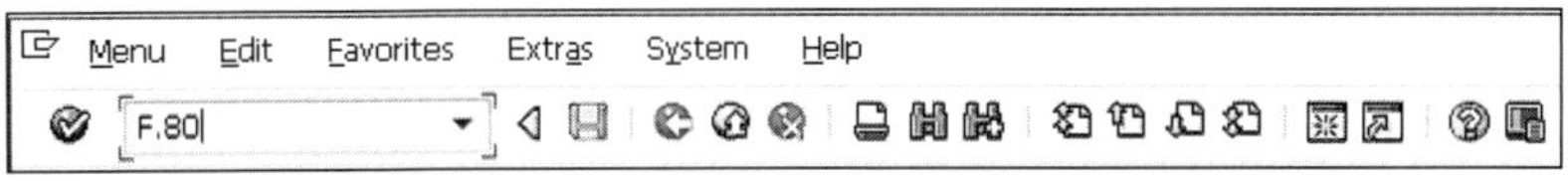

Figure 6.68 Entering "F.80" in the Command Field

The **Mass Reversal of Documents: Initial Screen** opens (Figure 6.69). As in Transaction FB08, the **Company code**, **Document Number**, **Fiscal Year**, and **Reason for reversal** fields are required. Note that in Transaction F.80, you can enter a range of values for these fields, whereas in Transaction FB08, you can only enter a single value for each field. In Transaction F.80, you also have a **Ledger** field, which in most cases will be your leading ledger.

Transaction F.80 has some additional features as well. Under **General selections,** there are several useful input fields, and in the **Reverse posting details** area, there is a **Test Run** checkbox. For mass reversals, it's always a good idea to run the program in test mode first.

When all the required fields are entered, click the **Execute** icon or press F8 to post the AP reversal documents. Detailed results are provided in the **Mass Reversal of Documents** output screen (Figure 6.70).

That concludes our discussion of the individual and mass reversals of non-clearing AP documents. Next, we'll look at the reversal of clearing documents.

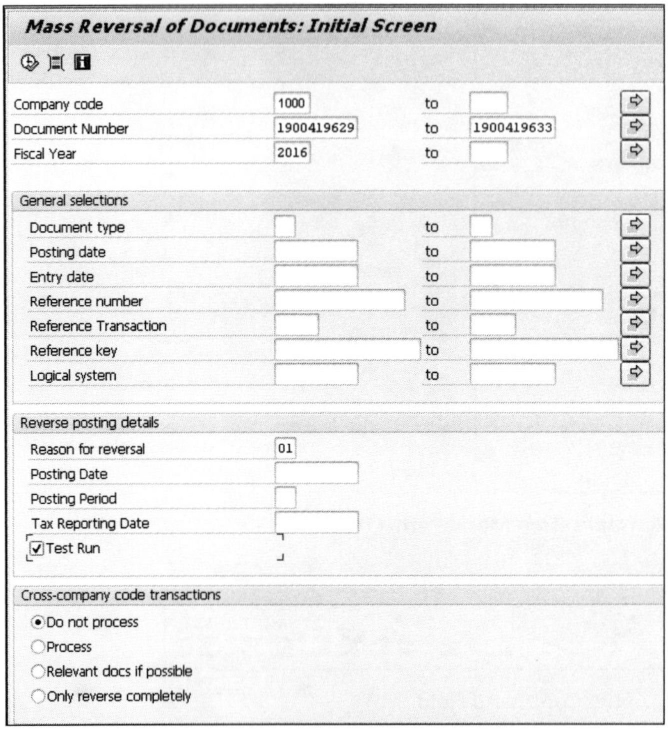

Figure 6.69 Mass Reversal of Documents: Initial Screen

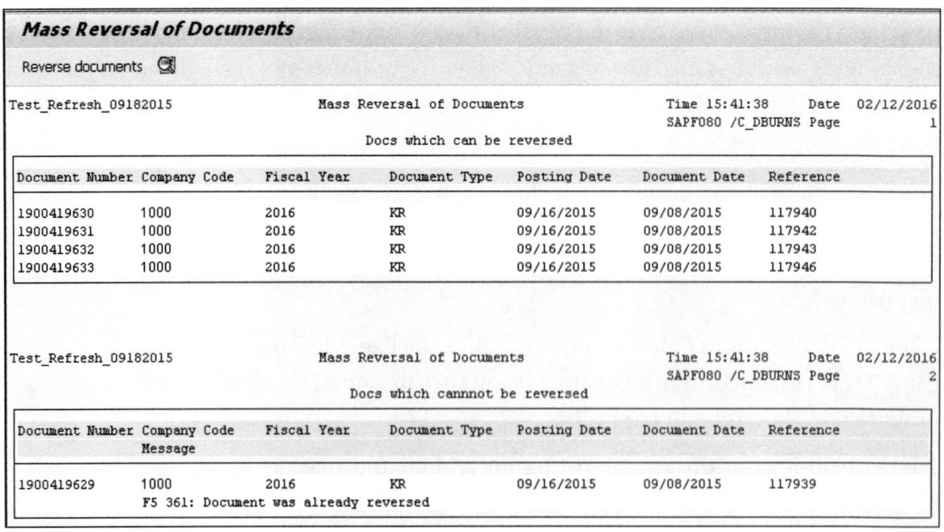

Figure 6.70 Mass Reversal of Documents Output Screen

6.4.2 Reversing a Clearing Document

To reverse an AP clearing document, use Transaction FBRA or application menu path, **Accounting • Financial Accounting • General Ledger • Document • FBRA – Reset Cleared Items**, as shown in Figure 6.71.

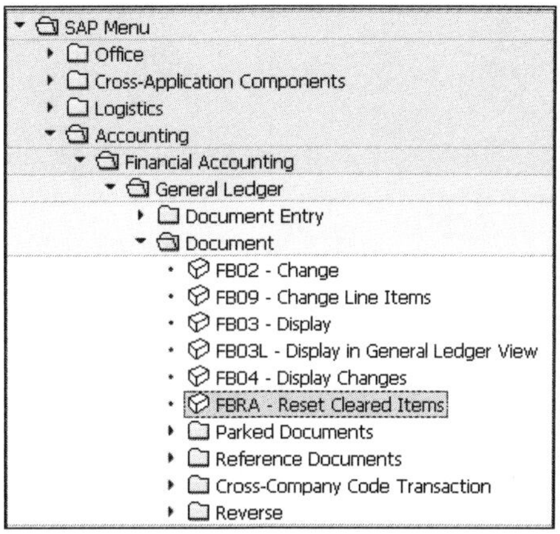

Figure 6.71 Transaction FBRA Application Menu Path

Double-click **FBRA – Reset Cleared Items** from the menu path, or enter "FBRA" in the **Command** field (as shown in Figure 6.72) and press [Enter].

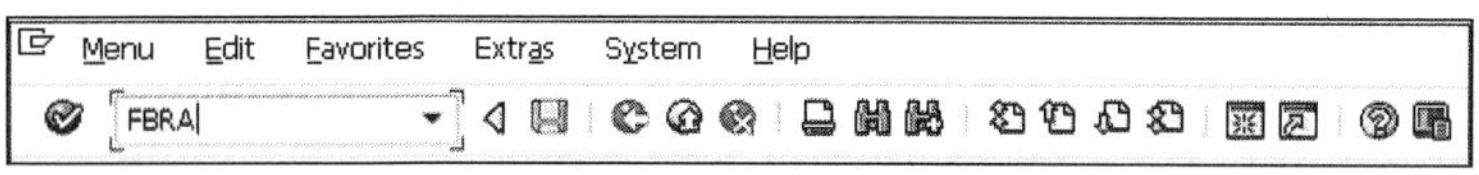

Figure 6.72 Entering "FBRA" in the Command Field

The **Reset Cleared Items** screen opens (Figure 6.73). The **Clearing Document**, **Company Code**, and **Fiscal Year** fields are all required.

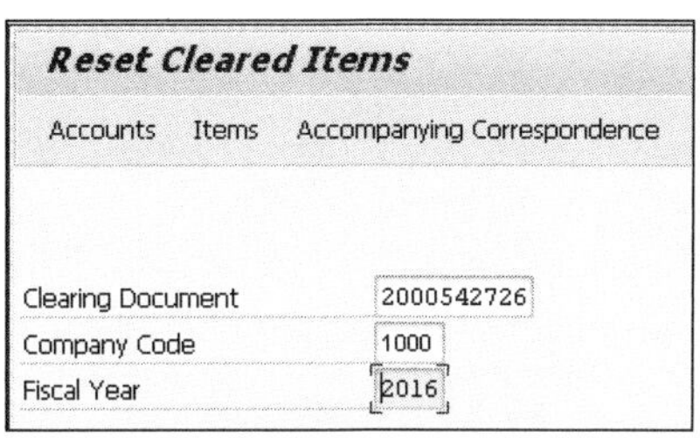

Figure 6.73 Reset Cleared Items

After entering the required screen elements, click the **Reset Cleared Items** icon 💾 or press [Ctrl]+[S]. This will bring up the **Reversal of clearing document** dialog box (Figure 6.74), in which you must choose one of three options: **Only resetting**, **Resetting and revers**, or **Cancel**.

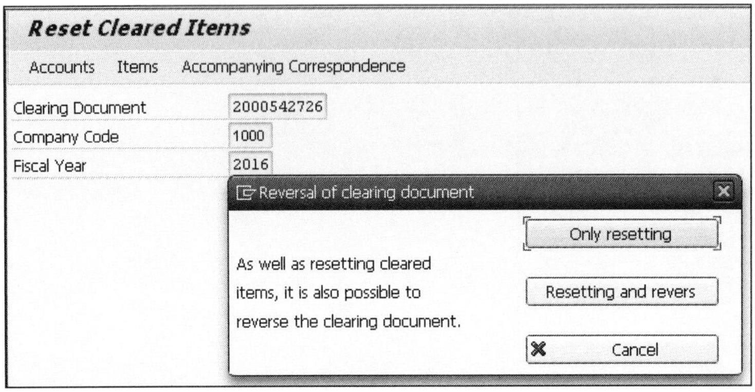

Figure 6.74 Reversal of Clearing Document Dialog Box

The **Only resetting** option doesn't reverse the clearing document. Instead, it breaks the reference between a clearing document and the AP item it cleared and changes the status of the cleared AP item back to **Open**. Only use this option when the AP item selected for clearing was the wrong line item. The clearing document becomes an open item and needs to be reassigned to clear the correct AP open item.

The **Resetting and revers** option (Figure 6.74) not only resets the cleared item back to **Open** status but also reverses the clearing document. For this example, select this option to open the **Reversal Data** dialog box (Figure 6.75).

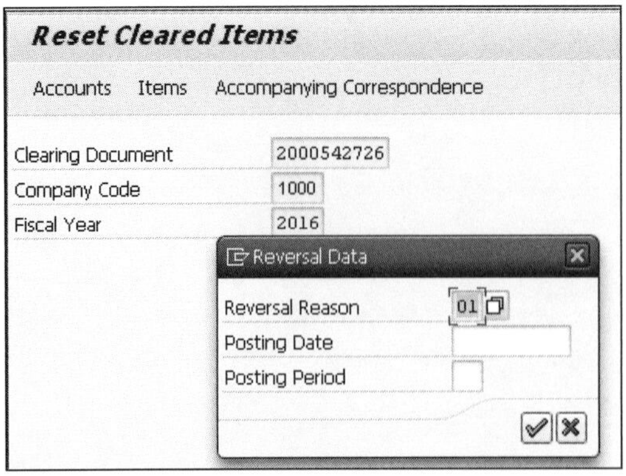

Figure 6.75 Reversal Data Dialog Box

The **Reversal Reason** field provides the reason a document is reversed. As previously stated, the reversal reason also determines whether an alternative posting date is allowed and whether the reversal can be created from a negative posting. In this example, the **Reversal Reason** field is populated with a value of **01**, signifying that the reversal will take place in the current period.

Click the **Continue** icon ✅ or press [Enter]. Two subsequent information dialog boxes appear. The first message, shown in Figure 6.76, states that the clearing document was reset. The second message, shown in Figure 6.77, provides the number of a new document that was posted, which is the document that reversed the clearing document.

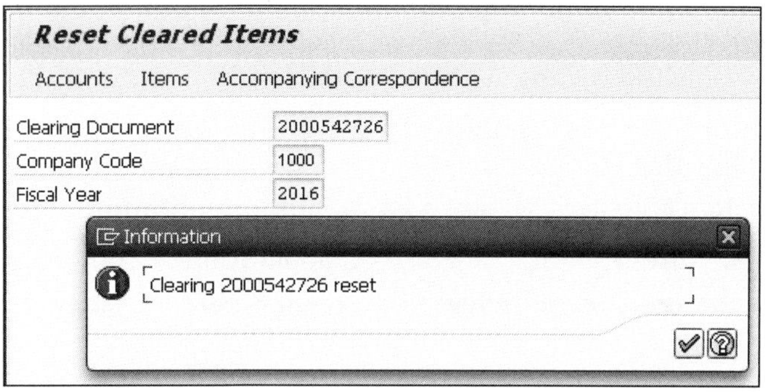

Figure 6.76 Clearing Document Reset Message

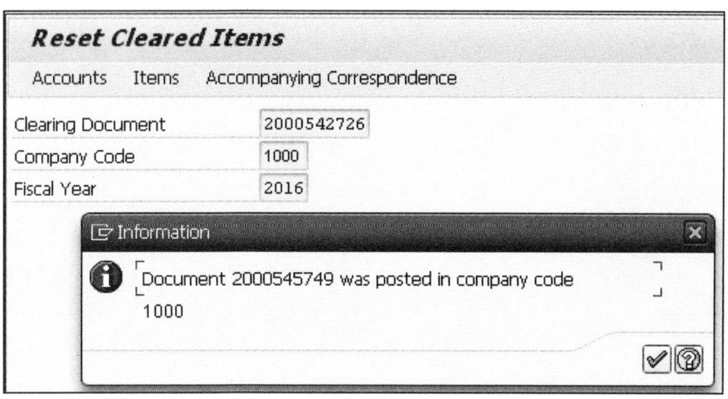

Figure 6.77 Reversal Document Posted Message

This concludes our discussion of AP document reversals. In this section, you learned the differences between clearing and non-clearing documents and saw examples for each. Now, let's discuss the topic of changing and displaying AP documents.

6.5 Changing and Displaying Documents

This section covers the change and display capabilities for AP accounting documents. The scope of this section is limited to Transaction FB60, but the same principles apply for other AP and FI documents.

Rules for changing field values in FI documents are defined in configuration, and separate rules are defined for header and line item fields. In other words, you have some configuration options available that determine which fields in a posted document can be changed.

It's important to note that there are some limits to this. SAP will never allow you to change fields considered central to the principle of orderly accounting. These are fields that are material to AP and G/L account balances, posting dates, and integration. Such fields include not only the **Posting Date**, **D/C** (debit/credit) indicator, and **Amount** fields but also update objects (i.e., cost center). If an AP accounting document contains an incorrect value of this sort, the document should be reversed using Transaction FB08 or Transaction FBRA (see Section 6.4).

To change an AP document, use Transaction FB02 or application menu path, **Accounting • Financial Accounting • General Ledger • Document • FB02 – Change**, as shown in Figure 6.78.

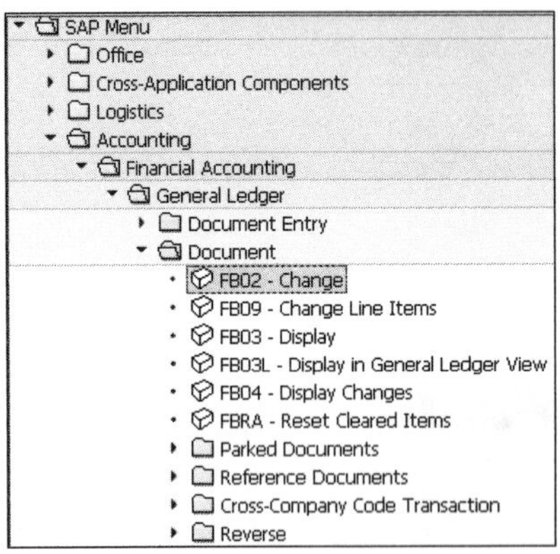

Figure 6.78 Transaction FB02 Application Menu Path

Double-click **FB02 – Change** from the menu path, or enter "FB02" in the **Command** field (as shown in Figure 6.79) and press [Enter].

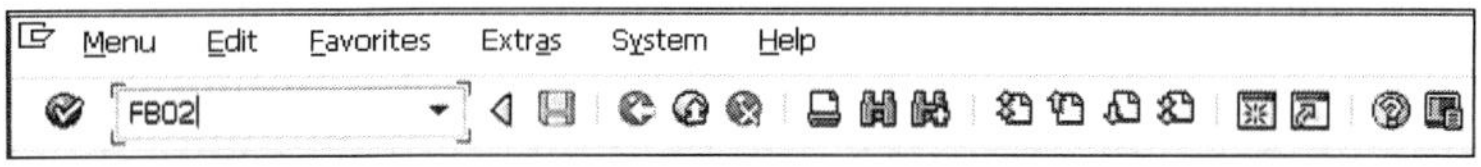

Figure 6.79 Entering "FB02" in the Command Field

The **Change Document: Initial Screen** opens (Figure 6.80). The **Document Number**, **Company Code**, and **Fiscal Year** fields require values to be input.

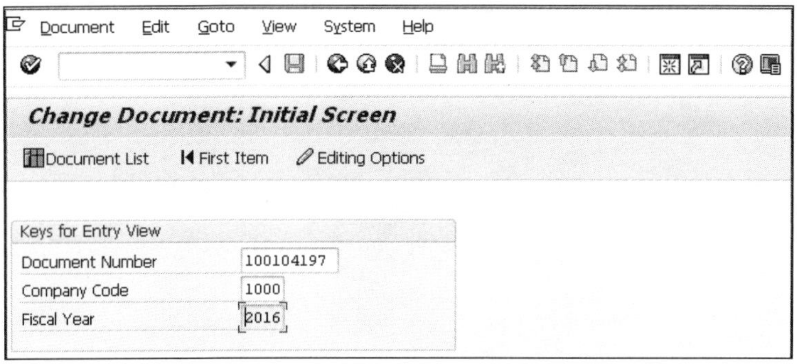

Figure 6.80 Change Document: Initial Screen

After entering all field values, press Enter. The **Change Document: Data Entry View** screen opens (Figure 6.81).

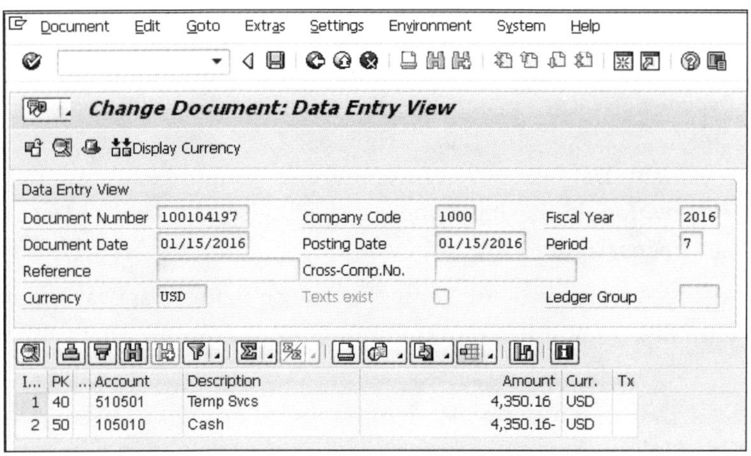

Figure 6.81 Change Document: Data Entry View

To change a header field, click the **Header** icon to open the **Document Header** dialog box (Figure 6.82). Fields that can't be changed are grayed out. Fields that can be changed appear white and are ready for field values to be entered or changed.

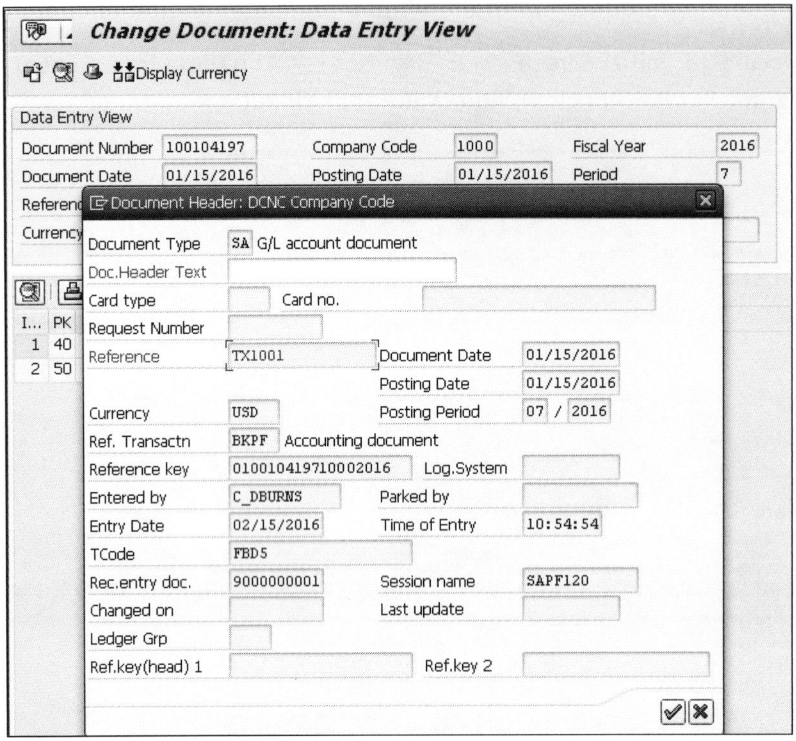

Figure 6.82 Change Document Header

From the **Change Document: Data Entry View** screen (refer to Figure 6.81), you can change line item fields by double-clicking a line. After doing so, the **Change Document: Line Item** screen opens (Figure 6.83).

Fields that can't be changed are grayed out. Those that can be changed appear white and are ready for field values to be entered or changed. For this example, change the **Text** field (Figure 6.84).

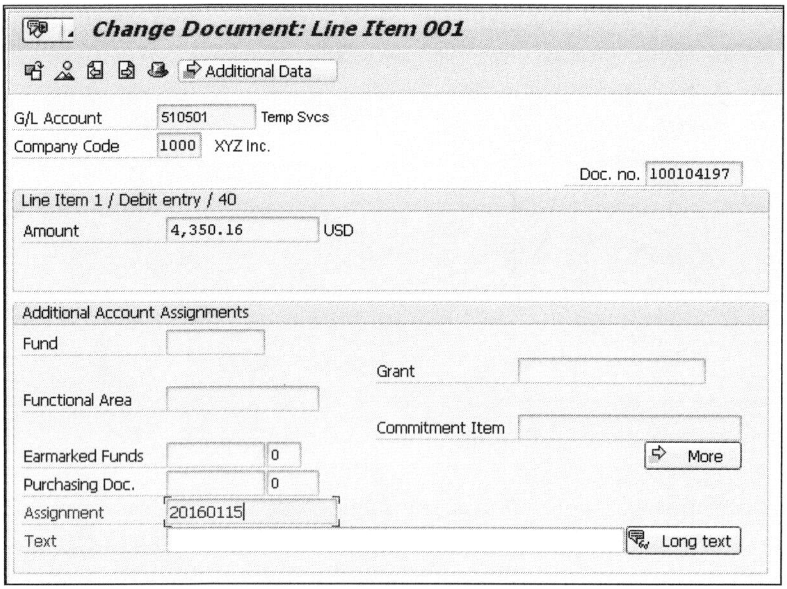

Figure 6.83 Change Document: Line Item

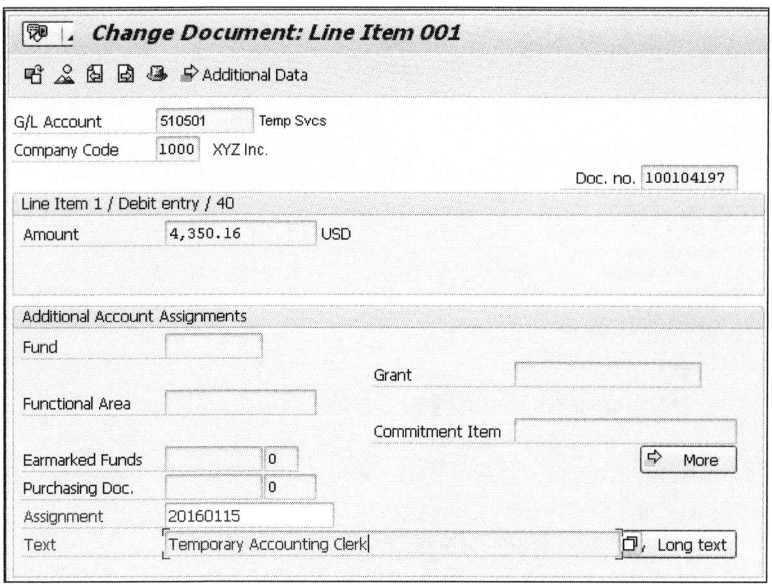

Figure 6.84 Change Line Item with Text Field Change

After changing field values, click the **Save** icon or press [Ctrl]+[S]. A message indicates that the document changes have been saved (Figure 6.85).

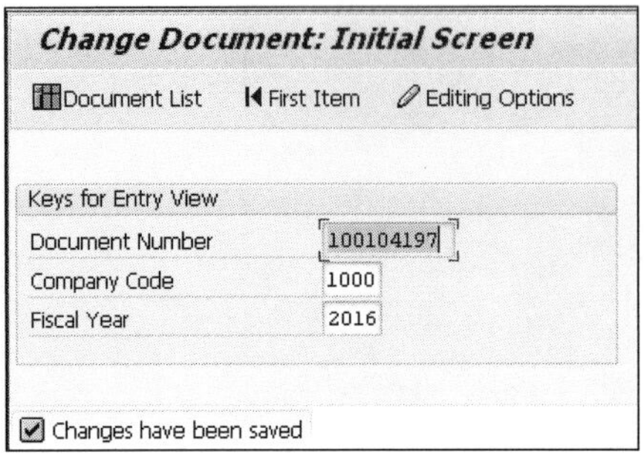

Figure 6.85 Changes Have Been Saved Message

To display an AP accounting document, use Transaction FB03 or application menu path, **Accounting • Financial Accounting • General Ledger • Document • FB03 – Display**, as shown in Figure 6.86.

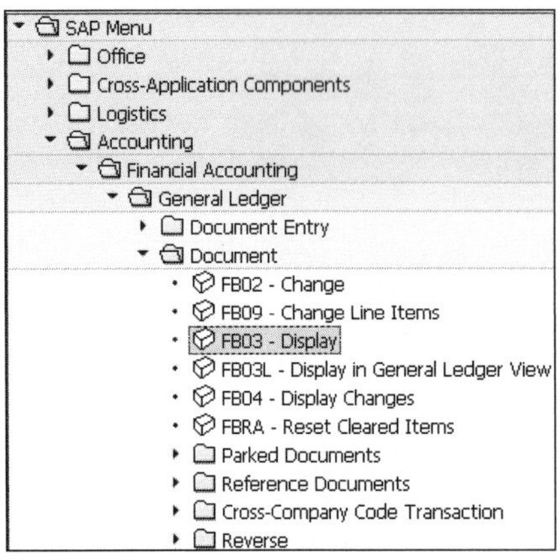

Figure 6.86 Transaction FB03 Application Menu Path

Double-click **FB03 – Display** from the menu path, or enter "FB03" in the **Command** field (as shown in Figure 6.87) and press [Enter].

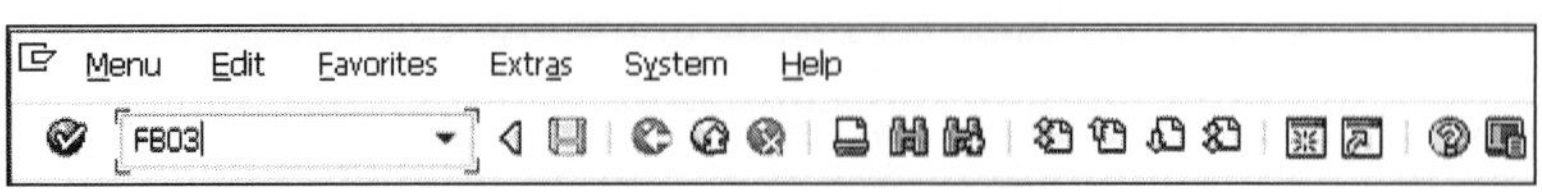

Figure 6.87 Entering "FB03" in the Command Field

The **Display Document: Initial Screen** opens (Figure 6.88). The **Document Number**, **Company Code**, and **Fiscal Year** fields are required.

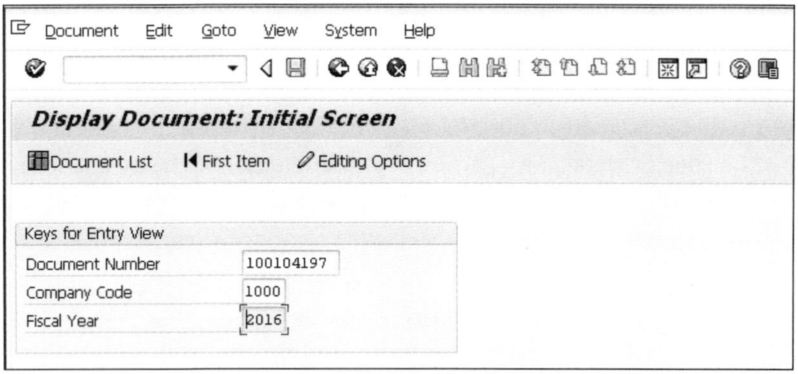

Figure 6.88 Display Document: Initial Screen

After entering field values, press `Enter`. The **Display Document: Data Entry View** screen opens (Figure 6.89).

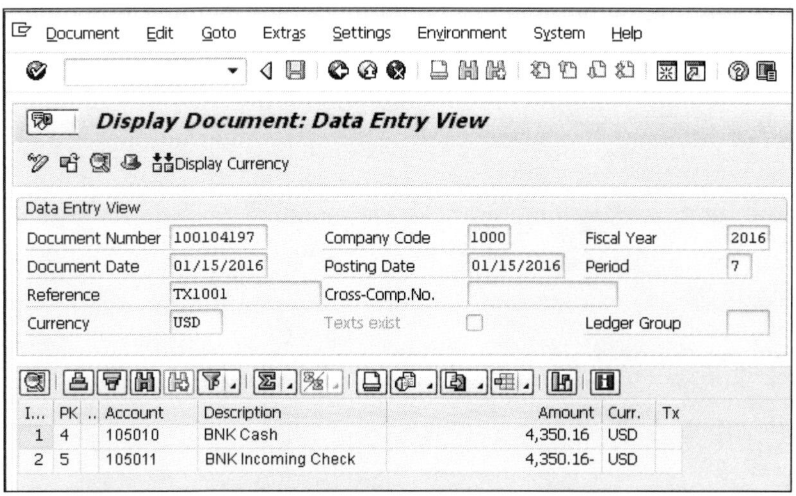

Figure 6.89 Display Document: Data Entry View

From this screen, you can double-click a line to view line item details, or click the **Header** icon to view header details.

This concludes our discussion of changing and displaying AP documents. In the next section, we'll discuss the topic of issuing outgoing payments.

6.6 Issuing Outgoing Payments

The basics of AP are that you create vendor invoices and issue payments. The vendor invoice contains the specific details (e.g., amount and due date) of the outstanding payable owed to a vendor. Issuing payment is the physical transfer of funds from your company to the vendor.

In the AP module, issuing outgoing payments can be accomplished in mass using the automated payment program (Transaction F110) or individually using Transaction F-53 (i.e., post payment) or Transaction F-58 (i.e., post and print forms).

Most accounting departments set up a regular schedule to issue payments in mass using Transaction F110. This transaction is covered in detail in Chapter 7. For one-off payments, use Transaction F-53 or Transaction F-58.

Let's begin with an example of posting a manual outgoing payment using Transaction F-53. It can be executed in the AP module from application menu path, **Accounting • Financial Accounting • Accounts Payable • Document Entry • Outgoing Payment • F-53 – Post**, as shown in Figure 6.90.

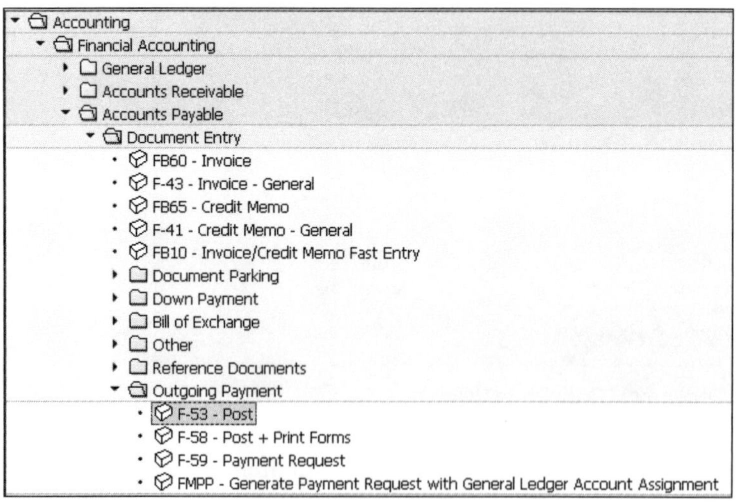

Figure 6.90 Transaction F-53 Application Menu Path

Double-click **F-53 – Post** from the menu path, or enter "F-53" in the **Command** field (as shown in Figure 6.91) and press Enter.

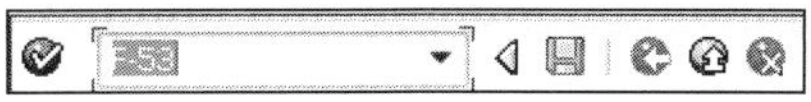

Figure 6.91 Entering "F-53" in the Command Field

The **Post Outgoing Payments: Header Data** screen opens (Figure 6.92). In the top portion of the screen, most field values should contain default values, depending on your configuration and editing options. Make sure to input all required fields that don't contain default values.

In this example, default values are populated into the **Posting Date**, **Type** (i.e., document type), **Period**, **Company Code**, and **Currency/Rate** fields. We manually entered a value in the **Document Date** field.

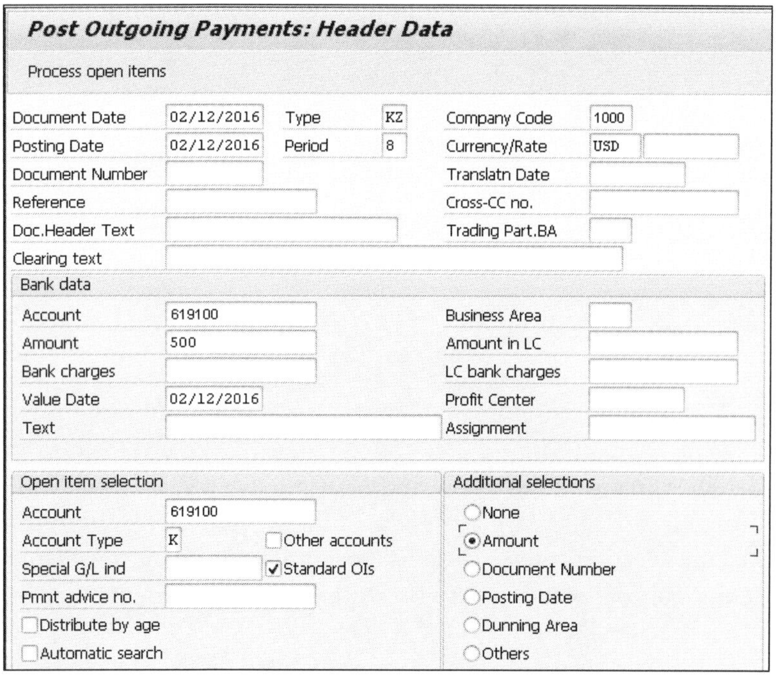

Figure 6.92 Post Outgoing Payments: Header Data

In the **Bank data** section, enter values for **Account**, **Amount**, and any other fields that are required. In the **Open item selection** section, enter the vendor number in **Account.**

Finally, in the **Additional selections** section, select a radio button that indicates how the program should select an open invoice. For this example, we selected the **Amount** radio button.

With all relevant fields entered, click the **Process open items** button at the top-left portion of the screen (Figure 6.92). The **Post Outgoing Payments Enter selection criteria** screen opens (Figure 6.93). In this example, we entered the amount of the invoice to be paid ($500) in the **From** and **To** fields.

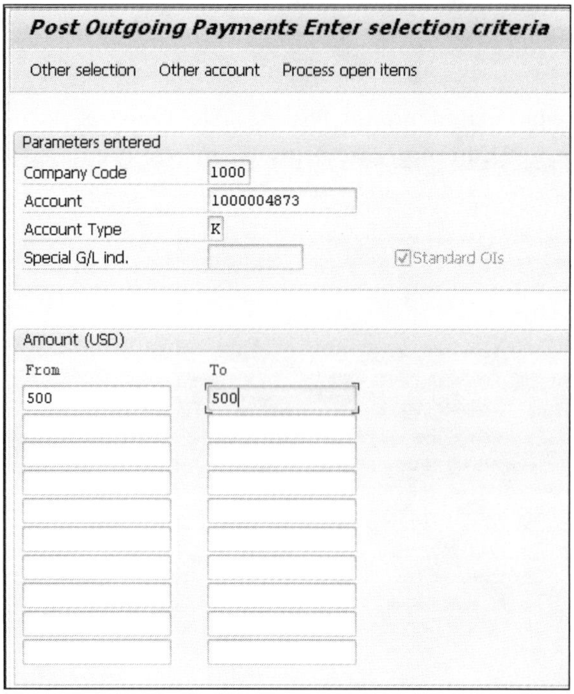

Figure 6.93 Enter Selection Criteria Screen

After you've entered the selection criteria, click the **Process open items** button (Figure 6.93) in the top-center portion of the screen. The **Post Outgoing Payments Process open items** screen opens (Figure 6.94).

Click the **Save** icon or press Ctrl+S. The program posts the payment document and issues the message shown in Figure 6.95.

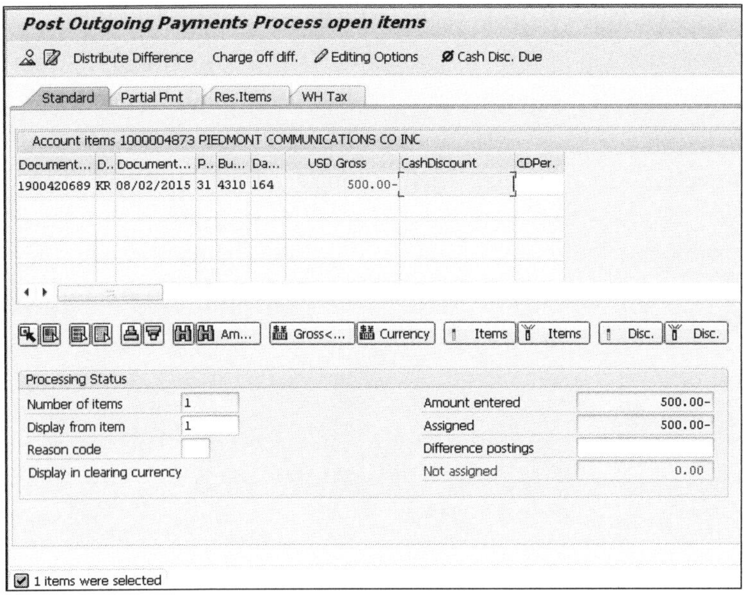

Figure 6.94 Post Outgoing Payments Process Open Items

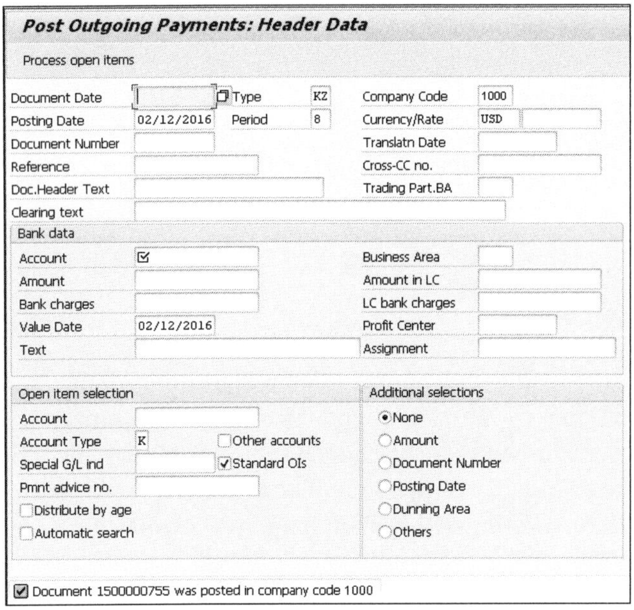

Figure 6.95 Document Posted Message

This concludes our example of issuing a vendor payment using Transaction F-53.

Transaction F-58 is another single-payment transaction. Like Transaction F-53, Transaction F-58 creates a payment entry that credits a bank account balance and clears an open AP invoice. In addition, Transaction F-58 allows you to print a check.

We won't cover Transaction F-58 in detail in this section because it's similar to Transaction F-53. However, if you want to try it for yourself, the transaction can be accessed in the AP module from application menu path, **Accounting • Financial Accounting • Accounts Payable • Document Entry • Outgoing Payment • F-58 – Post + Print Forms**, as shown in Figure 6.96.

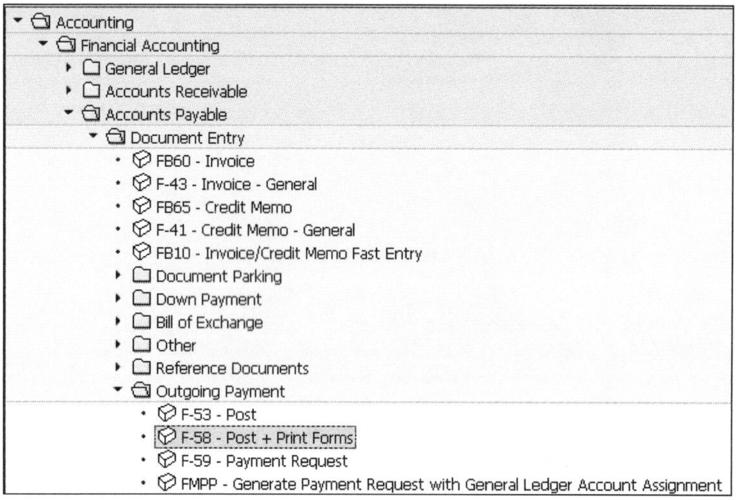

Figure 6.96 Transaction F-58 Application Menu Path

6.7 Summary

In this chapter, we covered AP account transactions originating in the AP module. The most common AP transaction is the entry of a vendor invoice using Transaction FB60. Vendor invoices are the documents that create open vendor liabilities and ultimately get paid. We also walked through examples of other AP transactions, including the creation of a credit memo, down payment request, manual outgoing payment, and document reversals.

This chapter covered not only the creation of different AP document types but also document display, change, reverse, park, saved as completed, and hold. These are all important concepts in the day in the life of an AP clerk or accounting supervisor.

In this chapter, the examples shown enabled you to learn the differences among document posting, parking, save as completed, and hold. Once again, these concepts aren't unique to AP. They are also applicable to G/L, AR, and some additional accounting transactions.

Some other functions were discussed, as they relate to Transaction FB60 and other AP transactions, such as the tree display, screen variants, account assignment templates, editing options, and post with reference. All are useful tools and are universal concepts in FI.

Although the content of this chapter focused on transactions originating in AP, make sure you review Chapter 5 as well to learn about procurement transactions originating in MM. Chapter 5 also covers the procure-to-pay process and key integration points.

This concludes our discussion of AP transactions. The next chapter is a detailed discussion of the AP automated payment program (Transaction F110).

Chapter 7
Automated Payment Program

In this chapter, one of the more complex transactions in Financial Accounting (FI) is discussed in detail: the automated payment program.

7

At first glance, the Accounts Payable (AP) automated payment program (Transaction F110) seems complicated—but don't worry. In this chapter, we'll walk you through each step in the process and cover the knowledge you need to issue outgoing payments in mass. Repetition is key. As you work through the complete payment program a few times, you'll begin to recognize the key points needed to complete a successful payment run. The more you practice, the easier it becomes.

Completing a successful payment run requires a mix of various configurations, master data, document settings, and detailed settings in Transaction F110. When errors occur, the key is to pinpoint the source quickly and accurately. This chapter focuses specifically on the settings within the payment program, not on configuration, master data, or AP documents. Becoming familiar with the payment program settings is the best way to help you identify the root cause of errors quickly.

Note

In most companies, Transaction F110 is set up as a regularly scheduled job. However, it falls on the AP team to ensure that the payment program settings are accurate. When functional errors occur in an automatic payment run, the AP department is responsible for identifying the root cause and fixing problems. Knowing the setup of Transaction F110, parameter maintenance, and vendor master data is essential. You also need to know how to execute Transaction F110 manually. Even if you have the transaction set up as a schedule job, there will be times when you need to execute it manually.

This chapter walks you through all the major components of the automated payment program, including maintaining payment parameters, creating a payment proposal, and executing a payment run. Other important topics covered include a review of additional payment run logs and payment output.

Let's start by discussing how to access the automated payment program and enter the payment parameters needed to run it.

7.1 Automated Payment Program Process

The process steps for executing the automated payment program include maintaining payment program parameters, creating a payment proposal, and executing a payment run, in that order.

Begin by using Transaction F110 or application menu path, **Accounting • Financial Accounting • Accounts Payable • Periodic Processing • F110 – Payments**, as shown in Figure 7.1.

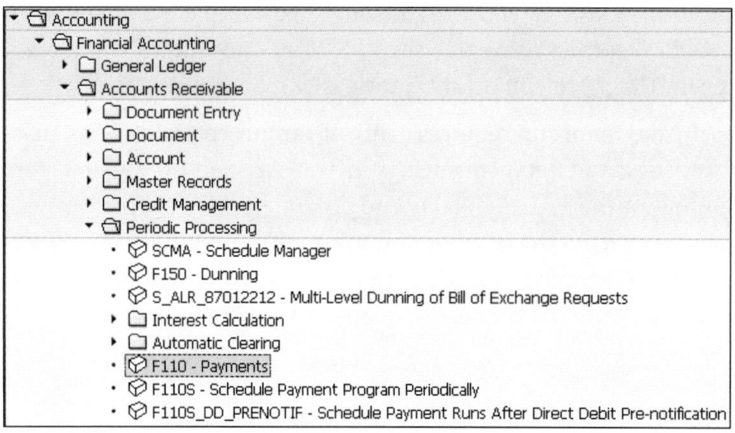

Figure 7.1 Transaction F110 Application Menu Path

Double-click **F110 – Payments** from the menu path, or enter "F110" in the **Command** field (Figure 7.2) and press [Enter].

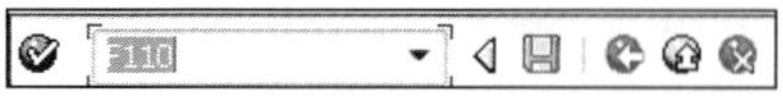

Figure 7.2 Entering "F110" in the Command Field

The **Automatic Payment Transactions: Status** screen opens (Figure 7.3). On this screen, you must enter values for the **Run Date** and **Identification** fields. The **Identification** field is limited to five characters, so building logic into the field value is important for reference. The logic you use will depend on the frequency and makeup of payment runs. You might also build in logic based on geography or your company's organizational structure. For example, you could use "US001" to represent a payment run for the United States. Other examples include naming logic based on function. For example, you could use "HR001" for issuing payroll or "AP001" for vendor payments.

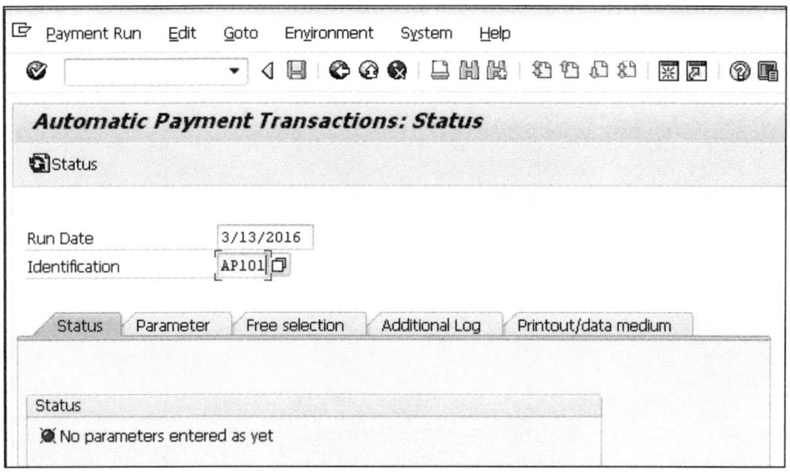

Figure 7.3 Automatic Payment Transaction: Status

7.1.1 Maintain Parameters

After entering values for **Run Date** and **Identification**, click on the **Parameter** tab to open the **Automatic Payment Transactions: Parameters** screen (Figure 7.4). On this screen, the **Posting Date** field defaults to the **Run Date**. In this example, field values were manually entered for **Docs entered up to**, **Company Codes**, **Pmt meths** (payment methods), **Next p/date** (next payment date), and **Vendor**. For simplicity, this example only includes one company code, payment method, and vendor, but an automatic payment run can be executed with multiple values for each of these fields.

Of particular importance is the **Next p/date** field. The date you enter is the next date you expect to run the automatic payment program. This date is important for the program to determine what invoices will come due between the run date and the next payment date so that these invoices can be included in this payment run.

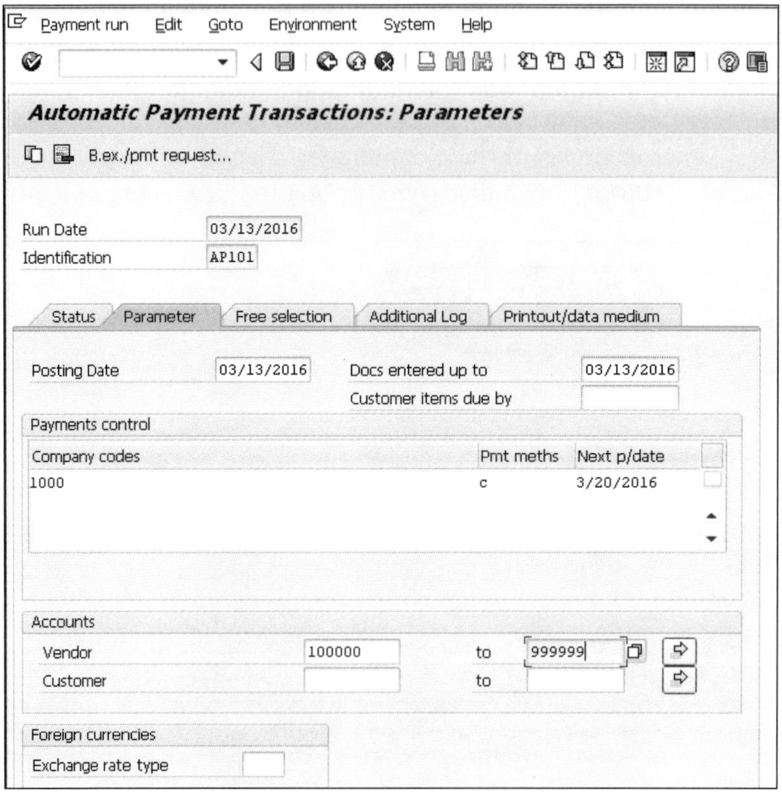

Figure 7.4 Automatic Payment Transactions: Parameters

After all parameters have been entered, click the **Save** icon to the right of the **Command** field, or press [Ctrl]+[S]. A message will indicate that the details have been saved (Figure 7.5).

> **Note**
>
> Additional settings can be made while maintaining parameters. Please see Section 7.2 for a complete discussion of additional settings.

After the parameter details have been saved, click on the **Status** tab. The **Automatic Payment Transactions: Status** screen reopens (Figure 7.6) but this time with a green status indicator that says **Parameters have been entered**. In the header, you'll see buttons for **Proposal** and **Payment Run**.

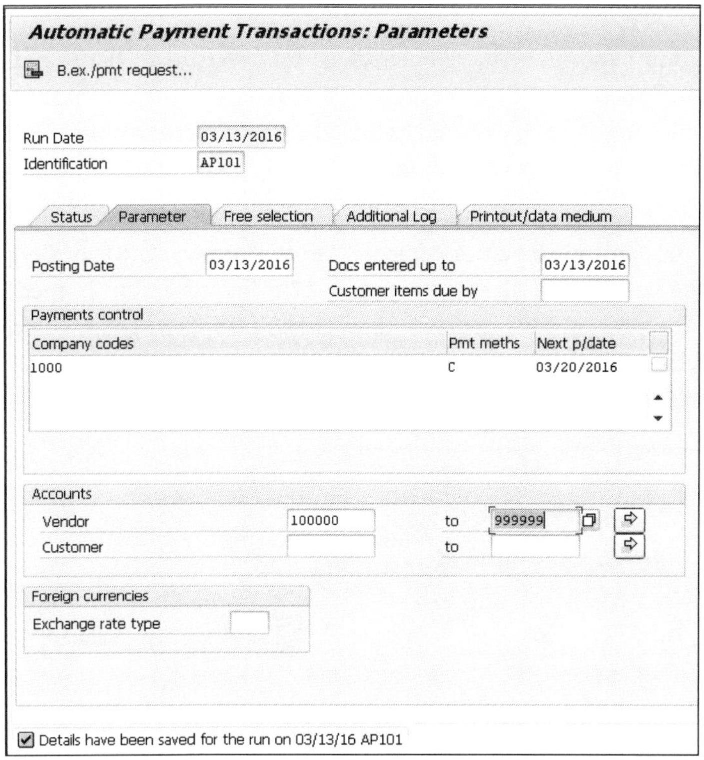

Figure 7.5 Parameter Details Have Been Saved Message

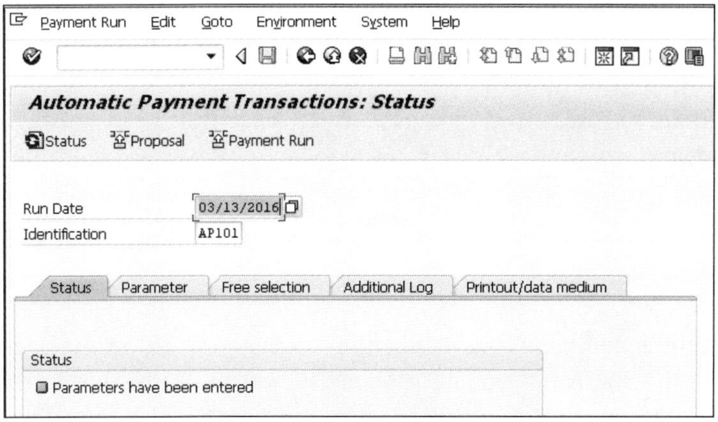

Figure 7.6 Automatic Payment Transactions: Status Screen with Parameters

7.1.2 Create Payment Proposal

After all payment program parameters have been saved (see Section 7.1.1), the next step is to create a payment proposal. This is the step in which the automated payment program determines which invoices will be paid based on the parameters entered and then generates a list of these items for your review. This list is referred to as the *payment proposal*.

To create the payment proposal, click on the **Proposal** button shown at the top of Figure 7.6 to open the **Schedule Proposal** dialog box (Figure 7.7). Check the **Start immediately** box to generate the proposal immediately and the **Create Payment Medium** box to automatically schedule the creation of the payment medium (e.g., check, ACH file, etc.). Then, click the **Execute** icon or press Enter.

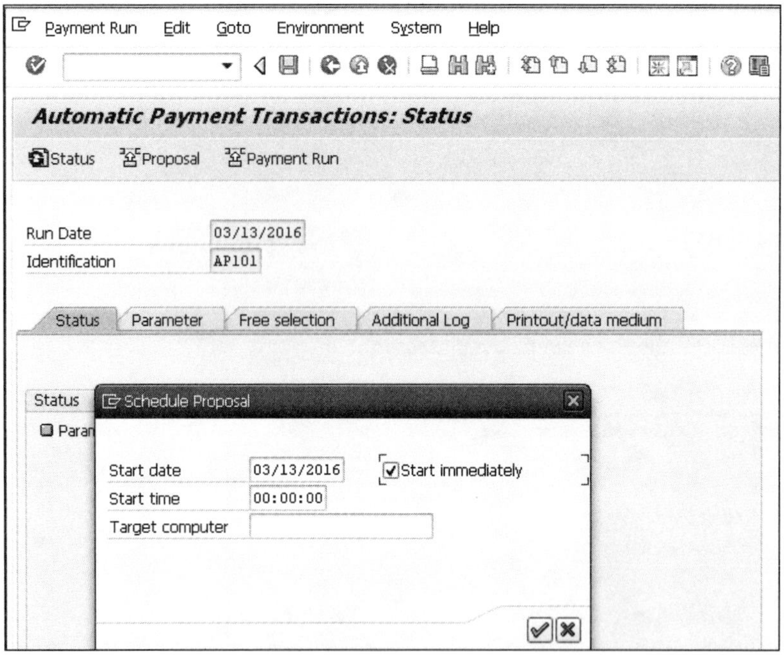

Figure 7.7 Schedule Proposal Dialog Box

When proposal creation is complete, the payment proposal completion message appears (Figure 7.8). In the **Status** tab, you'll see a green status indicator that reads, **Payment proposal has been created.**

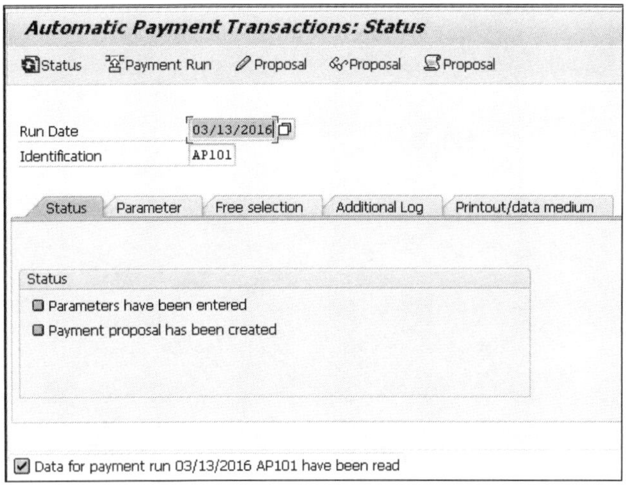

Figure 7.8 Payment Proposal Completion Messsage

To view the items contained in the proposal, click the **Proposal** icon shown in Figure 7.8, and the **Display Payment Proposal: Payments** screen opens (Figure 7.9). The top line with a green indicator in the type field indicates an item is selected for payment, whereas a bottom line with a red indicator indicates an item isn't selected for payment.

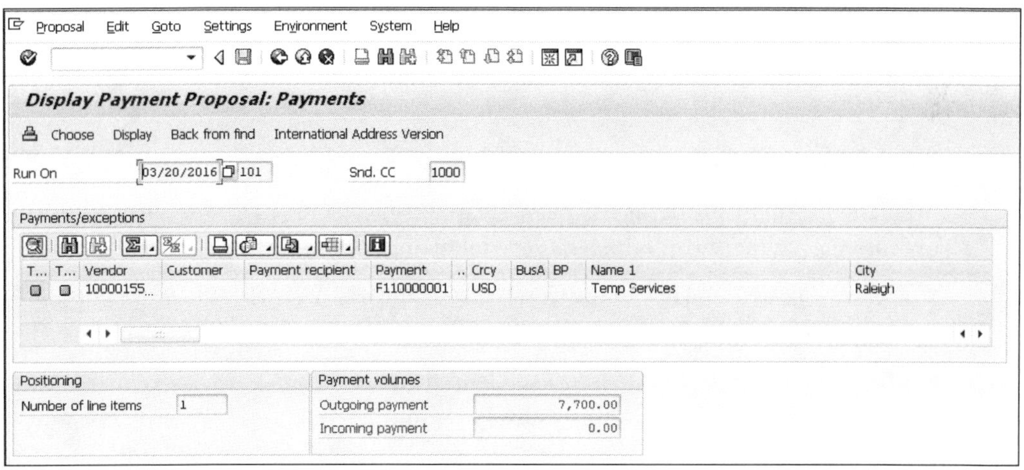

Figure 7.9 Display Payment Proposal: Payments

In this example, double-click the line with the green **Type** indicator to see the details making up the payment amount. The **Display Payment Proposal: Open Items** screen opens (Figure 7.10) showing individual documents, which can consist of open invoices, credit memos, and down payments.

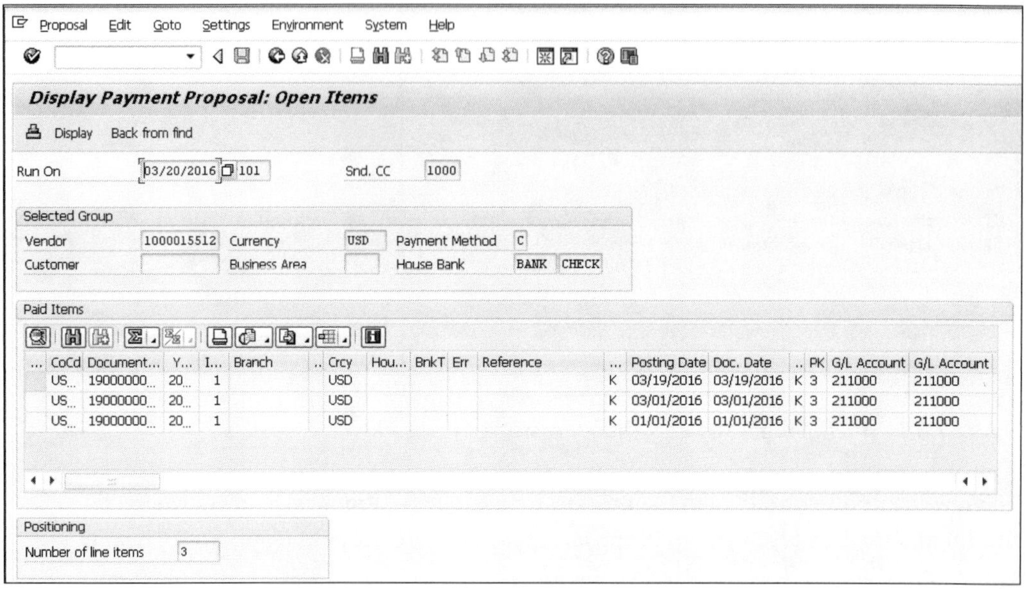

Figure 7.10 Display Payment Proposal: Open Items

Click on the **Back** icon to return to the **Automatic Payment Transactions: Status** screen (refer to Figure 7.8).

7.1.3 Execute Payment Run

After the payment proposal has been created (see Section 7.1.2), the next step is to execute the payment run, which has the following results:

- Creates payment entries in the General Ledger (G/L)
- Creates payment documents
- Changes the status of open items to **Cleared** status
- Creates the payment medium to transfer funds

To execute the payment run, click on the **Payment Run** button shown earlier in the top left of Figure 7.8, and the **Schedule Payment** dialog box appears (Figure 7.11). Check the **Start immediately** box to generate the payment run immediately and the **Create payment medium** box to automatically schedule the creation of the payment medium. Then, click the **Execute** icon or press Enter.

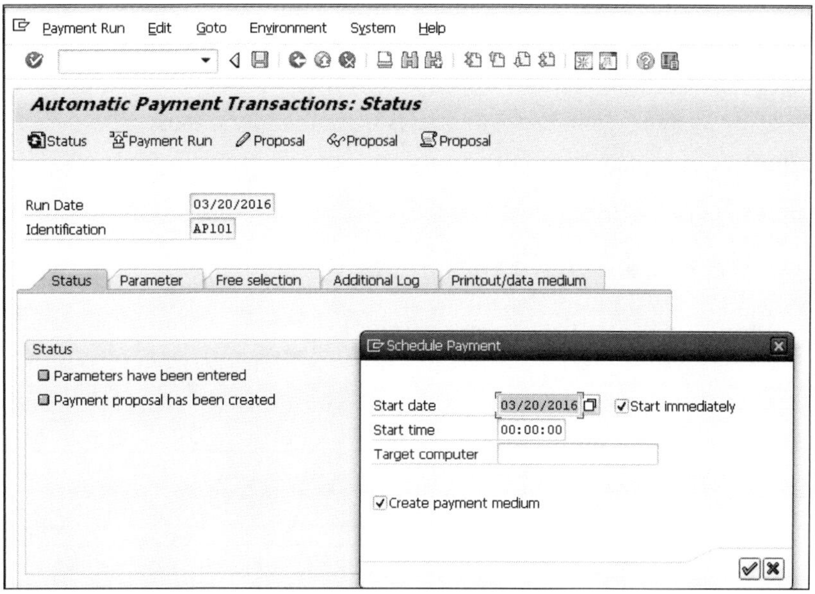

Figure 7.11 Schedule Payment Dialog Box

When the payment run is complete, a green status indicator appears in the **Status** screen saying **Payment run has been carried out** (Figure 7.12); it will include a list of the number of payment orders generated and completed.

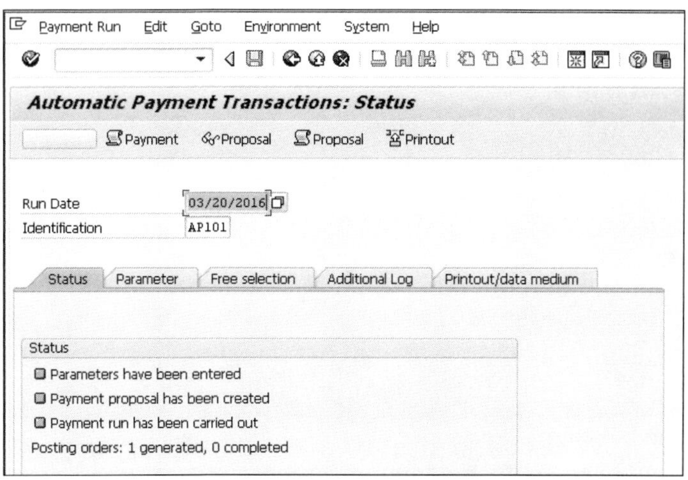

Figure 7.12 Payment Run Has Been Completed Message

In this example, the payment method is a check, which requires the physical printing of a check. Earlier (refer to Figure 7.11), we checked the **Create payment medium** box, which automatically created a spool request to print the checks. View the spool request by choosing **System • Own Spool Requests** from the menu bar.

The **Job Overview** screen opens (Figure 7.13).

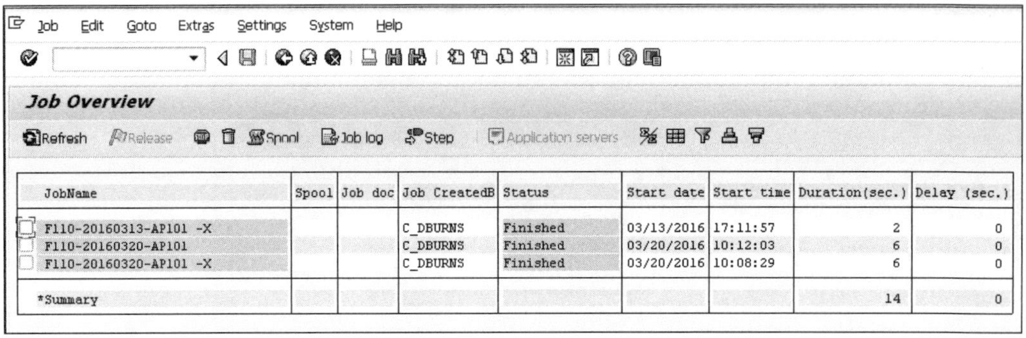

Figure 7.13 Output Controller: List of Spool Requests

To review the spool request details, check the box in the **JobName** column, and either click the **Display Contents** icon or press F6. In this example, we select the checkbox for job name **F110-20160320-AP101 -X**, and the **Display Job** screen appears (Figure 7.14). From here, you can review the job conditions, steps, details, and logs.

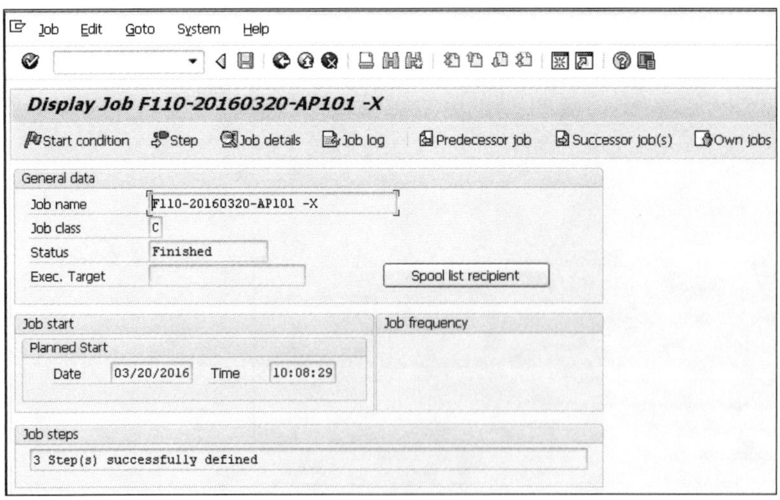

Figure 7.14 Print Preview Payment Output

7.2 Additional Settings

In Section 7.1 we covered the basic settings to execute Transaction F110, the automated payment program. In this section, we'll explore additional settings you can make to customize your payment run. These settings include free selection for field names and values, an additional log, and variants for printout/data medium.

7.2.1 Free Selection

In Section 7.1.1, we covered the topic of maintaining payment parameters for a payment run. When entering payment parameters, as shown in Figure 7.15, the selection criteria can be narrowed further by clicking the **Free selection** tab, which makes the **Automatic Payment Transactions: Free Selection** screen appear (Figure 7.15).

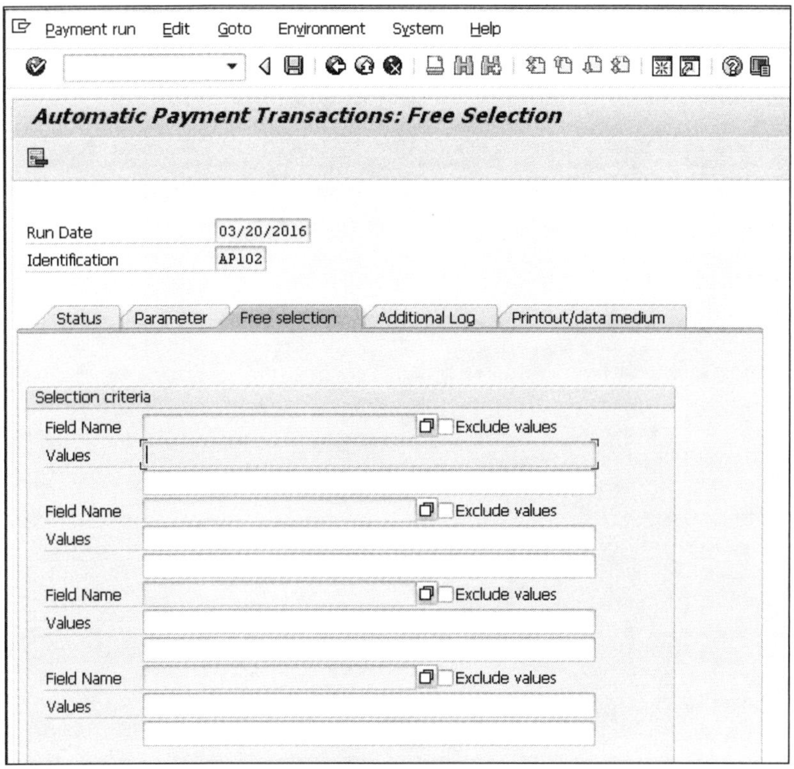

Figure 7.15 Payment Program Free Selection

From this screen, you can select additional single or multiple field values to include or exclude in the payment run. First, select a field name, and then click on the **Field Name** selection icon to view available field selections. By default, only two **Field Label** choices appear: **Sp. G/L Trans.type** (special G/L transaction types) and **Others**.

For this example, double-click the **Others** field label, and a dialog box opens with three options: **Document**, **Vendor master record**, and **Cust. master record** (Figure 7.16). This dialog box allows you to choose the source of additional field selections, which include financial documents, vendor master data, or customer master data. This field selection capability gives you many more fields to choose from than are typically practical to use, but it's better to have too many choices than not enough.

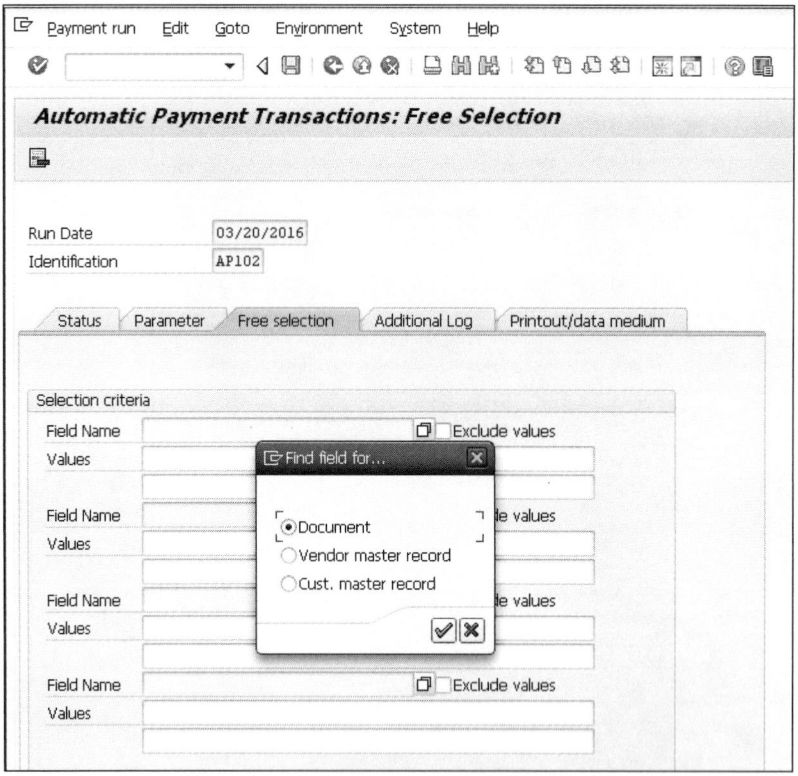

Figure 7.16 Free Selection Dialog Box for Other Fields

For this example, select **Document** from the dialog box and press Enter. A list of all specific field selection options appears on the next screen (Figure 7.17).

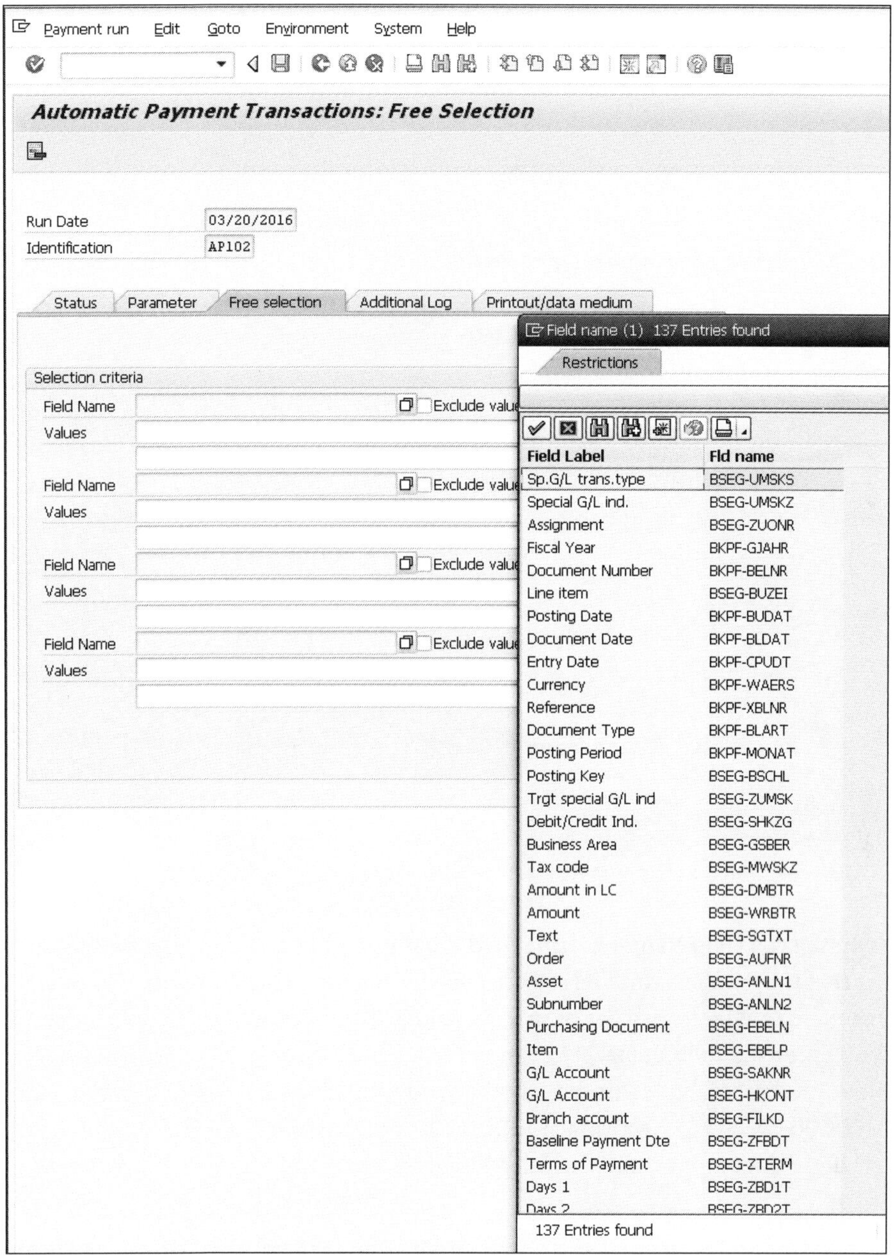

Figure 7.17 Field Name Entries for Documents

From the field entry selection, double-click the field you want to use. For this example, double-click on the **Document Number** field to return to the **Automatic Payment Transactions: Free Selection** screen, where the **Field Name** value is now populated (Figure 7.18).

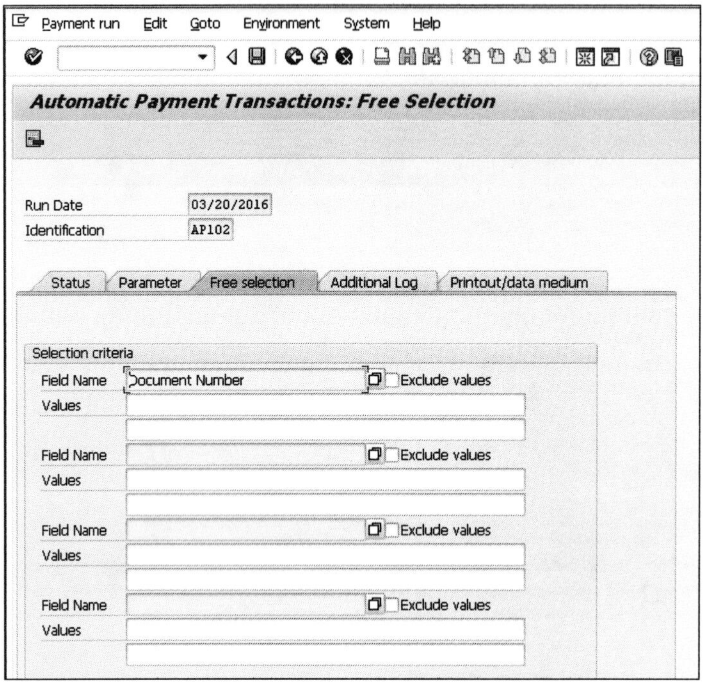

Figure 7.18 Free Selection Screen with Field Name Value

After you select a **Field Name**, specific field **Values** must be entered. The first notable point is that these values can't be selected via dropdown. In other words, you need to enter them manually from a list of specific values. The second notable point is about how you enter the field value. You can enter a single value, a range of values, or a combination thereof. For example, say that you want to enter four document numbers: 1900000001, 1900000004, 1900000005, and 1900000006. You can enter each of these document numbers individually, separated by commas, as shown in Figure 7.19.

The second method is to enter the consecutive range of document numbers within parentheses, with the start and end range separated by a comma, as shown in Figure 7.20.

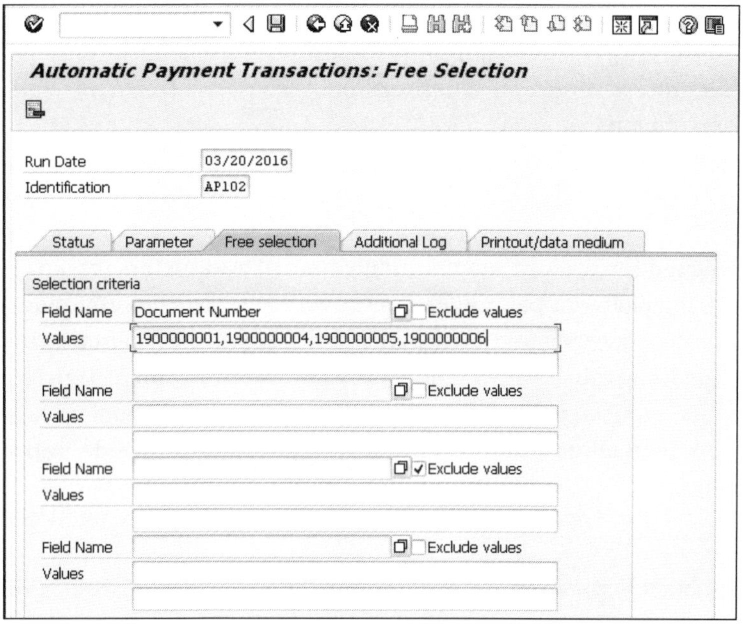

Figure 7.19 Free Selection Single Field Value Entry

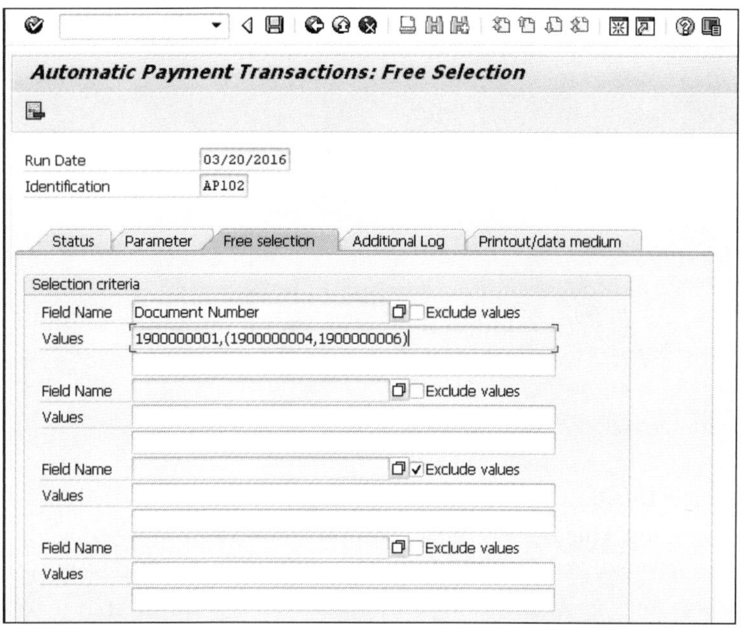

Figure 7.20 Free Selection with Single Value and Range Value Entry

After all free selections are entered, click the **Save** icon to the right of the **Command** field or press [Ctrl]+[S]. Notice that multiple **Selection Criteria** can be entered, so you can repeat the process shown for additional field selections to narrow your selection of items for payment.

7.2.2 Additional Logs

In Section 7.1.1, we covered the topic of maintaining payment parameters for a payment run. When entering payment parameters, as shown earlier in Figure 7.5, additional trace elements can be selected for the logs created during the payment process by clicking the **Additional Log** tab. When you do so, the **Automatic Payment Transactions: Additional Log** screen opens (Figure 7.21). The checkboxes in the **Required logging type** area of the screen allow you to choose additional data to include in the program execution logs.

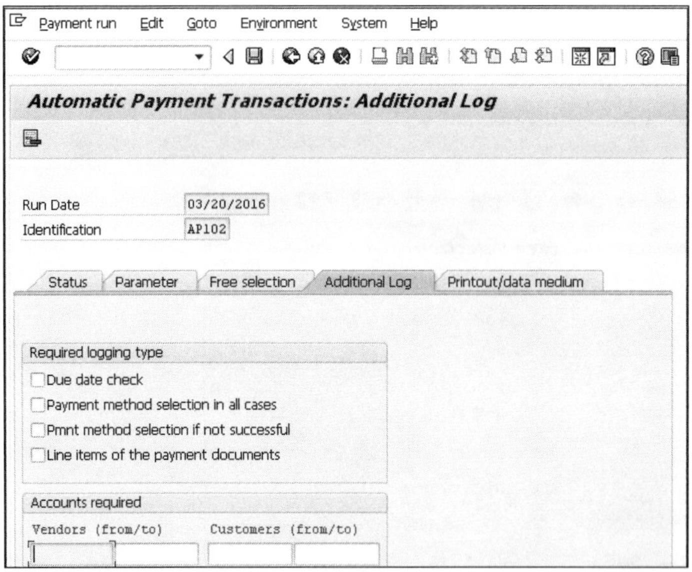

Figure 7.21 Payment Program Additional Log /Tab

For example, if you select **Due date check** (Figure 7.22), the due date for open items is captured in the payment log. This trace is most useful if there is any question about the accuracy of the due date calculation and why an open item isn't being selected for payment. The due date check is an example of an additional log option that is frequently used.

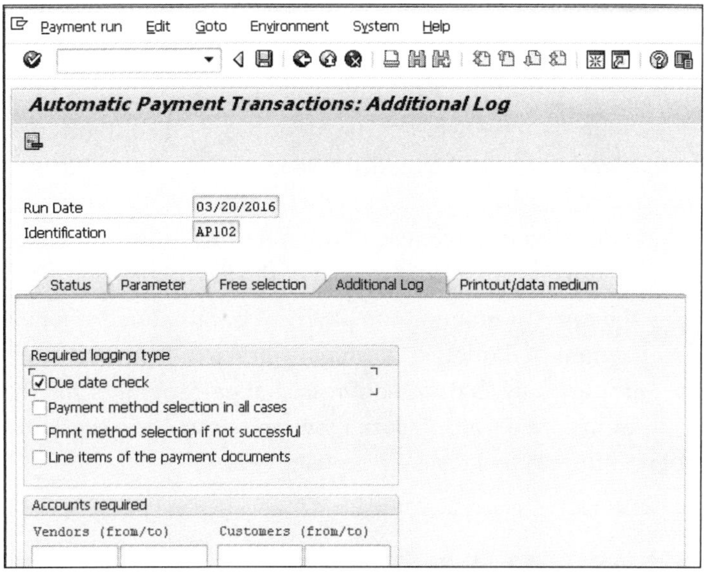

Figure 7.22 Additional Log with Due Date Check

There are three other checkboxes in the **Required logging type** area (Figure 7.22):

- **Payment method selection in all cases**
  This records the payment method and bank in the log for all items selected for payment.
- **Pmnt method selection if not successful**
  This records the payment method and bank that aren't permitted in the payment run. This option is particularly useful for troubleshooting errors in the payment run. It can point you to corrections that need to be made in either the vendor master record or the payment program configuration. This indicator can also help you determine why an open item may not be selected for payment with the payment program parameters you entered.
- **Line items of the payment documents**
  This records payment document numbers and line items in the execution log. This information can be useful for tracking down a clearing document for an open item that was paid in error.

In Figure 7.22, the **Accounts required** area at the bottom of the screen allows you to narrow your trace selection by vendors and customers. Note that you can enter individual vendor/customer numbers or a range of values.

7.2.3 Variants for Data Medium

In the payment method configuration, the format of the outgoing payments is set by assigning a payment medium program. You can also create your own payment formats using the Payment Medium Workbench. The payment program configuration and the Payment Medium Workbench are beyond the scope of this book, but you need to know that when you run the automated payment program, the payment methods assigned in the payment parameters each have a data medium exchange (DME) program assigned that controls the output format of the payments.

In Section 7.1.1, we covered the topic of maintaining payment parameters for a payment run. When entering payment parameters, as shown earlier in Figure 7.5, variants are assigned to the **Form Printing/Data Medium Exchange** programs for the payment methods specified. Click the **Printout/data medium** tab to open the **Automatic Payment Transactions: Printout and DME** screen (Figure 7.23).

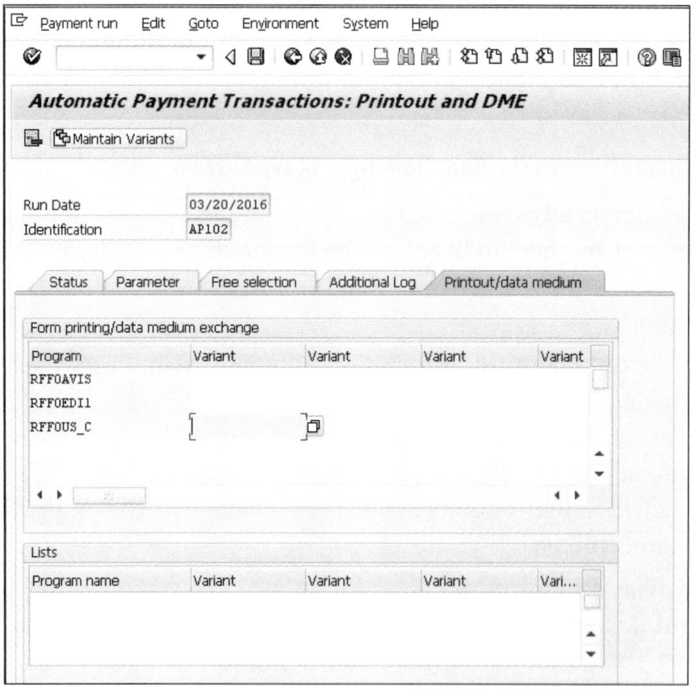

Figure 7.23 Payment Program Printout and DME Screen

Here, we'll review a variant for program RFFOUS_C. RFFOUS_C is a standard DME program for checks. To select a variant from the **Automatic Payment Transactions:**

Printout and DME screen, click the variant selection dropdown icon shown in Figure 7.23, and choose your variant. In this example, we selected variant **PRINT_US** (Figure 7.24).

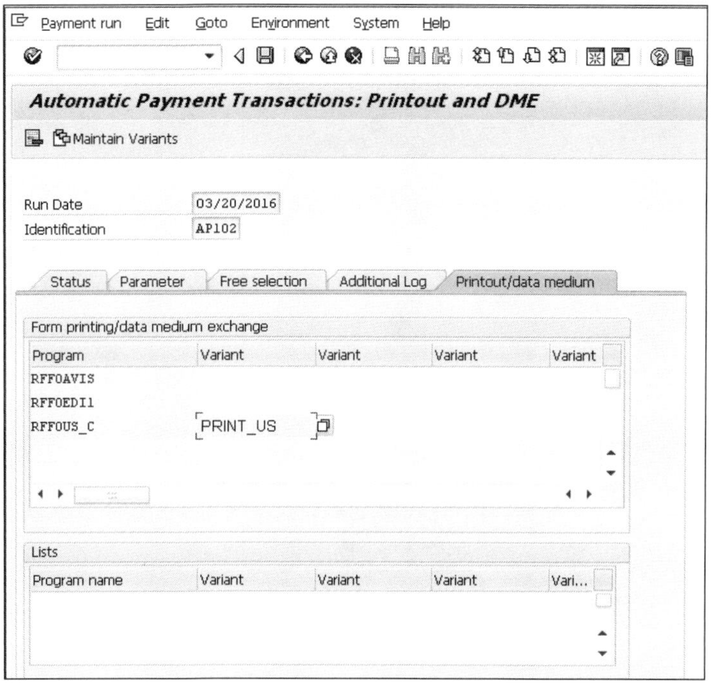

Figure 7.24 Payment Program Printout and DME with Variant Assigned

To review and maintain a variant, position your cursor on the one you want to view, and click the **Maintain Variants** button. In the **Maintain Variant** screen that opens (Figure 7.25), there are many different field selections to maintain. In the remainder of this section, we'll discuss the essential fields for program RFFOUS_C and highlight some of the other, more commonly used fields. Note, however, that the **Maintain Variant** screen will differ based on the DME program used.

In this variant for program RFFOUS_C, the essential fields to maintain are **Paying company code**, **Payment method**, **House Bank**, **Account ID**, **Check lot number**, and **Print checks** with a **Printer** specified. All these fields are essential for the program to know how to post to the G/L, the relevant bank account to credit, what check numbers to assign, and the printer to use.

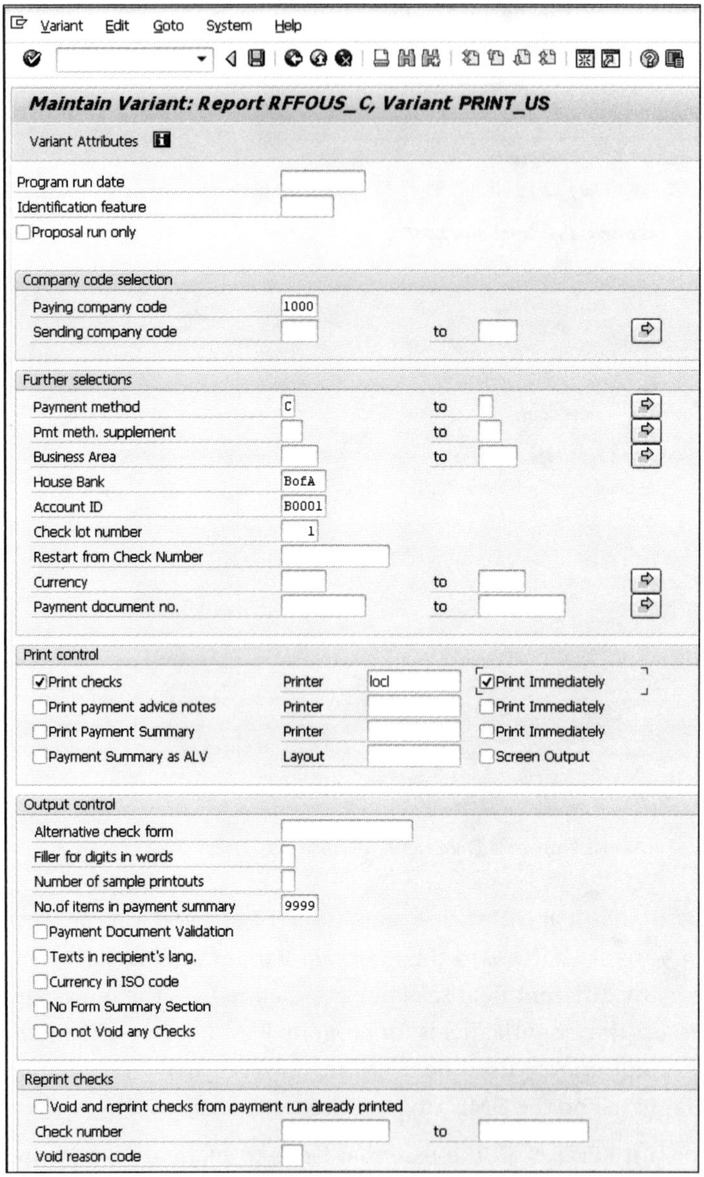

Figure 7.25 Payment Program Maintain Variant Screen

This variant has some other features that you should be aware of and fields that aren't necessarily required but may be applicable depending on your configuration and business processes. The header fields in this variant (Figure 7.26) consist of the following:

- **Program run date**
  This field lists the date on which you plan for the program payment run to take place, although you can run the program at an earlier or later date than the one specified here. This field may be useful for a one-time payment run that requires unique settings in the variant. For recurring payment runs, you may choose to leave this field blank.

- **Identification feature**
  This field is a freely defined six-character field. It's not a required field, but it can be useful as a unique identifier if you use multiple DME variants with the same payment method.
- **Proposal run only**
  This checkbox specifies that this variant can't be used for payment executions; it can only be used for payment proposals. This poses some risks, and we don't suggest using this option without a valid need and with thorough testing. As a rule of thumb, only use fields on a variant if you need them.

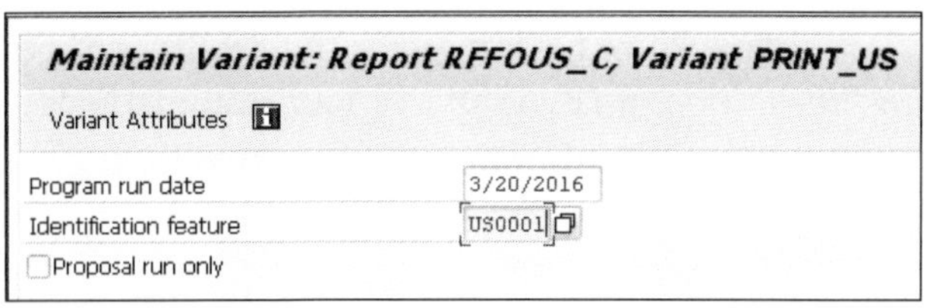

Figure 7.26 Payment Program Variant Header Fields

The fields in the **Further selections** area of a variant (Figure 7.27) that may be of use to you include **Pmt meth. supplement** and **Business Area**. The usefulness of these fields depends on your business requirements and how you use these fields in financial transactions. The main takeaway is that if you do use these fields, additional options exist for their use in the payment variant.

This concludes our discussion of additional settings in the automated payment program. In the next section, we'll discuss how to find details about and run inquiries on automatic payment runs that have been executed.

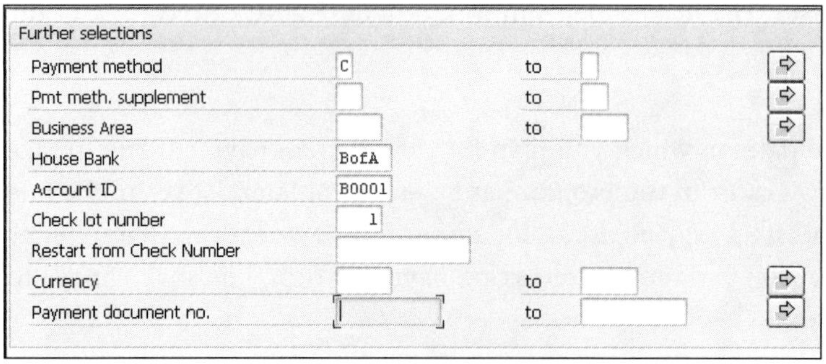

Figure 7.27 Payment Program Variant Further Selections

7.3 Automatic Payment Run Inquiries

During an automatic payment run or after one has been executed, an AP clerk or supervisor may need to provide summary-level detail about payment run output. CFOs, controllers, and treasury managers all need to know about impact to cash flow, and specific vendor inquiries may be requested for high-visibility vendors. The payment process plays a part in other vital business decisions as well.

For all these reasons and more, you should know how to report the details of a specific automatic payment run. In this section, we'll discuss various automatic payment lists and overviews that you can use to provide this useful information.

7.3.1 Proposal Lists

It's common to receive a request from an AP supervisor for the list of invoices in a payment proposal. The best practice is to thoroughly review each payment proposal and have it approved before an automatic payment run is completed. On review of a payment proposal, a supervisor may decide to exclude certain payments by blocking invoices or vendors. By reviewing a proposal list, you may also find errors with the payment terms assigned in an AP invoice or vendor master record. Whatever the issue, the payment proposal allows you to adjust transactions prior to finalizing your automatic payment run.

To generate a payment proposal list from Transaction F110, choose **Edit • Proposal • Proposal List** from the menu bar, as shown in Figure 7.28.

The **Payment List** screen opens (Figure 7.29) with a list of payment proposal items for the automatic payment run. More details are contained in the report than are shown in Figure 7.29, including a list of blocked items and totals broken out by each of the following categories: business area, company code, country, currency, payment method, and bank account. From this screen, you can also change the layout, download the list to a local file, or email the output.

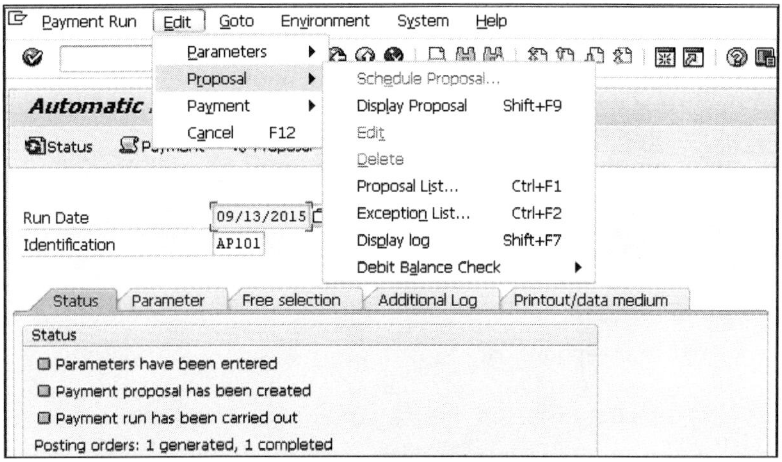

Figure 7.28 Payment Proposal List Dropdown Menu

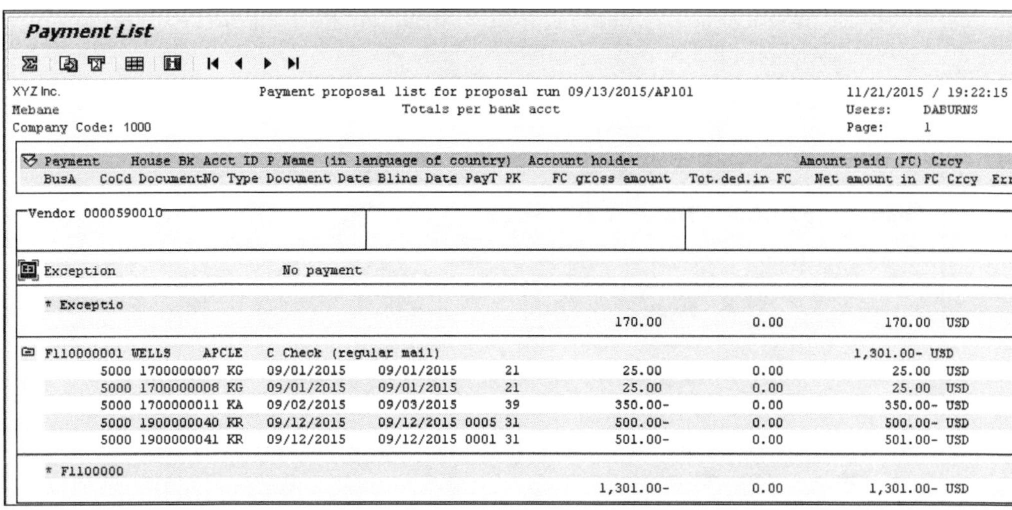

Figure 7.29 Payment Proposal List

To view a list of exceptions in the automated payment run, use the same report; the list of exceptions is provided, as shown in Figure 7.30.

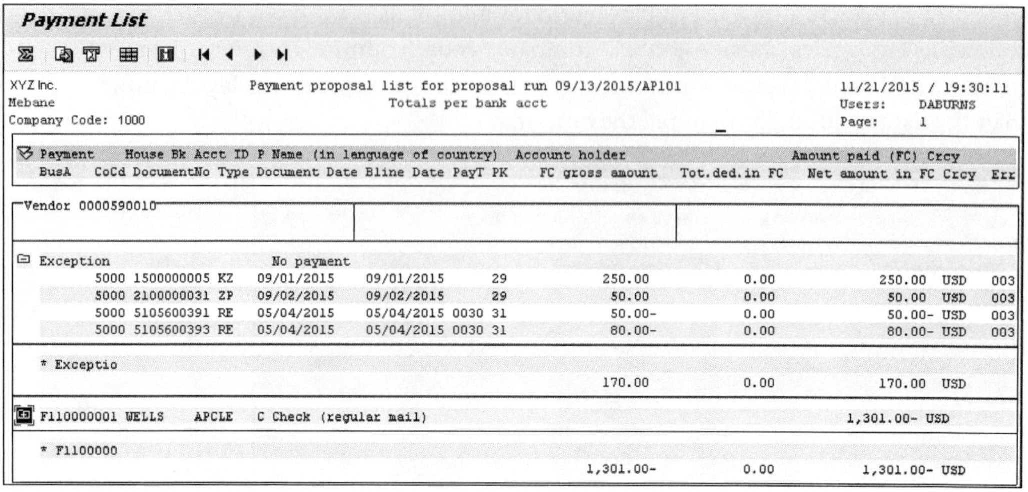

Figure 7.30 Payment Proposal Exceptions List

7.3.2 Payment Lists

It's also a common practice for an AP supervisor to request the list of invoices paid after the payment run is completed. This should be part of your standard business process. To produce the payment list from Transaction F110 (Figure 7.31), choose **Edit • Payment • Payment list**.

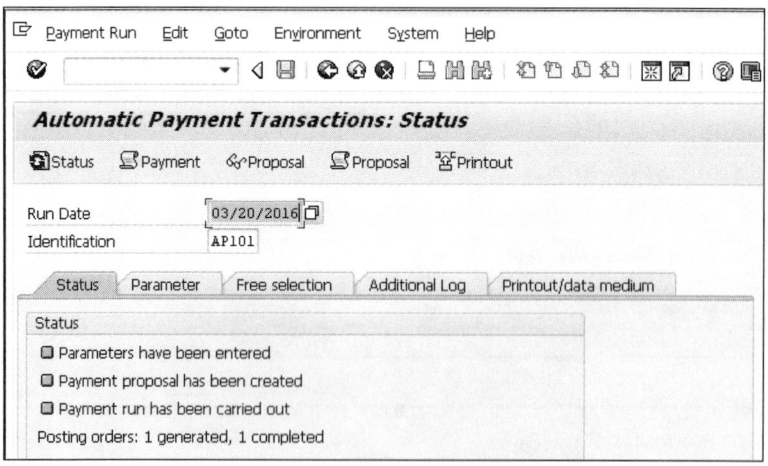

Figure 7.31 Automatic Payment Transactions Screen

The **Payment List** screen opens (Figure 7.32), providing a list of payment items settled in your payment run. More details are contained in the report shown in Figure 7.32, including totals broken out by each of the following categories: business area, company code, country, currency, payment method, and bank account. From this screen, you can also change the layout, download the list to a local file, or email the output.

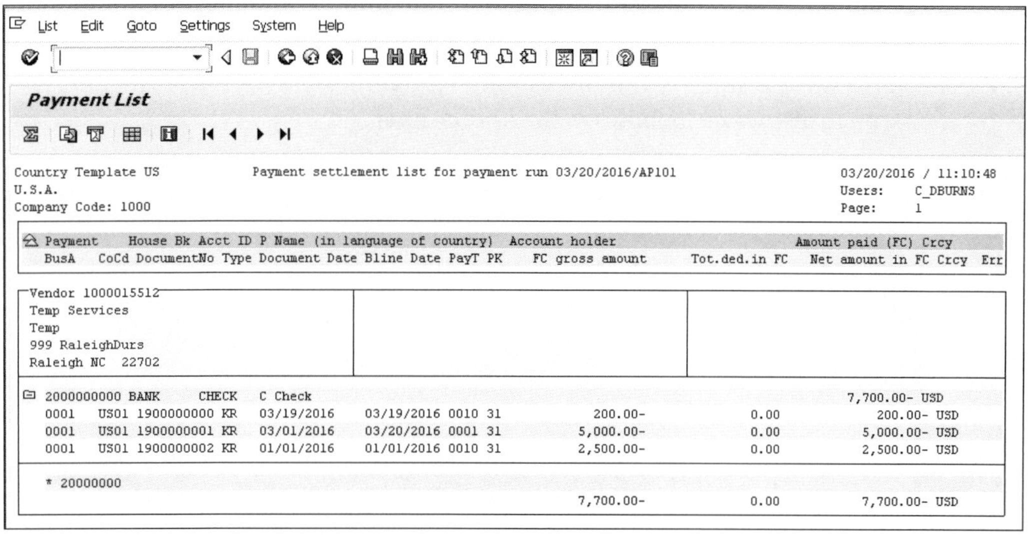

Figure 7.32 Payment Settlement List

7.4 Summary

The automated payment program (Transaction F110) is one of the most complicated transactions in FI. Several aspects of the system come together to make it run successfully, including configuration, master data, and transaction settings.

In this chapter, we covered the main steps in executing the automated payment program. The first of these is the entry of payment parameters, which involves specifying what is going to be paid through the use of selection criteria. The next step is the creation of payment proposals. The payment proposal is a list of vendor open items selected for payment, based on the payment parameters entered. The last step is the execution of the payment run. In this step, payment documents are created, the G/L is updated, and a data medium is ready to be produced for the physical transfer of funds.

This chapter also went into greater detail on certain settings that may be useful to end users, including free selection, additional logs, and variants for DME, all of which play an important role in the automatic payment process.

We also discussed how to produce payment lists and proposal lists. These lists can be generated directly from Transaction F110. Within each list, you can change the report layout, download to a local file, or send the list via email. A thorough review of these lists is important to the validation of outgoing payments.

Now that we've completed our discussion of the automated payment program, let's move on to discuss AP inquiries in the next chapter.

Chapter 8
Accounts Payable Account Inquiries

In this chapter, we'll explore transactions and reports you can use on a daily basis for Accounts Payable (AP) account maintenance. Often, these tools simply validate vendor account details and payments, but they can also reveal errors and discrepancies in vendor account balances and line item details.

Accounts Payable (AP) account inquiry and validation are essential job functions of an AP clerk or supervisor. Often, you can use these functions to uncover data entry and other posting errors. Knowing how to perform the transactions in this chapter provides you with essential skills needed in the day-to-day operations of an AP department.

These functions can be useful in the following ways:

- To reconcile AP reconciliation balances with vendor subledger balances
- For month-end and year-end account analysis
- To assist with cash management forecasting
- For vendor account inquiries

One of the ongoing challenges faced by an AP department is the barrage of inquiries from vendors regarding their account balances and expected payment dates. This chapter provides you with the basic tools you need to address these types of inquiries and more.

The following sections will discuss AP account inquiry and maintenance functions that will help you research individual transactions, display account balances, view account transaction details, and run reports and queries. We'll start with the different types of vendor account balance displays in detail.

8.1 Vendor Account Displays

The AP vendor account display allows you to view individual or collective vendor account balances and transaction details (i.e., individual AP documents and line items). The primary transactions used to view vendor account details are Transaction FK10N and Transaction FBL1N.

One powerful feature of SAP is its drilldown capability. Specifically, within certain views of summary data, you can drill down directly from that view to the line item details making up an account balance. Transactions FK10N and FBL1N provide good examples of this drilldown functionality. Starting directly in Transaction FK10N, you can double-click any account balance and automatically transfer to Transaction FBL1N to see a detailed view of the transaction details that make up the balance.

Now that we've discussed the basic capabilities of vendor account balances, let's look at specific examples in the following sections.

8.1.1 Vendor Account Balance

Transaction FK10N is the vendor account balance display transaction that allows you to view the account balance of one or more vendors by accounting period. The display screen breaks down the vendor account balance into debit balance, credit balance, period balance, cumulative balance, and sales/purchases amounts, and you can double-click any of these numbers to drill down to the detailed transactions making up the balance.

To display vendor balances, use Transaction FK10N or application menu path, **Accounting • Financial Accounting • Accounts Payable • Account • FK10N – Display Balances**, as shown in Figure 8.1.

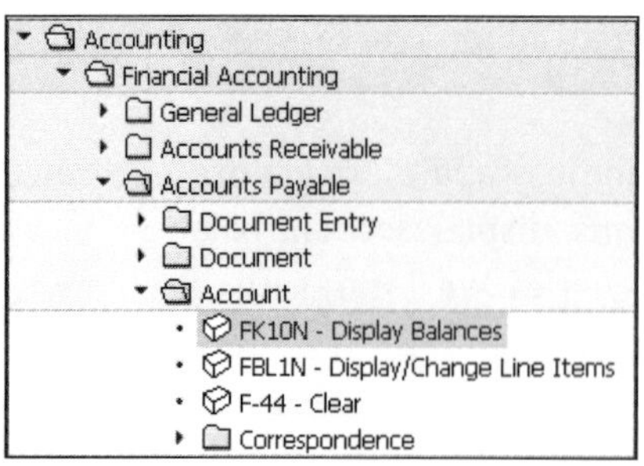

Figure 8.1 Transaction FK10N Application Menu Path

Double-click **FK10N – Display Balances** from the menu path, or enter "FK10N" in the **Command** field (as shown in Figure 8.2) and press [Enter].

Figure 8.2 Entering "FK10N" in the Command Field

The **Vendor Balance Display** selection screen appears (Figure 8.3). Enter values for the **Vendor**, **Company code**, and **Fiscal year** fields, and then click the **Execute** icon.

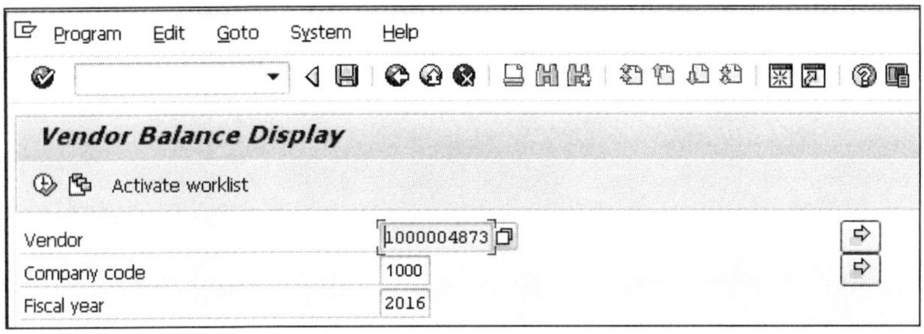

Figure 8.3 Vendor Balance Display Screen

The **Vendor Balance Display** output screen appears (Figure 8.4). From this screen, you can double-click any account display to view balance details, or you can click the **Special G/L** tab to view balances for specific special G/L transactions, such as down payments.

Transaction FK10N is frequently used to reconcile AP with G/L liabilities. At a high level, it also provides the period breakdowns needed for reconciling month-end activities for financial close.

Although there are several standard reports from which you can obtain vendor account balances, Transaction FK10N is by far the most powerful and flexible tool available.

This concludes our discussion of vendor account balances. In the next section, vendor account line item displays are discussed.

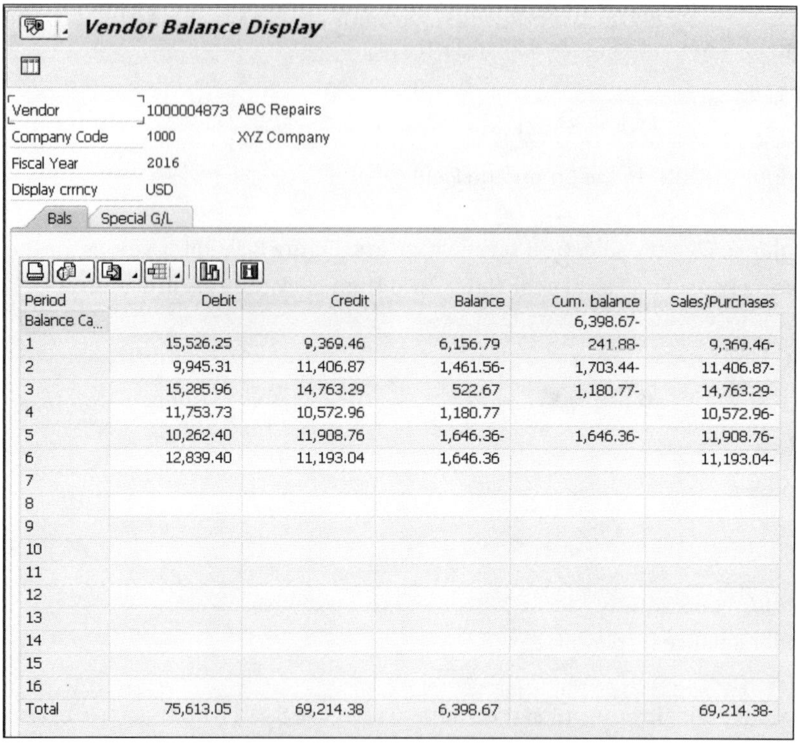

Period	Debit	Credit	Balance	Cum. balance	Sales/Purchases
Balance Ca...				6,398.67-	
1	15,526.25	9,369.46	6,156.79	241.88-	9,369.46-
2	9,945.31	11,406.87	1,461.56-	1,703.44-	11,406.87-
3	15,285.96	14,763.29	522.67	1,180.77-	14,763.29-
4	11,753.73	10,572.96	1,180.77		10,572.96-
5	10,262.40	11,908.76	1,646.36-	1,646.36-	11,908.76-
6	12,839.40	11,193.04	1,646.36		11,193.04-
7					
8					
9					
10					
11					
12					
13					
14					
15					
16					
Total	75,613.05	69,214.38	6,398.67		69,214.38-

Figure 8.4 Vendor Balance Display Output

8.1.2 Vendor Account Line Items

Transaction FBL1N is the vendor line item display that provides all the individual documents and accounting line items posted to a vendor account. When using this transaction code, selection screens give you the flexibility to filter data by vendor account, company code, posting date, type of transaction, and many other fields. These selection options can be saved as variants, making them reusable. In addition, you can filter, search, sort, and subtotal from the output screen. The output can be downloaded into various file formats (e.g., Excel) making further analysis outside SAP possible when needed.

Before going any further, it's important to understand the concept of open item management (which we introduced in Chapter 2, Section 2.1.3). This SAP concept is how the system tracks, matches, and manages vendor line items that are supposed to be offset (i.e., cleared) by other accounting entries and net to zero. For example, when a vendor invoice is received, an accounting document posts a line item credit to the vendor account. This credit is considered an open item because it has created an open payable (i.e., liability) due to the vendor. After payment is issued to the vendor, the open liability is matched with an offsetting debit to the vendor account, and its status is changed from **Open** to **Cleared**.

Issuing an outgoing vendor payment creates a payment document that also acts as a system clearing document. This clearing document creates a debit entry to the vendor account and a credit to cash. Therefore, the vendor liability is matched with the outgoing payment and nets to zero, indicating that the open liability no longer exists.

With the concept of open item management in mind, Transaction FBL1N is particularly useful for showing the status of an invoice (i.e., **Open** or **Cleared**) and the due date for each invoice. It's an essential tool for handling vendor inquiries regarding the status of invoices and payments. Often, when a vendor claims that a payment is overdue, an AP clerk's first response is to use Transaction FBL1N to verify that the invoice does indeed have an **Open** status.

> **Note**
>
> Transaction FBL1N is often a frequently used tool during month-end and year-end close processes. For details, see Chapter 16 and Chapter 17.

To display vendor line items using Transaction FBL1N, follow application menu path, **Accounting • Financial Accounting • Accounts Payable • Account • FBL1N – Display/ Change Line Items**, as shown in Figure 8.5.

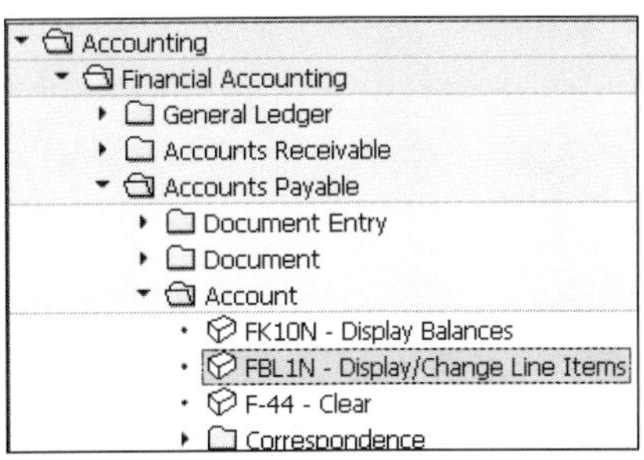

Figure 8.5 Transaction FBL1N Application Menu Path

Double-click **FBL1N – Display/Change Line Items** from the menu path, or enter "FBL1N" in the **Command** field (as shown in Figure 8.6) and press Enter.

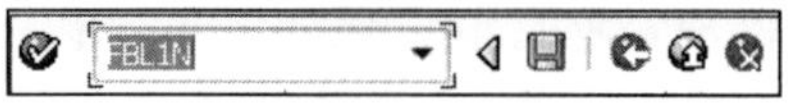

Figure 8.6 Entering "FBL1N" in the Command Field

The **Vendor Line Item Display** selection screen opens (Figure 8.7). Enter values in the **Vendor account** and **Company code** fields. The most notable components of this selection screen are the **Status** and **Type** areas under **Line item selection.** The **Status** buttons allow you to choose to see **Open items**, **Cleared items**, or **All items**. You can also narrow your data selection by entering relevant date parameters.

The checkboxes in the **Type** section allow you to choose the types of documents to display on the output screen.

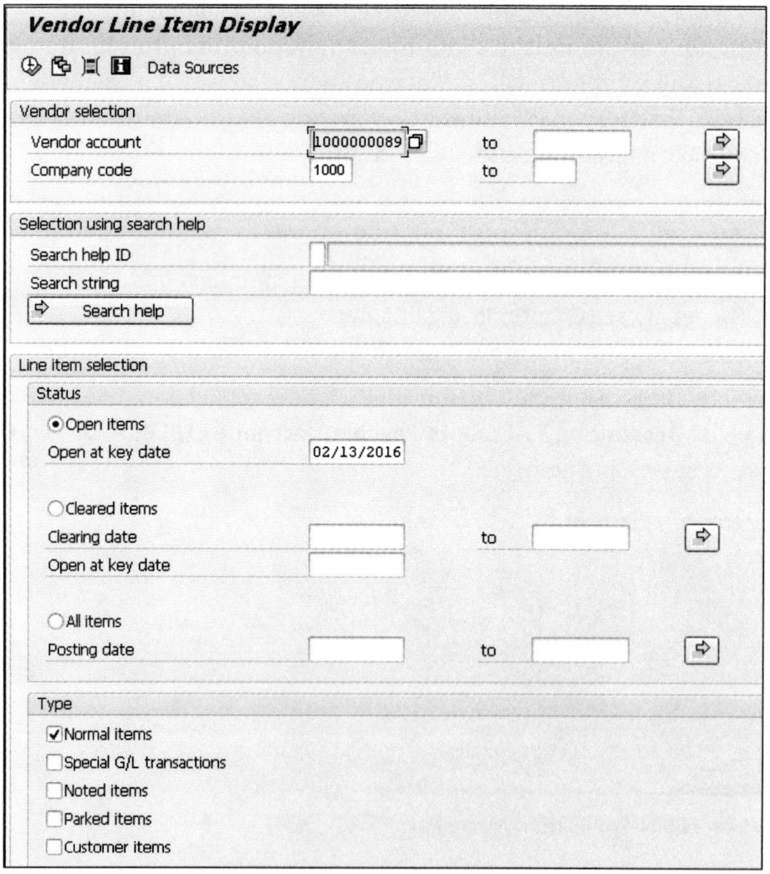

Figure 8.7 Vendor Line Item Display Selection Screen

After you've entered all your selection parameters, click the **Execute** icon. The **Vendor Line Item Display** output screen opens (Figure 8.8).

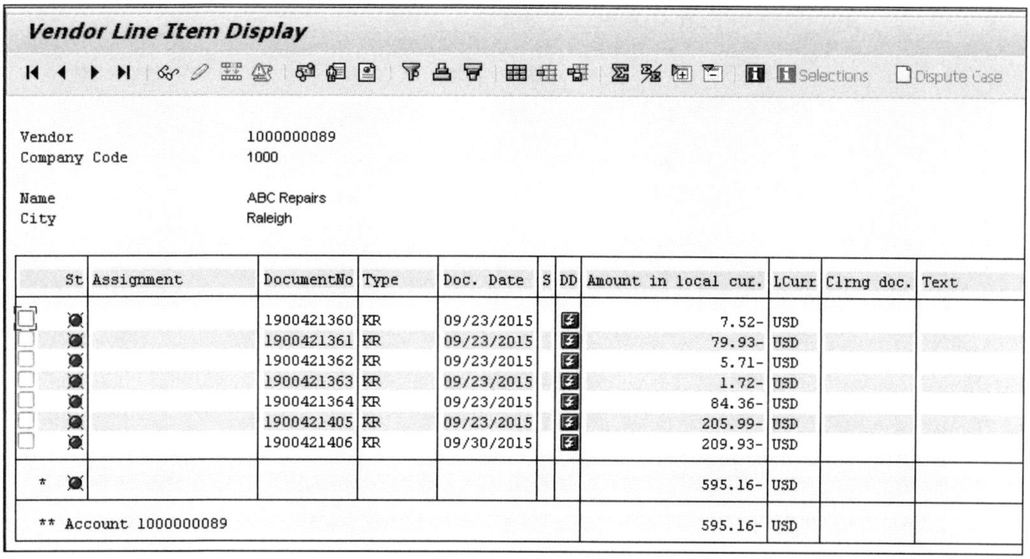

Figure 8.8 Vendor Line Item Display Output Screen

Now, you can change the layout, sort, filter, total, subtotal, and so on using icons on the toolbar. Transaction FBL1N also allows you to double-click an individual line item to drill down directly into an AP invoice or other AP document, such as a credit memo or down payment. After you're in an AP document, you can then drill down into individual line item details.

Table 8.1 lists some useful icons frequently used in Transaction FBL1N.

Icon	Description
	Click once on the document you want to display, and then click on this **Display Document** icon.
	Click once on the document you want to change, and then click on this **Change Document** icon.
	If a vendor invoice was paid by check, click once on the document, and then click on this **Display Check Information** icon.

Table 8.1 Frequently Used Icons in Transaction FBL1N

Icon	Description
	To filter data in the view, click on this icon, and then define your field criteria (i.e., select fields to filter and values).
	To sort data in ascending order, click once on a column header, and then click this **Sort in Ascending Order** icon.
	To sort data in descending order, click once on a column header, and then click this **Sort in Descending Order** icon.
	To change the screen layout, click on the **Change Layout** icon, and then select fields and the order of display.
	To select a different predefined screen layout, click on the **Select Layout** icon. In the popup window, double-click on the screen layout you want to use.
	Use the **Save Layout** icon to save changes you've made to the screen layout.
	To total data, click once on a column header, and then click on this **Display Sum** icon.
	To subtotal data, click once on a column header, and then click on this **Subtotal** icon.

Table 8.1 Frequently Used Icons in Transaction FBL1N (Cont.)

In addition to these icons, several additional actions are available from the dropdown menu. For example, choosing **List • Export • Spreadsheet** allows you to export vendor line item details from the screen to a spreadsheet.

The vendor line item display is the most powerful tool at your disposal for checking the status of an invoice or payment. AP clerks and supervisors use it frequently, and it's often the first stop when fielding an inquiry about a vendor account balance, the status of an invoice, or the status of a payment.

8.2 Due Date Analysis

One of the most common inquiries sent to an AP department regards when a specific invoice is due for payment. The quickest and easiest way to find the answer is using Transaction FBL1N, which is covered in detail in Section 8.1.2.

Within the vendor line item display, two fields are most relevant to due date determination: **Net Due Date** and **Net Due Date Symbol**. The **Net Due Date Symbol** graphically represents whether a payable isn't due, is due, or is overdue. All three symbols are represented in Figure 8.9 in the column **DD**.

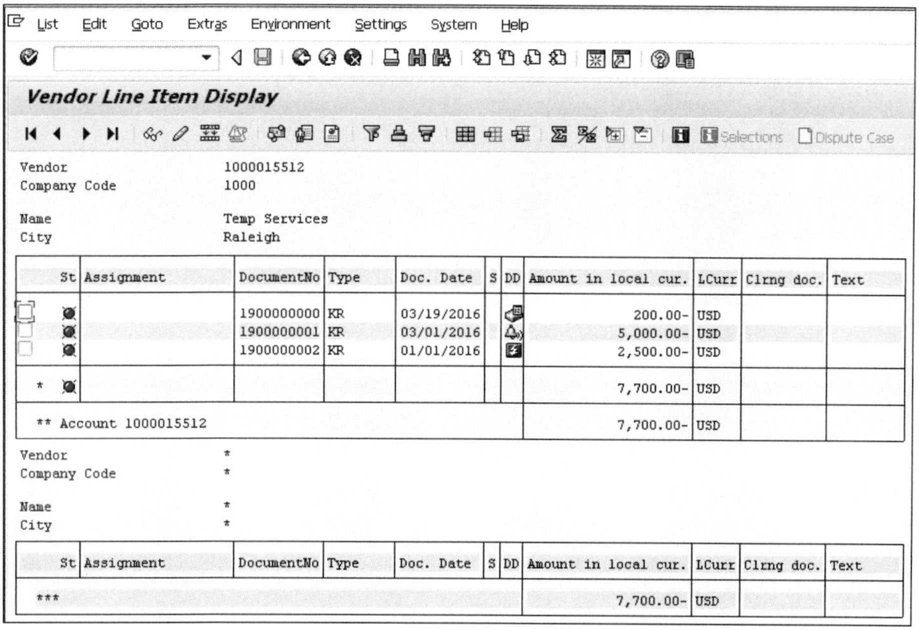

Figure 8.9 Output with Due Date Symbols

They have the following meanings:

- **Overdue**
  This symbol appears anytime an invoice is unpaid and the current date is past the payment due date.
- **Due**
  This symbol appears anytime an invoice is unpaid and the current date equals the payment due date.
- **Not Due**
  This symbol appears anytime an invoice is unpaid and the current date is less than the payment due date.

See Section 8.5.1 for further discussion of due date analysis.

8.3 Payment History

After a vendor invoice has been paid, it shows up as a cleared item in Transaction FBL1N. A paid invoice appears in the vendor line item display with a clearing document, payment date, and payment method.

To view a cleared vendor line item using Transaction FBL1N, follow application menu path, **Accounting • Financial Accounting • Accounts Payable • Account • FBL1N – Display/Change Line Items**, as shown in Figure 8.10.

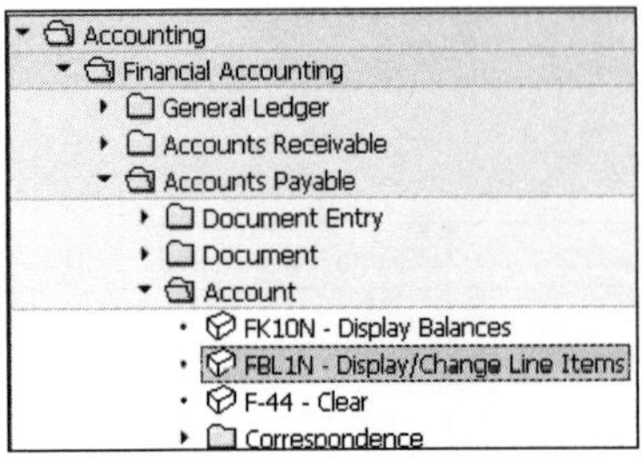

Figure 8.10 Transaction FBL1N Application Menu Path

The **Vendor Line Item Display** selection screen opens (Figure 8.11). Enter values in the **Vendor account** and **Company code** fields. For this example, to see a payment issued, we selected the **Cleared items** status option and must enter a value in the **Clearing date** field.

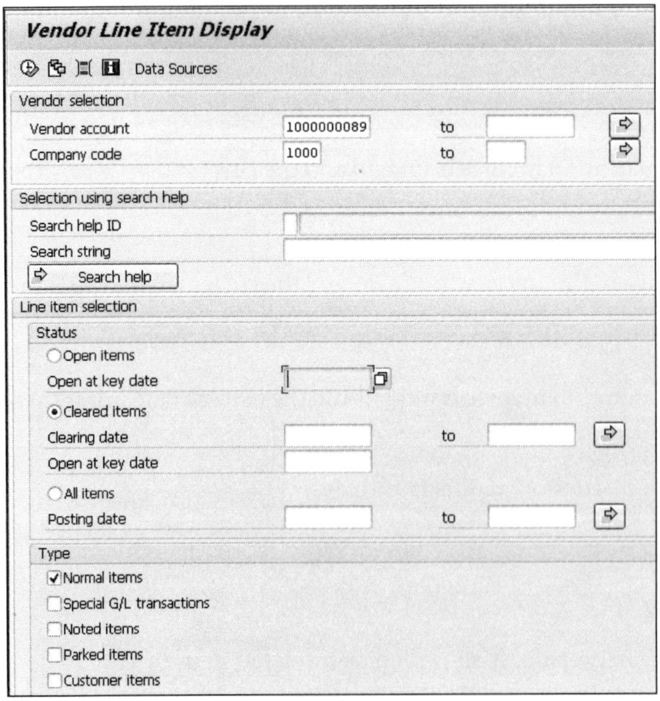

Figure 8.11 Vendor Line Item Display with Cleared Items Selected

With all field values entered, click the **Execute** icon. The **Vendor Line Item Display** screen opens, showing the date the vendor invoice was paid, the payment method, and the clearing document number (Figure 8.12).

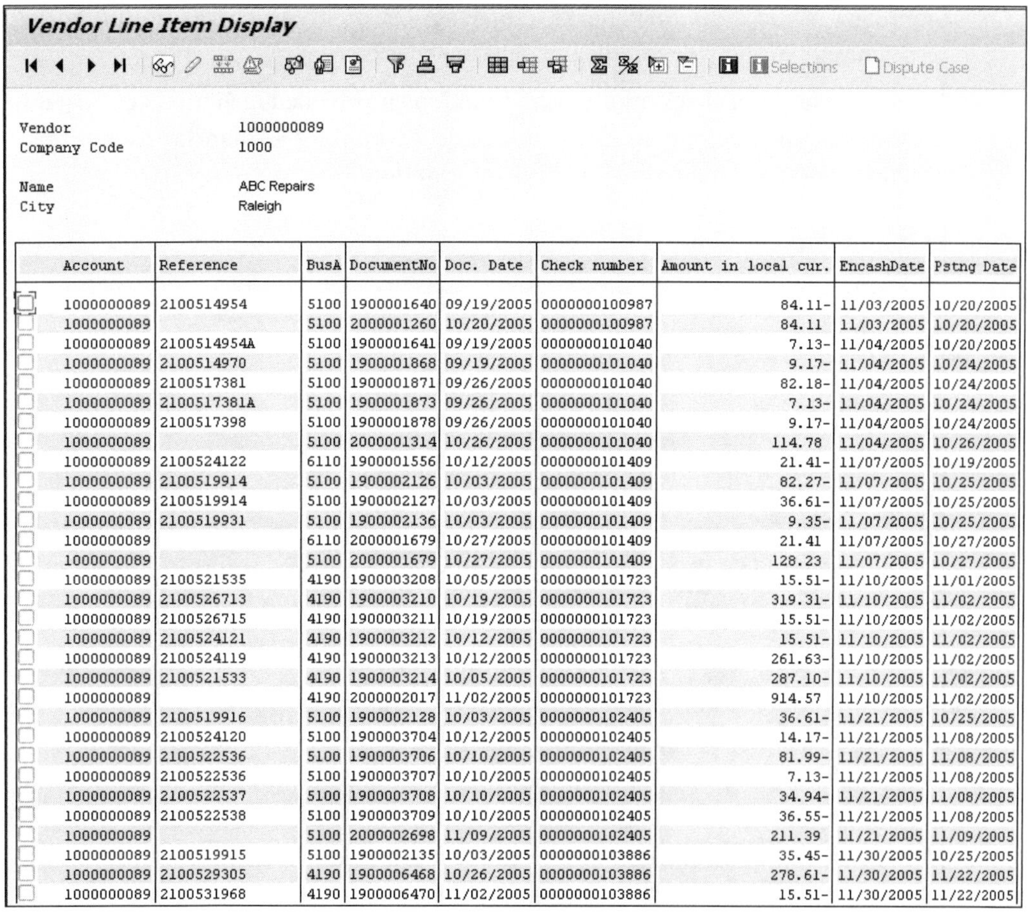

Account	Reference	BusA	DocumentNo	Doc. Date	Check number	Amount in local cur.	EncashDate	Pstng Date
1000000089	2100514954	5100	1900001640	09/19/2005	0000000100987	84.11-	11/03/2005	10/20/2005
1000000089		5100	2000001260	10/20/2005	0000000100987	84.11	11/03/2005	10/20/2005
1000000089	2100514954A	5100	1900001641	09/19/2005	0000000101040	7.13-	11/04/2005	10/20/2005
1000000089	2100514970	5100	1900001868	09/19/2005	0000000101040	9.17-	11/04/2005	10/24/2005
1000000089	2100517381	5100	1900001871	09/26/2005	0000000101040	82.18-	11/04/2005	10/24/2005
1000000089	2100517381A	5100	1900001873	09/26/2005	0000000101040	7.13-	11/04/2005	10/24/2005
1000000089	2100517398	5100	1900001878	09/26/2005	0000000101040	9.17-	11/04/2005	10/24/2005
1000000089		5100	2000001314	10/26/2005	0000000101040	114.78	11/04/2005	10/26/2005
1000000089	2100524122	6110	1900001556	10/12/2005	0000000101409	21.41-	11/07/2005	10/19/2005
1000000089	2100519914	5100	1900002126	10/03/2005	0000000101409	82.27-	11/07/2005	10/25/2005
1000000089	2100519914	5100	1900002127	10/03/2005	0000000101409	36.61-	11/07/2005	10/25/2005
1000000089	2100519931	5100	1900002136	10/03/2005	0000000101409	9.35-	11/07/2005	10/25/2005
1000000089		6110	2000001679	10/27/2005	0000000101409	21.41	11/07/2005	10/27/2005
1000000089		5100	2000001679	10/27/2005	0000000101409	128.23	11/07/2005	10/27/2005
1000000089	2100521535	4190	1900003208	10/05/2005	0000000101723	15.51-	11/10/2005	11/01/2005
1000000089	2100526713	4190	1900003210	10/19/2005	0000000101723	319.31-	11/10/2005	11/02/2005
1000000089	2100526715	4190	1900003211	10/19/2005	0000000101723	15.51-	11/10/2005	11/02/2005
1000000089	2100524121	4190	1900003212	10/12/2005	0000000101723	15.51-	11/10/2005	11/02/2005
1000000089	2100524119	4190	1900003213	10/12/2005	0000000101723	261.63-	11/10/2005	11/02/2005
1000000089	2100521533	4190	1900003214	10/05/2005	0000000101723	287.10-	11/10/2005	11/02/2005
1000000089		4190	2000002017	11/02/2005	0000000101723	914.57	11/10/2005	11/02/2005
1000000089	2100519916	5100	1900002128	10/03/2005	0000000102405	36.61-	11/21/2005	10/25/2005
1000000089	2100524120	5100	1900003704	10/12/2005	0000000102405	14.17-	11/21/2005	11/08/2005
1000000089	2100522536	5100	1900003706	10/10/2005	0000000102405	81.99-	11/21/2005	11/08/2005
1000000089	2100522536	5100	1900003707	10/10/2005	0000000102405	7.13-	11/21/2005	11/08/2005
1000000089	2100522537	5100	1900003708	10/10/2005	0000000102405	34.94-	11/21/2005	11/08/2005
1000000089	2100522538	5100	1900003709	10/10/2005	0000000102405	36.55-	11/21/2005	11/08/2005
1000000089		5100	2000002698	11/09/2005	0000000102405	211.39	11/21/2005	11/09/2005
1000000089	2100519915	5100	1900002135	10/03/2005	0000000103886	35.45-	11/30/2005	10/25/2005
1000000089	2100529305	4190	1900006468	10/26/2005	0000000103886	278.61-	11/30/2005	11/22/2005
1000000089	2100531968	4190	1900006470	11/02/2005	0000000103886	15.51-	11/30/2005	11/22/2005

Figure 8.12 Vendor Line Item Display with Paid Invoice

Transaction FBL1N is frequently used to find out when a vendor invoice was paid. The program's flexibility makes it a valuable tool in making these kinds of inquiries. You can search for cleared items for one or more vendors by using a specific date or by referencing a specific invoice or clearing document number.

8.4 Check Register

Check management is an important function in AP. You can issue checks using the automated payment program or you can issue a check manually. Check management also includes voiding checks, replacing lost or stolen checks, renumbering, reassigning, canceling payment, and deleting checks.

The complete list of check information functions is provided in Figure 8.13. To get to these folders, follow application menu path, **Accounting • Financial Accounting • Accounts Payable • Environment • Check Information**.

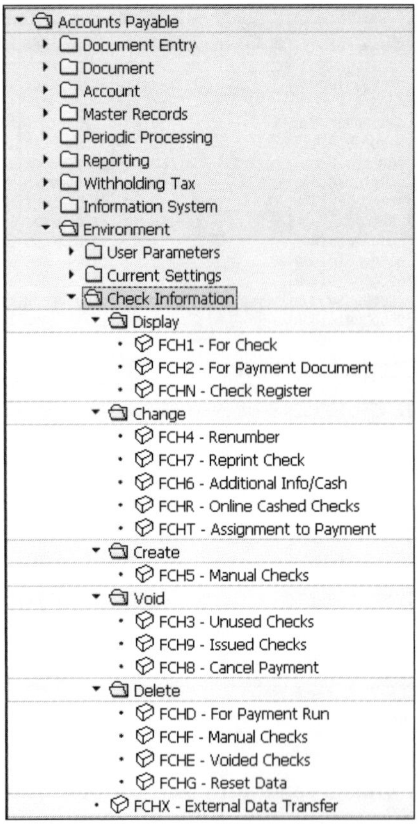

Figure 8.13 Application Menu Path for Check Information

You need to be aware of these functions and transactions. There are many circumstances where you'll need to reprint a check using Transaction FCH7 or cancel a check using Transaction FCH8.

The remainder of this section focuses on the central check management tool: the *check register*. This program generates a list of all check registers belonging to a company code based on the selection criteria you choose. It also allows you to create checklists, which may consist of outstanding checks, voided checks, payroll checks, or other options.

The check register is a one-stop shop for information about checks on an individual or collective basis. It allows you to see all the information associated with a check, including payment date, amount, vendor, encashment/void date, and more.

To view the check register, follow application menu path, **Accounting • Financial Accounting • Accounts Receivable • Environment • Check Information • Display • FCHN – Check Register**, as shown in Figure 8.14.

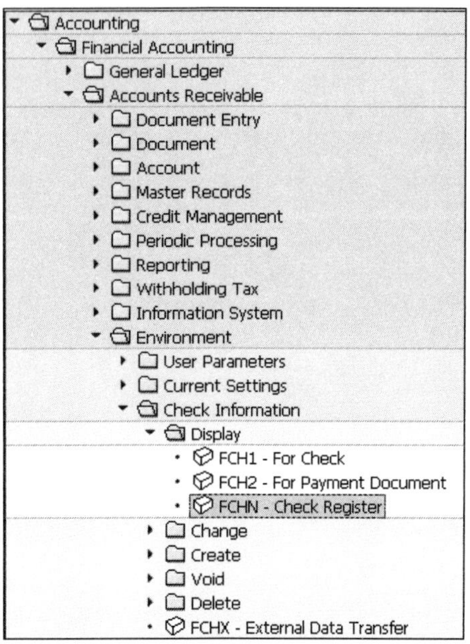

Figure 8.14 Transaction FCHN Application Menu

Double-click **FCHN – Check Register** from the menu path, or enter "FCHN" in the **Command** field (as shown in Figure 8.15) and press [Enter].

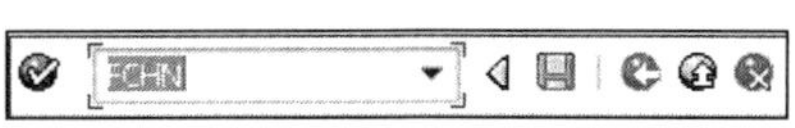

Figure 8.15 Entering "FCHN" in the Command Field

The **Check Register** selection screen opens (Figure 8.16). In the header, enter field values for the **Paying Company Code**, **House Bank**, and **Account ID** fields; you also have the option to include **Payroll checks**.

In the main body of the selection screen, you'll see two selection tabs. Under **General Selections**, you can narrow your search by bank, bank account, specific check number, currency, or amount, and you'll see selection options that influence output control and layouts. If you want to narrow your selection even more, move to the **Further Selections** tab for additional field selection options.

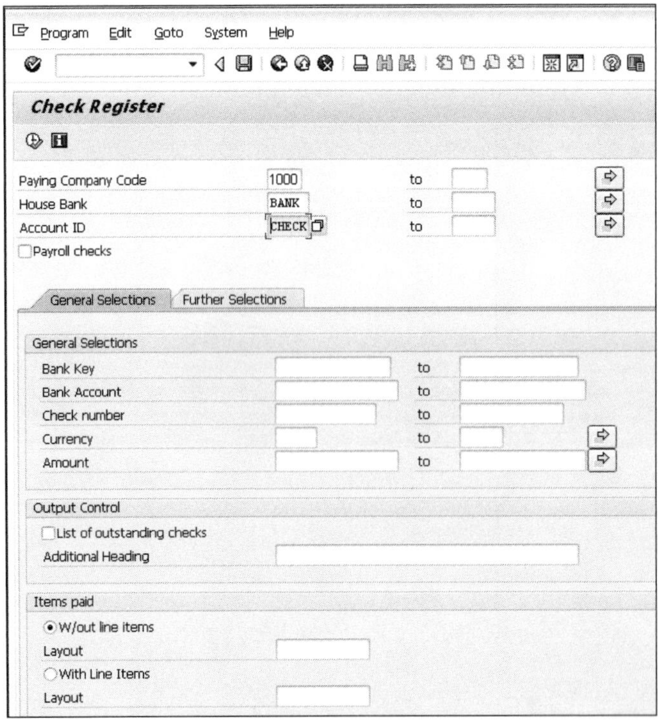

Figure 8.16 Check Register Selection Screen

After you've entered all your selection parameters, click the **Execute** icon . The **Check Register** output screen opens (Figure 8.17).

From this screen, you can see virtually any data associated with a check. You can also drill down, sort, filter, total, subtotal, export, and change the line layout.

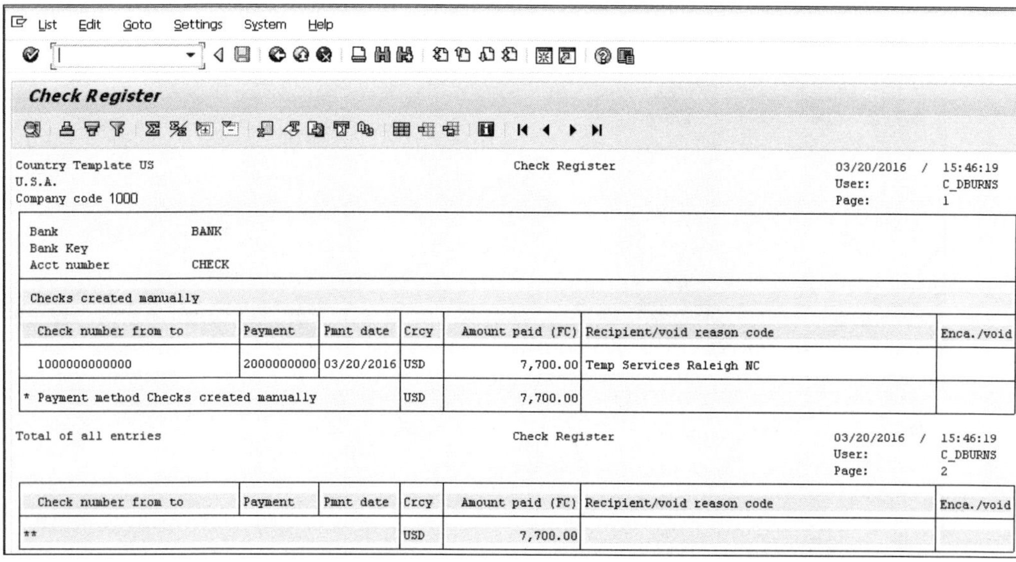

Figure 8.17 Check Register Output Screen

Double-click on a line item within the check registry, and the **Display Check Information** screen appears (Figure 8.18).

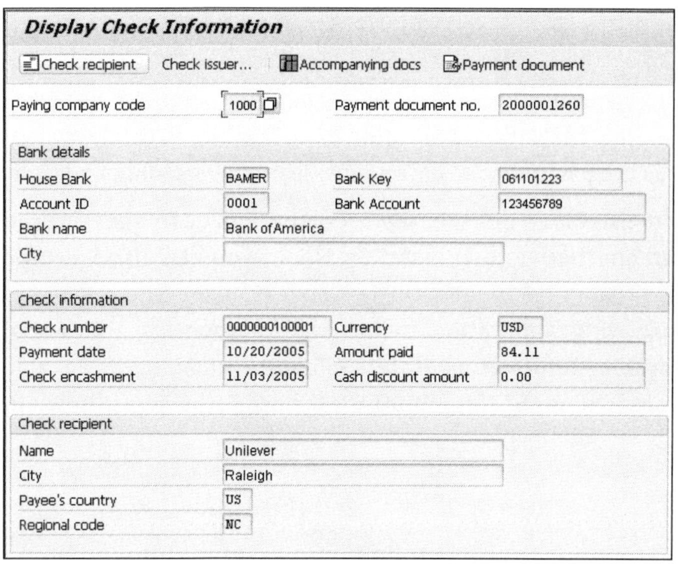

Figure 8.18 Display Check Information Screen

Click on the **Check recipient** button to display the name and address where the check was sent (Figure 8.19).

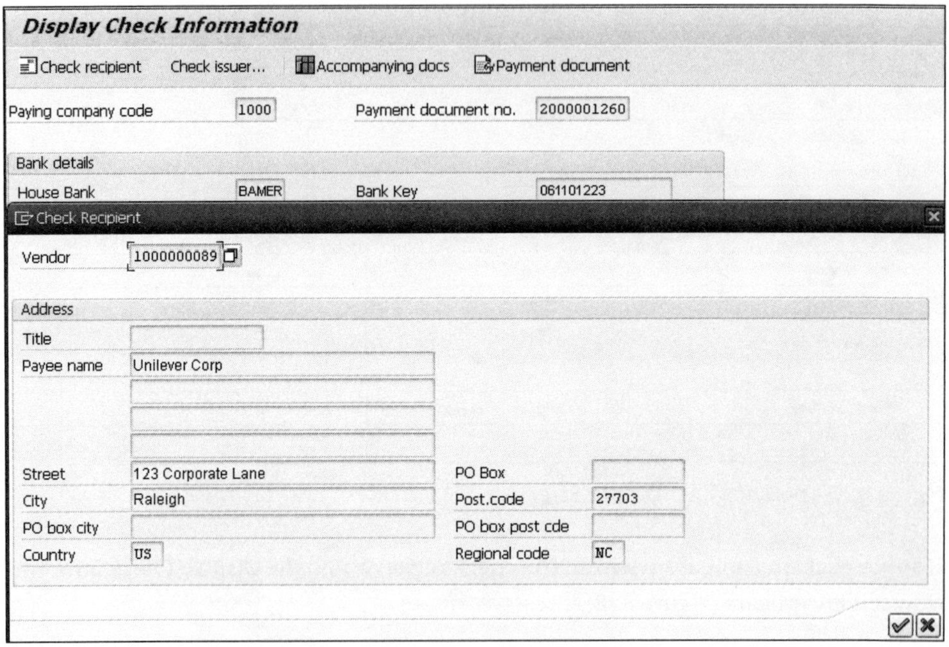

Figure 8.19 Check Recipient Dialog Box

From Figure 8.18, click on the **Check issuer** icon to display the payment run from which the check was generated, as displayed in Figure 8.20. The screen displays associated information, such as the payment run date, identification, user, date and time.

As you can see, the check register is an indispensable tool that will be frequently used by AP departments. As an alternative to Transaction FCHN, you can also view the check register via standard report S_P99_41000101 – Check Register. You can access this report using the following application menu path: **Accounting • Financial Accounting • Accounts Payable • Information System • Reports for Accounts Payable Accounting • Payment Transactions • S_P99_41000101 – Check Register**, as shown in Figure 8.21.

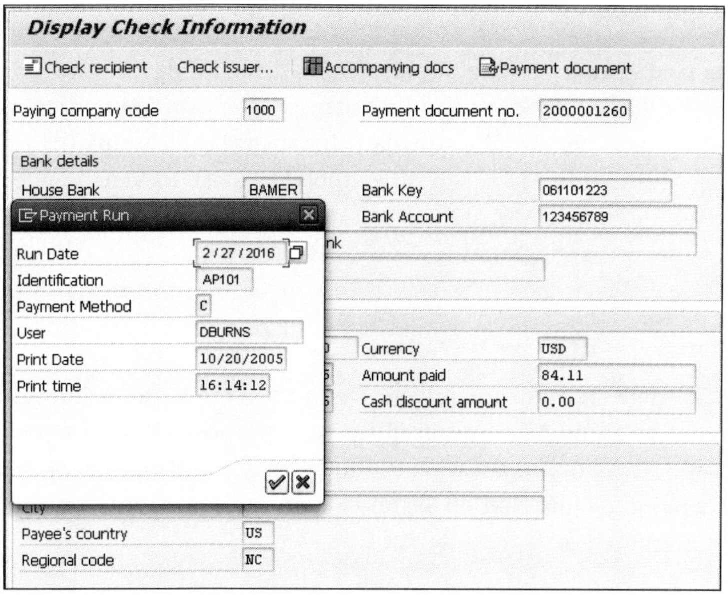

Figure 8.20 Payment Run Dialog Box

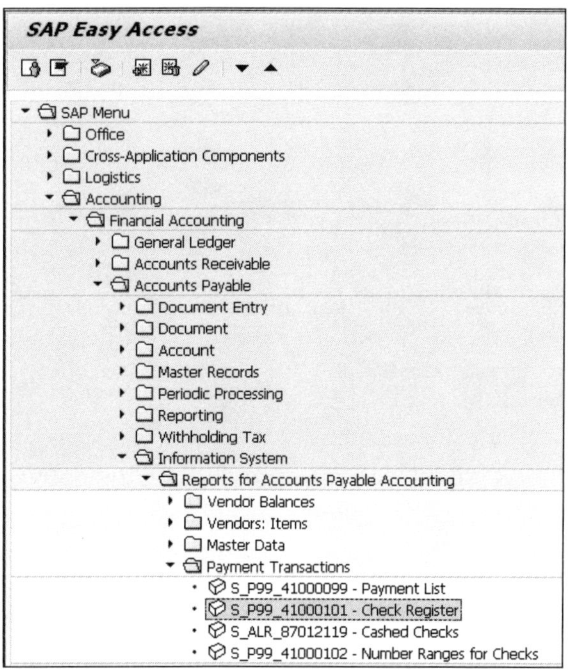

Figure 8.21 Check Register Report Application Menu Path

8.5 Reports and Queries

In Section 8.1, we discussed vendor account displays in detail, including Transactions FK10N and FBL1N. For validating vendor account balances and transaction details, these transactions are the most beneficial, particularly because of their ability to drill down into accounting documents. However, other tools do exist to view vendor account balances and transaction details. In this section, we'll show you where to find these alternatives in AP reports and queries.

8.5.1 Standard Reports

Standard reports are SAP delivered and are universally found in the **Information System** folder of the application menu. The most useful general-purpose AP account balance reports can be accessed from application menu path, **Accounting • Financial Accounting • Accounts Payable • Information System • Reports for Accounts Payable Accounting**, as shown in Figure 8.22.

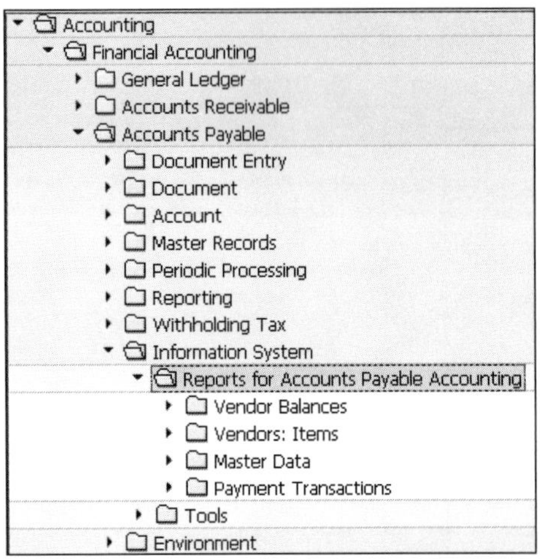

Figure 8.22 AP Reports Application Menu Path

Many standard reports exist for viewing vendor balances, line items, payment transactions, and master data. Let's look at two reports in more detail as examples.

Due Date Analysis for Open Items

Vendor due date analysis is the process of determining how much is due to be paid in each period. The most comprehensive tool is report S_ALR_87012078 – Due Date Analysis for Open Items.

To perform AP due date analysis, use Transaction S_ALR_87012078 or application menu path, **Accounting • Financial Accounting • Accounts Payable • Information System • Reports for Accounts Payable Accounting • Vendors: Items • S_ALR_87012078 – Due Date Analysis for Open Items**, as shown in Figure 8.23.

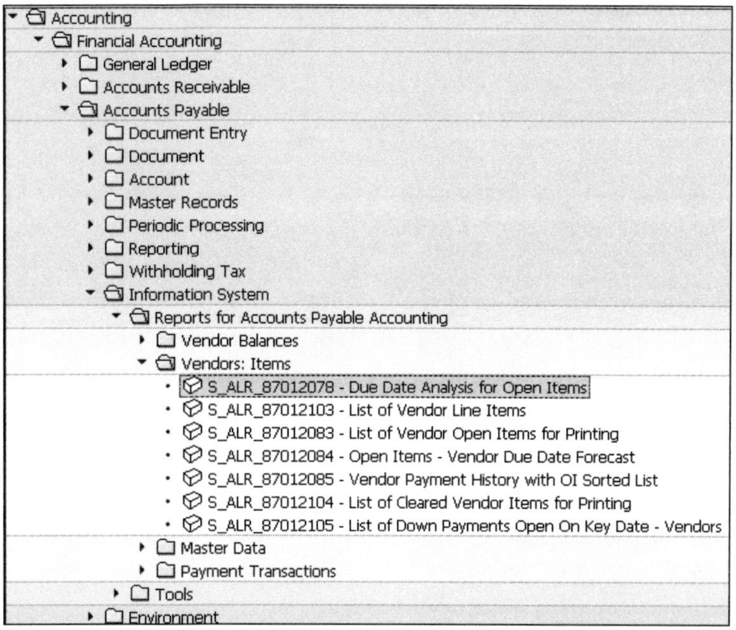

Figure 8.23 Report S_ALR_87012078 Application Menu Path

Double-click **S_ALR_87012078 – Due Date Analysis** from the menu path, and the selection screen for report S_ALR_87012078 opens (Figure 8.24). For this example, we entered one value each for **Vendor account** and **Company code**, although multiple values are permitted. The field value for **Open items at key date** defaults to the current date, but it can be overwritten. In the **Output type** area, multiple choices exist, and you should try them all. For this example, we selected the first option: **Graphical report output**.

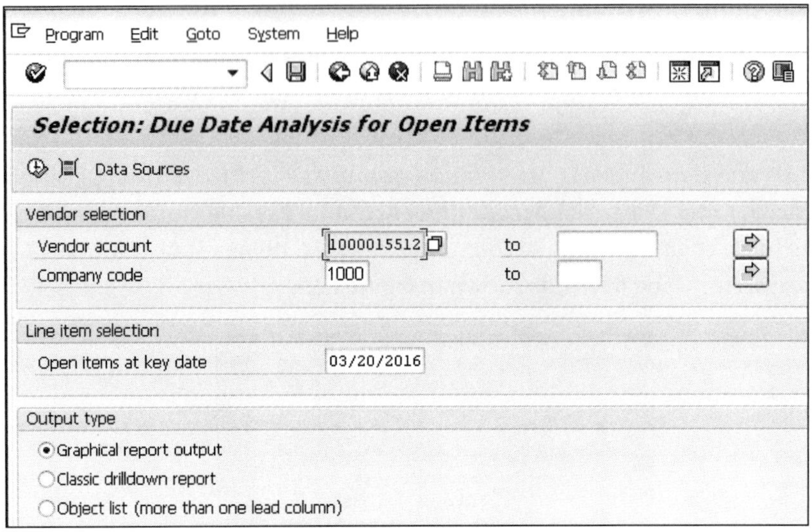

Figure 8.24 Due Date Analysis Report Selection Screen

When all screen field values are entered, click the **Execute** icon. The output screen for the due date analysis report opens (Figure 8.25), showing amounts currently due for the vendor selected.

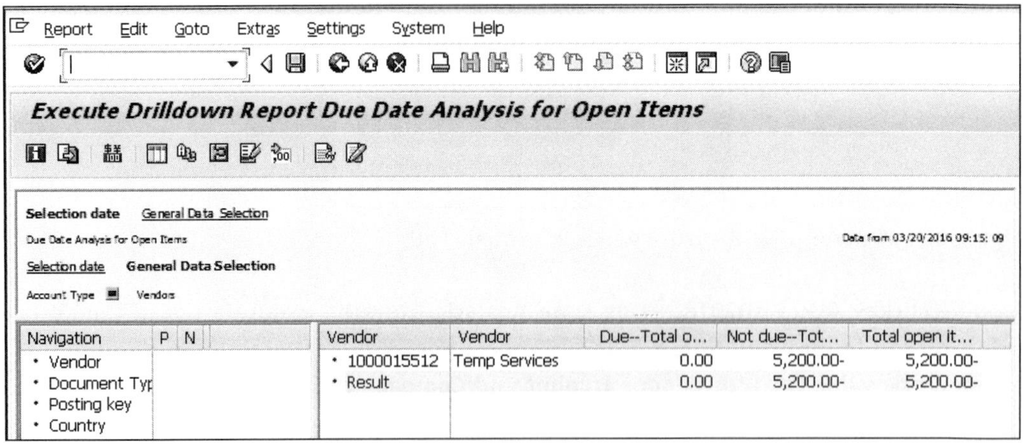

Figure 8.25 Due Date Analysis Report Output Screen

From the output screen, you can drill down, navigate using other objects, or export the data.

Vendor Balances in Local Currency

A frequent activity in accounting departments is to check account balances. Sometimes this is done to reconcile system data with reports. Other times, it's just the normal course of executing business functions, such as financial close. A useful standard AP report for this purpose is report S_ALR_87012082 – Vendor Balances in Local Currency. You can access report S_ALR_87012082 using application menu path, **Accounting • Financial Accounting • Accounts Payable • Information System • Reports for Accounts Payable Accounting • Vendor Balances • S_ALR_87012082 – Vendor Balances in Local Currency**, as shown in Figure 8.26.

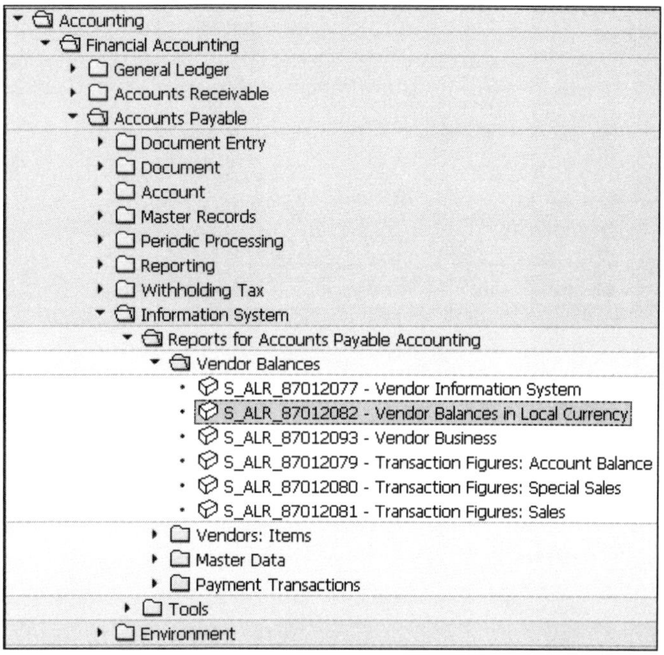

Figure 8.26 Report S_ALR_87012082 Application Menu Path

Double-click **S_ALR_87012082 – Vendor Balances in Local Currency** from the menu path, and the **Vendor Balances in Local Currency** selection screen opens (Figure 8.27). For this example, we entered values for the **Vendor account** and **Company code** fields. Values will default into the **Fiscal Year** and **Reporting periods** fields.

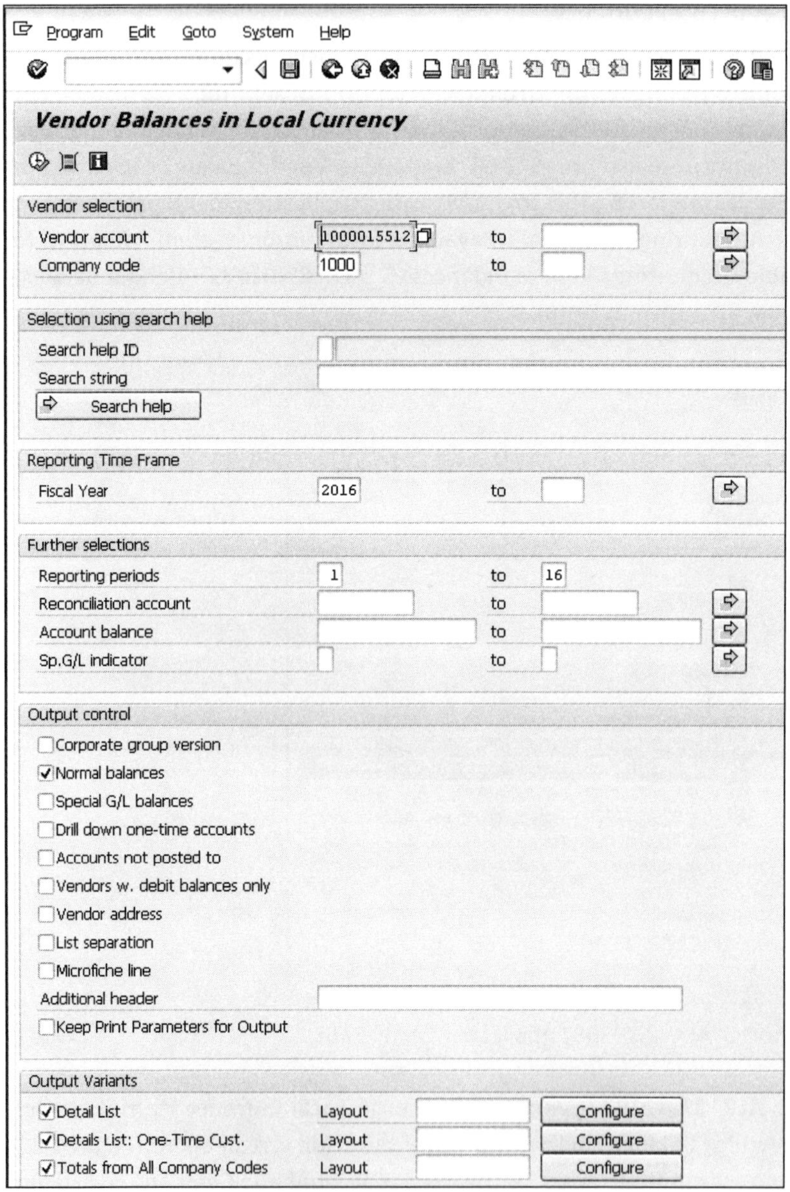

Figure 8.27 Vendor Balances Report Selection Screen

When all screen field values are entered, click the **Execute** icon. The output screen for the report opens (Figure 8.28), showing vendor balances.

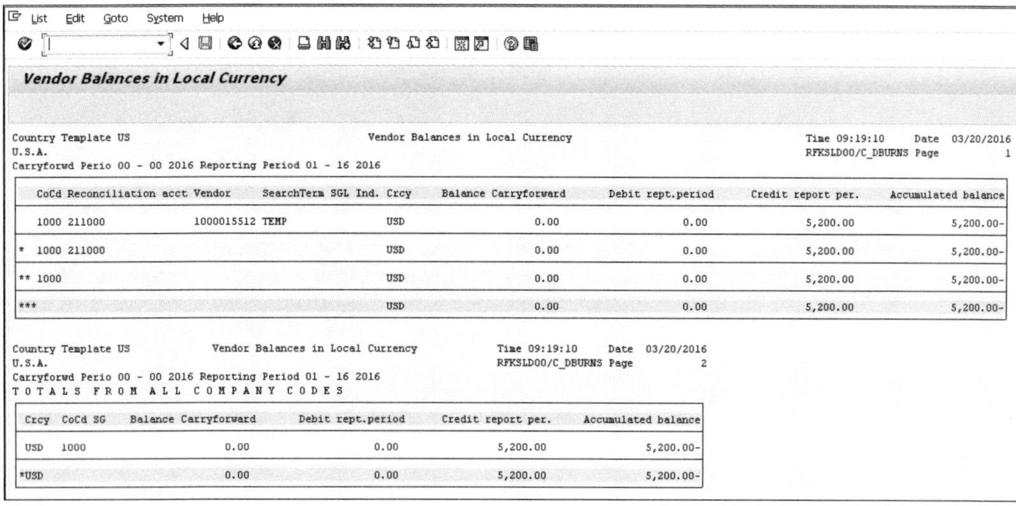

Figure 8.28 Vendor Balances Report Output Screen

Drilldown capability doesn't exist in report S_ALR_87012082, but for a nice view of vendor balances, this report serves the purpose well.

8.5.2 Direct Table Queries

We've looked at the use of standard reports in AP; now, let's discuss how to make direct table queries to view AP data. There are two transactions that allow you to do so: Transaction SE11 and Transaction SE16.

> **Note**
>
> End users are typically not given authorization to use direct table access via Transaction SE11 because it's targeted specifically for use by developers. Transaction SE16 is more commonly authorized with restriction to specific tables.

Let's take a closer look at each transaction.

Transaction SE11

The first approach is to use Transaction SE11, which can be accessed via the following application menu path: **Tools • ABAP Workbench • Development** (see Figure 8.29).

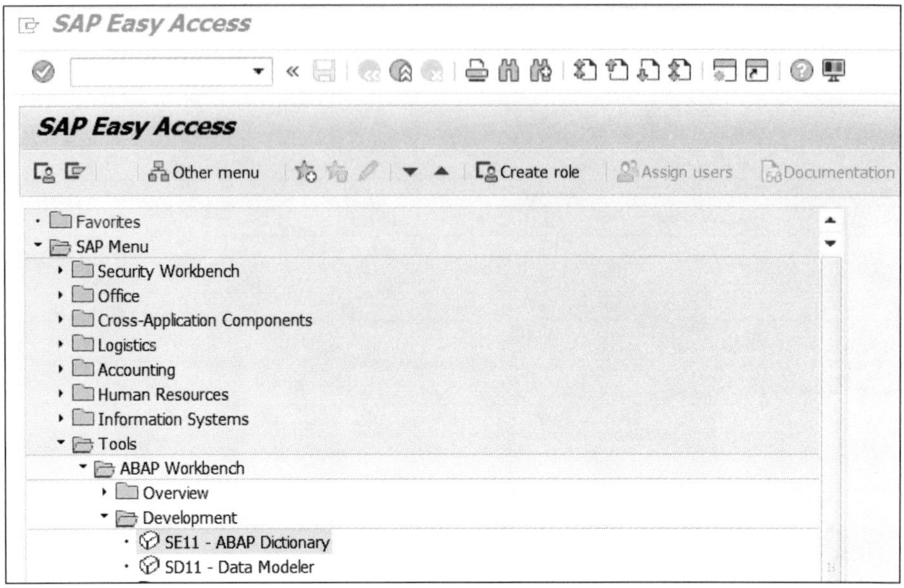

Figure 8.29 Transaction SE11 Application Menu Path

Double-click on **SE11 – ABAP Dictionary,** and the **ABAP Dictionary: Initial Screen** popup screen appears (see Figure 8.30).

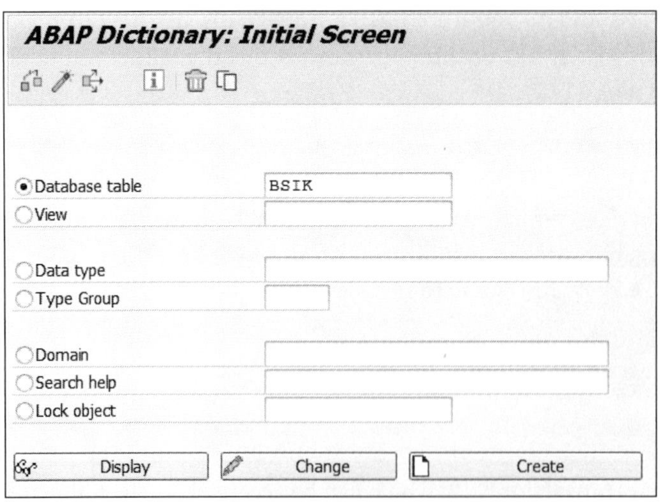

Figure 8.30 Initial Screen for AP Table

Enter a **Database table,** and click on the **Display** icon. For this example, the AP secondary index table "BSIK" was entered.

Press [Enter] or click the **Display** icon to open the **Dictionary: Display Table** screen (see Figure 8.31).

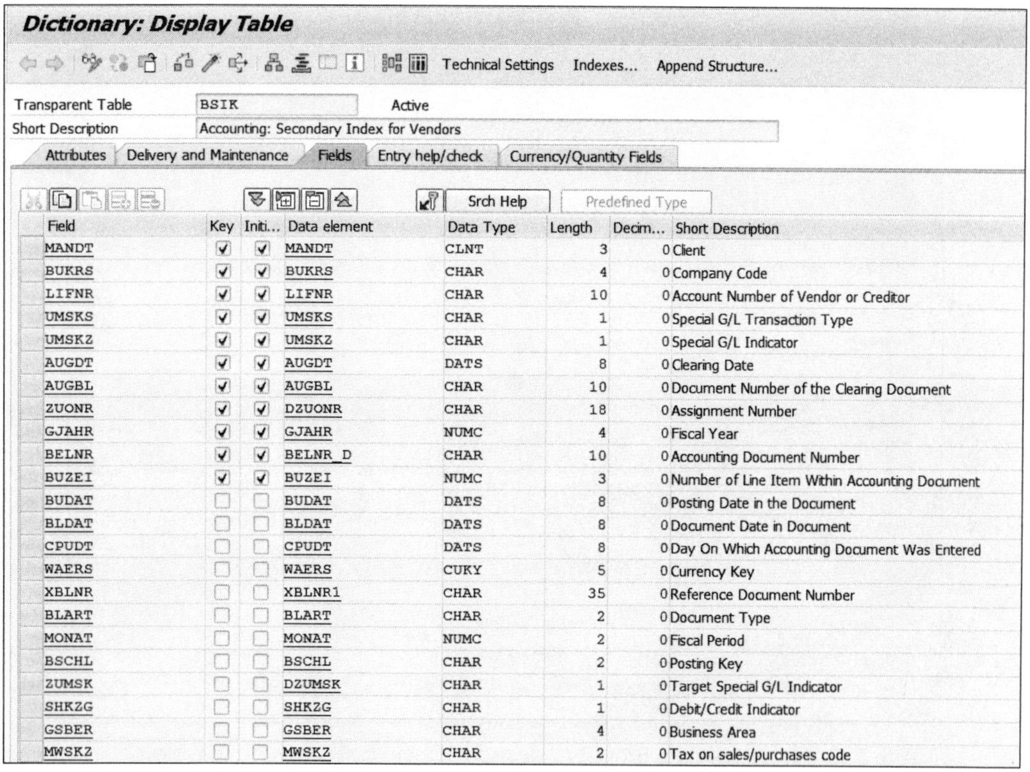

Field	Key	Initi...	Data element	Data Type	Length	Decim...	Short Description
MANDT	✓	✓	MANDT	CLNT	3	0	Client
BUKRS	✓	✓	BUKRS	CHAR	4	0	Company Code
LIFNR	✓	✓	LIFNR	CHAR	10	0	Account Number of Vendor or Creditor
UMSKS	✓	✓	UMSKS	CHAR	1	0	Special G/L Transaction Type
UMSKZ	✓	✓	UMSKZ	CHAR	1	0	Special G/L Indicator
AUGDT	✓	✓	AUGDT	DATS	8	0	Clearing Date
AUGBL	✓	✓	AUGBL	CHAR	10	0	Document Number of the Clearing Document
ZUONR	✓	✓	DZUONR	CHAR	18	0	Assignment Number
GJAHR	✓	✓	GJAHR	NUMC	4	0	Fiscal Year
BELNR	✓	✓	BELNR_D	CHAR	10	0	Accounting Document Number
BUZEI	✓	✓	BUZEI	NUMC	3	0	Number of Line Item Within Accounting Document
BUDAT			BUDAT	DATS	8	0	Posting Date in the Document
BLDAT			BLDAT	DATS	8	0	Document Date in Document
CPUDT			CPUDT	DATS	8	0	Day On Which Accounting Document Was Entered
WAERS			WAERS	CUKY	5	0	Currency Key
XBLNR			XBLNR1	CHAR	35	0	Reference Document Number
BLART			BLART	CHAR	2	0	Document Type
MONAT			MONAT	NUMC	2	0	Fiscal Period
BSCHL			BSCHL	CHAR	2	0	Posting Key
ZUMSK			DZUMSK	CHAR	1	0	Target Special G/L Indicator
SHKZG			SHKZG	CHAR	1	0	Debit/Credit Indicator
GSBER			GSBER	CHAR	4	0	Business Area
MWSKZ			MWSKZ	CHAR	2	0	Tax on sales/purchases code

Figure 8.31 Display AP Table BSIK

As you can see, Transaction SE11 allows you to view the database table before viewing its contents. Next, click on the **Contents** icon in the toolbar to begin viewing detail in the table.

The **Data Browser: Selection Screen** appears (see Figure 8.32). Here, there are several field values that you can enter in order to pare down your data selection, making it easier to find what you're looking for. In this example, a value was entered for **Fiscal Year**.

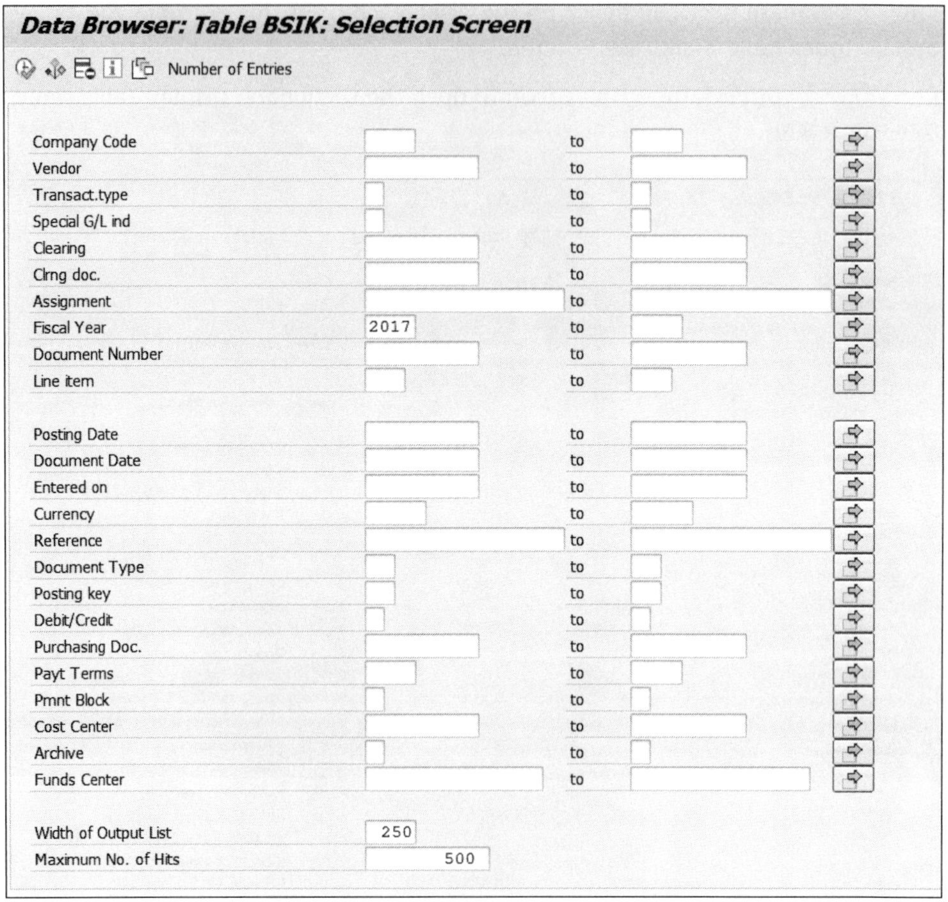

Figure 8.32 Table BSIK Data Browser Selection Screen

After entering field values in the selection screen, click on the **Execute** icon at the top left of the screen. The AP table entries appear (see Figure 8.33).

The toolbar at the top of Figure 8.33 contains options to change the layout, sort, filter, download, and more. From the AP table BSIK display, you can also double-click on any row and display all the field values in the AP line.

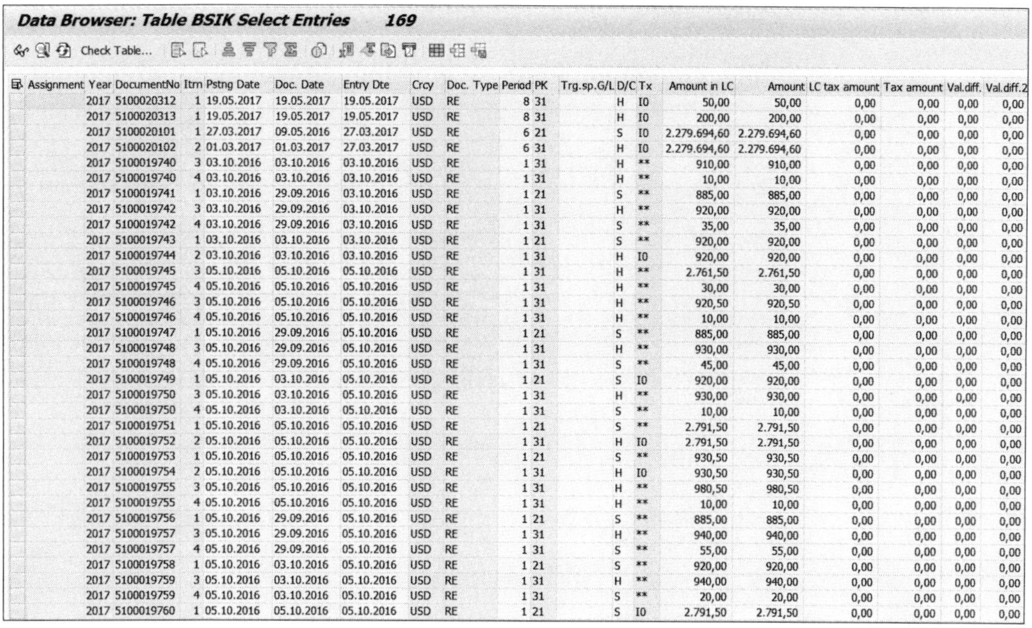

Assignment	Year	DocumentNo	Itm	Pstng Date	Doc. Date	Entry Dte	Crcy	Doc. Type	Period	PK	Trg.sp.G/L	D/C	Tx	Amount in LC	Amount	LC tax amount	Tax amount	Val.diff.	Val.diff.2
	2017	5100020312	1	19.05.2017	19.05.2017	19.05.2017	USD	RE	8	31		H	I0	50,00	50,00	0,00	0,00	0,00	0,00
	2017	5100020313	1	19.05.2017	19.05.2017	19.05.2017	USD	RE	8	31		H	I0	200,00	200,00	0,00	0,00	0,00	0,00
	2017	5100020101	1	27.03.2017	09.05.2016	27.03.2017	USD	RE	6	21		S	I0	2.279.694,60	2.279.694,60	0,00	0,00	0,00	0,00
	2017	5100020102	2	01.03.2017	01.03.2017	27.03.2017	USD	RE	6	31		H	I0	2.279.694,60	2.279.694,60	0,00	0,00	0,00	0,00
	2017	5100019740	3	03.10.2016	03.10.2016	03.10.2016	USD	RE	1	31		H	**	910,00	910,00	0,00	0,00	0,00	0,00
	2017	5100019740	4	03.10.2016	03.10.2016	03.10.2016	USD	RE	1	31		H	**	10,00	10,00	0,00	0,00	0,00	0,00
	2017	5100019741	1	03.10.2016	29.09.2016	03.10.2016	USD	RE	1	21		S	**	885,00	885,00	0,00	0,00	0,00	0,00
	2017	5100019742	3	03.10.2016	29.09.2016	03.10.2016	USD	RE	1	31		H	**	920,00	920,00	0,00	0,00	0,00	0,00
	2017	5100019742	4	03.10.2016	29.09.2016	03.10.2016	USD	RE	1	31		S	**	35,00	35,00	0,00	0,00	0,00	0,00
	2017	5100019743	1	03.10.2016	03.10.2016	03.10.2016	USD	RE	1	21		S	**	920,00	920,00	0,00	0,00	0,00	0,00
	2017	5100019744	2	03.10.2016	03.10.2016	03.10.2016	USD	RE	1	31		H	I0	920,00	920,00	0,00	0,00	0,00	0,00
	2017	5100019745	3	05.10.2016	05.10.2016	05.10.2016	USD	RE	1	31		H	**	2.761,50	2.761,50	0,00	0,00	0,00	0,00
	2017	5100019745	4	05.10.2016	05.10.2016	05.10.2016	USD	RE	1	31		H	**	30,00	30,00	0,00	0,00	0,00	0,00
	2017	5100019746	3	05.10.2016	05.10.2016	05.10.2016	USD	RE	1	31		H	**	920,50	920,50	0,00	0,00	0,00	0,00
	2017	5100019746	4	05.10.2016	05.10.2016	05.10.2016	USD	RE	1	31		H	**	10,00	10,00	0,00	0,00	0,00	0,00
	2017	5100019747	1	05.10.2016	29.09.2016	05.10.2016	USD	RE	1	21		S	**	885,00	885,00	0,00	0,00	0,00	0,00
	2017	5100019748	3	05.10.2016	29.09.2016	05.10.2016	USD	RE	1	31		H	**	930,00	930,00	0,00	0,00	0,00	0,00
	2017	5100019748	4	05.10.2016	29.09.2016	05.10.2016	USD	RE	1	31		S	**	45,00	45,00	0,00	0,00	0,00	0,00
	2017	5100019749	1	05.10.2016	03.10.2016	05.10.2016	USD	RE	1	21		S	I0	920,00	920,00	0,00	0,00	0,00	0,00
	2017	5100019750	3	05.10.2016	03.10.2016	05.10.2016	USD	RE	1	31		H	**	930,00	930,00	0,00	0,00	0,00	0,00
	2017	5100019750	4	05.10.2016	03.10.2016	05.10.2016	USD	RE	1	31		S	**	10,00	10,00	0,00	0,00	0,00	0,00
	2017	5100019751	1	05.10.2016	05.10.2016	05.10.2016	USD	RE	1	21		S	**	2.791,50	2.791,50	0,00	0,00	0,00	0,00
	2017	5100019752	2	05.10.2016	05.10.2016	05.10.2016	USD	RE	1	31		H	I0	2.791,50	2.791,50	0,00	0,00	0,00	0,00
	2017	5100019753	1	05.10.2016	05.10.2016	05.10.2016	USD	RE	1	21		S	**	930,50	930,50	0,00	0,00	0,00	0,00
	2017	5100019754	2	05.10.2016	05.10.2016	05.10.2016	USD	RE	1	31		H	I0	930,50	930,50	0,00	0,00	0,00	0,00
	2017	5100019755	3	05.10.2016	05.10.2016	05.10.2016	USD	RE	1	31		H	**	980,50	980,50	0,00	0,00	0,00	0,00
	2017	5100019755	4	05.10.2016	05.10.2016	05.10.2016	USD	RE	1	31		H	**	10,00	10,00	0,00	0,00	0,00	0,00
	2017	5100019756	1	05.10.2016	29.09.2016	05.10.2016	USD	RE	1	21		S	**	885,00	885,00	0,00	0,00	0,00	0,00
	2017	5100019757	3	05.10.2016	29.09.2016	05.10.2016	USD	RE	1	31		H	**	940,00	940,00	0,00	0,00	0,00	0,00
	2017	5100019757	4	05.10.2016	29.09.2016	05.10.2016	USD	RE	1	31		S	**	55,00	55,00	0,00	0,00	0,00	0,00
	2017	5100019758	1	05.10.2016	03.10.2016	05.10.2016	USD	RE	1	21		S	**	920,00	920,00	0,00	0,00	0,00	0,00
	2017	5100019759	3	05.10.2016	03.10.2016	05.10.2016	USD	RE	1	31		H	**	940,00	940,00	0,00	0,00	0,00	0,00
	2017	5100019759	4	05.10.2016	03.10.2016	05.10.2016	USD	RE	1	31		S	**	20,00	20,00	0,00	0,00	0,00	0,00
	2017	5100019760	1	05.10.2016	05.10.2016	05.10.2016	USD	RE	1	21		S	I0	2.791,50	2.791,50	0,00	0,00	0,00	0,00

Figure 8.33 Table BSIK Entry Selection Results

Transaction SE16

You can also view AP data directly in tables via Transaction SE16, which can be accessed via the following application menu path: **Tools • ABAP Workbench • Overview • Application Hierarchy** (see Figure 8.34).

Double-click on **SE16 – Data Browser**, and the **Data Browser: Initial Screen** appears (see Figure 8.35).

Enter a table name (e.g., "BSIK") and press Enter, or click on the **Contents** icon in the left side of the screen shown in Figure 8.35. The same screen shown earlier in Figure 8.32 appears.

The toolbar at the top of Figure 8.35 allows you to change the layout, sort, filter, download, and more. From the AP table display (refer to Figure 8.33), you can also double-click on any row and display all the field values in AP for that entry.

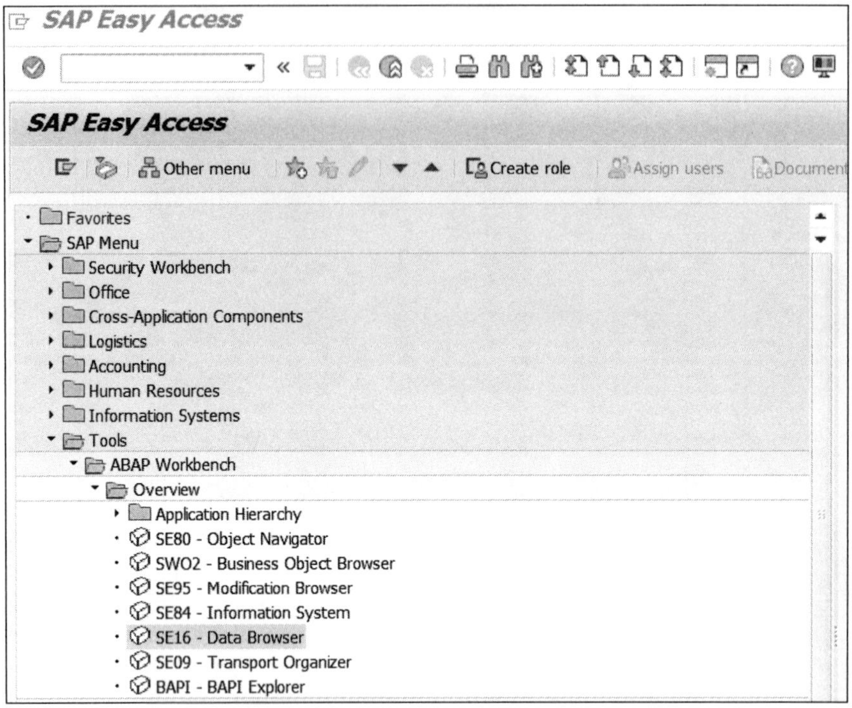

Figure 8.34 Transaction SE16 Application Menu Path

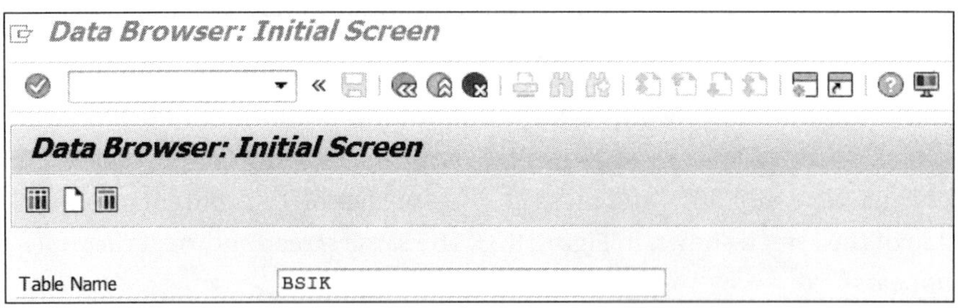

Figure 8.35 Data Browser: Initial Screen

8.6 Summary

In this chapter, we demonstrated transactions and reports you can use in your day-to-day work in vendor account maintenance. The topics covered in this chapter also assist you in making inquiries and troubleshooting problems based on vendor transaction details in the AP module. Often, you'll use these tools simply to validate vendor account details and payments, but these are essential tools used daily in an accounting department.

Transactions FK10N and FBL1N are used to view account balances and line item details. These are among the most common AP transactions executed in the system. Frequent use of these transactions and reports is essential to understanding the activity in AP. Their drilldown capability makes them powerful and flexible tools.

In an AP department, it's essential to quickly track down the status of invoices, payments, and other vendor account transactions. Vendor account displays and standard reports give you the ability to do this. Check management is another important function, and the check register (Transaction FCHN) is a one-stop shop for check information.

In addition to covering the topics of standard AP reports and transactions to display AP data, this chapter covered two ways to display financial information directly from tables. The first is using Transaction SE11, which allows you to display the table and its contents. The second way is using Transaction SE16, which takes you directly into table contents.

Account maintenance is the name of the game in AP. The tools discussed in this chapter provide you with the ability to answer inquiries, adjust vendor account balances, and perform account maintenance. AP isn't a static event, and you need programs at your disposal to handle inquiries and account maintenance.

This concludes our discussions of AP. In the next chapter, we look at the Accounts Receivable (AR) module and AR processes.

Chapter 9
Accounts Receivable Processes

In this chapter, we discuss Accounts Receivable (AR) business processes and integration with the Sales and Distribution (SD) module through the order-to-cash business process.

The purpose of the Accounts Receivable (AR) module is to manage customer accounts and incoming payments. From a financial perspective, this is a critical part of the business—some would argue the most important part—because without customers and revenue, there is no business.

In many ways, this argument holds true. The sustainability of a company depends on a solid business model and revenue generation. This doesn't mean that you should ignore other aspects of business operations. However, revenue is necessary to build and sustain a business and is fundamental to profitability.

The AR module includes several business processes, such as customer invoices, incoming payments, credit management, and dunning. These business functions are all important, but they aren't the focus of this chapter. For more details on AR subprocesses, see Chapter 10. The objective of this chapter is to focus on the order-to-cash business process, which consists of the following steps:

1. Create a sales order (SO).
2. Create an outbound delivery.
3. Bill the customer.
4. Manage receivables.
5. Receive payment.

As we explore the order-to-cash process in detail, we cover two distinct business functions:

- **Sales**
  Sales involves customer interaction that ultimately results in a commitment from customers via a purchase order (PO) to buy goods or services from your company. When the PO is received by your company, a SO is created in your SAP system using the Sales and Distribution (SD) module.
- **AR management**
  AR management is the operational management of customer accounts and outstanding receivables. This accounting function involves maintaining customer accounts, monitoring credit, collections management, customer service, and reporting.

Together, sales and AR management influence revenue forecasts, profitability, cash flow, human capital management, and budgeting.

Now that you understand the basics, let's begin to discuss the order-to-cash process in detail. SAP business processes often consist of steps that are cross-modular, and the order-to-cash process is a great example of the integration between finance and logistics. This process is the focus of this chapter, specifically in demonstrating the integration between the SD module and AR.

There are many transactions in SD, and we won't attempt to discuss them all in detail in this chapter. Instead, the intention is to provide you with enough knowledge to understand the basic integration of AR and SD.

It's important for accountants and financial managers to understand the dependencies AR has with SD; this knowledge will serve you well in better performing certain functions, such as financial close.

We'll start by considering the frontend of the order-to-cash process before moving on to direct invoices, account maintenance, and exceptions.

9.1 Logistics

The order-to-cash process begins in SD, which is a component of Logistics. Logistics functionality in SAP covers a broad spectrum of capabilities and SAP modules. Some of the modules in Logistics include SD, Material Management (MM), Production, Plant Maintenance (PM), and Quality Management (QM), as listed in Figure 9.1.

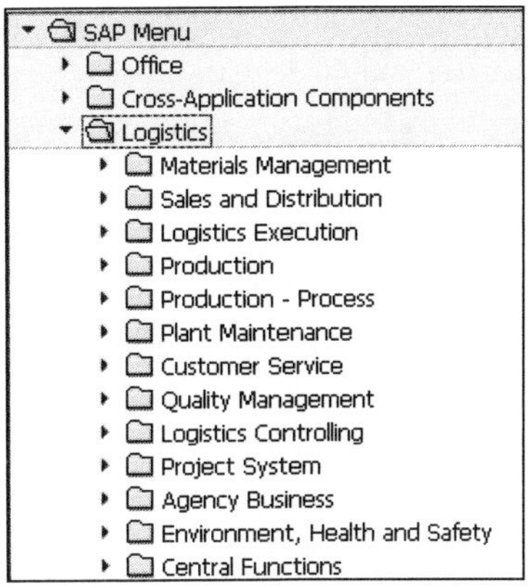

Figure 9.1 Logistics Application Menu

Within the SD module, there are also numerous capabilities. As you can see in Figure 9.2, the capabilities that exist in SD include **Sales Support**, **Sales**, **Shipping and Transportation**, **Billing**, and more.

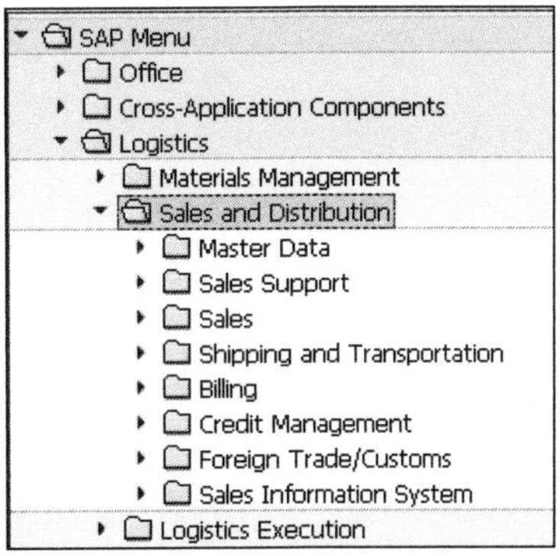

Figure 9.2 Sales and Distribution Application Menu Path

In this chapter, our discussions are limited to those portions of SD relevant to the sale, delivery, and billing of goods or services—specifically, transactions in SD-Sales and SD-Billing.

Sometimes, as finance and accounting professionals, we have a tendency to think that revenue just shows up at our doorstep, and all we have to do is tend to the accounting and customer service aspects of it. In reality, much occurs at the frontend of the order-to-cash process. For example, there are many aspects to the customer relationship side of revenue management. Some challenges include incorrect shipments of goods, shipping damaging goods, returns, and collection disputes. The point is that AR management is a dynamic function, and understanding the moving parts is key to knowing how to manage AR overall. Furthermore, to effectively manage sales accounting, you need a complete understanding of the order-to-cash process and the integration between SD and AR.

Let's start at the beginning. A customer sale is the starting point of the order-to-cash business process and takes the form of the sales order (SO) mentioned previously. SOs are handled in the portion of Logistics referred to as SD-Sales, which is where transactions exist for sales inquiries, quotations, scheduling agreements, contracts, and more. SD-Sales is also where outbound deliveries are created. The application menu path **Logistics • Sales and Distribution • Sales** for SD-Sales is shown in Figure 9.3.

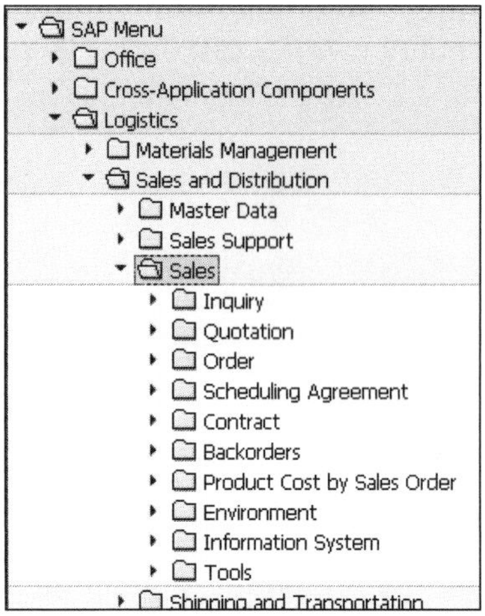

Figure 9.3 SD-Sales Application Menu Path

Note

The setup and configuration of SD is more complex than AR. It requires special expertise in areas such as pricing. Therefore, your company should ensure it has specialized SD expertise in house.

In the following sections, we'll discuss steps in the order-to-cash process, starting with the creation of an SO.

9.1.1 Sales Orders

According to SAP, an SO is a request from a customer to a company to deliver a defined quantity of products or provide a service at a certain time. The SO is typically considered a contractual agreement between a buyer and seller to deliver goods or services of a particular price and quantity by a set date.

There is a lot of complexity behind the creation of a SO, which is beyond the scope of this book. Keep in mind that companies have entire customer service departments whose job is to create SOs all day. This process involves taking customer orders over the phone or electronically, manually entering SOs, and handling customer inquiries. The point is that creating SOs is a specialized function that requires knowledge of customers, products, pricing, and the sales organization.

The job of finance and accounting is to have a basic understanding of the sales process and to know when and how it affects accounting. Furthermore, it's important to communicate with sales and customer service on questions of revenue recognition, status of orders, and billing.

The intent of this book isn't to teach you how to create SOs or other Logistics transactions. To obtain an understanding of the integration between SD and AR in the order-to-cash process, displaying Logistics documents will suffice. For purposes of our discussion, you should know that SOs contain pricing information, materials and quantities, shipping methods, and much more.

The transactions used for SOs are as follows:

- Transaction VA01 Create Sales Order
- Transaction VA02 Change Sales Order
- Transaction VA03 Display Sales Order

Figure 9.4 shows an example SO displayed using Transaction VA03. An SO contains a header and several tabs, and the bottom section shows all SO line items and line item tabs. To an accountant, the complexity of SOs can seem overwhelming. What's most important for you is to understand the key pieces of information that impact the financials. Note that the SO itself doesn't update accounting until subsequent steps are performed; the primary impact to accounting occurs when an SD billing document is created. This billing function also produces an open receivable in the customer's account in AR.

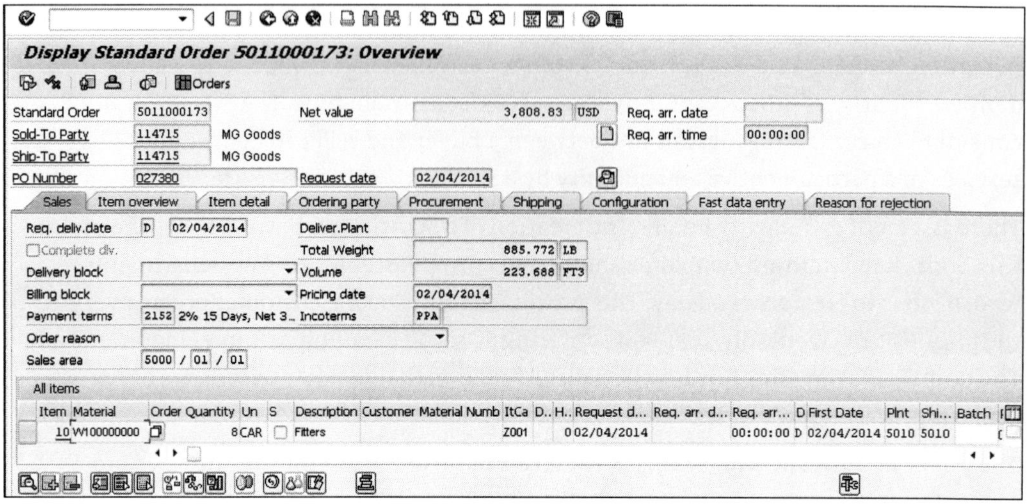

Figure 9.4 Display Sales Order

9.1.2 Outbound Deliveries

After an SO has been created, the next step is to deliver the goods or services. This is referred to as a *goods issue* and results in an inventory posting in accounting.

A user creates an outbound delivery using Transaction VL01N, referencing the SO. When an outbound delivery is created, the SO will display an outbound delivery document number in **Document Flow** (Figure 9.5).

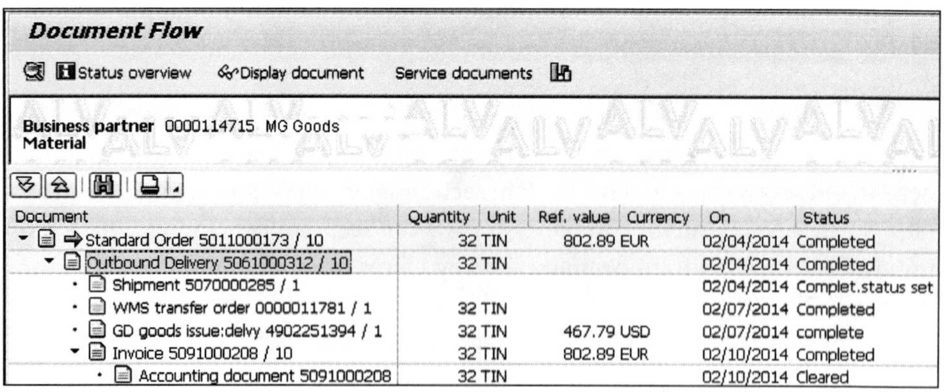

Figure 9.5 Outbound Delivery in Document Flow

Click on the outbound delivery document number and then the **Display document** button to enter the outbound delivery document (Figure 9.6). Note that the outbound delivery document number highlighted in Figure 9.5 is the same as the outbound delivery document number shown in the header of Figure 9.6.

Figure 9.6 Display Outbound Delivery Document

In Figure 9.6, tabs exist for several logistical functions relevant to the selection of goods, shipping, and transport: **Picking**, **Loading**, and **Transport**. One other tab of particular importance to Financial Accounting (FI) is **Goods Movement Data**. Movement of goods reduces inventory and produces a financial document. This is one of the key integration points between SD and FI.

9.1.3 Billing Documents

Following outbound delivery, the next step is the creation of a customer billing document. In accounting, the term *bill* is synonymous with *invoice*. An SD billing document is created in either SD-Sales or SD-Billing using Transaction VF01. When a customer bill is created in SD, it always references an SO. See the example billing document in Figure 9.7.

An SD billing document has a unique feature: Once created, it doesn't automatically transfer information to accounting. To transfer information, use Transaction VF02, and choose **Billing document • ReleaseToAccounting.** Once released, **ReleaseToAccounting** will be grayed out, indicating this step has already been completed.

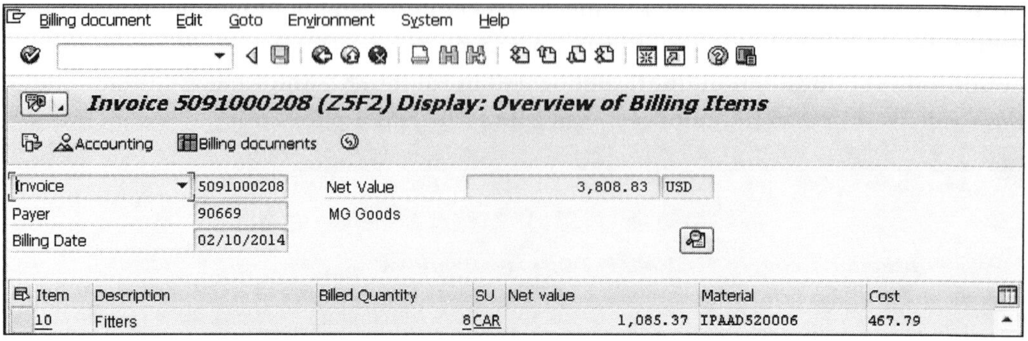

Figure 9.7 Display Billing Document Screen

After outbound delivery items have been released to accounting, click the **Accounting** button in Transaction VF02 or Transaction VF03 to view the AR invoice.

9.1.4 Automatic Creation of Accounting Invoice

When a billing document has been posted, as shown in Section 9.1.3, a corresponding AR invoice is automatically created after the bill has been released to accounting. At the end of the bill creation process, the billing document created using Transaction VF01 creates two documents: an SD invoice (i.e., a bill) and an AR invoice. Things become a little tricky here. Both documents can have the same document number and typically do for many SAP customers. Let's take a look using the example shown earlier in Figure 9.7.

Within **Document Flow** in Transaction VF03, you can see both the SD invoice number (i.e., billing document) and the accounting document invoice number (Figure 9.8).

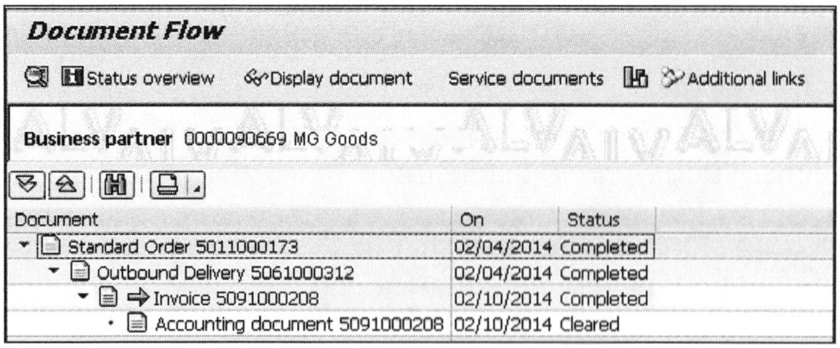

Figure 9.8 Transaction VF03 Display Document Flow

View the invoice document in AR by clicking the accounting document number and then the **Display document** button. You'll see the open receivable created in AR and awaiting payment receipt (Figure 9.9).

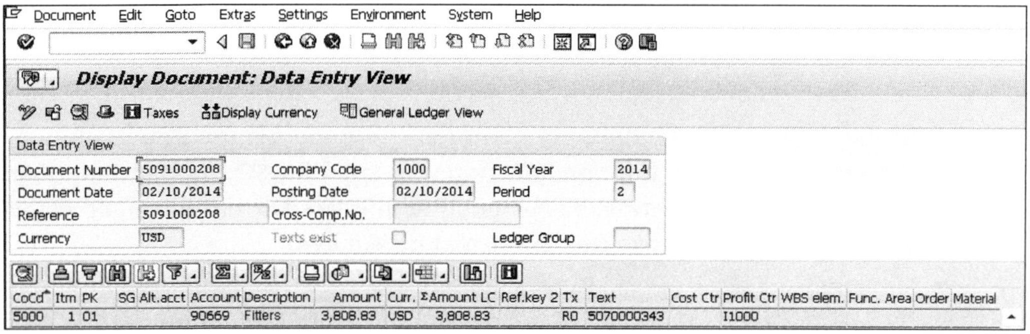

Figure 9.9 Display Acccounts Receivable Invoice Document

Now that you've learned about the frontend of the order-to-cash business process, let's discuss the creation of a direct invoice in the AR module next. It's important to understand that accounting integration from SD to AR is a one-way street, meaning that updates to accounting documents can flow from SD to AR but not from AR to SD.

9.2 Direct Invoices

Direct invoices is often used to refer to AR invoices created using Transaction FB70. These are AR invoices created directly in the AR module, independent of SD-Sales and the creation of billing documents.

There are a few distinguishing features of direct invoices. First, they have no corresponding SD billing document. SD billing documents are only created using Transaction VF01, either in SD-Sales or SD-Billing. Another difference is that the standard document type for direct AR invoices is DR, whereas those from SD are document type RV. Using Transaction FBL5N, you can therefore distinguish direct invoices from those transferred from SD. The document number ranges are also different because number ranges are assigned to document types.

When do you use direct invoices? There are several different scenarios that are applicable, as follows:

- **Outside sales ordering system**
  It would be nice to think that every company takes advantage of the full integration that SAP has to offer, but this isn't always the case. Sometimes, a company will use a sales ordering system outside of SAP. It could be that this system was already in place when SAP was implemented, and the decision was made to keep it. In a situation like this, management may have decided to keep the sales ordering system because the sales force and customer service representatives were already trained on it. The cost of transitioning to SD may have been another deciding factor.

  Whatever the reason, if a non-SAP system is used for SO management, then accounting data for receivables may simply be interfaced to the AR module. In this situation, some direct invoicing in SAP may be required.
- **No SO exists**
  It's a best practice to create an SO for any sale. However, sometimes one size does not fit all. For various reasons, a company may decide not to create SOs for all sales. There are several factors that come into play, including lines of business, size of the company, and industry. Moreover, for small or one-time purchases, a company may decide that creating an SO is neither necessary nor worth the effort. In such situations, a company may decide to create invoices directly in AR instead.
- **Miscellaneous receivables**
  Business models have become very creative over the years. Although the majority of businesses generate revenue by providing goods, there are a lot of service-based business models that don't require shipping and inventory movement. A collection agency is a good example. Other examples include the collection of a service fee, fines, tax, or subscription fees. For some business models, it makes more sense to create direct invoices and fully manage receivables in the AR module.

For more information on direct AR invoices, see Chapter 10, Section 10.1.1.

Now that you've learned about AR invoices, let's discuss customer account maintenance and payment receipt.

9.3 Customer Account Maintenance and Incoming Payments

Within an accounting department, there is typically a group responsible for customer account maintenance. One metric the AR department is responsible for is the days sales outstanding (DSO). DSO is a measure of the average number of days it takes a company to collect revenue after a sale has been made. DSO is a key performance indicator (KPI) that is monitored at the C-Suite of a company.

Keeping DSO at acceptable levels involves several moving parts, such as monitoring customer accounts through account statements, dunning, credit management, and more. Processes need to be in place for collecting on overdue accounts, establishing customer credit ratings, and setting payment terms.

Regarding terms of payment, it's important to establish favorable payment terms with customers. Usually there are standards such as *net 30*. However, important customers often demand payment terms that are more favorable to them and their cash flow. Balancing this aspect of the business can be tricky. Many companies offer payment terms with discounts that reward early payment. This all plays into cash management and liquidity forecasting. The quicker you receive payment from your customers, the better the health of the business.

In addition, the form of payment and your ability to process payments quickly make a big difference. Most companies have lockboxes to centrally process incoming check payments quickly. In addition, receiving payment electronically (e.g., direct deposit) reduces processing costs and makes the funds available quicker.

There are a couple ways to post incoming payments electronically in SAP. The first is a *lockbox*, that is, a post office box accessible by your bank. Your customers send their payments to the post office box, and then the bank collects and processes these payments directly and deposits them into your bank account. You can obtain an electronic file from your bank to process lockbox transactions in SAP. A more detailed look at the lockbox is beyond the scope of this book, but it's an important concept to understand.

Your company can also receive an electronic bank statement (EBS) from your bank and automatically clear customer invoices in SAP. For further details on EBS, see Chapter 15. This method is useful on accounting for electronic payments (e.g., ACH, wire transfers).

Finally, you can create incoming payments manually in AR. Whether an AR invoice is created as a follow-on document from SD or created as a direct invoice using Transaction FB70, the next step in the order-to-cash process is to receive payment from the customer.

Incoming payments are created in AR using Transaction F-28. This transaction is covered in detail in Chapter 10, Section 10.6. When an incoming payment is posted, a clearing document is created, and the status of the AR invoice changes from **Open** to **Cleared**.

9.4 Process Exceptions

Throughout the order-to-cash business process, exceptions happen. Goods sent to your customers may arrive damaged and need to be returned. Invoices may contain an incorrect amount or quantity. Documents may be posted with incorrect information. Although we won't attempt to identify all the possible exceptions that can occur, we'll discuss three transactions in the AR module that are frequently used to correct errors and make adjustments: credit memos, document reversals, and changing documents.

9.4.1 Credit Memos

A *credit memo* is exactly what it appears to be: a credit back to a customer's account. A credit memo may be created because of a defective good, overcharge, or other adjustment needed to a customer's account. Credit memos net against open receivable amounts at the time of payment receipt to properly net the balance in the customer account.

There are two ways to create credit memos. The first is in the AR module using Transaction FB75. This is covered in detail in Chapter 10, Section 10.2. Transaction FB75 should be used for general customer account credit adjustments not specific to sales transactions originating in SD. When you need to issue a credit memo for a transaction originating in SD, the best approach is to create it using Transaction VF01.

Figure 9.10 shows the Transaction VF01 **Billing Type** dropdown box, with the **Credit Memo** option highlighted.

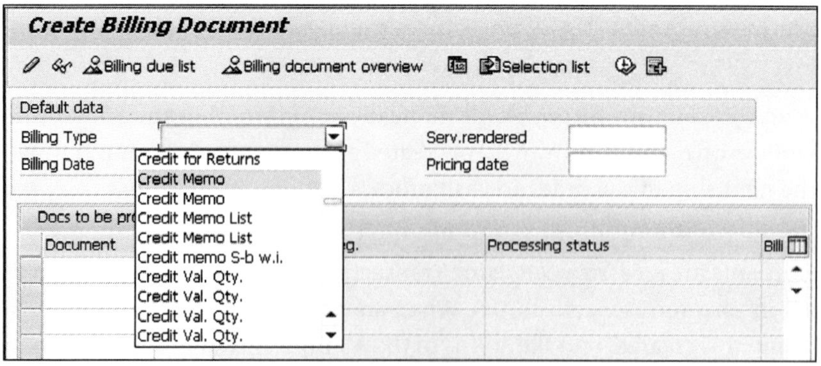

Figure 9.10 Transaction VF01 Billing Type Dropdown List

After you create a credit memo, the SO referenced in the credit memo displays the credit memo document number in **Document Flow**. A credit memo originating in SD also transfers to FI so that the customer account reflects the credit. These credit memos can be seen in AR using Transaction FBL5N.

As noted earlier, credit memos can be created both in AR and SD. Remember, SD and AR integration is a one-way street: financial information flows from SD to AR, but not vice versa. Therefore, if the credit memo needs to tie back to an SO, create the credit memo in SD, not in AR.

Next, let's discuss document reversals.

9.4.2 Document Reversals

An SAP best practice is to reverse documents in the module in which they originate. This concept is important for keeping modules in sync.

In Chapter 10, Section 10.4, we discuss resetting and reversing AR documents in detail. However, for documents originating in SD, document reversals should be made in that module rather than reversing follow-on documents in AR.

In this chapter, we discuss several SD transactions. The first, Transaction VA01, creates a SO. To cancel an SO, use Transaction VA02. To delete an SO using Transaction VA02, choose the **Delete** option from the **Sales document** dropdown menu (Figure 9.11). You can only do so if no subsequent documents have been created.

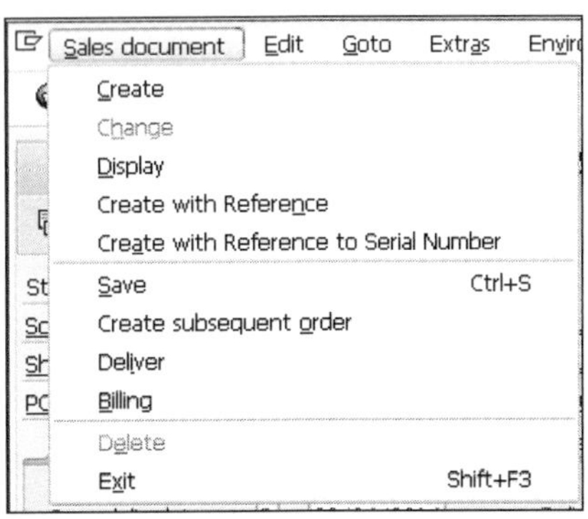

Figure 9.11 Transaction VA02 Dropdown Selection Menu

Keep in mind that SOs can be large documents with numerous line items. Just because there is an error or issue in one line of the SO doesn't mean that you must cancel the entire SO. SO line items can be changed, deleted, and inserted, so before canceling an entire SO due to a line item issue, make sure you attempt to fix the document first. If a customer truly cancels an order, then the delete option is applicable.

The next SD transaction discussed is an outbound delivery that is created using Transaction VL01N in SD-Sales. Changes to the outbound delivery document cancel or modify all subsequent documents, ensuring that the outbound delivery document shows the current status of the entire outbound delivery. To reverse or cancel the goods movement portion of an outbound delivery, use Transaction VL09.

The third SD transaction discussed in this chapter is the billing document. To cancel the billing document, use Transaction VF11. In this way, the AR invoice is also reversed, and the current status is correctly updated for the SO. Remember, reversing a document in the module of origin also triggers a reversal in FI. You can validate this in an AR customer accounting using Transaction FBL5N.

9.4.3 Change Posted Documents

As noted previously, SAP best practice is to change posted documents in the module in which they originated. However, there is an exception to this rule with the AR invoice, which we'll discuss toward the end of this section. See Chapter 10, Section 10.5, for more on changing AR documents.

Transaction VA01 is used for the creation of an SO. SOs can be canceled, and SO line items can be deleted or added. The transaction to change an SO is Transaction VA02. Any change to an SO should be made by the office responsible for entering and managing SOs in the system.

Note

An accountant or accounting supervisor may request that a change to an SO be made but should not make the change directly unless it's part of his job responsibilities and he has been trained. Before making any change, it's important to understand the dependency on subsequent documents and the impact any change will have to the statuses of an SO.

Another important SD transaction is outbound delivery. To make a subsequent adjustment to an outbound delivery, you can use Transaction VL02N. Keep in mind that outbound deliveries involve several other steps related to transportation and shipping. Other steps or transactions may be needed to perform the changes you require.

The last transaction discussed is the billing document, which is created using Transaction VF01. To change the billing document, use Transaction VF02. In this transaction, you release billing information to accounting. Certain accounting information can't be changed in SD after this release has taken place. In the case of an AR invoice, you need to make any change directly in the AR invoice that was created as a follow-on document when the release to FI took place. The FI transaction to change the AR invoice is Transaction FB02.

One of the more commonly changed fields in an AR invoice is the **Baseline Date**. You may also need to change the payment terms or the payment method assigned in the document. These are simple changes that cause no reconciliation problems between AR and SD.

Throughout this chapter, we've mentioned numerous times that SD to AR is a one-way street as far as integration and the exchange of financial information. It's important to keep the integrated documents in sync as much as possible. Moreover, keeping all documents centrally tied to the SO makes life a lot easier. However, we must stress the different business functions between SD and AR because these differences are relevant to changing customer invoices directly in AR.

In the order-to-cash business process, the frontend steps are executed in SD. When a customer bill is created and transferred to accounting, a customer invoice is created in AR. From this point on, customer account maintenance and collections are the responsibility of accounting.

There are times when it's necessary for an AR clerk to change an invoice in AR (i.e., document type RV) that was created as a follow-on document from SD. Reviewing the typical responsibilities of an AR department is helpful in framing the reasons why such a change may be necessary. AR departments may be responsible for the following tasks:

- Keeping DSO at acceptable levels
- Monitoring customer accounts
- Dunning
- Managing credit
- Collecting on overdue accounts
- Establishing customer credit ratings

- Setting payment terms
- Processing incoming payments
- Blocking customer accounts

If the AR department needs to make a change to a posted document to fulfill these responsibilities, and the change can't be made in SD, then the department will make the changes necessary in the AR module.

9.5 Summary

In this chapter, we focused on AR business processes and integration with the SD module. The steps that make up the sale of goods and services aren't isolated to the AR module but rather reach back into transactions in the SD module. Sales functions originate in SD-Sales. The complete business process includes creating SOs, outbound deliveries, billing, and payment receipts. Together, these make up the order-to-cash process.

The significance of the order-to-cash process is that it begins with the receipt of a customer order via PO, and it ends with payment receipt from the customer. The process demonstrates integration between SD and FI, which is an essential link between Logistics and FI.

SD supports the business in taking customer orders, revenue recognition, goods movements, shipping and transportation, pricing, and more. It's important for any accountant, particularly AR clerks and supervisors, to have a base knowledge of SD and FI integration.

The first step in the sales process is a customer SO. After an order has been placed, the goods must be picked, packed, and shipped. These functions involve the creation of an outbound delivery document in SD, with several subsequent documents associated with it and displayed in **Document Flow**.

Following outbound delivery, the next step is the creation of a customer bill via Transaction VF01 in either SD-Sales or SD-Billing. The result is the creation of an SD billing document. After a billing document is released to accounting, a partner invoice is created in AR. This invoice in AR is referred to as a subsequent or follow-on document and is displayed in **Document Flow**.

It's an SAP best practice to change or reverse a document in the module in which it was created. Both SOs and outbound deliveries can be changed in SD, with limitations based on the subsequent steps already performed.

Transactions in both SD and FI make the order-to-cash process complete. In this chapter, you learned about each step in the process, integration points, and when and how to reverse or change documents.

This concludes the discussion of AR processes and integration with SD. In the next chapter, we'll discuss AR transactions in detail.

Chapter 10

Accounts Receivable Transactions

In this chapter, we cover Accounts (AR) transactions in detail. These transactions consist of line items that include a customer subledger entry. A customer invoice can be created directly in the AR module or as a part of a document chain created in the Sales and Distribution (SD) module through the order-to-cash business process.

This chapter covers Accounts Receivable (AR) transactions originating in the AR module. The most common of these is the entry of a customer invoice document using Transaction FB70. This chapter covers not only the creation of AR customer invoices but also associated AR functions, such as document display, change, reverse, park, and more.

The AR module serves to manage customer receivables and accounts for incoming payments. First, you create a customer invoice. Then, you receive payment and apply the amount received against an open invoice. However, this seemingly straightforward process can take many twists and turns. Posting credit memos and down payments received, clearing accounts, making document corrections, and reconciling balances are just some of the functions that need to be performed by accountants in the AR department.

This chapter begins by covering the basics of creating a customer invoice in the AR module. We then take a deep dive into each associated function.

Some of the transactions covered in this chapter, such as the creation of a customer invoice, are tasks you're likely to perform on a daily basis. Other transactions, such as document reversal, are executed less frequently. This chapter can be revisited as a reference point for less frequently used transactions and can provide you with an overall refresher on the AR module. Let's begin our discussion by looking at AR customer invoices.

10.1 Customer Invoices

This section covers the AR customer invoice creation process, which includes document entry, park, post, save as complete, and hold. It also covers the Transaction FB70 tree display, screen variants, account assignment templates, editing options, and post with reference—all of which provide valuable insights to help you be more productive and organized within the AR module.

To create a customer invoice in SAP using Transaction FB70, you must enter document header details (e.g., posting date) and at least one noncustomer line item that nets the document balance to zero. You may find that you can't complete a document while you're in the middle of processing it or that a field you need to enter is not present on the screen; this section gives you the tools you need to deal with these and other challenges and provides you with the knowledge to enter AR transactions more efficiently.

10.1.1 Document Entry

To create an AR customer invoice document, use Transaction FB70 or application menu path, **Accounting • Financial Accounting • Accounts Receivable • Document Entry • FB70 – Invoice**, as shown in Figure 10.1.

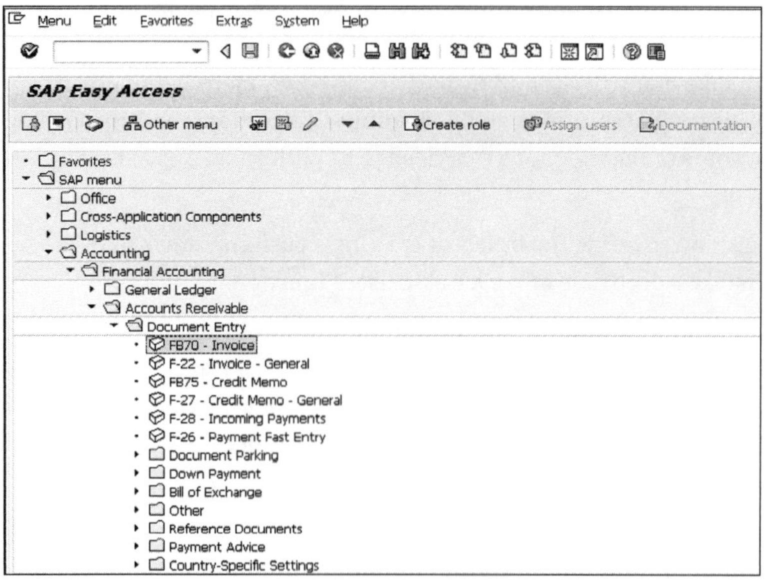

Figure 10.1 Transaction FB70 Application Menu Path

Double-click on **FB70 – Invoice** from the menu path, or enter "FB70" in the **Command** field (as shown in Figure 10.2) and press [Enter].

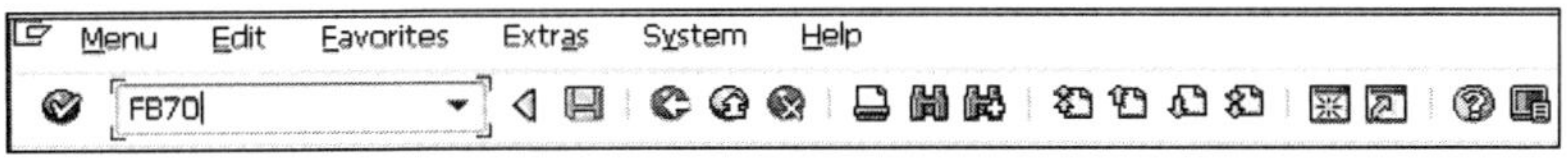

Figure 10.2 Entering "FB70" in the Command Field

The **Enter Customer Invoice** entry screen opens (Figure 10.3). The fields that appear on the header with prepopulated values may vary, depending on your system configuration and editing options. In this example, field values defaulted into the **Posting Date**, **Document Type**, currency, and **Company Code** fields, whereas field values were manually entered into the **Customer**, **Invoice date**, **Reference**, and **Amount** fields.

10

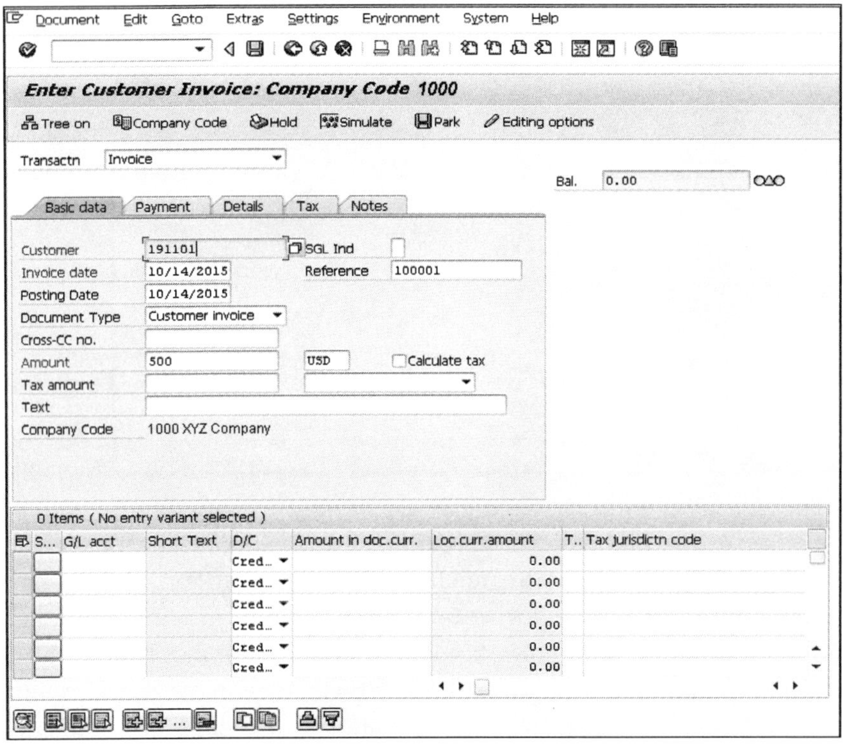

Figure 10.3 Enter Customer Invoice Entry Screen

The customer invoice **Reference** field can contain the document number of the customer or a different value. This field is used as a search criterion when displaying or changing documents. In addition, take special note of the **Invoice date** field. The **Invoice date** is the start date of the due date calculation. In other words, if the payment terms are net 30, the clock starts ticking based on the date in the **Invoice date** field, not the **Posting Date** field. After entering header details, the next step is to enter at least one line item, as shown in Figure 10.4.

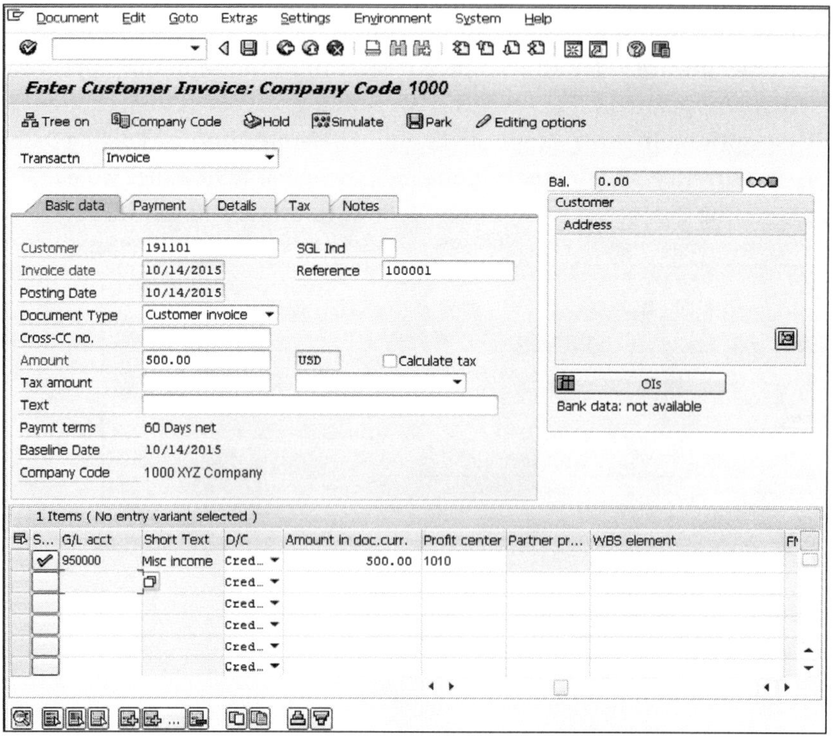

Figure 10.4 Enter Customer Invoice Screen with Line Item Entry

In Figure 10.4, the line item entered is a credit to a revenue account. For a revenue line item, you're required to enter values for the **G/L acct**, **D/C** (debit/credit indicator), and **Amount in doc.curr.** fields at a minimum. In addition, **Profit center** may be required if Profit Center Accounting (PCA) is activated in your system. We entered a profit center in this example. Your SAP system may have additional field entry requirements based on the configuration of your field status settings.

After entering document line items, click the **Simulate** button in the top center of the entry screen. This initiates simulation of the customer invoice posting logic to determine if the document can be properly posted. If the simulation is unsuccessful, an error message appears. If successful, the **Document Overview** screen appears, as shown in Figure 10.5.

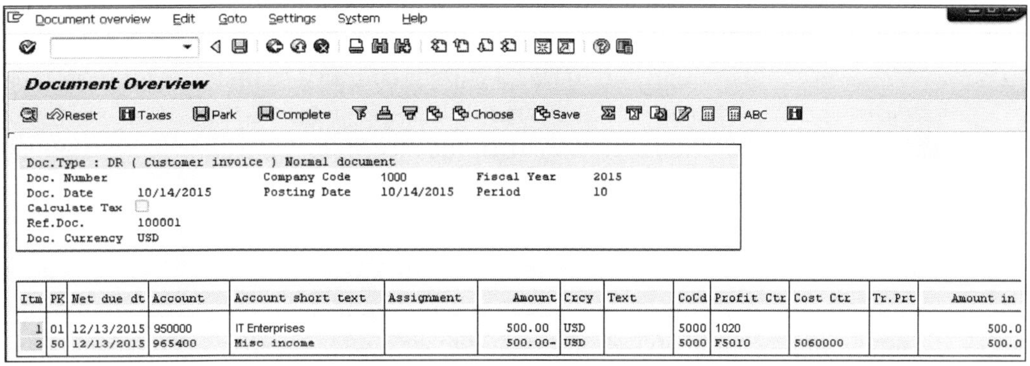

Figure 10.5 Document Overview Screen

After simulation is complete, click the **Post** icon to the right of the **Command** field in the upper-left corner of the screen. This will post the customer invoice, and a message appears with the new document number, as shown in Figure 10.6.

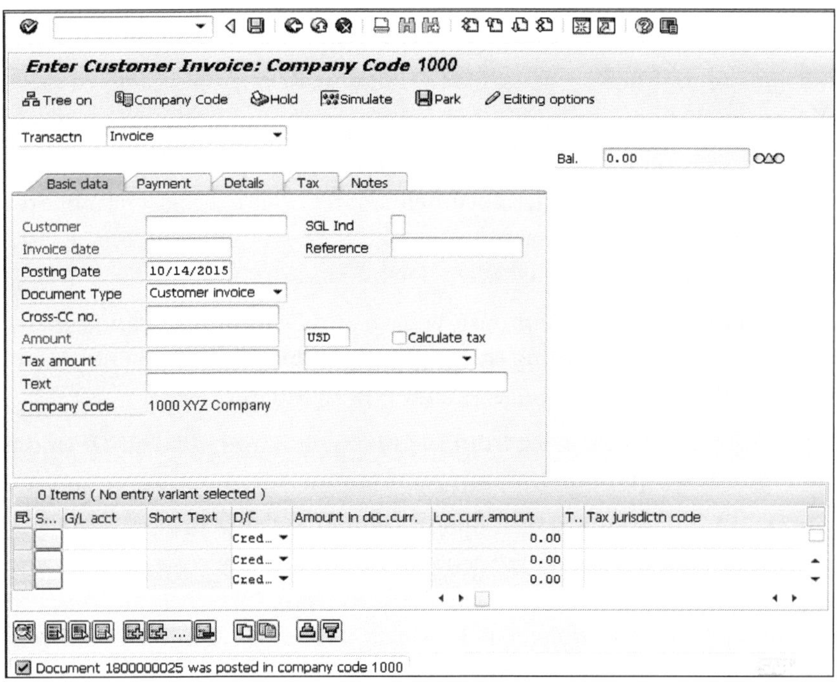

Figure 10.6 Document Posted Message

10.1.2 Post, Park, Save as Complete, and Hold

This section describes the different ways to create customer invoice documents: post, park, save as complete, and hold. All are universal concepts within Financial Accounting (FI) and therefore aren't unique to customer invoices and Transaction FB70; however, their discussion in this section is confined to their use for customer invoices. These functions work the same in General Ledger (G/L) and AP, so if you read Chapter 3 and Chapter 6, you'll see that the content in this section is very similar.

Post

Posting a customer invoice was covered in its entirety in Section 10.1.1. A posted document is a customer invoice that is considered complete, produces an accounting document number, and updates the customer account and G/L account balances.

After a customer document is posted, the only way to reverse its impact on the customer account and G/L account balances is to reverse the document. Reversing G/L documents is covered in Section 10.4.

Park

Document parking allows you to save a customer invoice document without impacting the customer account and G/L account balances. This may be necessary if the document is incomplete or if further edits, data validation, or document approval are required prior to posting.

Because parked documents are considered incomplete, they can be changed or deleted. When parked, these customer documents don't update transaction figures and account balances. Moreover, a parked document doesn't go through the extensive document entry checks performed when documents are posted.

To park a customer invoice document, use Transaction FV70 or application menu path, **Accounting • Financial Accounting • Accounts Receivable • Document Entry • Document Parking • FV70 – Park/Edit Invoice**, as shown in Figure 10.7.

Double-click **FV70 – Park/Edit Invoice** from the menu path, or enter "FV70" in the **Command** field (as shown in Figure 10.8) and press [Enter].

The **Park Customer Invoice** entry screen opens (Figure 10.9). The fields that default values into the document header vary depending on your system configuration and editing options. In this example, the **Customer, Invoice date, Reference**, and **Amount** fields were manually entered, whereas field values were defaulted for the **Posting Date, Invoice Date**, currency, and **Company Code** fields.

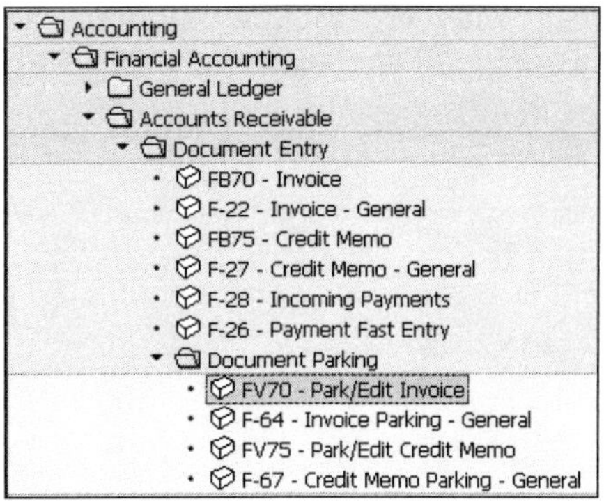

Figure 10.7 Transaction FV70 Application Menu Path

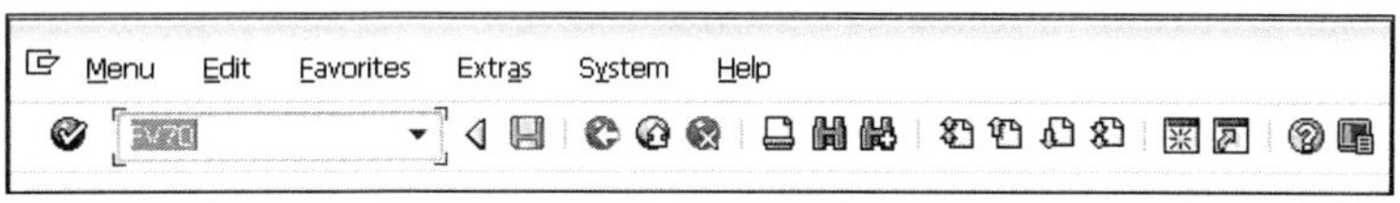

Figure 10.8 Entering "FV70" in the Command Field

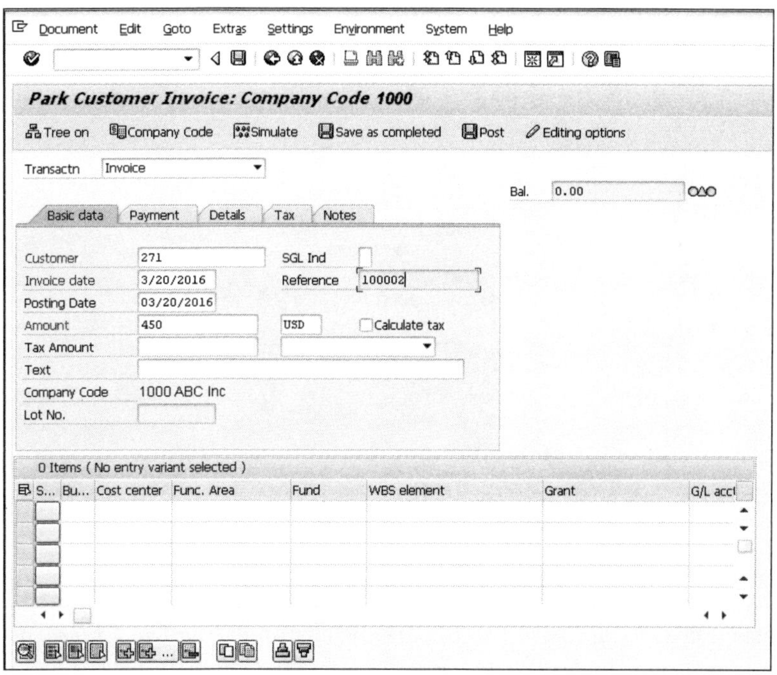

Figure 10.9 Park Customer Invoice Initial Screen

After inputting field values on the header screen, enter at least one line item, as shown in Figure 10.10.

Figure 10.10 Entry Screen with Line Items

After the line items are entered, click the **Park** icon to the right of the **Command** field in the upper-left portion of the screen to park the customer invoice. A message appears with the new parked document number, as shown in Figure 10.11.

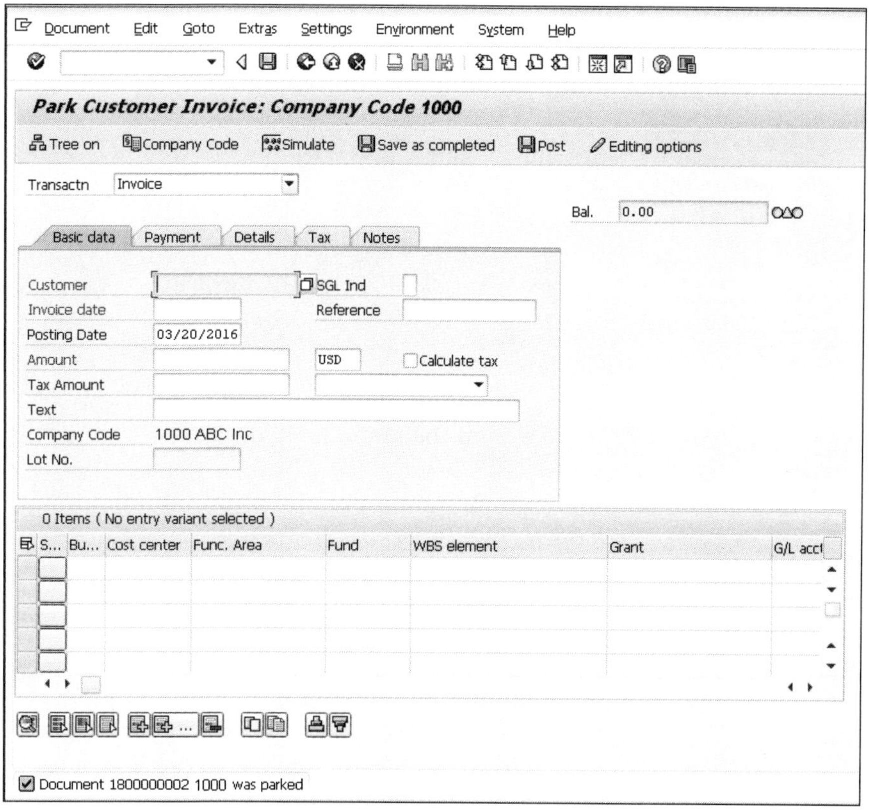

Figure 10.11 Document Parked Message

Save as Completed

The *save as completed* function is similar to document parking, but with some key distinctions. When you save a document as completed, the program goes through more extensive document check logic, just as if the document were being posted. Like parked documents, however, documents that are saved as completed can be edited and changed prior to posting.

Although the park and save as completed functions are similar, the latter should generally only be used when you're sure the document is accurate, complete, and only needs final approval before being posted.

To save a customer invoice as completed, use Transaction FV70 or application menu path, **Accounting • Financial Accounting • Accounts Receivable • Document Entry • Document Parking • FV70 – Park/Edit Invoice**, as shown in Figure 10.12.

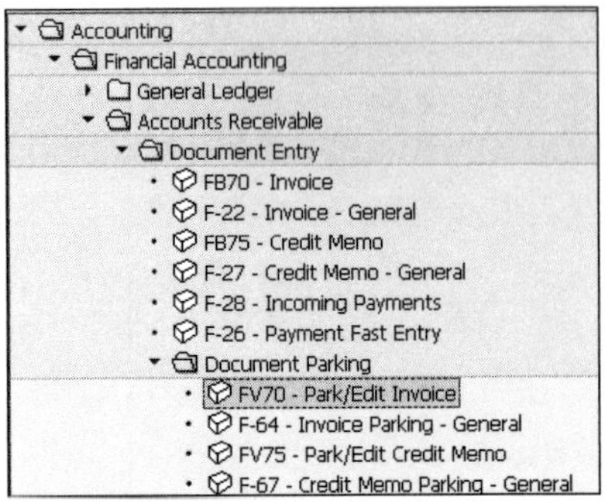

Figure 10.12 Transaction FV70 Application Menu Path

Double-click **FV70 – Park/Edit Invoice** from the menu path, or enter "FV70" in the **Command** field (Figure 10.13) and press Enter.

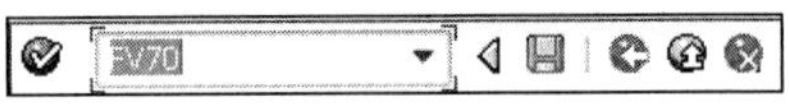

Figure 10.13 Entering "FV70" in the Command Field

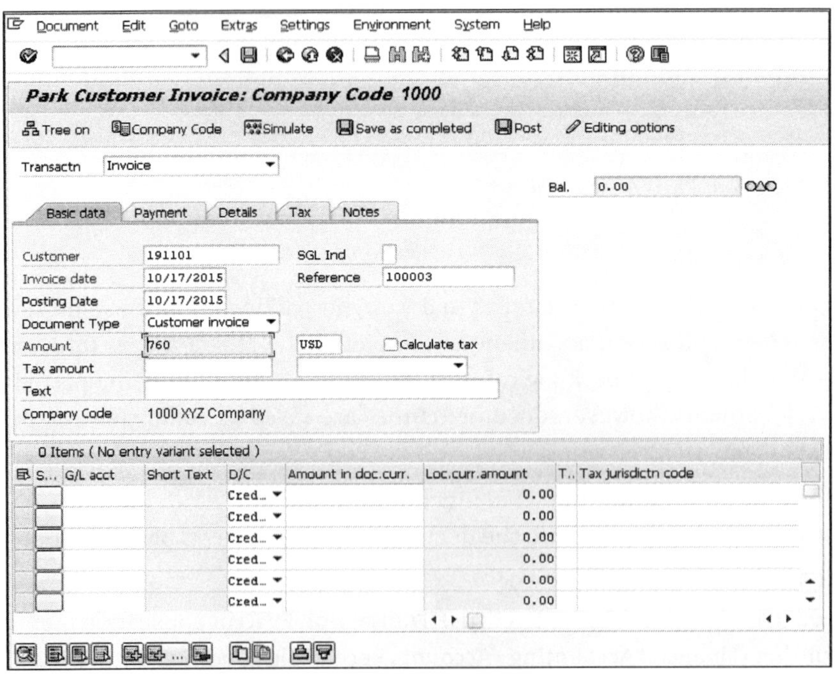

Figure 10.14 Entry Screen for Save as Complete Function

The **Park Customer Invoice** entry screen opens (Figure 10.14). The fields that appear on the header with prepopulated values may vary depending on your system configuration and editing options. In this example, the **Customer**, **Invoice date**, **Reference**, and **Amount** fields were manually entered, whereas field values were defaulted for the **Posting Date**, **Document Type**, currency, and **Company Code** fields.

After the **Park Customer Invoice** header screen is complete, enter at least one line item, as shown in Figure 10.15.

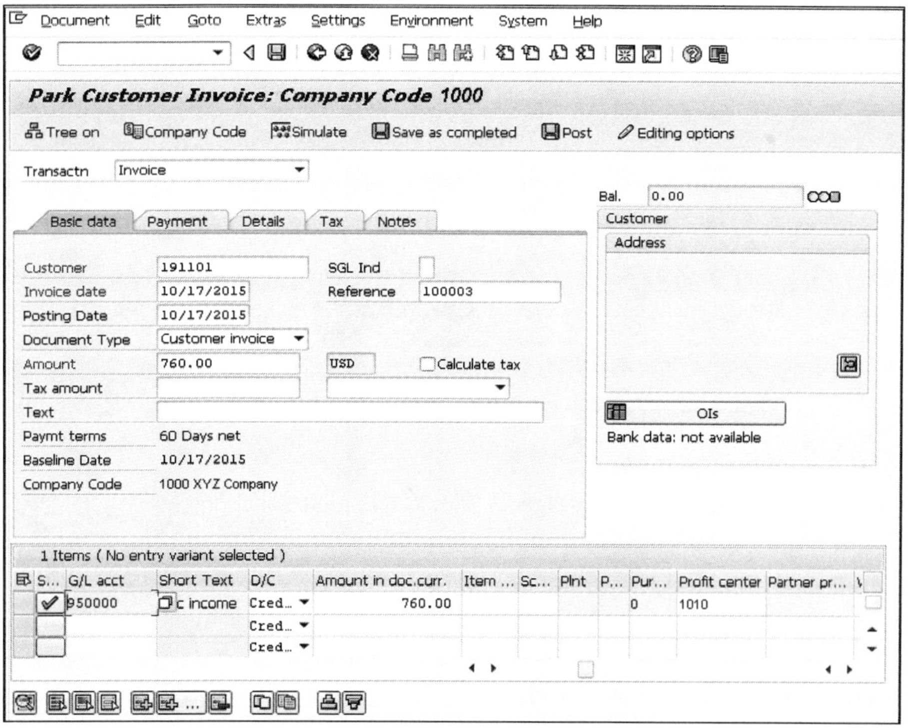

Figure 10.15 Line Item Entry for Save as Complete Function

After entering line items, click the **Save as completed** icon at the top-center portion of the screen to save the customer invoice as completed. A message appears with the new document number, as shown in Figure 10.16.

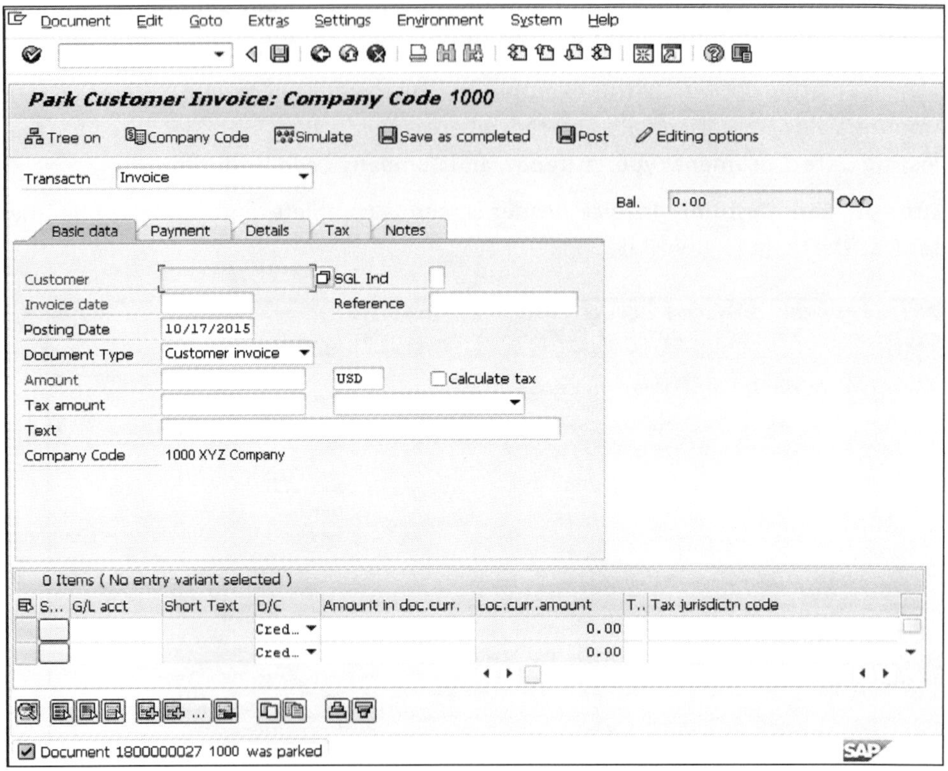

Figure 10.16 Document Created Message for Save as Complete Function

Hold

Document hold allows you to temporarily save your data. It's most useful when you're interrupted during document entry. Because held documents are temporary, they don't update AR and G/L transactions and balances. Furthermore, in subsequent processing, they can be edited, deleted, parked, or posted. Unlike post, park, and save as completed, the hold function produces no permanent document number until the document is parked or posted.

To hold an AR accounting document, use Transaction FB70 or application menu path, **Accounting • Financial Accounting • Accounts Receivable • Document Entry • FB70 – Invoice**, as shown in Figure 10.17.

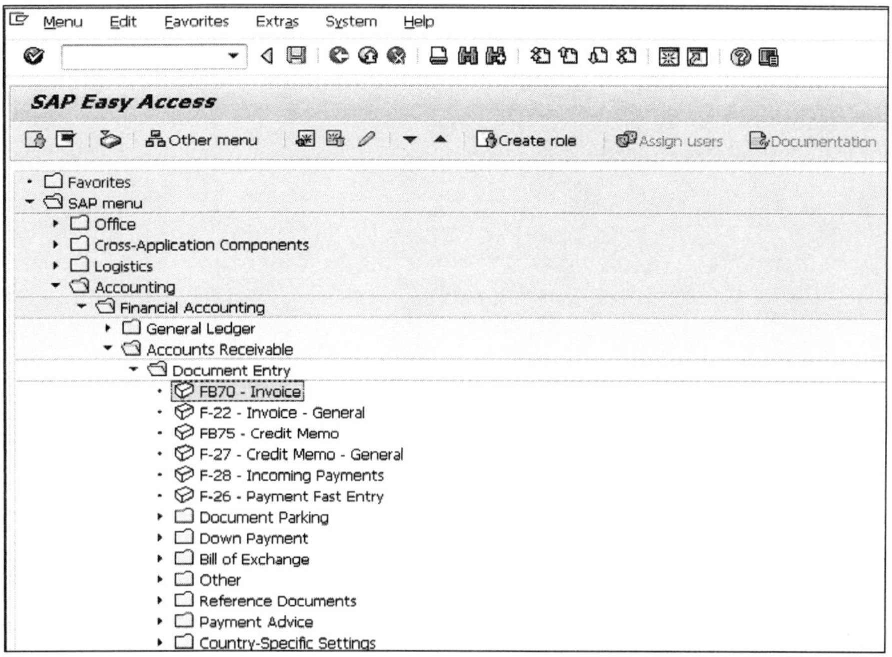

Figure 10.17 Transaction FB70 Application Menu Path

Double-click **FB70 – Invoice** from the menu path, or enter "FB70" in the **Command** field (Figure 10.18) and press [Enter].

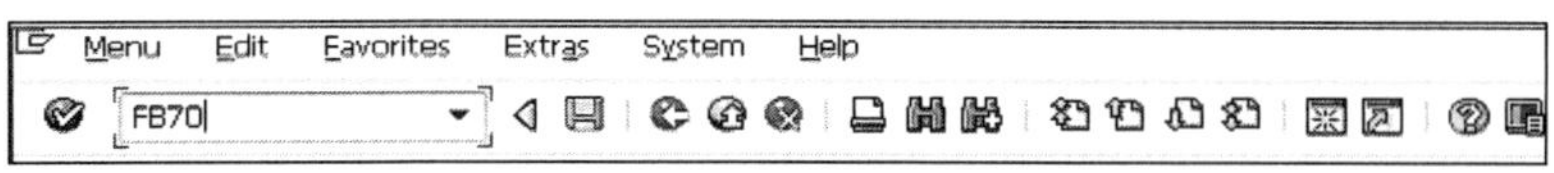

Figure 10.18 Entering "FB70" in the Command Field

At any point in Transaction FB70, you can use the hold function. You can do so regardless of how much or little information has been entered because no system checks take place when you hold an AR document.

In the example shown in Figure 10.19, the **Customer**, **Invoice date**, **Reference**, and **Amount** fields were manually entered, along with one partially complete line item. In the screen header, field values were prepopulated with values for the currency, **Posting Date**, **Document Type**, and **Company Code** fields.

At any point, the document can be held by pressing [F5] or selecting **Document • Hold** from the menu bar, as shown in Figure 10.20.

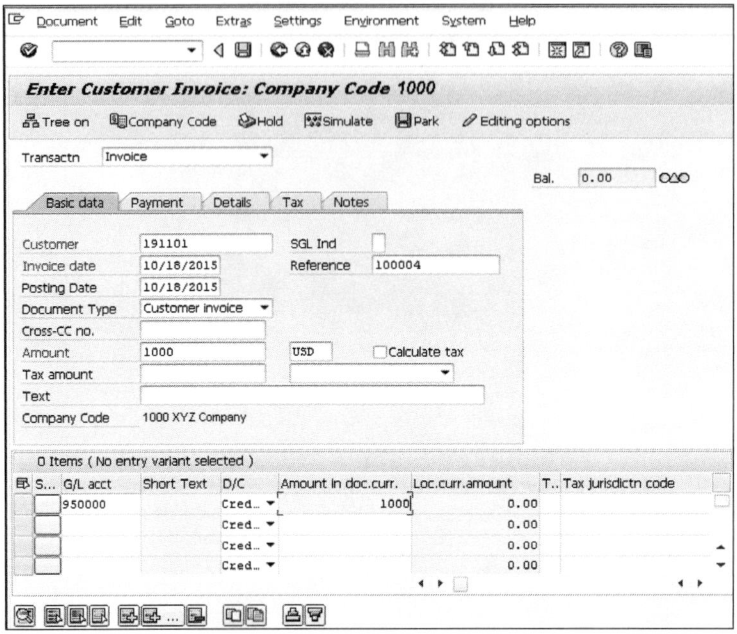

Figure 10.19 Entry Screen for Document Hold Function

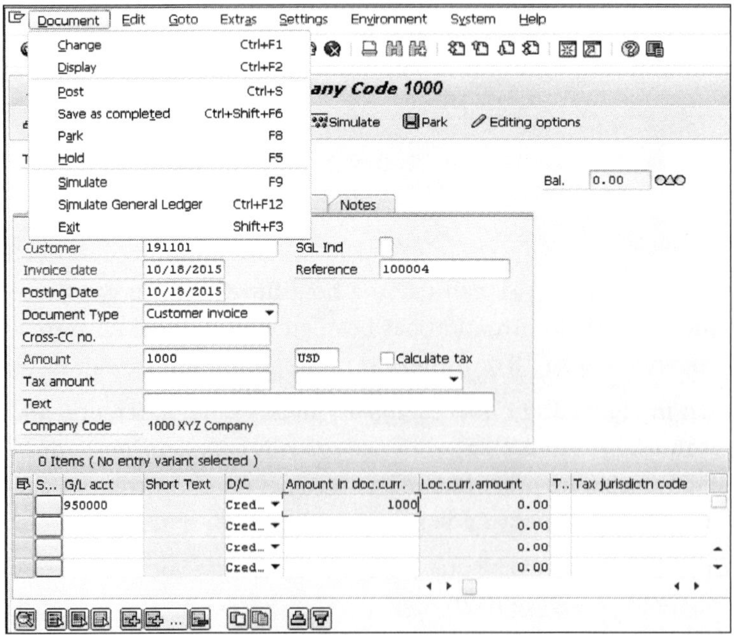

Figure 10.20 Document Hold Menu Choice

When you select **Document • Hold**, a dialog box opens (Figure 10.21) and prompts you to enter a temporary document number. This 10-character preliminary document number can contain numbers, letters, and special characters. This is a temporary document number, meaning that it's no longer valid when a permanent number is assigned, such as when the document is posted, parked, or saved as completed.

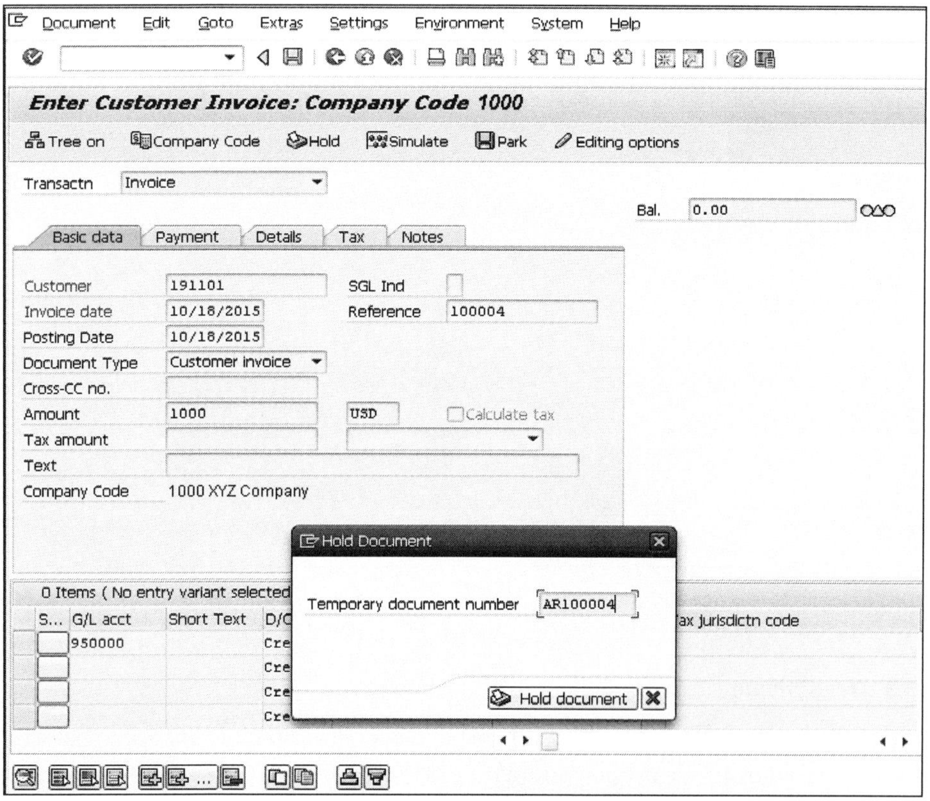

Figure 10.21 Temporary Document Number Dialog Box

After entering a temporary document number, press [Enter] or click on the **Hold document** button. A temporary accounting document is created, and a message appears with the held document number, as shown in Figure 10.22.

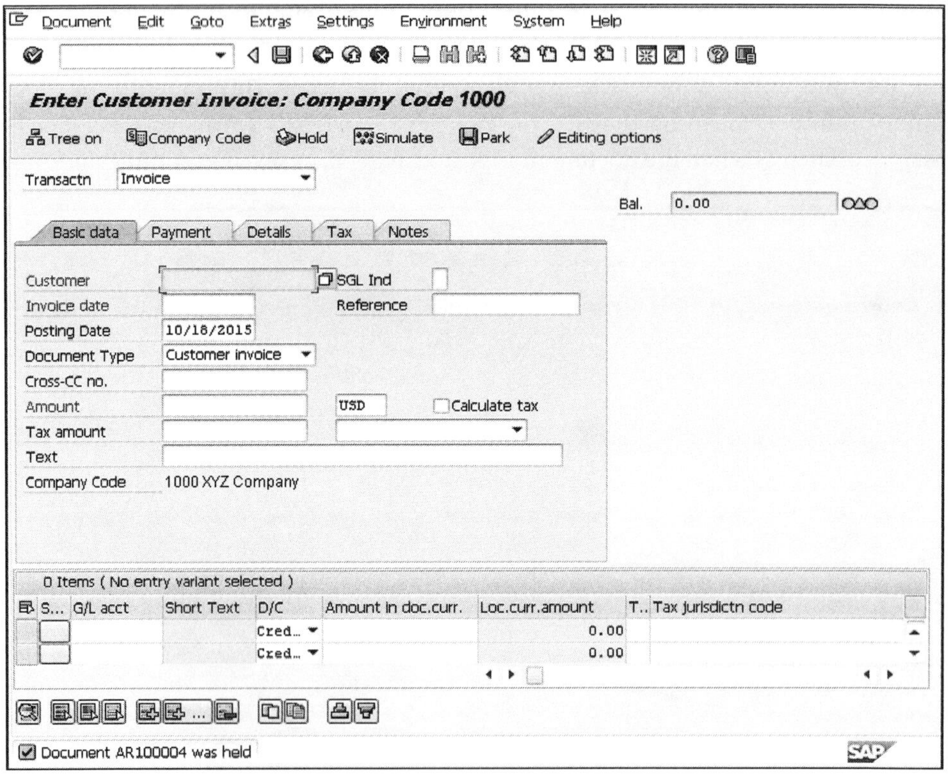

Figure 10.22 Document Held Message

10.1.3 Tree Display

The *tree display* provides an easy-to-use visual display for several functions that can also be accessed from the dropdown menu in Transaction FB70. The tree display is a universal concept, or shortcut, for accessing accounting documents and document entry tools in FI. In this section, we'll confine the discussion of the tree display to Transactions FB70 and FV70, but this capability can be used in some other FI transaction for which the tree display is available, such as Transaction FB50 and Transaction FB60.

The tree display is a toggle function, meaning that it can be turned on (i.e., made visible) or off (i.e., made invisible) with the click of a button or via a keyboard combination.

Figure 10.23 shows Transaction FB70 with the tree display on, visible as a panel on the left side of the transaction screen.

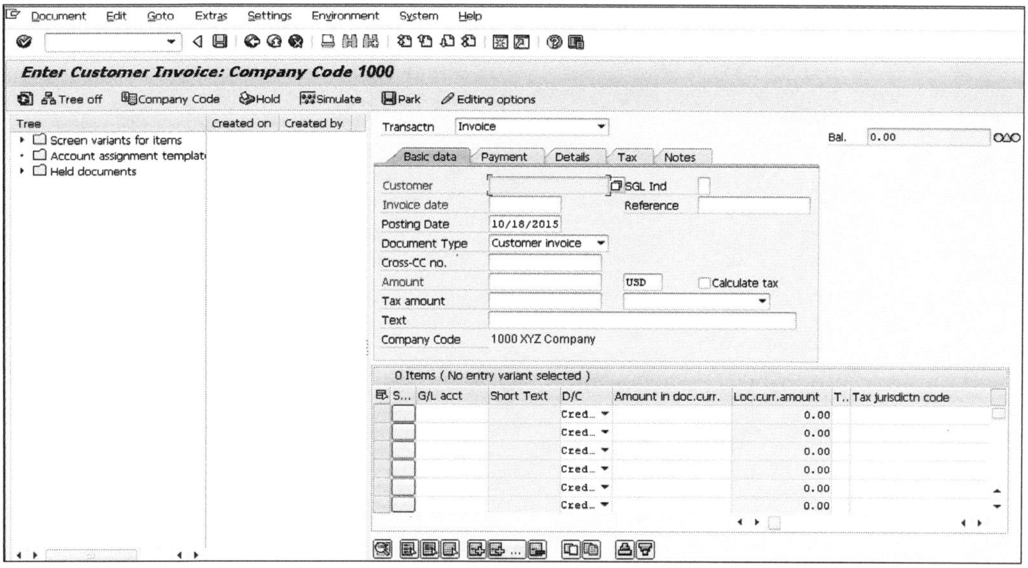

Figure 10.23 Enter Customer Invoice with Tree Display On

With the tree display on, you'll see a panel containing folders on the left. The folders that appear in the display vary by transaction code. In Transaction FB70, you'll see the following folders:

- **Screen variants for items**
- **Account assignment templates for items**
- **Held documents**

Screen variants and account assignment templates are covered in detail in Section 10.1.4.

In Section 10.1.2, we demonstrated how to hold a customer invoice document. You can view held documents in the tree display by clicking on the triangle to the left of the **Held documents** folder. This action opens the folder and displays all the held documents created by the user. By double-clicking on a held document in the tree display, the details appear in the **Enter Customer Invoice** entry screen, as shown in Figure 10.24. Once displayed, held document details can be edited, parked, or posted.

The tree display function in Transaction FV70 is the same as in Transaction FB70 and has the same toggle capability. Transaction FV70 with tree display on is shown in Figure 10.25.

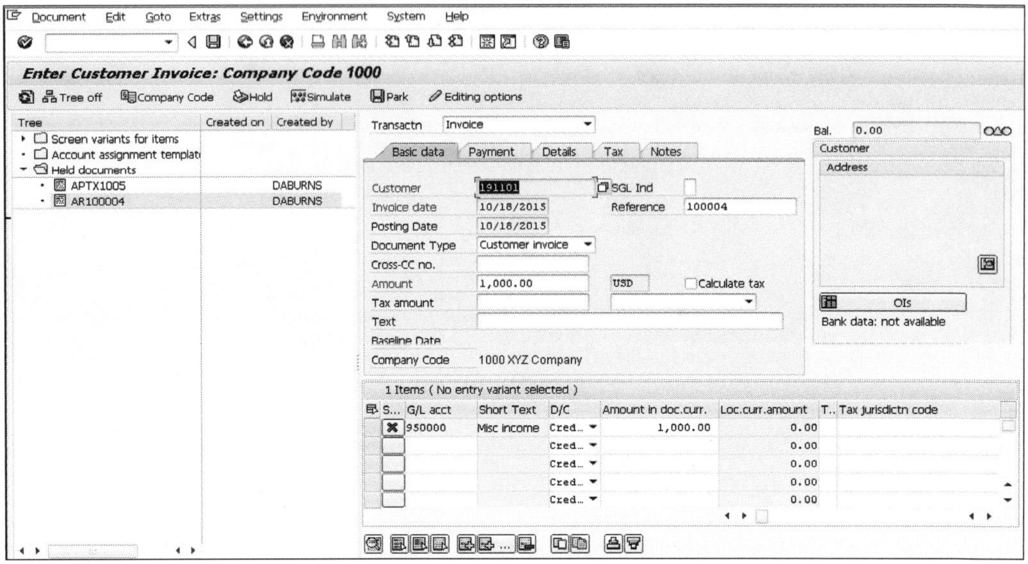

Figure 10.24 Held Documents with Tree Display On

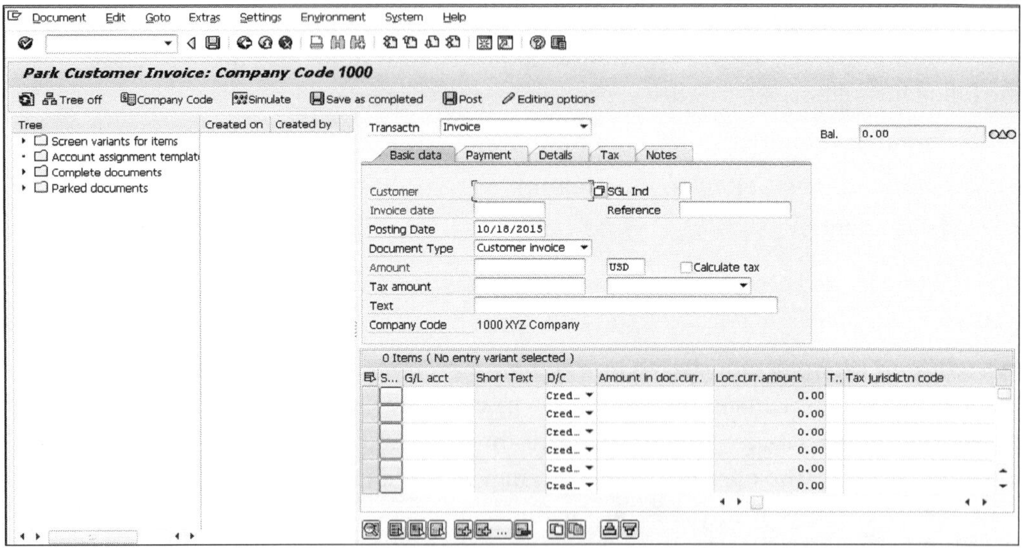

Figure 10.25 Transaction FV70 with Tree Display On

In Transaction FV70, you'll see the following folders:

- **Screen variants for items**
- **Account assignment templates for items**
- **Complete documents**
- **Parked documents**

In the Transaction FV70 tree display, folders for screen variants and account assignment templates appear at the top, as they did in Transaction FB70. However, folders for complete and parked documents appear in Transaction FV70, but didn't in the Transaction FB70 tree display. The folder for held documents, which appeared in Transaction FB70's tree display, doesn't appear in Transaction FV70. As you can see, the tree display default folders vary by transaction.

10.1.4 Using Screen Variants and Account Assignment Templates

Screen variants and *account assignment templates* are tools available in FI to simplify entry of customer documents. They aren't unique to AR or Transaction FB70, but we'll confine our discussion of them to this transaction in this section. Note that both screen variants and account assignment templates can be accessed and maintained from both the tree display in Transaction FB70 and the dropdown menu. In this section, we focus on using the tree display, which is the most user-friendly and frequently used method.

Use of Screen Variants

A screen variant sets the columns for line item entry in Transaction FB70 (Figure 10.26). In other words, it controls the fields displayed on the screen and the order in which they appear.

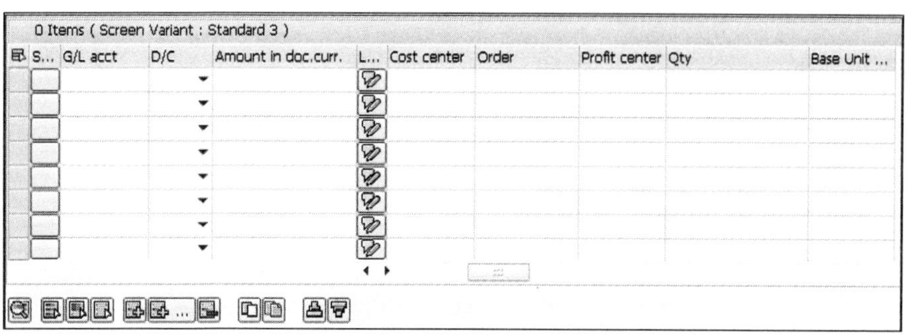

Figure 10.26 Transaction FB70 Screen Variant

A well-developed screen variant reduces data entry time and the number of data entry errors. Your goal is to have on the screen only the fields you need to enter or display. For example, if you use PCA, your AR screen variants should make the **Profit center** field available and prominently placed. In addition, if you use the **Segment** field for reporting by line of business, you should make **Segment** a prominently placed field in the screen layout, even if it's derived from the profit center.

Transaction FB70 has a default screen variant assigned, which is displayed each time you execute the transaction. However, the default may not be your preferred line item entry screen, or you may prefer different screen variants depending on the type of customer document you're creating. In Transaction FB70, you can select different screen variants at any time via the tree display or the dropdown menu. In AR, you may want different screen variants created based on the major types of customer invoices created. If you work for a multinational corporation, you may need multiple AR screen variants set up for intercompany receivables, regional invoices, and other recurring types of scenarios.

Let's look at screen variant selection in action. Go to Transaction FB70, and make sure the tree display is on (see Section 10.1.3). Click on the triangle next to the **Screen variants for items** folder to see a list of available variants to choose from (Figure 10.27).

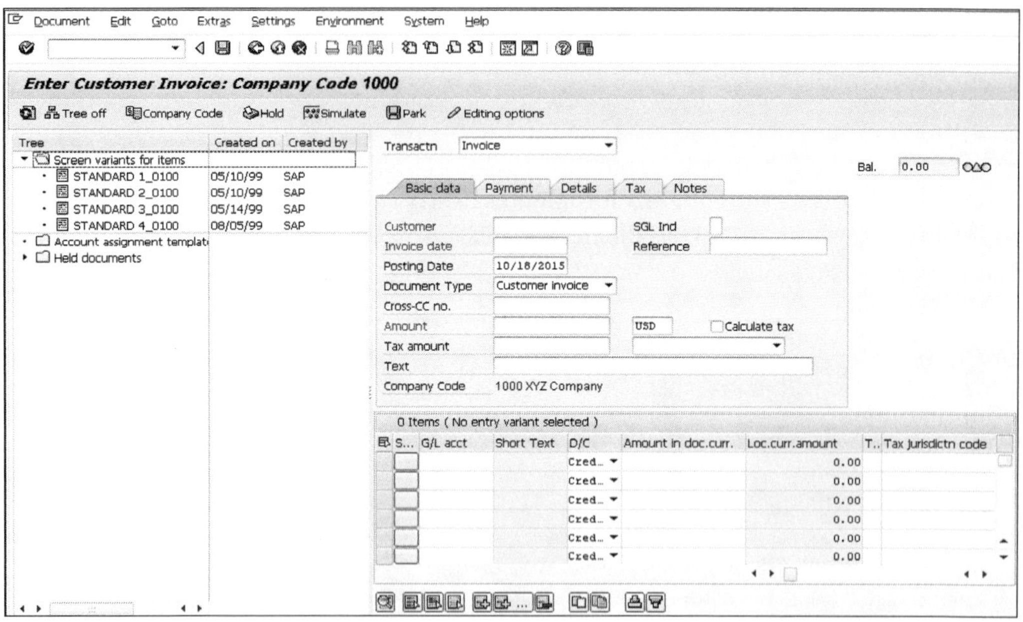

Figure 10.27 Screen Variant List

Double-click the screen variant you want to use (Figure 10.28), and the line layout in the bottom right of the screen will change.

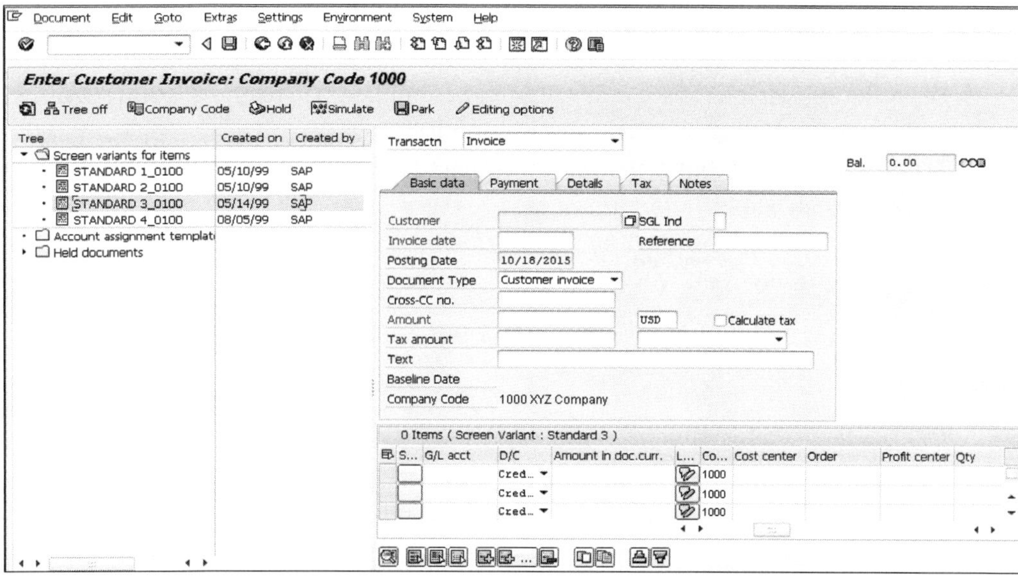

Figure 10.28 Screen Variant Selection

> **Note**
>
> The creation and maintenance of screen variants is beyond the scope of this book. They are cross-client dependent, meaning that if a screen variant change is made in one SAP client, the change is reflected in every other client within that SAP instance. For this reason, screen variant creation and maintenance are a function usually restricted to an SAP support team or system administrator.

Use of Account Assignment Templates

Account assignment templates are prepopulated field values in document line items. This is a useful concept in AR that helps reduce data entry requirements for customer invoices, which are frequent and consistent in their makeup. These templates allow you to quickly enter customer invoices without the hassle of reentering all the necessary field values each time you create a new document.

In AR, account assignment templates are used heavily for repetitive transactions that post to the same line of accounting (e.g., G/L accounts, profit centers, etc.). They may also be used for intercompany transactions. Account assignment templates in AR not only make data entry easier but also ensure consistency in your AR accounting entries.

The next time you find yourself entering a customer invoice from scratch that you've created multiple times in the past, consider creating an account assignment template.

Let's take a closer look at account assignment templates. Go to Transaction FB70, and make sure the tree display is on (see Section 10.1.3). Click on the triangle next to the **Account assignment template for items** folder to see a list of available templates to choose from (Figure 10.29).

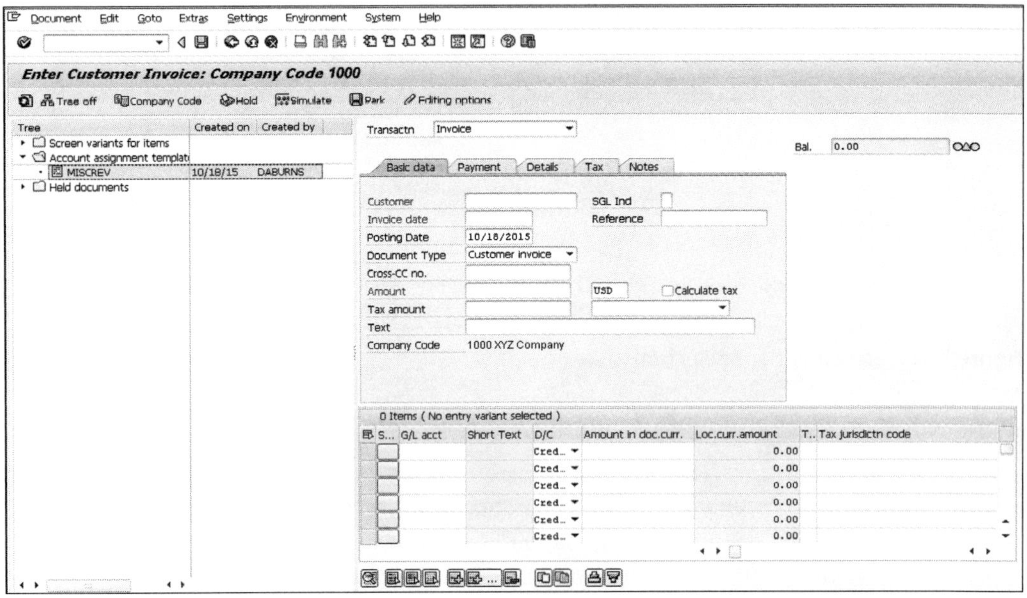

Figure 10.29 Account Assignment Template List

Double-click the template you want to use (Figure 10.30), and the line layout in the line item entry screen changes to reflect the prepopulated values contained in the account assignment template. Afterward, you can add or edit these prepopulated field values.

In this example, account assignment template **MISCREV** contains prepopulated values for the **G/L acct**, **D/C** (debit/credit indicator), and **Tax Code** fields. With these fields prepopulated, let's manually enter additional fields to walk through completing an AR customer invoice from an account assignment template.

In the header, the **Customer**, **Reference**, and **Invoice date** fields were manually entered. In the line item, **Profit center** was manually entered. With all the other required fields populated, you simply need to enter a value in the **Amount** field to complete the document entry requirements (Figure 10.31).

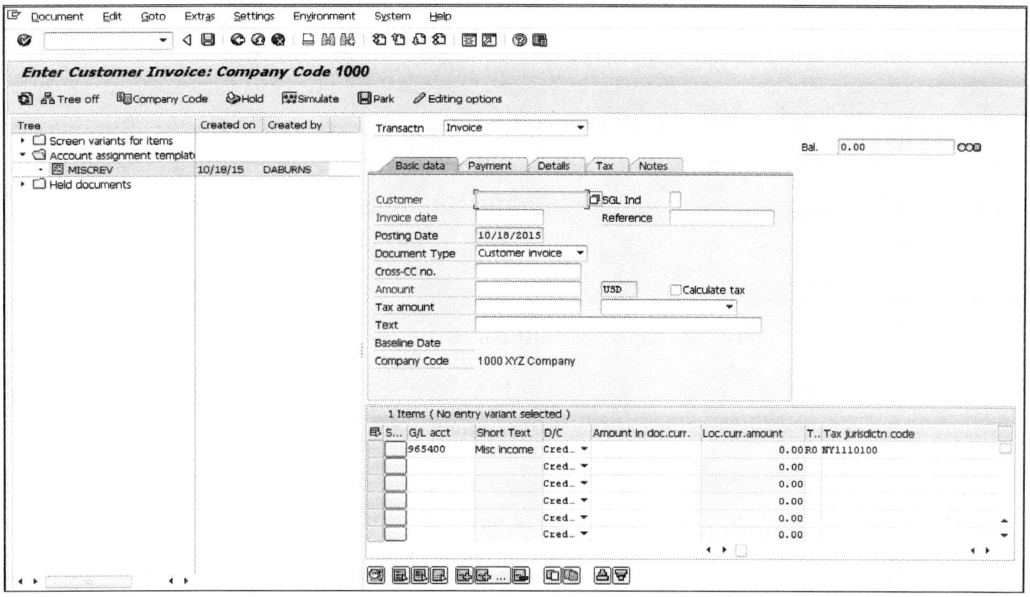

Figure 10.30 Account Assignment Template Selection

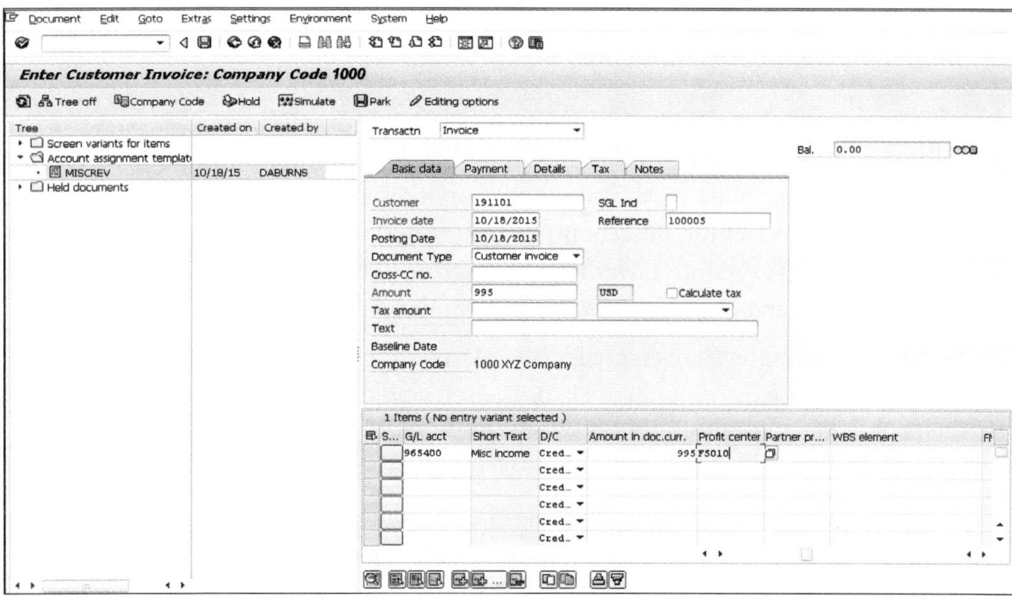

Figure 10.31 Account Assignment Template Entry Complete

With document entry complete, you can post, park, or hold this vendor invoice. In this example, we posted the document (Figure 10.32).

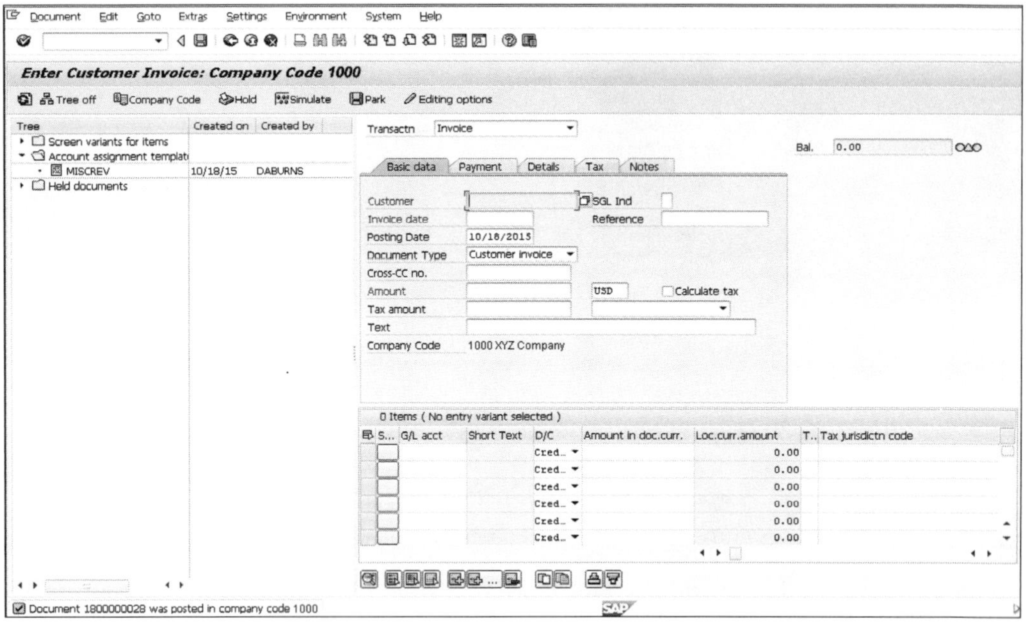

Figure 10.32 Posted Document Using Account Assignment Template

10.1.5 Controlling Document Entry with Editing Options

Controlling document entry with editing options allows you to make user-specific settings for transactions in accounting. Editing options are useful tools that give you some level of field control over the entry screen, what is displayed, and values that are defaulted, and they determine the interpretation of certain field entry values.

Editing options are a universal concept in FI, but our discussion in this section is limited to their use in Transaction FB70. The settings you make aren't transaction-specific, meaning that after you've made an editing option in Transaction in FB70, it also applies to other accounting transactions, such as Transactions FB50 and FB60.

In this section, we'll demonstrate some of the most commonly used settings and provide a complete list of all editing options and their descriptions (see Table 10.1 later in this section).

To access editing options from Transaction FB70 (Figure 10.33), click on the **Editing options** button at the top of the **Enter Customer Invoice** screen, or press Shift+F4.

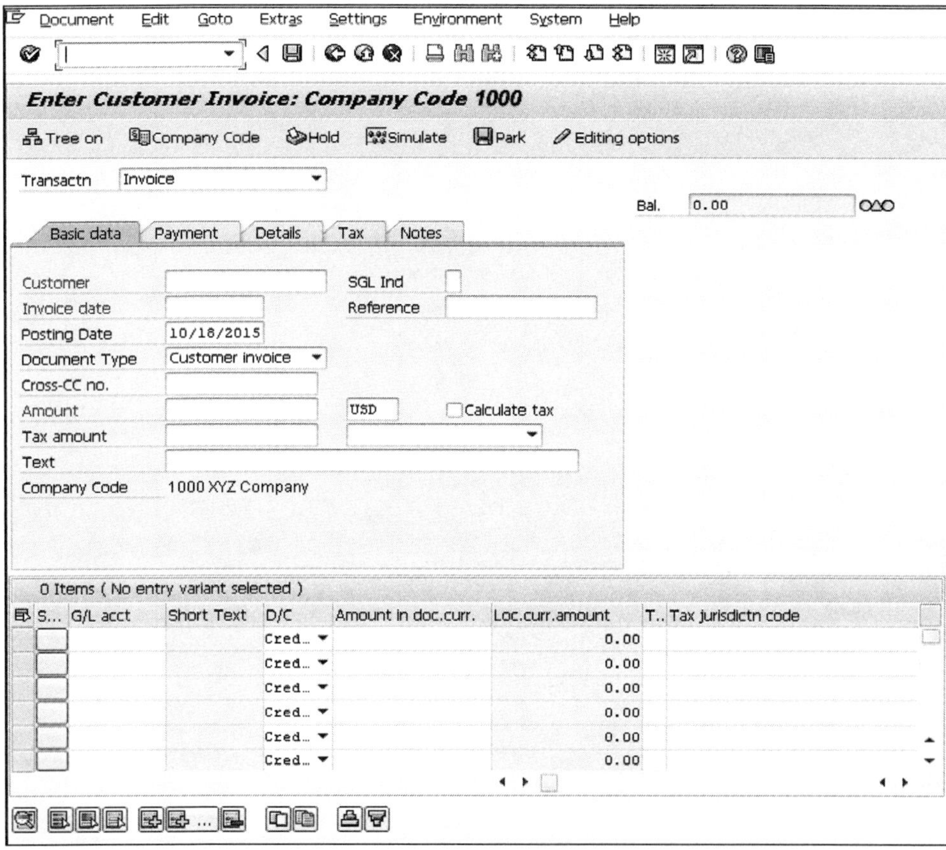

Figure 10.33 Enter Customer Invoice Screen for Editing Options

The **Accounting Editing Options** screen opens (Figure 10.34). Editing options fall into four general categories, each with its own area of the screen:

- **General Entry Options**
- **Special options for single screen transactions**
- **Default document currency**
- **Default Company Code**

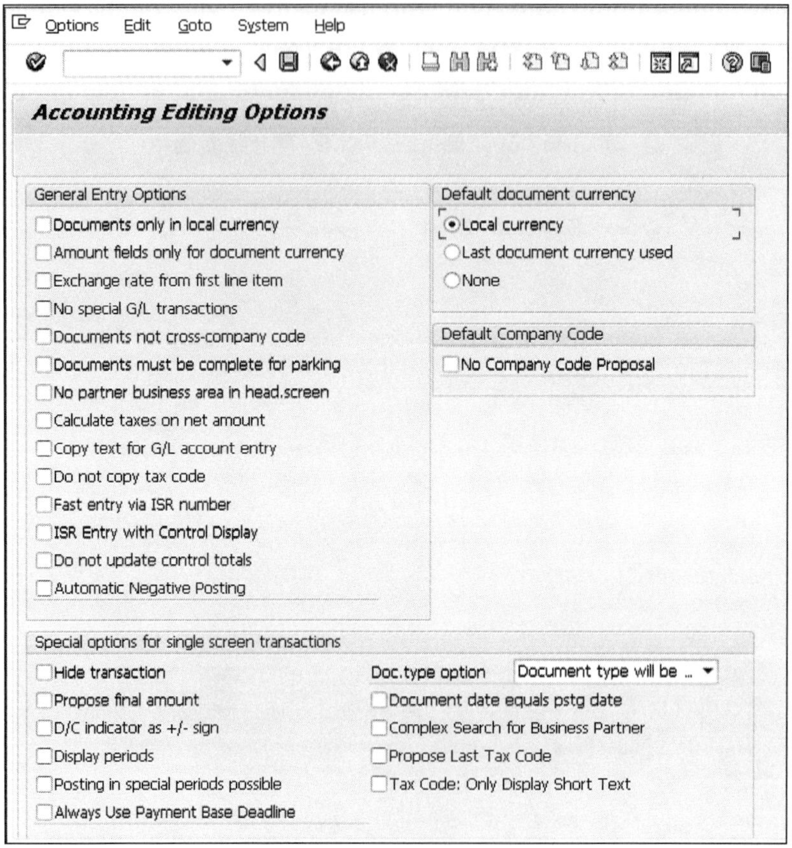

Figure 10.34 Accounting Editing Options

In the upper-right corner of Figure 10.34, the **Local currency** radio button is selected in the **Default document currency** area. With this setting, the local currency of the company code will default into Transaction FB70.

For this example, change the **Default document currency** to **None** (Figure 10.35), and then click the **Save** icon or press Ctrl + S.

After the editing options are saved, return to Transaction FB70 to find that the currency field (next to the **Amount** field) in the header is now blank (Figure 10.36), meaning that no value defaulted into this field. This currency setting is relevant to AR when posting receivable transactions for multiple regions. It forces you to think about the correct currency to use, instead of using the local currency by default.

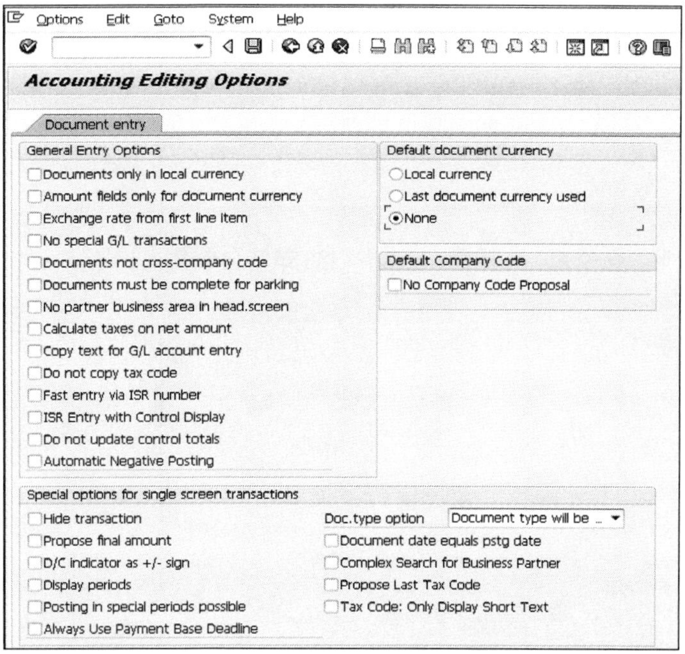

Figure 10.35 Accounting Editing Options with No Default Currency

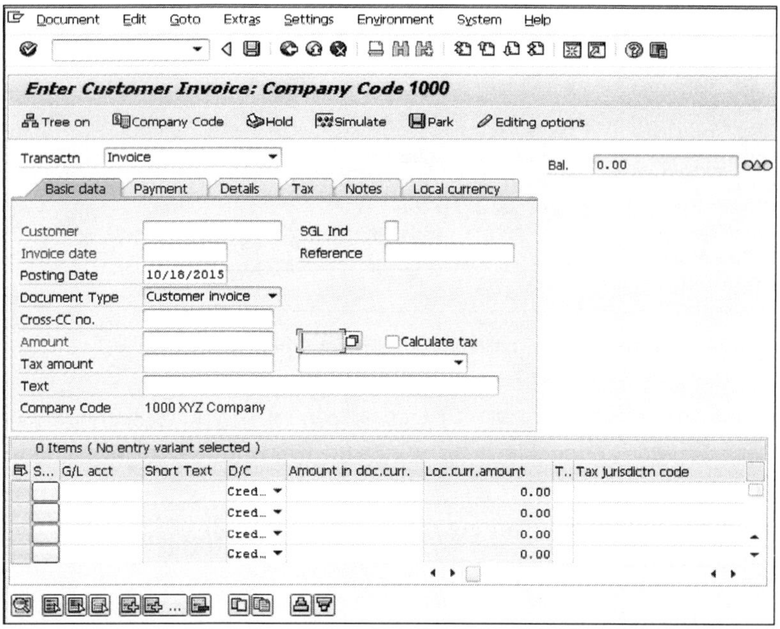

Figure 10.36 Enter Customer Invoice Screen with Blank Currency Field

Similarly, you can use editing options to change the transaction entry screen so that no company code is proposed. In this example, do so by selecting the **No Company Code Proposal** checkbox of the **No Default Company Code** in the **Accounting Editing Options** screen (Figure 10.37). After this selection is made, click the **Save** icon or press Ctrl+S.

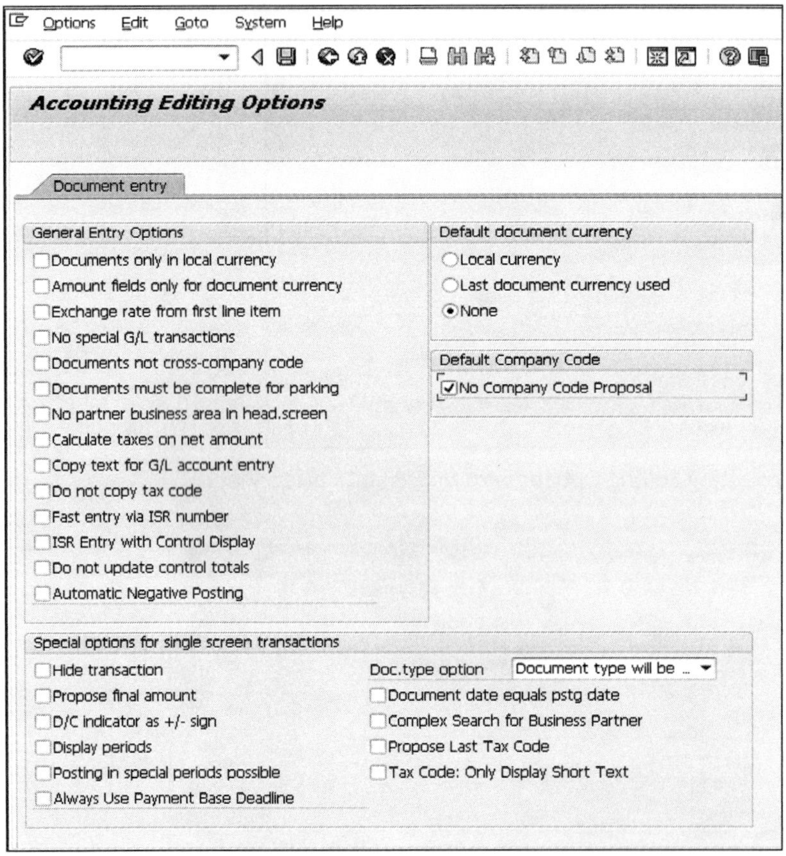

Figure 10.37 Accounting Editing Options with No Company Code Proposal

After the editing options are saved, return to Transaction FB70; you're immediately prompted to enter a **Company Code** (Figure 10.38). Again, this option may be useful in AR when you're responsible for creating receivable entries in multiple regions represented as separate company codes in SAP.

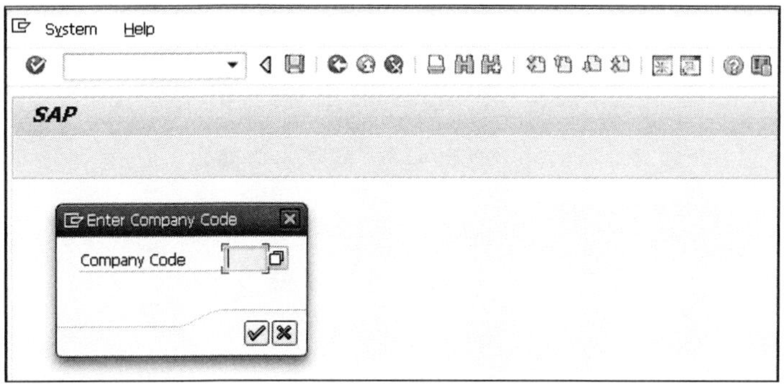

Figure 10.38 Enter Company Code Dialog Box

Another common use of editing options is to change the document type setting. In this example, change the **Doc.type option** field to **Document type hidden** (Figure 10.39), and then click the **Save** icon or press Ctrl + S.

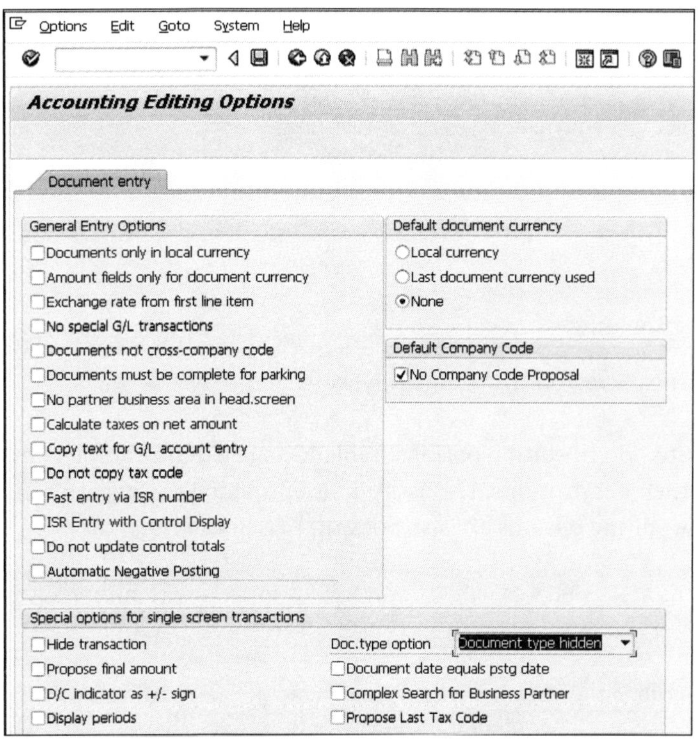

Figure 10.39 Accounting Editing Options with Hidden Document Type

After the editing options are saved, return to Transaction FB70, and you'll see that the **Document Type** field is now hidden from view (Figure 10.40).

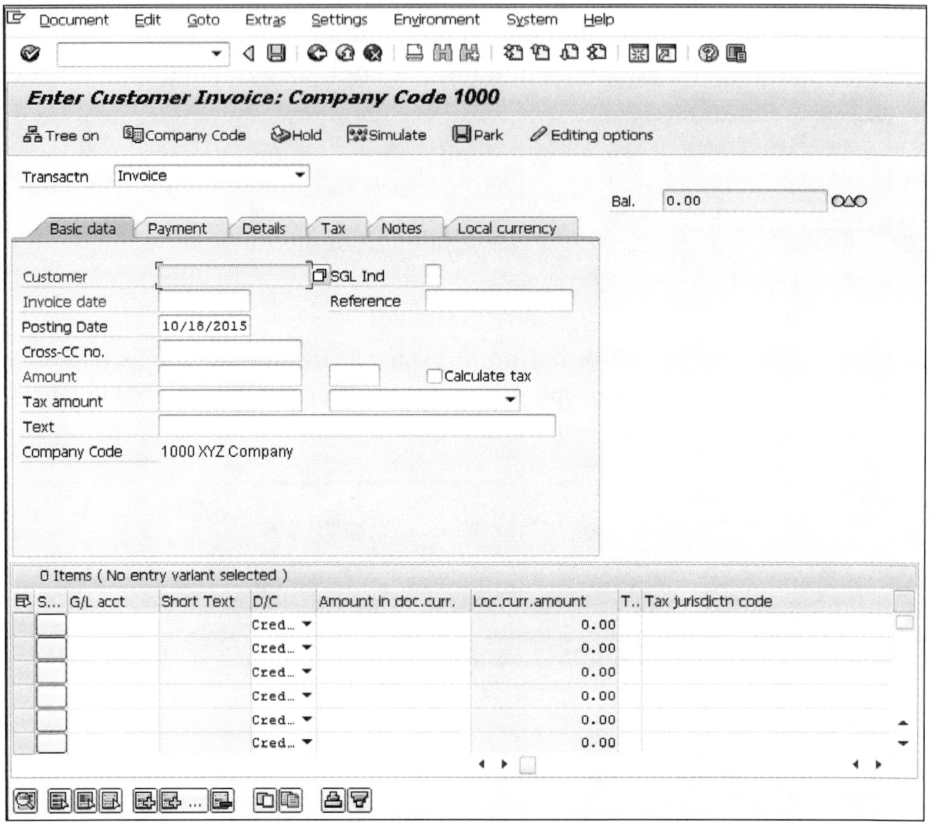

Figure 10.40 Document Entry Screen with Document Type Hidden

That concludes our discussion of editing options. Table 10.1 provides a complete list of editing options and their descriptions. This table is also provided in Chapter 3 and Chapter 6 because these editing options are also relevant to G/L and AP.

Editing Option	Description
Documents only in local currency	Only allows entry of documents in local currency
Amount fields only for document currency	Only allows entry amounts in foreign currency when entering documents in foreign currency

Table 10.1 Editing Options and Descriptions

Editing Option	Description
Exchange rate from first line item	Corrects the exchange rate in the document header automatically using the amounts in the first line item when posting foreign currency documents
No special G/L transactions	Prevents entry of special G/L transactions
Documents not cross-company code	Prevents cross-company code entries
Documents must be complete for parking	Prevents incomplete documents from being parked
No partner business area in head.screen	Prevents the default partner business area from being entered in the document header
Calculate taxes on net amount	Indicates that the G/L account amounts entered are net of taxes
Copy text for G/L account entry	Automatically copies text from last G/L line item to subsequent line items
Do not copy tax code	Deactivates the setting that the last tax code entered is automatically copied to G/L account line items
Fast entry via ISR number	Enables the fast entry of incoming invoices using the ISR subscriber number
ISR Entry with Control Display	Provides the ability to enter an alternative vendor number in cases where several vendors may have the same ISR number
Do not update control totals	Prevents control totals from being updated
Automatic Negative Posting	Makes any automatically generated lines negative postings when the negative postings indicator is set for at least one manually entered line
Default document currency	▪ **Local currency**: Defaults local currency used in header currency field ▪ **Last document currency used**: Defaults last currency used in header currency field ▪ **None**: Defaults no currency in the header currency field

Table 10.1 Editing Options and Descriptions (Cont.)

Editing Option	Description
Default Company Code	Forces manual selection of the company code to be used when the **No Company Code Proposal** check-box is checked
Hide transaction	Hides the **Transaction** field on the entry screen
Propose final amount	Proposes the final invoice amount in the customer or vendor line after a G/L line has been entered
D/C indicator as +/- sign	Allows the entry of +/- sign with amounts, which derives the debit/credit indicator
Display periods	Enables the display of period on the entry screen under basic data
Posting in special periods possible	Enables the period field for data input
Always use payment base deadline	Only permits payment deadline calculation based on the baseline date
Doc.type option	■ Displays document type in header ■ Document type ready for input ■ Displays document type using short name ■ Document type ready for input using short name ■ Document type hidden
Document date equals pstg date	Defaults the document date from the posting date
Complex Search for Business Partner	Specifies when entering a vendor invoice if a complex search is possible for the number of the trading partner
Propose last tax code	Proposes the last tax code used the next time the transaction is called
Tax Code: Only display short text	Changes the tax code dropdown list in the transaction to only display the short text of the tax code

Table 10.1 Editing Options and Descriptions (Cont.)

This concludes our discussion of editing options. In the next section, we'll present material on the post with reference functionality.

10.1.6 Post with Reference

Post with reference is a quick and easy way to create a new customer invoice or other document by replicating most of the accounting data from a document that has already been posted. It's much like a document copy function, except for flow control indicators provided by SAP that allow you to select specific actions to control in the process. For example, there is a **Do not propose amounts** flow control indicator. When this indicator is selected, you must reenter dollar amounts for each document line item rather than having the amount field values adopted from the reference document.

Post with reference is a universal concept in FI, but the scope of our discussion in this section is limited to its use in Transaction FB70. We'll demonstrate its use with a simple example and provide a complete list of flow control options and their descriptions (see Table 10.2 later in this section). Bear in mind that post with reference offers no unique functionality to AR. If in Chapter 3 and Chapter 6 you found the post with reference useful for G/L and AP transactions, you're likely to find it useful for AR transactions as well.

Post with reference can be used when you enter a customer invoice document via Transaction FB70 or application menu path, **Accounting • Financial Accounting • Accounts Receivable • Document Entry • FB70 – Invoice**, as shown in Figure 10.41.

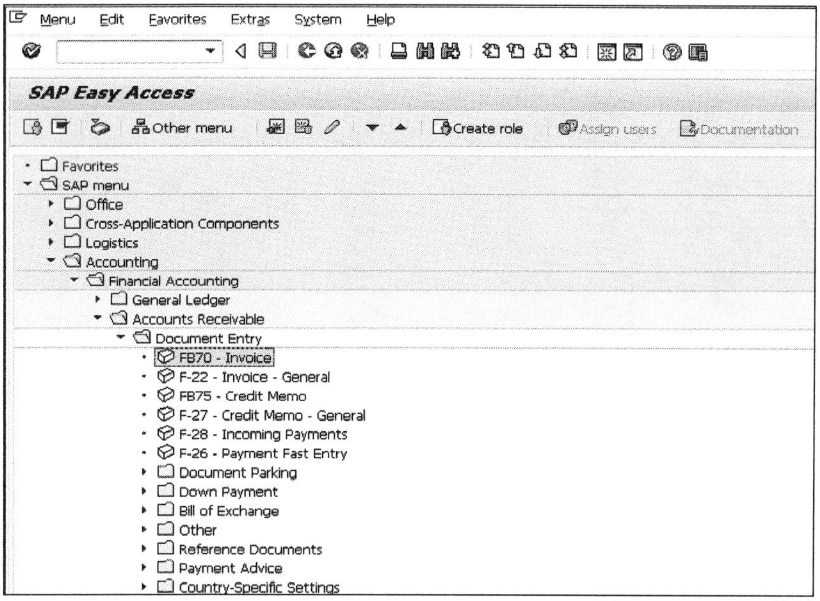

Figure 10.41 Transaction FB70 Application Menu Path

Double-click **FB70 – Invoice** from the menu path, or enter "FB70" in the **Command** field (Figure 10.42) and press [Enter].

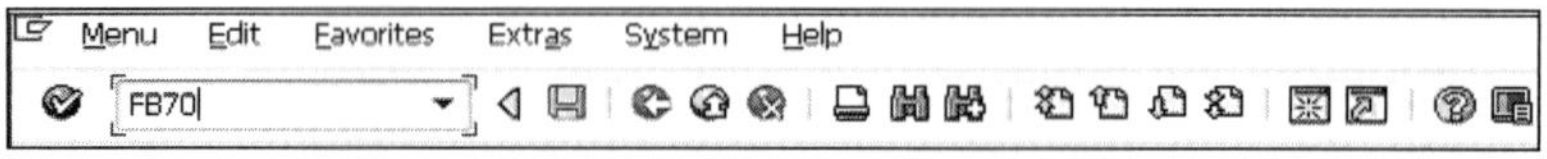

Figure 10.42 Entering "FB70" in the Command Field

From the **Enter Customer Invoice** entry screen (Figure 10.43), initiate the post with reference function by choosing **Goto • Post with reference**, or press [Shift]+[F9].

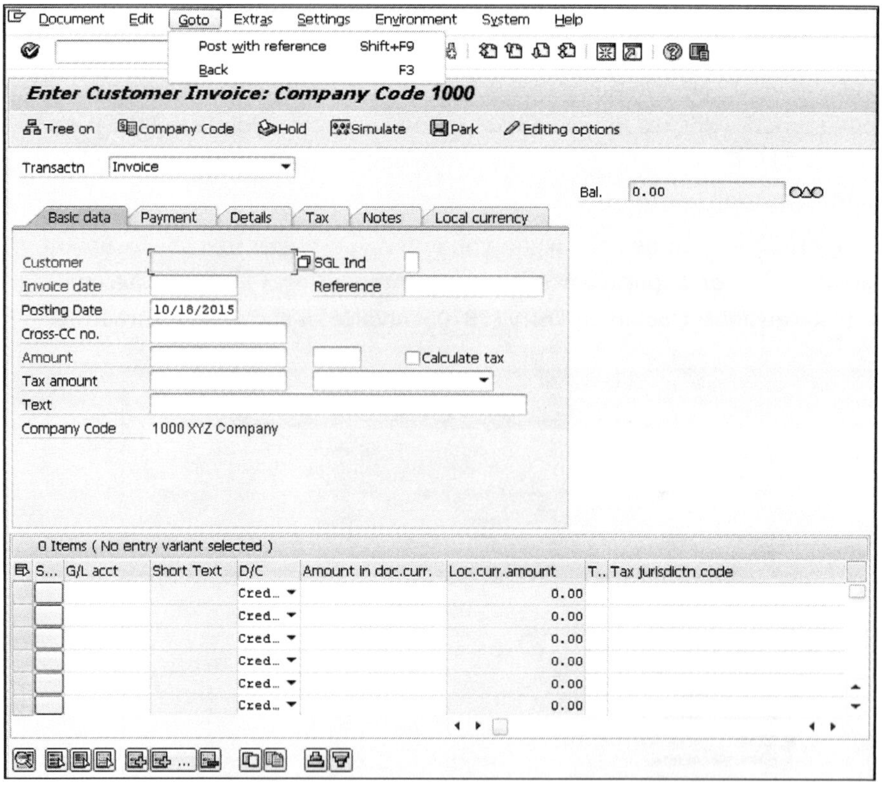

Figure 10.43 Post with Reference Dropdown Menu

The post with reference **Post Document: Header Data** selection screen opens (Figure 10.44). Here, enter the **Document Number**, **Company Code**, and **Fiscal Year** fields in the **Reference** area. For this example, select the **Do not propose amounts** checkbox in the **Flow control** area.

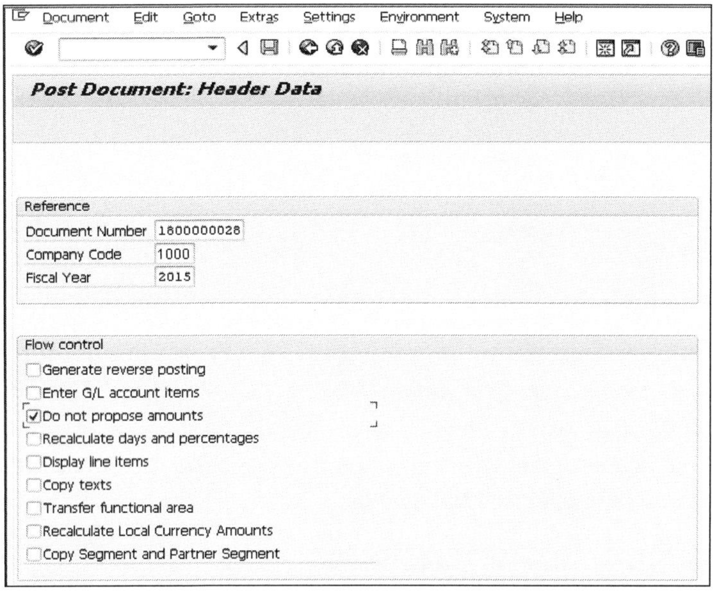

Figure 10.44 Post with Reference Post Document Header Data

After the relevant fields are populated in the **Post Document: Header Data** screen, press Enter to access the first screen of the new customer invoice document (Figure 10.45). Header data in this new document contains the field values copied from the reference document. Note that you can edit many field values at this point.

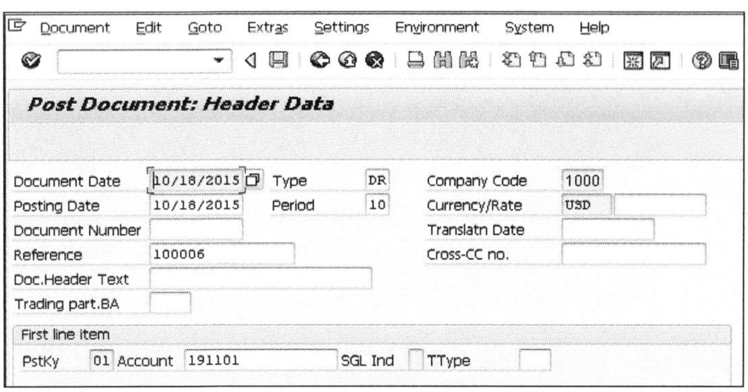

Figure 10.45 Post with Reference Header Data

In this example, we changed the **Document Date**, **Posting Date**, and **Reference** fields (Figure 10.46).

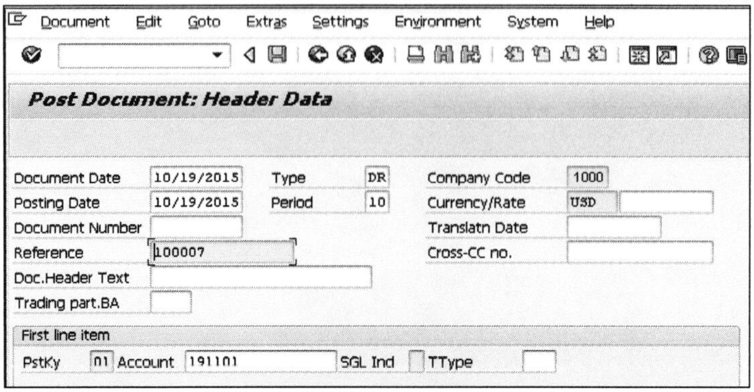

Figure 10.46 Post with Reference Header Data with Changes

After you've changed the header fields as needed, press [Enter], and the **Post Document Add Customer item** screen opens (Figure 10.47).

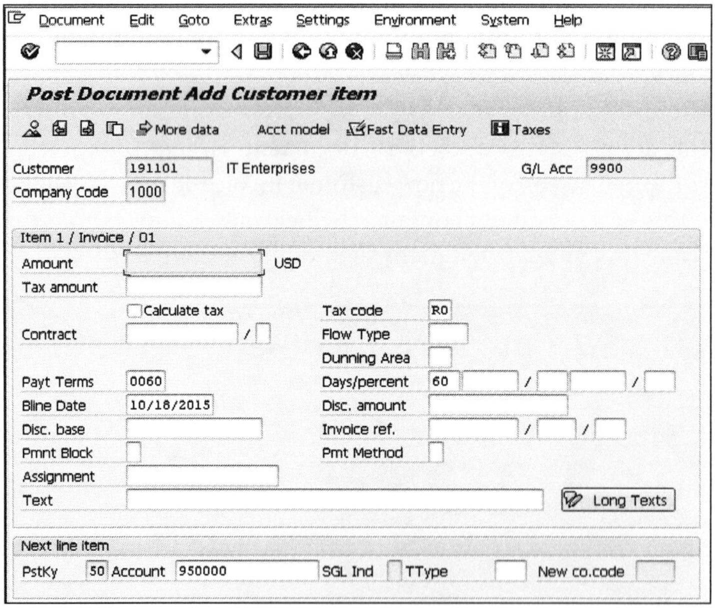

Figure 10.47 Post with Reference Add Customer Item

Note that the **Amount** field is blank because you selected the **Do not propose amounts** indicator in the **Flow control** area (refer to Figure 10.44) when you initiated the post with reference transaction.

For this example, enter "2000" in the **Amount** field (Figure 10.48).

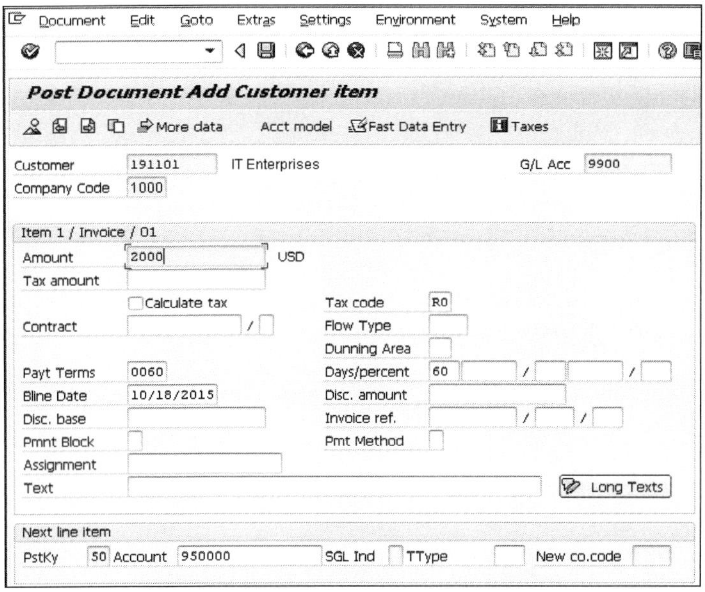

Figure 10.48 Post with Reference Add Customer Item with Amount Change

After the **Amount** field is entered, press [Enter], and a second **Post Document Add G/L account item** screen opens (Figure 10.49). Again, the **Amount** field is blank.

For this example, again enter "2000" in the **Amount** field (Figure 10.50).

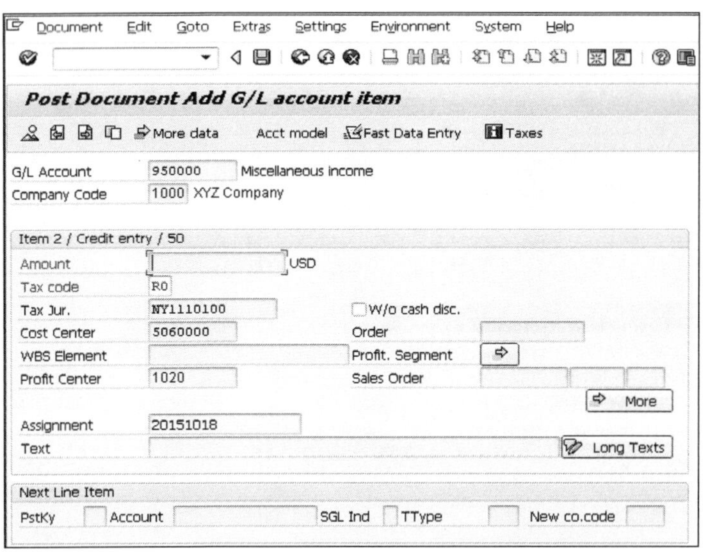

Figure 10.49 Post with Reference Add G/L Account Item with Amount Blank

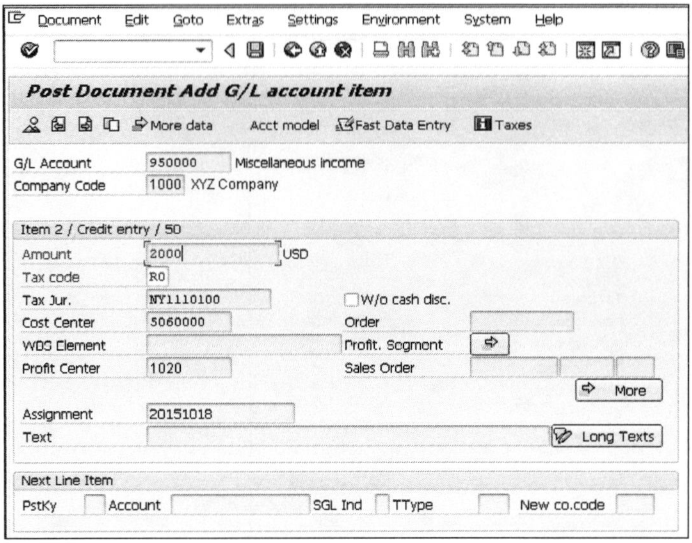

Figure 10.50 Post with Reference Add G/L Account Item with Amount Change

After entering all G/L account line items, click the **Post** icon or press Ctrl+S to post the customer invoice document (Figure 10.51). A message appears with the new customer invoice document number.

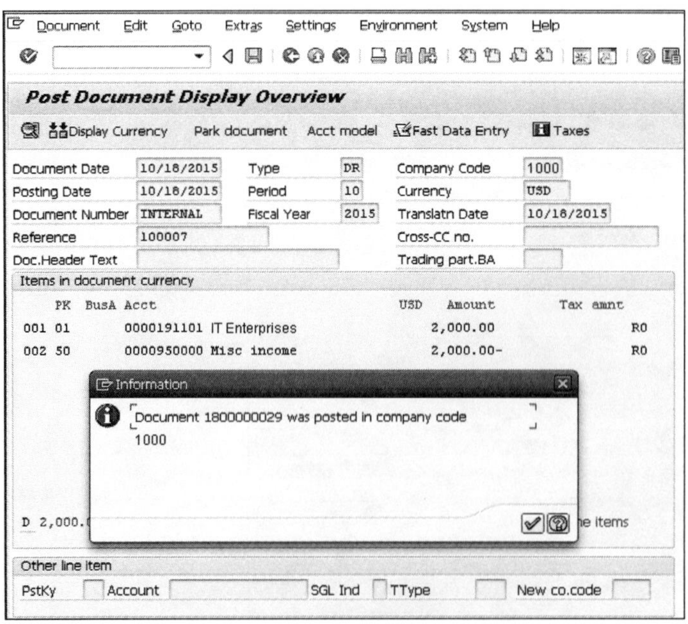

Figure 10.51 Post with Reference Document Created Message

This completes our post with reference example in AR. Table 10.2 provides a complete list of flow control options and their descriptions (as shown earlier in Figure 10.44). Flow control indicators are the same for all post with reference transactions, so you won't see any unique indicators for AR.

Flow Control Checkbox	Description
Generate reverse posting	Automatically generates reverse debit/credit indicators to offset the reference document
Enter G/L account items	Transfers line items to the fast entry screen for G/L accounts so that several line items can be displayed and processed from one screen
Do not propose amounts	Requires line item amounts to be manually entered in the new document
Recalculate days and percentages	Recalculates days and percentages from payment terms
Display line items	Displays each individual line item separately so that default field values can be changed if necessary
Copy texts	Copies long texts from the reference document to the new document
Transfer functional area	Transfers the reference functional area instead of re-deriving it because the functional area is normally derived
Recalculate local currency amounts	Recalculates local currency amounts to account for changes in exchange rates
Copy segment and partner segment	Transfers the fields instead of re-deriving their values because they are normally derived

Table 10.2 Flow Control Checkboxes and Descriptions

10.2 Credit Memos

Customer invoices are amounts owed to you by customers for goods or services purchased. *Credit memos*, on the other hand, are credits issued back to the customer's account (in the AR context; for credit memos in the AP context, see Chapter 6). A credit may be due for any number of reasons, such as overpayment, damaged goods, additional discounts, and erroneous bill amounts.

Credit memos allow you to correct erroneous customer balances and offset incoming payment balances. In other words, the amount paid to you is the invoice amount less any credit memos posted to the customer's account.

In the AR module, you can post a credit memo via Transaction FB75 or application menu path, **Accounting • Financial Accounting • Accounts Receivable • Document Entry • FB75 – Credit Memo**, as shown in Figure 10.52.

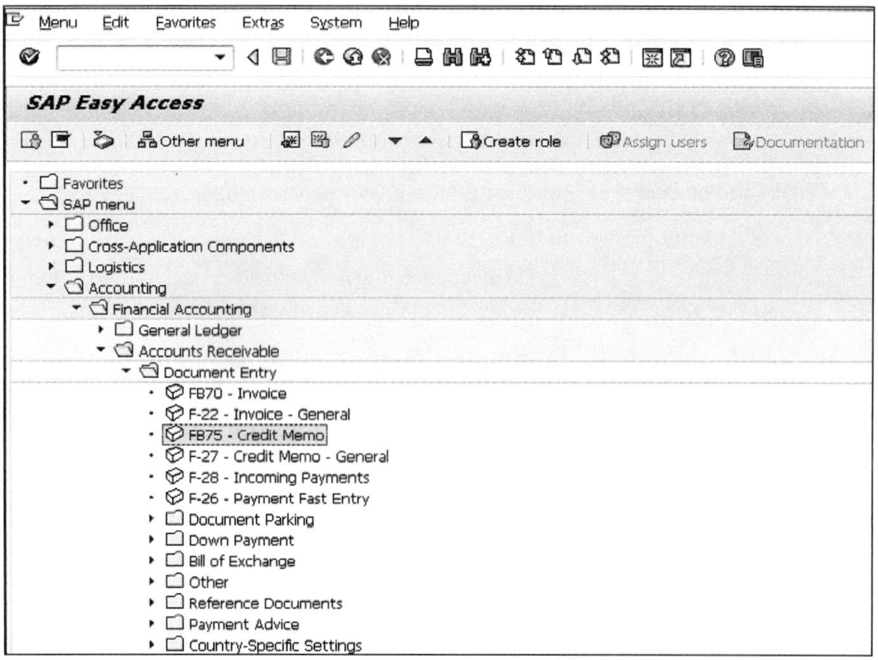

Figure 10.52 Transaction FB75 Application Menu Path

Double-click **FB75 – Credit Memo** from the menu path, or enter "FB75" in the **Command** field (Figure 10.53) and press Enter.

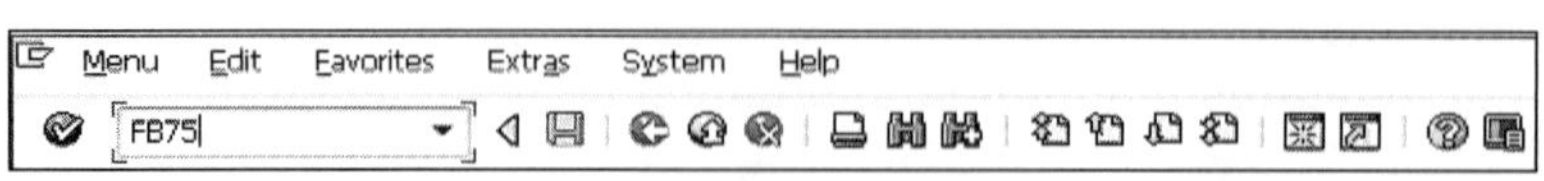

Figure 10.53 Entering "FB75" in the Command Field

The **Enter Customer Credit Memo** screen opens (Figure 10.54). In the document header, enter values for the **Customer**, **Document date**, **Amount**, and any other fields that are required, but don't prepopulate a value. In this example, field values defaulted for **Posting Date**, **Company Code**, and currency.

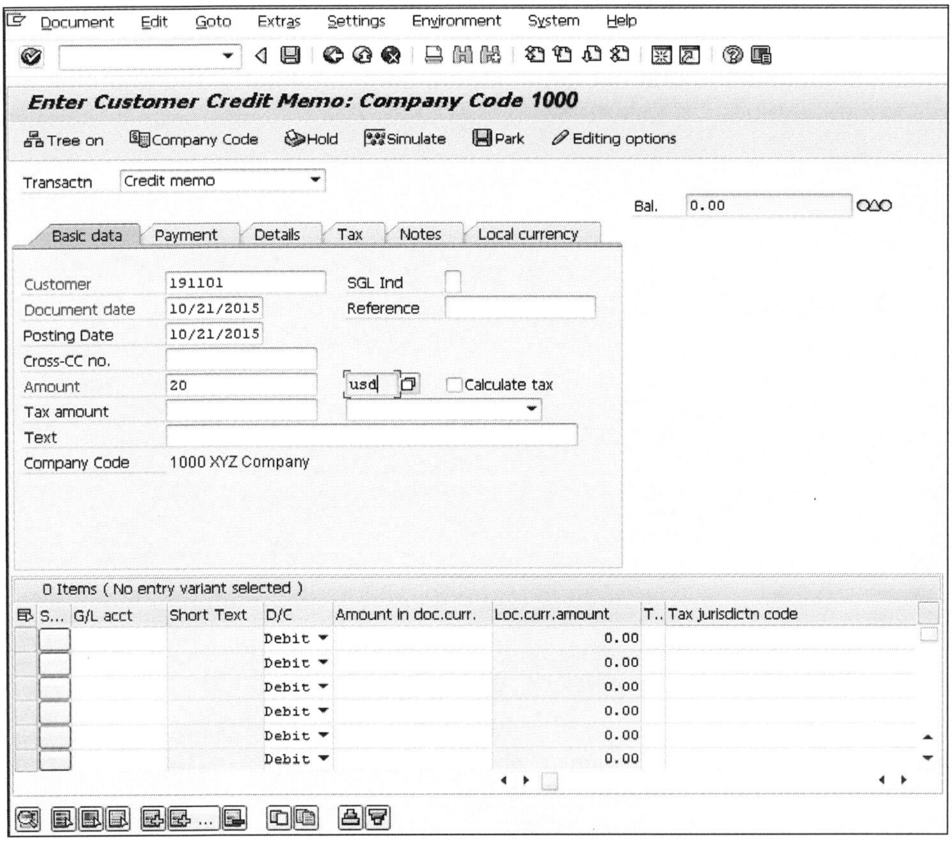

Figure 10.54 Enter Customer Credit Memo

With the header entry complete, enter at least one G/L line item (Figure 10.55). In this example, the line item is an offset (i.e., debit) to a revenue account. Values were manually entered here in the **G/L acct**, **D/C** (i.e., debit/credit indicator), **Amount in doc.curr.**, **Tax Code**, and **Profit center** fields.

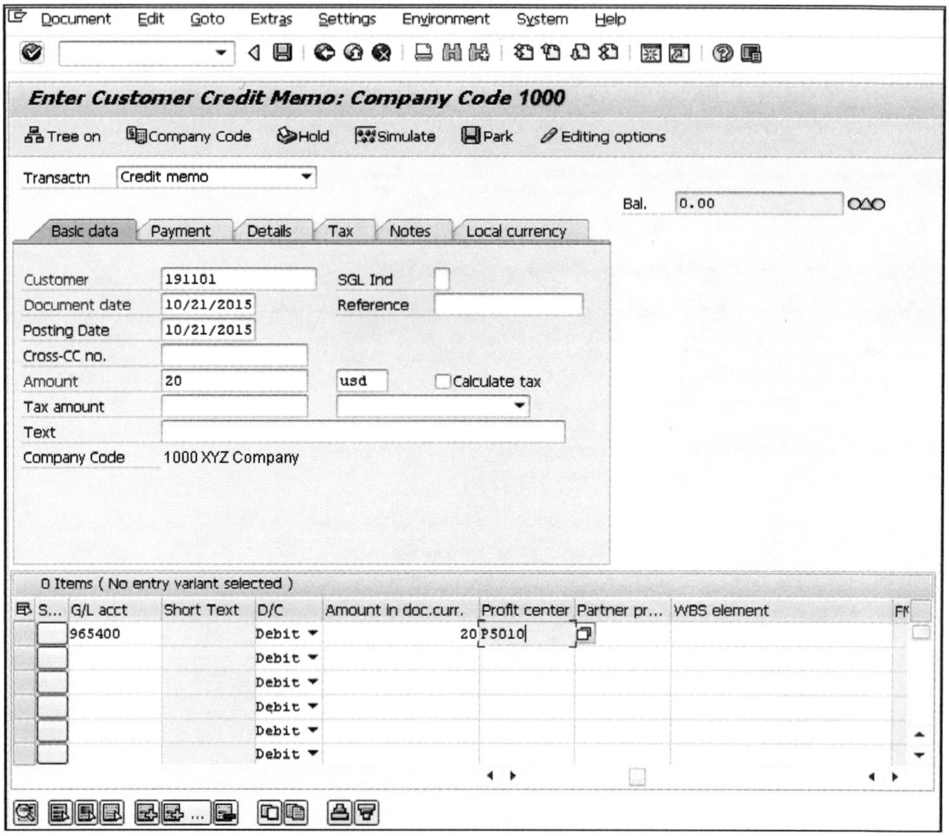

Figure 10.55 Enter Customer Credit Memo Screen with Line Item Entry

After entering document line items, click the **Simulate** button in the top center of the **Enter Customer Credit Memo** screen to initiate simulation of the customer credit memo posting logic, which will determine if the document can be properly posted. If the simulation is unsuccessful, an error message appears. If successful, the **Document Overview** screen opens, as shown in Figure 10.56.

After simulation is complete, click the **Post** icon to the right of the **Command** field in the upper-left corner of the screen. This posts the customer credit memo, and a message appears with the new document number, as shown in Figure 10.57.

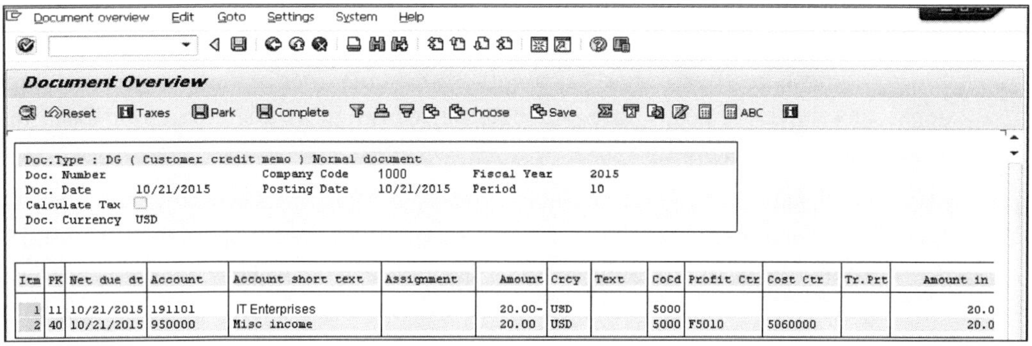

Figure 10.56 Enter Customer Credit Memo Document Overview

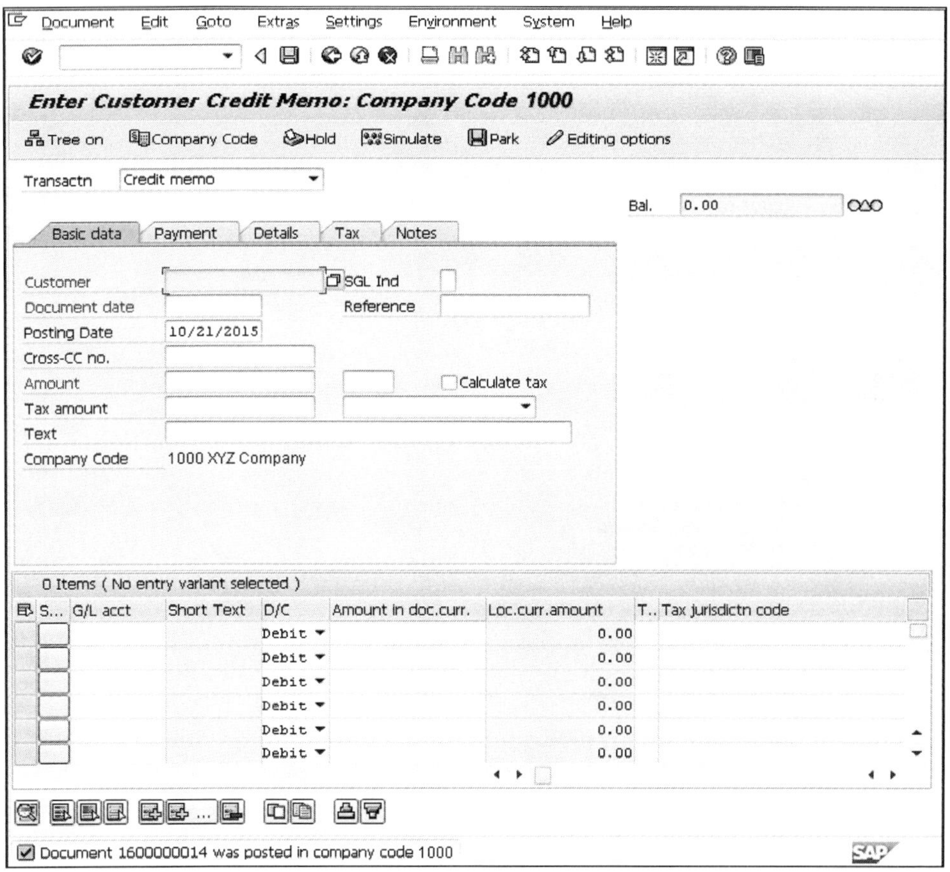

Figure 10.57 Customer Credit Memo Document Posted Message

10.3 Down Payments Received

Down payments received are prepayments from a customer in advance of receiving goods or services. A down payment may be requested as a sign of good faith or required to reserve a product.

An optional step in the down payment process in AR is the *down payment request*. You enter a customer down payment request and then clear it against an incoming down payment. Down payment requests are *noted items* in FI, meaning that they don't update G/L account balances. In other words, down payment requests aren't reflected in either the transaction figures or the balance displays. They can only be viewed in line item displays by specifying that you want to see noted items.

To enter a customer down payment request in the AR module, use Transaction F-37 or application menu path, **Accounting • Financial Accounting • Accounts Receivable • Document Entry • Down Payment • F-37 – Request**, as shown in Figure 10.58.

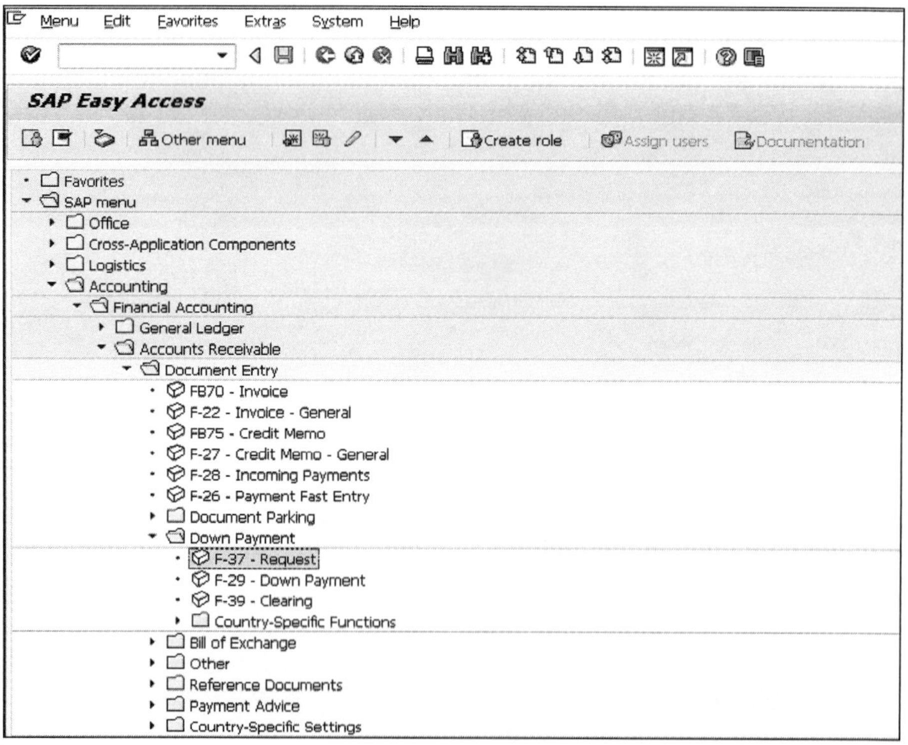

Figure 10.58 Transaction F-37 Application Menu Path

Double-click **F-37 – Request** from the menu path, or enter "F-37" in the **Command** field (Figure 10.59) and press Enter.

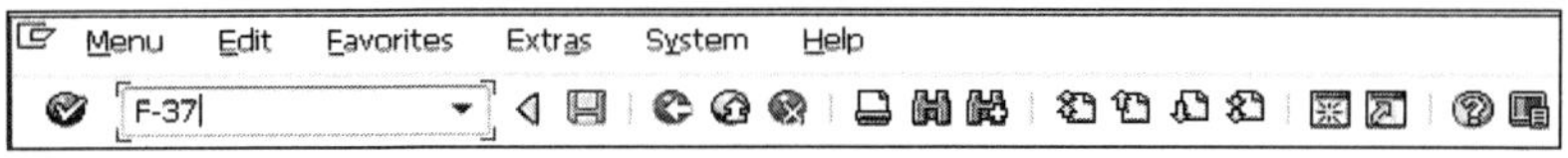

Figure 10.59 Entering "F-37" in the Command Field

The **Customer Down Payment Request: Header Data** screen opens (Figure 10.60). In the document header, enter a value for **Document Date** and any other fields that are required, but don't prepopulate a field value. In this example, field values defaulted for **Posting Date**, **Type** (i.e., document type), **Period**, **Company Code**, and **Currency/ Rate**.

In the **Customer** area at the bottom of the screen, you must also enter an **Account** and special G/L indicator (in the **Trg.sp.G/L ind.** field).

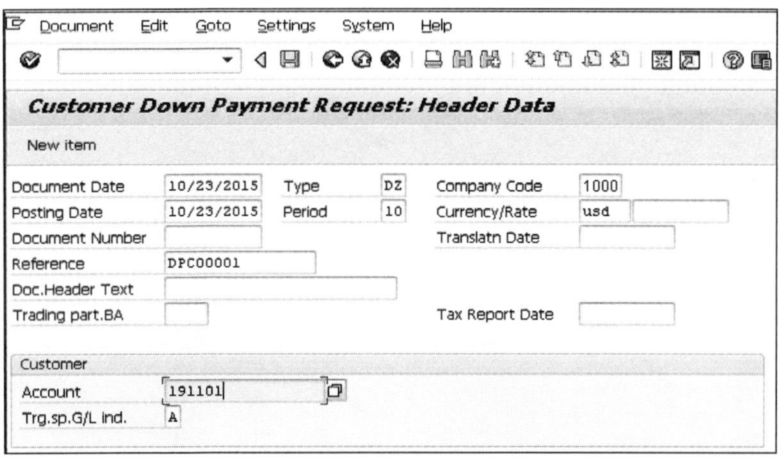

Figure 10.60 Customer Down Payment Request Header Data

With the header data complete, click on the **New Item** button. The **Customer Down Payment Request Correct Customer Item** screen opens (Figure 10.61). Here, enter values for the **Amount**, **Due on**, and any other required fields.

After entering the customer line item, click the **Save** icon in the top of the entry screen to the right of the **Command** field. This posts the customer down payment request, and a message appears with the new document number, as shown in Figure 10.62.

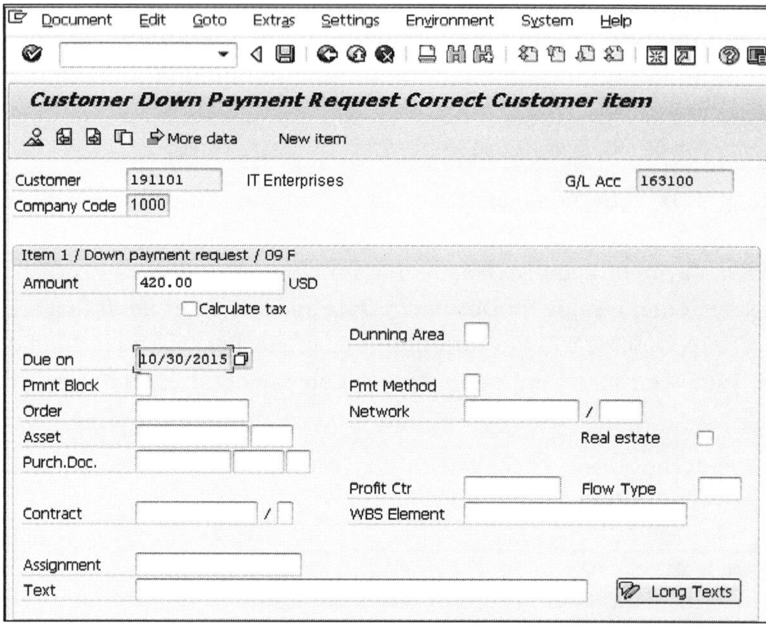

Figure 10.61 Add Customer Item to Customer Down Payment Request

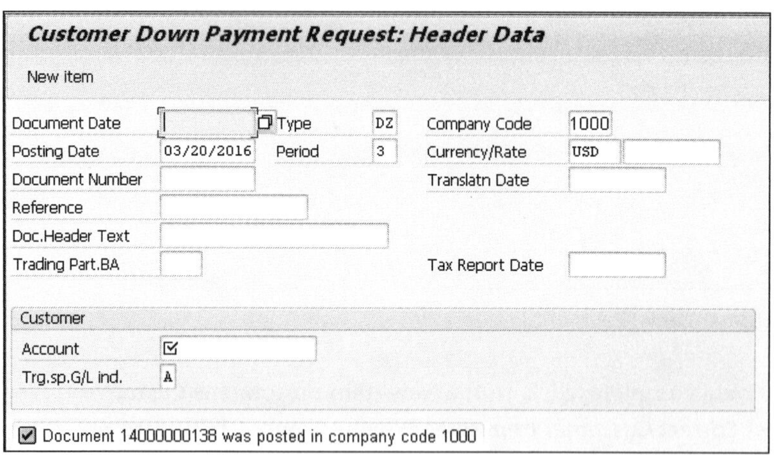

Figure 10.62 Customer Down Payment Request Document Posted Message

When a down payment is received, enter the customer down payment in the AR module using Transaction F-29 or application menu path, **Accounting • Financial**

Accounting • Accounts Receivable • Document Entry • Down Payment • F-29 – Down Payment, as shown in Figure 10.63.

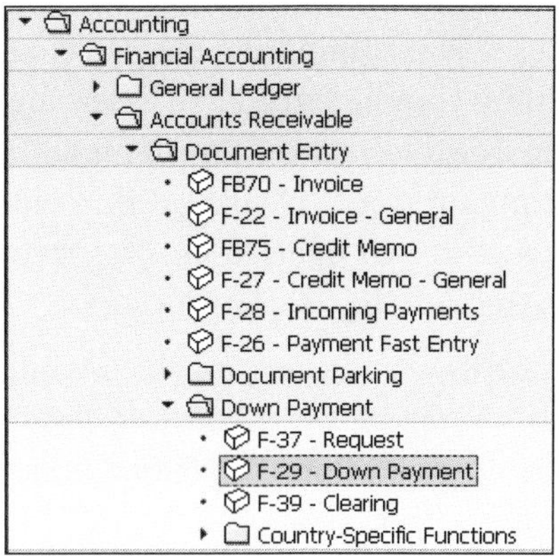

Figure 10.63 Transaction F-29 Application Menu Path

Double-click **F-29 – Down Payment** from the menu path, and the **Post Customer Down Payment Request: Header Data** screen opens. In the document header, enter a value for **Document Date** and any other fields that are required but that don't contain a default value.

In the **Customer** area, at the bottom of the screen, you must also enter an **Account** and special G/L indicator (in the **Trg.sp.G/L ind.** field). In the **Bank** area, you must enter an **Account** and **Amount**.

When all field values are entered, click the **Requests** button at the top of the screen. The **Post Customer Down Payment Choose Requests** screen opens. Select your request, and click the **Create Down Payments** button in the top-left portion of the screen. The **Post Customer Down Payment Display Overview** screen opens. Click the **Save** icon to post the customer down payment.

Now that you understand customer down payments, let's move on to the next topic: resetting and reversing AR documents.

10.4 Resetting and Reversing Documents

The most important thing to know before attempting to reverse an AR document is what type of document it is. It may be a customer invoice or credit memo, and these documents can be classified as either clearing or non-clearing documents for reversal purposes.

Clearing documents are those produced through a post with clearing transaction, such as Transaction F-04 (see Chapter 3, Section 3.2), or incoming payments using Transaction F-28. These documents have two technical components: First, a clearing document contains complete header data and at least two completed line items with debit/credit amounts netting to zero. The second component of a clearing document is account clearing. Through the clearing process, a customer open item is selected and its status changed from **Open** to **Cleared** when the clearing document posts.

A *non-clearing accounting document* has the same attributes as a clearing document, except that it doesn't clear a customer open item. Therefore, a non-clearing document doesn't change the status of a customer line item from **Open** to **Cleared**. Non-clearing documents are the simplest to reverse.

10.4.1 Reversing a Non-Clearing Document

To reverse a single AR document, use Transaction FB08 or application menu path, **Accounting • Financial Accounting • Accounts Receivable • Document • Reverse • FB08 – Individual Reversal**, as shown in Figure 10.64.

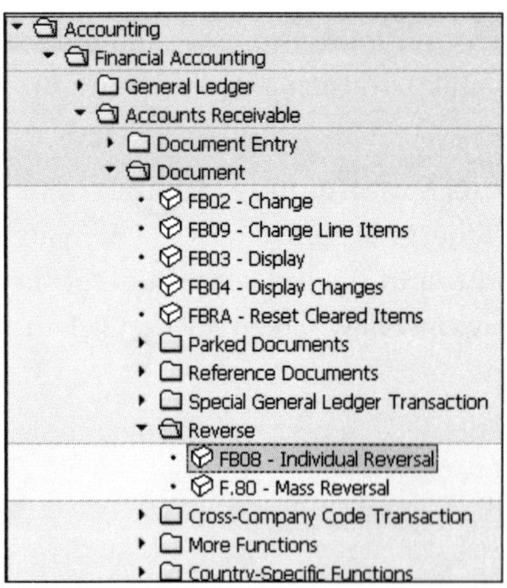

Figure 10.64 Transaction FB08 Application Menu Path

Double-click on **FB08** from the menu path, or enter "FB08" in the **Command** field (Figure 10.65) and press [Enter].

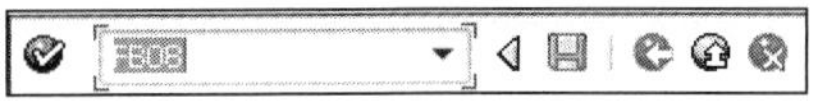

Figure 10.65 Entering "FB08" in the Command Field

The **Reverse Document: Header Data** screen opens (Figure 10.66). At a minimum, the **Document Number**, **Company Code**, **Fiscal Year**, and **Reversal Reason** fields are required.

The **Reversal Reason** field is noted in the reversed document. It also determines whether an alternative posting date is allowed or whether the reversal can be created from a negative posting. In this example, the **Reversal Reason** field is populated with a value of **01**, indicating that the reversal will take place in the current period.

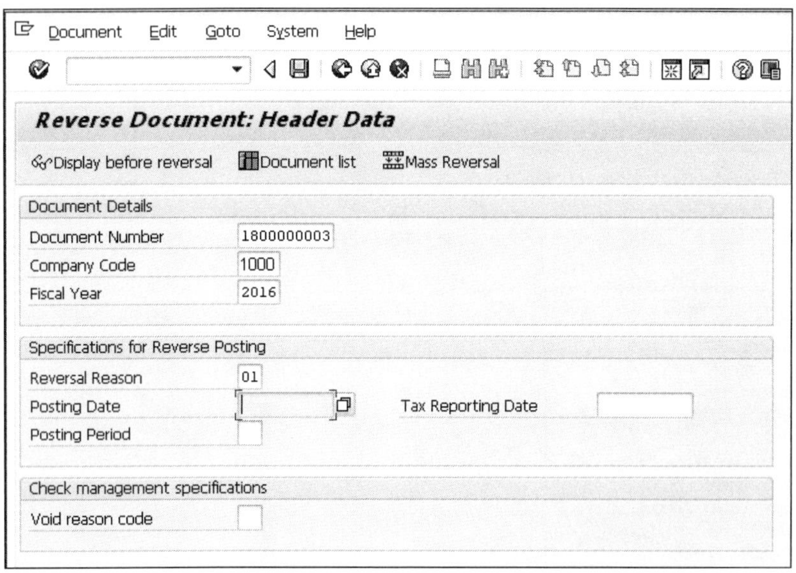

Figure 10.66 Reverse Document Header Data Screen

When all the required fields are entered, click the **Post** icon or press Ctrl+S to post the AR reversal document. A message appears with the new G/L document number (Figure 10.67).

If you have more than one non-clearing document to reverse, use Transaction F.80 or application menu path, **Accounting • Financial Accounting • Accounts Receivable • Document • Reverse • F.80 – Mass Reversal**, as shown in Figure 10.68.

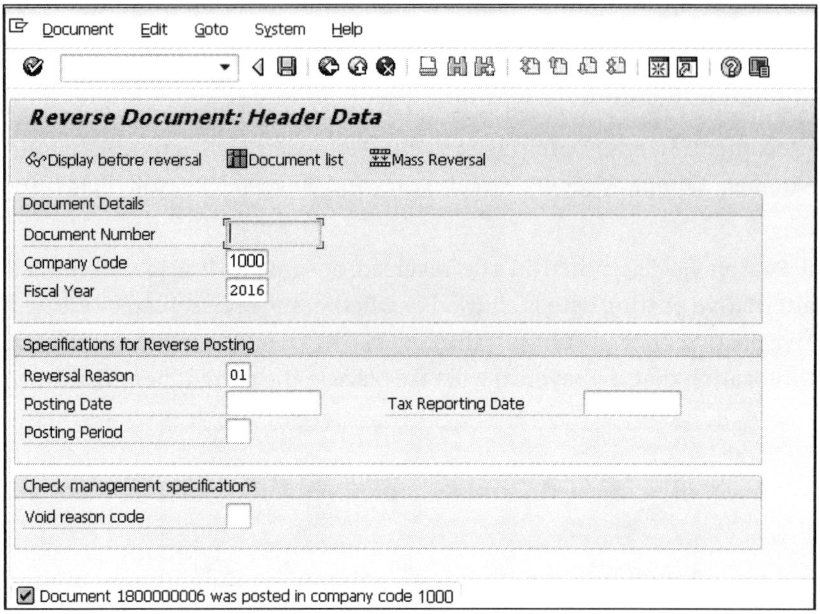

Figure 10.67 Reversal Document Created Message

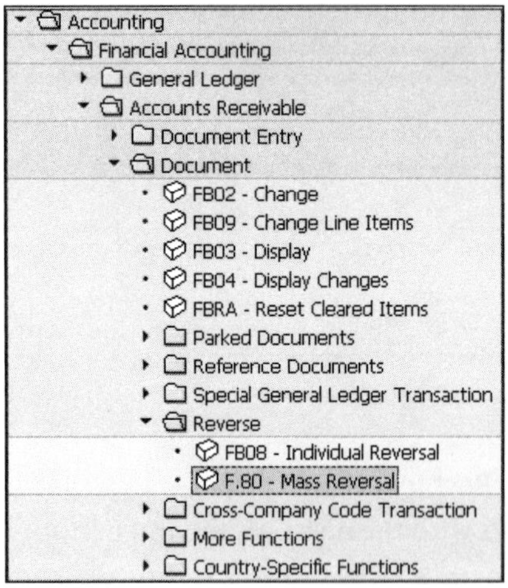

Figure 10.68 Transaction F.80 Application Menu Path

Double-click **F.80 – Mass Reversal** from the menu path, or enter "F.80" in the **Command** field (Figure 10.69) and press Enter.

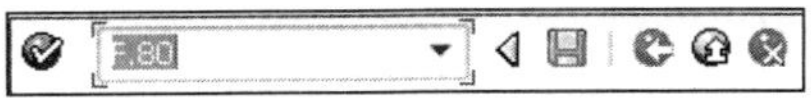

Figure 10.69 Entering "F.80" in the Command Field

The **Mass Reversal of Documents: Initial Screen** opens (Figure 10.70). As in Transaction FB08, the **Company Code**, **Document Number**, **Fiscal Year**, and **Reason for reversal** fields are required. Note that you can enter a range of values for these fields in Transaction F.80, whereas in Transaction FB08 you can only enter a single value for each. In Transaction F.80, you also have a **Ledger** field, which in most cases will reflect your primary ledger.

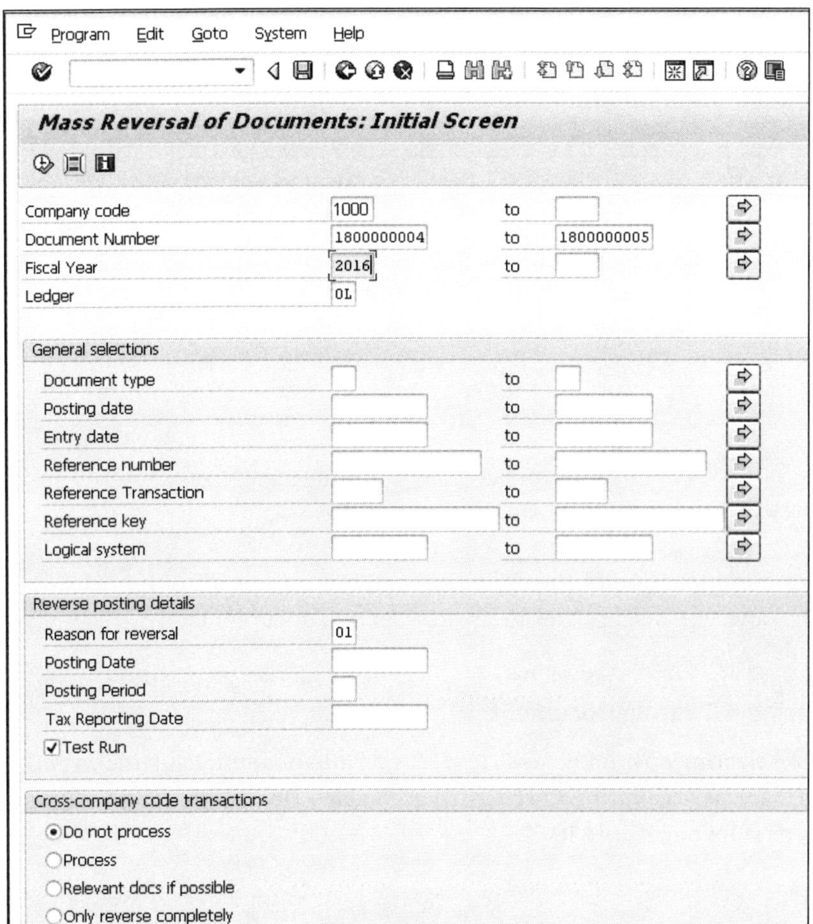

Figure 10.70 Mass Document Reversal Screen

Transaction F.80 has other notable features. Under **General selections**, you'll see several input fields that may be useful. In addition, in the **Reverse posting details** area, you'll see a **Test Run** checkbox. For mass reversals, it's always a good idea to run the program in test mode first.

When all the required fields are entered, click the **Execute** icon or press F8 to post the AR reversal documents. Detailed results are provided on the **Mass Reversal of Documents** output screen (Figure 10.71).

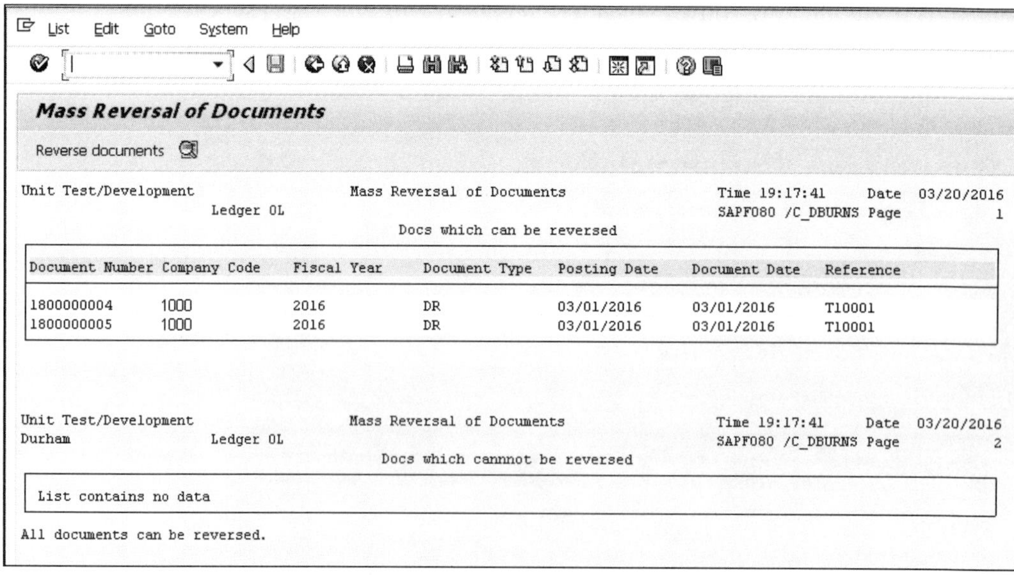

Figure 10.71 Massive Reversal of Documents Overview Screen

That concludes our discussion of the individual and mass reversals of non-clearing AR documents. Now, let's discuss how to reverse clearing documents.

10.4.2 Reversing a Clearing Document

To reverse an AR clearing document, use Transaction FBRA or application menu path, **Accounting • Financial Accounting • Accounts Receivable • Document • FBRA – Reset Cleared Items**, as shown in Figure 10.72.

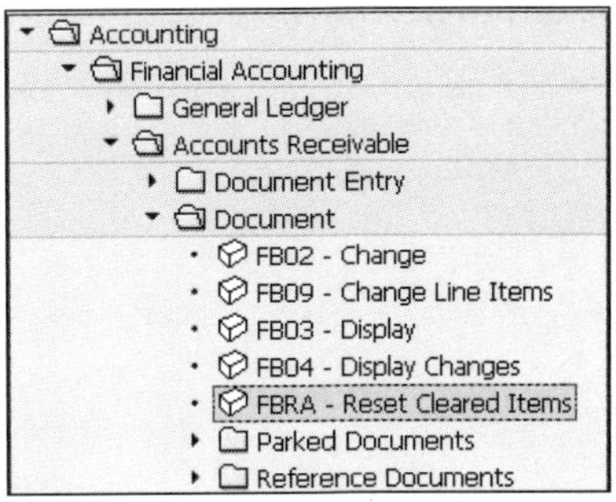

Figure 10.72 Transaction FBRA Application Menu Path

Double-click **FBRA – Reset Cleared Items** from the menu path, or enter "FBRA" in the **Command** field (Figure 10.73) and press [Enter].

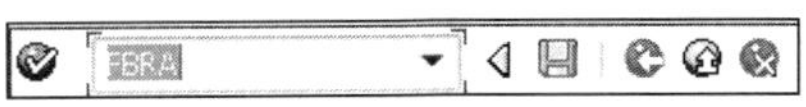

Figure 10.73 Entering "FBRA" in the Command Field

The **Reset Cleared Items** screen opens (Figure 10.74). The **Clearing Document**, **Company Code**, and **Fiscal Year** fields are all required.

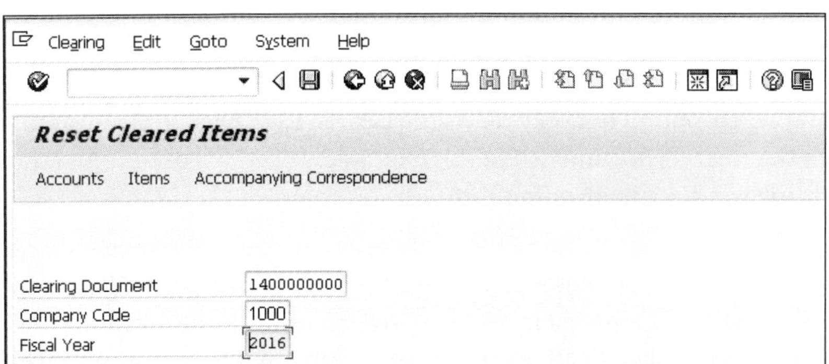

Figure 10.74 Reset Cleared Items

After entering the required fields, click the Save button, or press [Ctrl]+[S]. This prompts the **Reversal of clearing document** dialog box (Figure 10.75) to pop up. In this box, you must choose one of three options: **Only resetting**, **Resetting and revers**, or **Cancel**.

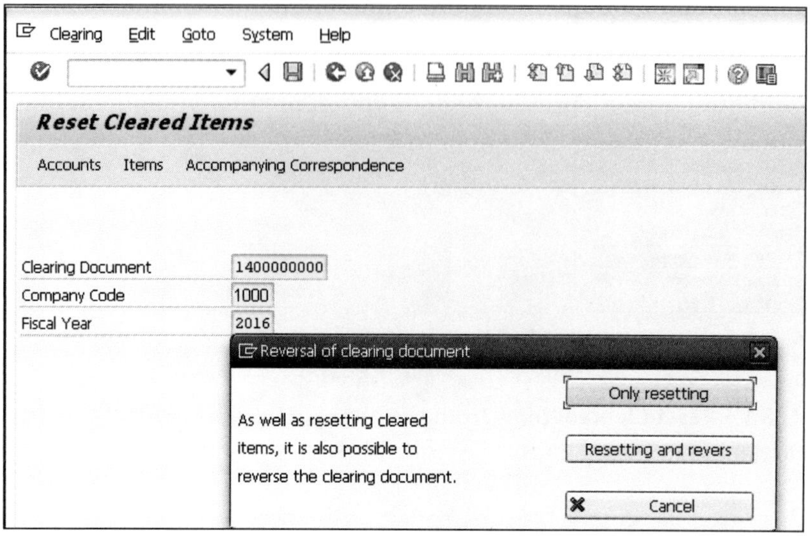

Figure 10.75 Reversal of Clearing Document Dialog Box

The **Only resetting** option doesn't reverse the clearing document. Instead, it breaks the reference between a clearing document and the AR item it cleared and changes the status of the cleared AR item back to **Open**. Only use this option when the AR item selected for clearing was the wrong line item. The clearing document thus becomes an open item and can be reassigned to clear the correct AR open item.

The **Resetting and revers** option not only resets the cleared item back to **Open** status but also reverses the clearing document. For this example, select this option, and the **Reversal Data** dialog box pops up (Figure 10.76).

The **Reversal Reason** field is required, and the value selected is noted in the reversed document. This value also determines whether an alternative posting date is allowed or whether the reversal can be created from a negative posting. In this example, the **Reversal Reason** field is populated with a value of **01**, signifying that the reversal will take place in the current period.

Click the **Continue** icon, or press Enter. Two subsequent information dialog boxes appear. The first, shown in Figure 10.77, states that the clearing document was reset. The second, shown in Figure 10.78, provides the number for a new document that has been posted, which is the document that reversed the clearing document.

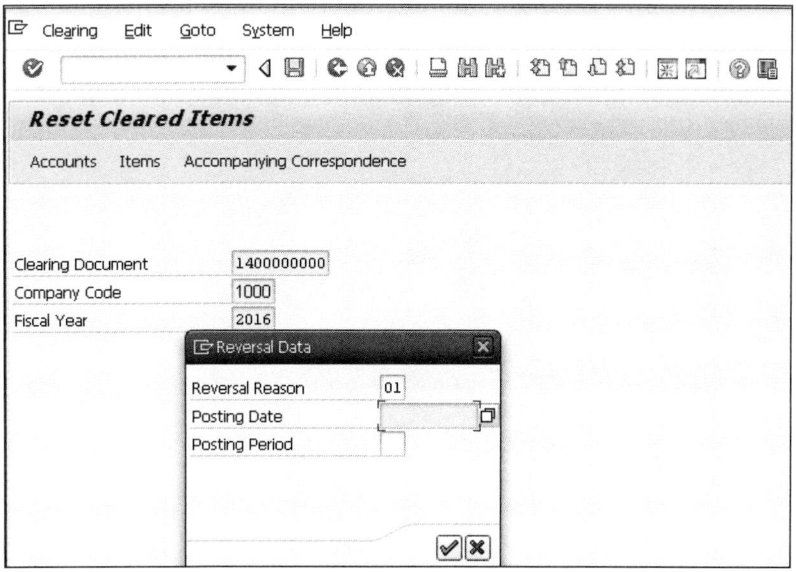

Figure 10.76 Reversal Data Dialog Box

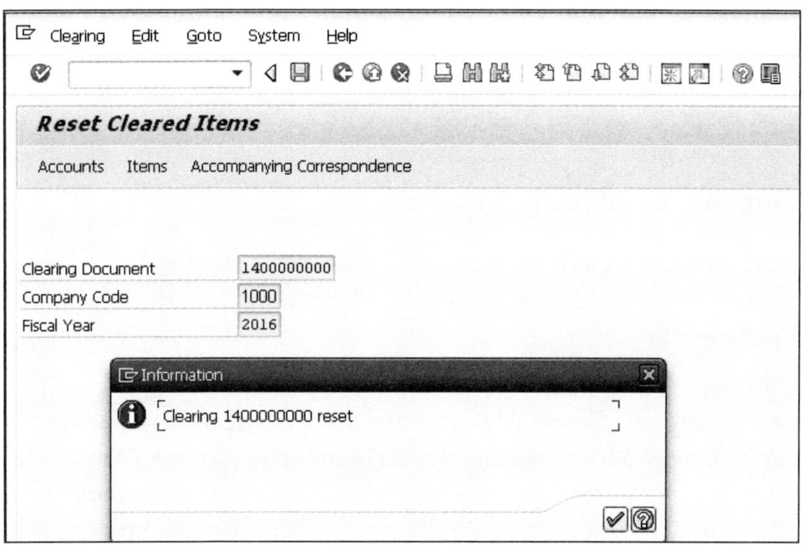

Figure 10.77 Clearing Document Reset Message

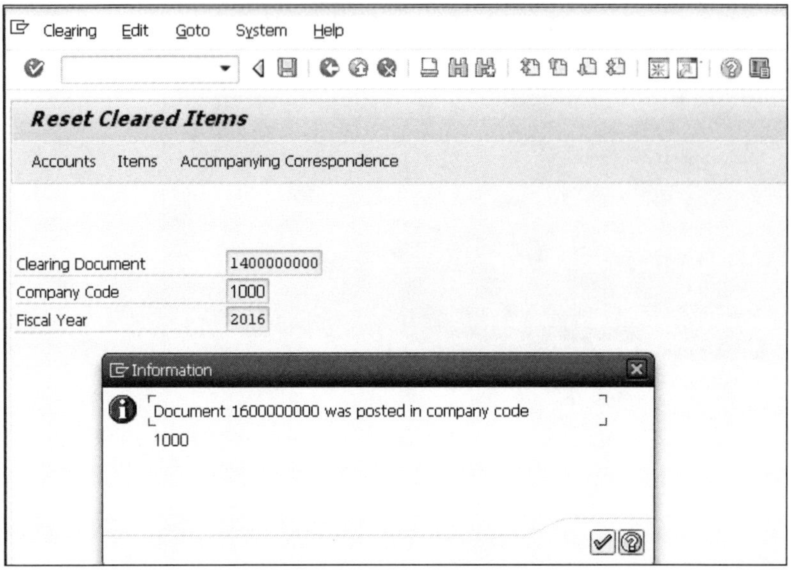

Figure 10.78 Reversal Document Posted Message

You should now have a good understanding of clearing versus non-clearing documents, how to reverse individual AR documents, and reversing multiple documents. In the next section, the topic of changing and displaying documents is discussed.

10.5 Changing and Displaying Documents

This section covers the change and display capabilities for AR accounting documents. The scope of this section is limited to Transaction FB70, but the same principles apply for other AR documents.

Rules for changing field values in SAP accounting documents are defined in configuration, and separate rules are defined for header and line item fields. Note, however, that SAP will never allow you to change fields considered central to the principle of orderly accounting. In other words, fields that are material to AR and G/L account balances, posting dates, and integration can't be changed after an AR accounting document has been posted. These include not only the **Posting Date**, **D/C** (debit/credit indicator), and **Amount** fields but also update objects (i.e., cost center). If an AR accounting document contains an incorrect value of this sort, the document should be reversed using Transaction FB08 or Transaction FBRA (see Section 10.4).

Note that the principle of orderly accounting is applicable to more than just AR documents. It holds true for G/L, AP, asset accounting, banking, and any accounting entry. To change an AR document, use Transaction FB02 or application menu path, **Accounting • Financial Accounting • Accounts Receivable • Document • FB02 – Change**, as shown in Figure 10.79.

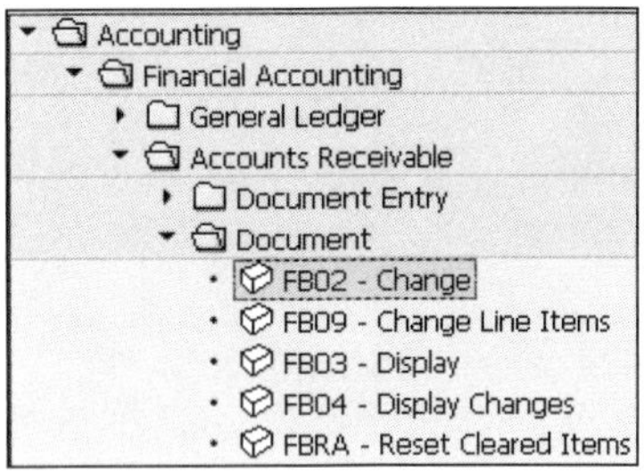

Figure 10.79 Transaction FB02 Application Menu Path in AR

Double-click **FB02 – Change** from the menu path, and the **Change Document: Initial Screen** opens (Figure 10.80). The **Document Number**, **Company Code**, and **Fiscal Year** fields are required.

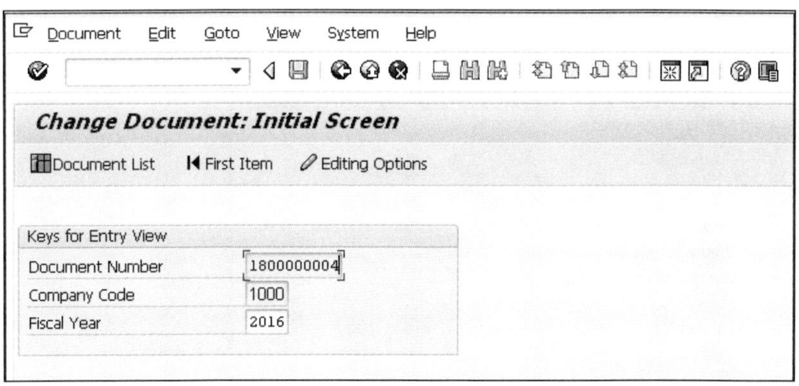

Figure 10.80 Change Document: Initial Screen

After entering all field values, press Enter. The **Change Document: Data Entry View** screen opens (Figure 10.81).

To change a header field, click on the **Header** icon, and the document header dialog box pops up (Figure 10.82). Fields that can't be changed are grayed out. Fields that can be changed appear white and are ready for field values to be entered or changed.

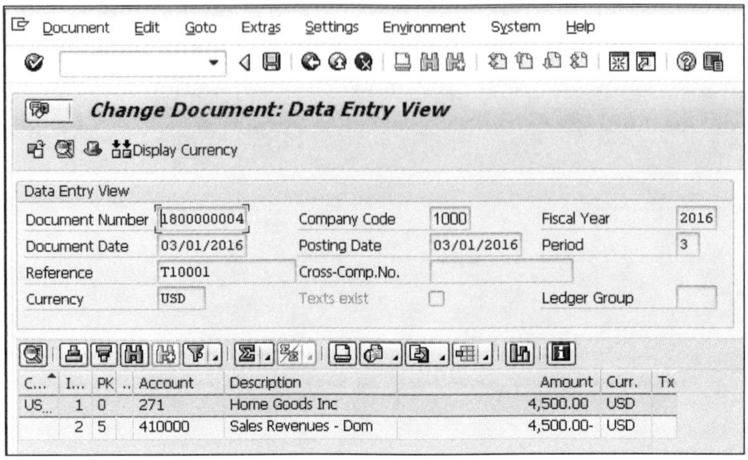

Figure 10.81 Change Document: Data Entry View

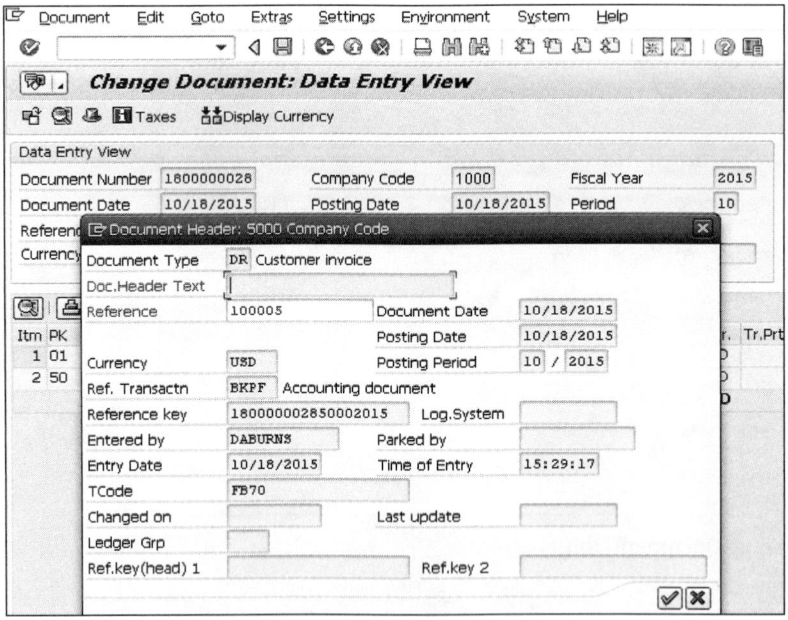

Figure 10.82 Change Document Header Screen

From the **Change Document: Data Entry View** screen (refer to Figure 10.81), you can change line item fields by double-clicking a line. After doing so, the **Change Document: Line Item** screen opens (Figure 10.83).

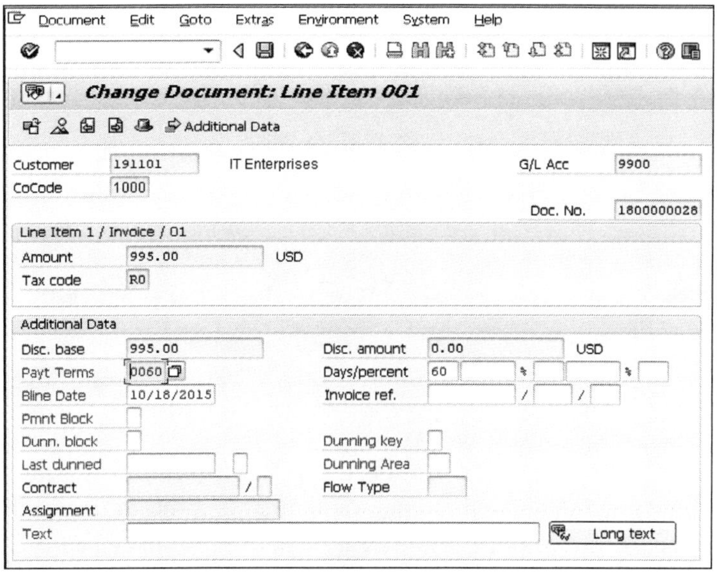

Figure 10.83 Change Document: Line Item

Fields that can't be changed are grayed out. Those that can be changed appear white and are ready for field values to be entered or changed. In this example, we changed the **Text** field (Figure 10.84).

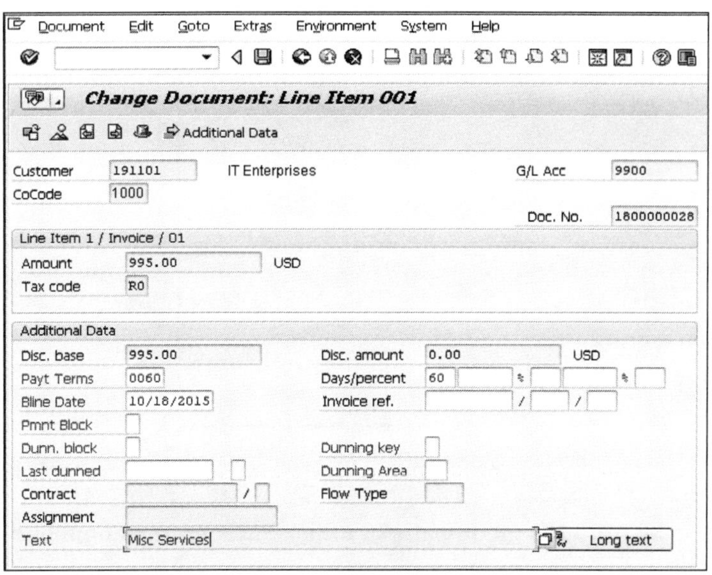

Figure 10.84 Change Document with Line Item Text Change

After changing field values, click the **Save** icon, or press `Ctrl`+`S`. A message indicates that the document changes have been saved (Figure 10.85).

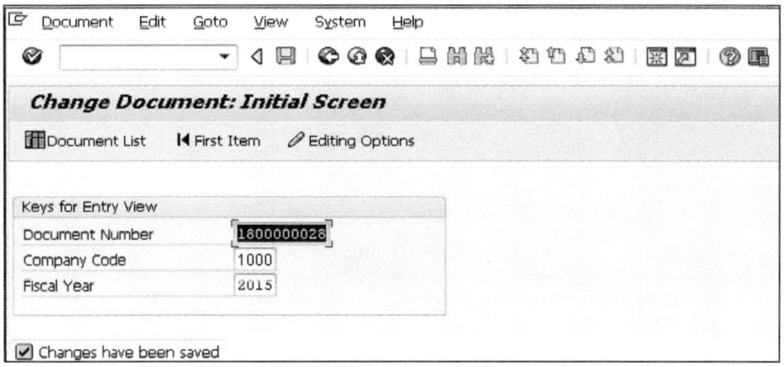

Figure 10.85 Document Changes Have Been Saved Message

To display an AR accounting document, use Transaction FB03 or application menu path, **Accounting • Financial Accounting • Accounts Receivable • Document • FB03 – Display**, as shown in Figure 10.86.

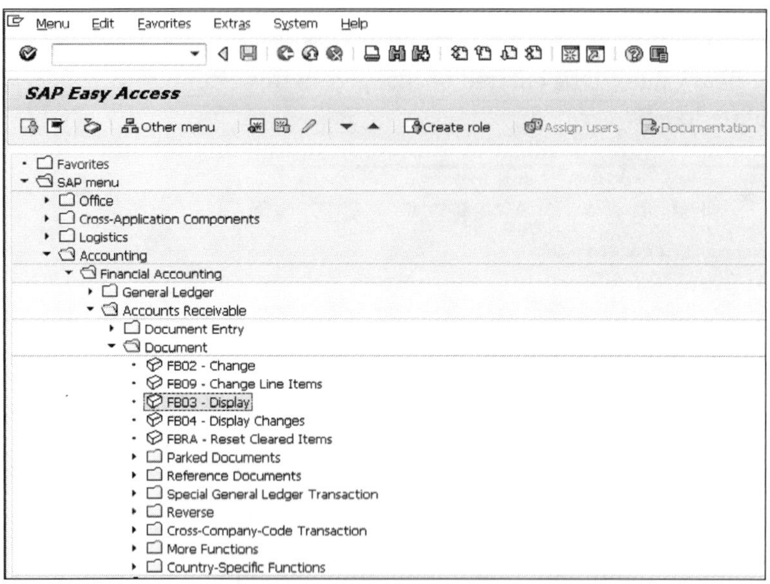

Figure 10.86 Transaction FB03 Application Menu Path in AR

Double-click **FB03 – Display** from the menu path, or enter "FB03" in the **Command** field (Figure 10.87) and press `Enter`.

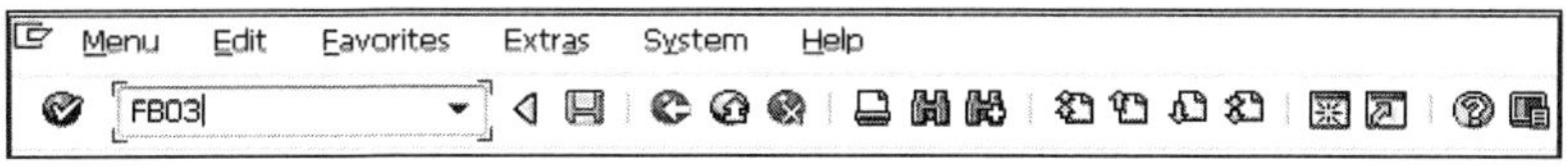

Figure 10.87 Entering "FB03" in the Command Field

The **Display Document: Initial Screen** opens (Figure 10.88). The **Document Number**, **Company Code**, and **Fiscal Year** fields are required.

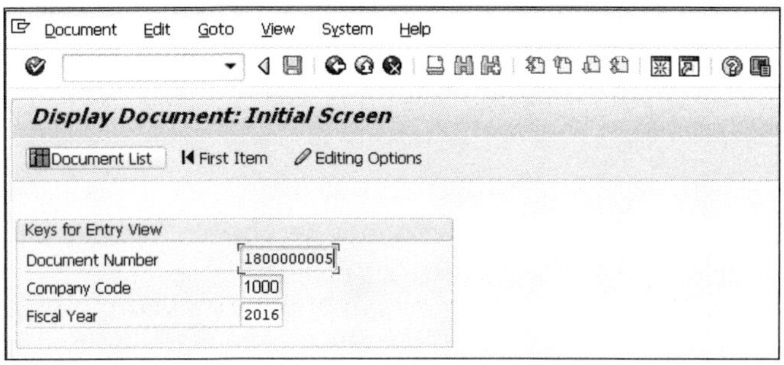

Figure 10.88 Document Display: Initial Screen

After entering the required field values, press Enter. The **Display Document: Data Entry View** screen opens (Figure 10.89).

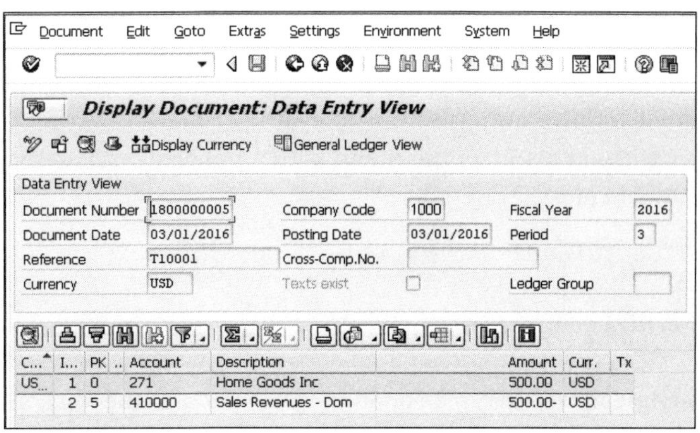

Figure 10.89 Display Document: Data Entry View

From this screen, you can double-click a line to view line item details, you can or click the **Header** icon to view header details.

10.6 Process Incoming Payments

At the core of the AR module is its ability to create a customer invoice and post a payment receipt. The customer invoice includes specific details (e.g., amount, due date) about the receivable owed by a customer. Processing an incoming payment involves the physical transfer of funds from a customer to your company.

Several payment methods are available, including check, wire transfer, and direct deposit. Electronic payments can automatically clear open customer invoices through the electronic bank reconciliation process in SAP, which is beyond the scope of this chapter. This section covers the manual creation of an incoming payment using Transaction F-28.

To post a manual incoming payment using Transaction F-28, follow the application menu path, **Accounting • Financial Accounting • Accounts Receivable • Document Entry • F-28 – Incoming Payments**, as shown in Figure 10.90.

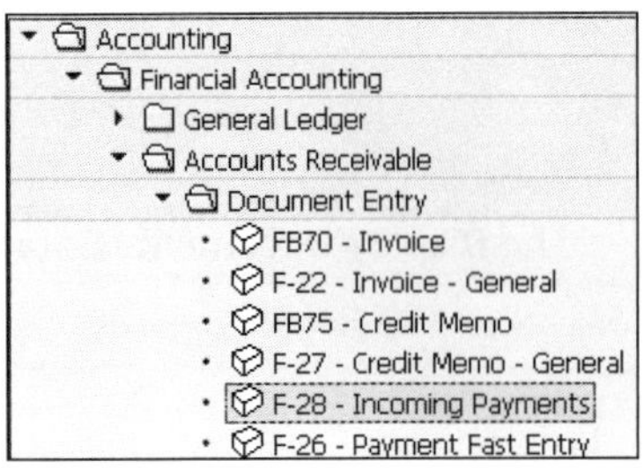

Figure 10.90 Transaction F-28 Application Menu Path

Double-click **F-28 – Incoming Payments** from the menu path, or enter "F-28" in the **Command** field (Figure 10.91) and press [Enter].

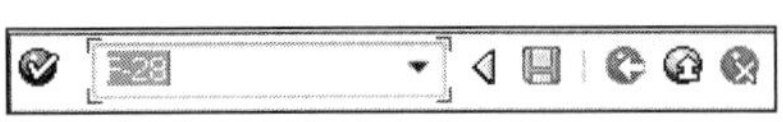

Figure 10.91 Entering "F-28" in the Command Field

The **Post Incoming Payments: Header Data** screen opens (Figure 10.92). In the top portion of the screen, most field values should contain default values, depending on your configuration and editing options. Make sure to input all required fields that don't prepopulate values. In this example, default values populated into the **Posting Date**, **Type** (i.e., document type), **Period**, **Company Code**, and **Currency/Rate** fields. We manually input a value into the **Document Date** field.

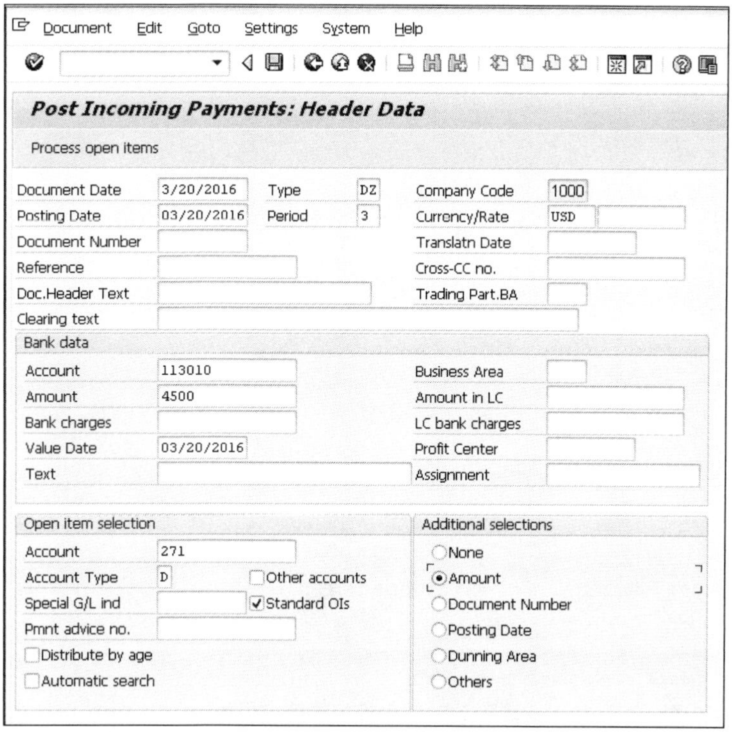

Figure 10.92 Post Incoming Payments: Header Data

In the **Bank data** area, enter values for **Account**, **Amount**, and any other fields that are required. In this example, we also entered a value in the **Profit Center** field. In the **Open item selection** area, enter the customer number in **Account**.

Finally, in the **Additional selections** area, choose a button that indicates how the program should search for and select open invoices. For this example, select the **Amount** button.

With all relevant fields entered, click the **Process open items** button in the top-left portion of the screen (Figure 10.92). The **Post Incoming Payments Enter selection criteria** screen opens (Figure 10.93). In this example, we entered the amount of our invoice to be paid ($2000) in the **From** and **To** fields.

After your selection criteria are entered, click the **Process open items** button (Figure 10.93) in the top-center portion of the screen. The **Post Incoming Payments Process open items** screen opens (Figure 10.94).

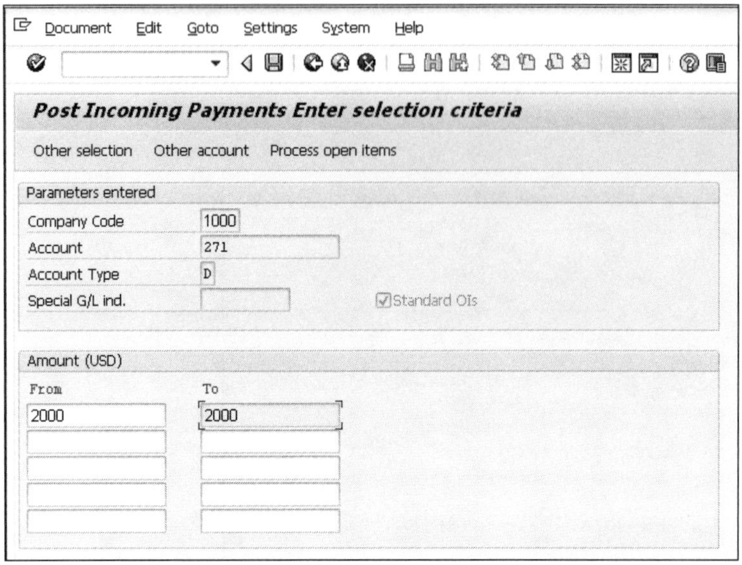

Figure 10.93 Post Incoming Payments Selection Criteria Screen

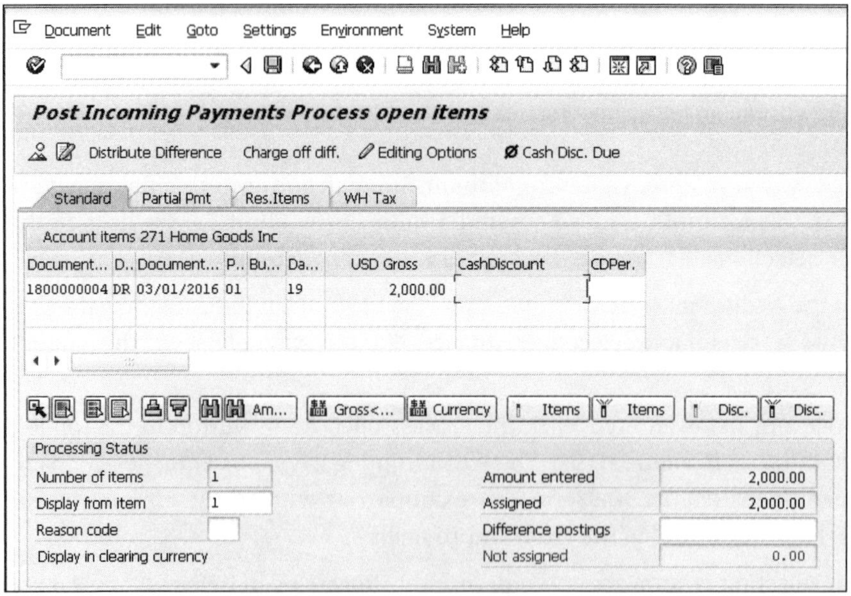

Figure 10.94 Incoming Payments Process Open Items Screen

If the correct open items have been selected, click the **Save** icon , or press Ctrl+S. The program posts the payment document and issues a "document posted" message (Figure 10.95).

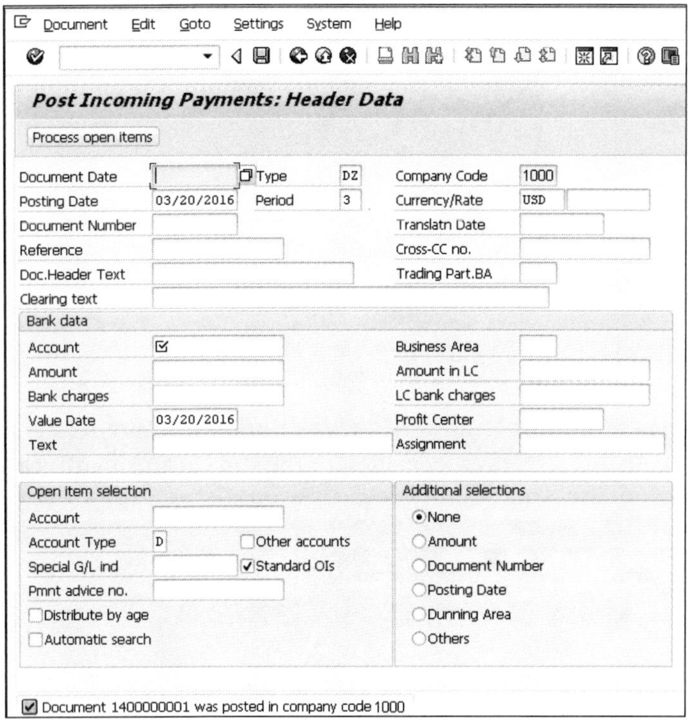

Figure 10.95 Incoming Payment Document Posted Message

This ends our discussion of incoming payments. The next topic, dunning, is important when customers aren't paying their invoices on time. Let's move on to discuss the details in the next section.

10.7 Dunning

Dunning is the process of sending periodic notices to customers regarding overdue payments. Setting up dunning requires configuration and settings within customer master data that are beyond the scope of this book. However, it's essential for an AR clerk to know how to execute the dunning program, which is a process we cover in the remainder of this section.

To execute a dunning run, follow application menu path, **Accounting • Financial Accounting • Accounts Receivable • Periodic Processing • F150 – Dunning**, as shown in Figure 10.96.

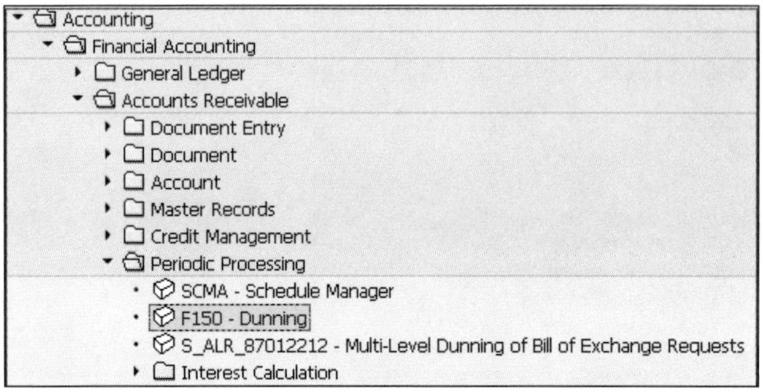

Figure 10.96 Transaction F150 Application Menu Path

Double-click **F150 – Dunning** from the menu path, and the **Dunning** program initial screen opens (Figure 10.97). In this screen, enter values for the **Run On** and **Identification** fields.

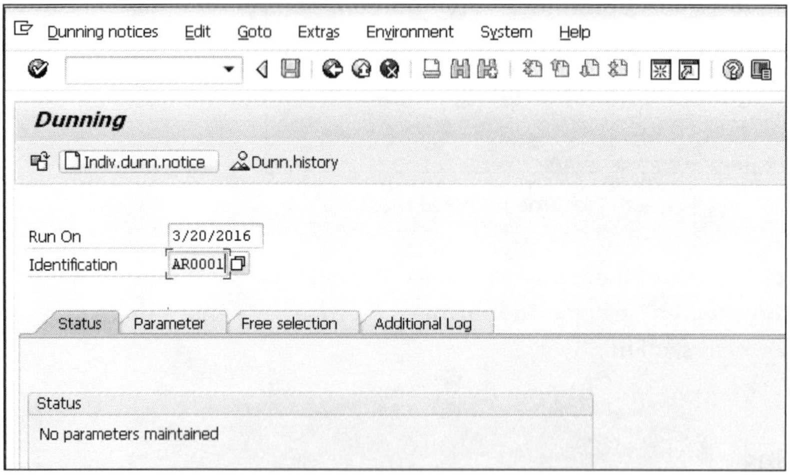

Figure 10.97 Dunning Program Initial Screen

Click on the **Parameter** tab. The **Dunning: Parameters** screen opens (Figure 10.98). Enter values for the **Dunning date**, **Docmnts posted up to**, **Company Code**, and **Customer** (or **Vendor** in some circumstances) fields.

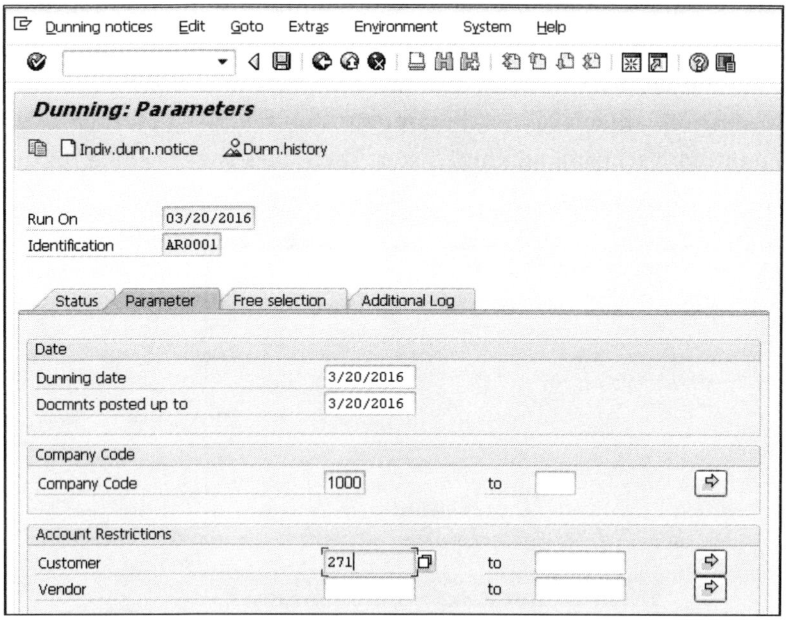

Figure 10.98 Dunning Parameters Screen

After all the parameters are entered, click the **Save** icon or press [Ctrl]+[S] to return to the **Status** tab (Figure 10.99). A message now appears: **Parameters were maintained**.

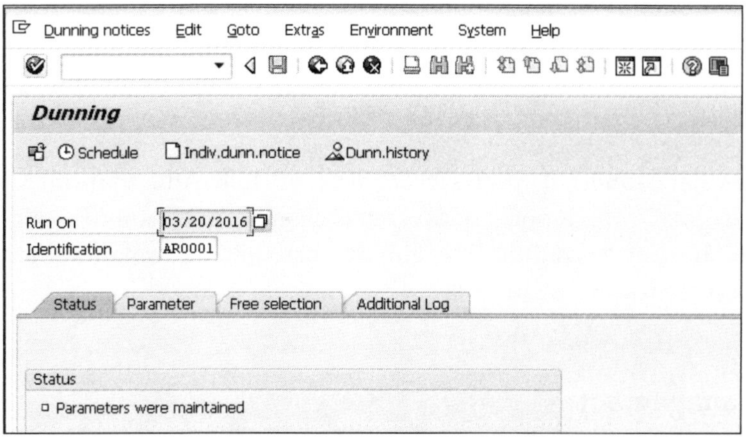

Figure 10.99 Dunning Status with Parameters Maintained

Now, click on the **Schedule** button in the top-left portion of the screen. The **Schedule Selection and Print** dialog box pops up (Figure 10.100) and immediately prompts you to enter a value for **OutputDevice**. To schedule the dunning run and print the dunning notices immediately, enter a value for **Start date,** and select the **Start immediately** and **Dunn.print with scheduling?** checkboxes. Then, click the **Schedule** button in the dialog box.

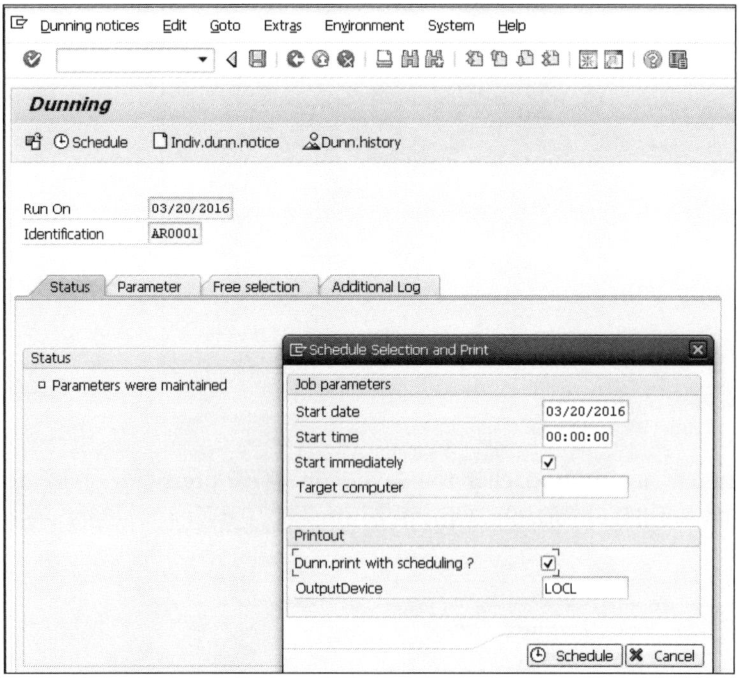

Figure 10.100 Dunning Schedule Selection and Print Dialog Box

A message indicates that dunning has been scheduled successfully. After the printing is complete, you can email your dunning notices or set them up to be automatically emailed to your customers. In addition, the dunning date and dunning level are updated in the SAP customer master record.

10.8 Credit Management

Credit management is an essential part of working in AR. The detailed setup is beyond the scope of this book, but we do want to discuss a few key points.

There are several parts to the credit management setup, one of which is the definition of groups (e.g., accounting clerk groups) and categories (e.g., risk categories). Customers are allocated to these groups for purposes of reporting and monitoring.

The credit management setup is highly personalized from company to company. Many factors can influence how it's configured. Much depends on your risk tolerance and exposure, credit limits, and customer history.

To see the standard tools and reports available in AR credit management, follow application menu path, **Accounting • Financial Accounting • Accounts Receivable • Credit Management**, as shown in Figure 10.101.

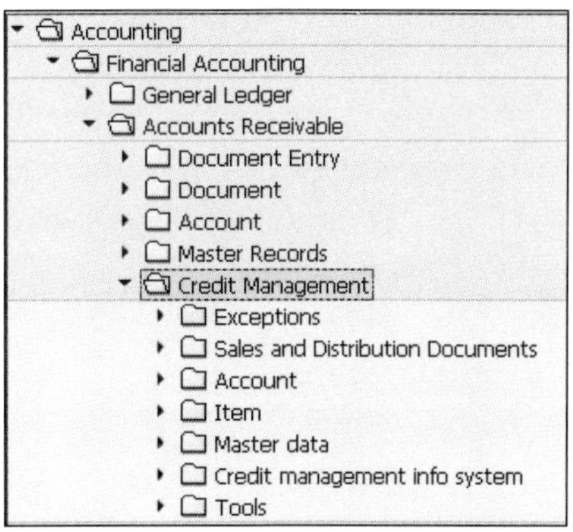

Figure 10.101 Credit Management Application Menu Path

10.9 Summary

In this chapter, we covered AR account transactions originating in the AR module. In Chapter 9, during our discussion of the order-to-cash process, you learned about sales transactions originating in SD-Sales. The discussion in this chapter is limited to AR transactions, not the sales cycle and the complete order-to-cash process.

The most common AR transaction is the entry of a customer invoice using Transaction FB70. Customer invoices are the documents that create open customer receivables and ultimately impact revenue recognition. We also walked through examples of other AR transactions, including the creation of a credit memo, down payment request, incoming payment, and document reversal.

Like the other FI modules, AR requires a host of tools to correct errors and to keep accurate track of receivables and revenue. Resetting and reversing, changing, and displaying documents are just some of the essential tasks of an AR clerk and AR supervisor. In addition, dunning and credit management are used for monitoring, management, and risk mitigation. Although they don't produce transactions per se, dunning and credit management are important AR business processes.

In addition to transactions and tools specific to AR, several pieces of standard functionality are available in AR that exist in other modules as well. These include the ability to park, hold, and save documents as completed, along with the tree display, account assignment templates, screen variants, and more. By learning these functions in AR, you've also acquired knowledge that transcends other areas of FI.

This concludes our discussion of AR transactions. In the next chapter, we'll discuss AR account inquiries.

Chapter 11
Accounts Receivable Account Inquiries

In this chapter, we explore transactions and reports you can use to make inquiries about customer accounts and balances in Accounts Receivable (AR). The transactions and reports in this chapter can be used to reconcile balances, identify errors, and perform other customer account maintenance functions.

Accounts Receivable (AR) account maintenance is an essential job function of AR personnel. In performing this function, you may uncover data entry and posting errors. Knowing how to perform the transactions in this chapter provides you with essential skills required in the day-to-day operations of an AR department. We'll discuss the basic tools of the trade and provide guidance about the best transactions to use in different scenarios.

One of the ongoing challenges faced by an AR department is the large number of inquiries from customers regarding their account balances, discounts, expected due dates, and payment receipts. This chapter provides you with the basic tools needed to satisfy these types of inquiries and more.

These functions can be useful in the following ways:

- To reconcile General Ledger (G/L) accounts receivable balances with customer subledger balances
- For month-end and year-end account analysis
- To assist with cash management forecasting
- To perform customer account inquiries

The following sections will discuss AR account inquiry and maintenance functions that help you research individual transactions, display account balances, view account transaction details, and run reports and queries. Many of the tools discussed in this chapter have practical application not only in month-end and year-end closing but also in the day-to-day functions performed by AR clerks and supervisors.

We'll begin by discussing the different types of customer account displays in detail, including customer balances and line item displays.

11.1 Customer Account Displays

The AR customer account display allows you to view individual or collective customer account balances and transaction details (i.e., individual AR documents and line items). The primary transactions used to view customer account balances and account details are Transaction FD10N and Transaction FBL5N.

Drilldown capability is particularly powerful within these two transactions. From Transaction FD10N, you can double-click on a balance and immediately drill down into a customer line item display in Transaction FBL5N. Then, within Transaction FBL5N, you can double-click an individual customer line item and immediately be taken into the individual accounting document that contains that customer line item.

Let's look at the customer account balance transaction and line items.

11.1.1 Customer Account Balance

Transaction FD10N is the customer account balance display, which is used frequently in AR to reconcile with G/L receivables account balances. At a high level, this transaction provides the period breakdowns needed for reconciling month-end activities, and it's also useful if you need to drill down into a specific account balance to see the documents that make up that balance.

Transaction FD10N allows you to view the account balance by accounting period for one or more customers. The display screen breaks the customer account balance down into a debit balance, credit balance, period balance, cumulative balance, and sales/purchases amounts. By double-clicking any of these numbers, you can drill down to see the detailed transactions that make up the balance.

To display customer balances, use Transaction FD10N or application menu path, **Accounting • Financial Accounting • Accounts Receivable • Account • FD10N – Display Balances**, as shown in Figure 11.1.

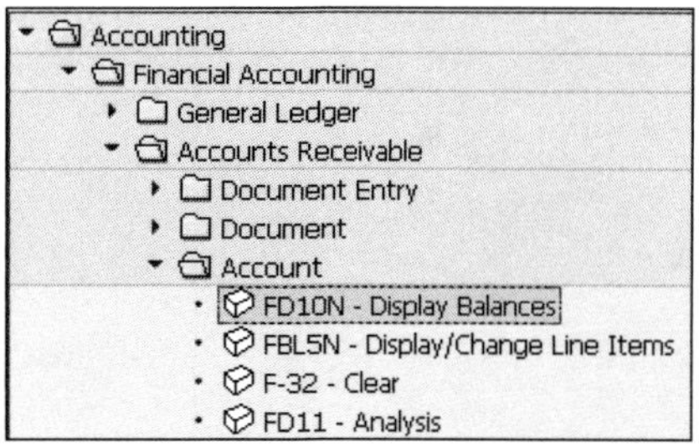

Figure 11.1 Transaction FD10N Application Menu Path

Double-click **FD10N – Display Balances** from the menu path, or enter "FD10N" in the **Command** field (Figure 11.2) and press [Enter].

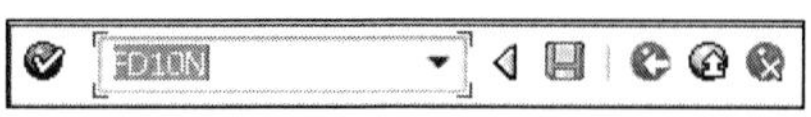

Figure 11.2 Entering "FD10N" in the Command Field

The **Customer Balance Display** selection screen opens (Figure 11.3). Enter values for the **Customer**, **Company code**, and **Fiscal year** fields, and then click the **Execute** icon.

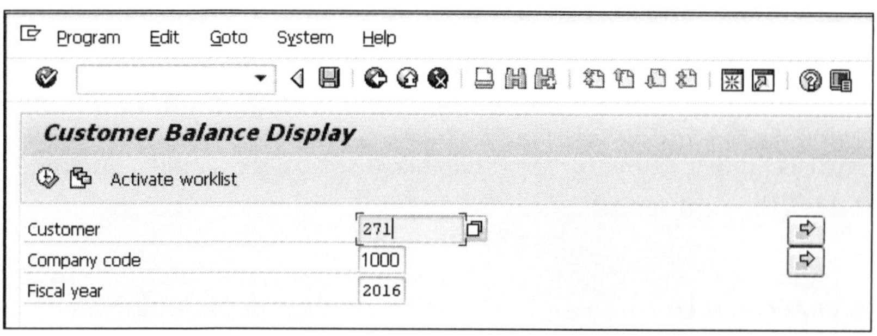

Figure 11.3 Customer Balance Display Screen

The **Customer Balance Display** output screen opens (Figure 11.4). From this screen, you can double-click any number to display balance details, or you can click on the **Special general ledger** tab to view balances for specific special G/L transactions, such as down payments.

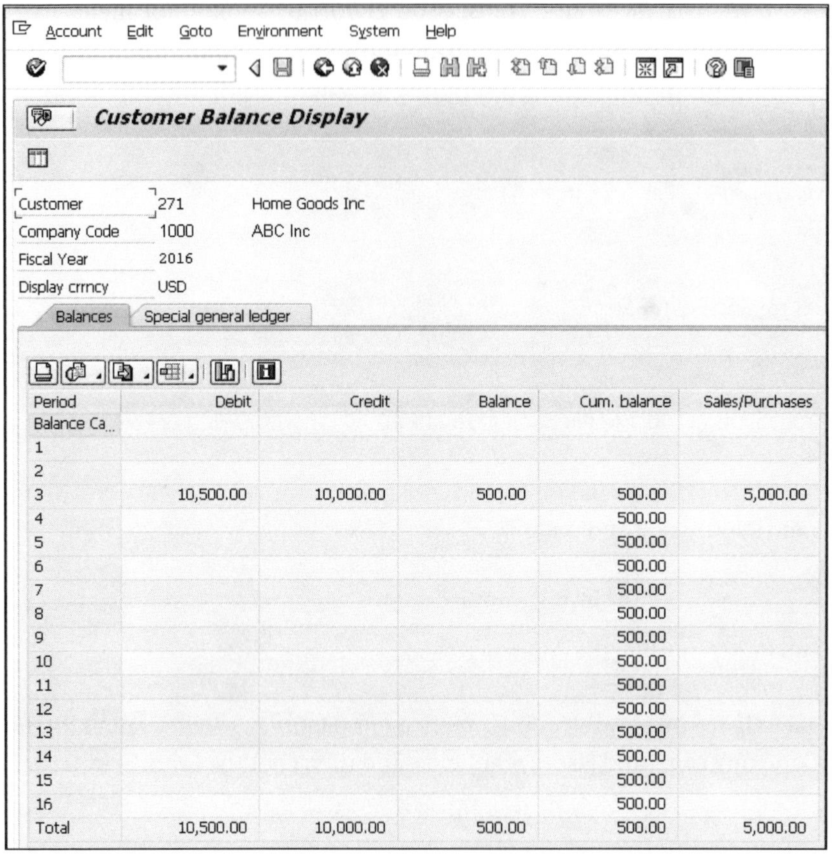

Figure 11.4 Customer Balance Display Output

Now that we've discussed customer account balance displays, let's look at customer line item displays in the next section.

11.1.2 Customer Account Line Items

Transaction FBL5N is the customer line item display, which provides all the individual documents and account line items posted to a customer account. When using this transaction, the selection screens give you the flexibility to filter data by customer account, company code, posting date, type of transaction, and more. These selection options can be saved as variants, making them reusable. In addition, from the output screen, you can filter, search, sort, subtotal, and more. The output can be downloaded into various file formats (e.g., Excel), making further analysis outside

SAP possible when needed. This functionality uses Transaction FBL3N and Transaction FBL1N, and works similarly in AR as it does in G/L and AP (which we discussed in Chapter 4 and Chapter 8, respectively).

Note

Believe it or not, spreadsheets are more in use than ever before in accounting and finance. It's very common to use Transaction FBL5N to query, filter, and sort data, only to export the results into a spreadsheet for further analysis.

The SAP concept of open item management is inherent in AR, just as it is in G/L (Chapter 2), Accounts Payable (AP) (Chapter 4), and fixed assets (which we'll discuss in Chapter 14). Open item management in AR is a way of tracking, matching, and managing customer accounting line items that are supposed to be offset (i.e., cleared) by other items and net to zero. For example, when a customer invoice is received, an accounting document posts a debit to the customer account. The debit entry to the customer account is considered an open item because it has created an open receivable due from the customer. After payment is received, the open receivable is matched with an offsetting credit to the customer account, and its status is changed from **Open** to **Cleared**.

With the concept of open item management in mind, Transaction FBL5N is particularly useful in showing the status of an invoice (i.e., open or cleared) and the due date for each invoice. It's an essential tool for handling customer inquiries regarding the status of invoices and payments. Moreover, Transaction FBL5N can be very telling in finding common errors in a customer account, such as duplicate invoice posting.

To display customer line items using Transaction FBL5N, follow application menu path, **Accounting • Financial Accounting • Accounts Receivable • Account • FBL5N – Display/Change Line Items**, as shown in Figure 11.5.

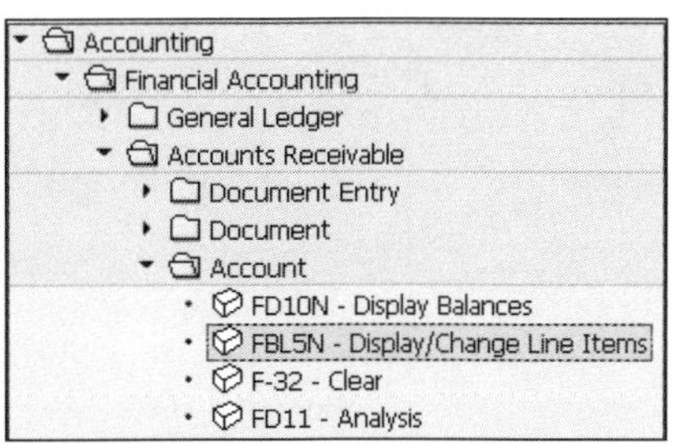

Figure 11.5 Transaction FBL5N Application Menu Path

Double-click **FBL5N – Display/Change Line Items** from the menu path, or enter "FBL5N" in the **Command** field (as shown in Figure 11.6) and press Enter.

Figure 11.6 Entering "FBL5N" in the Command Field

The **Customer Line Item Display** selection screen opens (Figure 11.7). Enter values in the **Customer account** and **Company code** fields. The most notable components of this selection screen are the **Status** and **Type** areas under **Line item selection**. The **Status** buttons allow you to choose **Open items**, **Cleared items**, or **All items** as the output. You can also narrow your selection of data by entering relevant date parameters.

The checkboxes in the **Type** area allow you to choose the types of documents to display on the output screen.

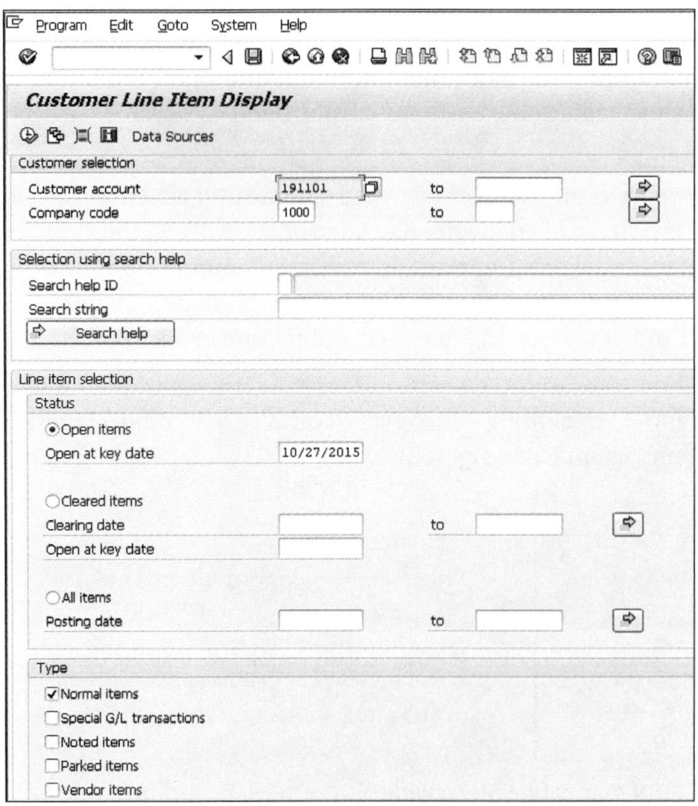

Figure 11.7 Customer Line Item Display Selection Screen

After you've entered all your selection parameters, click the **Execute** icon. The **Customer Line Item Display** output screen opens (Figure 11.8).

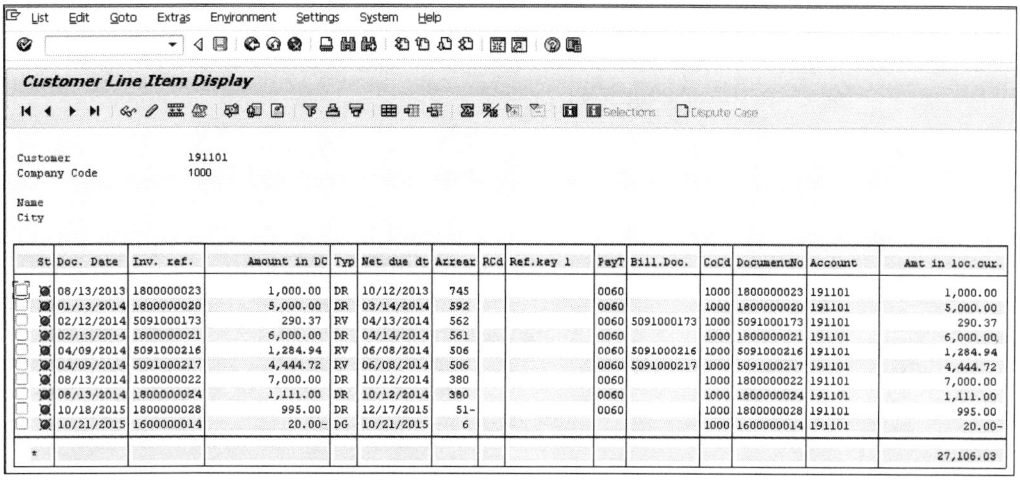

St	Doc. Date	Inv. ref.	Amount in DC	Typ	Net due dt	Arrear	RCd	Ref.key 1	PayT	Bill.Doc.	CoCd	DocumentNo	Account	Amt in loc.cur.
	08/13/2013	1800000023	1,000.00	DR	10/12/2013	745			0060		1000	1800000023	191101	1,000.00
	01/13/2014	1800000020	5,000.00	DR	03/14/2014	592			0060		1000	1800000020	191101	5,000.00
	02/12/2014	5091000173	290.37	RV	04/13/2014	562			0060	5091000173	1000	5091000173	191101	290.37
	02/13/2014	1800000021	6,000.00	DR	04/14/2014	561			0060		1000	1800000021	191101	6,000.00
	04/09/2014	5091000216	1,284.94	RV	06/08/2014	506			0060	5091000216	1000	5091000216	191101	1,284.94
	04/09/2014	5091000217	4,444.72	RV	06/08/2014	506			0060	5091000217	1000	5091000217	191101	4,444.72
	08/13/2014	1800000022	7,000.00	DR	10/12/2014	380			0060		1000	1800000022	191101	7,000.00
	08/13/2014	1800000024	1,111.00	DR	10/12/2014	380			0060		1000	1800000024	191101	1,111.00
	10/18/2015	1800000028	995.00	DR	12/17/2015	51-			0060		1000	1800000028	191101	995.00
	10/21/2015	1600000014	20.00-	DG	10/21/2015	6					1000	1600000014	191101	20.00-
*														27,106.03

Figure 11.8 Customer Line Item Display Output

After the output is displayed, you can change the layout, sort, filter, total, subtotal, and so on, and your layouts can be saved and reused. In Transaction FBL5N, you can also double-click an individual line item to drill down directly into an AR invoice or another AR document. When you're in an AR document, you can then drill down into individual line items in the document. This demonstrates the power of system integration and drilldown capability.

In Chapter 8, a table of frequently used icons in line item display is provided. For your convenience, this table is also provided here (Table 11.1). Nothing new or unique to AR is provided in this table. In fact, you'll discover that most of the icons you need to use repetitively in AP are the same ones you use regularly in AR.

Icon	Description
	Click once on the document you want to display, and then click on this **Display Document** icon.
	Click once on the document you want to change, and then click on this **Change Document** icon.
	To filter data in the view, click on this icon. Then define your field criteria (i.e., select fields to filter and values).

Table 11.1 Frequently Used Icons in Transaction FBL1N

Icon	Description
	To sort data in ascending order, click once on a column header, and then click this **Sort in Ascending Order** icon.
	To sort data in descending order, click once on a column header, and then click this **Sort in Descending Order** icon.
	To change the screen layout, click on the **Change Layout** icon, and then select fields and the order of display.
	To select a different predefined screen layout, click on the **Select Layout** icon. In the popup window, double-click on the screen layout you want to use.
	Use the **Save Layout** icon to save changes you've made to the screen layout.
	To total data, click once on a column header, and then click this **Display Sum** icon.
	To subtotal data, click once on a column header, and then click this **Subtotal** icon.

Table 11.1 Frequently Used Icons in Transaction FBL1N (Cont.)

The customer line item display is the most powerful tool at your disposal for checking the status of an invoice or payment. AR clerks and supervisors use it frequently, and it's often the first stop when fielding an inquiry about a customer account balance, the status of an invoice, or the status of a payment. Several standard reports can provide the same or similar output, but these standard reports may not have the same drilldown capability.

11.2 Customer Analysis

When it comes to analyzing details of a customer account, there are several useful transactions available in AR. In this section, we'll cover three common scenarios in the day-to-day work of an AR clerk or supervisor and discuss the best tool to use in each.

11.2.1 Due Date Analysis

The first scenario is finding the due date and status of an open AR invoice. One of the most frequent tasks requested of an AR department is to find out when a specific invoice is due for payment. One way to find the answer is via Transaction FBL5N, which was covered in detail in Section 11.1.2.

Within the customer line item display (Transaction FBL5N), there are two fields most relevant to due date determination: **Net Due Date** and **Net Due Date Symbol**. The **Net Due Date Symbol** graphically represents whether a customer receivable isn't due, is due, or is overdue. All three symbols are shown in Figure 11.9, each with an individual open customer invoice.

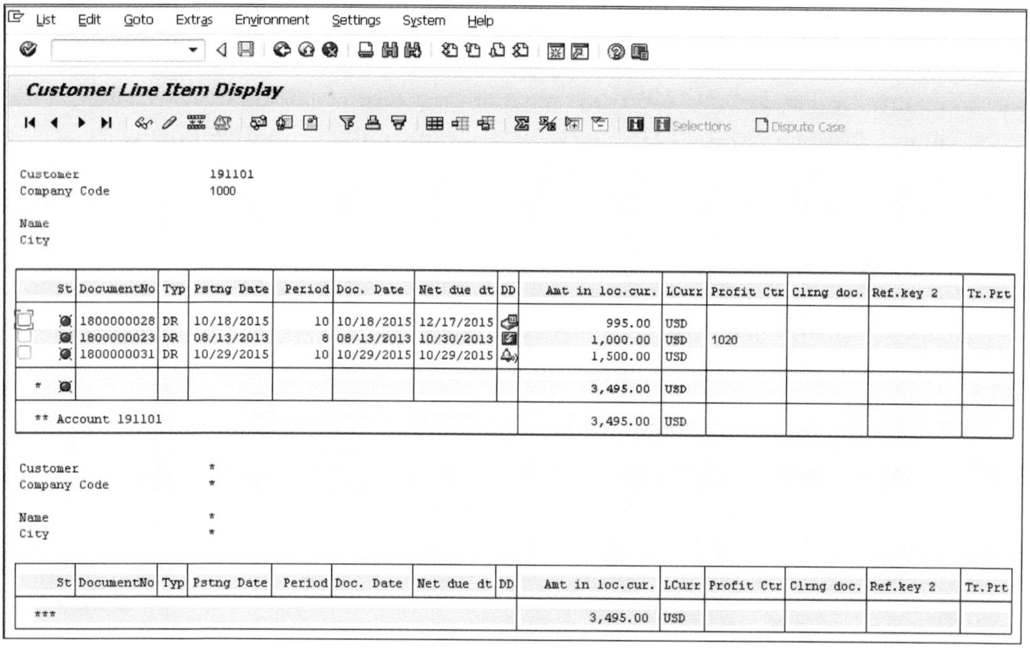

Figure 11.9 Transaction FBL5N Output with Due Date Symbols

The symbols have the following meanings:

- **Overdue**
  This symbol appears anytime an invoice is unpaid and the current date is past the payment due date. This is the symbol you want to watch out for because it means a customer account is past due.
- **Due**
  This symbol appears anytime an invoice is unpaid and the current date equals the payment due date. This is also one you want to keep an eye on, particularly if the customer has a history of making late payments.
- **Not Due**
  This symbol appears anytime an invoice is unpaid and the current date is less than the payment due date.

11.2.2 Searching for Cleared Customer Items

A second common AR task is to find the payment date of a customer invoice for which payment has been received and applied against a customer account. After a customer payment has been received and applied against an open invoice, that invoice will show up as a cleared item in Transaction FBL5N. A paid invoice appears in the customer line item display with a clearing document number and payment date.

Searching for cleared customer items in Transaction FBL5N is frequently used to determine if and when a customer payment was received. You can search for cleared items for one or more customers, on a specific date, or by referencing a specific invoice or clearing document number. These are just some of the ways to search for cleared customer items.

To view a cleared customer line item using Transaction FBL5N, follow application menu path, **Accounting • Financial Accounting • Accounts Receivable • Account • FBL5N – Display/Change Line Items**, as shown in Figure 11.10.

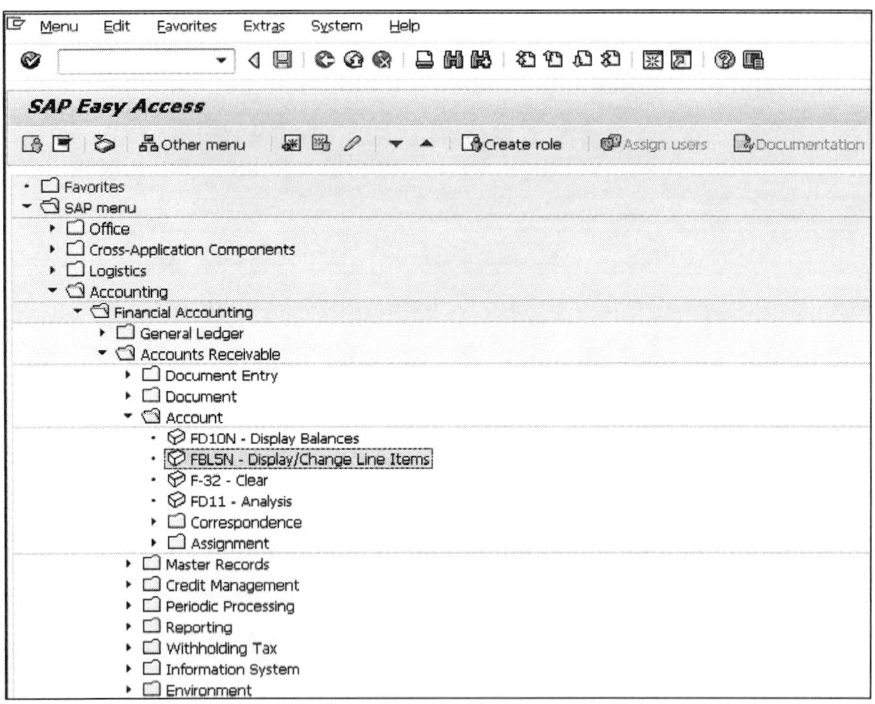

Figure 11.10 Transaction FBL5N Application Menu Path

The **Customer Line Item Display** selection screen opens (Figure 11.11). Enter values in the **Customer account** and **Company code** fields. For this example, to see a payment received, we selected the **Cleared items** status option and entered a date range in the **Clearing date** field. Note that this isn't the only way to see if a customer payment has been received, but it's the most frequent method used in accounting departments because it's the most flexible and powerful tool available.

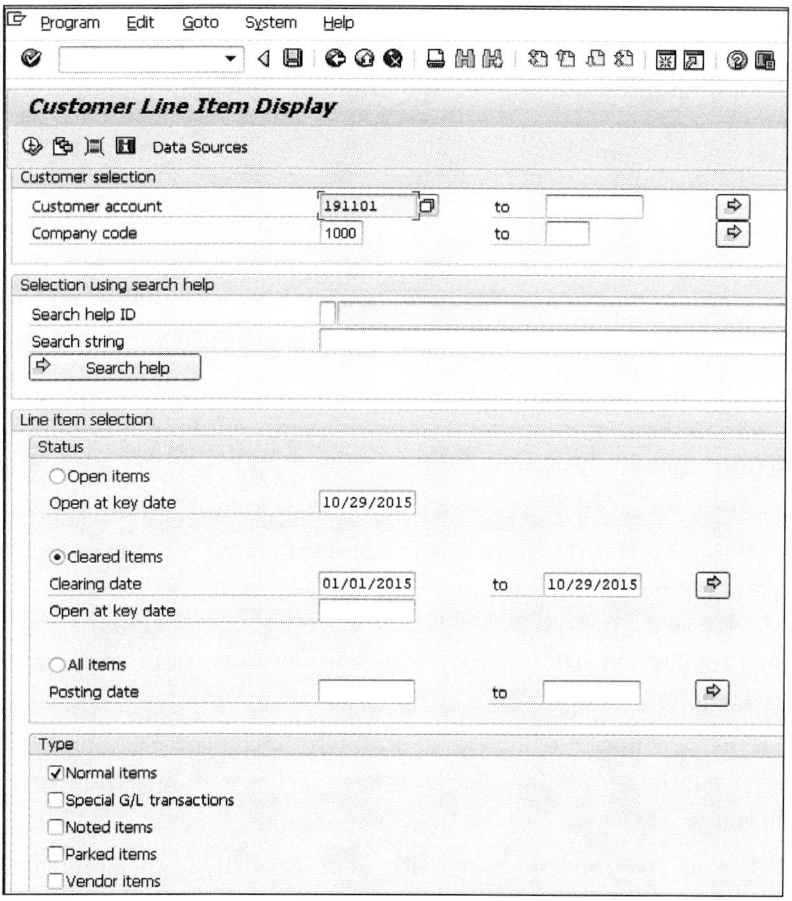

Figure 11.11 Selection Screen with Cleared Item Selections

With all field values entered, click the **Execute** icon ⊕. The **Customer Line Item Display** output screen appears, showing the payment date the customer payment was received and the clearing document number (Figure 11.12).

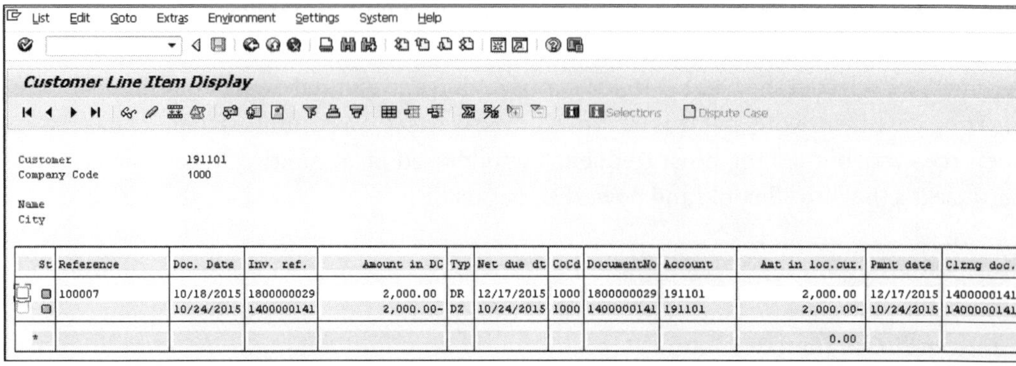

Figure 11.12 Output with Paid Invoice

Using Transaction FBL5N to search for cleared invoices and payments received is also valuable when looking for a misapplied payment, that is, an incoming payment that was applied to the wrong invoice or to the wrong customer account altogether. The best way to identify misapplied payments is to validate the customer number and reference number of the cleared invoice.

11.2.3 General Customer Analysis

The third common task covered in this section is performing general customer analysis using Transaction FD11. This transaction isn't necessarily used for only one specific purpose. Instead, it provides a breadth of information on a customer account. It's a one-stop shop to view balances, look at special G/L transactions, view payment history, and more. Transaction FD11 is designed to show the most common types of customer analysis required.

To review a customer accounting using Transaction FD11, follow application menu path, **Accounting • Financial Accounting • Accounts Receivable • Account • FD11 – Analysis**, as shown in Figure 11.13.

Double-click **FD11 – Analysis** from the menu path, or enter "FD11" in the **Command** field (Figure 11.14) and press Enter.

The **Customer: Initial Screen Account Analysis** selection screen opens (Figure 11.15). Enter values in the **Customer**, **Company Code**, and **Fiscal Year** fields.

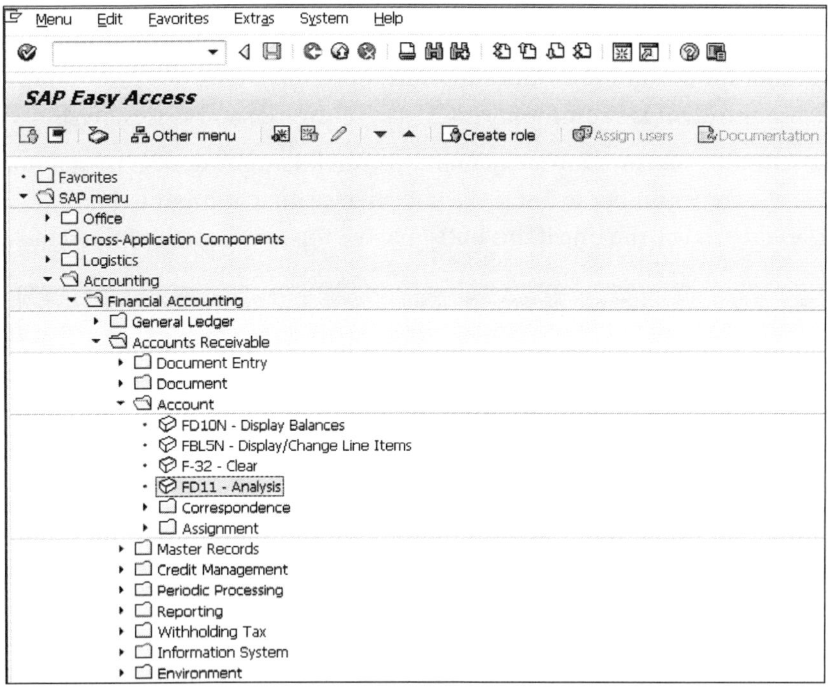

Figure 11.13 Transaction FD11 Application Menu Path

Figure 11.14 Entering "FD11" in the Command Field

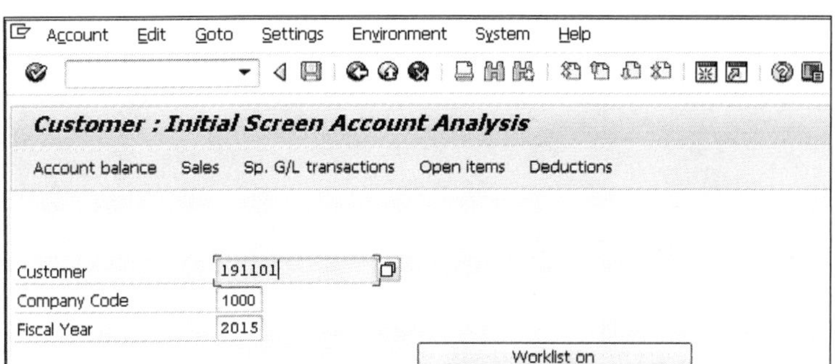

Figure 11.15 Customer: Initial Screen Account Analysis

With all field values entered, press Enter, and the **Account Balance Account Analysis** screen opens (Figure 11.16). Seven different tabs exist to take you directly to the type of data that you want to see. These tabs filter certain types of data (e.g., sales, down payments, discounts) that are commonly needed for customer account analysis.

Transaction FD11 also has drilldown capability to see line item detail. To see this detail, double-click any number in a screen, or click once on a number to place your cursor on it, and then click the **Line items** button in the top-left portion of the screen.

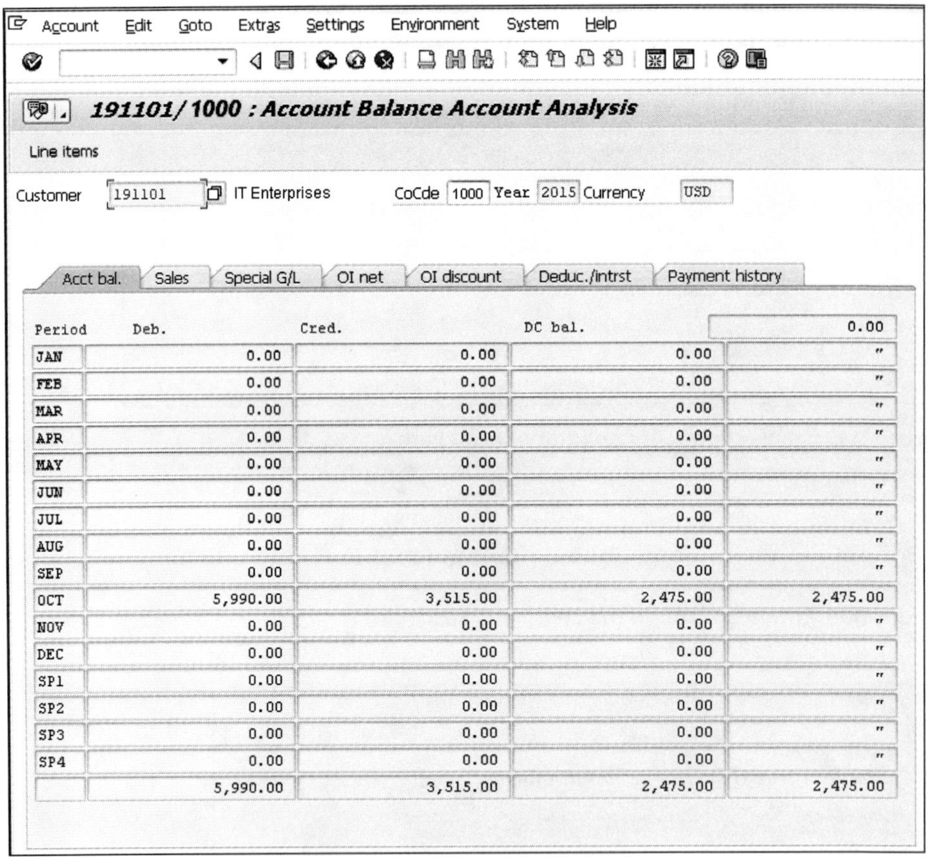

Period	Deb.	Cred.	DC bal.	0.00
JAN	0.00	0.00	0.00	"
FEB	0.00	0.00	0.00	"
MAR	0.00	0.00	0.00	"
APR	0.00	0.00	0.00	"
MAY	0.00	0.00	0.00	"
JUN	0.00	0.00	0.00	"
JUL	0.00	0.00	0.00	"
AUG	0.00	0.00	0.00	"
SEP	0.00	0.00	0.00	"
OCT	5,990.00	3,515.00	2,475.00	2,475.00
NOV	0.00	0.00	0.00	"
DEC	0.00	0.00	0.00	"
SP1	0.00	0.00	0.00	"
SP2	0.00	0.00	0.00	"
SP3	0.00	0.00	0.00	"
SP4	0.00	0.00	0.00	"
	5,990.00	3,515.00	2,475.00	2,475.00

Figure 11.16 Account Balance Account Analysis

Now that we've completed our discussion on customer account displays and customer account analysis, let's move on to discuss some standard reporting capabilities in AR.

11.3 Reports and Queries

In Section 11.1, we discussed customer account displays in detail, including a discussion of Transaction FD10N and Transaction FBL5N. For validating customer account balances and transaction details, these transactions are the most beneficial, particularly because of their ability to drill down all the way to accounting documents and line item detail. However, other tools do exist to view customer account balances and transaction details. In this section, you'll see where to find these alternatives in AR reports and queries.

11.3.1 Standard Reports

Standard reports are SAP delivered and universally found in the **Information System** folder of the application menu. The most useful general-purpose AR reports can be accessed from application menu path, **Accounting • Financial Accounting • Accounts Receivable • Information System • Reports for Accounts Receivable Accounting**, as shown in Figure 11.17.

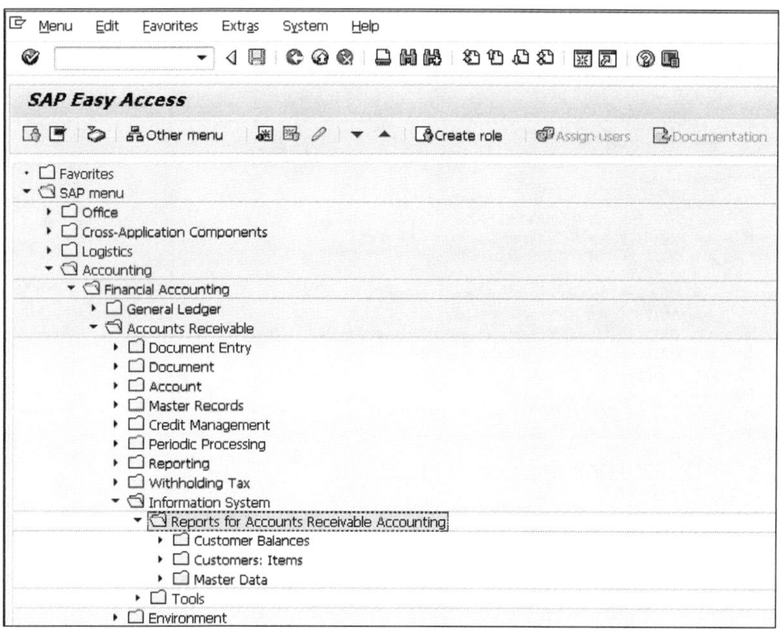

Figure 11.17 AR Reports Application Menu Path

Many standard reports exist for viewing customer balances, line items, and master data; let's take a closer look at two examples.

Due Date Analysis for Open Items

Customer due date analysis is the process of determining how much is due to be paid by a customer in each period. The most comprehensive tool for this task is report S_ALR_87012168 – Due Date Analysis for Open Items.

To perform AR due date analysis, use Transaction S_ALR_87012168 or application menu path, **Accounting • Financial Accounting • Accounts Receivable • Information System • Reports for Accounts Receivable Accounting • Customer: Items • S_ALR_87012168 – Due Date Analysis for Open Items**, as shown in Figure 11.18.

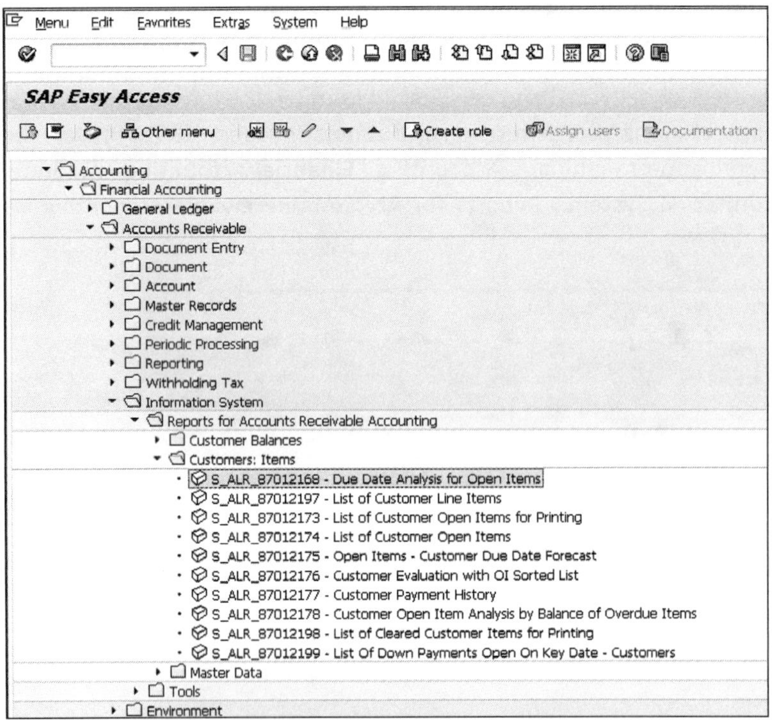

Figure 11.18 Report S_ALR_87012168 Application Menu Path

Double-click **S_ALR_87012168 – Due Date Analysis for Open Items** from the menu path, and the selection screen for report S_ALR_87012168 opens (Figure 11.19). For this example, we entered one **Customer account** and **Company code**, although multiple values are permitted. The field value for **Open items at key date** defaults to the current date, but it can be overwritten. In the **Output type** area, multiple choices exist, and you should try them all. For this example, we selected the first option: **Graphical report output**.

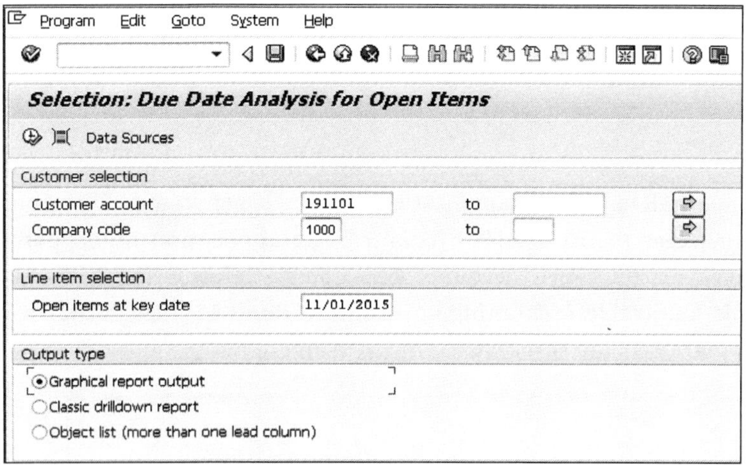

Figure 11.19 Selection Screen

With all screen field values entered, click the **Execute** icon. The output screen for the due date analysis report opens (Figure 11.20), showing amounts currently due for the customer selected.

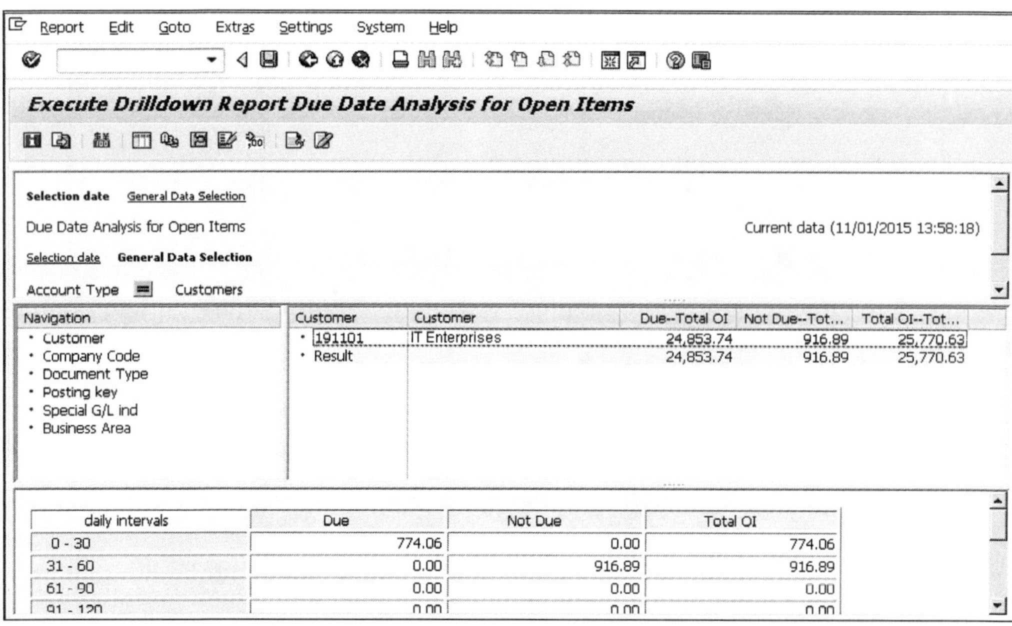

Figure 11.20 Output Screen

From the output screen, you can drill down, navigate using other objects, export the data, and more. Report S_ALR_87012168 can be a valuable tool in forecasting cash balances.

Customer Due Date Forecast

Another useful standard AR report is report S_ALR_87012175 – Open Items – Customer Due Date Forecast. Access report S_ALR_87012175 using application menu path, **Accounting • Financial Accounting • Accounts Receivable • Information System • Reports for Accounts Receivable Accounting • Customers: Items • S_ALR_87012175 – Open Items – Customer Due Date Forecast**, as shown in Figure 11.21.

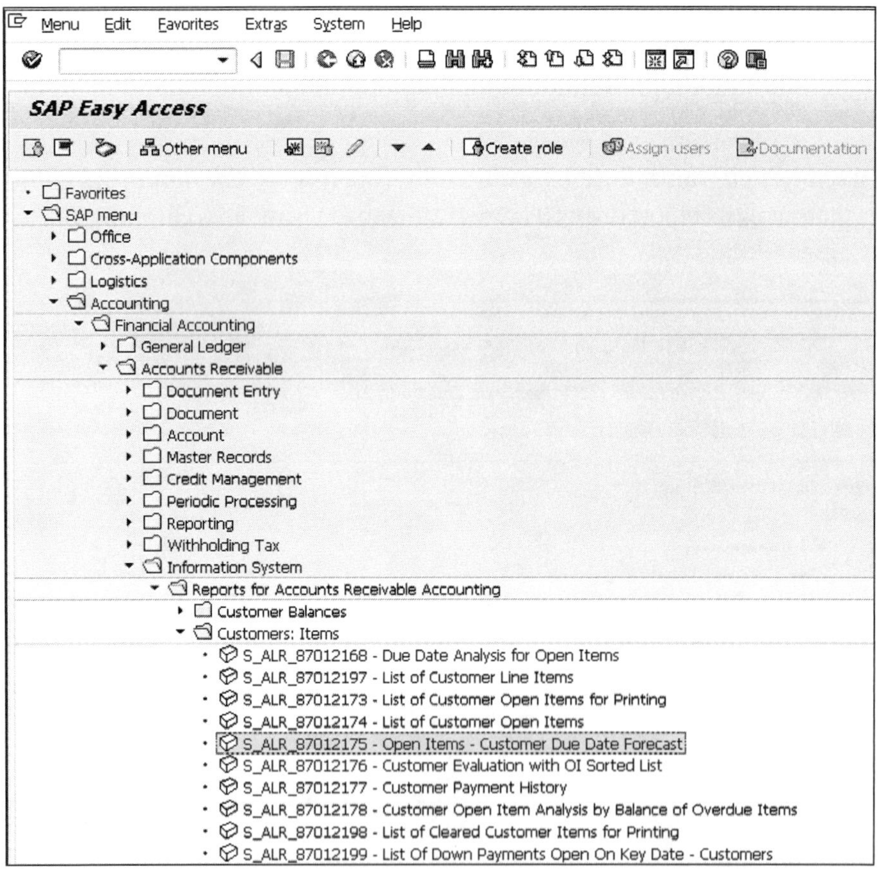

Figure 11.21 Report S_ALR_87012175 Application Menu Path

Double-click **S_ALR_87012175 – Open Items – Customer Due Date Forecast** from the menu path, and the **Open Items – Customer Due Date Forecast** selection screen opens (Figure 11.22). For this example, we entered values for the **Customer account** and **Company code** fields. A value defaulted into the **Open items at key date** field. Additional output selections can be made in the **Further selections** and **Output control** areas.

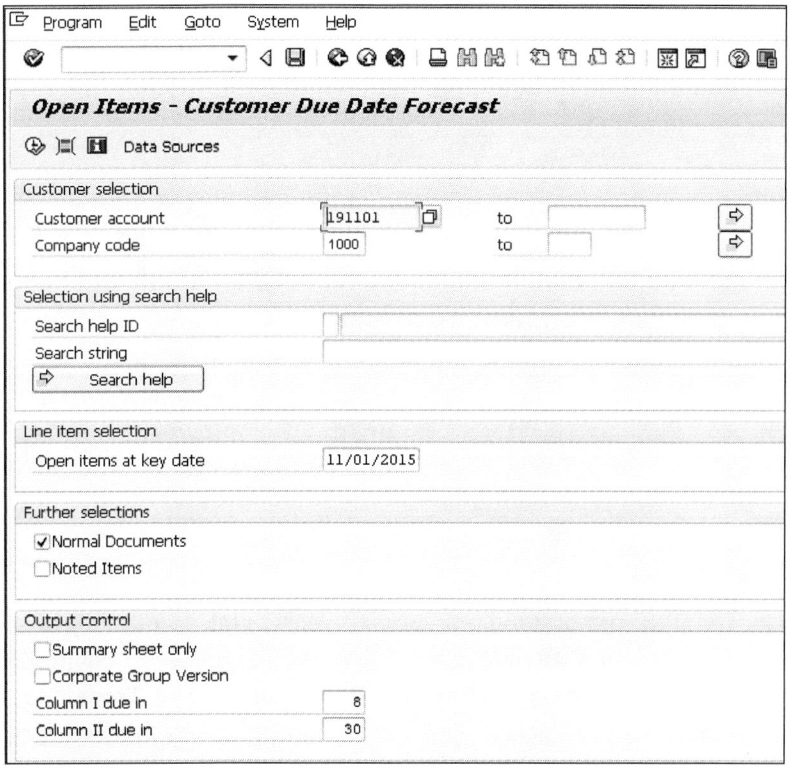

Figure 11.22 Selection Screen

With all screen field values entered, click the **Execute** icon. The output screen for the report appears (Figure 11.23), showing customer due date forecasts.

Drilldown capability doesn't exist in report S_ALR_87012175, but for a nice summary view of customer balances, this report serves the purpose well.

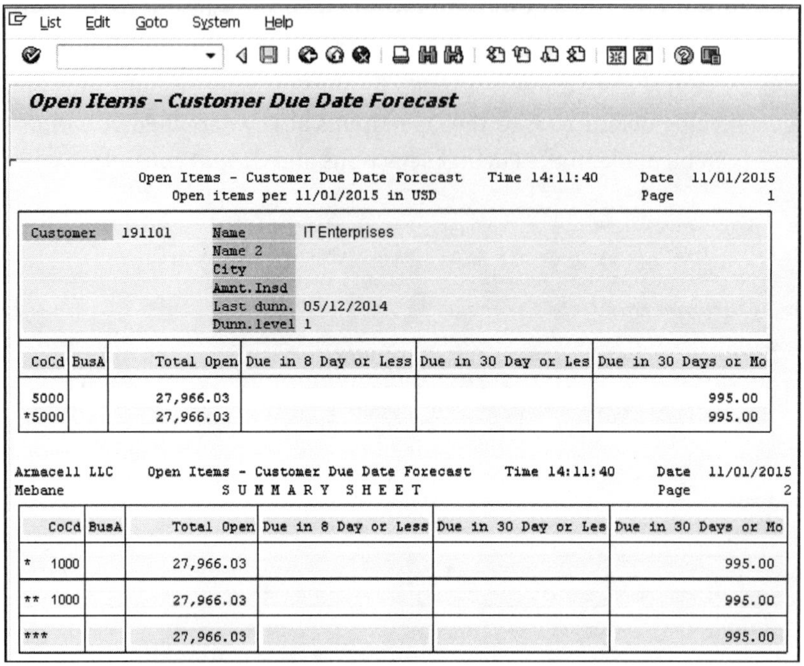

Figure 11.23 Initial Output Screen

11.3.2 Direct Table Queries

Now that we've looked at the use of standard reports in AR, let's take a look at how to make direct table queries to view AR data. As we discussed for the G/L in Chapter 4 and AP in Chapter 8, there are two transactions that allow you to do so: Transaction SE11 and Transaction SE16.

> **Note**
>
> Transaction SE11 is specifically targeted for use by developers; end users typically don't have authorization. It is more common for end users to be authorized to use direct table access via Transaction SE16, with restrictions to specific tables.

We'll explore each in the following sections.

Transaction SE11

Transaction SE11 is the first approach, which can be accessed via the following application menu path: **Tools • ABAP Workbench • Development** (see Figure 11.24).

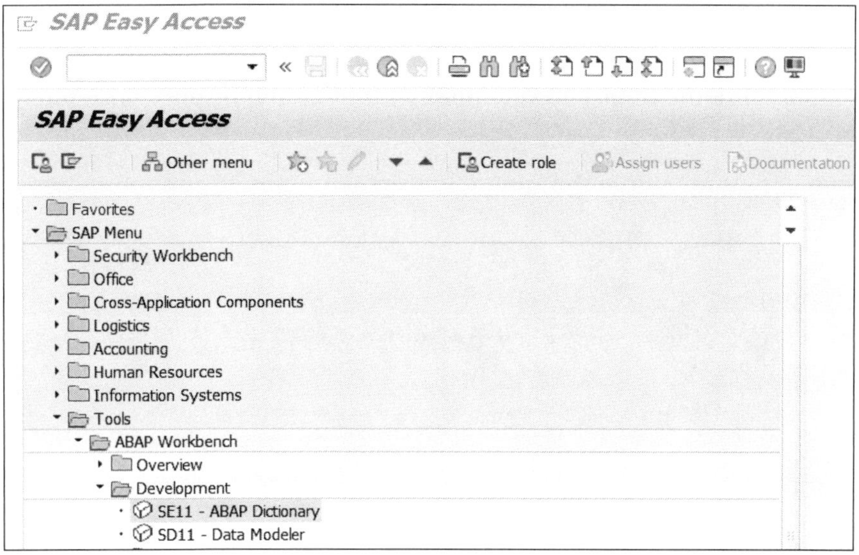

Figure 11.24 Transaction SE11 Application Menu Path

Double-click on **SE11 – ABAP Dictionary**, and the **ABAP Dictionary: Initial Screen** popup appears (see Figure 11.25).

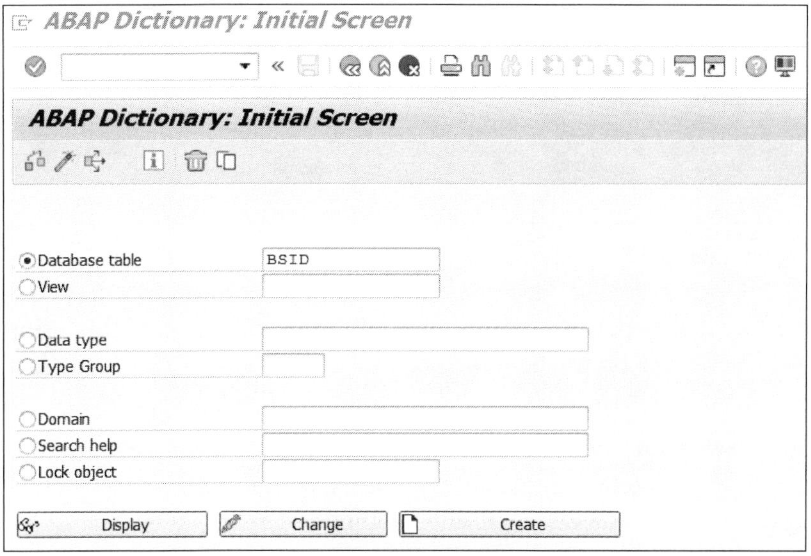

Figure 11.25 ABAP Dictionary: Initial Screen

Enter a **Database table,** and click on the **Display** icon. For this example, the AR secondary index table "BSID" was entered.

Press Enter or click the **Display** icon to open the **Dictionary: Display Table** screen (see Figure 11.26).

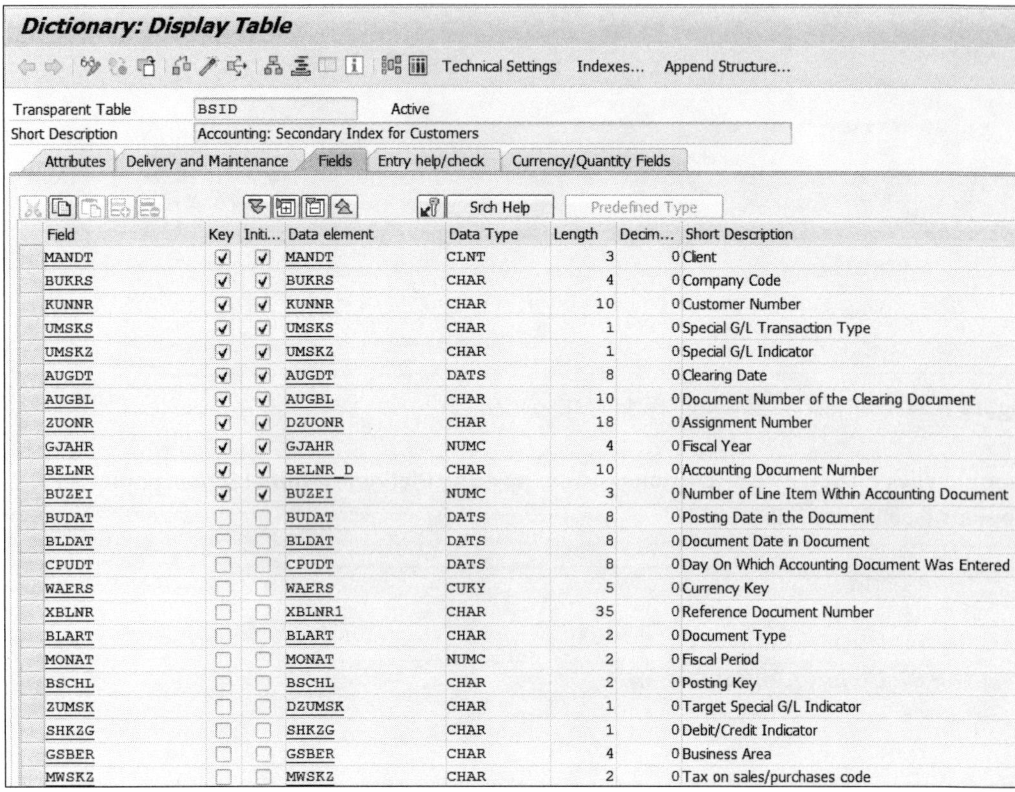

Figure 11.26 Display Table BSID

As you can see, you can view the database table before viewing its contents using Transaction SE11. Now, click on the **Contents** icon in the toolbar. This is the first step toward viewing detail in the table.

The **Data Browser Selection Screen** appears (see Figure 11.27). You can enter various field values to reduce your selection of data and make it easier to find what it is that you're looking for. In this case, a value was entered for **Fiscal Year**.

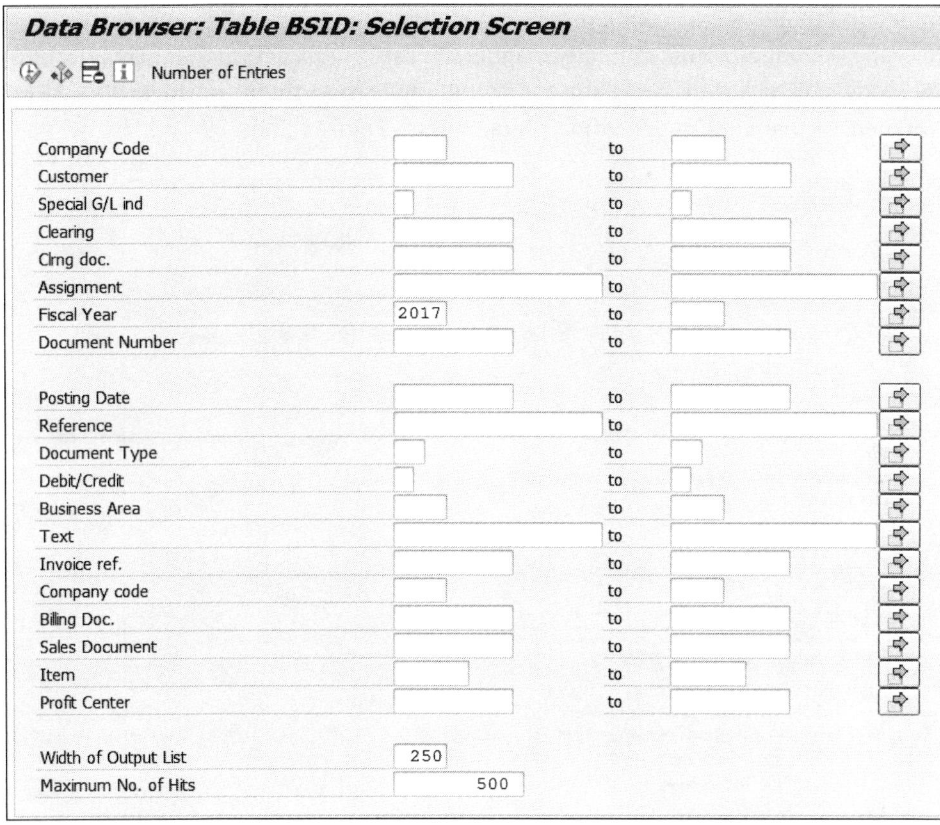

Figure 11.27 AR Table BSID Selection Screen

After entering field values in the selection screen, click on the **Execute** icon at the top left of the screen (see Figure 11.27). The AR table entries appear (see Figure 11.28).

Customer	Trans.type	SG	Clearing	Clrng doc.	Assignment	Year	DocumentNo	Itm	Pstng Date	Doc. Date	Entry Dte	Crcy	Reference	Doc. Type	Period	PK	Trg.sp.G/L	D/C	Tx	Amount in LC
3000001424					0090017520	2017	0090017520	1	23.11.2016	23.11.2016	09.02.2017	USD	0090017520	RV	2	01		S		89,10
3000002292						2017	0090017686	1	09.05.2017	09.05.2017	09.05.2017	USD	0090017686	RC	8	01		S		2.000,00
3000002292						2017	0090017687	1	09.05.2017	09.05.2017	09.05.2017	USD	0090017686	RV	8	11		H		2.000,00
3000009478					0090017522	2017	0090017522	1	19.10.2016	19.10.2016	09.02.2017	USD	0090017522	RV	1	01		S		49,00
3000032238						2017	1800001900	1	30.05.2017	11.05.2017	30.05.2017	USD	TEST	DR	8	01		S		100,00
8050000180					0090017688	2017	0090017688	1	15.05.2017	15.05.2017	16.05.2017	USD	0090017688	RV	8	01		S		1.250,00

Figure 11.28 AR Table BSID Entries

Use the toolbar at the top of Figure 11.28 to change the layout, sort, filter, download, and more. From the AR table BSID display, you can also double-click on any row and display all the field values in the AR line.

Transaction SE16

You can also look at AR data directly in tables by using Transaction SE16. This transaction code can be accessed via the following application menu path: **Tools • ABAP Workbench • Overview • Application Hierarchy** (see Figure 11.29).

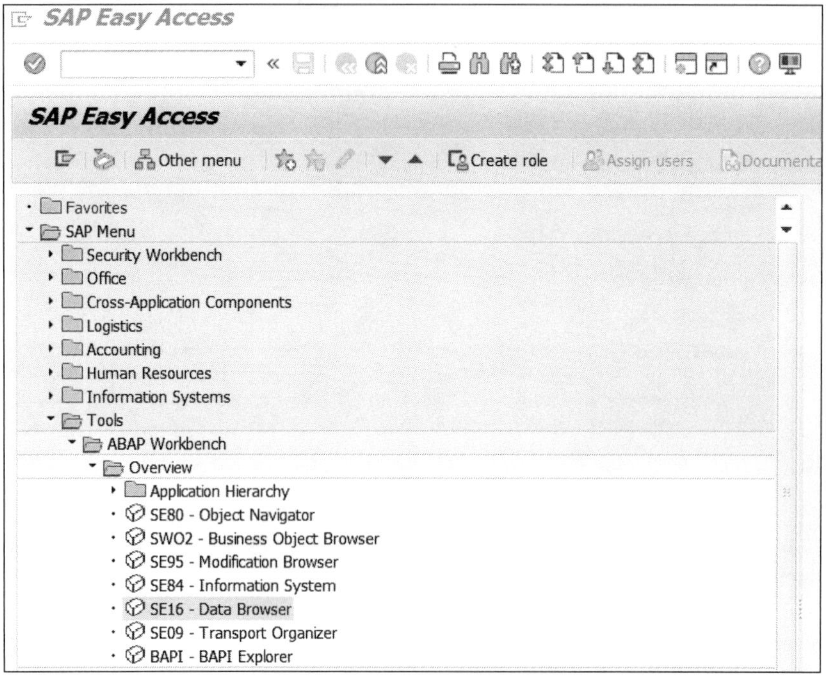

Figure 11.29 Transaction SE16 Application Menu Path

Double-click on **SE16 – Data Browser**, and the **Data Browser: Initial Screen** appears (see Figure 11.30).

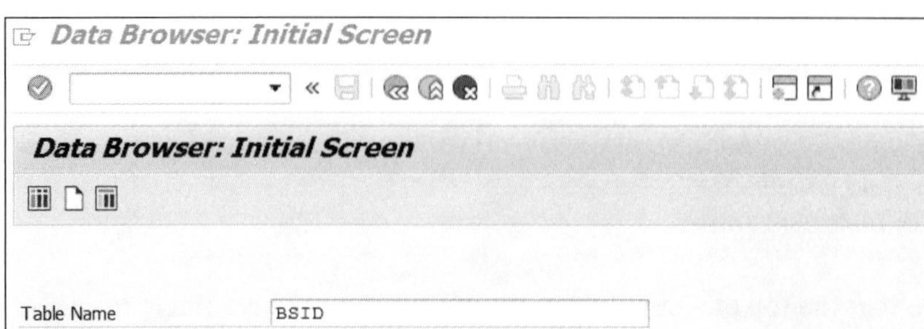

Figure 11.30 Data Browser: Initial Screen

Enter a table name (e.g., "BSID") and press Enter, or click on the **Contents** icon in the left side of the screen shown in Figure 11.31.

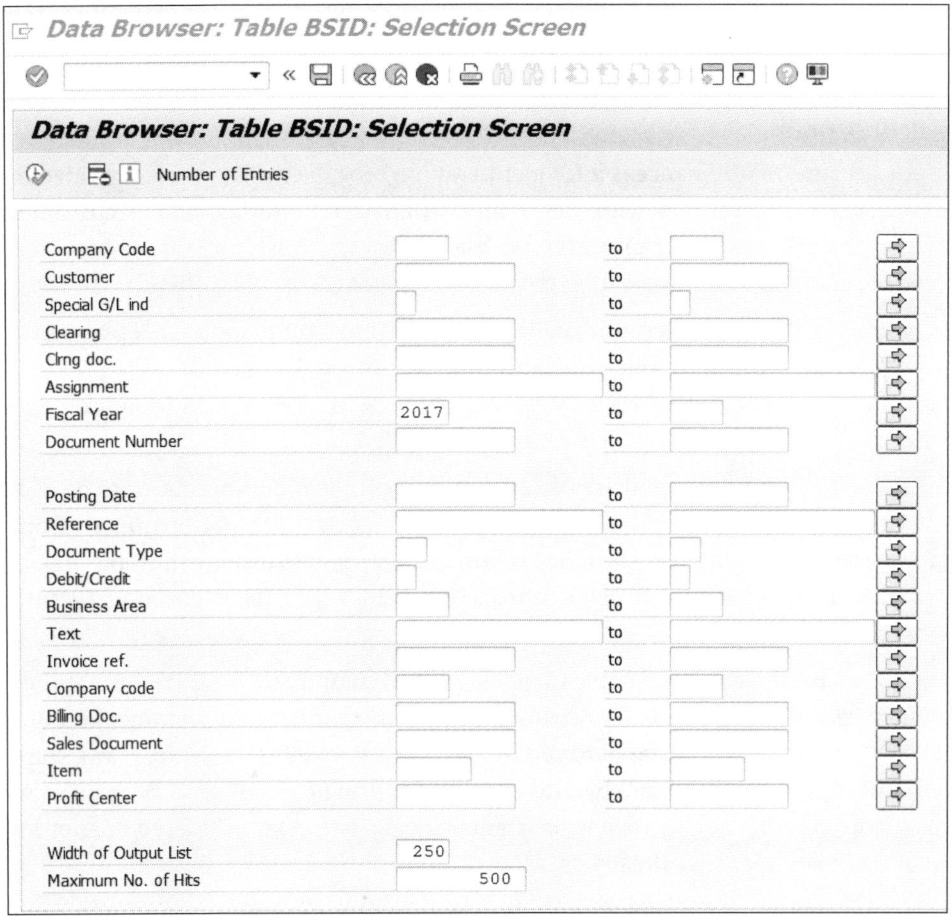

Figure 11.31 Table BSID Selection Screen

Use the toolbar at the top of Figure 11.31 to can change the layout, sort, filter, download, and more. From the AR table display, you can also double-click on any row and display all the field values in AR for that entry.

11.4 Summary

In this chapter, we covered some of the most essential tools for AR account inquiries. These tools include the AR account balances transaction (Transaction FD10N), the AR account line item display transaction (Transaction FBL5N), and standard AR reports. Frequent use of these transactions and reports is essential to understanding the activity in AR.

In AR, account maintenance is a frequent and ongoing event. The tools provided in this chapter provide you with the ability to answer inquiries, adjust customer account balances, and perform account maintenance. AR isn't a static event; you need programs at your disposal to remain on top of changes.

In performing customer account analysis, Transactions FD10K and FBL5N play a useful role because of their drilldown capability. Moreover, Transaction FD11 provides predefined subsets of data, such as payment history, that allow you to quickly and easily perform the customer account analysis needed.

In addition to covering the topics of standard AR reports and transactions to display AR data, this chapter covered two ways to display financial information directly from tables. The first is using Transaction SE11, which allows you to display the table and its contents. The second way is using Transaction SE16, which takes you directly into table contents.

In an AR department, it's essential to quickly and accurately track down the status of an invoice, a payment, and other customer account transactions. Customer account display transactions and standard reports give you the ability to do so. Many standard AR reports are delivered by SAP, so before writing custom reports or queries, make sure you thoroughly review the standard reports and know that you're not recreating capabilities that already exist.

This concludes our AR discussions. In the next chapter, we move on to the topic of fixed asset accounting and processes.

Chapter 12
Fixed Asset Processes

In this chapter, we discuss fixed asset business processes with an emphasis on integration in the asset lifecycle.

Business processes in Financial Accounting (FI) often consist of cross-modular steps. In other words, all steps in the business process aren't isolated to one SAP module. We saw this in Chapter 5 with the procure-to-pay process, where purchase requisitions, purchase orders (POs), and other logistics transactions are executed in Materials Management (MM) and Purchasing modules (MM-Purchasing), while vendor account maintenance and outgoing payments take place in Accounts Payable (AP). We also saw this in Chapter 9 with the order-to-cash business process, where sales orders, deliveries, and billing takes place in Sales and Distribution (SD) and Sales modules (SD-Sales), while customer account maintenance and incoming payments are managed in Accounts Receivable (AR).

Another great example of a business process that crosses SAP modules is acquire-to-retire in FI Asset Accounting (FI-AA), often referred to as the asset lifecycle. Throughout this chapter, you'll see the term acquire-to-retire used synonymously with asset lifecycle.

For those unfamiliar with asset accounting, FI-AA is the SAP module used for managing fixed assets that are depreciable and reported on the balance sheet. A fixed asset can be land, buildings, machinery, or other physical asset owned by your company.

Acquire-to-retire is a core business process within SAP composed of multiple transactions, some of which reside in FI-AA and others that are outside of FI-AA. Using this business process as the basis of our discussion, we'll cover the overall asset lifecycle and some of its key points of integration with other modules.

Note

Many accounting departments have a specific job position called asset accountant. From an accounting perspective, this makes sense. Accounting rules, reporting requirements, and asset valuation methods justify the need for specialized accounting expertise in fixed assets.

From an SAP ERP system perspective, it also makes sense to have a specialized job role for an asset accountant. This is the go-to person for questions on asset classes, account determinations (i.e., how FI-AA transactions post), and depreciation. At month-end and year-end, the asset accountant is responsible not only for running and validating depreciation but also for reconciling asset General Ledger (G/L) balances with fixed asset subledger balances. Keeping FI-AA reconciled can be a time-consuming task.

We'll discuss several key business process steps in the acquire-to-retire process, but we'll focus most heavily on the acquisition step. This is a process step with a great amount of potential integration, with several acquisition methods available. To keep this chapter centered on FI-AA integration, we'll begin with a discussion of the asset lifecycle and then delve into the specifics of asset acquisition. For details on FI-AA transactions, see Chapter 13.

Note

SAP ERP provides functionality for leased assets, but they are beyond the scope of this book.

12.1 Fixed Asset Lifecycle

FI-AA is used for acquiring, managing, valuing, and supervising fixed assets within SAP. FI-AA is a subledger to the G/L. The subledger is an important concept to understand, so we'll discuss it a little more before getting into the specifics of the fixed asset lifecycle. This isn't the first time in this book that subledgers are described. This concept was introduced in Chapter 2 and was also discussed in the context of AP and AR.

A subledger stores individual transaction detail in separate tables and is managed via individual master records, such as vendors, customers, and fixed assets. FI-AA is its own subledger, with all AA entries stored in separate tables. Transaction detail is managed and viewed via asset master records and the FI-AA subledger.

Like AR and AP, the FI-AA subledger links back to the G/L by means of G/L reconciliation accounts. Each subledger account must link back to a G/L reconciliation account. When an accounting entry is posted to the FI-AA subledger, the system automatically updates the balance in the corresponding G/L reconciliation account. Therefore, the transaction detail is stored in the subledger, but balances are updated in the G/L.

Now that you understand the concept of the FI-AA subledger, let's discuss some other asset-related topics, including the stages of the asset lifecycle, the structure of the application menu path, basic configuration items, and depreciation.

12.1.1 Stages of the Asset Lifecycle

An asset's lifecycle isn't always a straight line from acquisition to retirement. We won't attempt to discuss all the variations that can occur, but rather we'll highlight a few scenarios to provide a good understanding of the acquire-to-retire business process and the relationship of FI-AA to other modules.

To provide a basis for the remainder of this chapter, let's look at the major parts of the asset lifecycle in order:

1. **Acquisition**
   This is the first step in the acquire-to-retire business process. It's important that the acquisition value accurately reflect the true cost of the asset. This step in the lifecycle requires entering into a contractual agreement with a business partner to acquire goods. In FI-AA, it requires the creation of an asset master record and the capitalization of an asset.
2. **Maintenance**
   Many types of assets need periodic maintenance. Over the life of an asset, it may need repairs, improvements, and replacement parts. Routine maintenance and repair costs to sustain performance are considered expenses, unless major upgrades or overhauls improve the value of an asset.
3. **Depreciation**
   Depreciation is the consumption of the asset over a period of time. Depreciation methods in SAP determine the rate at which an asset is depreciated. An asset's net book value is the original cost less depreciation, amortization, and impairment costs.
4. **Retirement**
   Retirement is the final stage in the asset lifecycle. It's the removal of an asset or part of an asset from the asset portfolio. In FI-AA, asset retirement is done by either selling or scrapping the asset.

It's important to point out that prior to entering an asset acquisition FI-AA, you need to have a good understanding of your company's fixed asset types and valuation methods. Fixed assets types come in many varieties, including tangible assets, such as furniture and computers, and intangibles, such as software, copyrights, and trademarks.

Fixed asset valuations need to reflect the true and relevant cost of an asset. Asset values should be absolute costs, not estimates. These include purchase price and costs associated with bringing the asset into workable condition.

Regardless of how the asset is acquired, there are two steps in the fixed asset acquisition process: the creation of an asset master record and the posting of capitalization value. After these steps are complete, the life of the fixed asset begins. For more information on fixed asset master data, see Chapter 2.

As the lifecycle of an asset progresses, many events can cause a required adjustment to the asset or its value. For example, asset maintenance or improvements may change the value of the asset, or the asset could be damaged or destroyed. Whatever the circumstance, FI-AA provides the means to adjust an asset's valuation.

The final stages of the fixed asset lifecycle involve selling, transferring, or scrapping the asset. Figure 12.1 shows the application menu paths for FI-AA transfer and retirements.

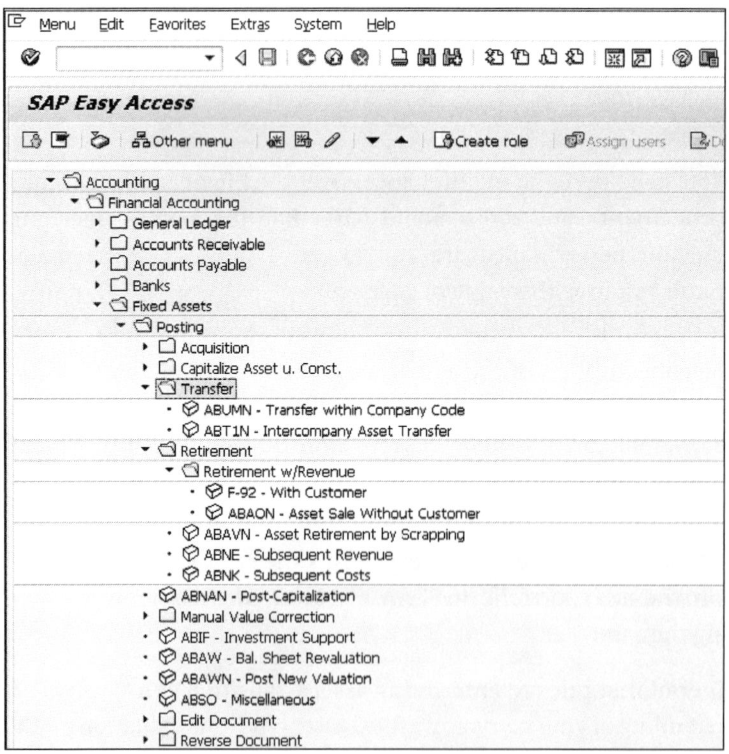

Figure 12.1 Application Menu Path for FI-AA Transfer and Retirements

For details on asset transfer and retirement transactions, see Chapter 13.

12.1.2 Structure of FI Asset Accounting Application Menu

Now, let's look at specific FI-AA transactions and show they are organized. Figure 12.2 shows the FI-AA application menu path, **Accounting • Financial Accounting • Fixed Assets**. You'll see the following relevant folders:

- **Posting**
  Contains transactions for acquisitions, capitalization, transfers, retirements, value corrections, and document edits and reversals. These are all core financial transactions relevant to the lifecycle of an asset (except depreciation).
- **Asset**
  Contains all the transactions for fixed asset master data, including fixed asset creation, change, and display. This folder also contains transactions to lock or delete fixed assets.
- **Periodic Processing**
  Contains many transactions, the most important of which is the transaction to execute depreciation (Transaction AFAB).
- **Information System**
  This is where the standard reports for FI-AA reside.

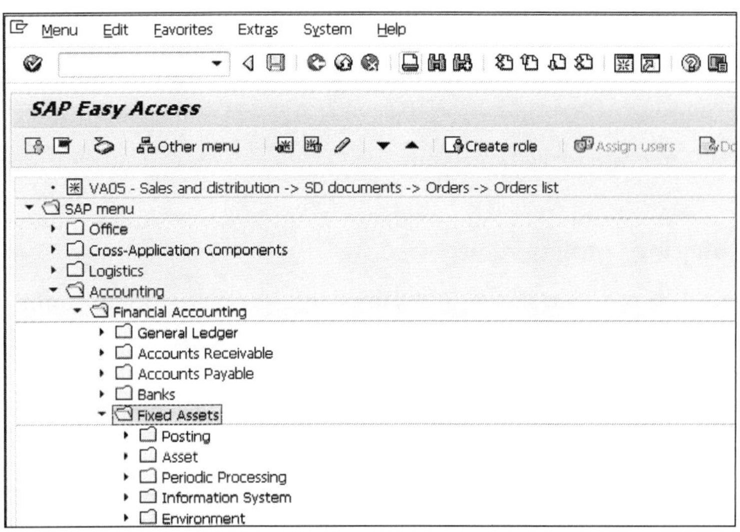

Figure 12.2 FI-AA Application Menu

Let's open the **Postings** folder as an example and explore the subfolders and transactions it contains. The first application subfolder shown is **Acquisition** (Figure 12.3). This folder contains transactions for the acquisition of a fixed asset. There are several ways a fixed asset can be acquired: produced in house, procured directly in FI-AA, transferred from an affiliate company, or procured and capitalized through MM-Purchasing.

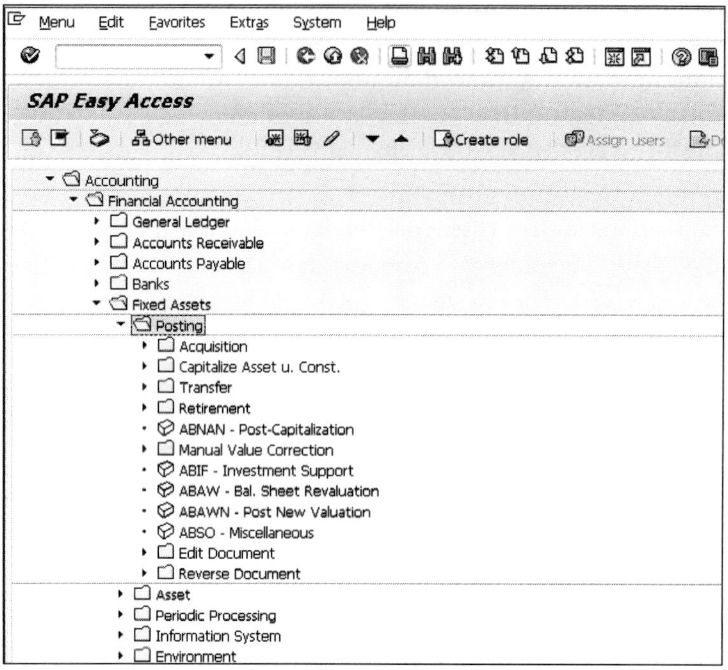

Figure 12.3 Application Menu Path for FI-AA Postings

12.1.3 FI Asset Accounting Configuration

At this point, it's important to mention that FI-AA involves a good amount of configuration. This book isn't a configuration guide, but it's important to know that FI-AA configuration is substantial. It includes asset classes, account determinations, depreciation areas, and much more. In this section, we discuss a few critical points of configuration to help in your overall understanding of FI-AA.

At the top of the list are asset classes. They are an important building block in FI-AA configuration in that they control such things as account determinations and screen layouts. Normally, asset classes correlate to specific asset types and fixed asset G/L accounts. They are configured to correlate with G/L accounts to meet the necessary reporting requirements on the balance sheet. In addition, an asset class determines the depreciation method used in calculating depreciation expense.

Following are some examples of typical asset classes:

- Land
- Buildings
- Machinery and equipment
- Furniture and fixtures
- Vehicles
- Computer hardware
- Computer software
- Leasehold improvements
- Low value assets
- Capital leases
- Assets under construction (AuC)

The next element of FI-AA configuration we'll discuss is account determinations, which establish the G/L accounts to post to for each FI-AA transaction type. Account determinations aren't unique to FI-AA; they exist throughout FI. They are of particular importance in FI-AA, however, because they automatically update the G/L for all relevant FI-AA transactions. Among these transactions are the following:

- Acquisition and production costs (APC)
- Down payments
- Gain/loss/revenue from sale
- APC revaluation
- Depreciation
- Transfer of reserves
- Depreciation revaluation
- Interest expense

See Chapter 14 for a more in-depth discussion on the topics of asset classes and FI-AA account determinations.

The last notable point on configuration has to do with depreciation expense. In configuration, a depreciation area and depreciation types are defined. They determine how depreciation will be calculated and posted to the G/L. Depreciation calculation is an important step in month-end and year-end close and in the calculation of an asset's net book value. For these reasons, accountants and accounting supervisors give depreciation a lot of attention. However, the preceding steps in the asset lifecycle are essential to achieve accurate depreciation postings.

Together, asset classes, account determinations, and depreciation are all critical areas of configuration, and a basic understanding of these areas goes a long way when troubleshooting errors in FI-AA.

12.1.4 Depreciation

Depreciation is covered at a high level in this section because of its special significance in the asset lifecycle. It's also covered in detail in Chapter 13.

As previously mentioned, depreciation is essential to the calculation of an asset's net book value. Net book value is the original cost of an asset less depreciation, amortization, and impairment costs.

Depreciation is calculated over the course of a fixed asset's lifetime. In configuration, you determine how the asset will depreciate. FI-AA configuration is designed to be flexible in accommodating the needs of any country and industry. In addition, the type of asset and its expected life play an important role in the setup of FI-AA and depreciation.

Let's put depreciation in perspective in terms of the overall accounting for fixed assets. Fixed asset master records are created in FI-AA. When capitalization occurs, the FI-AA subledger and G/L are updated with APC values. At this point, a fixed asset's value is reflected on the balance sheet. In FI-AA, ongoing adjustments are made to master data and asset values. Moreover, as depreciation is posted at regular increments (e.g., monthly), the balance sheet will contain accumulated depreciation amounts, whereas the profit and loss (P&L) statements will contain postings for depreciation expense amounts. All these postings are controlled through FI-AA account determinations.

Figure 12.4 shows the application menu path for Transaction AFAB, which executes depreciation. Most companies set up depreciation to run automatically as a scheduled job, and asset accountants are then responsible for reviewing the depreciation postings, validating them, and making any necessary adjustments. When the system posts depreciation, it creates collective documents. It doesn't create separate documents for each asset.

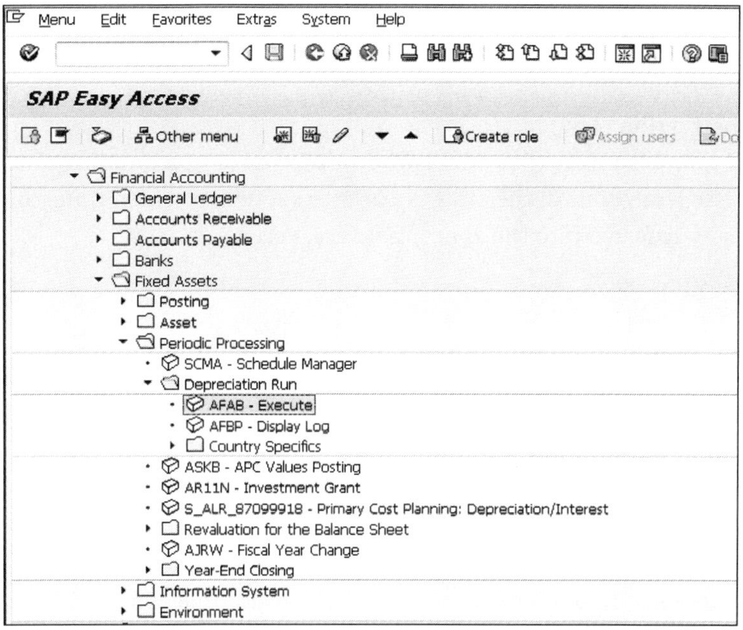

Figure 12.4 Transaction AFAB Depreciation Run Application Menu

Now that we've covered the basics of the overall asset lifecycle, let's discuss asset acquisition in more detail.

12.2 Asset Acquisition

Acquiring an asset is the first step in the acquire-to-retire business process. The focus of this section is on the various methods of acquiring fixed assets. An asset can be produced in house, procured directly in FI-AA, transferred from an affiliate company, or procured and capitalized through MM-Purchasing.

12.2.1 Fixed Asset Acquisition Types

It's important to understand each of these asset acquisition methods not only to gain an understanding of SAP's capabilities but also for insights into how your company's internal acquisition processes work.

There are three basic types of fixed asset acquisitions:

- **Internal acquisition**
  An acquisition of an asset from an affiliate company or an asset that is produced in house.
- **Assets under construction (AuC)**
  A special form of tangible assets that are being constructed (e.g., a building) and are accounted for separately until the asset is put into service, at which time, the cost of the asset is transferred into the appropriate asset class.
- **External acquisition**
  The acquisition of an asset from a business partner (i.e., vendor).

In this section, we don't attempt to cover these transactions in detail because a single chapter can't cover it all. Instead, we elaborate on external acquisition types to give you an understanding of FI-AA integration. In Section 12.2.2, an example is provided of an external acquisition using a PO. In addition, Chapter 13 provides a detailed example of an external procurement using Transaction F-90 and other FI-AA transactions.

Transaction F-90 is designed to debit an asset and credit a vendor account, thereby capitalizing the asset value, while at the same time producing an open payable (i.e., vendor invoice). This is a frequently used FI-AA external acquisition transaction.

Figure 12.5 also shows other external acquisition transaction types. There are several options to choose from, warranting some further discussion.

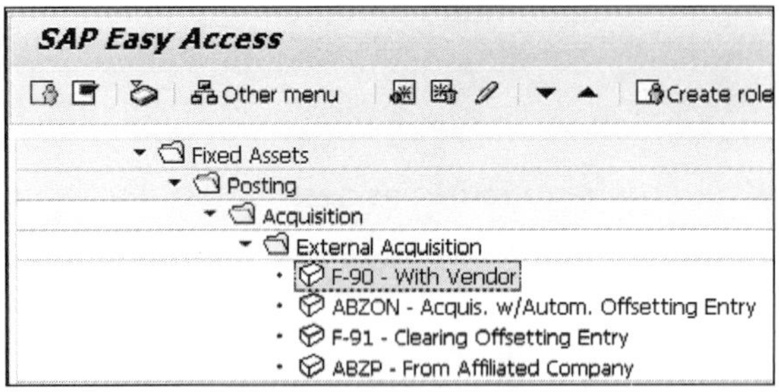

Figure 12.5 Transaction F-90 Application Menu

Transaction ABZON is used to capitalize an asset with an offsetting entry to the G/L. Using this transaction, a debit is made to an asset, and a credit is made to an offsetting G/L account. This transaction is used when there is no need to create an AP invoice, such as when a vendor has been prepaid for the asset. This may be the case for large-ticket assets for which vendors need to be prepaid to produce the asset.

Transaction F-91 will capitalize an asset with an offsetting entry to a G/L clearing account. Using this transaction, a debit is made to an asset, and a credit is made to an offsetting G/L clearing account.

For more details on these transactions, see Chapter 13.

12.2.2 External Asset Acquisition with Purchase Order

The final external fixed asset acquisition method we'll discuss in this section is the acquisition directly through a PO created in MM-Purchasing. If your company uses the MM-Purchasing module and creates POs for all asset acquisitions, this is the preferred method for capitalizing assets.

To use this method, when creating the PO, you must use account assignment category A in the line item of the PO. In configuration, you can designate a different account assignment category for use in POs, but category A is standard delivered by SAP.

Prior to creating the PO, the fixed asset master record must be created. Figure 12.6 shows an example PO with line items containing account assignment **A**. In the **Purchase Order History** tab, you can click the invoice receipt (IR) document to view the material invoice number associated with the procurement instance.

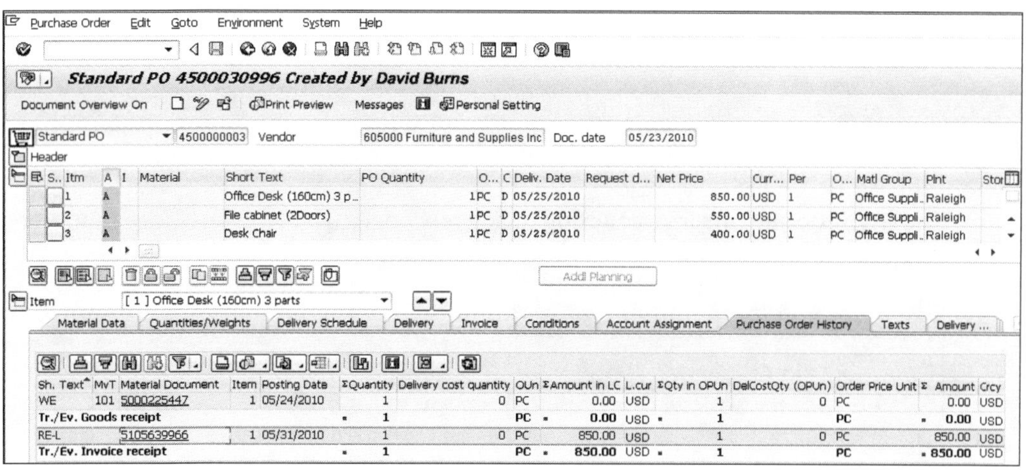

Figure 12.6 Example PO with Account Assignment A

Figure 12.7 shows the material invoice document number. Click the **Follow-On Documents** button to review the FI documents automatically created by Materials Management and Logistics Invoice Verification (MM-LIV).

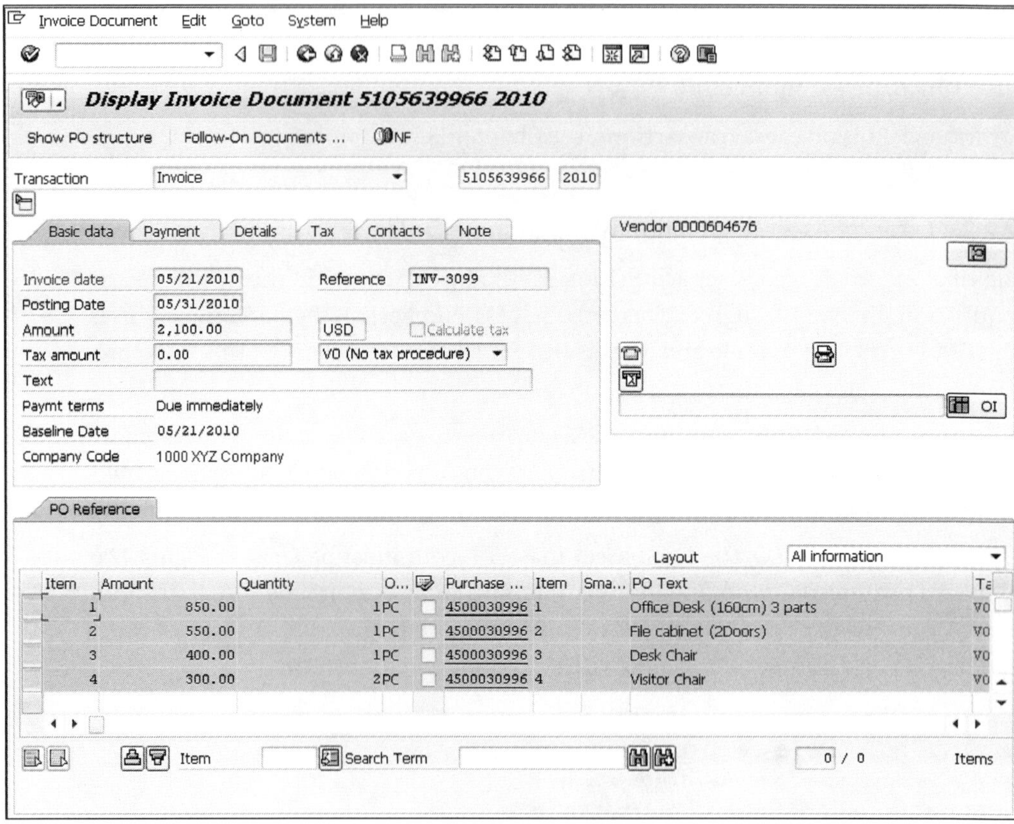

Figure 12.7 Display Material Invoice Document

The **List of Documents in Accounting** dialog box opens (Figure 12.8). Notice that there is one accounting document and one asset document.

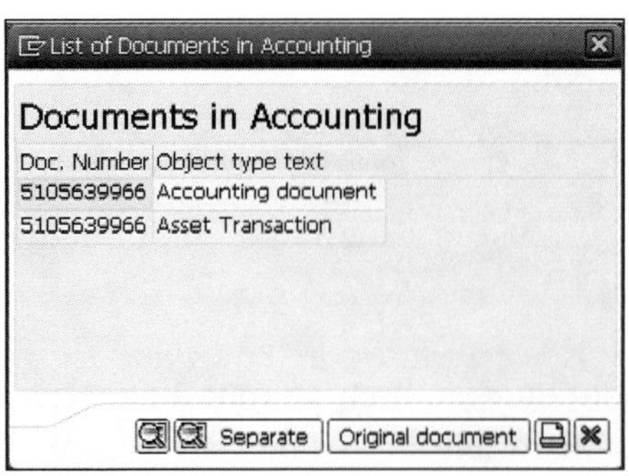

Figure 12.8 List of Documents in Accounting Dialog Box

Double-click the accounting document number to display the document (Figure 12.9). This document demonstrates that by using the procurement process in MM-Purchasing, you can produce an AP invoice that posts a credit to a vendor account and a debit to fixed assets.

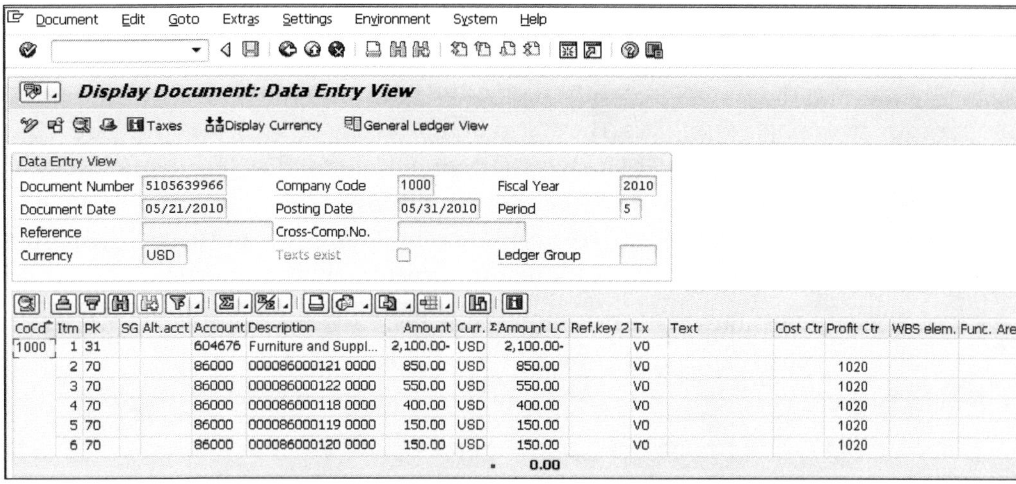

Figure 12.9 Display Accounting Document

This concludes our discussion of external fixed asset acquisitions. Next, we'll discuss internal acquisitions.

12.2.3 Internal Acquisition

As discussed in the previous section, there is a clear difference between internal and external asset acquisitions. An internal asset acquisition comes from an affiliate company or is produced in house, as opposed to an external acquisition, which is made from a business partner.

There are two standard transactions that fit under the category of an internal acquisition. The first occurs when a company acquires an asset from an affiliate company and uses Transaction ABZP. The second is for assets produced in house, in which case, Transaction ABZE is used.

Both Transactions ABZP and ABZE use standard transaction types. You only need to create custom transaction types if you need them to only post to certain depreciation areas in your chart of depreciation or if there is no standard transaction type with the necessary limitations.

12.2.4 Assets under Construction and Settlements

As straightforward as the acquire-to-retire process may seem, it's not this simple for all fixed assets, particularly during the acquisition phase. For example, AuCs can be cumbersome to manage. The difficulty lies in trying to put together all the pieces of the puzzle to ensure the accounting is correct.

Typically, AuCs need to be shown separately on the balance sheet. To begin using AuC, an asset class is required with specific AuC settings in configuration. Figure 12.10 shows an example asset class. The **Status of AuC** setting determines if the asset class is designated AuC or not. **Line item settlement** means that final line item settlement to an asset or cost center can be performed. The **Investment Measure** setting indicates that assets can't be created or posted to using FI-AA. Instead, the AuC are posted via internal orders (IOs) or Work Breakdown Structure (WBS) elements.

It's important to note that AuCs aren't final assets. Costs are accumulated in the AuC until the final settlement takes place. Then, the AuC value is transferred to a final asset.

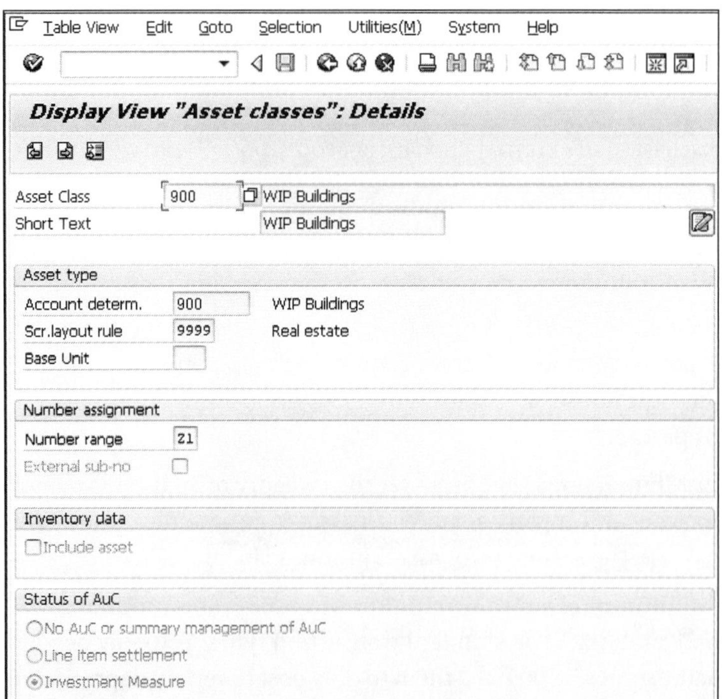

Figure 12.10 Example AuC Asset Class

There are several ways to accumulate costs that settle to AuC. For example, you can create an IO using Transaction KO01. The IO type **Investment Measure** should be selected when creating the IO. Subsequently, costs are accumulated using the IO as the cost collector. A settlement rule is created that designates the asset as the receiver, and the IO is settled to the asset using Transaction KO88.

There are multiple ways to accumulate and settle costs to AuCs, including the use of WBS elements. It's important that you understand the AuC cost collectors being used in your company, the timing of their settlement to AuC, and the process steps used during the settlement process.

12.3 Summary

Fixed assets are a major component of the balance sheet. Asset values and accumulated depreciation are broken down into their component parts, that is, asset classes correlating to G/L accounts. In addition, depreciation expense is posted at regular increments and reported on P&L statements.

There is no question that understanding AA is an essential part of the job in any accounting department. To understand AA in SAP, it's important to understand the integration between FI-AA and other modules. Such an understanding helps provide complete knowledge of the acquire-to-retire process.

In this chapter, we focused heavily on the FI-AA acquisition process, which is a step that has much variability. We introduced several fixed asset acquisition transactions, including Transactions F-90, F-91, ABZON, ABZP, and ABZE.

AuC is another important concept in FI-AA. AuCs are accounted for separately on the balance sheet, until a certain point in time when the asset is put into service. AuCs are an example of FI-AA flexibility in their integration with other modules. They need a separate asset class in which specific AuC settings are made, and cost collectors are needed (e.g., WBS, IO) that settle to an AuC.

When cost collectors for AuC are created, they won't work without specific settings. We introduced you to the settings specific to an IO for AuC. There are multiple ways to accumulate and settle costs to AuC, including use of WBS elements, IOs, and work orders. It's important that you understand the AuC cost collectors being used in your company, the timing of their settlement, and the process steps used during the settlement process.

This concludes our discussion of fixed asset processes. The next chapter discusses fixed asset transactions in detail.

Chapter 13
Fixed Asset Transactions

In this chapter, we discuss fixed asset transactions by covering the complete acquire-to-retire business process.

This chapter covers fixed asset transactions originating in the FI-Asset Accounting (FI-AA) module. It's important to understand the concept of a fixed asset's lifecycle, often referred to as the *acquire-to-retire* business process. The first step in this process in FI-AA is the creation of the asset master record. This is simply a shell until the asset is capitalized and the asset lifecycle begins.

13

After an asset master record is created, it can be capitalized, giving life to the asset. Throughout its lifetime, the asset depreciates until it's eventually sold, transferred, or retired. Along the way, an asset's lifecycle can take many twists and turns. It may be improved, damaged, revaluated, and maintained. End users must know the FI-AA transactions to make the necessary adjustments to asset values.

We discussed the asset lifecycle in Chapter 12. In this chapter, we'll take a more in-depth look at the lifecycle of an asset using FI-AA transactions.

Let's begin by discussing how to create a fixed asset master record.

13.1 Creating an Asset

To create an asset, use Transaction AS01 or application menu path, **Accounting • Financial Accounting • Fixed Assets • Asset • Create • AS01 – Asset**, as shown in Figure 13.1.

Double-click **AS01 – Asset** from the menu path, or enter "AS01" in the **Command** field (as shown in Figure 13.2) and press [Enter].

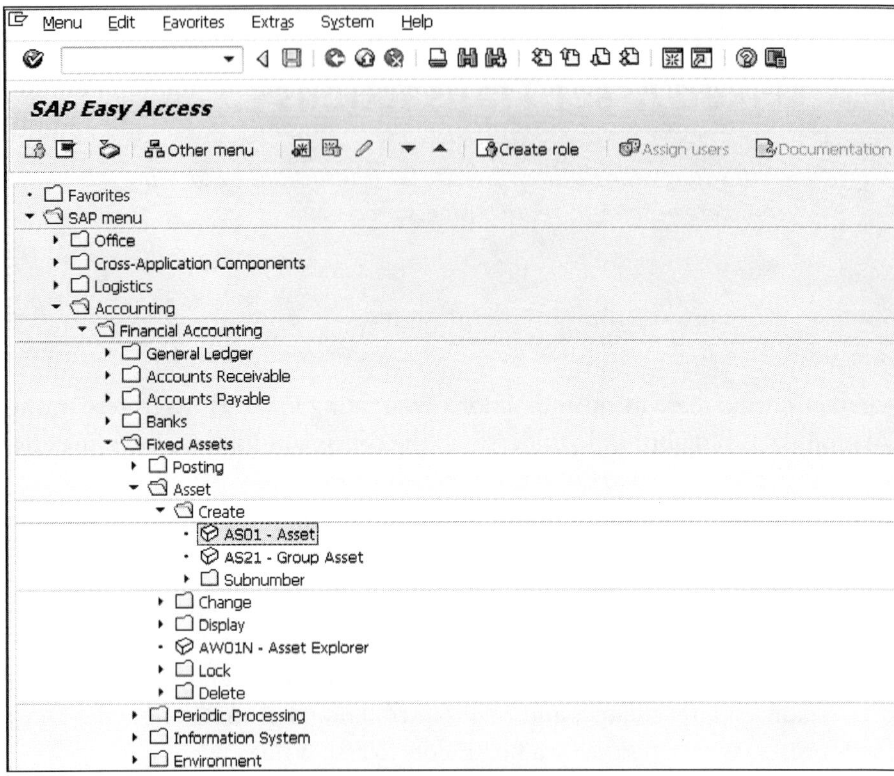

Figure 13.1 Transaction AS01 Application Menu Path

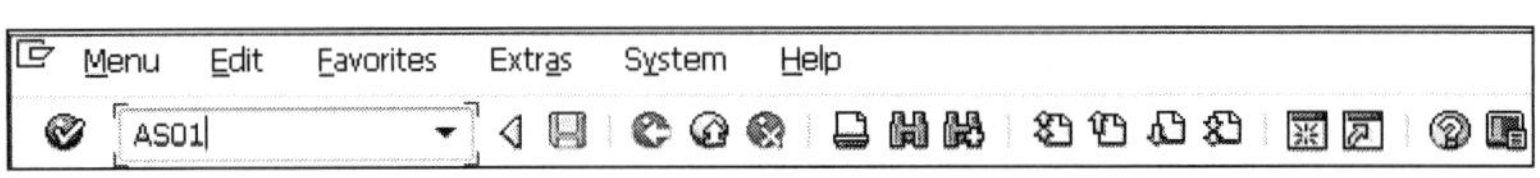

Figure 13.2 Entering "AS01" in the Command Field

The **Create Asset: Initial Screen** opens (Figure 13.3). Here, enter an **Asset Class**. Note that after an asset master record is created, the asset class can't be changed. If the wrong asset class is selected, the asset must be transferred to a new asset with the correct asset class. See Section 13.4 for more details on asset transfers.

In this example, the **Company Code** field defaults from the company code assigned to your user ID. The **Number of similar assets** field enables you to create multiple similar assets in one master transaction. These assets differ from each other only by their main and/or subnumber. For this example, we entered "1".

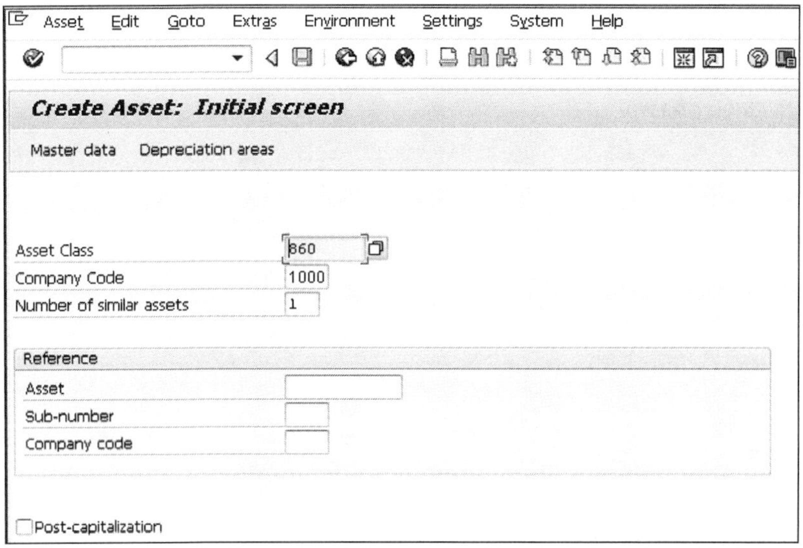

Figure 13.3 Create Asset: Initial Screen

The **Reference** area allows you to create a new asset referencing an existing one. In this way, many fields default into the new asset master record from the reference asset, thereby expediting the creation of a new asset master record.

Finally, selecting the **Post-capitalization** checkbox makes the capitalization date in the asset master record a required field, and the system automatically sets the acquisition date based on the capitalization date. When you check this field, you must also manually set the historical capitalization date and the acquisition date for the asset in the asset master record. For this example, leave it unselected, which gives you the most flexibility. Select this checkbox if you want an asset accountant or manager to manually set the acquisition and capitalization dates.

When all field values in Figure 13.3 have been added, press [Enter]. The **Create Asset: Master data** screen appears (Figure 13.4). Here, we entered values for **Description**, **Quantity**, and unit of measure (next to the **Quantity** field).

We also selected the **Manage historically** checkbox, which enables functionality that displays the asset in an asset chart. It also prevents reorganization of the asset and its transactions until the asset is deactivated.

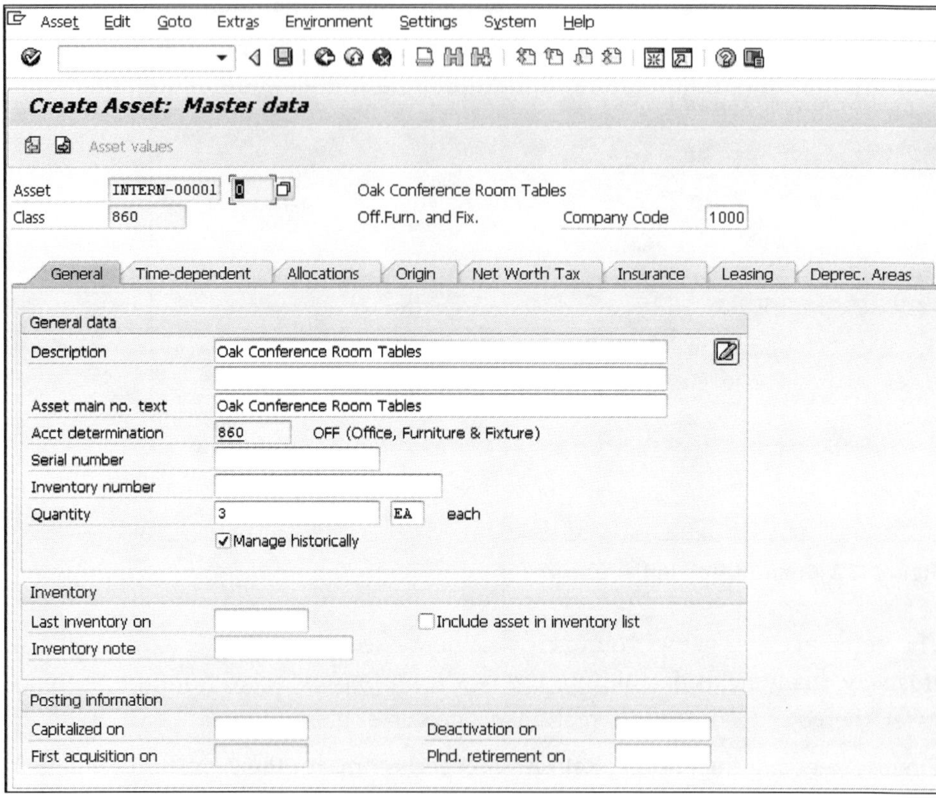

Figure 13.4 Create Asset: Master Data, General Tab

When all the information is entered in the **General** tab, click the **Time-dependent** tab (Figure 13.5). On this tab, the asset is assigned master data, organizational objects, and other specifications as required. In this example, the only assignment made is to a **Cost Center**.

> **Note**
>
> Although we won't cover the several other tabs on the asset master record in detail, but you should have a basic understanding of them. The **Allocations** tab is where evaluation groups and investment information are entered. The **Origin** tab contains information that further identifies specific attributes of the asset's origin and acquisition. The **Net Worth Tax** tab holds information on net worth valuation and fields relevant for real estate holdings. **Insurance** and **Leasing** have their own respective tabs.

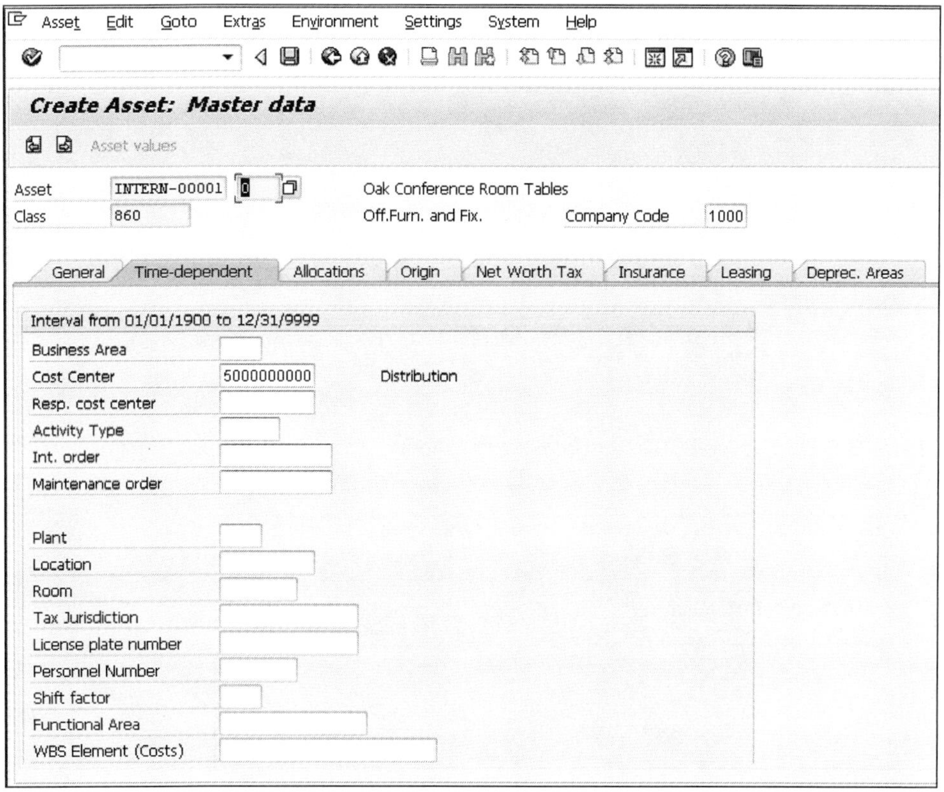

Figure 13.5 Create Asset: Master Data, Time-Dependent Tab

The last tab on the asset master screen is the **Deprec. Areas** tab (Figure 13.6). Depreciation areas are assigned to asset classes in configuration and default into the asset master record when created based on the asset class selected in Figure 13.3. However, flexibility exists within the asset master record to change depreciation areas and valuation attributes.

With all data entered in the asset master record, click the **Post** icon to the right of the **Command** field in the upper-left corner of the screen. This creates the asset master record, and a message appears with the new asset number, as shown in Figure 13.7.

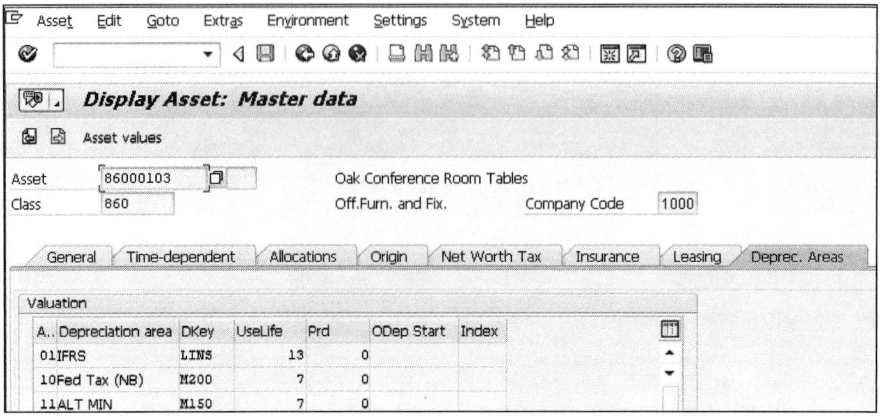

Figure 13.6 Display Asset: Master Data, Deprec. Areas Tab

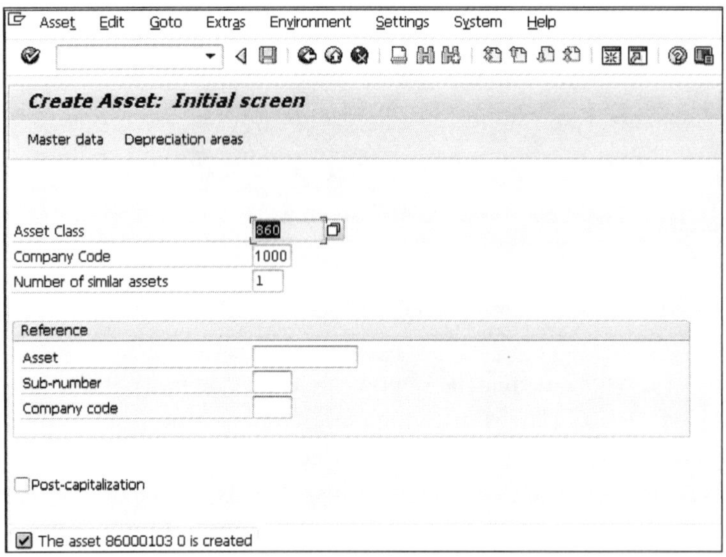

Figure 13.7 Asset Master Created Message

After an asset master record has been created, the asset can be capitalized. There are several ways to capitalize an asset, depending on how it's procured. The asset can be produced in house, procured directly in FI-AA, transferred from an affiliate company, or ordered through MM-Purchasing. In the remainder of this section, we focus on external acquisitions posted directly in FI-AA.

The external purchase of a fixed asset is a frequent event for most companies. As we discussed in Chapter 12, there are multiple transactions in FI-AA to accomplish this. Transaction F-90 was designed to debit an asset and credit a vendor account, thereby capitalizing the asset value while at the same time producing an open Accounts Payable (AP) invoice.

Next is Transaction ABZON, which is used to capitalize an asset with an offsetting entry to the General Ledger (G/L). Using this transaction, a debit is made to an asset, and a credit is made to an offsetting G/L account.

Finally, Transaction F-91 is used to capitalize an asset with an offsetting entry to a G/L clearing account. This transaction makes a debit entry to an asset and a credit entry to an offsetting G/L clearing account.

In the remainder of this section, we'll use Transaction F-90 to demonstrate asset capitalization. Transaction F-90 is used to post an external fixed asset acquisition with an external vendor. To see an example of fixed asset capitalization through a purchase order (PO), see Chapter 12.

To post an external asset acquisition, use Transaction F-90 or application menu path, **Accounting • Financial Accounting • Fixed Assets • Posting • Acquisition • External Acquisition • F-90 – With Vendor**, as shown in Figure 13.8.

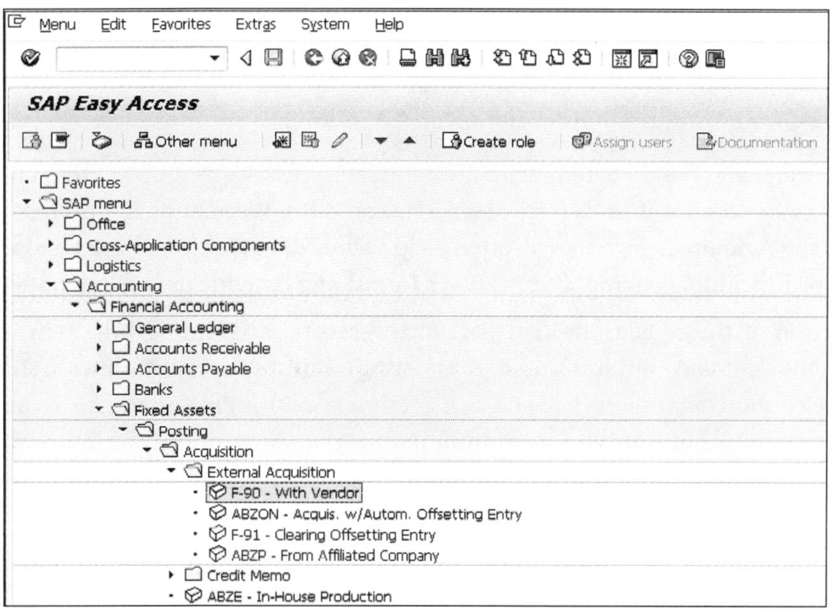

Figure 13.8 Transaction F-90 Application Menu Path

Double-click **F-90 – With Vendor** from the menu path, and the **Acquisition from purchase w. vendor: Header Data** screen opens (Figure 13.9). The fields on the header with prepopulated values may vary depending on your system configuration and editing options. In this example, the **Document Date** and **Reference** fields were manually entered, whereas field values were defaulted for the **Posting Date**, **Type**, **Period**, **Currency/Rate**, and **Company Code** fields.

At the bottom of the screen, the first part of the first accounting line item is entered. In the **First line item** area, enter a posting key (**PstKy**) and vendor number (**Account**). Posting key **31** indicates a credit to a vendor account.

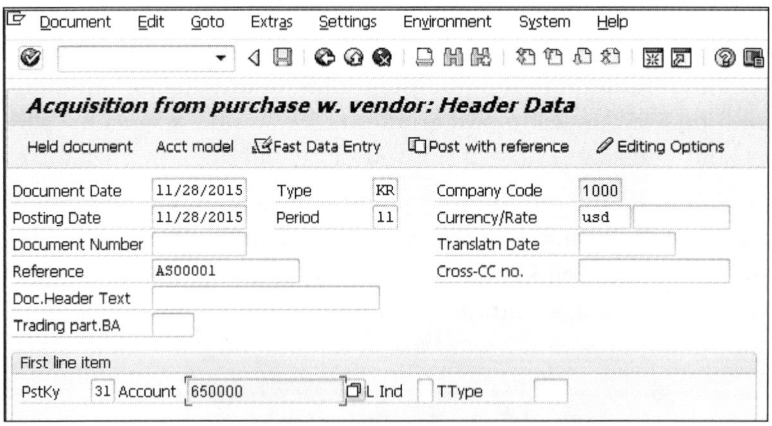

Figure 13.9 Asset Acquisition Header Data

When the header and **First line item** fields are complete, press `Enter`. The **Enter Vendor invoice: Add Vendor item** screen opens (Figure 13.10). We manually entered a value into the **Amount** field, whereas other field values defaulted from the vendor master record, including payment terms (**Payt Terms)** and baseline date (**Bline Date**).

At the bottom of the screen, the first part of the second accounting line item is entered. In the **Next line item** section, enter a posting key (**PstKy**), asset number in the **Account** field, and transaction type (**TType**). Posting key **70** indicates a debit to an asset account, and a value of **100** for the transaction type specifies that the line item is an external asset transaction.

With all field values entered as shown in Figure 13.10, press `Enter`. The **Enter Vendor invoice: Add Asset item** screen opens (Figure 13.11). In this example, we entered values in the **Amount** and **Tax code** fields.

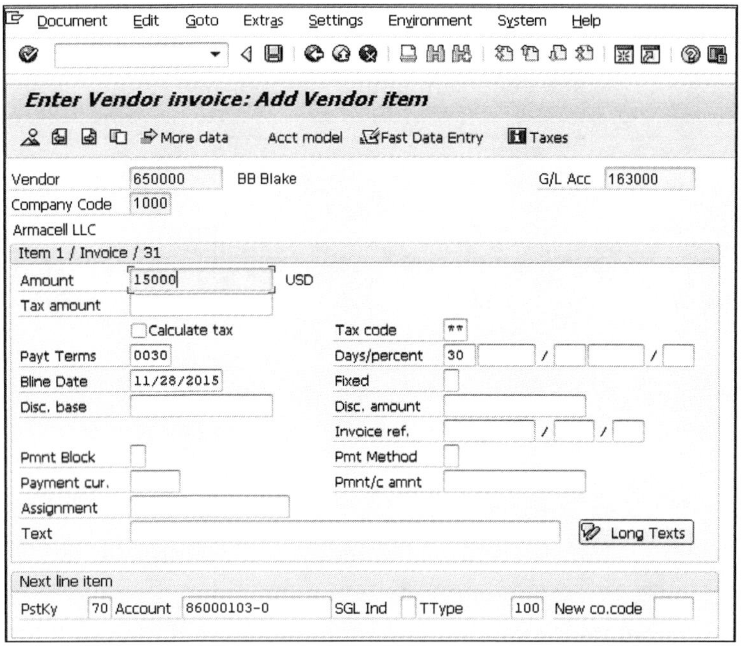

Figure 13.10 Add Vendor Item

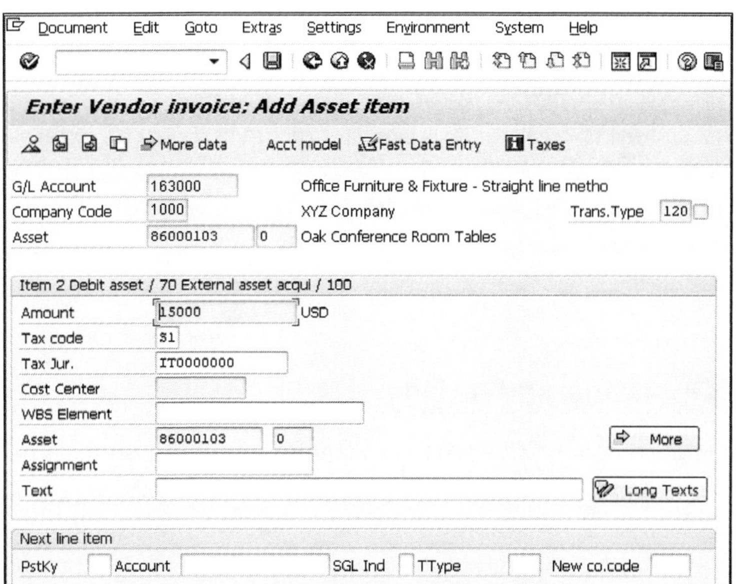

Figure 13.11 Add Asset Item

With all data entry complete, click the **Post** icon 🖫 to the right of the **Command** field in the upper-left corner of the screen. This creates the asset acquisition document, and a message appears with the new document number, as shown in Figure 13.12.

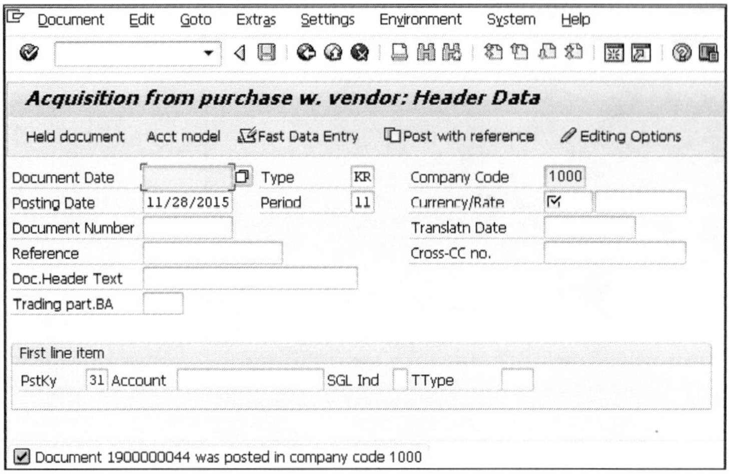

Figure 13.12 Document Created Message

Notice that the document type **KR** defaulted into Transaction F-90, which is a standard document type for AP invoices. This is because Transaction F-90 creates an open AP invoice. In addition, note that because document type **KR** was used, the document number created used the same number range as other AP invoices.

Now that you've learned how to create an asset master record and post an external fixed asset acquisition, let's discuss how to change, display, and lock asset master records. Regardless of the FI modules you use, master data maintenance is an important function that includes master data creation, change/edit, display, lock/block, and delete. FI-AA is no exception.

13.2 Changing, Displaying, and Locking

In Section 13.1, we demonstrated the creation of an asset master record. Some of the other day-to-day master data functions in FI-AA include changing, displaying, and locking asset master records. FI-AA also provides the capability to delete an asset master record but only when no transactions have been created (i.e., the asset hasn't been capitalized).

To change to an asset master record, use Transaction AS02 or application menu path, **Accounting • Financial Accounting • Fixed Assets • Asset • Change • AS02 – Asset**, as shown in Figure 13.13.

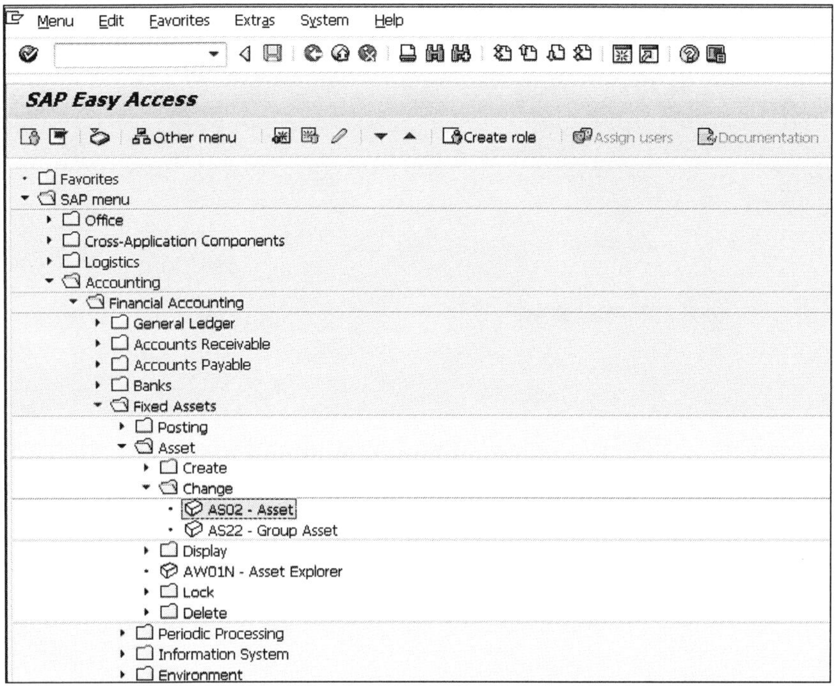

Figure 13.13 Transaction AS02 Application Menu Path

Double-click **AS02 – Asset** from the menu path, and the **Change Asset: Initial Screen** appears (Figure 13.14). Enter an **Asset** number and press Enter. Note that you also need to enter a **Subnumber** if applicable; otherwise, the field will default to **0**.

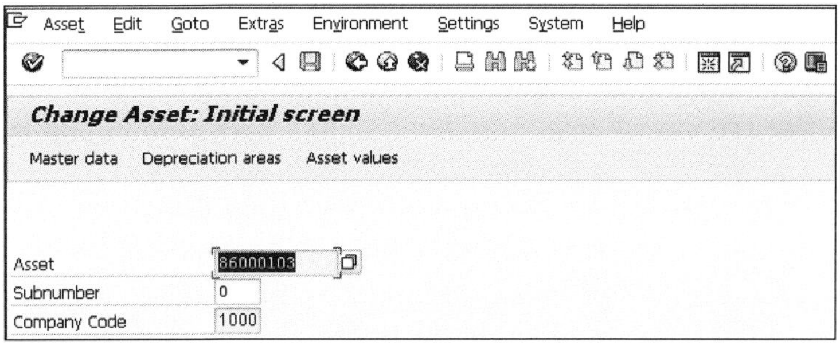

Figure 13.14 Change Asset: Initial Screen

After you press Enter, the **Change Asset: Master data** screen opens (Figure 13.15). Editable fields have white backgrounds.

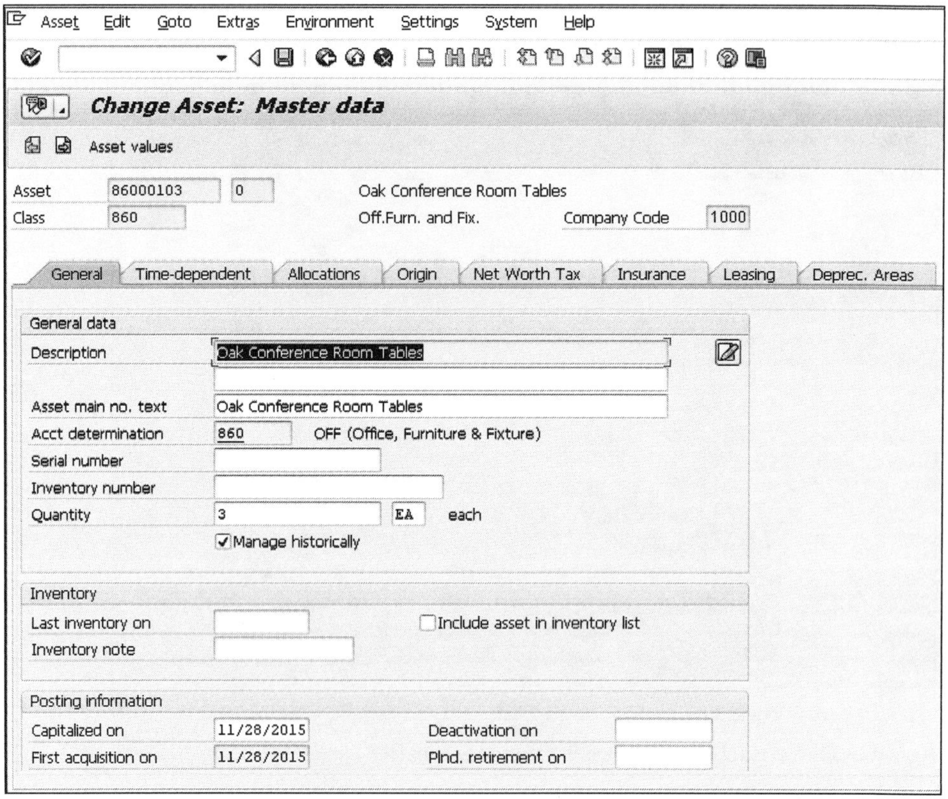

Figure 13.15 Change Asset: Master Data

For this example, click the **Origin** tab, and check the **Asset purch. new** box (Figure 13.16).

After asset master record changes have been made, click the **Save** icon to the right of the **Command** field in the upper-left corner of the screen. This saves changes to the asset master record, and a confirmation of change message appears, as shown in Figure 13.17.

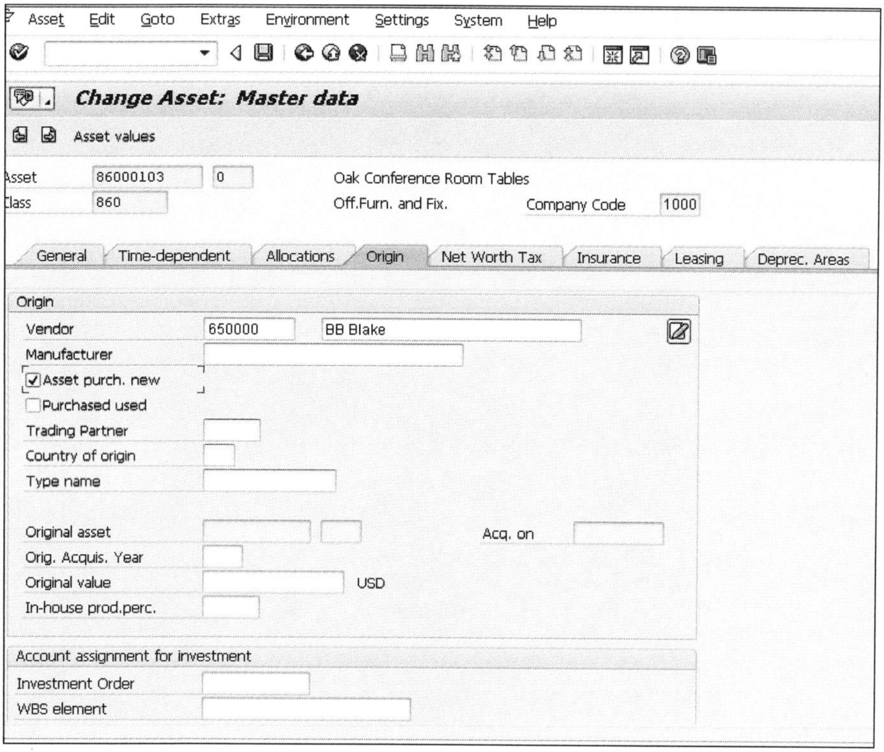

Figure 13.16 Change Asset: Master Data, Origin Tab

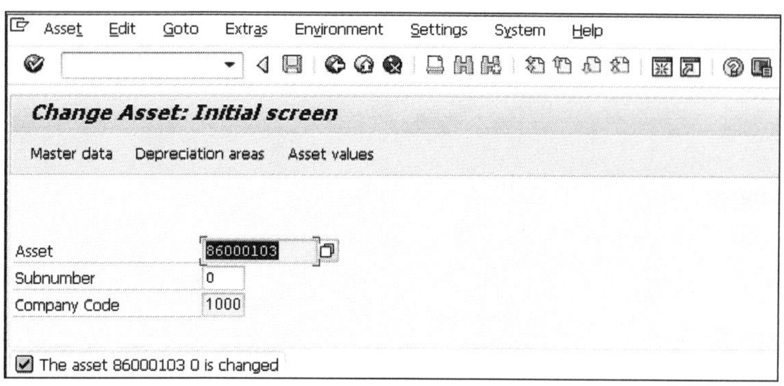

Figure 13.17 Asset Changed Message

To display an asset master record, use Transaction AS03 or application menu path, **Accounting • Financial Accounting • Fixed Assets • Asset • Display • AS03 – Asset**, as shown in Figure 13.18.

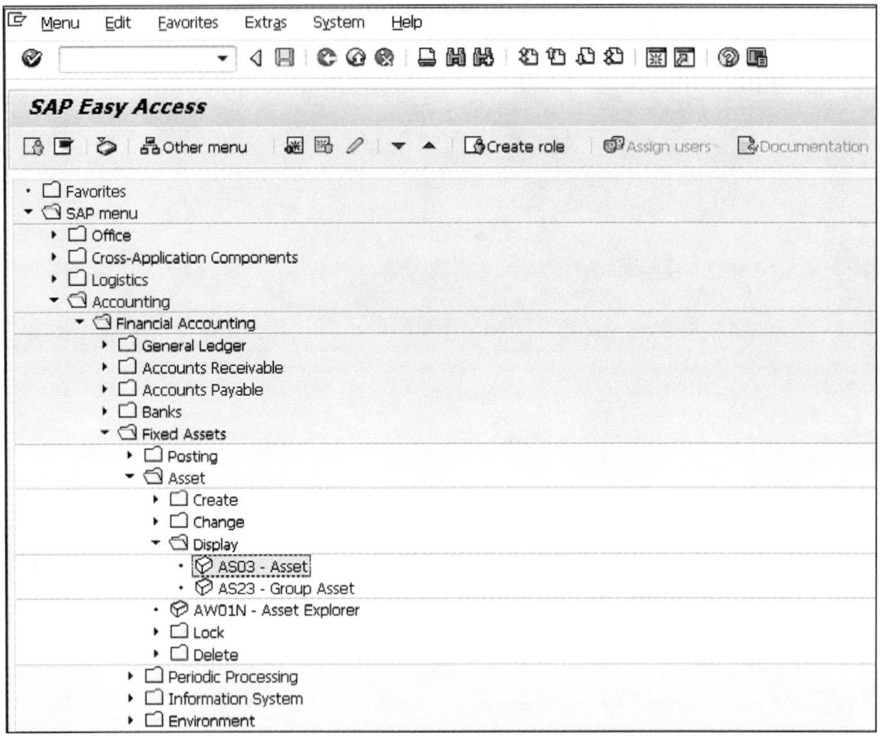

Figure 13.18 Transaction AS03 Application Menu Path

Double-click **AS03** from the menu path, and the **Display Asset: Initial screen** opens (Figure 13.19). Enter an **Asset** number and press Enter.

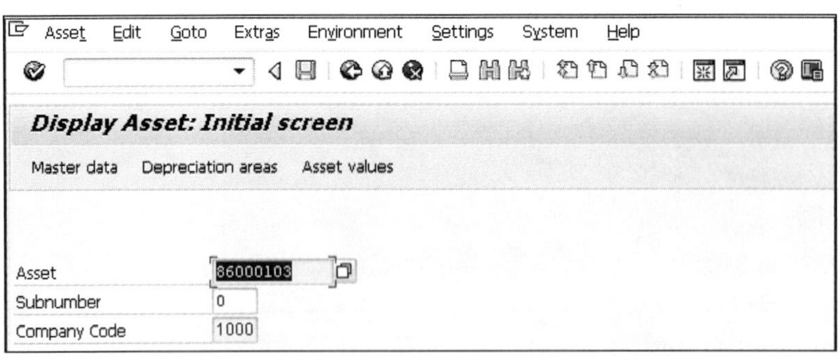

Figure 13.19 Display Asset: Initial Screen

The **Display Asset: Master data** screen opens (Figure 13.20). Click any of the available tabs to view relevant information.

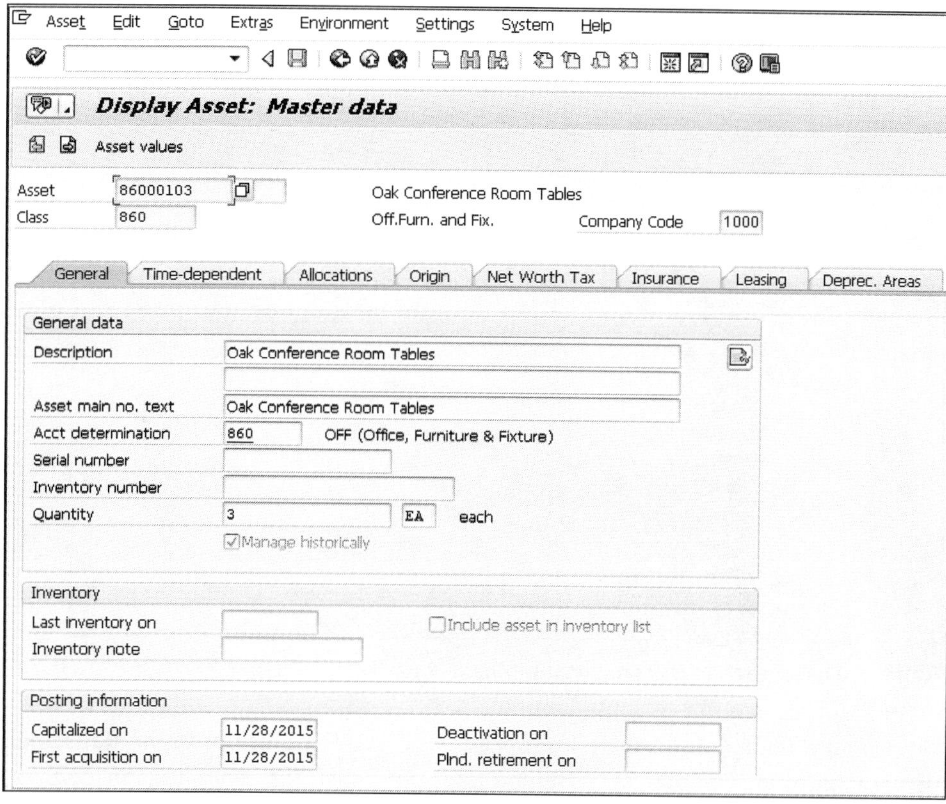

Figure 13.20 Display Asset: Master Data

The last topic we'll discuss in this section is locking an asset. In FI-AA, the terms *lock* and *block* are used synonymously. The lock transaction prevents further acquisition postings to an asset master record.

To lock an asset master record, use Transaction AS05 or application menu path, **Accounting • Financial Accounting • Fixed Assets • Asset • Lock • AS05 – Asset**, as shown in Figure 13.21.

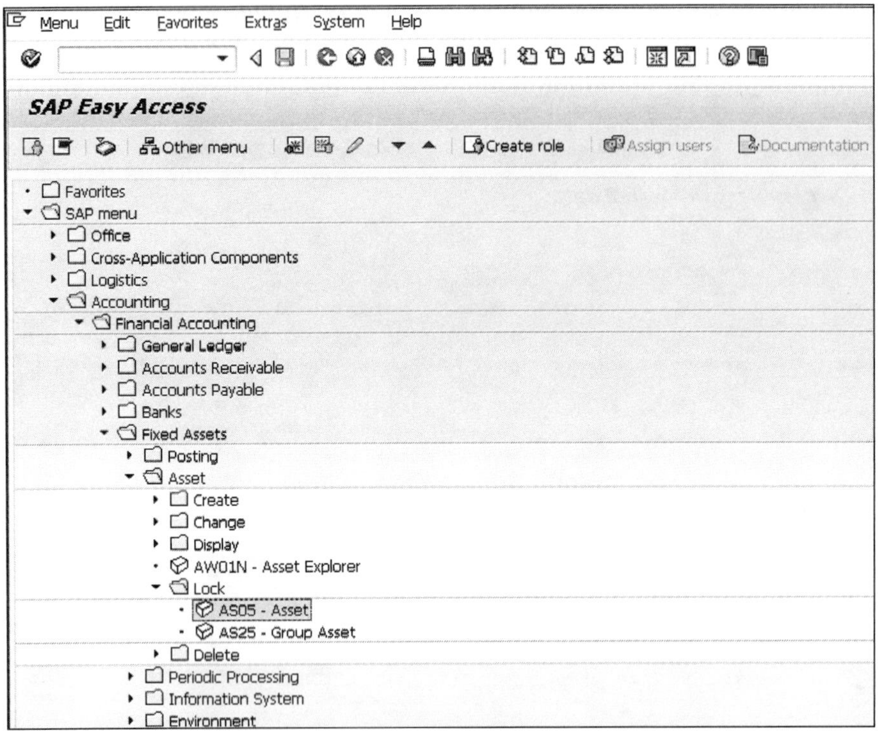

Figure 13.21 Transaction AS05 Application Menu Path

Double-click **AS05 – Asset** from the menu path, and the **Block Asset: Initial screen** opens (Figure 13.22). Enter an **Asset** number, and click the **Block** button or press Enter.

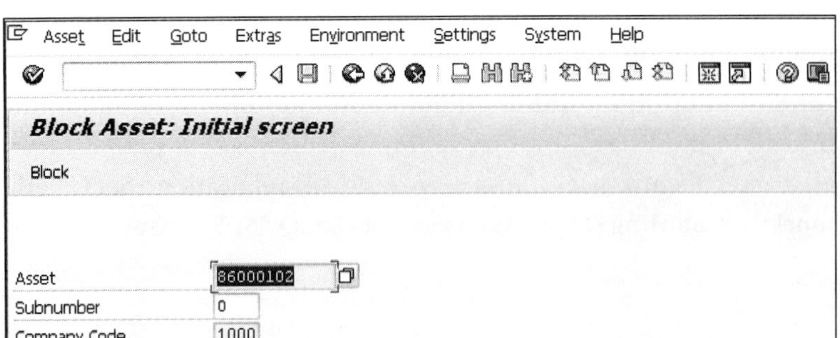

Figure 13.22 Block Asset: Initial Screen

The **Block Asset: Processing screen** opens (Figure 13.23).

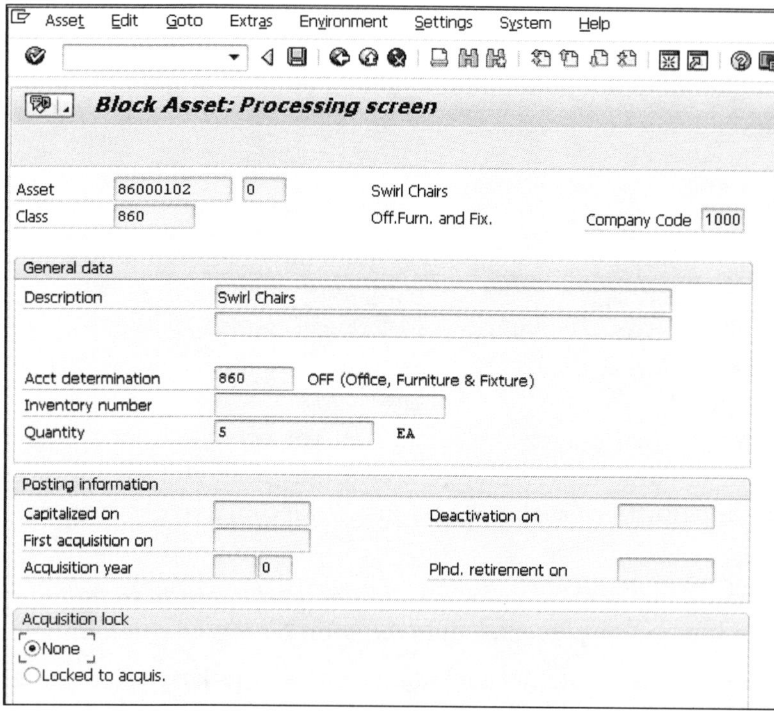

Figure 13.23 Block Asset: Processing Screen

As shown in Figure 13.24, change the **Acquisition lock** selection to **Locked to acquis**. This setting prevents any further acquisition transactions from posting to the asset master record.

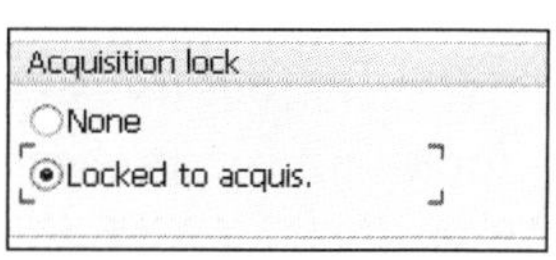

Figure 13.24 Acquisition Lock Selection

Click the **Save** icon to the right of the **Command** field in the upper-left corner of the screen. This saves the asset master record block, and a message confirming the block appears, as shown in Figure 13.25.

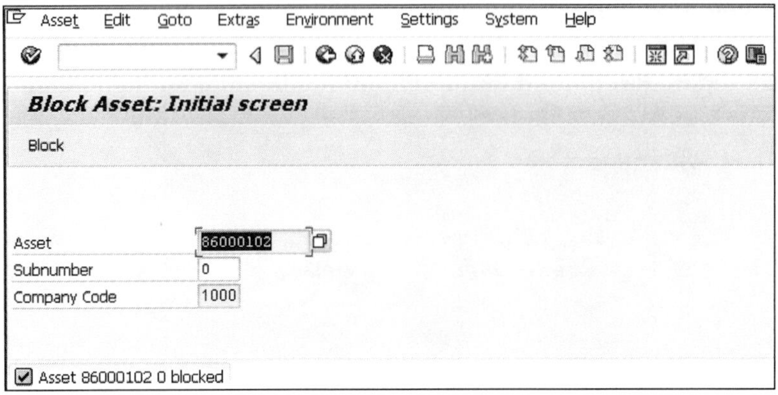

Figure 13.25 Asset Blocked Message

There are several reasons that you might block an asset. For example, when the asset master record is initially created, there may be information that is still missing, such as a serial number. In a situation like this, the asset master record is blocked for safety reasons.

Another reason for locking/blocking an asset is if a discrepancy has been found, in which case, further postings are prevented until the errors have been corrected.

This concludes our discussion of changing, displaying, and locking asset master records. In the next section, you'll learn how to best navigate assets using the Asset Explorer.

13.3 Navigating the Asset Explorer

Managing fixed assets isn't an easy job. The number of assets within a company can number in the thousands or tens of thousands and spread across numerous asset classes. Asset managers and accountants need user-friendly tools and comprehensive views of fixed assets and their financial information. SAP's primary solution is the Asset Explorer.

The Asset Explorer (Transaction AW01N) is an essential tool for any asset manager. Within this transaction, the system allows you to view all transactions tied to an asset as a one-stop shop. In addition, it allows you to see planned and actual depreciation, net book values over time, and depreciation parameters.

Now, let's take a closer look at the Asset Explorer in action by using Transaction AW01N or application menu path, **Accounting • Financial Accounting • Fixed Assets • Asset • AW01N – Asset Explorer**, as shown in Figure 13.26.

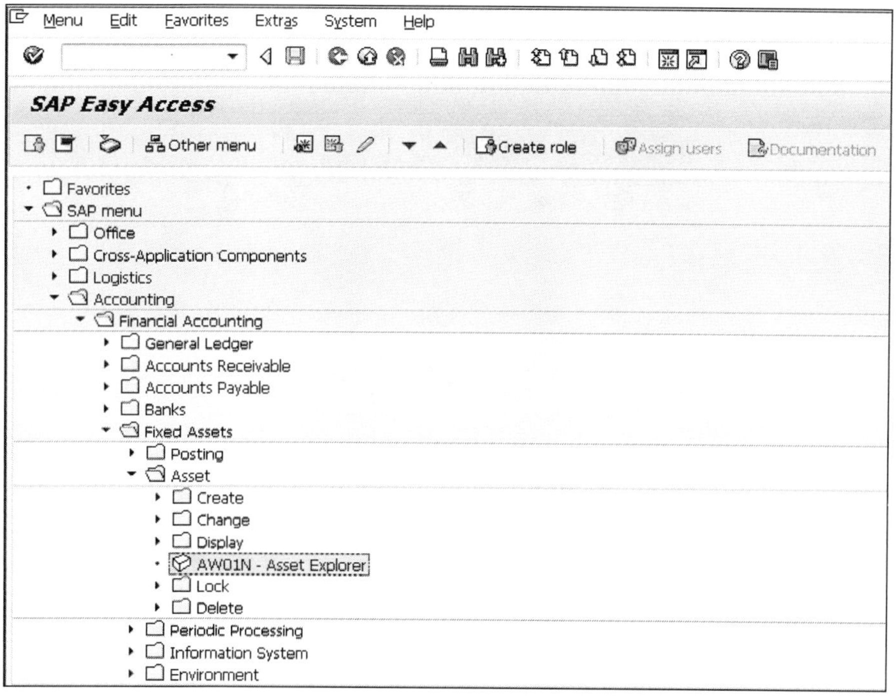

Figure 13.26 Transaction AW01N Application Menu Path

Double-click **AW01N – Asset Explorer** from the menu path, and the **Asset Explorer** screen opens (Figure 13.27). This initial screen defaults to the **Planned values** tab, where acquisition values and planned depreciation can be viewed by depreciation area. To change depreciation areas, use the navigation pane to the left of the screen.

In the **Transactions** area at the bottom of the screen, you'll see all transactions posted to this asset. The Asset Explorer has drilldown capability; double-click a transaction document number to view an individual document associated with the asset.

Click on the **Posted values** tab (Figure 13.28) to see all posted and planned depreciation for an asset by period. This powerful capability is used frequently by accountants, asset managers, and accounting supervisors.

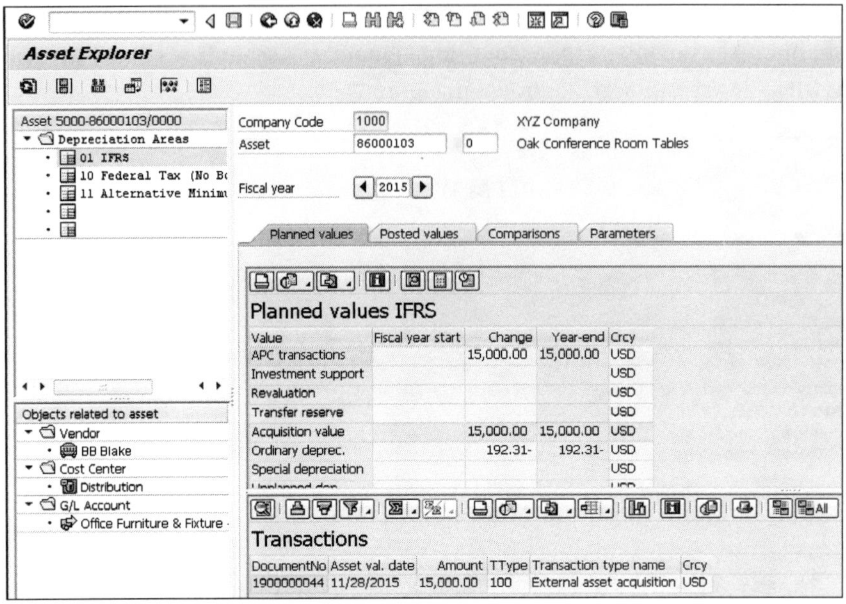

Figure 13.27 Asset Explorer Initial Screen

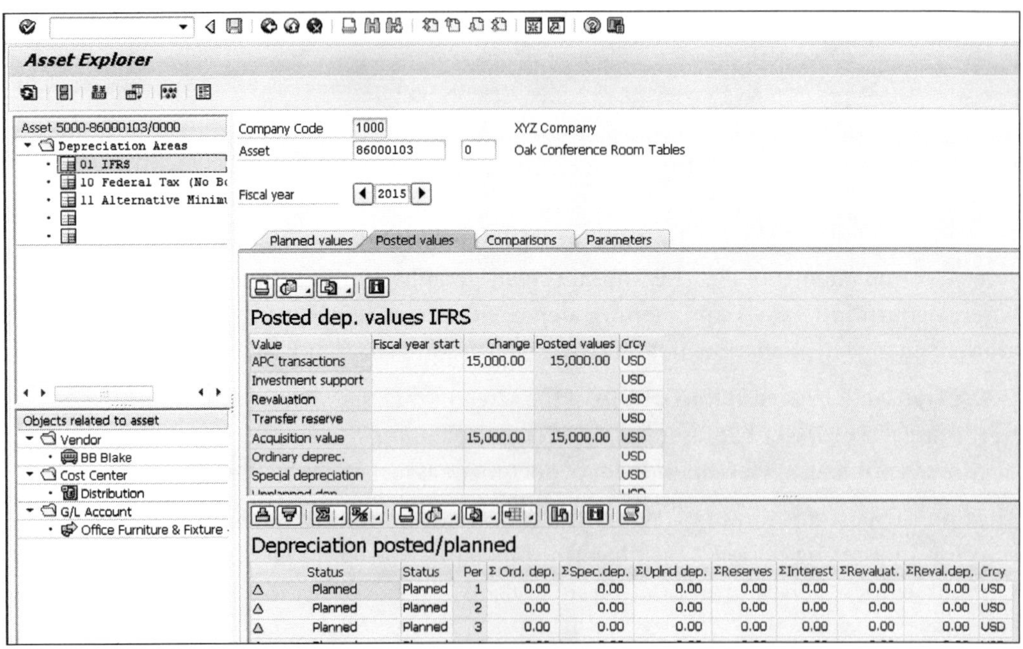

Figure 13.28 Asset Explorer: Posted Values Tab

Click on the **Comparisons** tab (Figure 13.29) to see annual breakouts for depreciation and net book value.

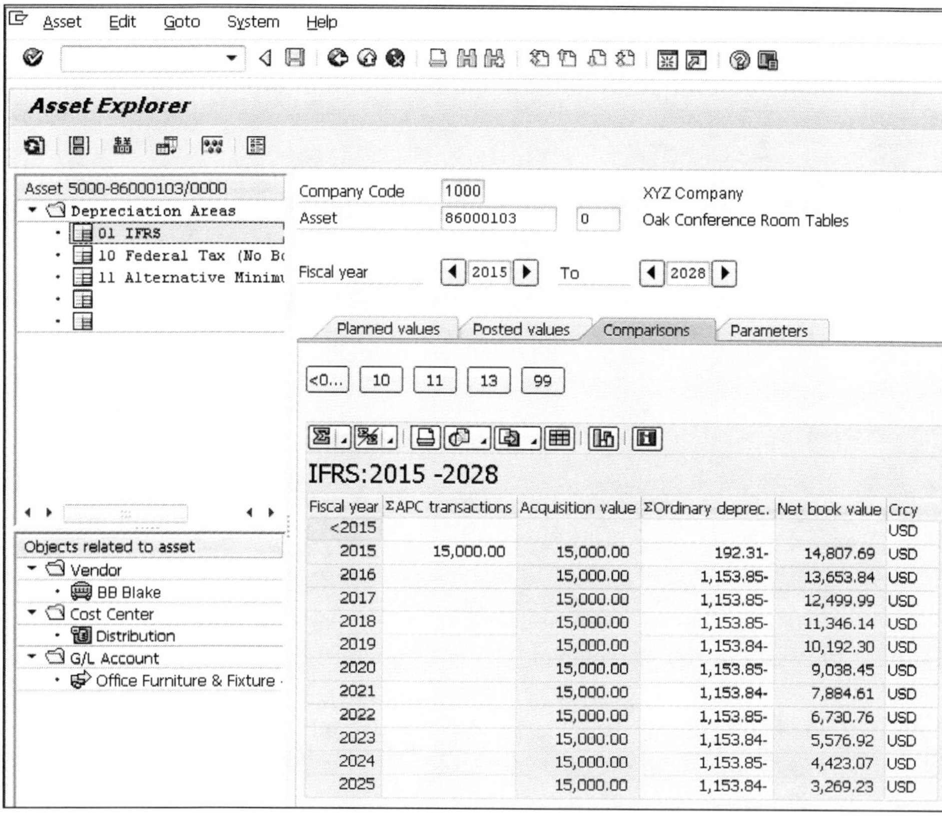

Figure 13.29 Asset Explorer, Comparisons Tab

Click on the **Parameters** tab (Figure 13.30) to see specific settings relevant to the depreciation of the asset. The **Dep. Key** (depreciation key) is fundamental, as it determines the asset's method of depreciation. **Useful life** and other relevant settings also can be viewed on this screen. Most of these settings are made in configuration and are associated with the asset class. However, if you ever question the validity of an asset's depreciation calculation, the **Parameters** tab is where you can go to validate an asset's depreciation settings.

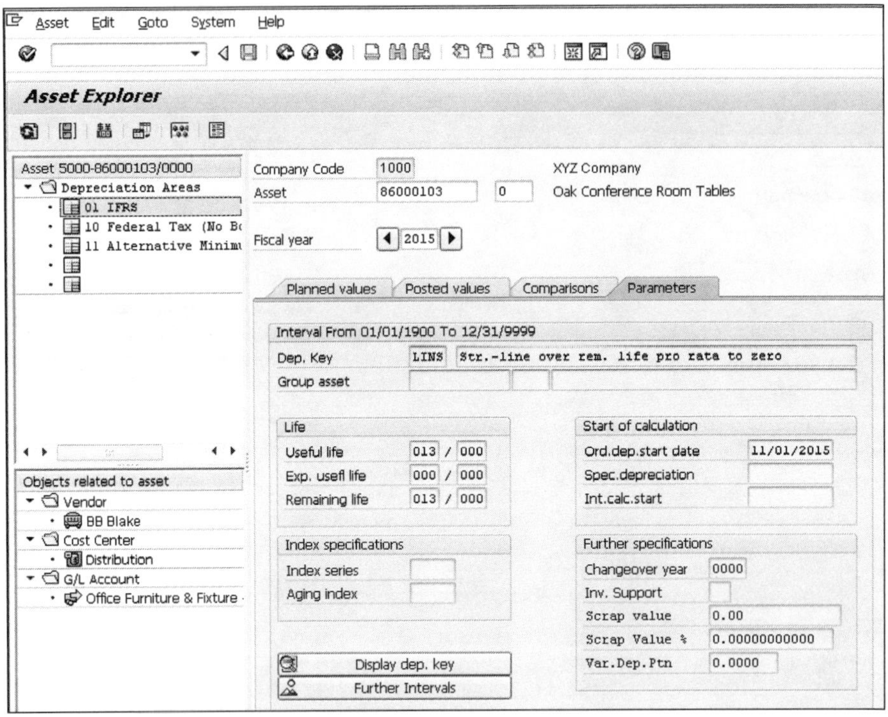

Figure 13.30 Asset Explorer: Parameters Tab

Now that you know how to navigate fixed assets using the Asset Explorer, let's discuss fixed asset transfers in the next section.

13.4 Transfers

There are two types of asset transfers in FI-AA: intracompany transfers and intercompany transfers.

The transactions used include the following:

- **Transaction ABUMN (Transfer within Company Code)**
  Use this transaction when you need to transfer an asset to another business unit or location (e.g., plant) within the same company code.
- **Transaction ABT1N (Intercompany Asset Transfer)**
  Use this transaction to transfer an asset to another company code within your organization.

In addition to transferring an asset to another business unit, Transaction ABUMN can be used to correct an asset that was created with the wrong asset class. In both situations, Transaction ABUMN is an asset transfer within the same company code.

Transaction ABUMN can also be used to perform a partial asset transfer. In this situation, you need to split up an asset or move part of it to another asset. This is common for assets with component or interchangeable parts.

Finally, you can use Transaction ABUMN to transfer an asset under construction (AuC) to a finished asset.

To access Transaction ABUMN, follow application menu path, **Accounting • Financial Accounting • Fixed Assets • Posting • Transfer • ABUMN – Transfer within Company Code**, as shown in Figure 13.31.

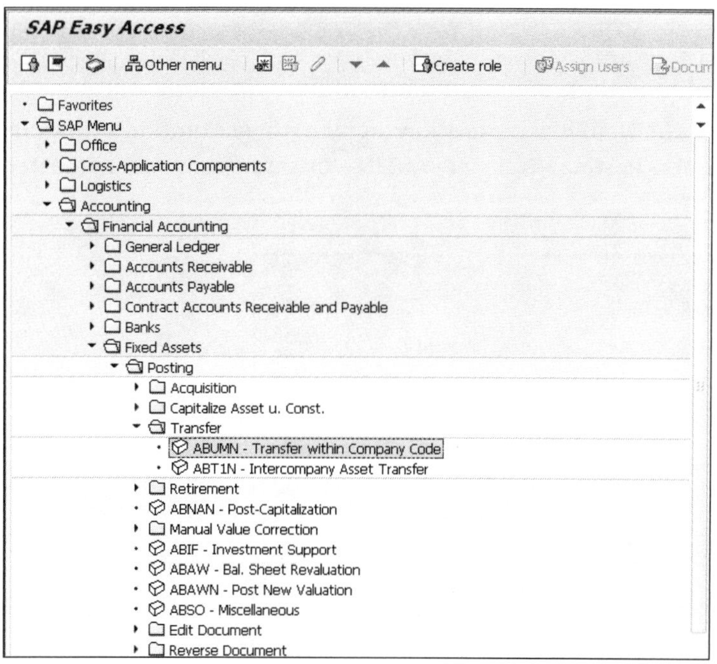

Figure 13.31 Transaction ABUMN Asset Transfer Application Menu Path

Double-click on **ABUMN – Transfer within Company Code**, and the **Enter Asset Transaction: Transfer within Company Code** selection screen appears (Figure 13.32). This is where you enter the details to transfer an asset.

Transaction ABT1N is used if the asset transfer takes place between company codes. This is required when another company code is taking ownership of the asset.

Figure 13.32 Enter Asset Transaction: Selection Screen

To access Transaction ABT1N, follow application menu path, **Accounting • Financial Accounting • Fixed Assets • Posting • Transfer • ABT1N – Intercompany Asset Transfer**, as shown in Figure 13.33.

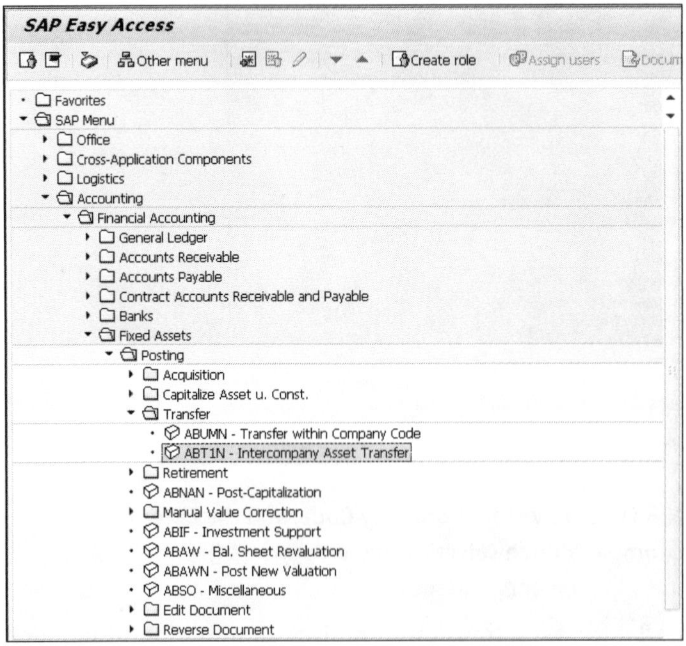

Figure 13.33 Transaction ABT1N Intercompany Asset Transfer Application Menu Path

Double-click on **ABT1N – Intercompany Asset Transfer,** and the **Enter Asset Transaction: Intercompany Asset Transfer** selection screen appears (Figure 13.34).

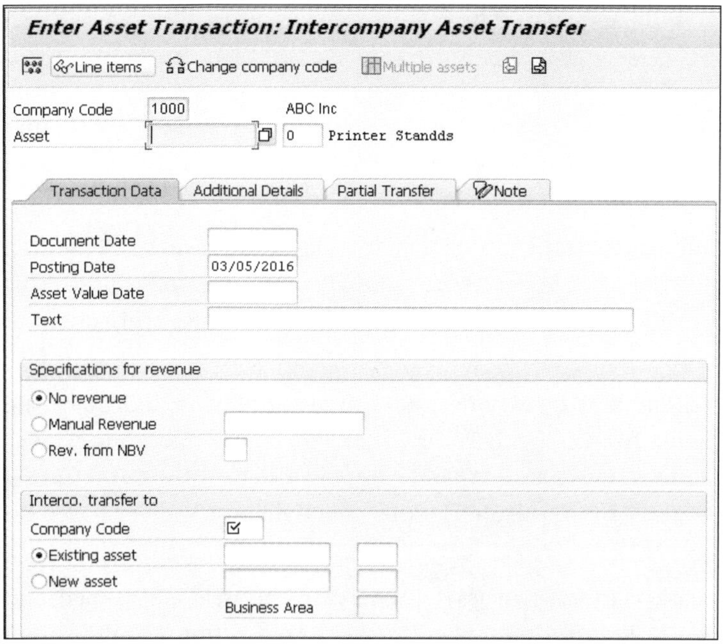

Figure 13.34 Enter Asset Transaction: Intercompany Asset Transfer

There are similarities between Transaction ABT1N and Transaction ABUMN, but there are some key differences. The most obvious difference is that Transaction ABT1N has different company codes for the sender and receiver assets. In other words, an asset is being transferred from the balance sheet of one company code to another.

In addition, intercompany asset transfers require that you make revenue specifications. You must specify if a revenue exchange will take place. Revenue may be associated with an intercompany transfer if it's sold to another part of the company with a separate company code.

Transaction ABT1N offers the following three options for revenue specification:

- **No revenue**
  No revenue is specified.
- **Manual Revenue**
  Manually specify the revenue associated with the asset transfer.
- **Rev. from NBV**
  Use the net book value (NBV) for revenue exchange.

This concludes our discussion of fixed asset transfers. In the next section, we'll discuss asset retirements.

13.5 Retirement

Most people think *asset retirement* means that the asset has no more value or future use. In actuality, asset retirement is simply the removal of an asset or part of an asset from the asset portfolio.

There are several FI-AA business transactions that are relevant to asset retirement. If an asset is sold to a customer and generates revenue, Transaction F-92 is used. This transaction creates a debit to AR through the creation of an AR invoice and a credit to the asset.

Instead of posting a retirement to a customer, you can instead post to a G/L clearing account using Transaction ABAON. Both Transaction F-92 and Transaction ABAON are considered asset sales. Transaction ABAON creates a debit to a G/L clearing account and a credit to the asset. Revenue is either manually specified or based on NBV.

Another common scenario is to scrap an asset. In this case, the asset is scrapped, and no revenue is associated with the retirement of the asset. Transaction ABAVN is used in this scenario.

In the next section, we discuss value adjustments to fixed assets.

13.6 Value Adjustments

There are many reasons that adjustments may need to be made to an asset's valuation. We don't intend to discuss them all here, but we'll highlight some key points.

A positive change to an asset value is referred to as a *write-up*. There are several reasons that a write-up may be necessary, such as when an asset wasn't capitalized in a fiscal year that is now closed, or when an incorrect depreciation key was used in the past, causing excess depreciation to be posted.

Several transactions exist in FI-AA to make value adjustments. These transactions, along with transaction types, provide you with the tools needed to make asset value adjustments for just about any circumstance.

Transaction ABZU is the primary transaction. It's used to post write-ups to ordinary depreciation, special depreciation, unplanned depreciation, and reserves by specifying the appropriate transaction type.

Other write-up transactions include Transaction ABMA for write-up of manual depreciation, Transaction ABAA for write-up of unplanned depreciation, and Transaction ABMR for write-up of transfer of reserves.

Another type of write-up is called *write-up to acquisition and production cost (APC)*. These are corrections to the acquisition and production costs of an asset. Transaction ABNAN is used to correct APC valuations.

Although each of these transactions has an intended purpose, the main differences among them are the transaction type defaults and selection options. We won't cover FI-AA transaction types in detail in this chapter, but for value adjustments, you should become familiar with them and understand when and how they are intended to be used.

This concludes our discussion of value adjustments. In the next section, the topic of depreciation is discussed.

13.7 Depreciation

Depreciation of an asset is typically referred to as *asset consumption*. In accounting terms, depreciation refers to the following:

- A decrease in the value of the asset
- The allocation of costs of an asset to periods in which the asset is used

Long-term assets are depreciated for both tax and accounting purposes. The former affects the balance sheet of a company, and the latter affects net income. Cost is allocated as depreciation expense in the periods in which the asset is expected to be used.

Depreciation expense is recognized by companies for financial reporting and tax purposes. Methods of computing depreciation, and the periods over which assets are depreciated, may vary among asset types, countries, and industries. Specific laws or accounting standards, which may vary by country, may dictate standards for depreciation.

There are several standard methods of computing depreciation expense, including fixed percentage, straight line, and declining balance methods. Depreciation expense begins when the asset is placed in service.

Now, let's see how depreciation expense is executed in FI-AA. The calculation of depreciation is an important step in the month-end and year-end closing processes. To execute an asset depreciation run, use Transaction AFAB or application menu path, **Accounting • Financial Accounting • Fixed Assets • Periodic Processing • AFAB – Execute**, as shown in Figure 13.35.

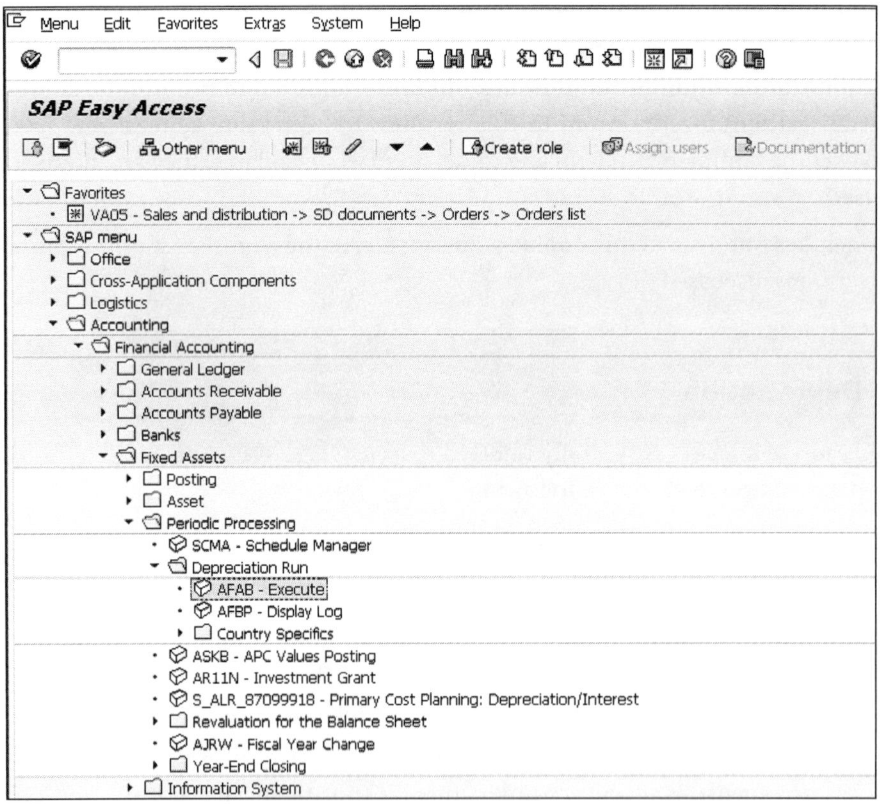

Figure 13.35 Transaction AFAB Application Menu Path

Double-click **AFAB – Execute** from the menu path, and the **Depreciation Posting Run** initial screen opens (Figure 13.36). Here, enter the parameters for your depreciation posting run. The **Company Code, Fiscal year**, and **Posting Period** fields are required.

The default selection in **Reason for posting run** is **Planned posting run**. However, occasionally there will be a need to repeat or restart a run, or to run unplanned depreciation.

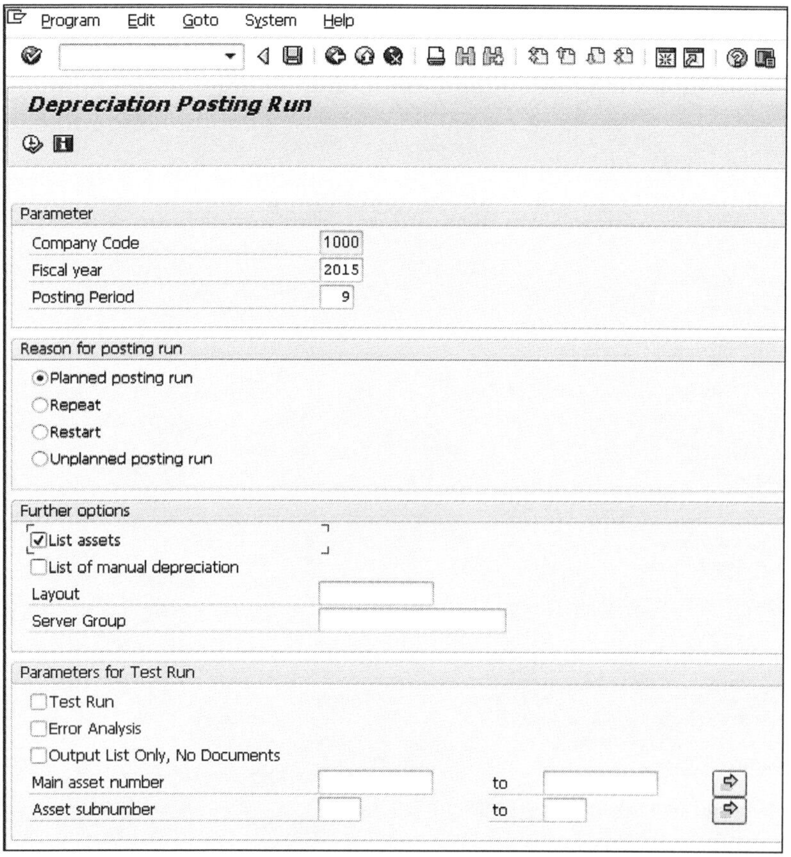

Figure 13.36 Depreciation Posting Run Initial Screen

The **Further options** area of the screen provides additional options for output. One common selection is **List assets**, which specifies that all assets will be listed for which depreciation is posted on the depreciation log.

It's always a good idea to run depreciation in test mode first. The **Parameters for Test Run** area at the bottom of the screen provides settings for you to do so.

With all the field values entered as in Figure 13.36, click the **Execute** icon. The depreciation run executes as a background job.

13

To view the results of a depreciation run, use Transaction AFBP or application menu path, **Accounting • Financial Accounting • Fixed Assets • Periodic Processing • Depreciation Run • AFBP – Display Log**, as shown in Figure 13.37.

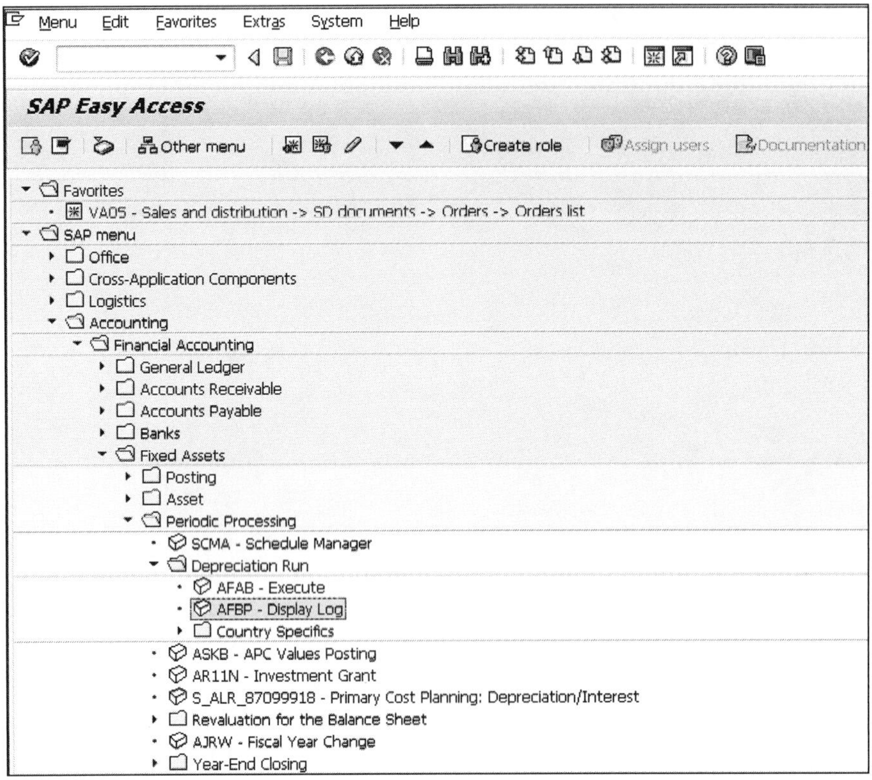

Figure 13.37 Transaction AFBP Application Menu Path

Double-click **AFBP – Display Log** from the menu path, and the **Log of Posting Run** screen opens (Figure 13.38). The **Company Code**, **Fiscal Year**, and **Posting Period** fields are required. Further options also are available, including the **List assets** checkbox, which indicates that all posted assets with depreciation will be listed on the output log.

With all field values entered, click the **Execute** icon. The **Log for Posting Run** screen opens (Figure 13.39). All the details from the depreciation run are provided. Within the log, you can change the layout, sort, filter, subtotal, download to Excel, and more.

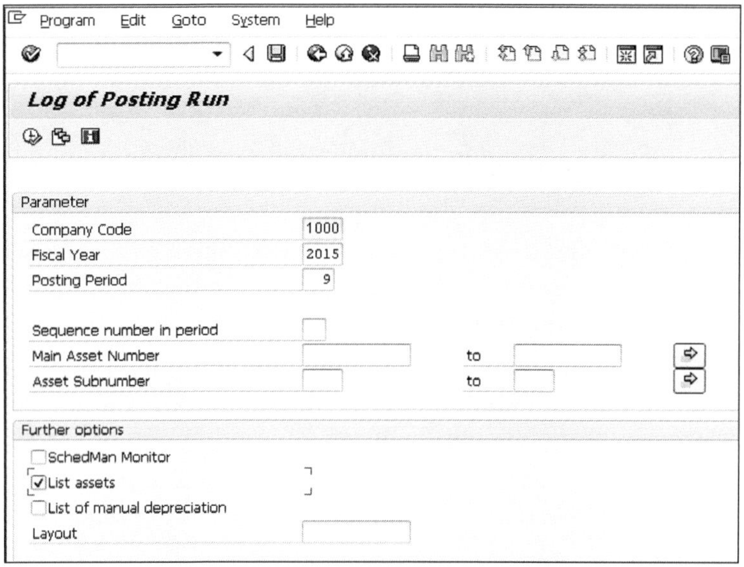

Figure 13.38 Log of Posting Run Initial Screen

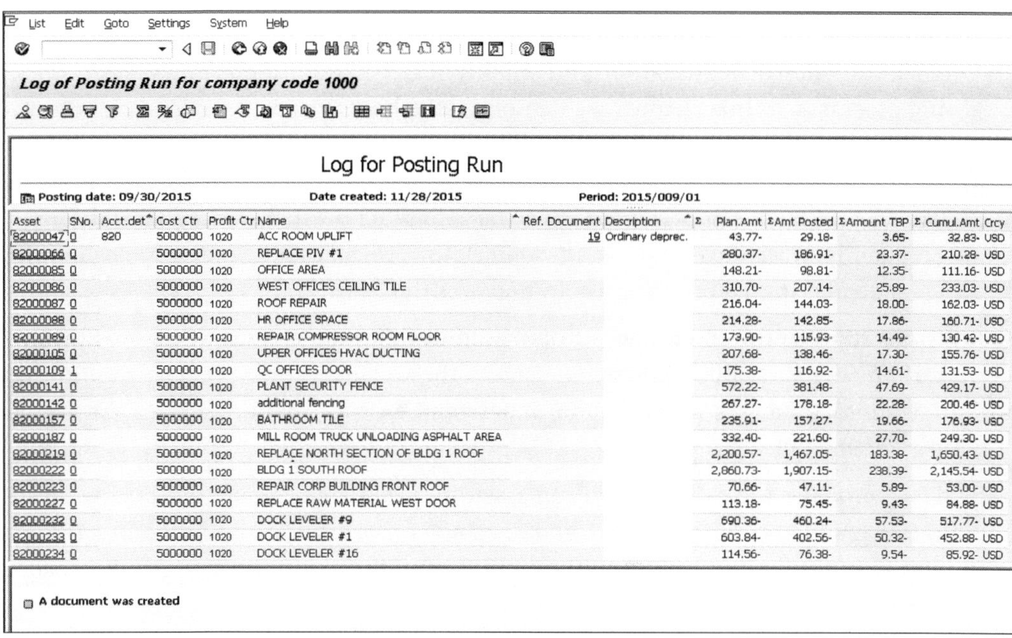

Figure 13.39 Log for Posting Run

This concludes our discussion of fixed asset depreciation. You should now have a good understanding of what depreciation is, how to execute a depreciation run in FI-AA, and how to view the log of a depreciation run.

13.8 Summary

The concept of the fixed asset lifecycle is important to understand. The fixed asset lifecycle is often referred to as the acquire-to-retire process. In this chapter, the different parts of the lifecycle were covered in detail.

The first step in the acquire-to-retire process is the creation of the asset master record using Transaction AS01. After an asset master record is created, the asset can be capitalized, giving life to the asset. In this chapter, capitalization of an asset was demonstrated using Transaction F-90 to debit an asset and credit a vendor account, thereby capitalizing the asset value, while at the same time producing an open payable (i.e., vendor invoice).

Throughout the lifecycle of an asset, the Asset Explorer (Transaction AW01N) is an indispensable tool for managing assets. In essence, it serves as a one-stop shop for asset information.

The calculation of depreciation is an important step in month-end and year-end closing processes. In this chapter, we demonstrated how to execute a depreciation run (Transaction AFAB) and how to view a depreciation run log (Transaction AFBP). In most companies, depreciation runs are scheduled jobs that run automatically at month-end, but it's important to know the details of how such a scheduled job works. Frequently, questions arise about depreciation calculations, and troubleshooting asset depreciation tends to be a common occurrence.

Other steps in the asset lifecycle discussed in this chapter include asset transfers, retirements, and value adjustments. Each of these transaction types have multiple FI-AA transactions. It's important to understand each of them and their associated transaction types.

FI-AA provides the capability for full asset lifecycle management, but business processes tend to be cross-modular, and fixed asset processes are no exception. Understanding the basics of FI-AA is an important first step for gaining a broader perspective on integrated asset processes.

This concludes our discussion of fixed asset transactions. In the next chapter, we'll discuss fixed asset posting logic and the validation of FI-AA postings.

Chapter 14

Fixed Asset Posting Logic

In this chapter, we cover useful topics in FI Asset Accounting (FI-AA) for understanding the validation of asset postings. Several factors make the validation of asset postings a challenge, including a large number of account determinations, transaction types, and General Ledger (G/L) accounts.

Trying to validate asset postings can often feel like wandering in the dark because, by the very nature of FI-AA, a lot happens in the background when you execute a transaction. When FI-AA is configured, there is a wide range of system settings and integration to sort out, requiring close collaboration with the chart of accounts, procurement, production, and core financials.

Asset accountants frequently encounter two types of issues. The first occurs when an asset transaction doesn't post to the expected General Ledger (G/L) account, for example, when an asset acquisition posts to the wrong asset class and G/L reconciliation account. The second common issue occurs when an asset manager finds that depreciation postings are incorrect. This is seen commonly during month-end or year-end close processes, when depreciation is run and postings are validated.

In this chapter, the intent is to give you a better understanding of the FI-AA design and posting logic, thereby empowering asset managers and accountants to execute their day-to-day job functions and to more easily validate FI-AA transactions.

Specific topics addressed in this chapter include fixed asset G/L accounts, asset classes, and account determinations, and covering these topics requires delving into configuration at times. We don't intend to cover the configuration but to provide you with a base level of understanding for how certain configurations influence the G/L account postings in FI-AA.

Let's begin by taking a look at G/L accounts.

14.1 General Ledger Accounts

Asset Accounting (AA) is a specialty. Numerous G/L accounts are needed to support FI-AA. It's a best practice to set up G/L reconciliation accounts in a one-to-one relationship with asset classes, which makes FI-AA more organized and easier to manage and streamlines FI-AA configuration with financial reporting.

Now, let's discuss some other aspects of G/L accounts in FI-AA. The specific G/L accounts you choose to use in FI-AA depend primarily on your business processes. Not all FI-AA steps are executed by every customer. Therefore, you need to carefully define your FI-AA business processes and implement the G/L accounts and configuration necessary to support those processes.

This chapter doesn't attempt to identify each possible G/L account you may need. Instead, we address the core G/L accounts to support acquisition and production cost (APC) and depreciation transactions. These include fixed asset balance sheet accounts (i.e., reconciliation and accumulated depreciation accounts) and profit and loss (P&L) accounts (i.e., depreciation expense).

Now, let's delve into balance sheet accounts in the next section.

14.1.1 Balance Sheet Accounts

In configuration, G/L account groups are defined prior to creating G/L accounts. These account groups determine the allowable number range for G/L accounts and control the layout of the G/L account master record and whether fields are required, optional, or suppressed. When creating a G/L account, an account group must be specified.

This is critical to know when your company is setting up its chart of accounts in SAP. Each type of G/L account (e.g., bank accounts, liabilities, assets) should have a distinct number range and account group. If your asset accounts aren't aligned but instead are scattered, then they will be more difficult to manage.

G/L account groups are especially important to FI-AA because a company must have at least one account group for fixed assets. This account group should designate an allowable number range consistent with your numbering scheme for asset classes. Asset classes are discussed in detail in Section 14.2. *Consistency* is the name of the game when setting up FI-AA in a way that is easy to understand and manage. Consistency between fixed asset G/L accounts and asset classes is especially important.

Figure 14.1 is an example of FI-AA balance sheet accounts.

Chart of Accounts ABC Inc

G/L acct	G/L Acct Long Text
140210	LAND
140211	EASEMENTS
140212	BUILDINGS
140213	OFFICE FURNITURE AND EQUIPMENT
140214	MACHINERY AND EQUIPMENT
140215	COMPUTER EQUIPMENT
140216	COMPUTER SOFTWARE
140217	VEHICLES
140218	CONSTRUCTION IN PROGRESS
140219	LEASEHOLD IMPROVEMENTS
140220	CAPITAL LEASES

Figure 14.1 FI-AA Balance Sheet Accounts

The core balance sheet fixed asset accounts include APC reconciliation accounts (Figure 14.1) and accumulated depreciation and amortization accounts.

Figure 14.2 is an example of accumulated depreciation accounts that correlate to the APC accounts in Figure 14.1.

Chart of Accounts ABC Inc

G/L acct	G/L Acct Long Text
140110	LAND
140111	EASEMENTS
140112	BUILDINGS
140113	OFFICE FURNITURE AND EQUIPMENT
140114	MACHINERY AND EQUIPMENT
140115	COMPUTER EQUIPMENT
140116	COMPUTER SOFTWARE
140117	VEHICLES
140118	CONSTRUCTION IN PROGRESS
140119	LEASEHOLD IMPROVEMENTS
140120	CAPITAL LEASES

Figure 14.2 FI-AA Accumulated Depreciation Accounts

A streamlined design will have a one-to-one relationship between fixed asset balance sheet accounts and asset classes (Figure 14.3).

There may be regulatory, industry, or country-specific requirements that dictate otherwise for some customers. Moreover, for each fixed asset reconciliation account, there should be a corresponding accumulated depreciation and amortization account.

Balance sheet accounts are designated in FI-AA account determinations and are discussed in detail in Section 14.3.

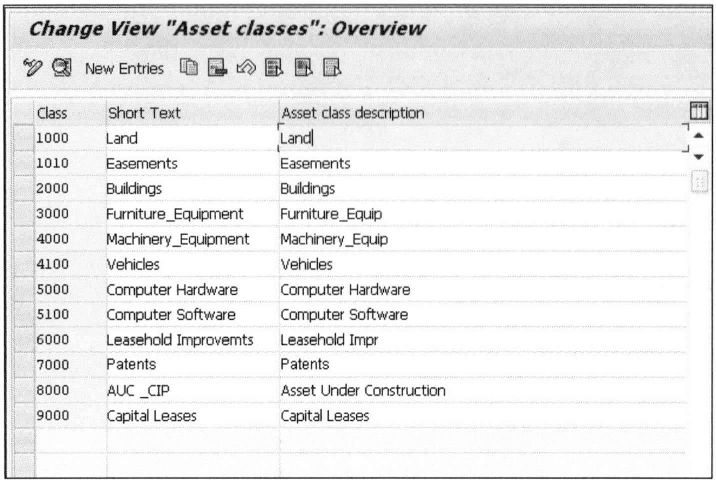

Figure 14.3 FI-AA Asset Classes

Now that you understand FI-AA balance sheet accounts, we'll discuss FI-AA P&L accounts in the next section.

14.1.2 Profit and Loss Accounts

In the P&L, many different G/L accounts may be used for fixed assets. These include G/L accounts for revenue, gain/loss, interest, and more. We'll focus on P&L depreciation expense accounts.

When a depreciation run is executed (Transaction AFAB), a debit is posted to a P&L depreciation and amortization expense account, and a credit is posted to a balance sheet accumulated depreciation account.

Depreciation expense accounts are designated in FI-AA account determination, which is discussed in detail in Section 14.3. From an accounting perspective, depreciation expense postings affect the net income of a company.

As you learned in this section, there is a close relationship between asset classes and FI-AA G/L accounts. In the next section, we'll discuss asset classes in detail.

14.2 Asset Classes

Asset classes are a fundamental part of the FI-AA design and provide a structure for fixed assets from an accounting point of view. Each asset master record is assigned to only one asset class. Asset classes serve other important functions in FI-AA, including assigning default values when creating assets (e.g., depreciation terms) and grouping assets for reporting. The asset class also determines the screen variant and account determinations.

> **Warning**
>
> An important system limitation to be aware of is that after an asset is created with an asset class, the asset class can't be changed on the fixed asset master record. To fix the error, you have to create a new asset with the proper asset class and transfer the misaligned asset to the new one. Be especially careful when you create a new asset master record to ensure that the correct asset class is selected.

Although asset classes are configurations and typically accessed via the IMG (Transaction SPRO), they also can be accessed using Transaction OAOA. This transaction opens the **Display View "Asset classes": Overview** screen (Figure 14.4).

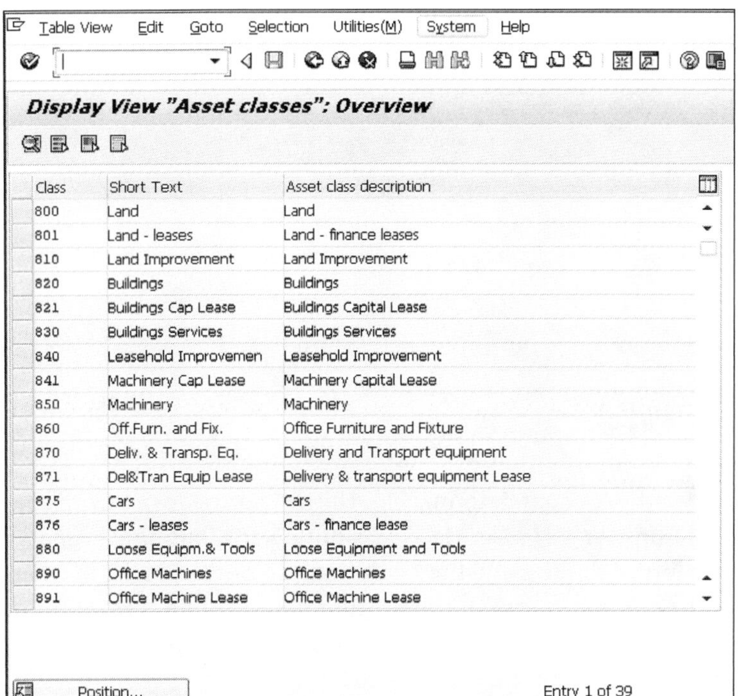

Class	Short Text	Asset class description
800	Land	Land
801	Land - leases	Land - finance leases
810	Land Improvement	Land Improvement
820	Buildings	Buildings
821	Buildings Cap Lease	Buildings Capital Lease
830	Buildings Services	Buildings Services
840	Leasehold Improvemen	Leasehold Improvement
841	Machinery Cap Lease	Machinery Capital Lease
850	Machinery	Machinery
860	Off.Furn. and Fix.	Office Furniture and Fixture
870	Deliv. & Transp. Eq.	Delivery and Transport equipment
871	Del&Tran Equip Lease	Delivery & transport equipment Lease
875	Cars	Cars
876	Cars - leases	Cars - finance lease
880	Loose Equipm.& Tools	Loose Equipment and Tools
890	Office Machines	Office Machines
891	Office Machine Lease	Office Machine Lease

Figure 14.4 Asset Classes: Overview

Double-click an asset class,, or highlight it and click the **Display** icon . The **Display View "Asset classes": Details** screen opens (Figure 14.5). Note that several important control parameters exist within the asset class, including screen layout rules for asset master records, number ranges, a setting to allow subasset numbers, and so on.

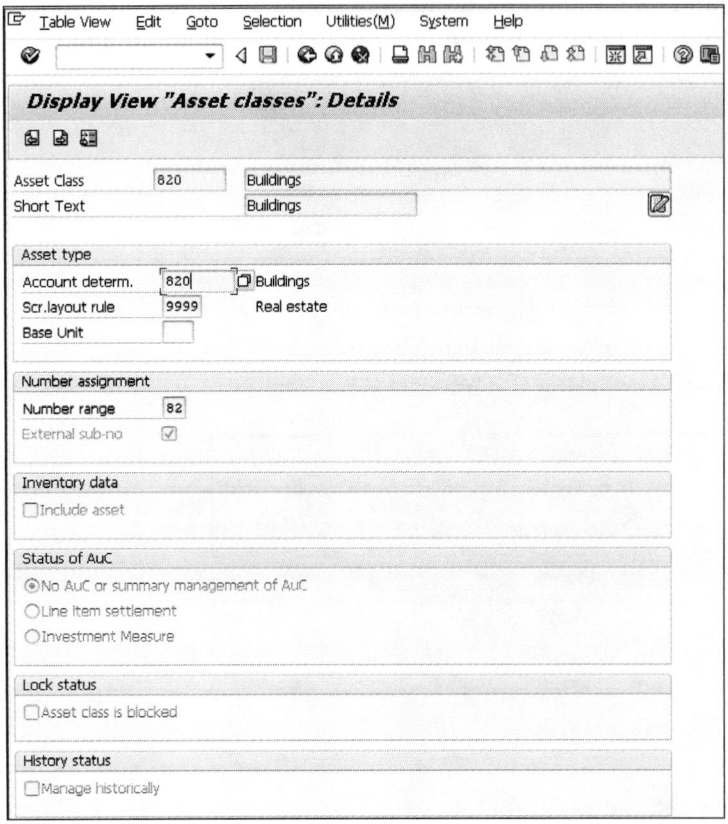

Figure 14.5 Asset Classes: Details

In Figure 14.5, take note of the **Account determ.** field. This field provides a link to specific account determinations for this asset class. Account determination designates the reconciliation accounts in the G/L and their offsetting accounts posted to when certain business transactions are executed. The **Account determ.** field is required in the asset class. Several asset classes can use the same account determination, but they must use the same chart of accounts and post in the same way to G/L accounts.

In this section, you've seen that asset classes are a fundamental structure in FI-AA. Moreover, through assignment of account determination, asset classes provide the link to G/L reconciliation accounts and offsetting accounts with certain business transactions. In the next section, we'll discuss FI-AA account determinations.

14.3 Account Determinations

Account determinations specify the G/L accounts posted to for specific FI-AA transaction types. They are required for the integration of FI-AA with the G/L.

Initially setting up and testing account determinations is no small task. Just think about all the different transaction types in FI-AA, and you'll get the picture. These transactions include acquisitions, retirements, revaluations, investment support, depreciation, and more.

Prior to setting up account determinations, a chart of depreciation must be created and assigned to a company code. This is an essential link between FI-AA and the G/L. Figure 14.6 shows an example chart of depreciation assigned to a company code. Although this assignment is made in configuration using Transaction SPRO, you can go directly to this setting using Transaction OAOB.

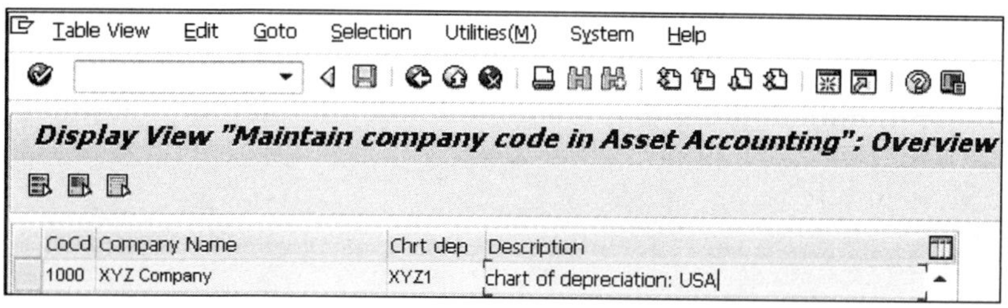

Figure 14.6 Assigning a Chart of Depreciation to a Company Code

The chart of depreciation contains a set of depreciation areas. Figure 14.7 shows an example chart of depreciation that contains multiple depreciation areas. Notice in the **G/L** column the value **1** in depreciation area **1**. This setting specifies that postings are to be made to the G/L in real time.

With this framework established, FI-AA account assignments can be made. Initially setting up FI-AA account assignments is tedious. Account determinations must be completed for each combination of transaction type and asset class, and these account determinations should be well documented in your company's accounting models, especially because any future changes to G/L asset accounts also need to be made in account determinations.

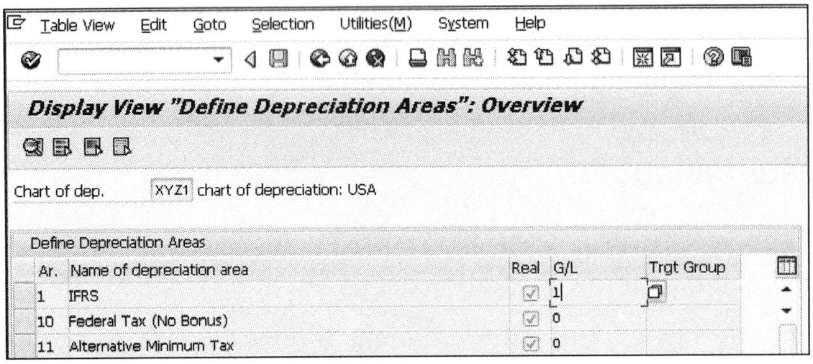

Figure 14.7 Define Chart of Depreciation

Several different account assignment transactions exist in FI-AA. They are broken out to allow account determinations by business transaction groupings. Table 14.1 provides a list of these transactions.

Transaction Code	Transaction Name
AO85	Acquisitions
AO86	Retirements
AO87	Revaluation of APC
AO88	Investment Support
AO89	Settlement AuC to CO Objects
AO93	Ordinary Depreciation
AO94	Special Depreciation
AO95	Unplanned Depreciation
AO96	Transfer of Reserves
AO97	Revaluation of Depreciation
AO98	Interest

Table 14.1 FI-AA Account Determination Transactions

Rather than going through each of the transactions in Table 14.1 individually, we'll focus on Transaction AO90, which provides a comprehensive view of FI-AA account determinations. Transaction AO90 includes account determinations for acquisitions, retirements, revaluations, balance sheet accounts, ordinary depreciation, special depreciation, unplanned depreciation, transfer of reserves, interest, and more. When you execute Transaction AO90, the **Display View "Chart of Accounts": Overview** screen opens (Figure 14.8).

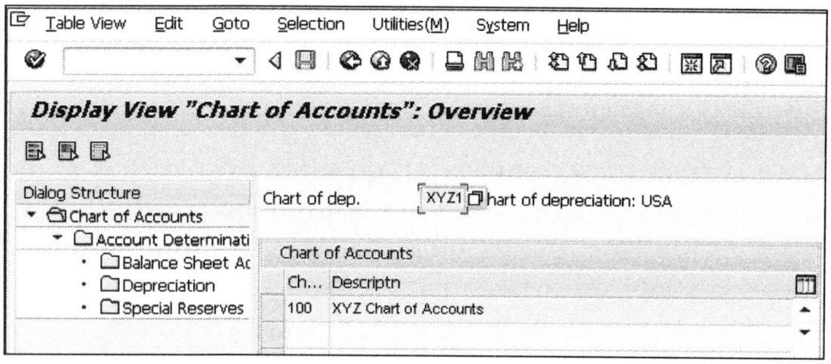

Figure 14.8 Chart of Accounts: Overview

By drilling down into the **Account Determination** folder, you'll open the **Display View "Account Determination": Overview** screen (Figure 14.9).

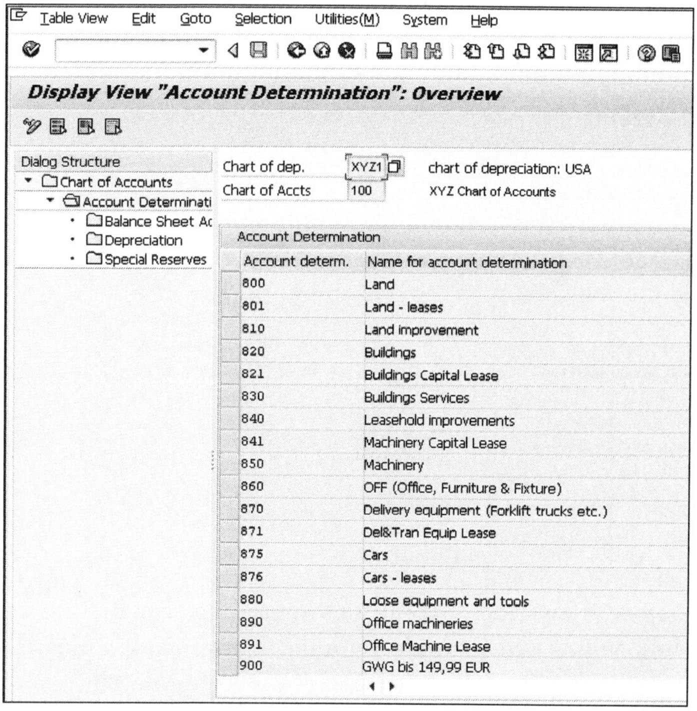

Figure 14.9 Account Determination: Overview

Notice that the **Account determ.** values and names directly mirror the asset classes discussed in Section 14.2. Although a one-to-one correlation isn't required, it helps keep your FI-AA setup organized and easy to manage.

Drilling down in the **Balance Sheet Accounts** folder lets you view specific account determination settings (Figure 14.10). It's important to note that not all G/L accounts are specified. More possibilities exist than are needed. A company typically only enters account determinations when it knows for certain they will be used. For example, if down payments aren't part of your company's acquisition process, you might choose not to enter a G/L account in the **Acquisition: down payments** field.

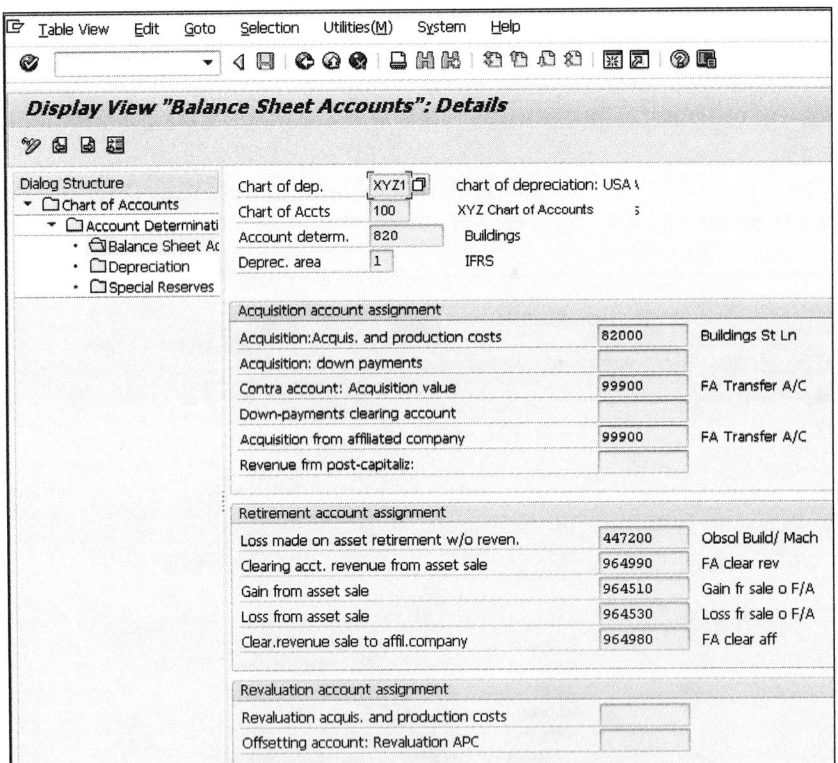

Figure 14.10 Balance Sheet Accounts: Details

Drilling down into the **Depreciation** folder, you can view specific account determination settings (Figure 14.11). Notice that separate account determinations must be made for ordinary, special, and unplanned depreciation. For accounting purposes, each type of depreciation may need to be accounted for separately.

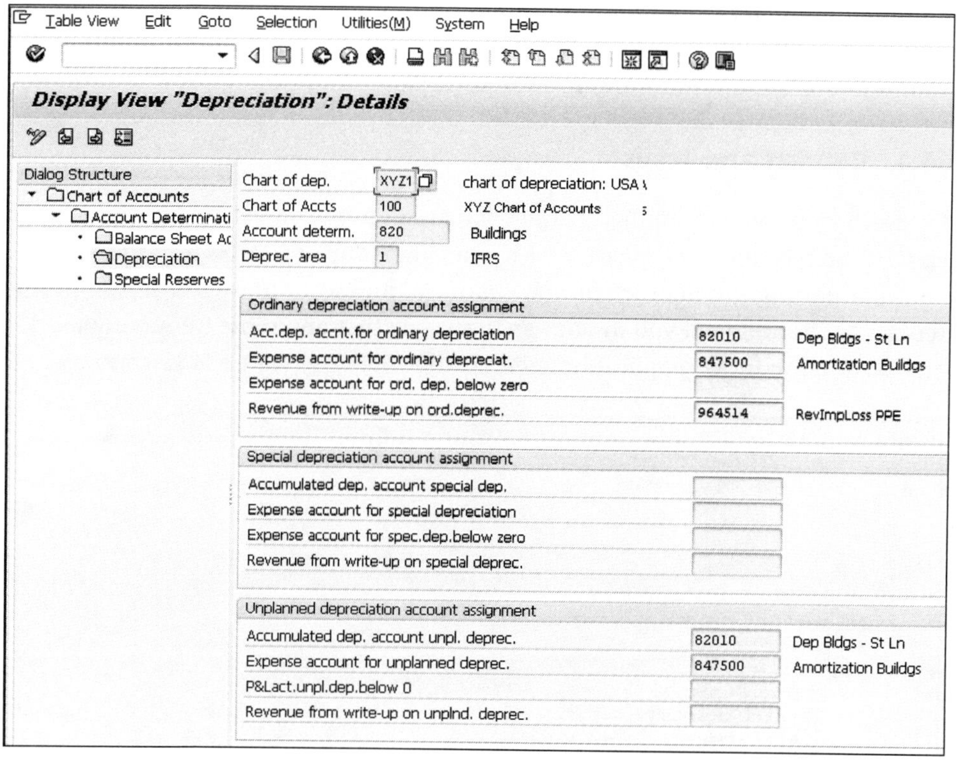

Figure 14.11 Depreciation: Details

A word of caution related to the setup of FI-AA account determinations and testing: Because so many FI-AA account determinations exist, it's important to keep FI-AA posting models with your expected results and to test all relevant account determinations before you go live with SAP. If you're already live on FI-AA and make a change to account determinations, the same applies.

In the world today, people are under a lot of pressure to complete tasks quickly. As a result, testing easily can be compromised or skipped altogether. Whether you're going live with FI-AA for the first time or making a change to account determinations, make sure to test all FI-AA postings before promoting a change to production. It's likely that fixing FI-AA posting errors in production will be a lot more time-consuming than testing.

In this section, you learned about FI-AA account determinations and how to view them, as well as the importance of testing them all and having good posting models with expected results. Understanding account determinations is critical for understanding

AA, and it gives you a greater understanding of the FI-AA posting logic necessary for validating and troubleshooting asset postings.

14.4 Reports and Tools

In the previous sections of this chapter, you learned about asset G/L accounts, asset classes, and account determinations. Knowing the setup of FI-AA is important to recognize a posting problem when you see it. In this section, we'll discuss specific reports and tools to aid you in your analysis. The first and most frequently used is Transaction AW01N. Its application menu path is shown in Figure 14.12.

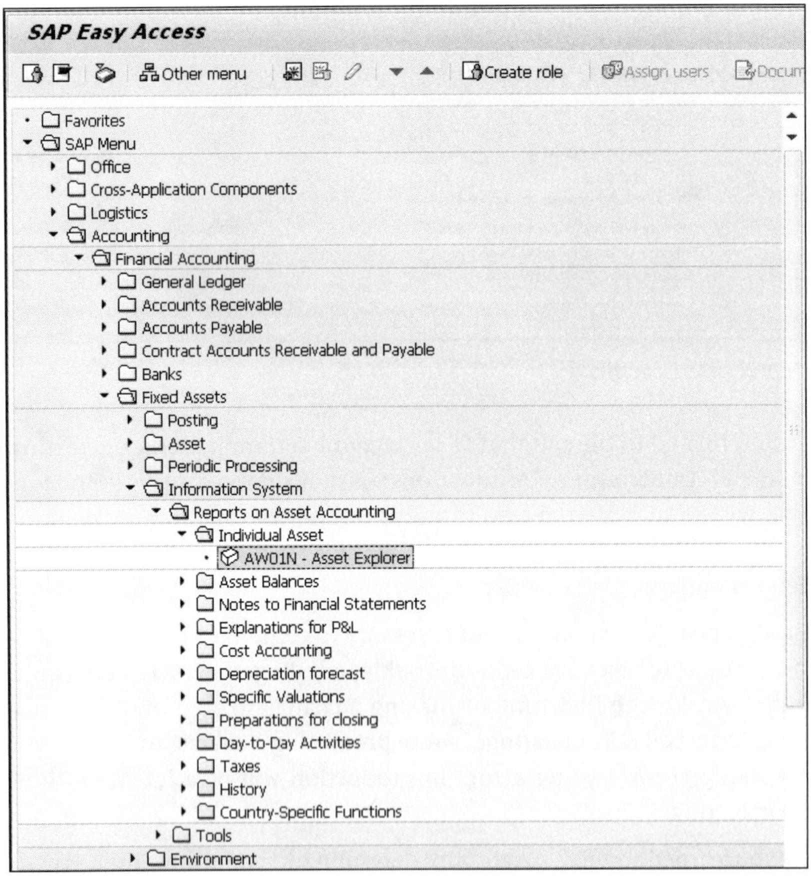

Figure 14.12 Asset Explorer Application Menu Path

Transaction AW01N is best used to get an overview of an asset, including posting history, planned depreciation, and net business value (NBV).

A multitude of additional standard reports exists to get details on asset balances. As shown in Figure 14.13, individual folders contain reports categorized as **Balance Lists**, **Inventory Lists**, **Leased Assets**, and **Country Specifics**.

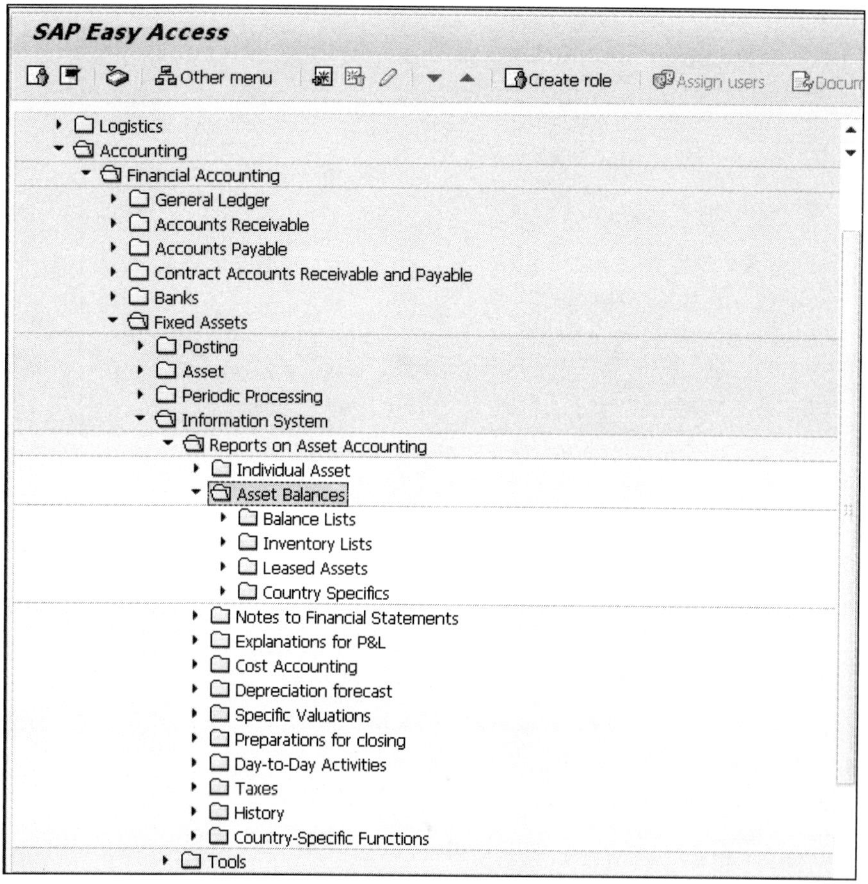

Figure 14.13 Asset Balances Application Menu Path

Within **Balance Lists** is the **Asset Balances** folder (Figure 14.14), where report selections exist by individual asset and other dimensions (e.g. **Business Area**, **Cost Center**, etc.).

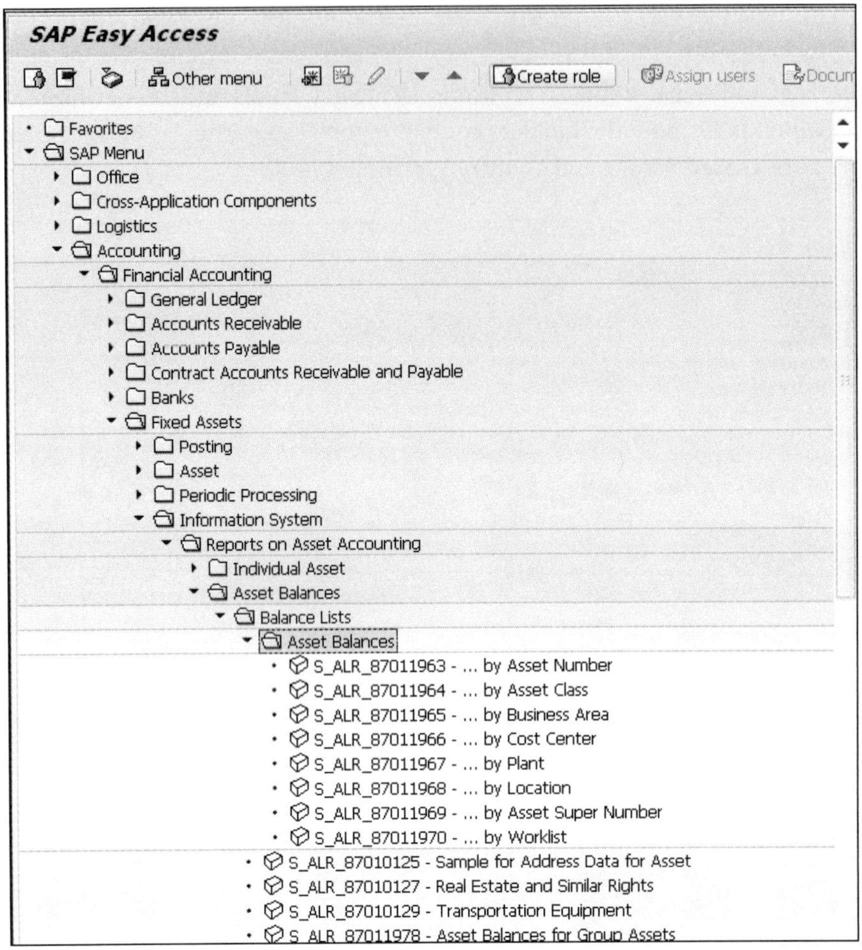

Figure 14.14 Asset Balances Reports Application Menu Path

Also within the **Balances List** folder is a compilation of **Physical Inventory List** reports (Figure 14.15).

Also available in asset reports are reports on **Cost Accounting** (Figure 14.16). These reports are particularly useful for inquiries into depreciation and revaluation.

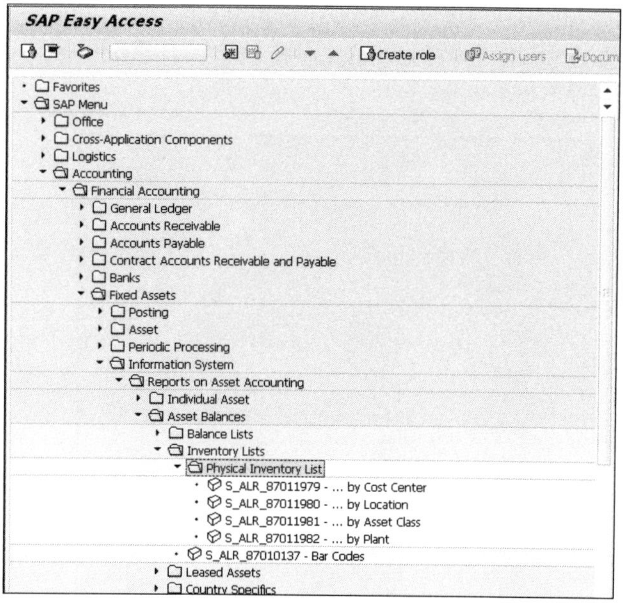

Figure 14.15 Physical Inventory List Application Menu Path

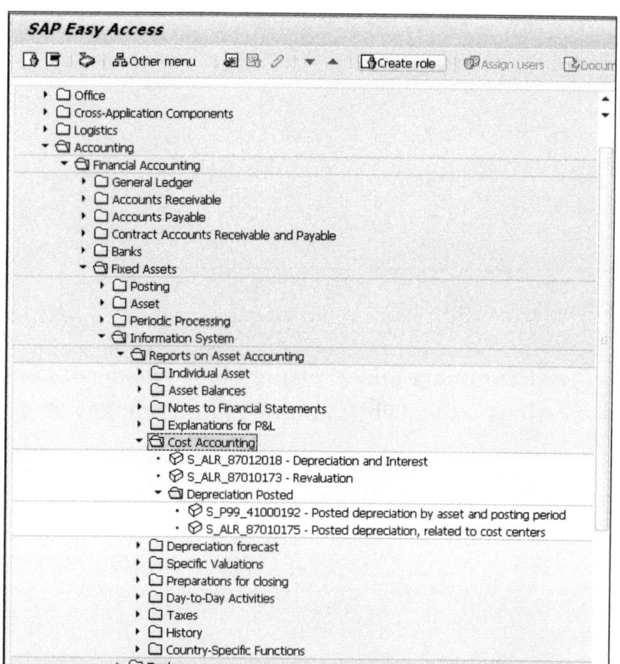

Figure 14.16 Asset Cost Accounting Reports Application Menu Path

If you still haven't found the reports you need, try looking in the **Problem Analysis** folder (Figure 14.17). Many useful tools exist here, such as Transaction ABST. Build this transaction into your financial close procedures.

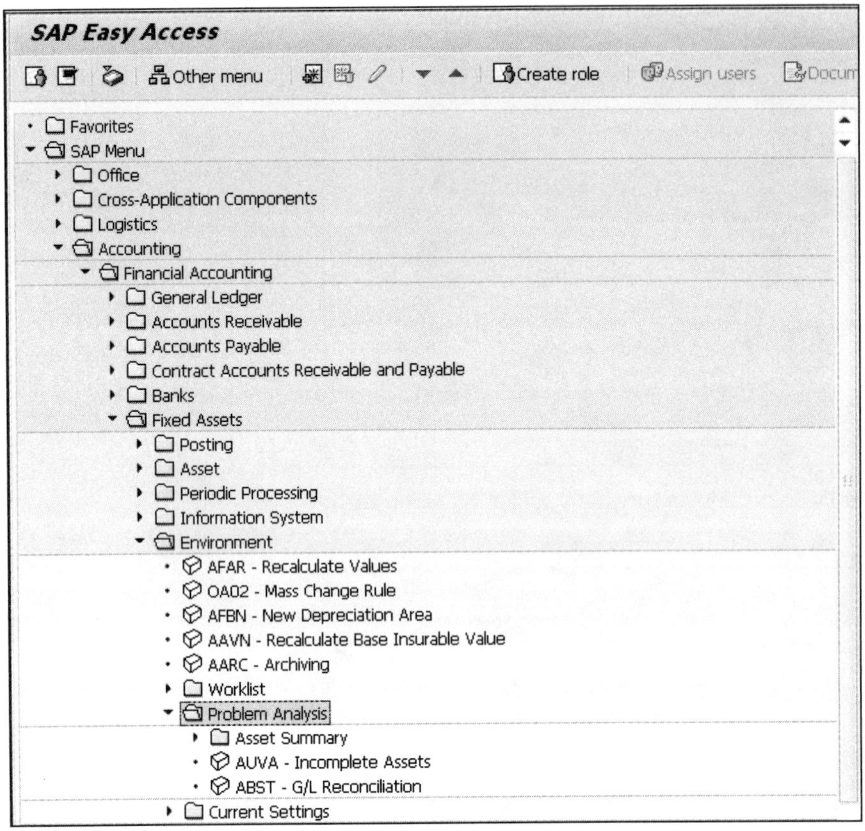

Figure 14.17 Problem Analysis Application Menu Path

Within **Problem Analysis** is the **Asset Summary** folder (Figure 14.18), which contains numerous transactions to view postings, value determination, intercompany transfers, and much more.

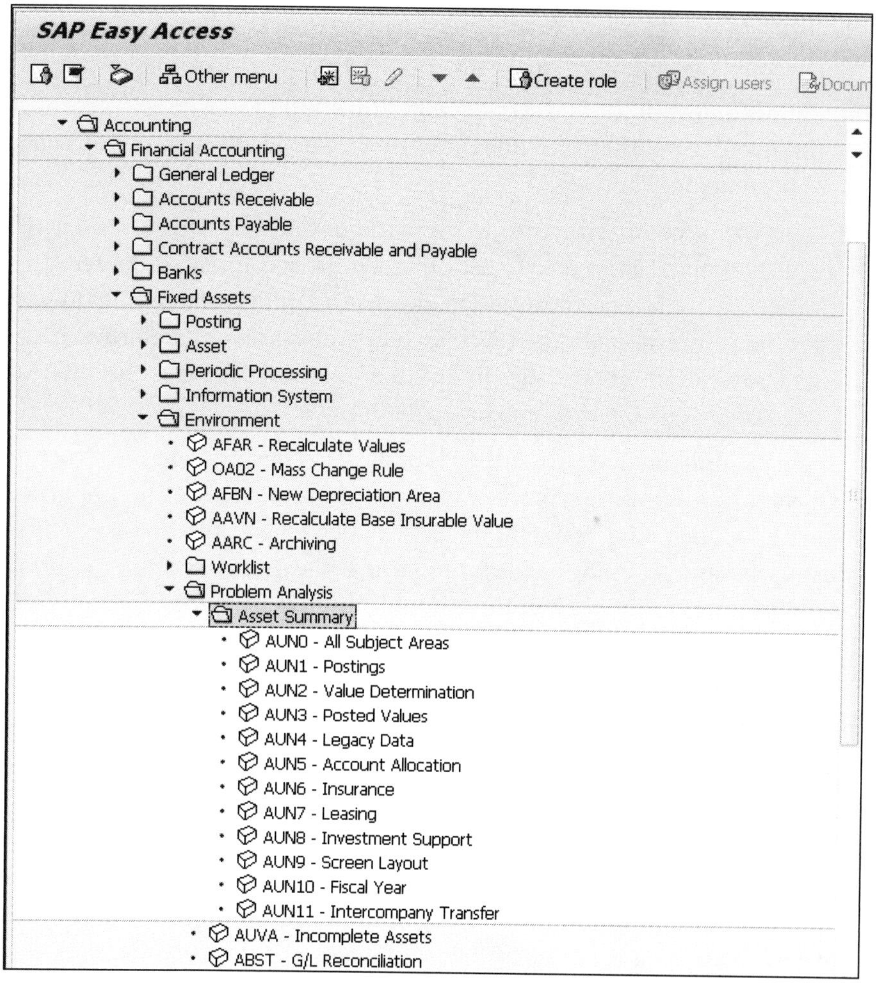

Figure 14.18 Asset Summary Application Menu Path

Now you should have a good grasp of the important elements required to understand and validate FI-AA postings.

14.5 Summary

This chapter discussed three topics in FI-AA essential to understanding asset postings: G/L accounts, asset classes, and account determinations. FI-AA consists of much more than these topics, but these provide the essential knowledge you need to identify potential posting problems.

The fixed asset G/L account structure is the backbone of AA. The essential G/L accounts needed are fixed asset reconciliation accounts, accumulated depreciation and amortization accounts, and depreciation expense accounts. Depending on your business processes, several additional G/L accounts and account determinations may be needed. Some of the possibilities that exist are accounts for revenue, interest, gain/loss, special depreciation, and unplanned depreciation.

Asset classes are a fundamental part of the FI-AA design. They provide the structure of fixed assets from an accounting point of view. Asset classes serve other important functions in FI-AA, including assigning default values when creating assets (e.g., depreciation terms) and grouping assets for reporting. The most important points to remember about asset classes are that they should correlate with your balance sheet reconciliation accounts and that all account determinations must be made for each combination of asset class and transaction type.

Account determinations specify the G/L accounts posted to for specific FI-AA transaction types. They are required for the integration of FI-AA with the G/L. Although several account determination transaction codes exist, the most useful is Transaction OA90, which provides the most comprehensive list of account determinations.

The topics of FI-AA G/L accounts, asset classes, and account determinations are important for gaining a greater understanding of asset posting logic and dependencies. Understanding them is essential for asset managers and accountants when validating and troubleshooting asset-related postings.

This completes the discussion of fixed assets. In the next chapter, we discuss bank master data and processes.

Chapter 15
Bank Master Data and Processes

In this chapter, we discuss bank master data and processes, including bank master records, house banks, and bank reconciliation.

In Chapter 2, we covered SAP Financial Accounting (FI) master data in detail. SAP defines *master data* as data that remains in your system unchanged over a long period of time. It contains information that is needed repeatedly in the same way. In FI, some examples of master data include General Ledger (G/L) accounts, vendors, customers, banks, and fixed assets. Each of these is important in its own way to specific business processes.

In this chapter, we'll cover house banks and vendor and customer bank accounts. The distinction between house banks and bank master records is simply that *house banks* are the banks with which your company has a bank account. That is, they are the banks with which your company does business. House bank accounts are used to hold cash, disburse payments, and receive money.

Customer and vendor bank accounts, on the other hand, are the bank accounts of your business partners. For external bank accounts that you send money to or receive money from, a bank account master record is created and assigned in your business partner's master record.

As you can imagine, several business processes use bank accounts. This includes any business process in which you send or receive money, calculate interest or fees, or manage cash and account balances. This chapter focuses on the bank reconciliation business process for demonstration and discussion purposes.

Let's begin with a detailed discussion of bank master data.

15.1 Bank Master Data

In this section, we'll discuss vendor and customer bank master records and house banks. It's important to understand how to create, maintain, and assign bank master records to customer and vendor accounts, as well as understand the relationship of the house bank to G/L accounts. These concepts are also a lead-in to a discussion of bank reconciliation, which relies on the proper relationship between G/L accounts and house banks.

15.1.1 Vendor and Customer Bank Data

For each business partner (i.e., vendors and customers), there is an expected exchange of money. You procure goods and services from vendors. In exchange, outgoing payments are made to the vendor to compensate them for the goods or services provided.

On the flip side, goods and services are sold to customers. Goods are issued, services provided, and payments received from a customer in exchange for these goods and services.

There are two steps necessary to set up and use vendor and customer bank data. First is the creation of a bank master record. The second is the assignment of bank master data to a vendor or customer account.

To access bank master record transactions, follow application menu path, **Accounting • Financial Accounting • Banks • Master Data • Bank Master Record**, as shown in Figure 15.1.

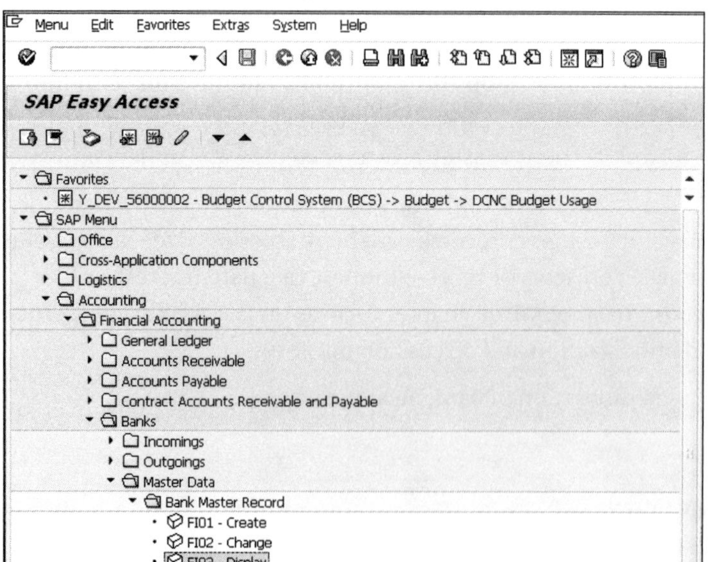

Figure 15.1 Bank Master Record Transactions Application Menu Path

As you can see, transactions exist to **Create** (Transaction FI01), **Change** (Transaction FI02), and **Display** (Transaction FI03) bank master records. Double-click **FI03 – Display** from the menu path, and the **Display Bank: Initial Screen** opens (Figure 15.2). After entering a **Bank Country** and **Bank Key**, press Enter.

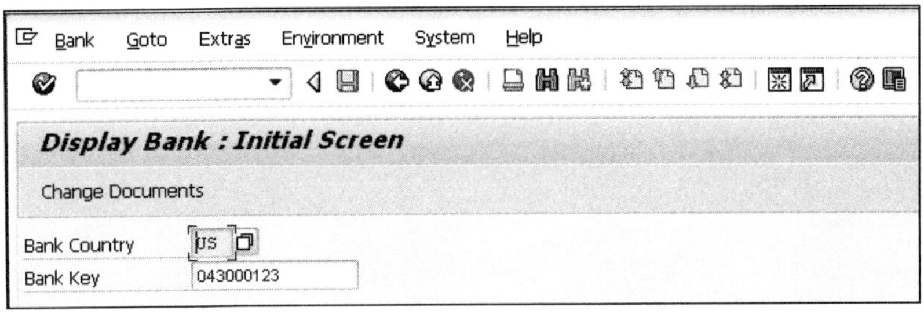

Figure 15.2 Display Bank: Initial Screen

The **Display Bank: Detail Screen** opens (Figure 15.3). After a bank with all its details has been created, the bank can be assigned in a vendor or customer master record.

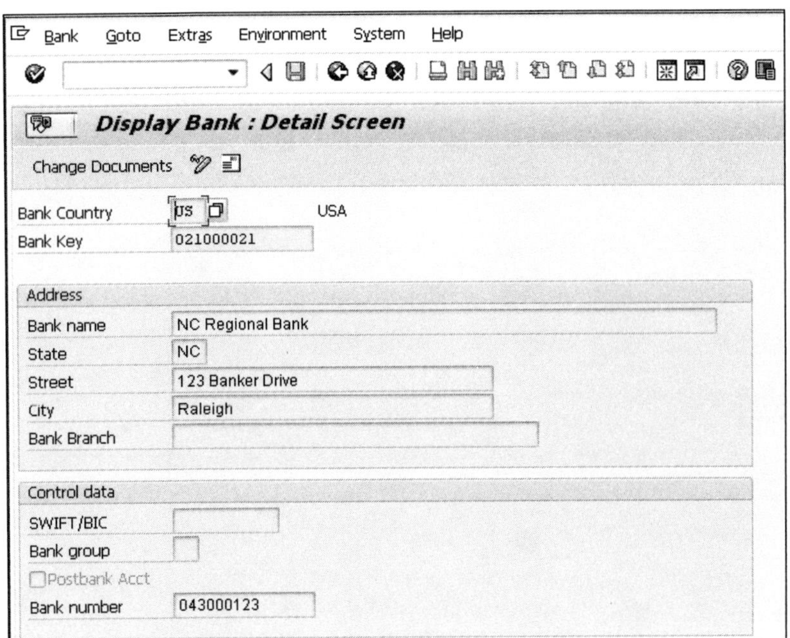

Figure 15.3 Display Bank: Detail Screen

Let's see an example of a bank assigned to a vendor master record. To view a vendor master record, follow application menu path, **Accounting • Financial Accounting • Accounts Payable • Master Records • FK03 – Display**, as shown in Figure 15.4.

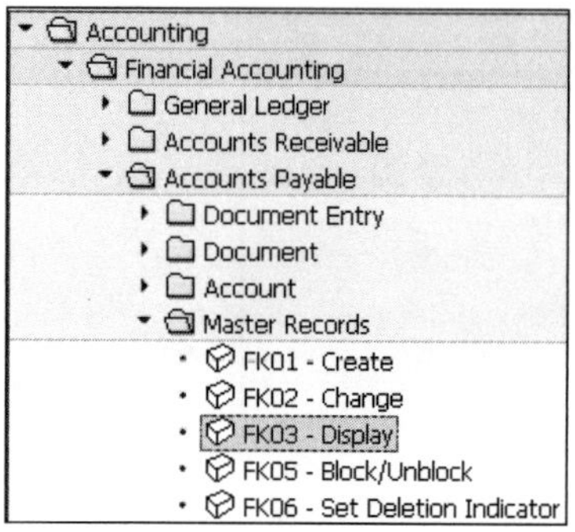

Figure 15.4 Transaction FK03 Application Menu Path

Double-click **FK03 – Display** from the menu path, and the **Display Vendor: Initial Screen** opens (Figure 15.5). Select the **Payment transactions** checkbox under **General data,** and press Enter.

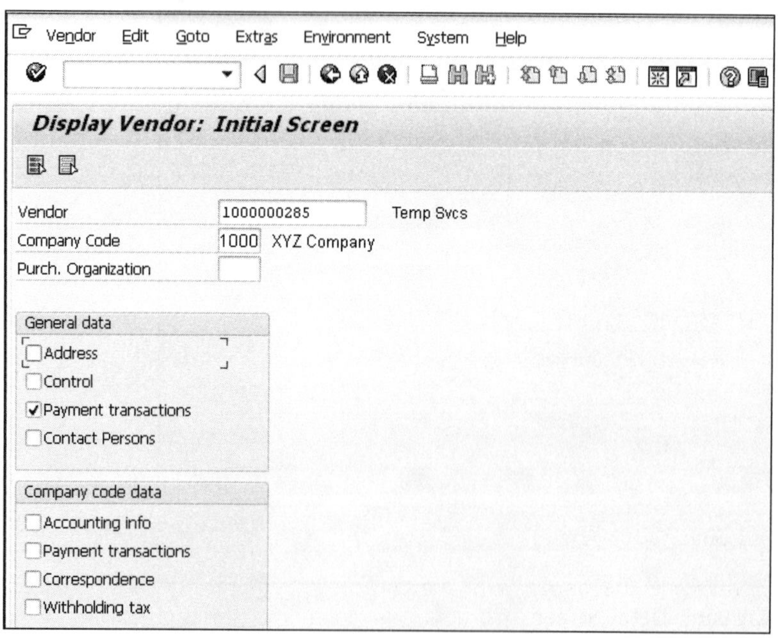

Figure 15.5 Display Vendor: Initial Screen

The **Display Vendor: Payment transactions** screen opens. In this example as shown in Figure 15.6, the **Bank Key** from the bank master record was entered into the vendor master record, along with a specific **Bank Account** number for the vendor.

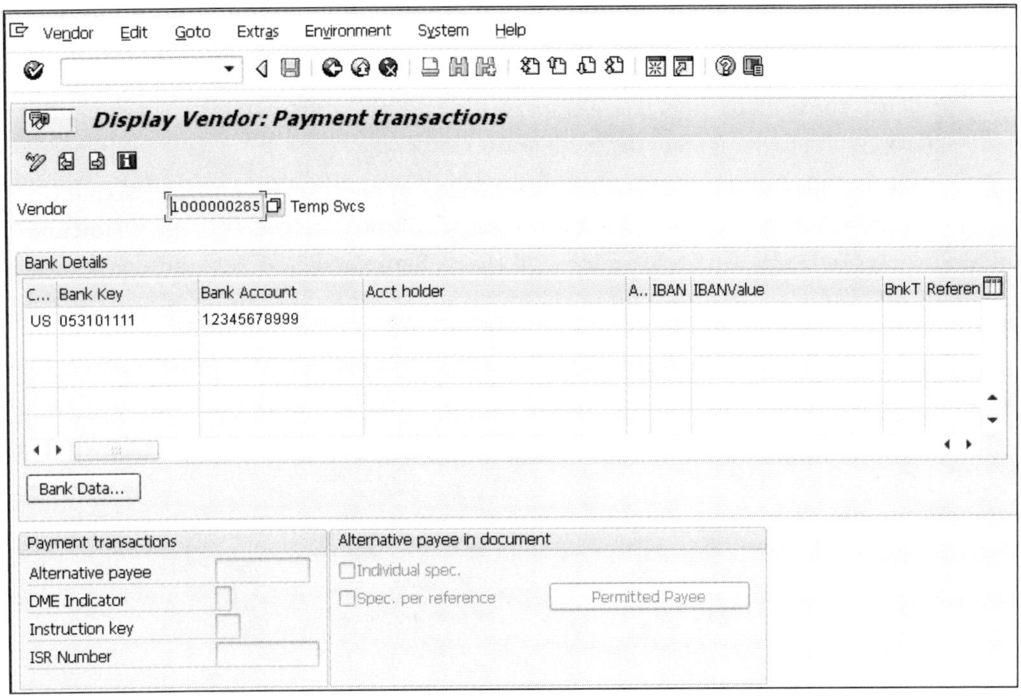

Figure 15.6 Display Vendor: Payment Transactions

These bank account details are needed in the vendor's account to transact electronic money transfers.

Entries in the bank directory (table BNKA) can be entered manually or uploaded from an electronic file using Transaction BAUP. Prior to using Transaction BAUP, the upload file must be registered in Transaction BA01 to convert the external structure to the SAP data structure.

15.1.2 House Banks

In SAP, house banks are the banks with which your company maintains a bank account. They are used to hold cash, disburse payments, and receive money. House banks are defined using an account ID that serves as a unique system identifier.

For each house bank account, you create a unique G/L account in the system. In addition, if you use SAP to reconcile bank statements, additional G/L subaccounts are created for each bank account. This bank account to G/L account structure is covered in detail in Section 15.2.

Bank master data is stored centrally. This includes address data and other control data, such as the SWIFT code. By specifying the country and a country-specific key, such as the bank number (i.e., ABA or routing number), you establish the connection between house banks and the bank master data.

To edit house banks and bank accounts, follow application menu path, **Accounting • Financial Supply Chain Management • Treasury Risk Management • Basic Functions • Master Data • House Banks • FI12 – Edit House Banks and Bank Accounts**, as shown in Figure 15.7.

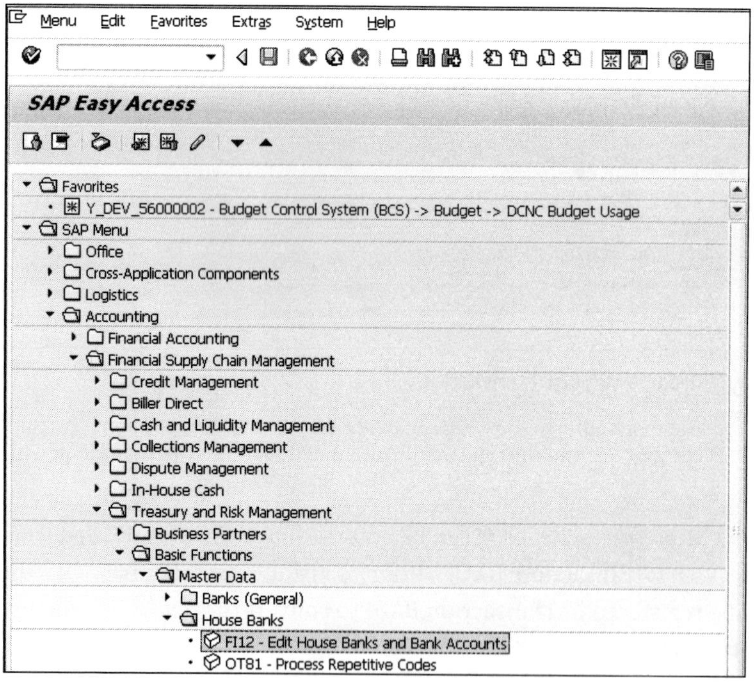

Figure 15.7 Transaction FI12 Application Menu Path

Double-click **FI12 – Edit House Banks and Bank Accounts** from the menu path, and the **Determine Work Area: Entry** screen opens (Figure 15.8). Here, enter your **Company Code**, and press Enter or click on the **Continue** button.

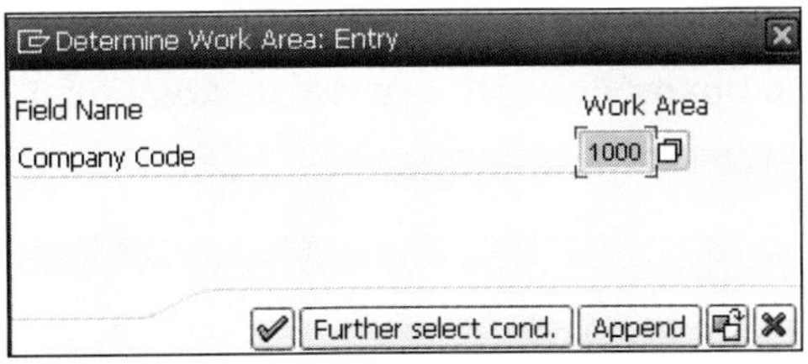

Figure 15.8 Determine Work Area: Entry

The **Change View "House Banks": Overview** screen opens (Figure 15.9). Click on a specific house bank in the **House Banks** area in the center of the screen, and then double-click the **Bank Accounts** folder.

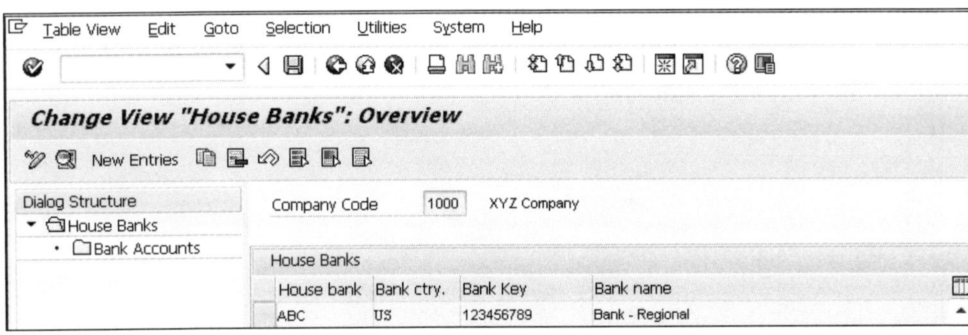

Figure 15.9 Change View "House Banks": Overview

The specific bank accounts at a house bank appear in the **Bank Accounts** area (Figure 15.10) in the center of the screen. Double-click a bank account, or single-click a bank account and then click the **Details** icon.

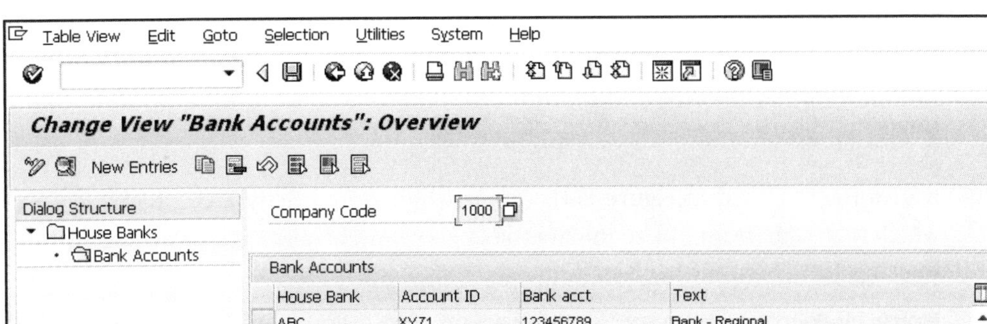

Figure 15.10 Bank Accounts Folder View

The **Change View "Bank Accounts": Details** screen opens (Figure 15.11). All the details for the bank account appear, including **Company Code**, **House Bank**, **Account ID**, **Description**, **Bank Account Number**, **Currency**, **Address**, and so on.

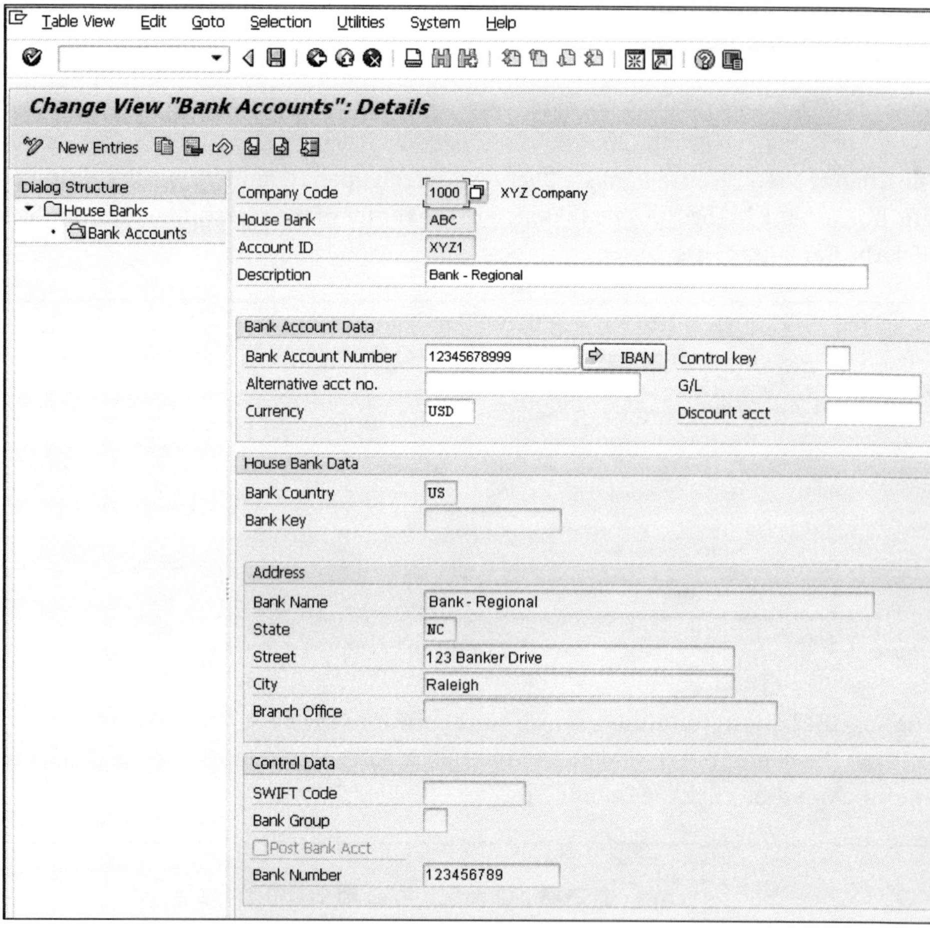

Figure 15.11 Change View "Bank Accounts": Details

Notice the **G/L** field in Figure 15.11. This is where you specify a G/L bank account, which is an important link to update the G/L account balance. It's also a prerequisite to using SAP electronic bank statements (EBS).

House bank accounts are specified in various places. For example, in the configuration of the automated payment program (Transaction F110), a house bank is linked to an individual payment method. This is accomplished using Transaction FBZP. When you execute Transaction FBZP, the **Customizing: Maintain Payment Program** screen appears (Figure 15.12).

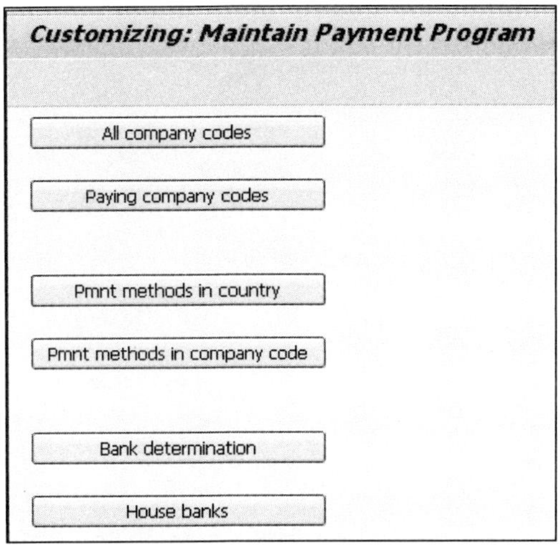

Figure 15.12 Customizing: Maintain Payment Program Screen

Click on the **Bank determination** button. The **Display View "Bank Selection": Overview** screen appears (Figure 15.13). Highlight your bank selection, and then double-click on the **Bank Accounts** folder in the **Dialog Structure** to the left of the screen.

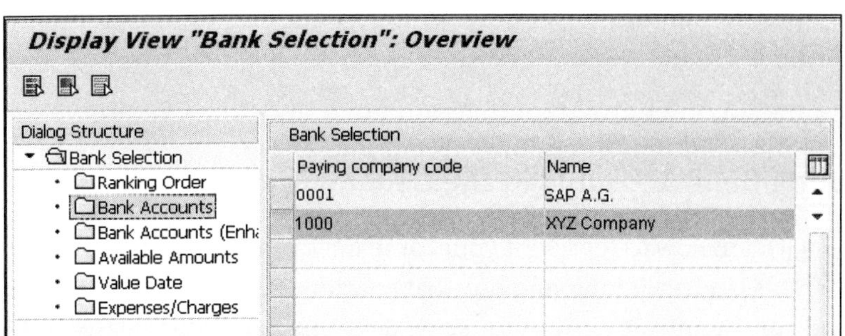

Figure 15.13 Display View "Bank Selection": Overview Screen

The **Change View "Bank Accounts": Overview** screen appears. In this screen, you can see the house bank and account specifications (Figure 15.14).

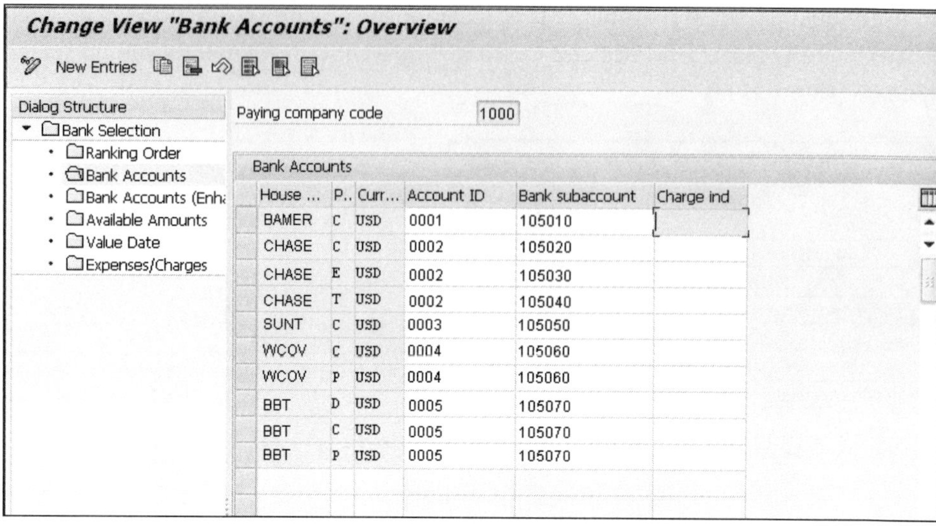

Figure 15.14 Change View "Bank Accounts": Overview Screen

House banks are also specified in bank reconciliation and the data medium exchange (DME) variants in Transaction F110.

Now that you understand house banks and bank master records, let's discuss how bank accounts are structured in the G/L for your company's bank accounts. As we walk through this material, keep in mind the distinction between bank master records in the system for your business partners, which are assigned in vendor and customer master records, and bank accounts owned by your company (i.e., house banks).

15.2 Structuring Bank Accounts in the General Ledger

In this section, you'll learn how to represent your company's bank accounts in the G/L chart of accounts. This is a tricky topic and one that continues to confuse even experienced users and consultants. It's tricky for several reasons: First, it forces you to think beyond how you're accustomed to seeing your bank accounts represented in your chart of accounts. Second, it requires you to organize your G/L bank account numbers in a methodical manner to plan for bank reconciliation in SAP, even if your company currently has no plans to do so. Lastly, if you do plan to use SAP's EBS functionality, setting up bank clearing accounts requires that you know all the types of transactions you expect to come through in your EBSs. Bank clearing accounts are discussed in detail in Section 15.2.2.

Note

The bank account structure in the chart of accounts and use of EBSs in SAP are springboards into using SAP Cash and Liquidity Management functionality. In turn, forecasting cash flow and liquidity are important functions for treasury managers, who need to know daily how much they can invest, what types of instruments to invest in, and how much cash needs to be kept on hand to cover upcoming expenses.

Cash management, liquidity forecasting, and treasury functions can be automated in SAP using the Financial Supply Chain Management (FIN-FSCM) solution. Although FIN-FSCM is beyond the scope of this book, it's important to understand the relationship it has with FI.

Now that you understand the importance of the G/L bank account structure, let's discuss the G/L bank accounts themselves in more detail.

15.2.1 Bank Balance Sheet Accounts

There are two main types of G/L bank accounts: main bank accounts, which have a one-to-one relationship with a house bank account, and bank clearing accounts, which are used for bank reconciliation. Both types are balance sheet accounts. The remainder of this section focuses on the main bank balance sheet accounts. Bank clearing accounts are discussed in detail in Section 15.2.2.

As noted, main G/L bank accounts are set up with a one-to-one relationship with house bank accounts. They are set up with a bidirectional link. In other words, the G/L account is specified in the house bank account, and the house bank and account ID are specified in the G/L bank account.

Figure 15.15 shows a house bank account using Transaction FI12. Notice in the **G/L** field that a G/L bank account number is linked to the bank account. This particular link designates the G/L account to which transaction figures will be updated.

Figure 15.16 shows a G/L bank account using Transaction FS03. Notice in the **House Bank** and **Account ID** fields that a link is provided back to the bank master record shown in Figure 15.15.

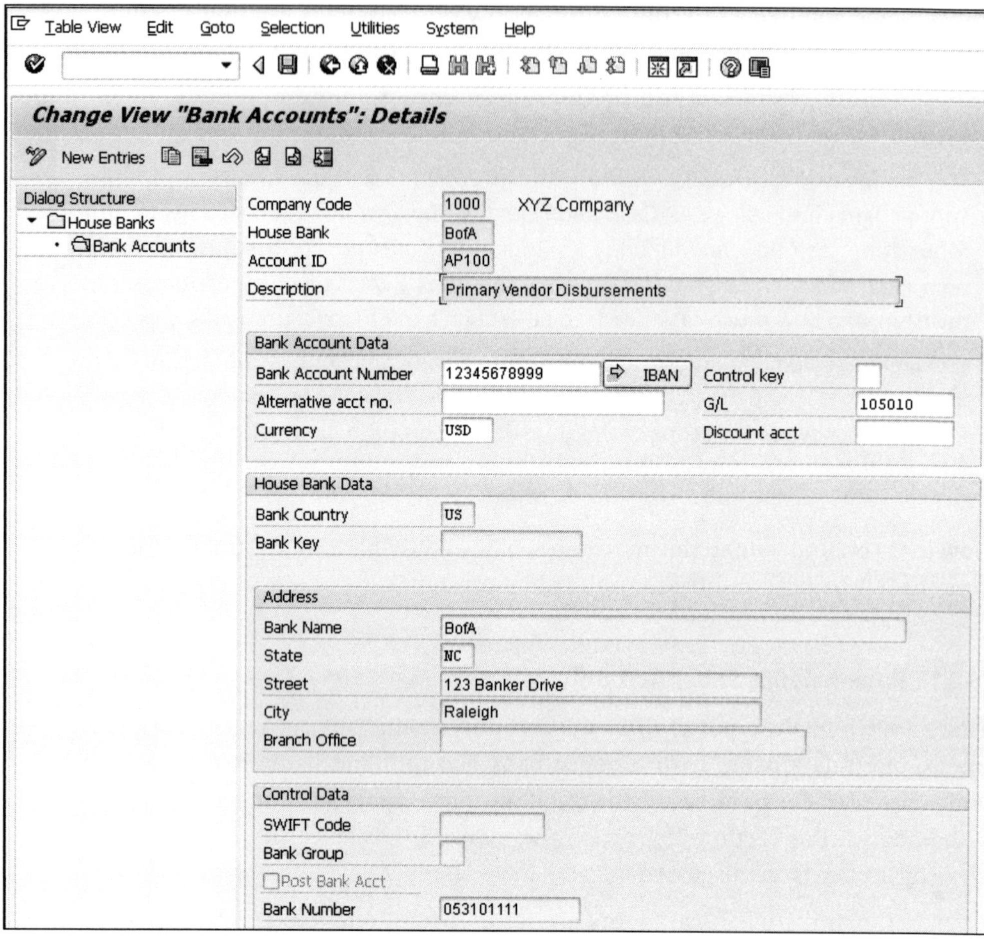

Figure 15.15 House Bank Account Display

Note

The main G/L bank accounts should end in "0" to allow the last digit of the account (i.e., 1–9) to be used for bank clearing accounts. We'll discuss this further in the next section.

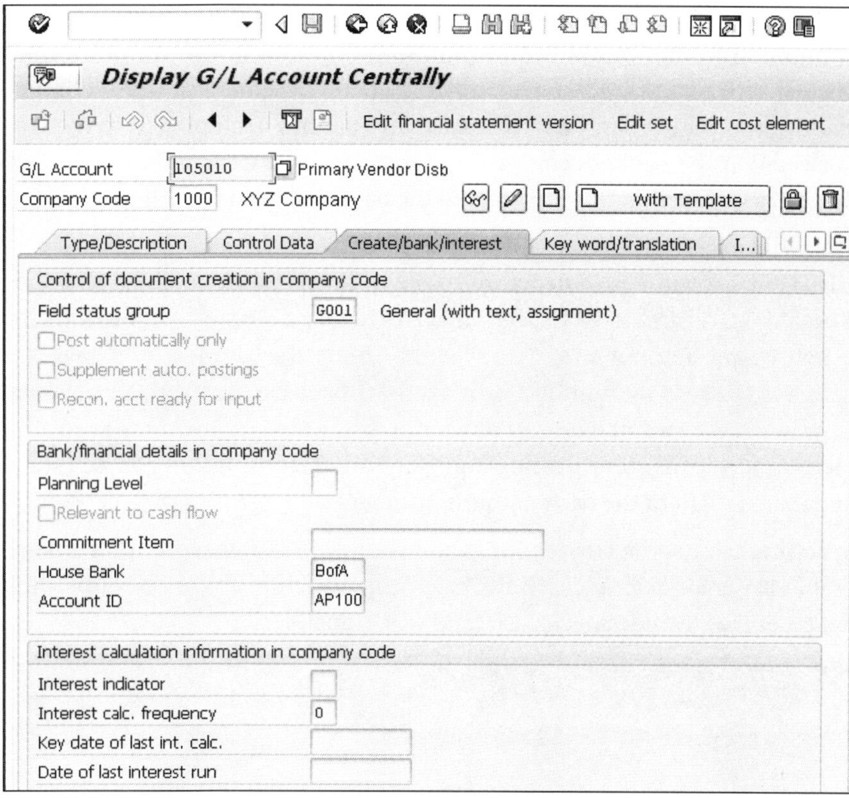

Figure 15.16 G/L Bank Account Display

Now that you understand the relationship of a house bank account and a main G/L bank account, let's move on to discuss bank clearing accounts.

15.2.2 Bank General Ledger Clearing Accounts

In SAP, a *G/L clearing account* is an open item managed account in which G/L transactions are posted with a status of **Open**, awaiting another G/L entry to offset and clear them. When this clearing process is complete, the status of an item in the G/L changes from **Open** to **Cleared**.

Open item management is an important concept to understand when using SAP's EBS functionality for bank reconciliation. G/L clearing accounts are used to account for in-transit transactions and book-to-bank matching.

Let's discuss this in a little more detail to ensure you understand the concept. G/L bank clearing accounts are used to house transactions posted in FI that haven't yet been reconciled with a transaction on an incoming bank statement. A transaction in a bank clearing account with an **Open** status is one that has been posted to the G/L but hasn't cleared at the bank. In contrast, a transaction in a clearing account with **Cleared** status is a transaction that has cleared the bank and been posted to the main G/L bank account.

Creating G/L bank accounts in a structured fashion is critical to keeping your G/L clean and organized. As discussed in Section 15.2.1, there is a one-to-one relationship between a house bank account and a G/L account. This G/L account should have "0" as the last digit in the account number. Moreover, G/L bank clearing accounts should be structured with a consistent naming convention using the last digit of the account (i.e., 1–9). In this way, consistent posting logic for bank reconciliation can be established using the last digit of the bank account number.

A clearing account should be created for each major type of transaction on a bank account. Table 15.1 is an example G/L bank account structure for an account with transaction types that include check, ACH, and wire transfer.

Account Structure	G/L Accounts
130100	Main Bank Account 1
130101	Outgoing Check
130102	Incoming Check
130103	Outgoing ACH
130104	Incoming ACH
130105	Outgoing Wire Transfer
130106	Incoming Wire Transfer
130109	Miscellaneous

Table 15.1 G/L Account Structure for Transaction Types

As you can see in this example, a G/L clearing account is created for each major transaction type. Using a consistent clearing account structure is important for account determinations. It also makes it easier to conduct postprocessing for bank items that don't clear automatically when an EBS is imported. See Section 15.4 for details on postprocessing of EBSs.

For each bank account, you need to create a clearing account for each of the relevant transaction types. However, the numbering convention should be used consistently across all bank accounts. For example, if another bank account is only used for outgoing wire transfers, the G/L accounts would be set up as shown in Table 15.2.

Account Structure	G/L Accounts
130110	Main Bank Account 2
130115	Outgoing Wire Transfer
130119	Miscellaneous

Table 15.2 G/L Account Numbering Convention

In these examples (Table 15.1 and Table 15.2), both main bank account numbers end in "0", outgoing wire clearing accounts end in "5", and the miscellaneous clearing accounts end in "9". As you can see, the numbering has remained consistent.

On a final note, not all bank transactions exist on the books when bank statements are imported into SAP. Examples include fees and interest. In such cases, it's advantageous to post these transactions to a miscellaneous clearing account to be manually reconciled at a later point in time.

That concludes the discussion of bank G/L accounts. In the next section, we discuss bank reconciliation.

15.3 Bank Reconciliation

The *bank reconciliation* process is all about matching bank statement transactions with those transactions posted in the G/L. In SAP, this matching process clears open items in the G/L bank clearing accounts and posts offsetting entries in the main bank account.

There are two methods of bank reconciliation in SAP. The first is the EBS option. With this option, EBSs are imported into SAP and automatically matched and reconciled. The second option is manual bank statement reconciliation, in which a user inputs each bank statement transaction manually.

Let's begin with a discussion of EBSs.

15.3.1 Electronic Bank Statements

As a tip, if you're just getting started with EBSs, knowing your bank data is just as important as knowing how to use the bank reconciliation features in SAP. Most importantly, become familiar with all the transaction types received in an electronic file from your bank. This is important to your G/L bank clearing account structure, account determinations, and mapping external to internal transactions.

With that said, let's dive into the details of importing an EBS in SAP. Importing EBSs is usually set up as a scheduled job to run daily. You don't have to reconcile bank statements daily, but it's a best practice.

To import a bank statement, follow application menu path, **Accounting • Financial Accounting • Banks • Incomings • Bank Statement • FF_5 – Import**, as shown in Figure 15.17.

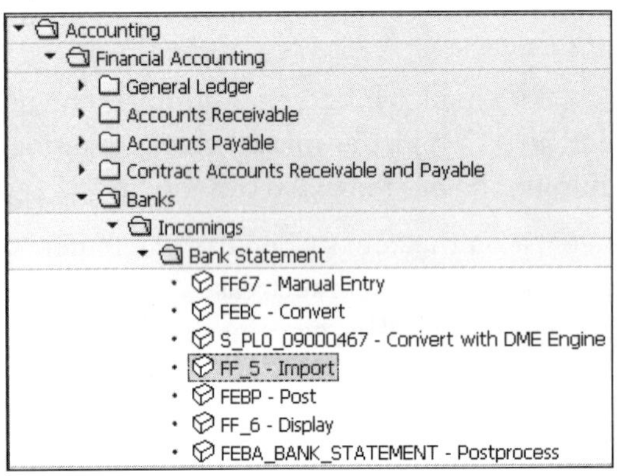

Figure 15.17 Transaction FF_5 Application Menu Path

Double-click **FF_5 – Import** from the menu path, and the **Bank Statement: Various Formats (SWIFT, MultiCash, BAI...)** screen opens (Figure 15.18). Numerous selection options and specifications exist on this screen within the following areas:

- **File specifications**
  Several basic selections must be made, including file format and file location. Note that the **Import data** checkbox must be selected to import the file into the system.
- **Posting parameters**
  These options determine if the bank statement creates postings immediately, creates a batch input session, or doesn't post. In addition, the **Only Bank Accounting** checkbox, when selected, causes the statement to post to the G/L bank accounts but blocks postings to subledgers.

- **Cash management**
  These options are only used if you're using the Cash Management module.
- **BAI Preprocessor**
  These options only exist when the BAI format is specified in the **Elect. bank statement format** field in the **File specifications** area. These options allow you to check, convert, and adjust data in the file prior to processing the file for bank reconciliation.
- **Algorithms**
  Allows you to specify or reference document number ranges. When this option is used, all other document numbers are ignored and can't be used to clear open items.
- **Output Control**
  This area provides additional output options.

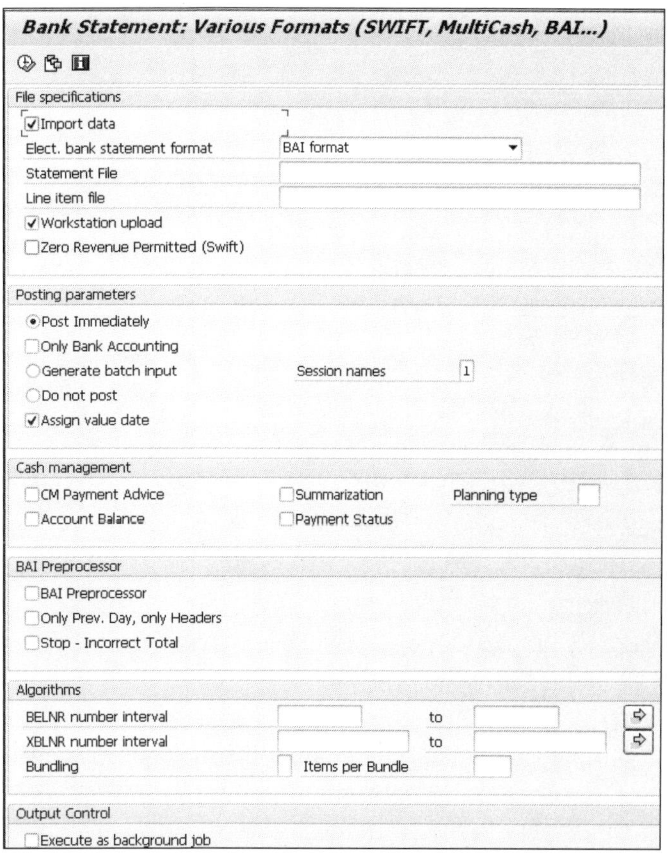

Figure 15.18 Import Electronic Bank Statement

After all your selections are made in Figure 15.18, you can save your choices as a variant and use it in a scheduled job.

Now let's walk through the complete import of an EBS using Transaction FF_5. After specifying the statement file location and making other selections (Figure 15.19), click the **Execute** icon.

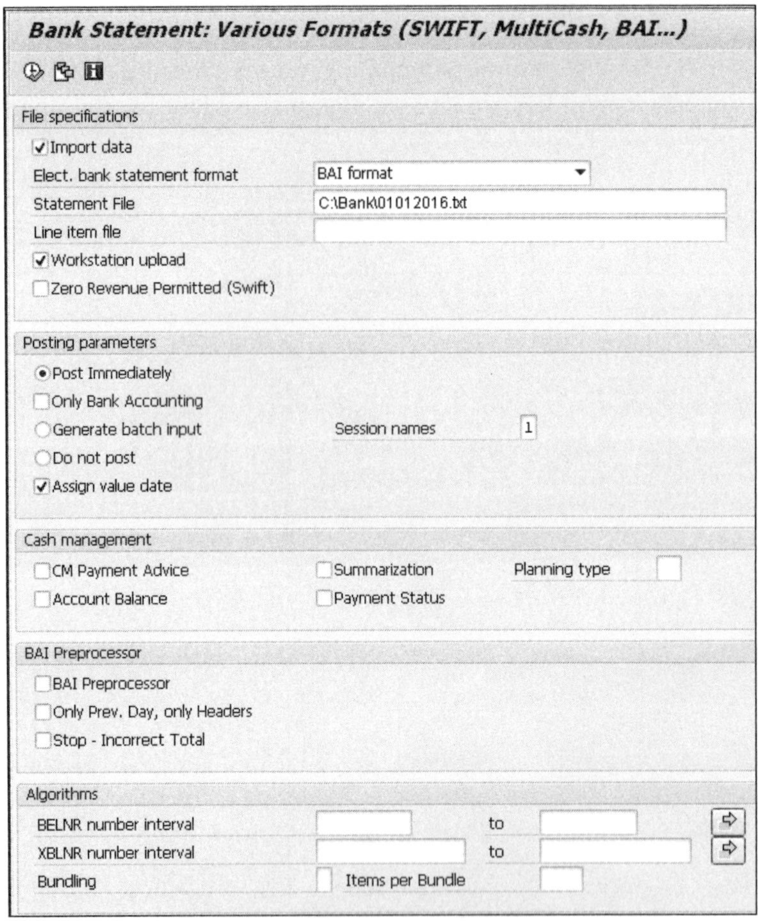

Figure 15.19 Example Import Electronic Bank Statement

After the import process is completed, the bank statement posting log is displayed (Figure 15.20).

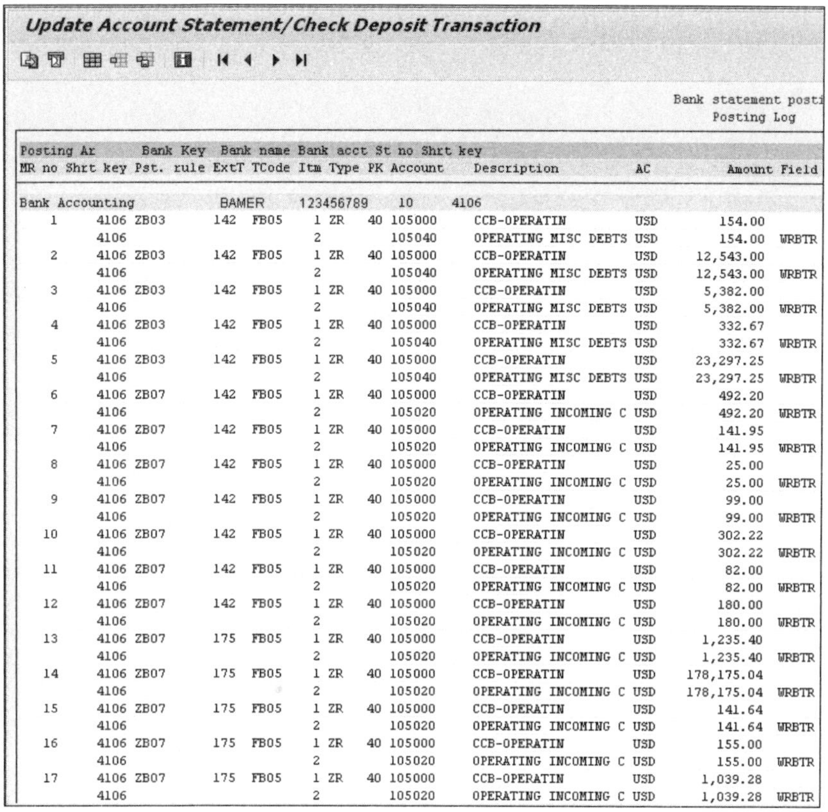

Update Account Statement/Check Deposit Transaction

Bank statement posti
Posting Log

Posting Ar		Bank Key	Bank name	Bank acct	St no	Shrt key						
MR no	**Shrt key**	**Pst. rule**	**ExtT**	**TCode**	**Itm**	**Type**	**PK**	**Account**	**Description**	**AC**	**Amount**	**Field**
Bank Accounting		BAMER	123456789	10	4106							
1	4106	ZB03	142	FB05	1	ZR	40	105000	CCB-OPERATIN	USD	154.00	
	4106				2			105040	OPERATING MISC DEBTS	USD	154.00	WRBTR
2	4106	ZB03	142	FB05	1	ZR	40	105000	CCB-OPERATIN	USD	12,543.00	
	4106				2			105040	OPERATING MISC DEBTS	USD	12,543.00	WRBTR
3	4106	ZB03	142	FB05	1	ZR	40	105000	CCB-OPERATIN	USD	5,382.00	
	4106				2			105040	OPERATING MISC DEBTS	USD	5,382.00	WRBTR
4	4106	ZB03	142	FB05	1	ZR	40	105000	CCB-OPERATIN	USD	332.67	
	4106				2			105040	OPERATING MISC DEBTS	USD	332.67	WRBTR
5	4106	ZB03	142	FB05	1	ZR	40	105000	CCB-OPERATIN	USD	23,297.25	
	4106				2			105040	OPERATING MISC DEBTS	USD	23,297.25	WRBTR
6	4106	ZB07	142	FB05	1	ZR	40	105000	CCB-OPERATIN	USD	492.20	
	4106				2			105020	OPERATING INCOMING C	USD	492.20	WRBTR
7	4106	ZB07	142	FB05	1	ZR	40	105000	CCB-OPERATIN	USD	141.95	
	4106				2			105020	OPERATING INCOMING C	USD	141.95	WRBTR
8	4106	ZB07	142	FB05	1	ZR	40	105000	CCB-OPERATIN	USD	25.00	
	4106				2			105020	OPERATING INCOMING C	USD	25.00	WRBTR
9	4106	ZB07	142	FB05	1	ZR	40	105000	CCB-OPERATIN	USD	99.00	
	4106				2			105020	OPERATING INCOMING C	USD	99.00	WRBTR
10	4106	ZB07	142	FB05	1	ZR	40	105000	CCB-OPERATIN	USD	302.22	
	4106				2			105020	OPERATING INCOMING C	USD	302.22	WRBTR
11	4106	ZB07	142	FB05	1	ZR	40	105000	CCB-OPERATIN	USD	82.00	
	4106				2			105020	OPERATING INCOMING C	USD	82.00	WRBTR
12	4106	ZB07	142	FB05	1	ZR	40	105000	CCB-OPERATIN	USD	180.00	
	4106				2			105020	OPERATING INCOMING C	USD	180.00	WRBTR
13	4106	ZB07	175	FB05	1	ZR	40	105000	CCB-OPERATIN	USD	1,235.40	
	4106				2			105020	OPERATING INCOMING C	USD	1,235.40	WRBTR
14	4106	ZB07	175	FB05	1	ZR	40	105000	CCB-OPERATIN	USD	178,175.04	
	4106				2			105020	OPERATING INCOMING C	USD	178,175.04	WRBTR
15	4106	ZB07	175	FB05	1	ZR	40	105000	CCB-OPERATIN	USD	141.64	
	4106				2			105020	OPERATING INCOMING C	USD	141.64	WRBTR
16	4106	ZB07	175	FB05	1	ZR	40	105000	CCB-OPERATIN	USD	155.00	
	4106				2			105020	OPERATING INCOMING C	USD	155.00	WRBTR
17	4106	ZB07	175	FB05	1	ZR	40	105000	CCB-OPERATIN	USD	1,039.28	
	4106				2			105020	OPERATING INCOMING C	USD	1,039.28	WRBTR

Figure 15.20 Bank Statement Posting Log

Click the **Back** icon to review bank statement statistics (Figure 15.21).

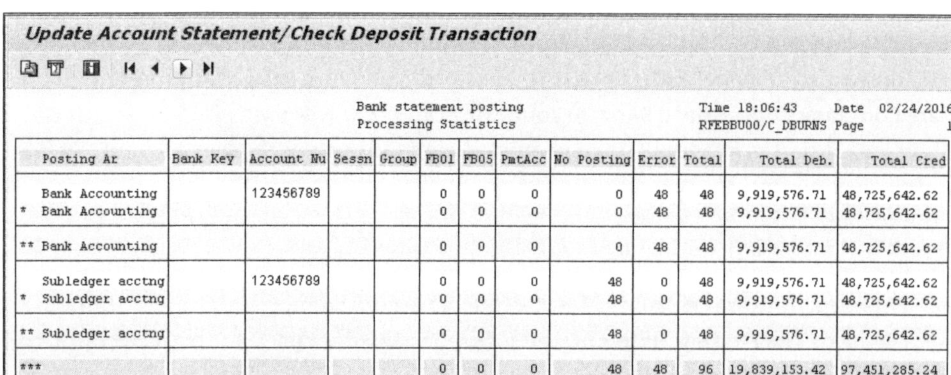

Update Account Statement/Check Deposit Transaction

Bank statement posting — Time 18:06:43 — Date 02/24/2016
Processing Statistics — RFEBBU00/C_DBURNS — Page 1

Posting Ar	Bank Key	Account Nu	Sessn	Group	FB01	FB05	PmtAcc	No Posting	Error	Total	Total Deb.	Total Cred
Bank Accounting		123456789			0	0	0	0	48	48	9,919,576.71	48,725,642.62
* Bank Accounting					0	0	0	0	48	48	9,919,576.71	48,725,642.62
** Bank Accounting					0	0	0	0	48	48	9,919,576.71	48,725,642.62
Subledger acctng		123456789			0	0	0	48	0	48	9,919,576.71	48,725,642.62
* Subledger acctng					0	0	0	48	0	48	9,919,576.71	48,725,642.62
** Subledger acctng					0	0	0	48	0	48	9,919,576.71	48,725,642.62
***					0	0	0	48	48	96	19,839,153.42	97,451,285.24

Figure 15.21 Bank Statement Statistics

After the process of importing an EBS is complete, the next step is the postprocessing of bank statement transactions that didn't clear automatically. For details, see Section 15.4.

15.3.2 Manual Bank Statements

For numerous reasons, your company may not opt to receive electronic files from your bank, perhaps due to cost or because an account has a small number of transactions. If this is the case, an alternative is to use manual bank statements. This approach may be used for smaller bank accounts for which the volume of transactions is so low that using EBSs isn't justifiable.

To manually enter a bank statement, follow application menu path, **Accounting • Financial Accounting • Banks • Incomings • Bank Statement • FF67 – Manual Entry**, as shown in Figure 15.22.

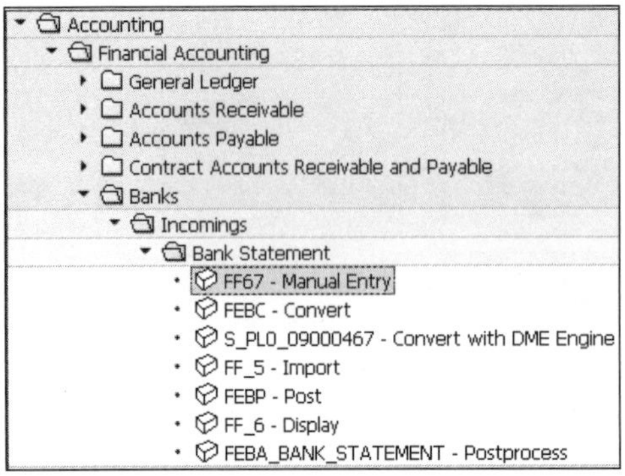

Figure 15.22 Transaction FF67 Application Menu Path

Double-click **FF67 – Manual Entry** from the menu path, and the **Process Manual Bank Statement** screen opens (Figure 15.23). The fields in the header area that require entry are **Company Code**, **House Bank**, **Account ID**, **Statement Number**, and **Statement Date**. Some variation in field control may exist, depending on your screen variant. Numerous selection options and specifications are also available in the following areas of the screen:

- **Control**
  Enter opening and closing balances to ensure consistency from one statement to the next. The **Posting Date** entered is the posting date used for bank account and subledger transactions created.

- **Selection of Payment Advices**
  These options are relevant if you use payment advices.
- **Further Processing**
  This area gives you the option, via the **Bank postings only** checkbox, to post to G/L bank accounts only. If this option is selected, subledger postings are blocked.

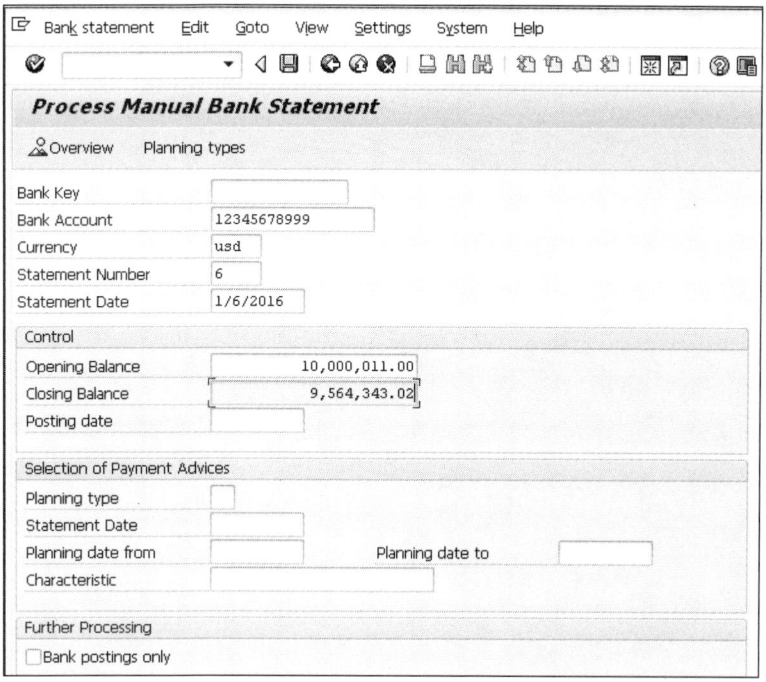

Figure 15.23 Process Manual Bank Statement

Manual bank statements may have little to no applicability in your company. However, for some organizations, they are a viable option. There is no doubt that the best option is to use EBSs whenever possible, but if there is a bank account with limited activity, or you need a temporary solution while your company restructures its bank accounts, then manual bank statements may be the answer.

15.4 Postprocessing of Electronic Bank Statements

When you import an EBS, SAP attempts to match individual transactions on the bank statement with G/L line items in bank clearing accounts. This matching process takes place based on interpretation algorithms.

The postprocessing program is used to check the status of bank statements and manually clear bank transactions that didn't clear automatically. To postprocess an EBS, follow the application menu path, **Accounting • Financial Accounting • Banks • Incomings • Bank Statement • FEBA_BANK_STATEMENT - Postprocess**, as shown in Figure 15.24.

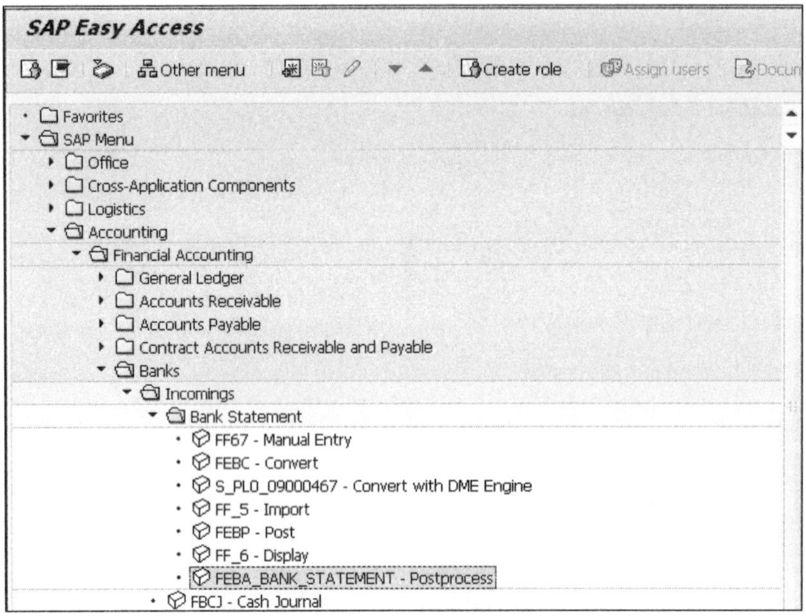

Figure 15.24 Transaction FEBA_BANK_STATEMENT Postprocess Application Menu Path

Double-click **FEBA_BANK_STATEMENT – Postprocess** from the menu path, and the **Bank Statement Subsequent Processing** screen opens (Figure 15.25). Numerous selection options and specifications exist on this screen. In the **Application** field, select **Electronic and manual bank statement** from the dropdown list. **Company code**, **House Bank**, and **Account ID** are required fields. In addition, you can enter a **Statement number**, **Statement Date**, or both.

The last field selection we'll discuss is the **Posting area.** If you're set up to clear vendors and customers, there is a selection option in the dropdown menu for subledger accounting. Otherwise, select **G/L accounting**.

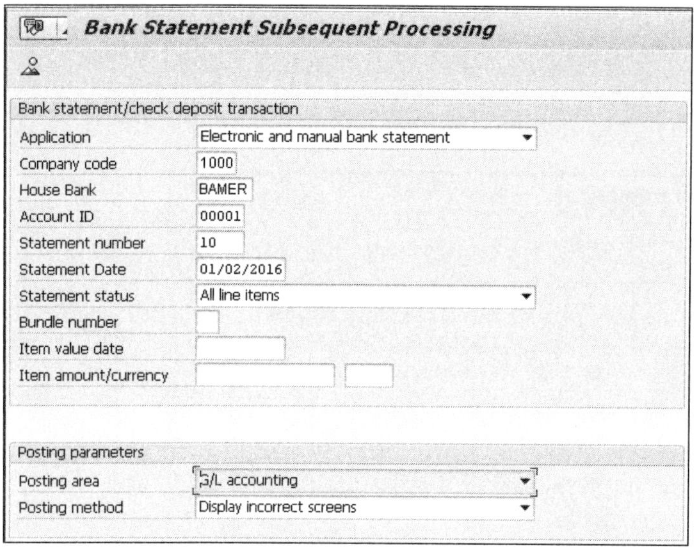

Figure 15.25 Bank Statement Subsequent Processing Screen

With all your field parameters entered, click the **Statement Overview** icon. The **Bank Statement Overview** screen appears (Figure 15.26).

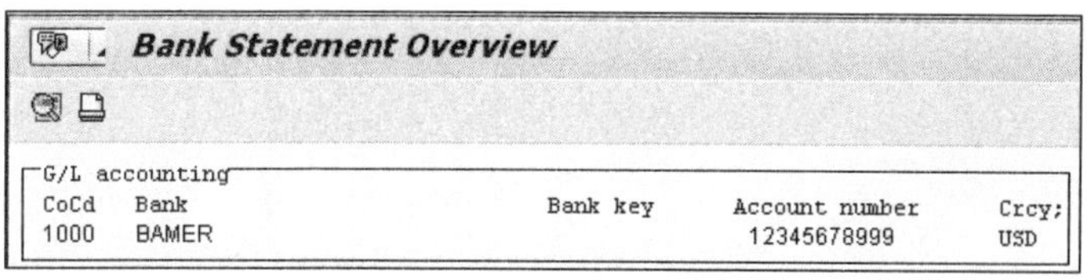

Figure 15.26 Bank Statement Overview Screen

Double-click on the statement line, and the **Bank Statement Overview** screen shows the statement number (Figure 15.27).

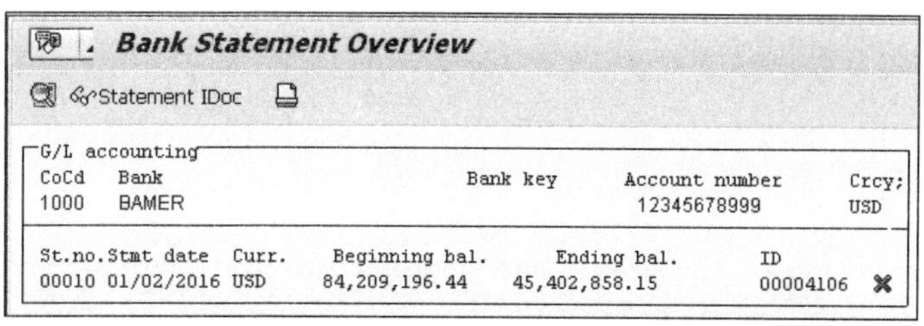

Figure 15.27 Bank Statement Overview: Statement Number

Double-click on the statement, and the **Bank Statement Overview** screen shows the statement transactions (Figure 15.28). This is where it gets interesting. On this screen, all the individual transactions on the bank statement are listed. Each has a status of **Posted** or **To be posted**.

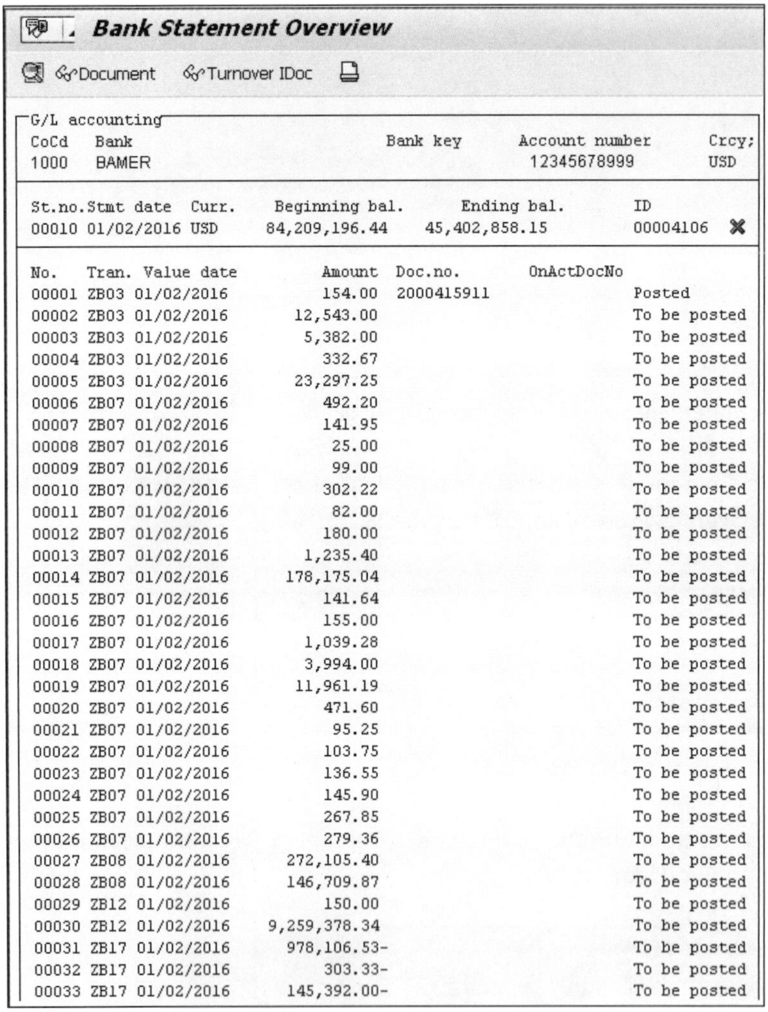

Bank Statement Overview

Document   Turnover IDoc

G/L accounting

CoCd	Bank	Bank key	Account number	Crcy;
1000	BAMER		12345678999	USD

St.no.	Stmt date	Curr.	Beginning bal.	Ending bal.	ID
00010	01/02/2016	USD	84,209,196.44	45,402,858.15	00004106

No.	Tran.	Value date	Amount	Doc.no.	OnActDocNo	
00001	ZB03	01/02/2016	154.00	2000415911		Posted
00002	ZB03	01/02/2016	12,543.00			To be posted
00003	ZB03	01/02/2016	5,382.00			To be posted
00004	ZB03	01/02/2016	332.67			To be posted
00005	ZB03	01/02/2016	23,297.25			To be posted
00006	ZB07	01/02/2016	492.20			To be posted
00007	ZB07	01/02/2016	141.95			To be posted
00008	ZB07	01/02/2016	25.00			To be posted
00009	ZB07	01/02/2016	99.00			To be posted
00010	ZB07	01/02/2016	302.22			To be posted
00011	ZB07	01/02/2016	82.00			To be posted
00012	ZB07	01/02/2016	180.00			To be posted
00013	ZB07	01/02/2016	1,235.40			To be posted
00014	ZB07	01/02/2016	178,175.04			To be posted
00015	ZB07	01/02/2016	141.64			To be posted
00016	ZB07	01/02/2016	155.00			To be posted
00017	ZB07	01/02/2016	1,039.28			To be posted
00018	ZB07	01/02/2016	3,994.00			To be posted
00019	ZB07	01/02/2016	11,961.19			To be posted
00020	ZB07	01/02/2016	471.60			To be posted
00021	ZB07	01/02/2016	95.25			To be posted
00022	ZB07	01/02/2016	103.75			To be posted
00023	ZB07	01/02/2016	136.55			To be posted
00024	ZB07	01/02/2016	145.90			To be posted
00025	ZB07	01/02/2016	267.85			To be posted
00026	ZB07	01/02/2016	279.36			To be posted
00027	ZB08	01/02/2016	272,105.40			To be posted
00028	ZB08	01/02/2016	146,709.87			To be posted
00029	ZB12	01/02/2016	150.00			To be posted
00030	ZB12	01/02/2016	9,259,378.34			To be posted
00031	ZB17	01/02/2016	978,106.53-			To be posted
00032	ZB17	01/02/2016	303.33-			To be posted
00033	ZB17	01/02/2016	145,392.00-			To be posted

Figure 15.28 Bank Statement Overview: Statement Transactions

In this example, we double-click on the second transaction in the amount of $12,543. The screen in Figure 15.29 appears, which shows the bank transaction to be posted.

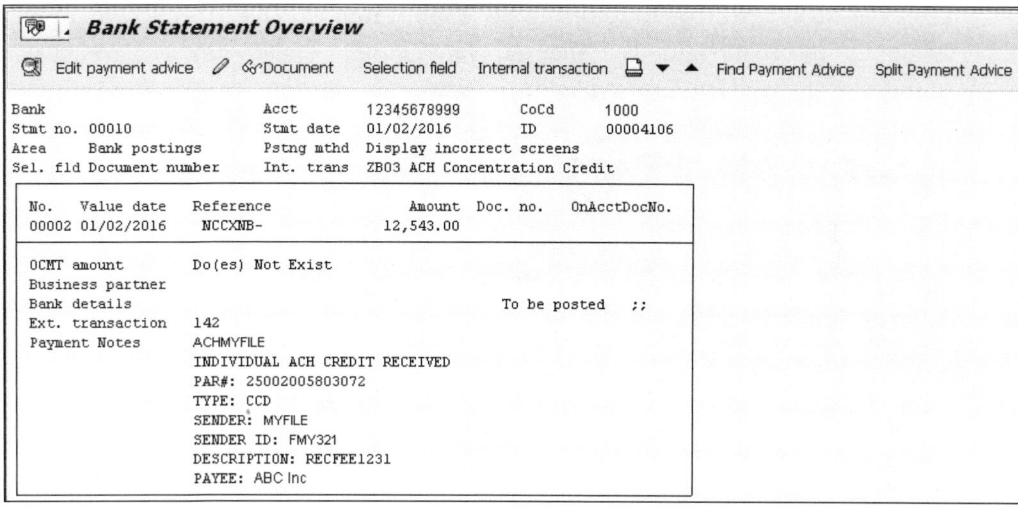

Figure 15.29 Bank Transaction to Be Posted

Click on the **Post** icon ☑. When you do so, the program attempts to find a matching entry in the G/L using Transaction FB05. If it's successful, a document posted message appears, as shown at the bottom of Figure 15.30. 15

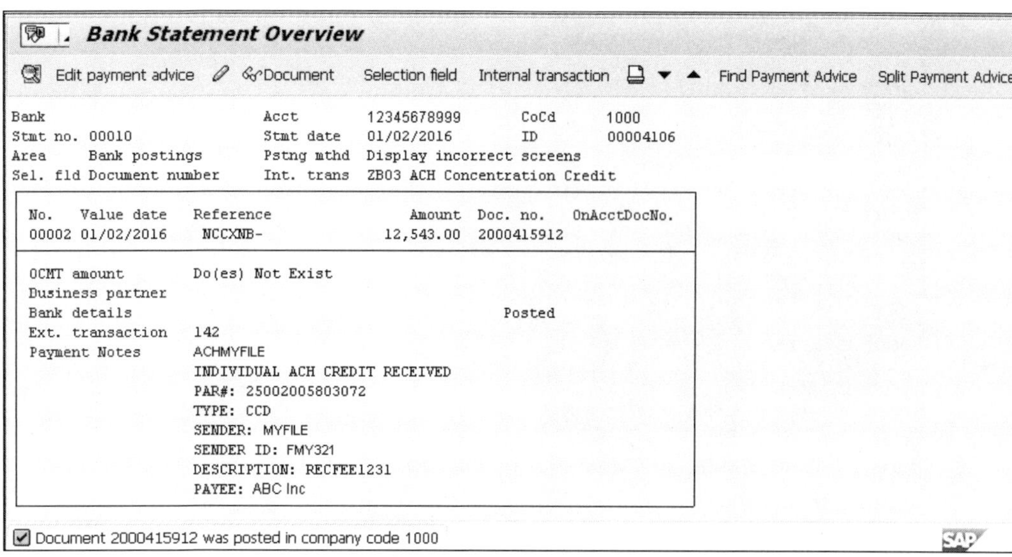

Figure 15.30 Bank Statement Transaction Document Posted

Click the **Back** button to return to the **Bank Statement Overview** screen. In this example, you see in Figure 15.31 that our transaction in the amount of $12,543 has a status that changed from **To be posted** to **Posted.**

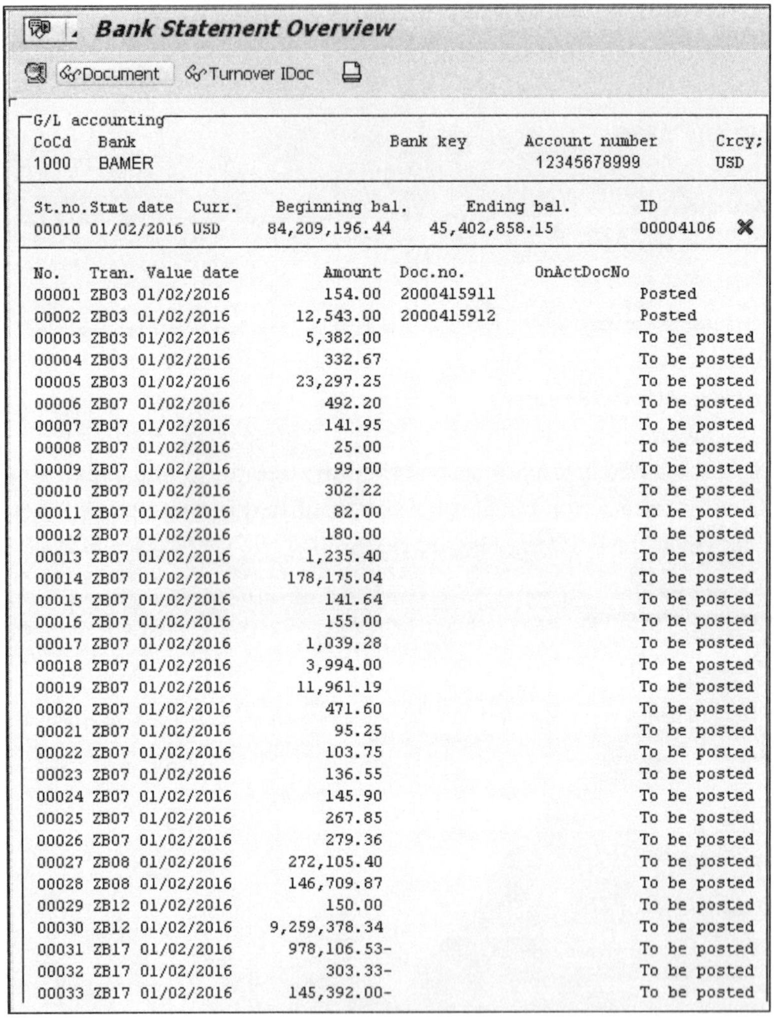

Bank Statement Overview

Document | Turnover IDoc

G/L accounting

CoCd	Bank	Bank key	Account number	Crcy;
1000	BAMER		12345678999	USD

St.no.	Stmt date	Curr.	Beginning bal.	Ending bal.	ID
00010	01/02/2016	USD	84,209,196.44	45,402,858.15	00004106

No.	Tran.	Value date	Amount	Doc.no.	OnActDocNo	
00001	ZB03	01/02/2016	154.00	2000415911		Posted
00002	ZB03	01/02/2016	12,543.00	2000415912		Posted
00003	ZB03	01/02/2016	5,382.00			To be posted
00004	ZB03	01/02/2016	332.67			To be posted
00005	ZB03	01/02/2016	23,297.25			To be posted
00006	ZB07	01/02/2016	492.20			To be posted
00007	ZB07	01/02/2016	141.95			To be posted
00008	ZB07	01/02/2016	25.00			To be posted
00009	ZB07	01/02/2016	99.00			To be posted
00010	ZB07	01/02/2016	302.22			To be posted
00011	ZB07	01/02/2016	82.00			To be posted
00012	ZB07	01/02/2016	180.00			To be posted
00013	ZB07	01/02/2016	1,235.40			To be posted
00014	ZB07	01/02/2016	178,175.04			To be posted
00015	ZB07	01/02/2016	141.64			To be posted
00016	ZB07	01/02/2016	155.00			To be posted
00017	ZB07	01/02/2016	1,039.28			To be posted
00018	ZB07	01/02/2016	3,994.00			To be posted
00019	ZB07	01/02/2016	11,961.19			To be posted
00020	ZB07	01/02/2016	471.60			To be posted
00021	ZB07	01/02/2016	95.25			To be posted
00022	ZB07	01/02/2016	103.75			To be posted
00023	ZB07	01/02/2016	136.55			To be posted
00024	ZB07	01/02/2016	145.90			To be posted
00025	ZB07	01/02/2016	267.85			To be posted
00026	ZB07	01/02/2016	279.36			To be posted
00027	ZB08	01/02/2016	272,105.40			To be posted
00028	ZB08	01/02/2016	146,709.87			To be posted
00029	ZB12	01/02/2016	150.00			To be posted
00030	ZB12	01/02/2016	9,259,378.34			To be posted
00031	ZB17	01/02/2016	978,106.53-			To be posted
00032	ZB17	01/02/2016	303.33-			To be posted
00033	ZB17	01/02/2016	145,392.00-			To be posted

Figure 15.31 Bank Statement Overview after Document Posted

This concludes our discussion of postprocessing of EBSs. You should now possess the basic understanding needed to perform this process.

15.5 Summary

This chapter covered bank master data in detail, including house bank accounts and vendor and customer bank master records. The distinction between house banks and other bank master records is simple: House banks are your company's accounts. Customer and vendor bank accounts, on the other hand, are the bank accounts of your business partners.

G/L bank accounts and their relationships to bank master data are of particular importance. G/L bank accounts should be set up with a one-to-one relationship with house bank accounts. The house bank account and G/L account are set up with a bidirectional link. In other words, the G/L account is specified in the house bank account, and the house bank and account ID are specified in the G/L bank account.

In banking, clearing accounts are used for bank reconciliation purposes. G/L clearing accounts are used to house transactions that posted in the G/L but aren't yet reconciled on a bank statement. G/L bank clearing accounts should be structured with a consistent naming convention; in this way, posting logic for bank reconciliation is most efficient.

This chapter also covered the bank statement reconciliation process. Bank reconciliation is the process of matching bank statement transactions with G/L transactions. In SAP, this matching process clears open items in the G/L bank clearing accounts and posts an offsetting entry to the main G/L bank account. We covered two methods for bank reconciliation: EBSs and manual bank statement reconciliation.

Regardless of whether you're using SAP bank reconciliation or not, the G/L account structure should be designed in a manner that allows your company to implement this capability down the road without having to restructure G/L bank accounts. Doing so also paves the way for additional functionality, such as using SAP Cash and Liquidity Management.

This concludes the discussion of bank master data and processes. In the next chapter, we'll discuss financial close processes.

Chapter 16
Financial Close Processes

In this chapter, we cover essential financial close processes for month-end and year-end, including opening and closing periods, carrying balances forward, periodic processing, and accruals.

Financial close is one of the most important business functions in Financial Accounting (FI). It requires knowledge of internal business processes, relevant SAP transactions, and financial reporting. Special attention is given to the timing of steps executed in the close process. In addition, don't underestimate the value of well-documented close procedures. If your company hasn't documented its close procedures, you should take the initiative to do so.

SAP developed a tool called the SAP Financial Closing cockpit to monitor, control, and increase efficiency when closing. The financial closing cockpit is beyond the scope of this chapter, but it's important to be aware of its existence and capabilities.

Whether you use a spreadsheet to track financial close steps or the financial closing cockpit, your financial close procedures should list steps and transactions in the order in which they need to be executed. In addition, throughout the close process, it's important to track the persons responsible for executing each step and expected completion dates.

For the most part, year-end financial close consists of month-end steps plus additional tasks, such as opening and closing fiscal years and carrying forward G/L balances. You may also be required to create additional master data, such as cost centers.

We'll begin our financial close discussions with the opening and closing accounting periods in FI.

> **Note**
> For details on integrated financial close processes, see Chapter 17.

16.1 Opening and Closing Financial Periods

This section discusses the opening and closing of accounting periods using Transaction OB52. Keep in mind that other modules (e.g., Materials Management [MM]) require opening and closing of periods, and these modules use transactions other than Transaction OB52. The scope of this section is limited to FI periods only. For further details on opening and closing periods in other modules, see Chapter 17.

16.1.1 Opening and Closing Periods

To open and close periods in FI, enter "OB52" in the **Command** field (as shown in Figure 16.1) and press Enter.

Figure 16.1 Entering "OB52" in the Command Field

The **Change View "Posting Periods: Specify Time Periods": Overview** screen opens (Figure 16.2). The periods open for postings are the range of periods in the **From per.2** and **To per. 2** fields shown on the right side of Figure 16.2. In this example, general users are allowed to post in period 12, 2015 (as shown in Figure 16.3).

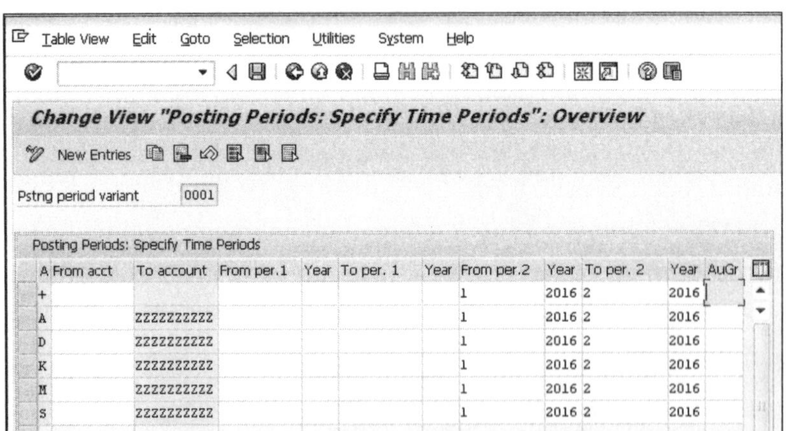

Figure 16.2 Change Posting Periods

Sometimes, a person with special privileges (e.g., director of accounting) needs to make accounting entries in a period not open to general users, or there may be a need to post a prior period that was closed or post to a special period (i.e., 13–16). To allow select individuals to perform these tasks, assign them to an authorization group.

Figure 16.3 shows an example of Transaction OB52 with an authorization group specified. This authorization group is entered in the **AuGr** field. The periods open for posting to individuals assigned to the authorization group are the range of periods in the **From per.1** and **To per. 1** fields shown on the left side of the screen.

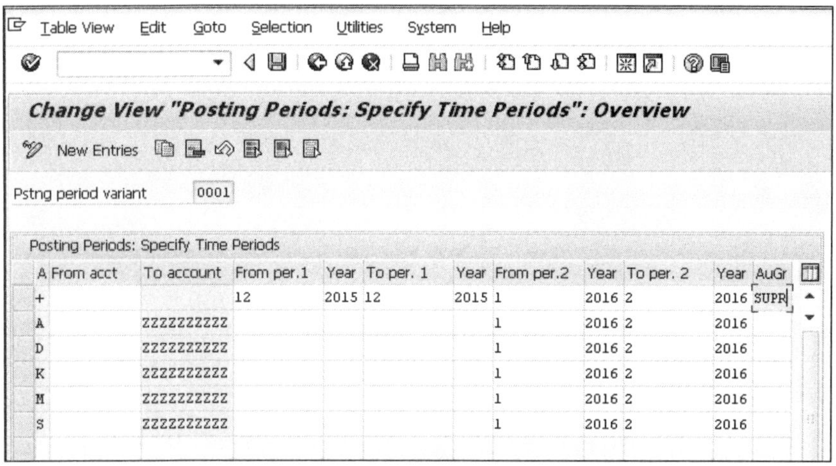

Figure 16.3 Change Posting Periods Screen with Authorization Group

To limit specific users with special posting privileges to a particular posting period, an authorization group must be created, and the posting period authorization (i.e., authorization object F_BKPF_BUP) must be added to the group members' security roles. If you use authorization groups, be diligent in your testing to ensure the groups are in line with your close procedures.

Now let's move on to discuss another feature of Transaction OB52: masking.

16.1.2 Masking

The Transaction OB52 masking feature, indicated in column **A** (second column from the left) in Figure 16.3, enables you to designate open periods by account type. The **+** sign indicates all account types, but it's overridden when more specific account designations are provided.

Available masking options are listed in Table 16.1.

Masking Option	Description
+	Valid for all account types
A	Assets
D	Customers
K	Vendors
M	Materials
S	G/L accounts
V	Contract accounts

Table 16.1 Transaction OB52 Masking Options

The masking feature provides flexibility in designating open FI periods by account type.

Now that we've discussed opening and closing financial periods, let's move on to discuss the carryforward of G/L account balances.

16.2 Balance Carryforward

Carrying forward balances to a new fiscal year is a core accounting concept and only relevant for year-end close.

When you think of carryforward balances, you probably think automatically of G/L account balances. It's true that G/L account balances are the primary target in the carryforward process, but you also need to perform carryforward functions for local ledgers, special ledgers, and subledgers. In this section, we'll begin with a discussion of G/L account balances and then address these other areas.

The primary balance carryforward step is for G/L account balances in the leading ledgers. It's executed using Transaction FAGLGVTR. In the same way, this step needs to be completed for each of your local ledgers. The program used to carry forward G/L balances can be run multiple times but doesn't normally need to be run more than once per year. After the program is run, postings to the previous fiscal year are automatically carried forward to the new fiscal year.

The process of G/L balance carryforward is twofold: First, balance sheet accounts are summarized with additional account assignments and transferred to the new fiscal year. Second, profit and loss (P&L) accounts are carried forward to the retained earnings account without additional account assignments. For both, the transaction currencies aren't transferred. The totals are carried over in local currency.

To carry forward G/L balances, use Transaction FAGLGVTR or application menu path, **Accounting • Financial Accounting • General Ledger • Periodic Processing • Closing • Carrying Forward • FAGLGVTR – Balance Carryforward (New)**, as shown in Figure 16.4.

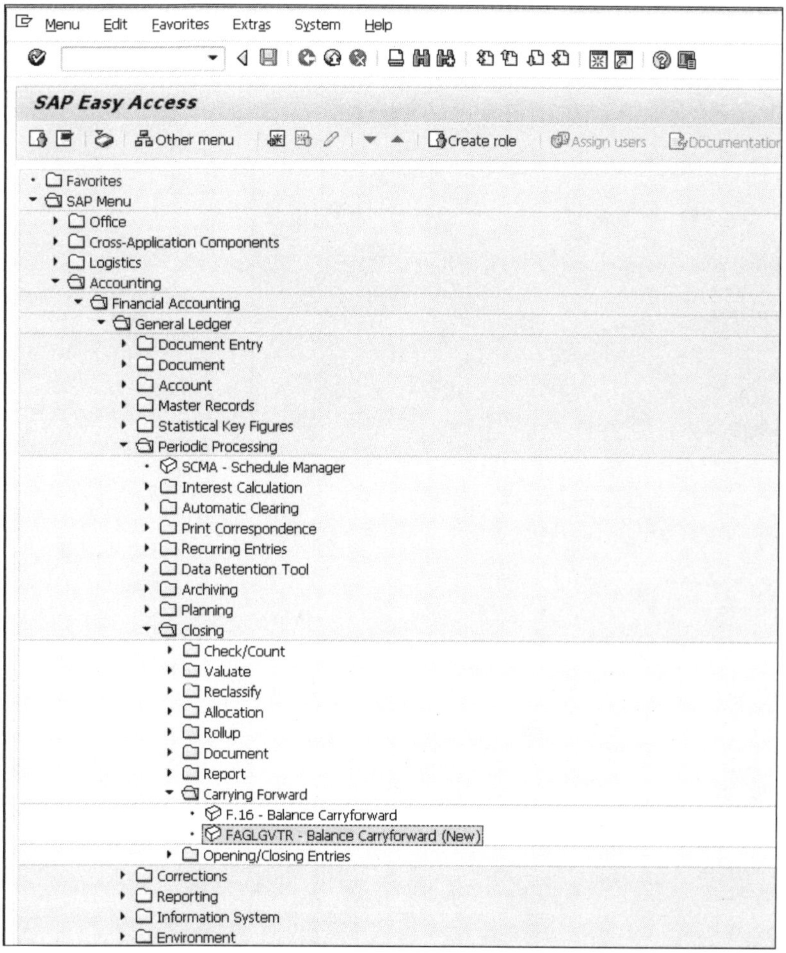

Figure 16.4 Transaction FAGLGVTR Application Menu Path

Double-click on **FAGLGVTR – Balance Carryforward (New)** from the menu path, and the **Balance carryforward** screen opens (Figure 16.5). Here, enter values in the **Ledger**, **Company code**, and **Carry forward to fiscal year** fields. In the **Processing options** area of the screen, notice the **Test run** option to run the program in test mode. In this example, we also selected options in the **List output** area at the bottom of the screen to output results and P&L balance transfers to retained earnings.

Note

The screen selection permits the entry of a range of company codes but only one ledger. This program has to be run separately for each of your ledgers.

With all field selections made, click the **Execute** icon.

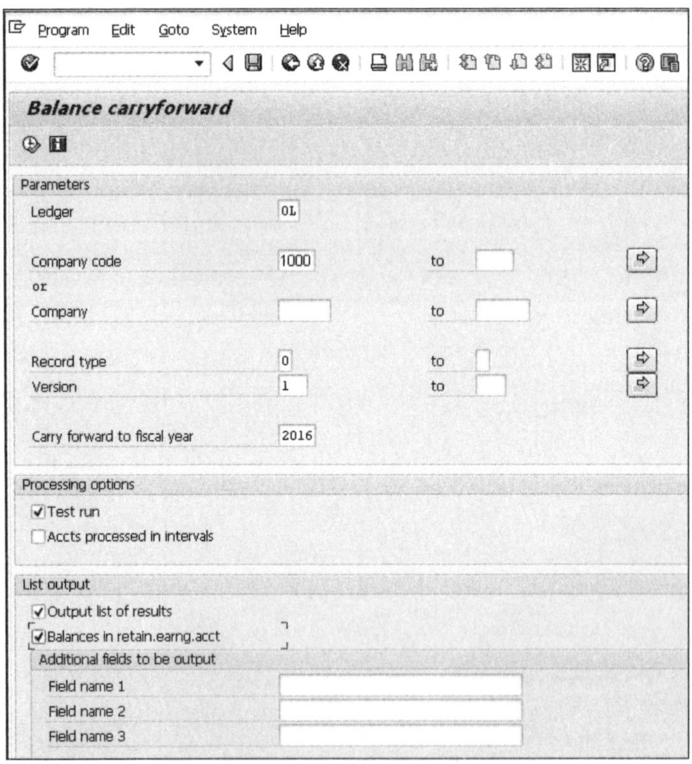

Figure 16.5 Balance Carryforward

The output screen opens (Figure 16.6).

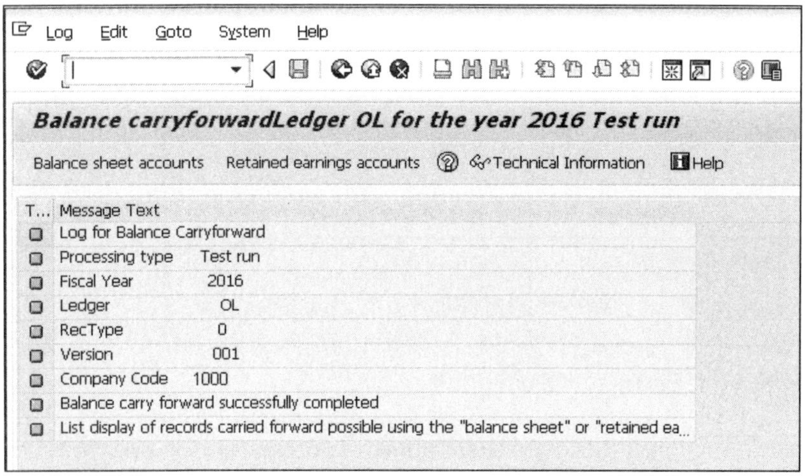

Figure 16.6 Balance Carryforward Output

Click on the **Balance sheet accounts** button, and the **Display of balance sheet accounts** screen opens (Figure 16.7). This screen shows individual balance sheet account balances, summarized by additional account assignment elements, being carried forward to the new fiscal year.

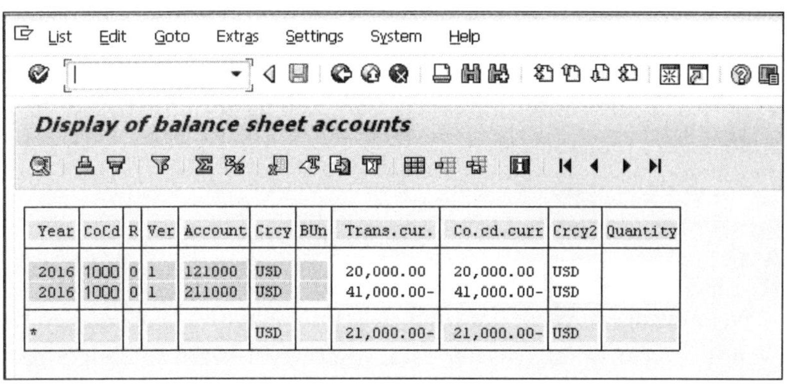

Figure 16.7 Display of Balance Sheet Accounts

Click on the **Back** button to return to the output screen (refer to Figure 16.6). Click on the **Retained earnings accounts** button, and the **Display of retained earnings accounts** screen opens (Figure 16.8). This screen shows individual P&L account balances to be carried forward to the new fiscal year.

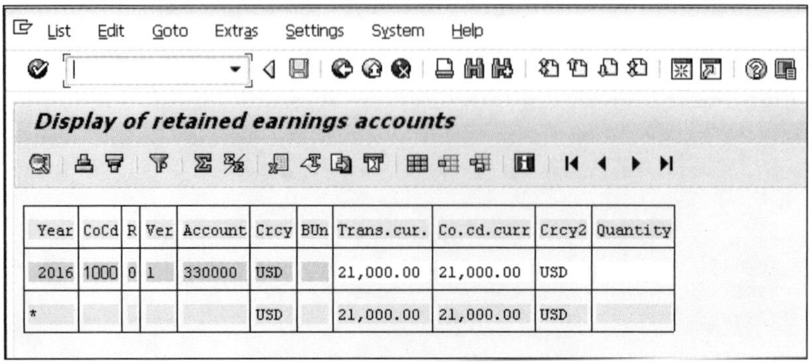

Figure 16.8 Display of Retained Earnings Accounts

In addition to Transaction FAGLGVTR, there are some other balance carryforward transactions for Special Purpose Ledger, Accounts Payable (AP), Accounts Receivable (AR), and classic G/L, as listed here:

- **Transaction GVTR**
  This transaction is used to carry forward balances in the Special Purpose Ledger.
- **Transaction F.07**
  This transaction is used to carry forward subledger balances in AR and AP.
- **Transaction F.16**
  This transaction is used to carry forward G/L balances in classic G/L (versus new G/L).

Now that you've learned about carrying forward G/L account balances in the G/L, let's discuss financial close steps for fixed assets.

16.3 Fixed Assets

Whenever you have subledgers, there are financial close activities that must take place. For both vendor and customer master data, you carry forward subledger balances using Transaction F.16 at year-end. At month-end, you also run dunning, issue payments, post accruals, post incoming payments, run billing, process bank statements, and perform other AP- and AR-related functions.

FI Asset Accounting (FI-AA) is also a subledger. As such, it has unique steps for financial close. For FI-AA at year-end, there are two primary steps that must be performed.

The first is to change the fiscal year using Transaction AJRW. This is a technical step required to carry forward assets into a new fiscal year.

To carry forward fixed assets, use Transaction AJRW or application menu path, **Accounting • Financial Accounting • Fixed Assets • Periodic Processing • AJRW – Fiscal Year Change**, as shown in Figure 16.9.

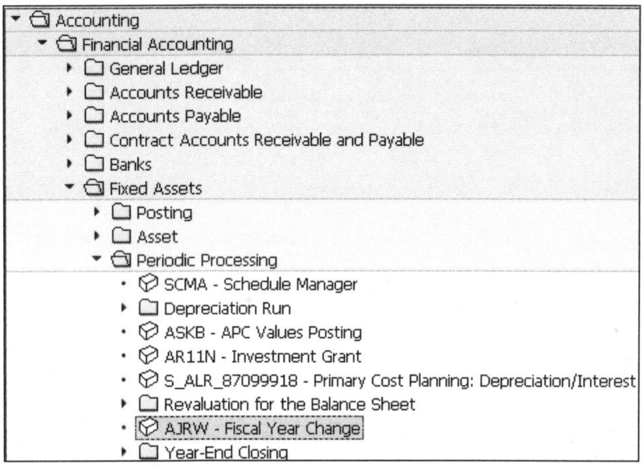

Figure 16.9 Transaction AJRW Application Menu Path

Double-click **AJRW – Fiscal Year Change** from the menu path, and the **Asset fiscal year change** screen opens (Figure 16.10). On this screen, enter values in the **Company code(s)** and **New fiscal year** fields. There is also a checkbox for **Test run**, giving you the ability to execute this program in test mode.

With all field selections made, click the **Execute** icon.

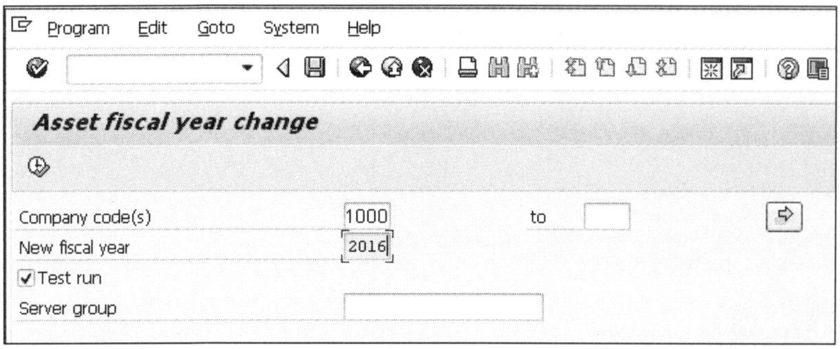

Figure 16.10 Asset Fiscal Year Change

The **Asset fiscal year change** output screen opens (Figure 16.11). If the **Status** column shows a green light, it indicates that the test run is successful, and the fixed assets can be carried forward into the new fiscal year specified.

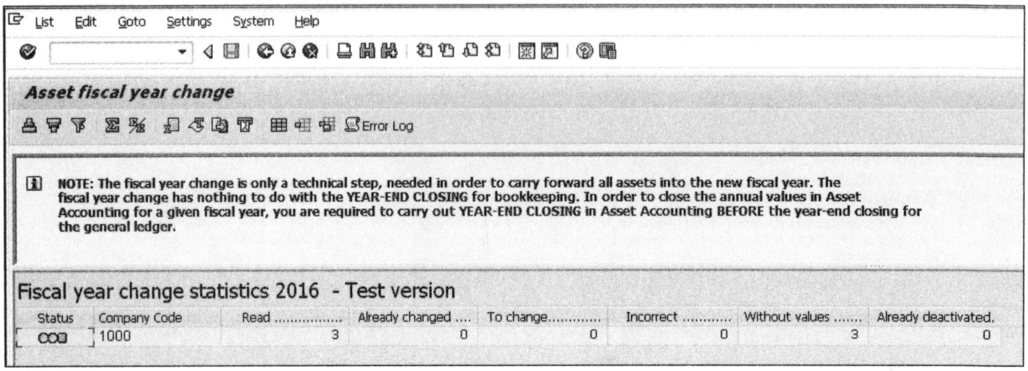

Figure 16.11 Asset Fiscal Year Change Output

While Transaction AJRW can be run in the foreground in test mode, it must be run in the background in production mode. This is also true of the next step in FI-AA: Transaction AJAB.

The second step for FI-AA at year-end is to change the fiscal year using Transaction AJAB or application menu path, **Accounting • Financial Accounting • Fixed Assets • Periodic Processing • Year-End Closing • AJAB – Execute**, as shown in Figure 16.12.

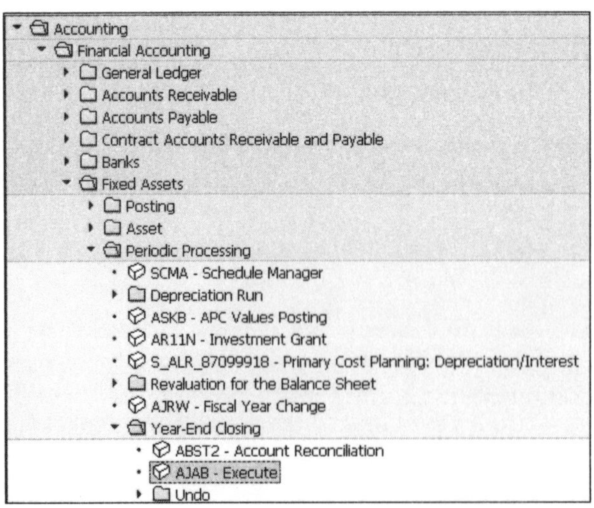

Figure 16.12 Transaction AJAB Application Menu Path

Double-click **AJAB – Execute** from the menu path, and the **Year-end closing Asset Accounting** screen opens (Figure 16.13). On this screen, enter values in the **Company code** and **Fiscal year to be closed** fields. You can also execute this program in test mode by selecting the **Test run** checkbox.

Transaction AJAB checks that there are no assets that have been posted (i.e., have an acquisition date) but not capitalized (i.e., no capitalization date). These assets are captured as errors when the program runs. This check doesn't make sense for assets under construction (AuC), and therefore you can specify AuC asset classes in the **Asset classes asset u. const.** field selection (Figure 16.13) to bypass the check and keep your error log clean.

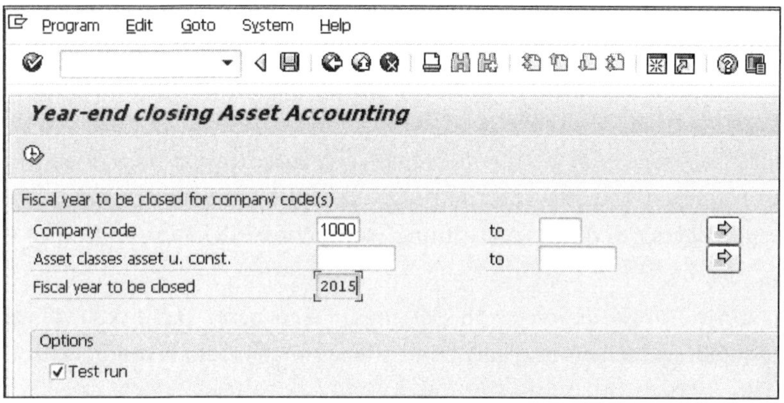

Figure 16.13 Year-End Closing Asset Accounting

You can execute Transaction AFAB in the foreground in test mode, but it must be executed as a background job when run in production mode. Enter your field values as shown in Figure 16.13, save as a variant, and work with your SAP Basis administrator to schedule the job to run automatically at each year-end. Now that we've covered fixed asset close processes, let's look at periodic processing functions in the next section.

16.4 Periodic Processing

Periodic processing is a classification of transactions that are executed at regular intervals. Some of them may be executed more frequently than at month-end or year-end, but they are included as closing steps because they are essential to producing financial statements.

Numerous transactions are considered to be periodic processing tasks. Which ones you need to execute in financial close depends on your business processes and the SAP modules implemented to support your business. The following are some of the more common transactions; this isn't a complete list, but it provides a good representation:

- **Recurring entries**
  Transaction F.14 creates financial documents from recurring entry documents. Recurring entry documents can be created for financial transactions with a fixed amount, interval (e.g., monthly), and life (e.g., 24 months).
- **Dunning**
  Transaction F150 creates dunning notices to send to customers for overdue payments and updates customer master data with the dunning level and a last dunned date.
- **Payments**
  Transaction F110 issues vendor payments in mass. It creates the payment medium necessary for monetary transfer and the financial postings necessary to update the G/L and subledgers. For details on running Transaction F110, see Chapter 7.
- **Depreciation**
  Transaction AFAB creates depreciation postings. Fixed asset net book values (NBVs) are updated, and accounting entries are made to accumulated depreciation and depreciation expense accounts.
- **Interest calculations**
  There are several types of interest calculations:
  - Transaction F.52 is used to calculate interest on G/L balances.
  - Transaction FINT is used for calculating interest in arrears for overdue customer accounts.
  - Transaction FINTAP is used for vendor interest calculation.
  - Other interest calculation transactions also exist for interest in arrears.

In addition to these transactions, periodic processing steps may include transactions for automatic clearing, printing correspondence, currency translation and valuation, manual accruals, and reverse accruals. Now that you understand what periodic processes are, let's walk through an example for recurring entries.

Note

The creation of a recurring document was demonstrated in Chapter 3. As discussed in that chapter, when a recurring document is saved, no accounting entries are created. It's only when the recurring entry program is run that accounting documents are created and G/L balances updated.

To create accounting documents from recurring entry reference documents, use Transaction F.14 or application menu path, **Accounting • Financial Accounting • General Ledger • Periodic Processing • Recurring Entries • F.14 – Execute**, as shown in Figure 16.14.

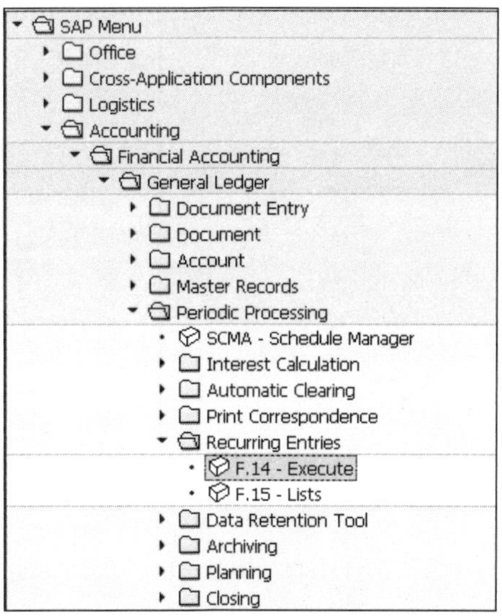

Figure 16.14 Transaction F.14 Application Menu Path

Double-click on **F.14 – Execute** from the menu path, and the **Create Posting Documents from Recurring Documents** screen opens (Figure 16.15).

Make sure to enter values for all required fields, such as **Company code, Document Number** (this is the reference document number), **Fiscal Year**, and **Batch input session name**. You can also enter additional field values in the **General selections** area of the screen to narrow your selection of recurring documents.

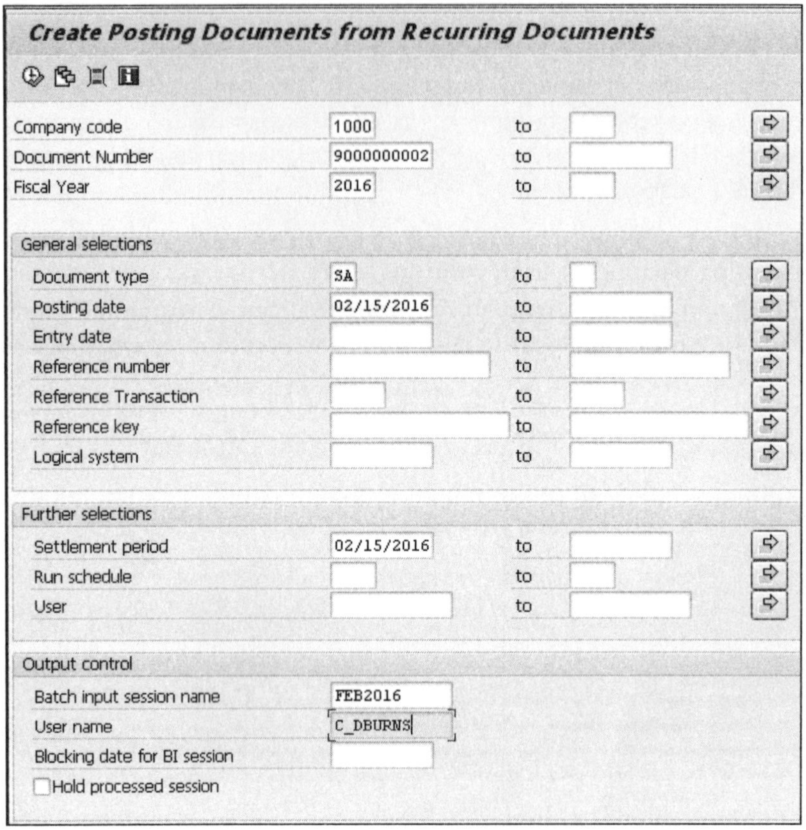

Figure 16.15 Create Posting Documents from Recurring Documents

The **Settlement period** field is particularly important. The date range provided must contain the date on which the next recurring entry is scheduled. If you're unsure, view the recurring entry document in your reference document using Transaction FBD3.

With all field values entered, click the **Execute** icon. A message appears that a session was created (Figure 16.16).

To view your session, use Transaction SM35. The **Batch Input: Session Overview** screen appears (Figure 16.17).

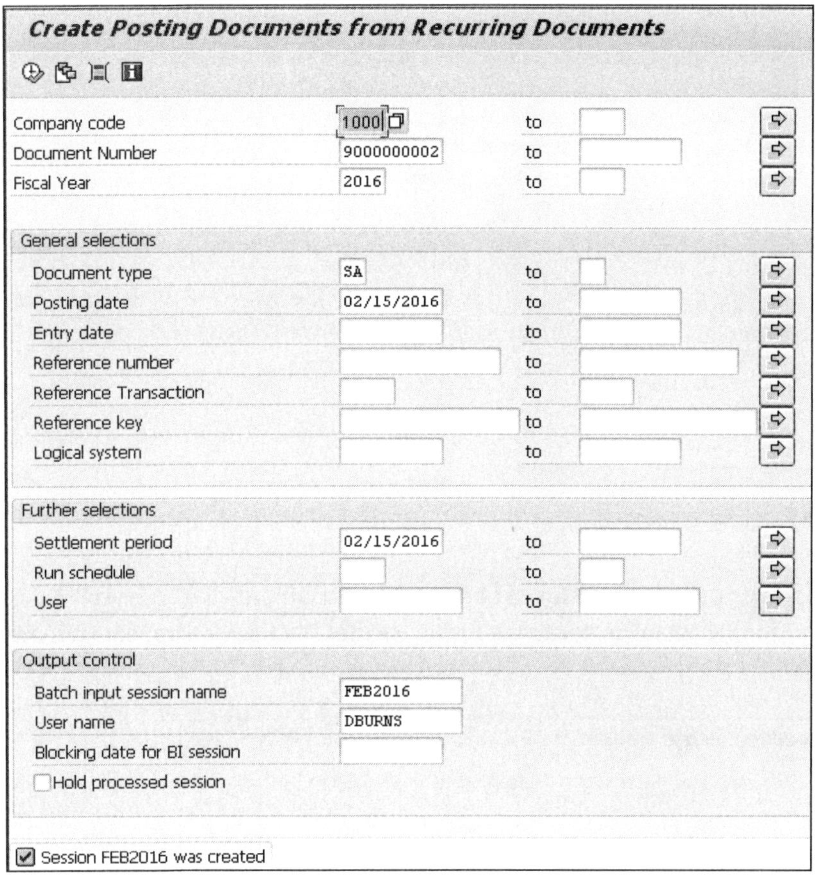

Figure 16.16 Recurring Documents Session Created

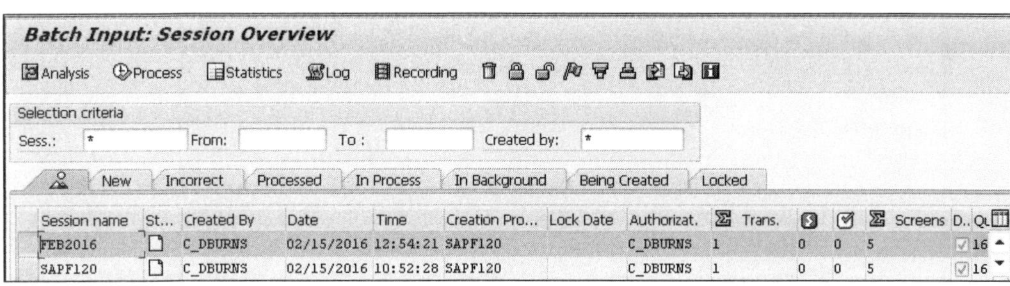

Figure 16.17 Batch Input: Session Overview Screen

Highlight your session name, and click the **Process** button. The **Process Session** dialog box appears (Figure 16.18).

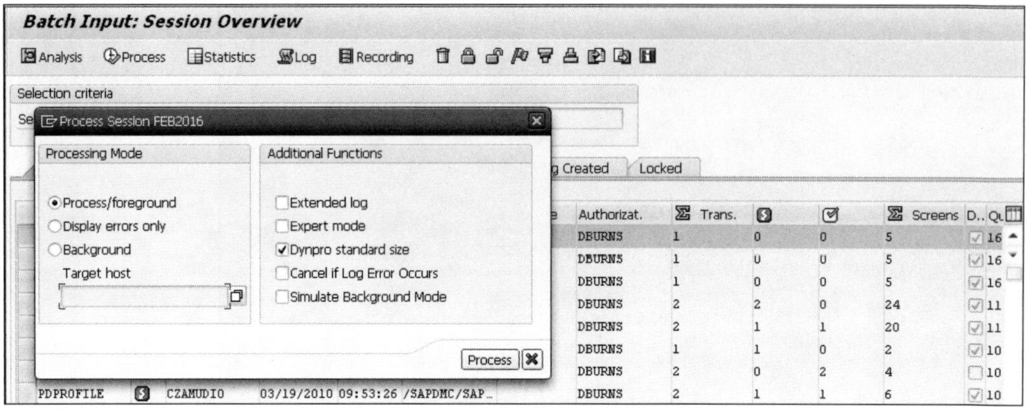

Figure 16.18 Process Session Dialog Box

Select **Process/foreground** to watch your accounting document as it's created. Click the **Process** button. The **Realize Recurring Entry: Header Data** screen appears (Figure 16.19).

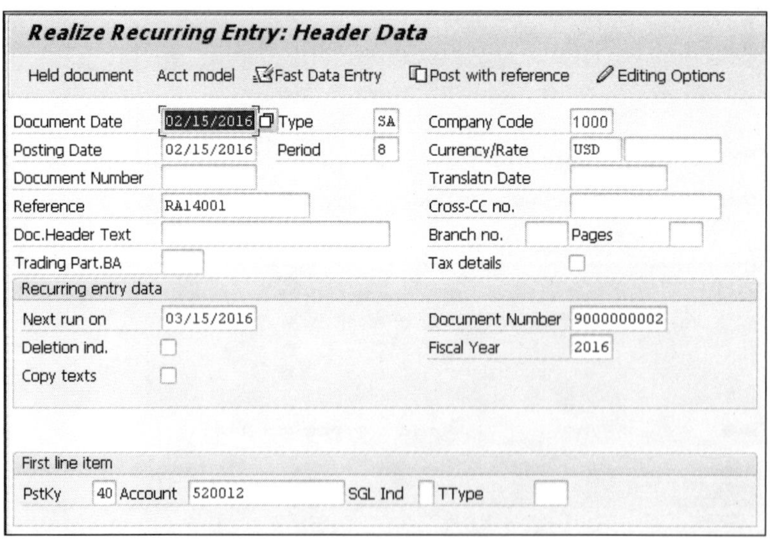

Figure 16.19 Realize Recurring Entry: Header Data Screen

Press Enter through the screens until your document is posted.

This concludes our discussion of periodic processes. As you can see, there are numerous types of periodic processes used during month-end and year-end close. It's important to know your company's business processes to understand which periodic processing transactions to use.

16.5 Foreign Currency Valuations

In this section, we'll discuss foreign currency valuation at a high level. To execute this process, several configuration steps are required. This book isn't a configuration guide, but you should be aware of this configuration because you depend on it to execute foreign currency valuation.

In configuration, a *valuation method* must be defined. In the valuation method, the *valuation procedure* must be specified. For example, one type of valuation procedure is the *lowest value principle*, which means the valuation will only be posted if it's a negative result. In the valuation method, specifications are also provided that determine how exchange rate differences should be posted and the basis for determining the exchange rate type used. In addition to defining the valuation method in configuration, you also define *valuation areas*, *accounting principles*, and specify *account determinations*. 16

When multiple currencies are used in a system, foreign currency valuation is needed to produce financial statements. It provides the ability to valuate account balances in your reporting currency using Transaction FAGL_FC_VAL (or Transaction F.05 if you're using the classic G/L). This step is relevant to G/L accounts managed in foreign currency and open items that were posted in foreign currency. You can perform the valuation in local currency or parallel currency. The result of the valuations can be stored per valuated document and posted to adjustment accounts and P&L accounts.

An example of G/L accounts managed in foreign currency is when your company processes incoming payments made in currencies other than your local currency. In this case, a G/L account can only be posted in this foreign currency, but the transaction figures and the account balance are kept in both the foreign currency and the local currency.

There are a couple different ways in which valuation takes place. For open items in customer, vendor, and G/L accounts, the items are read as of a specified key date and balanced by account or group and currency. For G/L account balances, reconciliation accounts and accounts managed on an open item basis aren't valuated, and P&L accounts are only valuated as required.

Documents are balanced by currency and account. The exchange rate type for the valuation is determined from this balance. Valuation differences are posted as determined by the valuation area configured and selected. Postings for accounts managed on an open item basis in the subledger and the G/L are posted to an adjustment account and a P&L account. Postings for G/L accounts not managed on an open item basis are posted to adjustment accounts or by account determination.

That concludes our discussion of foreign currency valuations. The next financial close topic we'll discuss is goods receipt/invoice receipt (GR/IR) clearing.

16.6 Goods Receipt/Invoice Receipt Clearing

GR/IR clearing computes price variances between GR and IR and allocates variances to inventory, price differences, or the assignment object based on the valuation procedure in the material master and the settings in the purchase order (PO) line item. The values are stored in a G/L GR/IR clearing account and settled periodically using the GR/IR clearing function.

> **Note**
>
> This topic is also discussed in Chapter 17. The content here, however, is more focused on FI, whereas Chapter 17 discusses GR/IR clearing from the broader perspective of integrated financial close.

GR/IR account maintenance is a process that should be performed regularly, although most consider it strictly as a month-end process. The system matches GRs with IRs based on the PO number, PO item, type of PO, indicator for invoice verification, and material or delivery costs.

Several tools are available for GR/IR clearing account analysis. The first is Transaction F.19, which can be found using application menu path, **Accounting • Financial Accounting • General Ledger • Periodic Processing • Closing • Reclassify • F.19 – GR/IR Clearing**, as shown in Figure 16.20.

Double-click on **F.19 – GR/IR Clearing**, and the **Analyze GR/IR Clearing Accounts and Display Acquisition Tax** screen appears (Figure 16.21).

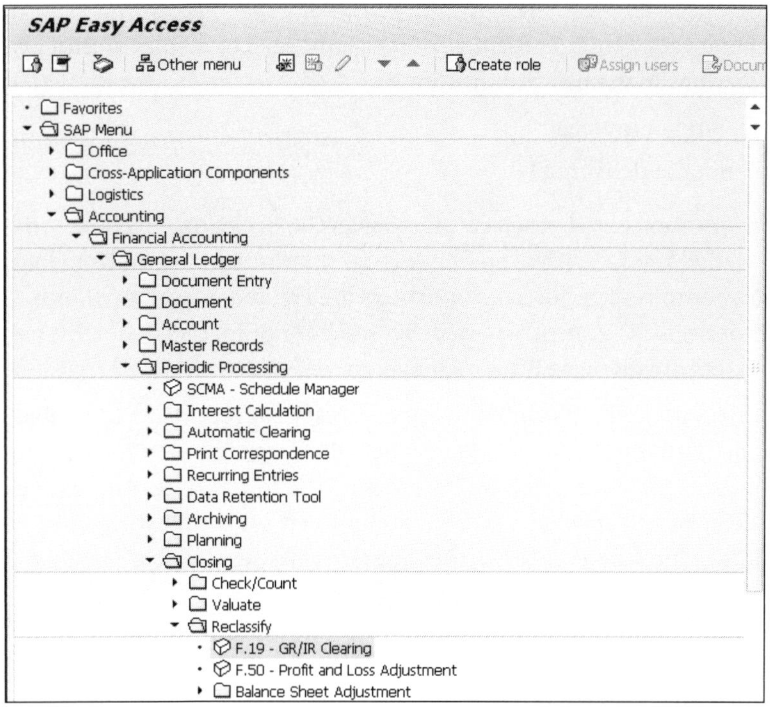

Figure 16.20 Transaction F.19 Application Menu Path

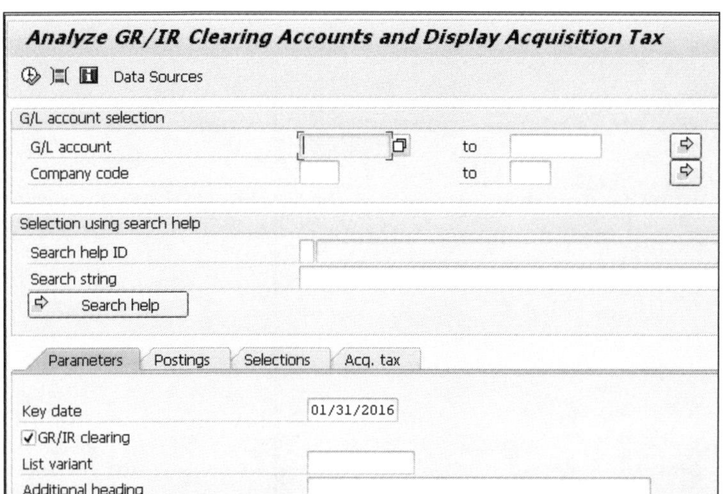

Figure 16.21 Analyze GR/IR Clearing Account and Display Acquisition Tax Selection Screen

This program is used to analyze GR/IR clearing accounts at a specified key date. It can also be used to generate adjustment postings, which are needed to display the following business transactions in the balance sheet:

- Goods delivered, but not invoiced
- Goods invoiced, but not delivered

When Transaction F.19 is executed, it selects all items in GR/IR clearing accounts that are open at the specified key date. If the open items per PO number and items in local currency don't balance to zero, adjustment postings are created. A credit balance in the GR/IR account reflects PO items that are delivered but not invoiced. A debit balance reflects items that are invoiced but not delivered.

Keep in mind that the adjustments to GR/IR are necessary for reporting, but subsequent purchasing activity will likely take place to net GR/IR line items to zero. Therefore, adjustment postings are intended to be reversed at a future date. All postings are reversed at the specified reverse posting date entered on the **Postings** tab, as shown in Figure 16.22. If no date is entered, the program reverses the postings on the day after the key date.

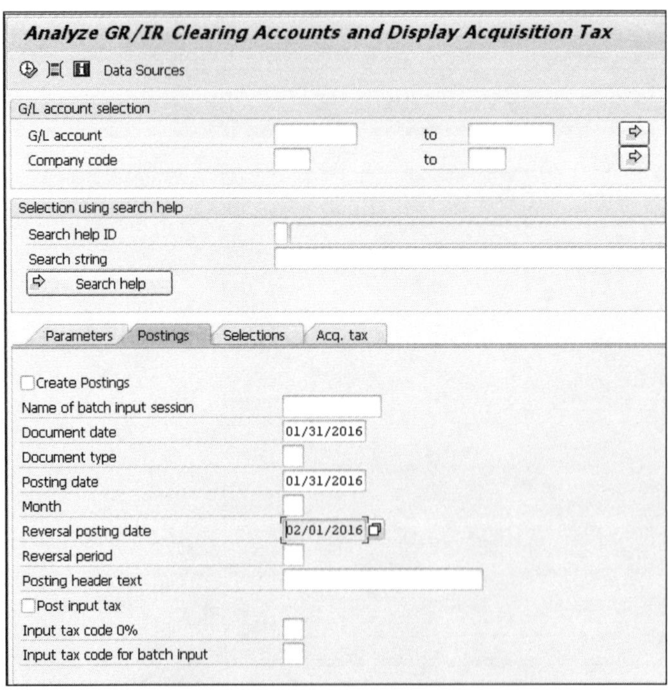

Figure 16.22 Analyze GR/IR Clearing Accounts: Postings Tab

Another tool in FI for GR/IR account maintenance is Transaction F.13. This can be found using application menu path, **Accounting • Financial Accounting • General Ledger • Periodic Processing • Automatic Clearing • F.13 – Without Specification of Clearing Currency**, as shown in Figure 16.23.

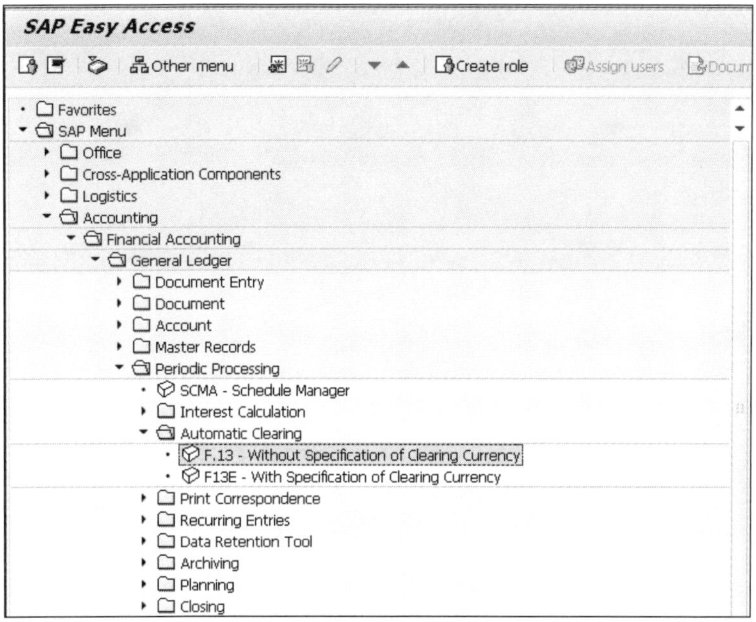

Figure 16.23 Transaction F.13 Application Menu Path

Double-click on **F.13 – Without Specification of Clearing Currency** and the **Automatic Clearing** screen appears (Figure 16.24).

Transaction F.13 isn't used exclusively for GR/IR clearing. It's also used to clear open items in customer, vendor, and G/L accounts. The logic, however, is the same for clearing GR/IR accounts. For GR/IR accounts, the program logic attempts to match documents that can be cleared and omit documents that can't.

There is one point to emphasize with GR/IR matching. There is a **GR/IR account special process.** checkbox (Figure 16.24) you can select. This special process is used when the assignment of GRs to the corresponding IRs is insufficient, based on the PO number and PO item. This indicator then not only matches GR/IR items by PO number and the PO item but also by the material document if a GR-related invoice verification is defined in the PO item.

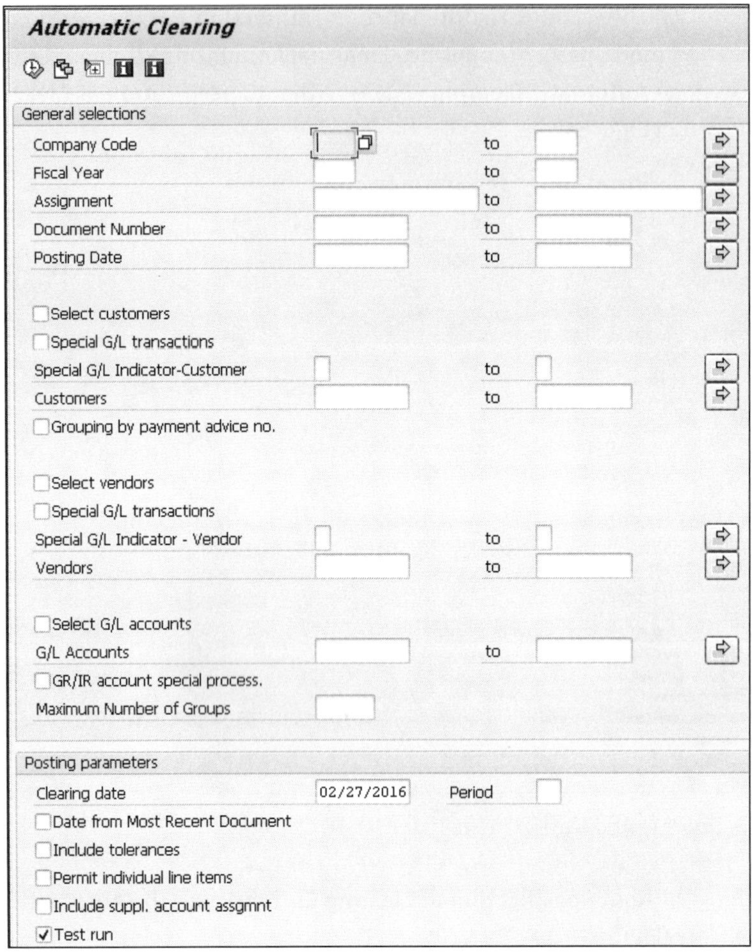

Figure 16.24 Automatic Clearing Screen for GR/IR Accounts

The next financial close item to be addressed is posting fixed asset depreciation.

16.7 Depreciation

Depreciation is covered in detail in Chapter 13. Rather than repeat the information already contained in that chapter, we'll summarize a few of the key points here as they relate to financial close.

Depreciation of an asset is typically referred to as *asset consumption*. It decreases the value of an asset and allocates costs of an asset to periods in which it's used. The primary output of an SAP depreciation run is a summary-level document with accounting entries that include credits to accumulated depreciation G/L accounts (on the balance sheet) and debits to asset expense G/L accounts (on the P&L statement).

Executing depreciation is an important step in financial close. It's done using Transaction AFAB or application menu path, **Accounting • Financial Accounting • Fixed Assets • Periodic Processing • AFAB – Execute**, as shown in Figure 16.25.

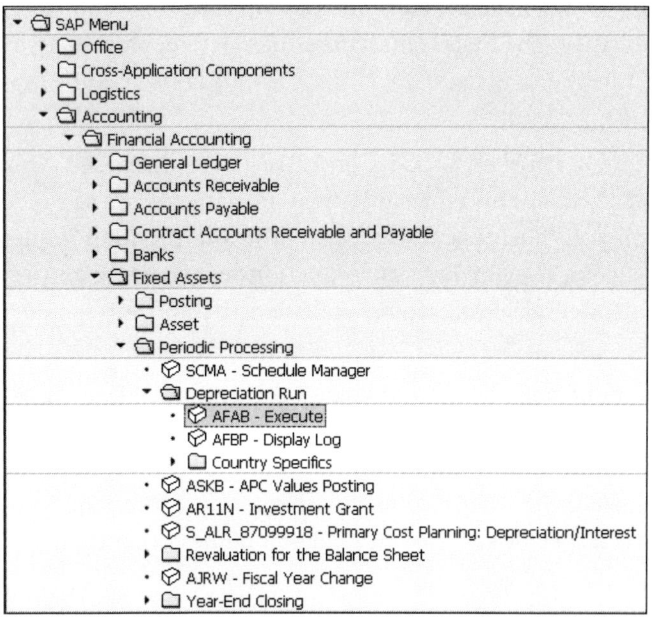

Figure 16.25 Transaction AFAB Application Menu Path

It's always a good idea to run depreciation in test mode first. To view the results of a depreciation run, use Transaction AFBP.

16.8 Summary

This chapter covered essential transactions in the month-end and year-end close processes. Financial close involves much more than the system mechanics of closing FI in SAP. Several manual steps, analyses, and accounting corrections need to be made to produce clean and accurate financial statements. Having a complete and organized process for closing the books is vital.

This chapter began with a discussion of opening and closing FI periods using Transaction OB52. This transaction is the control center to ensure general users are restricted to posting in a particular accounting period. G/L account balance carryforward is another important financial close process and is the critical step in year-end close. Transaction FAGLGVTR is the primary transaction in new G/L used to carry forward G/L balances.

Fixed assets are subledgers that need special consideration. During year-end close, two transactions must be executed. The first, Transaction AJRW, is a technical step to carry forward fixed assets into the new fiscal year. The second, Transaction AJAB, changes the fiscal year in FI-AA.

In this chapter, several different types of periodic processes were discussed. This includes numerous different transactions. Which ones you need to execute as a part of financial close depends on your business processes and the SAP modules implemented to support your business. They include such functions as recurring entries, dunning, outgoing payments, depreciation, interest calculations, and foreign currency revaluations.

This concludes our discussion of month-end and year-end close procedures in FI. Closing the books isn't isolated to FI. Any integrated process that crosses SAP modules may require a close step due to financial integration. In the next chapter, we build on the financial close processes discussed in this chapter by addressing integrated financial close, for which specific steps are needed in modules other than FI.

Chapter 17
Integrated Financial Close in SAP ERP

In this chapter, we cover integrated financial close processes. Financial Accounting (FI) practitioners must be able to step out of FI to understand integrated business scenarios and their dependencies in the close process.

Financial close at month-end and year-end doesn't happen in a vacuum. A common misconception is that financial close is only an FI process. In reality, coordinated close activities are required across teams that manage sales, production, logistics, accounting, planning, and analytics. Because finance and accounting departments are primarily responsible for financial close, they need to understand not only their own close processes but also integrated team close activities across business processes.

Understanding the broad reach of month-end and year-end close is important to a timely and coordinated financial close. Close steps need to be sequenced, and it's important to understand dependencies between close activities. Moreover, finance and accounting are on the hook if financial close isn't executed in a timely fashion. Therefore, an accounting department's ability to coordinate close activities with other teams is important for achieving the company's goals.

This chapter focuses on a few important integrated financial close steps in Controlling (CO), Materials Management (MM), and Sales and Distributions (SD). We won't provide a complete list of close activities in these modules, but rather we'll emphasize the importance of understanding the role of integration in the financial close process.

Let's begin with a discussion of financial close in the CO module.

17.1 Integrated Financial Close and Cost Accounting

Cost accounting, often referred to as *management accounting*, is executed in the CO module. Like FI, CO has its own posting periods and transactions that are relevant to financial close. In SAP ERP, FI and CO are separate modules, and, therefore, each has individual close tasks that must be performed.

CO provides an internal view of financial information and numerous capabilities, including Profitability Analysis (CO-PA), cost assessments and allocations, planning, and much more. Several books and resource materials are available on CO that you can reference to learn more about these topics.

The primary focus of this section is CO period locks, which are essentially the CO equivalent of opening and closing periods.

17.1.1 Controlling Period Locks

Period control in CO is managed through the period lock function. CO period control is unique in that it can be set by period *and* transaction type. Most companies don't use all the CO transaction types, so it's important to note in addressing this topic that you need to become familiar with the CO transaction types used in your organization.

To change CO period locks, use Transaction OKP1 or application menu path, **Accounting • Controlling • Cost Element Accounting • Environment • Period Lock • OKP1 – Change**, as shown in Figure 17.1.

Double-click **OKP1 – Change** from the menu path, and the **Change Period Lock: Initial Screen** opens (Figure 17.2). On this screen, you must enter a **Controlling Area, Fiscal Year**, and **Version**.

The **Version** field deserves further explanation. There is one specific version for actual and planned costs (i.e., version **0**) in each controlling area. This version is automatically created when you set up a controlling area. In addition to version 0, you can create any number of extra planning versions in which you can enter planning data. However, when posting actual costs, there is no option to enter a version because the actual values are automatically posted to version 0.

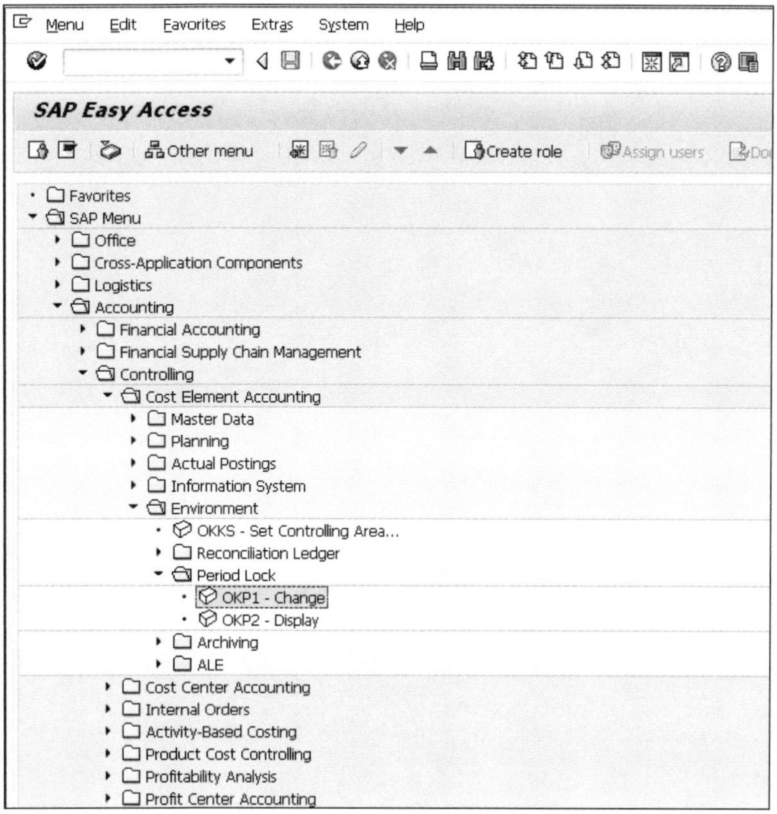

Figure 17.1 Transaction OKP1 Application Menu Path

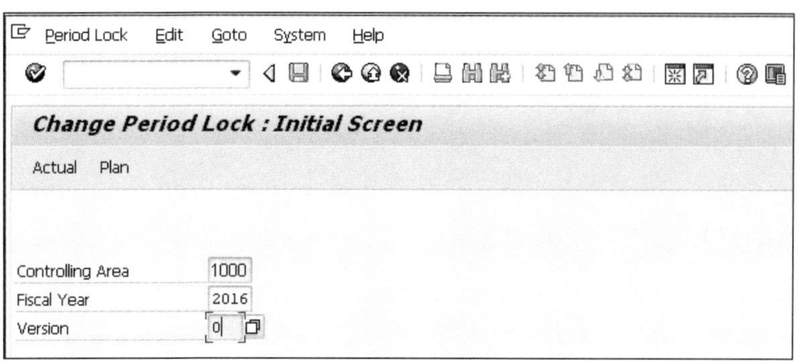

Figure 17.2 Change Period Lock: Initial Screen

With all the field values entered as in Figure 17.2, click the **Actual** button in the top left of the screen. The **Change Actual Period Lock: Edit** screen opens (Figure 17.3).

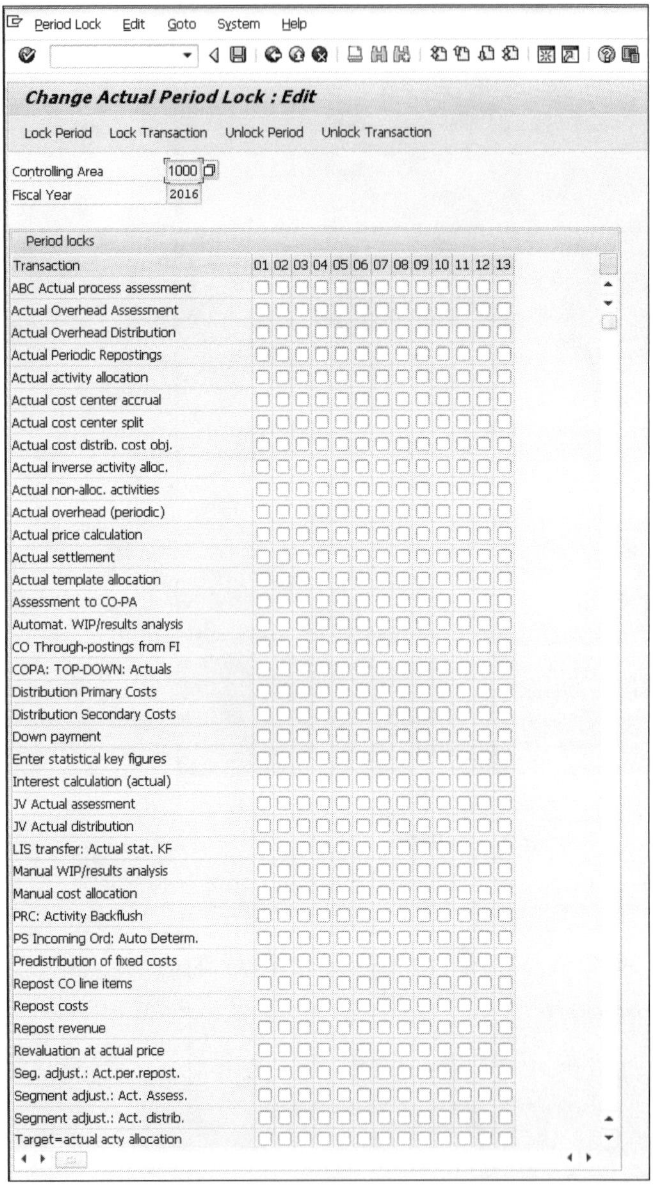

Figure 17.3 Change Actual Period Lock: Edit

CO periods can be locked by transaction, by period, or both. Figure 17.4 shows an example of a lock by period, meaning that a specific period (i.e., period **01**) is locked for all transaction types.

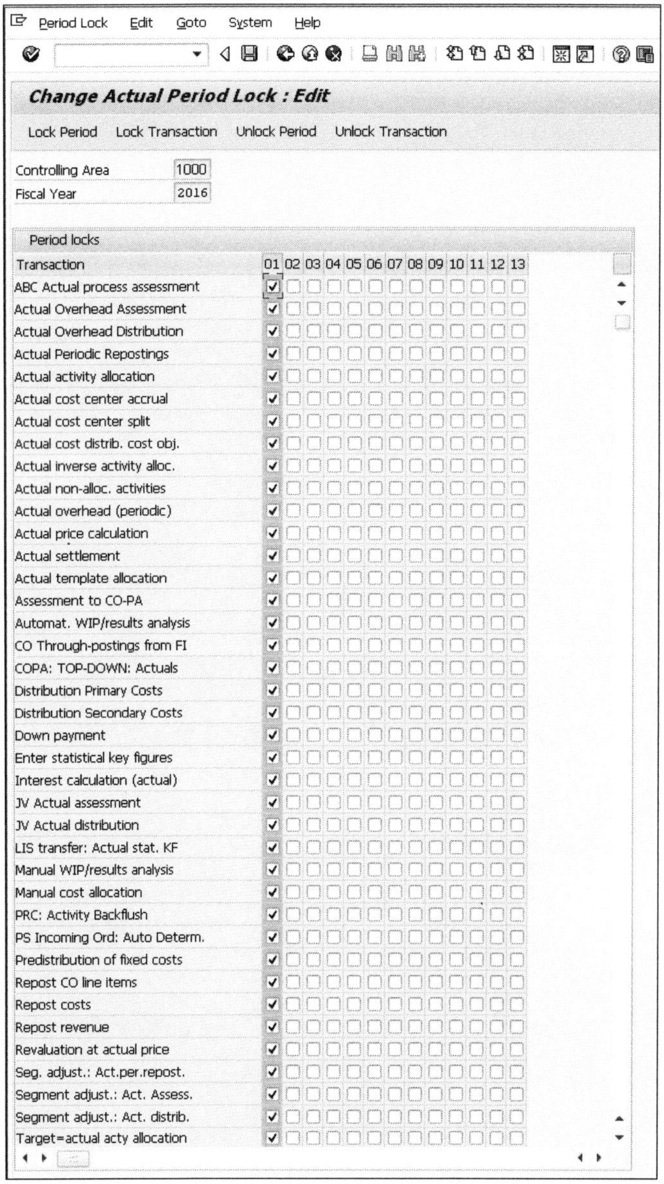

Figure 17.4 Period Lock by Period

Figure 17.5 shows an example period lock by transaction, meaning that a transaction (e.g., **ABC Actual process assessment**) is locked for all periods.

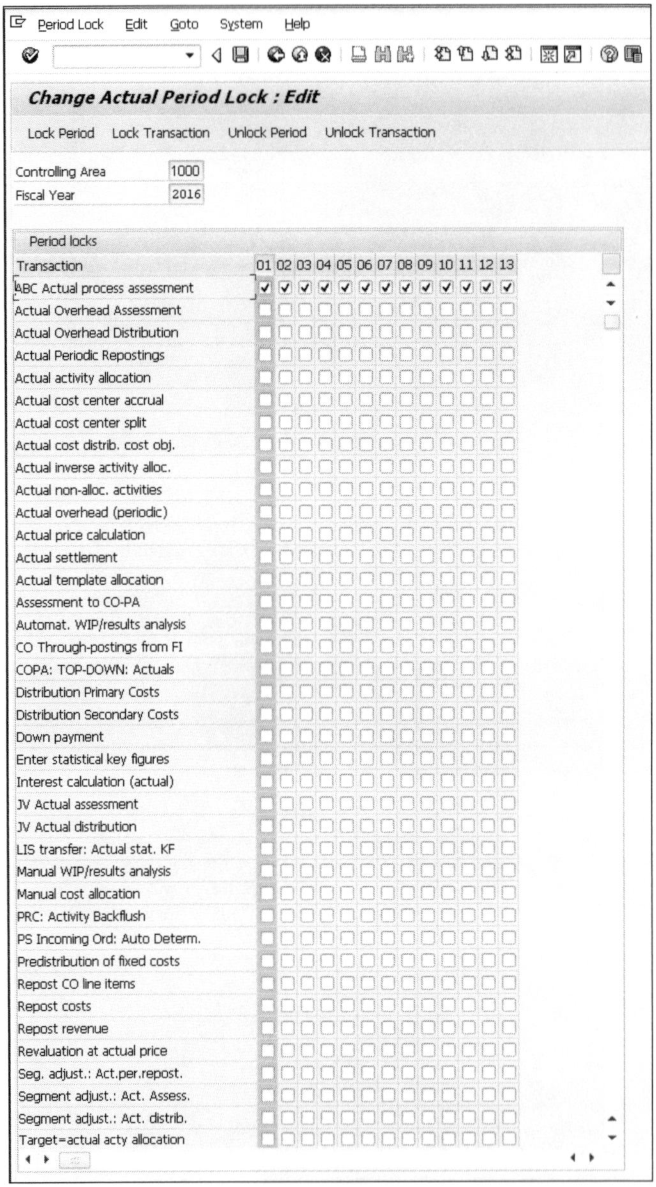

Figure 17.5 Period Lock by Transaction

Figure 17.6 shows an example of a period lock by transaction and period, meaning that specific periods are locked (e.g., periods **01–11**) for a specific transaction (e.g., **ABC**

Actual process assessment) while other periods (e.g., periods **12–16**) remain open for that same transaction.

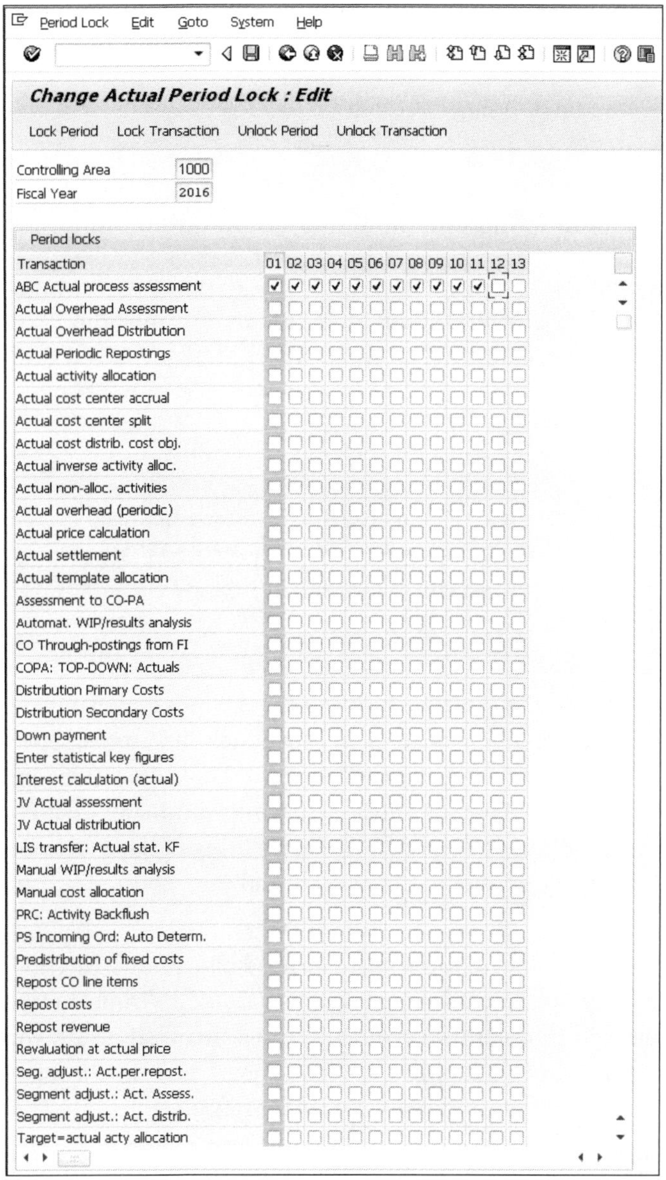

Figure 17.6 Period Lock by Transaction and Period

In this section, you learned the importance of locking periods in CO. Using Transaction OB52 to open and close FI periods isn't sufficient if you use CO. Period maintenance in CO is also required using Transaction OKP1. If you haven't done so already, make it a regular part of your close procedures to open/close CO periods in coordination with FI periods.

Now that you have a detailed understanding of CO period locks, let's discuss at a high level some other close tasks in CO.

17.1.2 Other Controlling Close Activities

In CO, there are several different period-end closing functions that can be executed. These transactions are spread across several submodules within CO, including Cost Element Accounting, Cost Center Accounting, Internal Orders, Activity-Based Costing, Product Cost Controlling, and CO-PA.

> **Note**
>
> The CO topics discussed in this section aren't exclusively considered financial close tasks. In fact, many CO transactions (e.g., settlements) can be executed many times throughout any given month. We emphasize them here simply because the timing of their execution at financial close is important to consider.

One of the most common functions in CO is the reposting of revenues and expenses. This activity includes the manual reposting of costs and revenues, line items, settlements, and activity allocations. If your company uses the reposting, allocation, and assessment functions in CO, you should make an effort to become familiar with these transactions. Even if you aren't the person responsible for executing CO transactions, you should be aware of when they are executed, by whom, and the expected impact on FI.

There are several types of cost allocations, including overhead allocations, distributions, and assessments. If your company uses these CO transactions, it's important to know the differences and how to troubleshoot errors when the financial result isn't what's expected. Build them into your close procedures and ensure that the timing of their execution is carefully coordinated with other close activities.

The main point to understand is that repostings, cost allocations, settlements, and several other CO functions need to be executed before financial close can be completed. The timing of all these close steps is important to ensure your internal and external financial reports accurately reflect the activity for the reporting period.

Let's briefly discuss in more detail the topic of CO *settlements*. The concept is relatively straightforward. When financial transactions are posted, a cost collecting object can be used to accumulate the costs, which at a later point in time will be settled to a final receiver. For example, an internal order (IO) is a short-lived cost collector whose costs will eventually be settled to a receiver, such as a material or cost center. Settlements can be executed for individual IOs using Transaction KO88 or collectively using Transaction KO8G.

The concept of settlements goes beyond CO. Some other examples of SAP objects that collect costs for settlement are Work Breakdown Structure (WBS) elements and Plant Maintenance (PM) orders. Furthermore, certain sales orders (SOs) may need to be settled to CO-PA. It's important to gain a full understanding of all your business processes to know the applicability of settlements across the SAP modules implemented at your company. There may be dependencies, so the timing of final settlements for a period needs to be coordinated across modules to coincide with financial close and the production of your financial statements. Think in terms of business processes when managing your company's month-end and year-end close activities.

This concludes our discussion of CO-related financial close activities. In the next section, we'll discuss integrated close and the MM module.

17.2 Integrated Financial Close and Materials Management

There is a close relationship between MM and FI-CO. Purchase requisitions (PRs), purchase orders (POs), goods receipts (GRs), and invoice receipts (IRs) are a string of related financial transactions, all of which are relevant to financial close. However, because MM is a separate module, it has its own tasks associated with financial close.

We begin with a discussion of period control.

17.2.1 Materials Management Period Maintenance

We've already seen separate period control transactions that exist in FI (i.e., Transaction OB52) and CO (Transaction OKP1). Now we'll introduce yet another, this one existing in the MM module.

At this point, you may be asking yourself, why does period control have to be managed separately in different modules? The simple answer is that each module was created separately with certain business processes in mind. For the finance professional, it's important to know that the ability to restrict financial activity exists in whatever module transactions are created that have a financial impact.

Now let's discuss the specifics of period control in MM. To open a new period, use Transaction MMPV or application menu path, **Logistics • Materials Management • Purchasing • Master Data • Subsequent Settlement • Vendor Rebate Arrangements • Environment • Condition/Arrangement • Environment • Material • Other • MMPV – Close Period**, as shown in Figure 17.7.

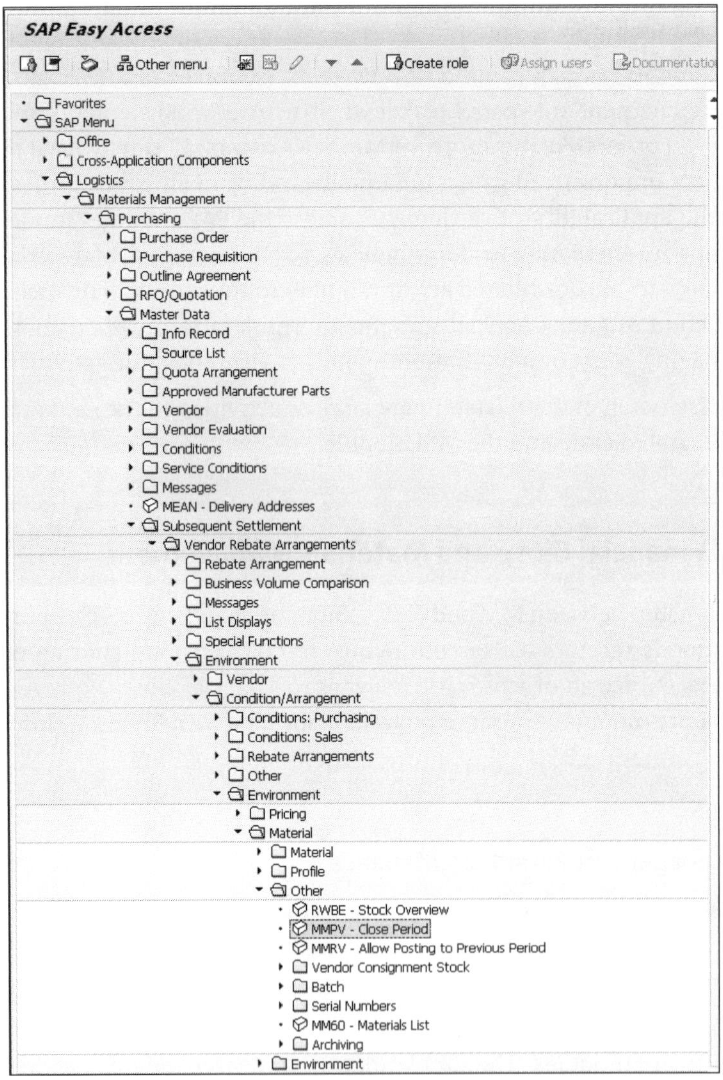

Figure 17.7 Transaction MMPV Application Menu Path

Double-click **MMPV – Close Period** from the menu path, and the **Close Period for Material Master Records** screen opens (Figure 17.8). On this screen, enter values in the **From company code/To company code**, **Period**, and **Fiscal year** fields. Notice that selection buttons exist for the following:

- **Check and close period**
- **Check period only**
- **Close period only**

You can also choose the following checkboxes:

- **Allow neg. qties in prev. per.** (allow negative quantities in previous period)
- **Allow neg. vals in prev. per.** (allow negative values in the previous period)

If negative quantities or values exist, and the respective checkbox isn't selected, the period check will fail, and the changing the period won't be permitted.

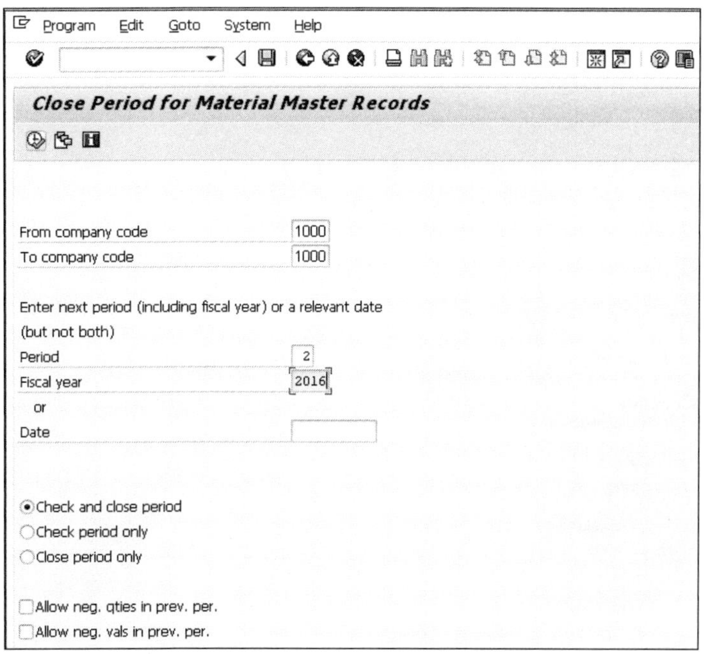

Figure 17.8 Close Period for Material Master Records

To display the current open MM period and to allow posting to the prior period, use Transaction MMRV or application menu path, **Logistics • Materials Management •**

Purchasing • Master Data • Subsequent Settlement • Vendor Rebate Arrangements • Environment • Condition/Arrangement • Environment • Material • Other • MMRV – Allow Posting to Previous Period, as shown in Figure 17.9.

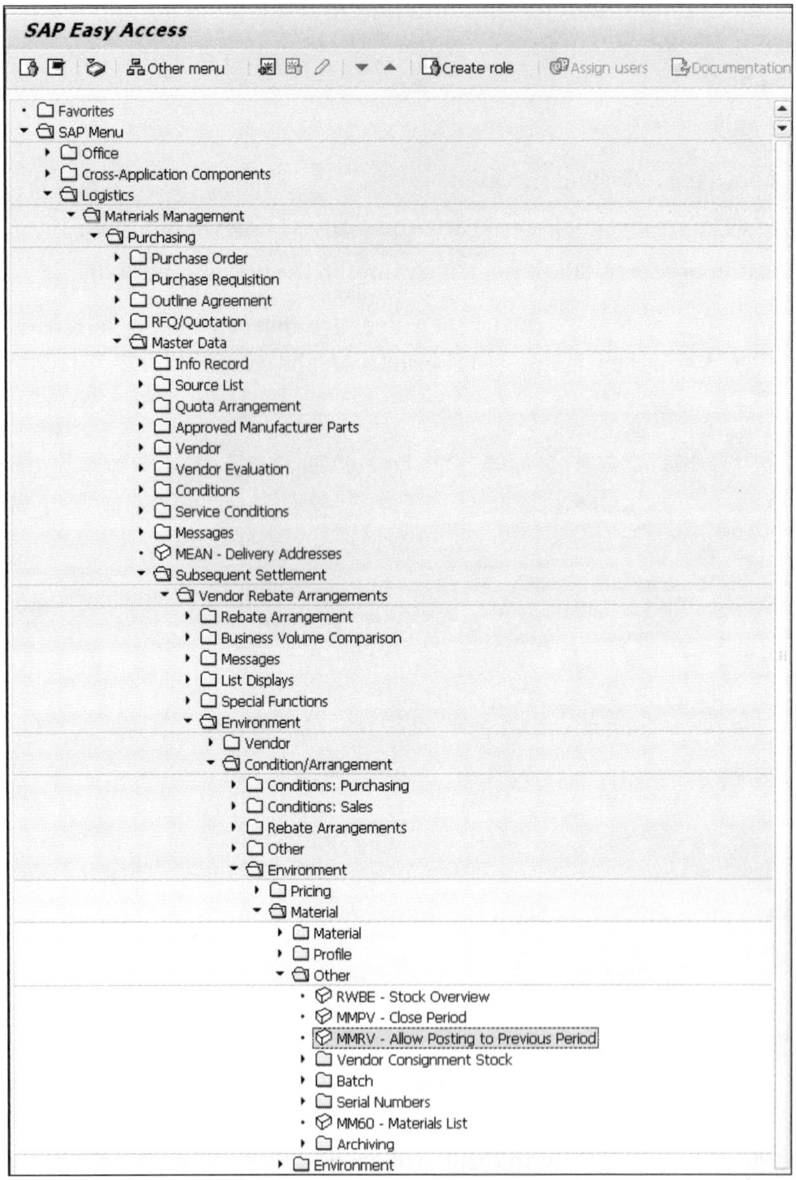

Figure 17.9 Transaction MMRV Application Menu Path

Double-click **MMRV – Allow Posting to Previous Period** from the menu path, and the initial screen in which to select a company code opens (Figure 17.10).

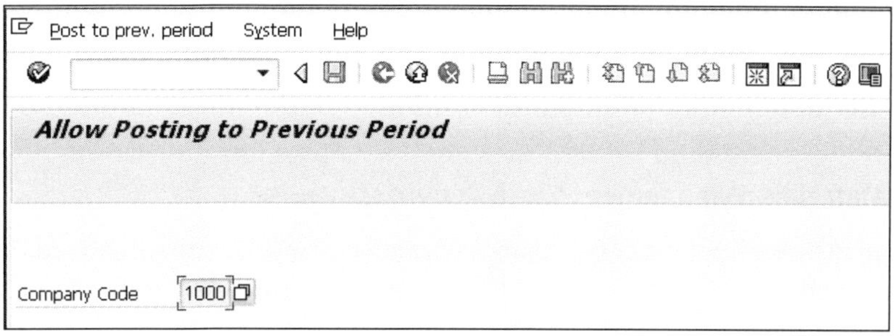

Figure 17.10 Company Code Selection Screen

Enter a company code and press `Enter`. The expanded **Allow Posting to Previous Period** screen opens (Figure 17.11). Notice that the current period, previous period, and last period in the previous year are listed. In addition, the **Post to previous period** area has two checkboxes. The first, **Allow posting to previous per.** allows postings to the previous MM period. By default, this option is selected, unless the second checkbox is chosen: **Disallow backposting generally**. This second checkbox prevents postings to the prior period and prevents the first checkbox (i.e., **Allow posting to previous per.**) from being set automatically during period close.

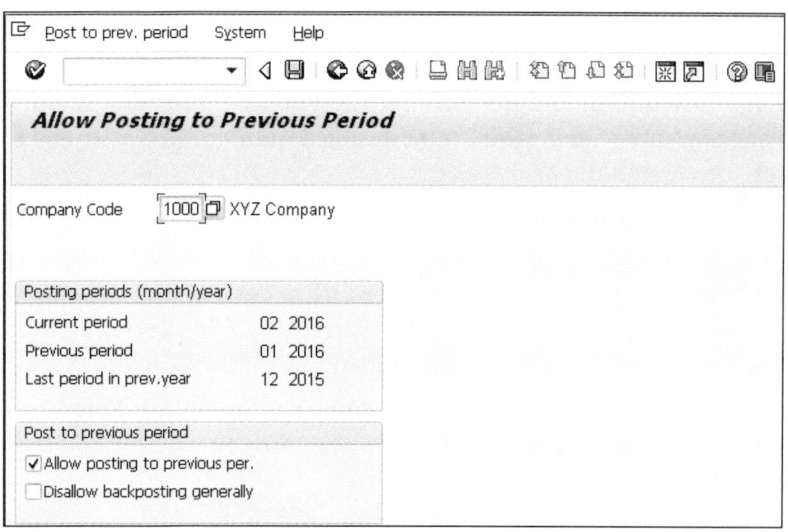

Figure 17.11 Allow Posting to Previous Period

As you can see, changing periods in MM is required. Opening and closing FI periods using Transaction OB52 isn't sufficient if you use MM. Make it a regular part of your close procedures to open/close MM periods along with the FI periods.

Now that you know how to manage period control in MM, we'll move on to some other MM activities that are important to integrated financial close.

17.2.2 Other Materials Management Close Activities

A review of open POs and PRs is a good business practice. These documents need to regularly be reviewed, edited, or canceled as the need arises. This activity should not be restricted to a time frame for month-end and year-end close, but it does become more important as you consider closing the books.

Follow-on transactions to open POs should also be reviewed. Are there GRs that haven't been processed? Have invoices been received that haven't been processed? Again, these steps aren't strictly month-end and year-end process steps, but just good business practices. Entering outstanding receipts and invoices in a timely fashion keeps the statuses of POs and PRs current and ensures that any financial impact is reflected in FI prior to closing the books.

Now let's discuss a few MM integration points that can have a substantial financial impact. These include the creation of AP invoices and the matching of GRs with IRs.

First, let's discuss AP invoices. It's important to make sure your company has good business processes in place to enter vendor invoices into AP. Processing IRs in a timely fashion has a downstream impact. It produces AP invoices in FI that are paid using the automated payment program (i.e., Transaction F110). Coordination between the FI and Logistics teams is important during month-end and year-end to ensure that all IRs are entered and paid.

The next topic we'll discuss is the GR/IR clearing function, which computes price variances between GR and IR and allocates variances to inventory, price differences, or the assignment object based on the valuation procedure in the material master and the settings in the PO line item. The values are stored in a G/L GR/IR clearing account and settled periodically using the GR/IR clearing function.

GR/IR account maintenance is a process that should be performed regularly, especially at month-end and year-end close. The system matches GRs with IRs based on the following information:

- PO
- PO item

- Type of PO item (e.g., standard PO, service PO)
- Indicator for invoice verification (e.g., GR-based invoice verification)
- Material or delivery costs

Variances are calculated by comparing each GR with its associated IR. IRs are recorded as a debit in the GR/IR clearing account, whereas GRs are recorded as credits. Price variances are computed using the lower of the GR quantity or the IR quantity. Because price variances are quantity based, it's possible to settle variances for partial deliveries and partial invoices.

There are several tools available for GR/IR maintenance:

- **Transaction MB5S – List of GR/IR Balances**
  This report compares the GR quantities and values relating to a PO with the invoice quantities and values for the same PO. The report is used to check GRs and IRs when the purchasing documents show some discrepancy.
- **Transaction MR11 – Maintain GR/IR Clearing Account**
  For differences between GR and IR with reference to a PO, entries in the GR/IR clearing account need to be cleared manually using Transaction MR11. There are many reasons that such a difference may occur. For example, an invoice may have been posted through AP instead of in procurement. Another example occurs if goods were received and returned for poor quality, but the vendor was accidently paid.
- **FI Clearing Transactions**
  When GR equals IR, both are still maintained in the G/L clearing account as open items until they are cleared. To clear open G/L items, FI transactions can be used, such as Transactions F.13 and F13E. After these GR and IR items are matched using a clearing program, individual line item statuses are changed from **Open** status to **Cleared**.

This concludes our discussion of MM. Next, let's move on to our final topic on integrated financial close: the Sales and Distribution (SD) module.

17.3 Integrated Financial Close and Sales and Distribution

Closing activities in the SD module are important for reporting sales and revenue. In some cases, billing documents don't post to costing-based CO-PA for the made-to-order scenario. In such a case, you need to settle to CO-PA using Transaction VA88.

In addition, other SD activities relevant to month-end and year-end close include the following:

- **Review open SOs**
  This is important to ensure that any sales cancellations, returns, or other follow-on functions have been entered into the system. Every effort should be made to ensure that SOs reflect their current status.
- **Execute billing**
  Using Transaction VF01, a billing run should be executed for relevant SOs. This ensures that customer invoices are created and that SO statuses are up to date and accurate at month-end and year-end close.
- **Open receivables**
  A review of open and overdue receivables is important for collections and cash forecasting. See Chapter 16 for more information on dunning. Make every effort to collect outstanding receivables and past due invoices prior to finalizing month-end and year-end close.

17.4 Summary

Financial close isn't isolated to FI. Many essential month-end and year-end close activities take place in FI, but SAP is an integrated system, which means that business processes cross modules and have dependencies. This chapter focused on some of the key FI financial close integration points with CO, MM, and SD.

Finance and accounting departments are usually the ones primarily accountable for financial close, but FI practitioners have to be able to step out of FI to understand integrated business scenarios and their dependencies in the close process. At a minimum, you need to be prepared to coordinate with logistics, sales, cost accounting, and other departments to ensure a smooth financial close.

In this chapter, we discussed period maintenance in MM and CO. Details of period maintenance in FI are covered in Chapter 16. Separate transaction codes exist in CO and MM for opening and closing periods. In MM, Transaction MMPV is used. In CO, the period maintenance transaction is Transaction OKP1. These transaction codes each operate differently.

In addition to period control, integrated close requires careful attention to transactions originating outside FI that have a financial impact. The specific non-FI document-related close tasks that need to be considered depend on your business processes and the SAP modules implemented.

Another common theme throughout integrated close is the need for document review, processing, reconciliation, and adjustments. For example, in both SD and MM, processes need to be in place to ensure the timeliness of posting follow-on documents. The accuracy of financial information and the status of SD and MM documents are dependent on the timely receipt and entry of documents.

We covered a lot of close steps in this chapter. The biggest takeaway is that as a financial professional, you need to understand your business processes. Many process steps take place outside of FI, yet can have a financial impact. As a result, your company depends on your cross-functional business process expertise to execute an accurate and timely financial close process.

Chapter 18
Understanding the Impact of SAP S/4HANA

In 2015, SAP introduced SAP S/4HANA, the next generation SAP Business Suite. This chapter presents several topics to help you understand what SAP S/4HANA is and the major changes in Financial Accounting in SAP. It's a resource that can help guide your journey into the digital era.

This chapter covers several major changes that have arrived with SAP S/4HANA, especially those relevant to FI. Prior chapters in this book covered SAP ERP 6.0 functionality through Enhancement Pack 8 (EHP 8), but SAP has announced that it will discontinue support of SAP ERP in 2025. Therefore, it's important for you to understand the direction SAP is going and to keep your knowledge of FI in SAP current. For those with even greater aspirations, this chapter can help you lead others in your company in this transformational journey into the digital era.

In this chapter, you'll learn what to expect in SAP S/4HANA. You'll understand how the underlying SAP HANA database enabled SAP to redesign the core code of the SAP Business Suite to be simpler, more efficient, and optimized. More importantly, this chapter gives you specific insights into the changes (i.e., simplifications) you'll encounter in the SAP S/4HANA design. No discussion on SAP S/4HANA would be complete without addressing the new embedded financial reporting capabilities, and the new user experience, SAP Fiori.

Note

This chapter covers SAP S/4HANA through the latest release as of the time of this writing, which is SAP S/4HANA 1709 (the on-premise version).

You'll be best prepared for a detailed discussion of specific finance and accounting changes in SAP S/4HANA after obtaining a basic knowledge of SAP HANA. Let's take a closer look at these changes in architecture.

18.1 Architectural Changes

The technologies available in SAP HANA are significant, and therefore the finance and accounting innovations in SAP S/4HANA are substantial, especially at the data structure level. Although the intent behind SAP S/4HANA was to minimize the impact to end users when migrating from SAP ERP, business process changes are required at times.

The foundational architecture change began at the database level with SAP HANA, which further evolved into a complete application development platform (ADP), SAP HANA. This enabled the other big architectural change, that is, the redesign of the business suite to optimize performance and eliminate redundant functionality.

Now, let's take a closer look at SAP HANA and examine how SAP S/4HANA compares to the classic SAP Business Suite.

18.1.1 SAP HANA Database

SAP S/4HANA is the new SAP Business Suite that came about due to innovations in database technology and architecture. Therefore, to fully grasp the concept of SAP S/4HANA, you need a basic understanding of the underlying technology: SAP HANA.

SAP HANA started with the SAP HANA database—an in-memory, columnar store, high-performance database. It was only through the innovations in the SAP HANA database that the limitations of online transactional processing (OLTP) databases could be overcome, which opened the doors to re-architect and optimize the SAP Business Suite. While OLTP databases are efficient at performing a multitude of tasks, such as inserting, reading, updating, and deleting records, online analytical processing (OLAP) databases are generally better suited for complex analytical queries and business intelligence.

Today, SAP HANA is marketed as an in-memory data platform. SAP HANA consists of the database and the ADP. It's much more than just a database, but the innovations in the database are critical to reaching new plateaus in computational performance. In turn, it increased computational performance and enabled the redesign of the classic SAP Business Suite.

SAP HANA's ADP includes database services, tools for advanced analytics, app development, data access, administration, security, and deployment option capabilities. In other words, SAP HANA and SAP S/4HANA together provide you with the capability to do transactional and analytical processing in a single database, all performed in-memory, real-time, and from a single source of truth for financial reporting.

18.1.2 New versus Classic SAP Business Suite

SAP S/4HANA is the next generation of SAP Business Suite. It should not be mistaken as the legal successor to any SAP Business Suite products. As the next generation software, SAP S/4HANA requires data migration from your legacy systems, unless you're already on a SAP HANA database. System migration is outside the scope of this book, but there are several SAP tools and migration paths available to make your transition to SAP S/4HANA a smooth one.

SAP Business Suite refers to functions in logistics and finance. SAP S/4HANA is referred to as the new business suite. SAP ERP 6.0 and prior versions are now referred to as the classic business suite.

Underlying the classic SAP ERP business suite are transactions, programs, tools, tables, and screens—essentially, everything you need for inputs, outputs, and basic reporting in a transactional system. There are many obstacles in attempting to do complex real-time analytics in an OLTP database, and more sophisticated analytics tools have been added to the SAP portfolio over the years.

The classic SAP Business Suite has evolved over a period of more than 25 years, with various pieces of system capabilities and integration created at different times. As a result, there is some redundancy in data structures and functionality.

Re-architecting the business suite, holistically, has its advantages. All the prior knowledge acquired in past product designs were comprehensively considered in the redesign. On top of that, the opportunity to optimize the business suite on an in-memory database with an innovative development platform (SAP HANA) is a formula for long-term success in the digital economy. SAP's vision was to create a combined OLTP and OLAP environment that is simpler and faster, and provides a single source of truth for real-time reporting. SAP HANA enabled SAP to completely redesign the business suite to accomplish this. In addition, with a holistic approach to the redesign of the business suite, SAP removed redundant functionality (referred to as the principle of one), eliminated many subledgers, and optimized the codebase.

For example, in SAP ERP, two General Ledgers (G/L) exist: classic G/L and new G/L. The new G/L was created mainly to allow multiple valuation methods. It also provided greater flexibility and began the process of eliminating some additional ledgers (for more information on the new G/L, see Appendix A). In SAP S/4HANA, SAP opted to go with the new G/L design and build on it further with the Universal Journal. In SAP S/4HANA, there is no classic G/L.

We've now covered some important design principles that explain why simply swapping out a legacy OLTP database with an SAP HANA database doesn't provide a fully optimized business suite. This approach, commonly known as SAP Business Suite on SAP HANA, is one that many SAP customers use to get a performance boost out of their systems. It also allows innovators to get a head start in learning about SAP HANA and gradually migrate to the new environment, rather than taking a big bang approach to system migration. However, achieving a fully optimized business suite is the end game that is achieved with SAP S/4HANA.

This concludes our discussion of the classic business suite in SAP ERP versus the new business suite in SAP S/4HANA. In the next section, we'll present specific types of simplifications in the SAP S/4HANA.

18.2 Financial Accounting Simplifications

Simplifications in SAP S/4HANA are re-architected product elements (i.e., tables, programs, screens, and other data structures) designed to eliminate redundant functionality, simplify the design, and optimize the core codebase for in-memory technology. Of course, there is a lot more software engineering behind it, which is beyond the scope of this book. The purpose of this section is to help you gain knowledge of specific SAP S/4HANA simplifications in Financial Accounting (FI).

Here, emphasis is placed on the more significant financial simplifications. However, financial processes don't operate in a vacuum. We introduce some discussion of SAP S/4HANA simplifications outside finance and accounting in Section 18.6.1 to lean your thinking toward system integration and business processes, rather than limiting your perspective to modular changes only.

Let's explore some of the specific SAP S/4HANA simplifications for FI, starting with the Universal Journal.

18.2.1 Universal Journal

Let's start this section by clarifying some terminology. The G/L in SAP S/4HANA is called the *Universal Journal*. Some sources also interchangeably refer to it as the Unified Journal. Both terms refer to the same thing: the new G/L line item table (table ACDOCA) in SAP S/4HANA. For consistency throughout this book, we'll only refer to the SAP S/4HANA G/L as the Universal Journal.

Before getting into the details of the Universal Journal, let's discuss the following limitations of the G/L in the classic business suite and the objectives in re-architecting it:

- **Classic G/L vs. new G/L**
  In SAP ERP, two versions of the G/L exist: the classic G/L and the new G/L (see Appendix A for details on the differences between the two). SAP's principle of one approach in building SAP S/4HANA is to provide one solution. In this case, SAP selected the new G/L. The classic G/L is no longer available in SAP S/4HANA.
- **Separate ledgers**
  Separate ledgers exist for material valuations, Controlling (CO), Asset Accounting (FI-AA), Fund Accounting, Special Purpose Ledgers, and more. This violates the single source of truth principle for financial reporting. It necessitates the need for ledger reconciliation and at times produces inconsistent financial results, depending on the data sources and subsets of data selected.
- **Scattered subledgers**
  Complicating matters further, subledgers were scattered about in the classic business suite (e.g., Accounts Payable [AP], Accounts Receivable [AR], FI-AA, etc.). All these separate ledgers and subledgers complicated reporting, increased the complexity of financial close, and introduced data integrity concerns.

The solution seems simple now that we have it available in SAP S/4HANA. That solution is the creation of a single line item table for all financial data with the data elements you need at the line item level to provide a single source of truth for financial reporting. The following are some additional benefits of the Universal Journal:

- Provides an extendable line item table so that custom fields can be added
- Allows on-the-fly data aggregations due to optimization on the SAP HANA in-memory database
- Enables real-time financial reporting on subsets of data filtered by any data element at the line item level in the ledger

In summary, the Universal Journal is a flexible single source of truth for financial reporting, which drastically simplifies the world of FI in SAP. By simplification of financial reporting, we refer to table ACDOCA as the single source of truth, the ability for real-time analysis, and flexibility in performing ad hoc queries.

It's important to realize that the advent of SAP HANA is what made the single ledger possible, as we discussed in Section 18.1.1.

Note

Refer to SAP Business Impact Note 2270339 for more details on changes to the G/L in SAP S/4HANA.

Now, let's dig into the details of the Universal Journal.

Figure 18.1 shows table ACDOCA, the Universal Journal. It incorporates data elements previously not housed in the G/L line item table, thereby providing a central source of financial information for housing transactions and reading data for reports.

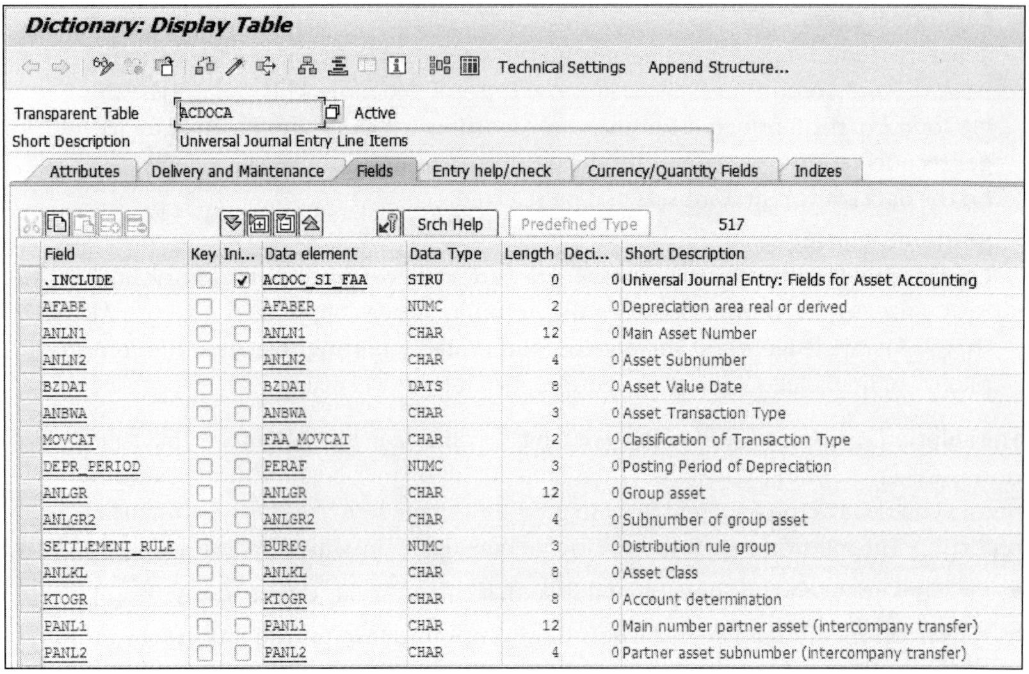

Figure 18.1 SAP S/4HANA Table ACDOCA

The Universal Journal is a significant change in the way financial transactions are stored and used for financial reporting. It not only houses core financial transactions but also incorporates line item detail for FI-AA, settlements, allocations, and more. This merging of cost accounting into the G/L is a huge accomplishment.

In re-architecting the business suite, SAP sought to minimize the impact to end users whenever possible. In FI terms, this means that even though the transactional data is stored in a single SAP S/4HANA table (table ACDOCA), most of the transactions end users are familiar with are the same or similar, with some exceptions.

The Universal Journal not only provides an extendable table (table ACDOCA) but is also optimized for SAP HANA. This makes it the central mantelpiece of SAP S/4HANA Finance and the new business suite in SAP S/4HANA.

Both classic G/L and new G/L types can be migrated to the Universal Journal in SAP S/4HANA, but there are additional considerations. For example, you can't introduce new ledgers or currencies during the migration.

If you plan to migrate from the classic G/L to the Universal Journal, you'll experience more changes in functionality, such as foreign currency evaluation and balance carryforwards. You may also need to reconsider your ledger design for future needs and consider new functionality such as document splitting. *Document splitting* is a system capability that splits document line items based on "characteristics" to achieve financial reporting capabilities at a lower level of detail, such as by segment, fund, business area, and so on.

One huge advantage of the Universal Journal, no matter your migration path, is that it includes the CO module. In essence, this means that CO transactions have been merged into the Universal Journal, with transaction data and documents for them stored in table ACDOCA. Moreover, the single source of truth concept for financial reporting comes into the picture because now FI and CO use the same data source for most financial reporting (see CO documents in Figure 18.2).

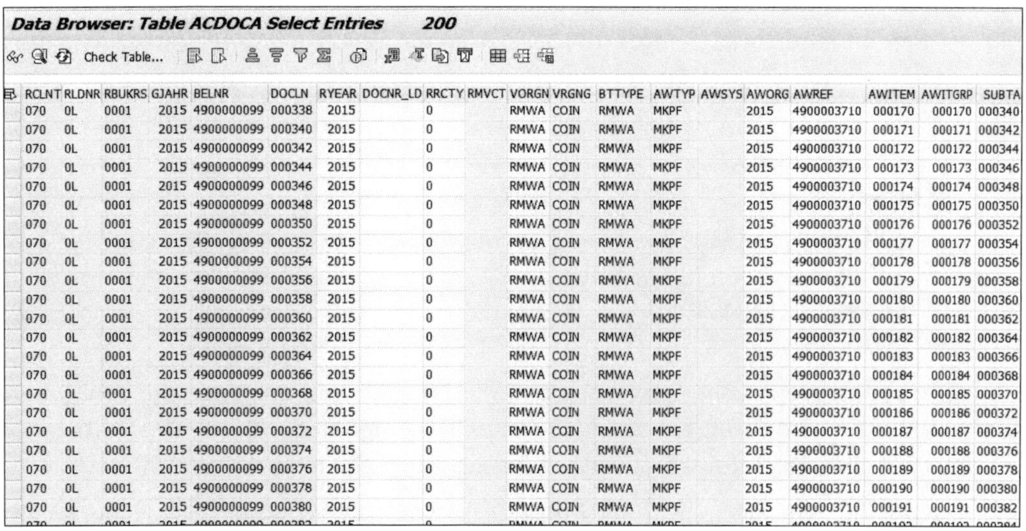
Data Browser: Table ACDOCA Select Entries 200

Check Table...

RCLNT	RLDNR	RBUKRS	GJAHR	BELNR	DOCLN	RYEAR	DOCNR_LD	RRCTY	RMVCT	VORGN	VRGNG	BTTYPE	AWTYP	AWSYS	AWORG	AWREF	AWITEM	AWITGRP	SUBTA
070	0L	0001	2015	4900000099	000338	2015		0		RMWA	COIN	RMWA	MKPF		2015	4900003710	000170	000170	000340
070	0L	0001	2015	4900000099	000340	2015		0		RMWA	COIN	RMWA	MKPF		2015	4900003710	000171	000171	000342
070	0L	0001	2015	4900000099	000342	2015		0		RMWA	COIN	RMWA	MKPF		2015	4900003710	000172	000172	000344
070	0L	0001	2015	4900000099	000344	2015		0		RMWA	COIN	RMWA	MKPF		2015	4900003710	000173	000173	000346
070	0L	0001	2015	4900000099	000346	2015		0		RMWA	COIN	RMWA	MKPF		2015	4900003710	000174	000174	000348
070	0L	0001	2015	4900000099	000348	2015		0		RMWA	COIN	RMWA	MKPF		2015	4900003710	000175	000175	000350
070	0L	0001	2015	4900000099	000350	2015		0		RMWA	COIN	RMWA	MKPF		2015	4900003710	000176	000176	000352
070	0L	0001	2015	4900000099	000352	2015		0		RMWA	COIN	RMWA	MKPF		2015	4900003710	000177	000177	000354
070	0L	0001	2015	4900000099	000354	2015		0		RMWA	COIN	RMWA	MKPF		2015	4900003710	000178	000178	000356
070	0L	0001	2015	4900000099	000356	2015		0		RMWA	COIN	RMWA	MKPF		2015	4900003710	000179	000179	000358
070	0L	0001	2015	4900000099	000358	2015		0		RMWA	COIN	RMWA	MKPF		2015	4900003710	000180	000180	000360
070	0L	0001	2015	4900000099	000360	2015		0		RMWA	COIN	RMWA	MKPF		2015	4900003710	000181	000181	000362
070	0L	0001	2015	4900000099	000362	2015		0		RMWA	COIN	RMWA	MKPF		2015	4900003710	000182	000182	000364
070	0L	0001	2015	4900000099	000364	2015		0		RMWA	COIN	RMWA	MKPF		2015	4900003710	000183	000183	000366
070	0L	0001	2015	4900000099	000366	2015		0		RMWA	COIN	RMWA	MKPF		2015	4900003710	000184	000184	000368
070	0L	0001	2015	4900000099	000368	2015		0		RMWA	COIN	RMWA	MKPF		2015	4900003710	000185	000185	000370
070	0L	0001	2015	4900000099	000370	2015		0		RMWA	COIN	RMWA	MKPF		2015	4900003710	000186	000186	000372
070	0L	0001	2015	4900000099	000372	2015		0		RMWA	COIN	RMWA	MKPF		2015	4900003710	000187	000187	000374
070	0L	0001	2015	4900000099	000374	2015		0		RMWA	COIN	RMWA	MKPF		2015	4900003710	000188	000188	000376
070	0L	0001	2015	4900000099	000376	2015		0		RMWA	COIN	RMWA	MKPF		2015	4900003710	000189	000189	000378
070	0L	0001	2015	4900000099	000378	2015		0		RMWA	COIN	RMWA	MKPF		2015	4900003710	000190	000190	000380
070	0L	0001	2015	4900000099	000380	2015		0		RMWA	COIN	RMWA	MKPF		2015	4900003710	000191	000191	000382

Figure 18.2 Transaction Types in Universal Journal

In SAP S/4HANA, secondary cost elements are in the chart of accounts and created using Transaction FS00, where there is a standard account group available for them. There is no longer a need for the reconciliation ledger or to transfer secondary postings from CO to G/L.

The introduction of the Universal Journal is a core design change in SAP S/4HANA. This ledger redesign impacts the G/L data structure significantly, while at the same time serving as the central hub for changes in SAP S/4HANA Finance. With the Universal Journal also comes some of the most profound benefits of SAP S/4HANA to users in finance, accounting, and controlling. These include one source of the truth for financial reporting, a flexible ledger, embedded analytics capabilities, faster close, and greater simplicity.

Note

For further reference, see SAP Note 2431747 on G/L incompatibility changes in SAP S/4HANA compared to classic SAP ERP releases.

This concludes our discussion of the Universal Journal. The next simplification item we'll discuss is Asset Accounting (FI-AA).

18.2.2 New Asset Accounting

There are substantial changes to FI Asset Accounting (FI-AA) in SAP S/4HANA, such as the inclusion of asset fields in the Universal Journal and replacement transaction codes.

Note

See Section 18.6.1 for additional discussion of changes to the FI-AA data structure as laid out in SAP Business Impact Note 2270387. We'll discuss business impact notes further in Section 18.6.3.

To use the new Asset Accounting in SAP S/4HANA, you must use the new G/L. If you're currently using the classic G/L and will be migrating to SAP S/4HANA, the new G/L is activated automatically in converting from SAP ERP to SAP S/4HANA.

A fundamental change from SAP ERP is that transaction types are no longer restricted to individual depreciation areas. In new Asset Accounting, you can create new postings to a specific depreciation area and accounting principle and adjust line items using the document change function. In addition, the user exit `APCF_DIFFERENT_AMOUNTS_GET` isn't supported in SAP S/4HANA.

> **Note**
>
> SAP Business Impact Note 2270388 provides a broad-based overview of the simplifications in FI-AA.

Like the Universal Journal, new Asset Accounting makes some significant changes in SAP S/4HANA to support the merging of FI-AA transaction detail into the Universal Journal. In addition, several other improvements and optimizations for SAP HANA were made. Let's explore these changes, as follows:

- **No more reconciliation**
  Reconciliation between FI-AA and G/L is no longer necessary because the asset subledger line item detail now exists in table ACDOCA. Therefore, the classic FI-AA to G/L reconciliation programs (e.g., program RAABST01) don't exist in SAP S/4HANA.
- **Parallel valuations**
  Functionality has been added to parallel valuations. In the new Asset Accounting, you must choose to use either the ledger approach or the accounts approach with parallel valuations—you can't use both. You're no longer restricted to using **Depreciation Area 01** to record your leading asset valuations. SAP S/4HANA posts in real time to both the actual leading valuations and parallel valuations. As a result, delta depreciation areas are no longer needed or supported. The new Asset Accounting posts real-time valuations for all accounting principles.
- **Subledger elimination**
  Often in discussions regarding SAP S/4HANA, you'll hear about how the Universal Journal reduces the need for subledgers. FI-AA is one example of a subledger that has been eliminated through the integration of transaction data into the Universal Journal. New Asset Accounting posts in real time for all accounting principles and no longer requires redundant data storage.
- **Transaction restrictions**
  Transaction codes in new Asset Accounting are no longer restricted to individual depreciation areas. Instead, when a transaction is entered, you can restrict it to an accounting principle or a specific depreciation area.

A point of emphasis with new Asset Accounting is that by putting together the new Asset Accounting with the Universal Journal, you've eliminated the need to reconcile the G/L to FI-AA subledgers. As previously stated, the FI-AA subledgers no longer exist. This can be a difficult concept to grasp. To put it simply, all asset financial transactions are posted in table ACDOCA (Universal Journal) with the asset number. By capturing the asset number at the line item level, the only limitation becomes the ability to obtain real-time access to that data and having the capability to efficiently aggregate the data however you like. This is, of course, possible through the SAP HANA in-memory database.

With the data structure changes and the elimination of subledgers in new Asset Accounting, there is an impact on financial close, which we'll discuss further in the next section.

There are numerous types of transactions in new Asset Accounting, including acquisition, revaluation, improvement, depreciation, retirement, and more. In SAP S/4HANA, all of them are updated in real time in the Universal Journal for all depreciation areas.

There are three types of transactions:

- New transactions
- Redirected transactions
- Obsolete transactions

Note

The **Transactions** section of SAP Business Impact Note 2270388 summarizes the changes in FI-AA transaction codes.

When appropriate, legacy transactions have been replaced with new transactions that end in "L". These new transactions have screens that allow for the input of **Depreciation Area** and **Accounting Principle**, which enables postings regarding specific accounting principles.

A complete list of these new transactions is as follows:

- Transaction AB01L: Create Asset
- Transaction ABAAL: Execute Unplanned Depreciation
- Transaction ABAKL: Last Retirement on Group Asset
- Transaction ABAOL: Asset Sale without Customer
- Transaction ABAVL: Asset Retirement by Scrapping
- Transaction ABAWL: Revalue Asset

- Transaction ABGFL: Enter Credit Memo in Year after Invoice
- Transaction ABGLL: Enter Credit Memo in Year of Invoice
- Transaction ABIFL: Investment Support
- Transaction ABMAL: Execute Manual Depreciation
- Transaction ABMRL: Manual Transfer of Reserves
- Transaction ABNAL: Post Capitalization
- Transaction ABNEL: Post Subsequent Revenue
- Transaction ABNKL: Subsequent Costs
- Transaction ABSOL: Miscellaneous Transactions
- Transaction ABSTL: Reconciliation Analysis FI-AA
- Transaction ABUML: Transfer within Company Code
- Transaction ABZEL: Acquisition from In-House Production
- Transaction ABZOL: Acquisition with Automatic Offsetting Entry
- Transaction ABZPL: Acquisition from Affiliated Company
- Transaction ABZUL: Writeup

An example of a redirected transaction is the legacy Transaction AB01 (Create Asset Transactions). If you attempt to use this system transaction in SAP S/4HANA, you're redirected to the new Transaction AB01L. An example of an obsolete transaction in SAP S/4HANA is Transaction AJRW, used in legacy to change the FI-AA fiscal year.

On a final note related to the new Asset Accounting, see SAP Note 2270388 for a complete list of FI-AA programs that are either obsolete programs or have been changed in SAP S/4HANA. You should familiarize yourself with them. This becomes more important as you do custom code analysis and find any custom programs that are cloned from obsolete programs.

This concludes our discussion of SAP S/4HANA FI-AA simplifications. We've only scratched the surface. Our hope is that by highlighting some of the key FI-AA changes here, you can grasp the extent of the changes in new Asset Accounting, will research further, and are directed to the right resources to plan accordingly.

In the next section, we'll discuss some ways in which financial simplifications in SAP S/4HANA have impacted financial close.

18.2.3 Financial Close

The SAP S/4HANA redesign does impact your close procedures in ways that are important to understand. The good news is that the changes will further simplify the financial close process.

Related to the new Asset Accounting, fiscal year-end close no longer requires that you execute Transaction AJRW (i.e., program RAJAWE00) to separately change the fiscal year in Asset Accounting. In other words, this one step in the fiscal year close process has been eliminated due to the integration of the balance carryforward functions for the Universal Journal and new Asset Accounting.

For those of you who are responsible for FI-AA, this should excite you. The balance carryforward process in G/L carries forward values for each asset and G/L account simultaneously. Gone are the hours spent reconciling fixed asset subledgers against G/L account balances. In addition, when balance carryforward has been executed for all the ledgers in SAP S/4HANA, the new year is automatically open for new Asset Accounting.

Now, let's move on to a key logistics change to the material ledger in SAP S/4HANA.

18.3 Change in Material Number Length

The objective of this chapter isn't simply to inform you about specific SAP S/4HANA changes within FI, but to broaden your perspective to consider holistically how SAP S/4HANA has changed from SAP Business Suite.

With that said, let's briefly touch on a big master data change in Logistics. In SAP S/4HANA, the length of the material master has been extended from 18 to 40 characters. This is the **MATNR** field in the database. SAP has adapted the standard data elements, structures, internal interfaces, and so on. However, somewhere in your business process, there is likely some custom code with material numbers that must be adapted.

> **Note**
>
> For more details on the material number, refer to SAP Note 2267140.

The extended material number in SAP S/4HANA is switched off by default. If it's not switched on, SAP S/4HANA still works with shorter versions of the extended fields.

Switching the extended material number on has widespread implications. For finance and accounting, the frontend procurement transactions use material numbers (e.g., Transaction ME21N Create Purchase Order). Therefore, we have a vested interest in ensuring the success of Logistics and need to be aware of significant changes that may impact the business process.

If your company intends to turn on the extended material number functionality, the capability is available for using the full length of 40 characters in the material master. The following are some examples of things to consider in relation to this change:

- Material numbers in external interfaces
- Multisystem landscapes that contain or exchange material numbers
- Reporting
- Master data maintenance and creation processes
- Functional modules, Business Application Programming Interfaces (BAPIs), IDocs, structures, and so on that SAP has adapted but need to be tested in your system
- Communication partners needing adjustment for new data formats

This concludes our discussion of specific business suite simplifications in SAP S/4HANA. In the next section, we discuss changes to financial reporting in SAP S/4HANA via embedded analytics.

18.4 Embedded Analytics

From a technical perspective, SAP S/4HANA embedded analytics is referred to as a set of analytical features that provide the capability of performing real-time analytics on transactional data. SAP delivers virtual data models (VDM) and core data services (CDS) views to present data. VDMs are structured SAP HANA database views with consistent modeling rules used for SAP S/4HANA. Data is accessed via SQL and OData requests. With SAP HANA extended application services, you can create views in a CDS document to allow you to view data in the new business suite in ways you're accustomed to in the classic business suite.

The intent of this section isn't to delve into the technical details, but rather to provide you with enough relevant information on the topic to assist you in working with FI in SAP S/4HANA Finance. First, let's begin with a brief description of how SAP S/4HANA embedded analytics is made possible.

Prior to SAP HANA and SAP S/4HANA, the OLTP database provided certain limitations within the SAP ERP data structure (as discussed in Section 18.1.1). In turn, processing limitations restricted your ability in FI to retrieve large quantities of financial data in a timely manner and restricted the ability to aggregate the data on the fly. With SAP S/4HANA, you have the tools and transactional data needed to do real-time analytical processing from one source of truth. The SAP HANA database provides the in-memory processing capability, and the Universal Journal gives you a central data source for financial reporting.

To sum up the concept of embedded analytics in SAP S/4HANA, you now have added capabilities embedded in FI-CO to enable direct reporting, data analysis, and data aggregations with real-time financial data pulling from a single source: the Universal Journal. While it's true that more reporting in SAP S/4HANA can be done directly out of the Universal Journal, it's wrong to assume that you can totally eliminate the need for additional reporting tools such as SAP Business Warehouse (SAP BW) and SAP BusinessObjects Business Intelligence (SAP BusinessObjects BI). The point is that when you convert to SAP S/4HANA, it's necessary to evaluate all your reporting requirements and to reassess when and how they will be provided.

Let's move on to an important topic related to reporting and viewing financial data: SAP compatibility views. A *compatibility view* is essentially a named query that seamlessly replaces a classic view. It transparently accesses the same data via the Data Dictionary and presents it to the user without the user experiencing any change.

As changes to the core data model of the business suite took place, SAP took into consideration the need to be nondisruptive regarding customers and the large amount of code that builds on top of the classic business suite data model. Compatibility views are the solution to still being able to use custom code where possible when reading from the database. Let's discuss this using FI-AA data as an example.

In the classic business suite, actual FI-AA transaction data posted in tables ANEP, ANEA, ANLOP, and so on are now posted in the Universal Journal (table ACDOCA). However, through compatibility views, you can continue using existing reports to view this asset data. The compatibility view does this by redirecting selections from the old tables to the new data store (i.e., table ACDOCA) and then presenting the data in the format from the original tables.

In this section, our discussion of SAP S/4HANA embedded analytics was just an introduction to the topic. It's important for your company to do a complete review of reporting requirements in its transition to SAP S/4HANA. A holistic analysis of reporting needs must be considered in the context of new capabilities in SAP S/4HANA tools, such as compatibility views, and SAP Fiori.

Now let's move on to discuss SAP Fiori in more detail.

18.5 SAP Fiori

SAP Fiori 2.0 is the latest user interface (UI) for SAP S/4HANA. SAP Fiori is a role-based, tile-driven user experience that is flexible and personalized.

One of the most obvious and notable changes brought by modern leaps in digital technology is in the UI, specifically SAP Fiori. Many users don't normally welcome changes to visual tools that take them away from what they are familiar with. However, there are many new features that make SAP Fiori an improved experience over SAP GUI. For example, in Figure 18.3, you see the SAP GUI standard menu.

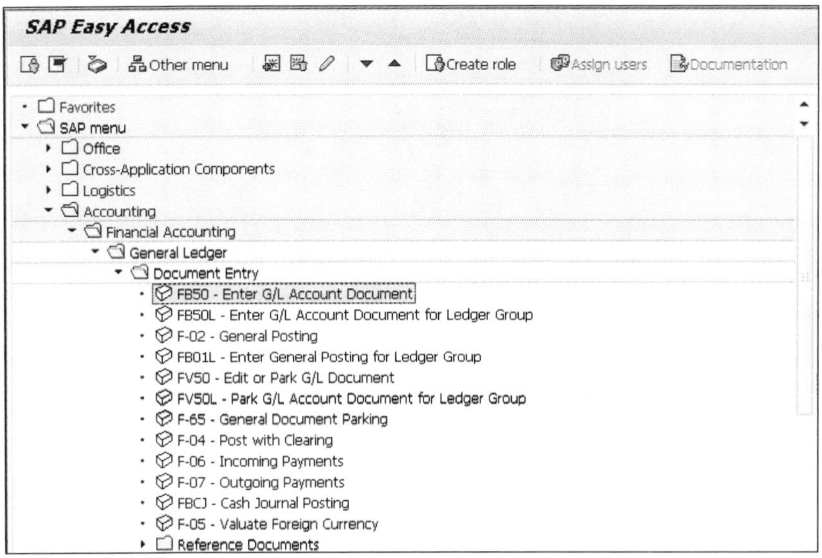

Figure 18.3 SAP GUI

Compare that to the SAP Fiori launchpad in Figure 18.4. The SAP Fiori launchpad is a key component of the solution. The launchpad is the web-based interface with all your available SAP Fiori apps, based on your role. It's your access point to SAP Fiori apps, regardless of the device you're using.

The launchpad home page displays tiles, which are business applications that you can launch. These business applications can be business transactions, reports, master data creation and maintenance, analytics applications, and more. As shown in the example launchpad in Figure 18.4, it has a flexible design regarding the placement and grouping of apps.

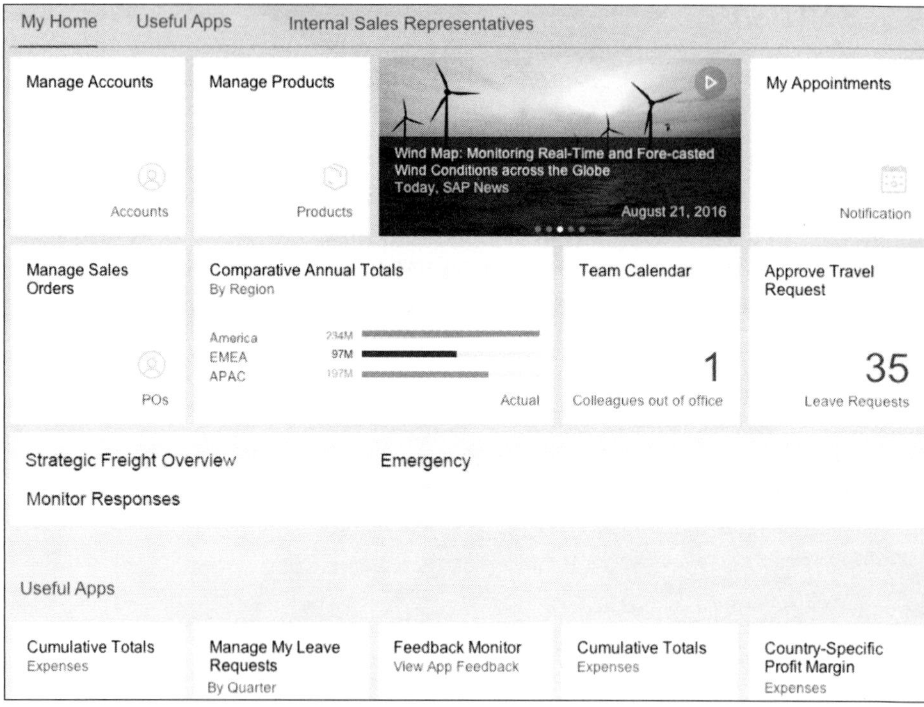

Figure 18.4 Example SAP Fiori Launchpad

As you can see, the user experience has evolved from a menu-driven approach based on transaction codes with the SAP GUI, to a personalize dashboard approach in SAP Fiori. Graphics, nice color schemes, and familiar tiles make the SAP Fiori launchpad an enjoyable user experience. It also presents you with work tasks that immediately need your attention and provides key performance indicators (KPIs) with real-time data at a glance.

Such a big change to the SAP user experience was long overdue, but don't think the SAP GUI is gone with SAP S/4HANA; it isn't. Most likely, you'll be able to access transactions the old way through the SAP GUI if your company's policy permits it and your platform supports access to it. For now, think of SAP Fiori as the best practice and SAP GUI as an alternative.

A key point to keep in mind is that the SAP user experience needs to change to accommodate the needs of today's end users who need access anywhere, anytime, and from any device. SAP Fiori meets these needs. When your company migrates from SAP ERP 6.0 to SAP S/4HANA, marrying that effort with the implementation of SAP Fiori is ideal.

Let's explore a bit further into SAP Fiori, from its design principles to the SAP Fiori apps reference library.

18.5.1 Design Principles

SAP Fiori was designed with the objectives to simplify the user experience, personalize it, and make it enjoyable. It's role based and designed around the way people work. This user-centered design concept is based on the premise that if users enjoy the experience, they will be more productive.

SAP Fiori is also designed with the idea in mind of being a harmonized user experience across SAP applications and platforms. In other words, the UI should have a consistent look and feel, regardless of whether you're accessing an SAP system from a laptop, tablet, or phone. The current SAP Fiori 2.0 release uses a visual theme named Belize. As an end user, you'll come to appreciate this. You'll be able to recognize SAP regardless of the application you're running and regardless of the device you're using. With SAP Fiori, you'll be able to look at a screen and recognize SAP and Belize.

The SAP design concept behind SAP Fiori consists of the five core design principles listed in Table 18.1.

Editing Option	Description
Role-based	Deliver the right information based on an individual's role at the right time and from any device.
Adaptive	Get instant, relevant insight from any device (e.g., mobile apps, desktop, laptop).
Simple	Highlight your most important tasks, functions, and activities.
Coherent	Deliver a consistent user experience across the enterprise (e.g., create sales order, issue goods to customer, process payment receipt, customer analytics, etc.).
Delightful	Enrich the end user experience to make it intuitive and easy with SAP Fiori apps.

Table 18.1 SAP Core Design Principles

Now that you have a basic understanding of how SAP Fiori was redesigned and why, let's discuss how you access available SAP Fiori apps and look at an example in SAP S/4HANA Finance.

18.5.2 SAP Fiori Apps Reference Library

A key reference point for SAP Fiori is the SAP Fiori apps reference library, where you can explore SAP Fiori apps currently available and find resources to help plan your SAP Fiori implementation. The SAP Fiori apps reference library is available at *https://fioriappslibrary.hana.ondemand.com/sap/fix/externalViewer/*. Figure 18.5 shows the welcome page with **Categories** to the left for filtering SAP Fiori apps.

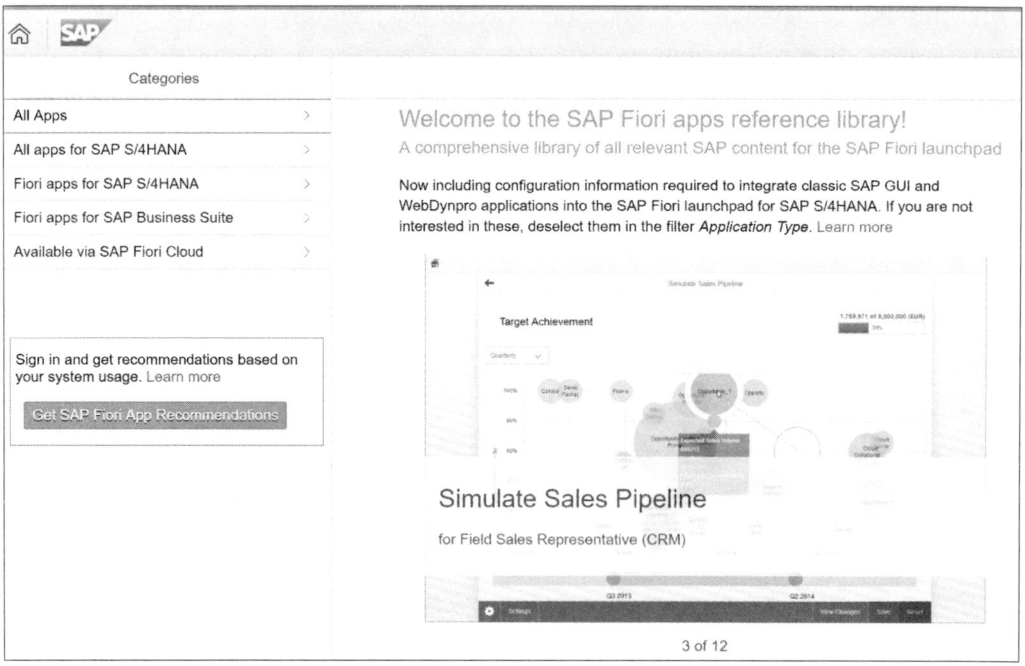

Figure 18.5 SAP Fiori Apps Reference Library

In addition to being able to find all the SAP Fiori apps available today in the SAP Fiori apps reference library, you can also find information on app installation, configuration, and other useful resources at this website.

Let's look at an example of a SAP Fiori app in SAP S/4HANA Finance so you get an understanding of how to navigate the SAP Fiori apps reference library. Under **Categories** in the top left of Figure 18.5, there are several ways to navigate the SAP Fiori apps reference library. For this example, select **Fiori apps for SAP S/4HANA**, which takes you to the screen shown in Figure 18.6.

Next, click on **by Product Version,** and the **Product Version** selection screen appears (Figure 18.7).

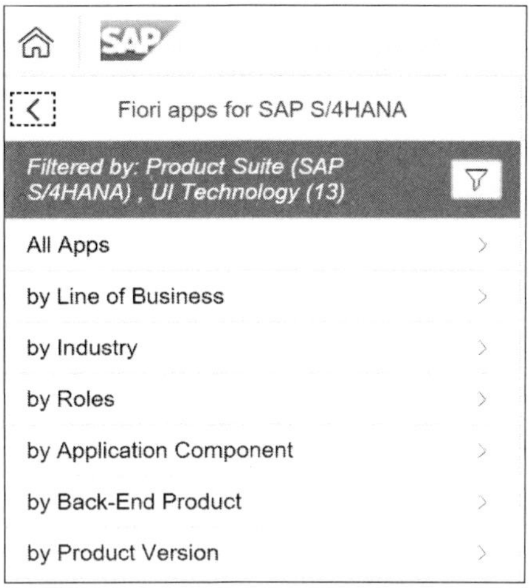

Figure 18.6 SAP Fiori Apps for SAP S/4HANA Screen

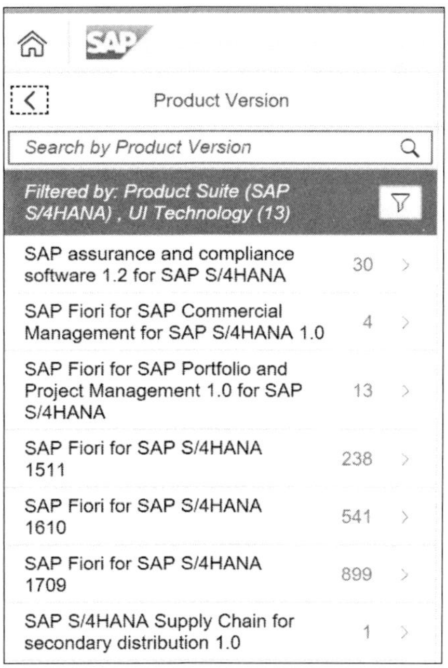

Figure 18.7 Product Version Selection Screen

Select the **SAP Fiori for SAP S/4HANA 1709** option, and the 899 apps available are listed by role (Figure 18.8).

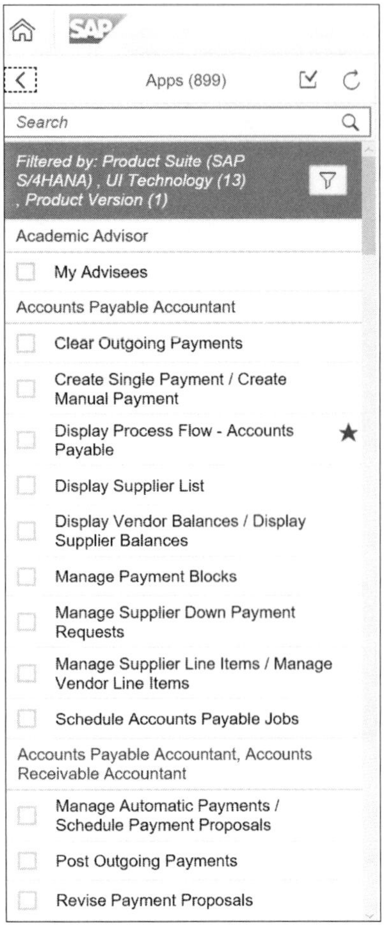

Figure 18.8 Available Apps for SAP S/4HANA 1709

Under the **Accounts Payable Accountant** role, select the **Create Single Payment/Create Manual Payment** checkbox in Figure 18.8, and click `Enter`. Details on the SAP Fiori app appear (Figure 18.9). In the header, next to **Application Type**, the Create Single Payment app is listed as a transaction. In the **PRODUCT FEATURES** area, a description of the app is provided, along with references to **App Documentation** and a link to additional resources on solution capabilities.

The **Implementation Information** area (Figure 18.10) of the Create Single Payment SAP Fiori app contains details and links useful to the installation, configuration, and extensibility of the app. It also describes the applicability of this app in SAP Fiori Cloud.

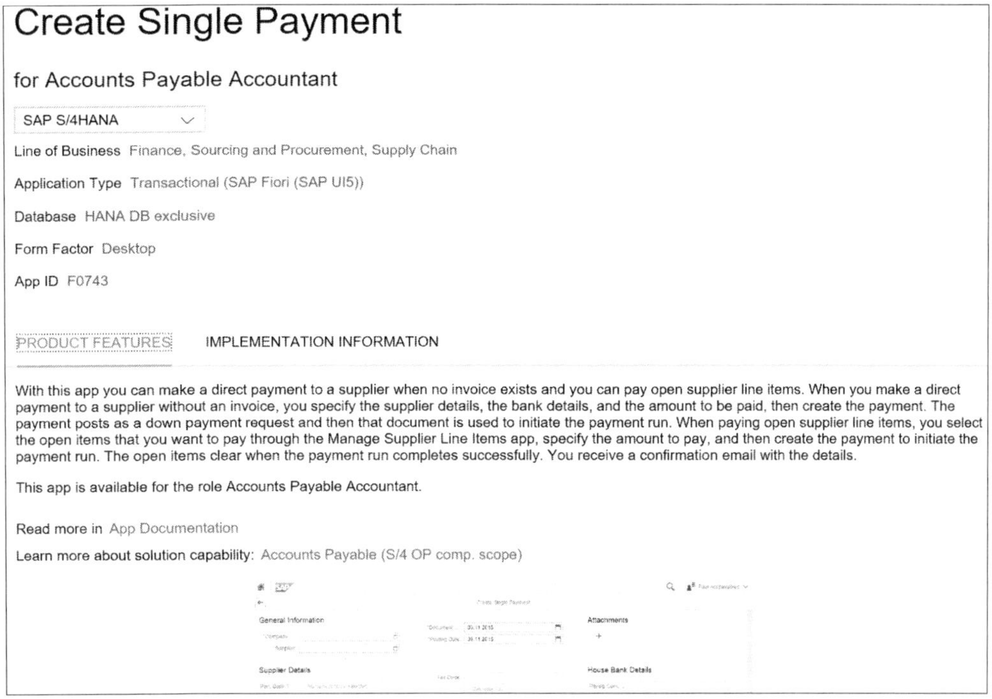

Figure 18.9 Create Single Payment SAP Fiori App

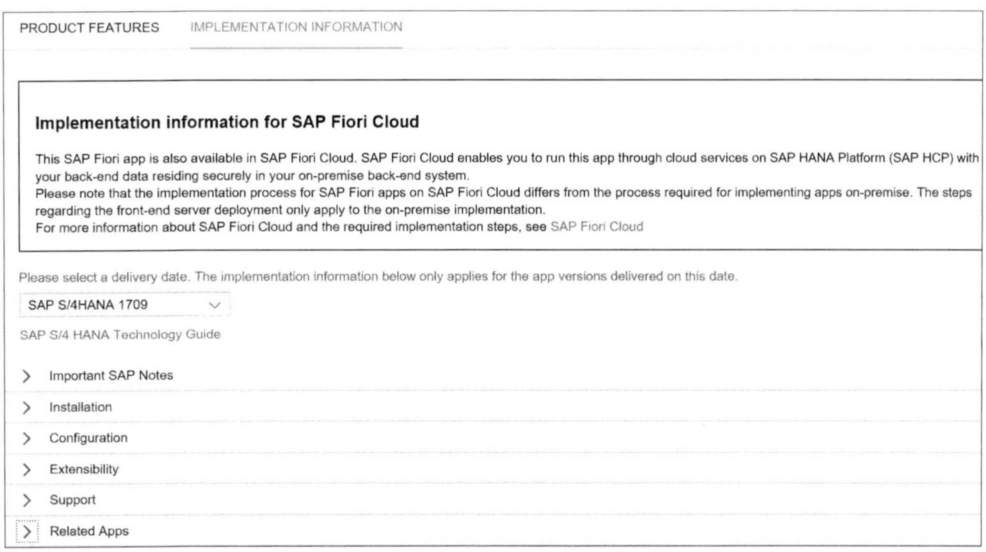

Figure 18.10 Implementation Information for the SAP Fiori App

This concludes our discussion of the SAP Fiori apps reference library. You should now be able to navigate the SAP Fiori apps reference library to explore SAP Fiori apps for SAP S/4HANA Finance and obtain useful information on their use, installation, configuration, and more.

In the next section, we'll discuss further reference materials.

18.6 Further Reference Materials for SAP S/4HANA Simplifications

This section introduces you to additional terminology and reference material useful to you in your journey to SAP S/4HANA. We'll discuss the SAP simplification list, simplification categories, and business impact notes. All of these will prove to be useful reference points, whether you're just beginning to plan your migration to SAP S/4HANA or are already an SAP S/4HANA user.

18.6.1 Simplification List

SAP catalogues all changes to the business suite in the simplification list for SAP S/4HANA. This list was created by SAP to assist customers in planning efforts. The simplification list is also a useful tool for assessing time, resources, and budget needed for project planning and conversion.

Each SAP S/4HANA release has its own list of simplifications. For example, SAP S/4HANA 1709 has a simplification list titled "Simplification List for SAP S/4HANA 1709 Initial Shipment Stack." The PDF document can be found at the following: *http://bit.ly/2GHtLA8*.

Note

These PDF versions of the simplification lists are officially published by SAP as white papers, with a document versioning nomenclature that contains the date the paper is released. In addition, there is a downloadable spreadsheet version provided as an attachment to SAP Note 2313884.

The simplification list covers all the capabilities in SAP S/4HANA, including industry solutions. The list of simplifications is quite extensive, but keep in mind that it's a complete inventory of changes to the business suite. As you review it, focus on the simplification items relevant to your business and map them to your existing environment. This is an important step in your journey to SAP S/4HANA.

In addition to the PDF and XLS versions of the simplification list, SAP has introduced a new web-based version. As shown in Figure 18.11, SAP Note 2313884 provides a link to the tool, with a disclaimer that for future releases of SAP S/4HANA, the XLS version of the simplification list will no longer be produced.

Figure 18.11 SAP Note 2313884 Link to Web-Based Simplification List

The web-based version of the simplification list is available at *https://launchpad.support.sap.com/#/sic/*.

This web version is very intuitive. You can use the search feature or click on the appropriate tile (see Figure 18.12) to select the SAP S/4HANA version you want to see.

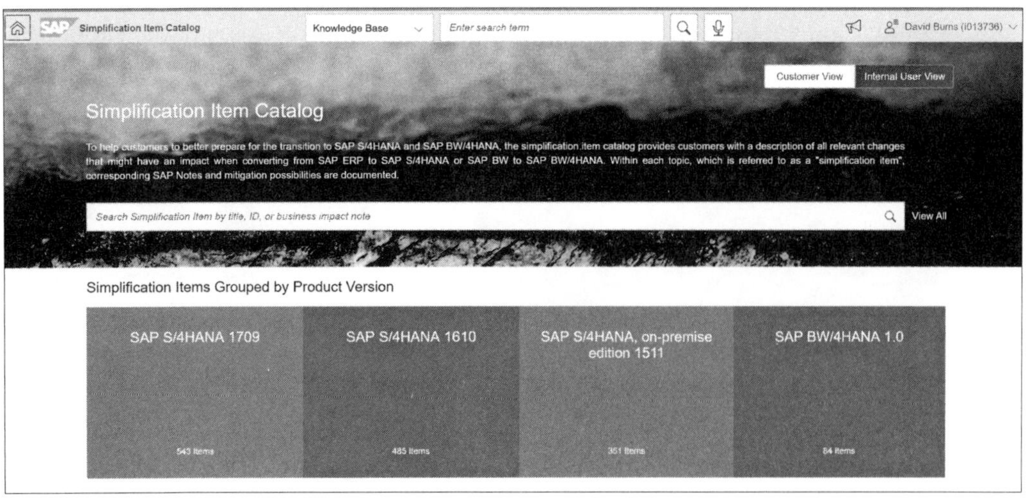

Figure 18.12 Web-Based Version Simplication List

For this example, click on **SAP S/4HANA 1709**, and the **Simplification Item Catalog** screen appears (Figure 18.13).

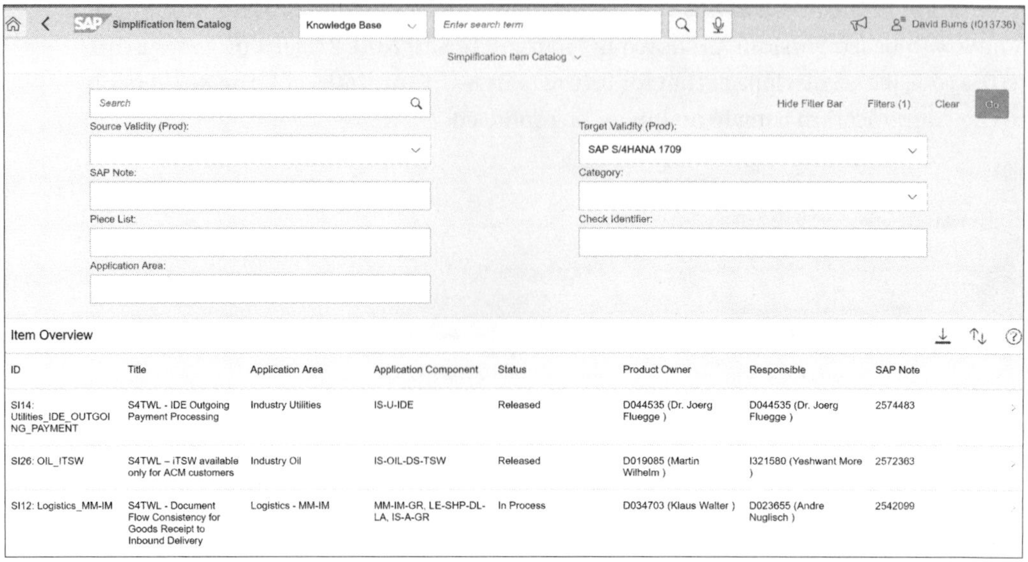

Figure 18.13 Simplification Item Catalog Screen

From here, you can search, sort, input more filters, or download the list. For this example, we entered "Financials" in the **Application Area** field to get the simplification list for financials (Figure 18.14).

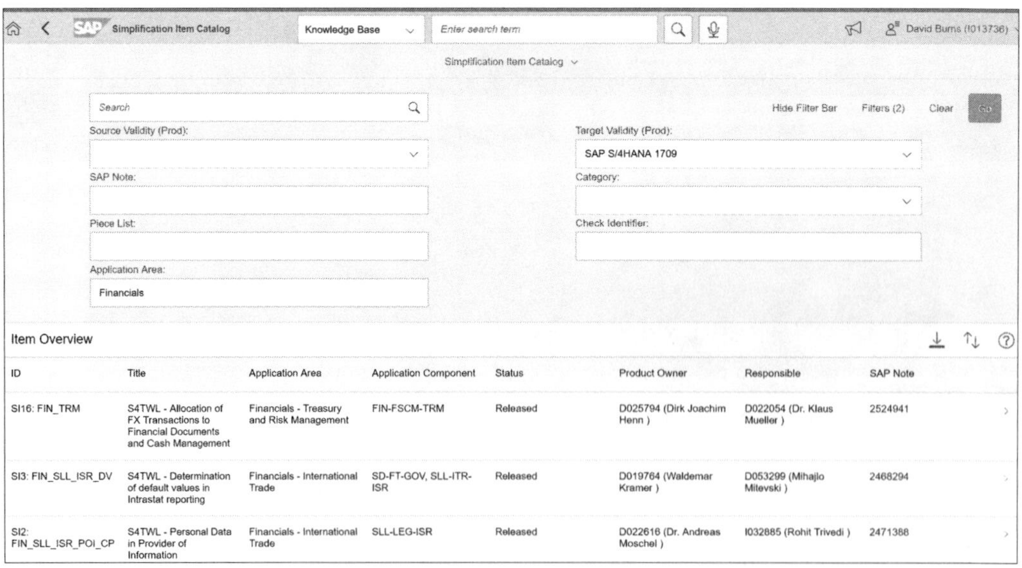

Figure 18.14 Web-Based Financials Simplification List

Now that you're familiar with the simplification list for SAP S/4HANA, we'll elaborate on two important points related to it. First are simplification categories and the second is SAP Business Impact Notes, both of which are referenced in the list for each individual simplification item.

18.6.2 Simplification Categories

The simplification list for SAP S/4HANA is a catalog of all individual changes (i.e., simplification items) to the business suite. SAP categorized each simplification item based on the type of impact. These are listed in Table 18.2.

Editing Option	Description
Re-architected for SAP HANA in-memory platform	Functionality that is optimized to leverage the capabilities of the SAP HANA database (i.e., new data model).
Consolidation of existing functionalities	Functionality that is unified and optimized in SAP S/4HANA, but basically remains the same.
No functional equivalent	Parts of the classic SAP Business Suite that may have no functional equivalent in SAP S/4HANA. Alternative functionality may already be available in SAP S/4HANA or on the roadmap.

Table 18.2 Simplification Categories

Each simplification item contains a description, business impact, recommendations, and related SAP Notes. The recommendations provide guidance from SAP on how to adapt related custom code.

In the next section, we'll discuss the relevant SAP Notes for SAP S/4HANA simplifications.

18.6.3 SAP Business Impact Notes

Each simplification item will reference one or more associated SAP Notes, referred to for SAP S/4HANA purposes as Business Impact Notes. These SAP Business Impact Notes are vital resources that provide additional information about each simplification, including changes to the data structure. SAP Business Impact Notes might also include additional reference material related to the change, such as how-to-guides, white papers, and references to additional SAP Notes.

The best way to demonstrate the value of SAP Business Impact Notes is with a specific example. Using the web-based simplification list (refer to Figure 18.12), we view the details of simplification item **DATA STRUCTURE CHANGES IN ASSET ACCOUNTING** (Figure 18.15) from the **Simplification Item Catalog** screen.

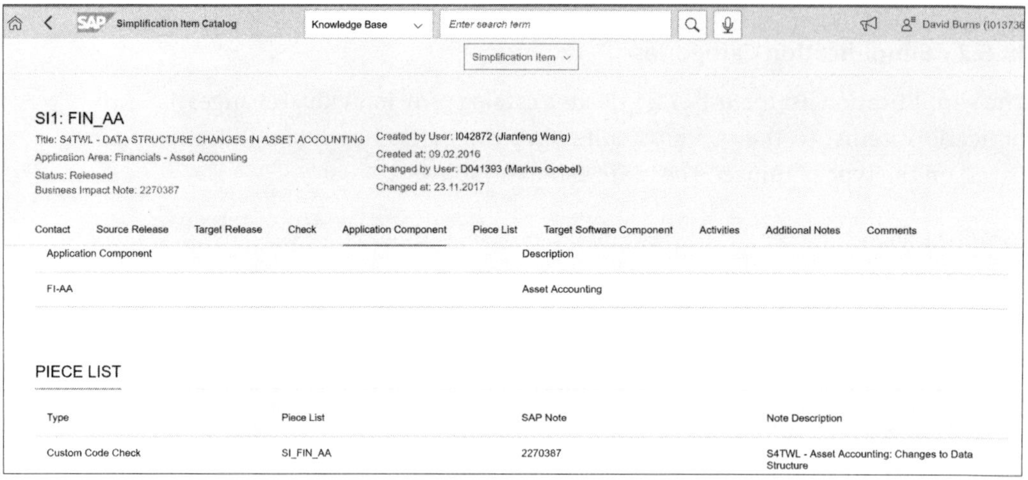

Figure 18.15 Simplification Item: Data Structure Changes in Asset Accounting

In the header, the **Business Impact Note** field is provided with a hyperlink note. For this example, we click on note number **2270387**, and the SAP Note opens in a new window (Figure 18.16).

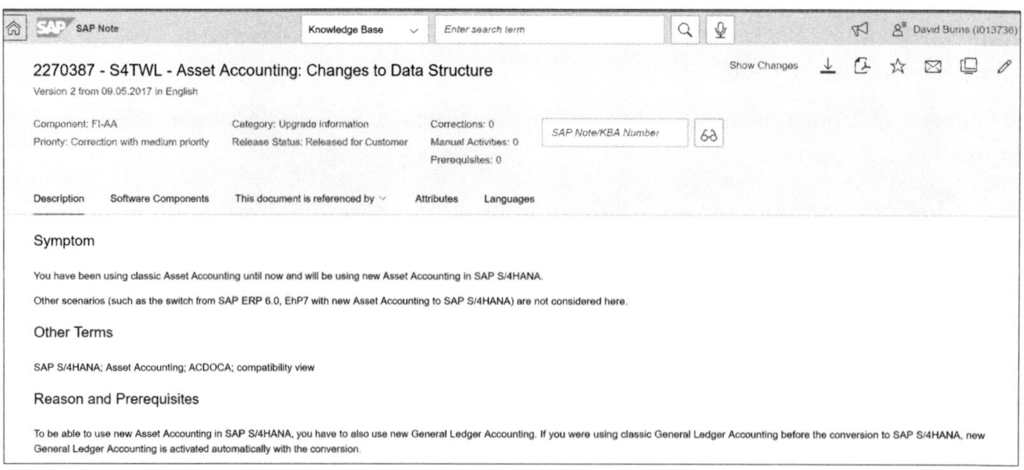

Figure 18.16 SAP Note 2270387: Top Section

In the **Symptom** and **Reason and Prerequisites** areas of SAP Note 2270387, we see that this note is relevant to the switch from classic FI-AA to new Asset Accounting in SAP S/4HANA, which requires the use of the new G/L.

Further down in the note's **Description**, detailed changes are provided in the **Solution** area (Figure 18.17). SAP Note 2270387 provides significant details on changes to FI-AA data structures and where different data is posted in new Asset Accounting. Such changes impact conversion and have a ripple effect on reports, queries, and some business processes (e.g., financial close).

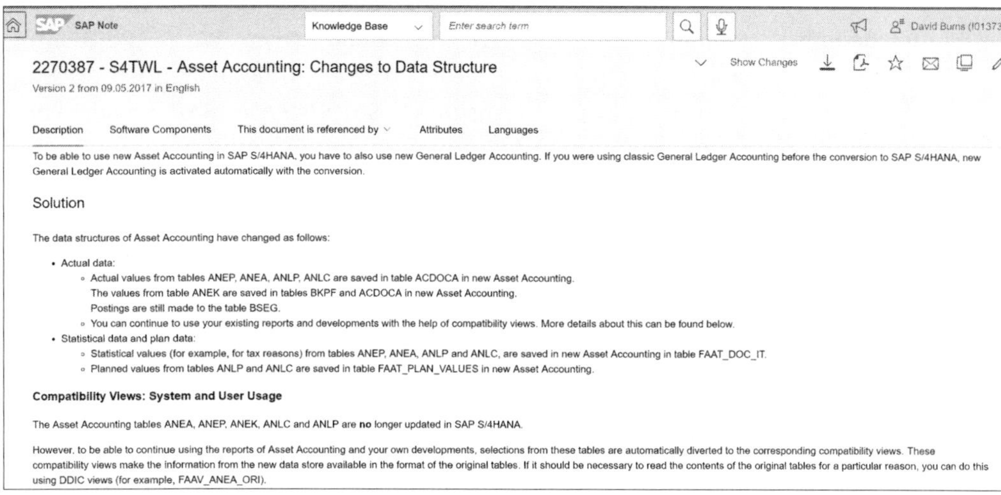

SAP Note | Knowledge Base | Enter search term | David Burns (I013736)

2270387 - S4TWL - Asset Accounting: Changes to Data Structure
Version 2 from 09.05.2017 in English

Show Changes

Description | Software Components | This document is referenced by | Attributes | Languages

To be able to use new Asset Accounting in SAP S/4HANA, you have to also use new General Ledger Accounting. If you were using classic General Ledger Accounting before the conversion to SAP S/4HANA, new General Ledger Accounting is activated automatically with the conversion.

Solution

The data structures of Asset Accounting have changed as follows:

- Actual data:
  - Actual values from tables ANEP, ANEA, ANLP, ANLC are saved in table ACDOCA in new Asset Accounting.
    The values from table ANEK are saved in tables BKPF and ACDOCA in new Asset Accounting.
    Postings are still made to the table BSEG.
  - You can continue to use your existing reports and developments with the help of compatibility views. More details about this can be found below.
- Statistical data and plan data:
  - Statistical values (for example, for tax reasons) from tables ANEP, ANEA, ANLP and ANLC, are saved in new Asset Accounting in table FAAT_DOC_IT.
  - Planned values from tables ANLP and ANLC are saved in table FAAT_PLAN_VALUES in new Asset Accounting.

Compatibility Views: System and User Usage

The Asset Accounting tables ANEA, ANEP, ANEK, ANLC and ANLP are **no** longer updated in SAP S/4HANA.

However, to be able to continue using the reports of Asset Accounting and your own developments, selections from these tables are automatically diverted to the corresponding compatibility views. These compatibility views make the information from the new data store available in the format of the original tables. If it should be necessary to read the contents of the original tables for a particular reason, you can do this using DDIC views (for example, FAAV_ANEA_ORI).

Figure 18.17 SAP Note 2270387: Bottom Section

18.7 Summary

The primary intent of this chapter was to create a guide as you journey into the digital era of FI in SAP. This chapter presented several topics to help you understand what SAP S/4HANA is and the major changes it brings to FI. We began with an overview of SAP HANA and introduced SAP S/4HANA, which is the new SAP business suite based on innovations in database technology and architecture.

The chapter then covered specific SAP S/4HANA changes (i.e., simplifications) relevant to end users. Among the most significant changes is the introduction of the Universal Journal, a single G/L line item table (table ACDOCA) providing a single source of truth for financial reporting, and new Asset Accounting, an example of an eliminated subledger through the integration of transaction data into the Universal Journal.

The introduction of the Universal Journal is a core design change in SAP S/4HANA. This ledger redesign impacts the G/L data structure significantly, while at the same time serving as the central hub for changes in FI. With the Universal Journal also comes some of the most profound benefits of SAP S/4HANA to users in finance, accounting, and controlling.

FI-AA is one example of a subledger that has been eliminated through the integration of transaction data into the Universal Journal. New Asset Accounting posts in real time to all accounting principles and no longer requires redundant data storage.

We then discussed SAP S/4HANA embedded analytics, focusing on key features that provide added capabilities in real-time performance and analysis. With SAP S/4HANA, we have the tools and transactional data needed to do real-time analytical processing from one source of truth. To ease the transition to SAP S/4HANA, SAP provides compatibility views so the changes to the data structures minimize the impact on reporting.

Critical to our discussion of SAP S/4HANA is the new SAP user experience: SAP Fiori. When your company migrates from SAP ERP 6.0 to SAP S/4HANA, it's best to combine that effort with implementation of SAP Fiori. SAP Fiori is designed with the idea in mind of being a harmonized user experience across SAP applications and platforms. In other words, the UI should have a consistent look and feel, regardless of whether you're accessing an SAP system from a laptop, tablet, or phone.

The chapter ended by opening the door to further SAP S/4HANA exploration via the simplification list. SAP catalogues all changes to the business suite in the simplification list for SAP S/4HANA. Each SAP S/4HANA release has its own list of simplifications. We discussed the various ways to access the list, the simplification categories, and the business impact notes, which provide additional information about each simplification and reference materials.

After reading this chapter, you should have a basic understanding of SAP HANA, SAP S/4HANA, SAP Fiori, and many of the resources available for you in understanding the impact to you as an end user. I wish you all the best as you move forward in your careers and sincerely hope this book helps you on your journey to SAP S/4HANA.

Appendices

Appendix A
The New General Ledger

The content of this book, in its entirety, was written and presented with the new G/L. However, there are still many SAP customers using the classic G/L. This appendix provides supplemental details about the new G/L for informational purposes rather than to demonstrate functionality or teach configuration.

There is so much new functionality available in the new G/L that there is no way a single chapter can do it justice. Therefore, only a subset of critical capabilities is presented in this appendix. Several books and reference materials exist on the topic that you should read to obtain a greater understanding.

Unlike the chapters in this book, this appendix isn't written from a transactional point of view. It's intended to provide supplemental information to enhance your understanding of the new G/L and its unique capabilities. Configuring Financial Accounting (FI) is beyond the scope of this book, but discussing some configuration concepts is necessary to assist in your understanding of the topic.

If you're installing SAP for the first time, the new G/L will be automatically activated. If your company is still on classic G/L and intends to upgrade to the new G/L, you'll need to launch a migration project. The content in this appendix will assist you with your preparations for both of these situations. If you're already using the new G/L, it will help you better understand its capabilities, and if you're migrating to the new G/L from the classic G/L, it will help you in making design decisions.

The *new G/L* is described as an enhanced version of the classic G/L, with greater flexibility and extensibility. A major accomplishment of the new G/L was to incorporate some functionality that resided outside the G/L, including Profit Center Accounting (PCA), reconciliation ledger, and Special Purpose Ledger. In doing so, the new G/L has also significantly reduced the time and effort required to close the books at period-end and year-end.

In this section, we'll begin with a discussion of the flexibility and extensibility of new G/L. After that, we'll discuss the key features of new G/L, including the following:

- Parallel ledgers
- Document splitting
- Segments
- PCA

A.1 Flexibility and Extensibility

To fully grasp how the new G/L is more flexible and extensible, you first need to understand some of the limitations of the classic G/L, such as the following:

- **No parallel ledgers**
  In the classic G/L, Special Purpose Ledger can be used to add additional dimensions to meet reporting requirements, and parallel accounting can be accomplished through the creation of additional G/L accounts.
- **No real-time reconciliation between Controlling (CO) and FI**
  Reconciliation was accomplished through a reconciliation ledger.
- **No ability to extend data structure with customer fields**
- **No segment reporting capability**
  In other words, you can't subdivide classic G/L balances by other characteristics to produce full financial statements.

This list is by no means a complete account of the limitations of the classic G/L. Removing these limitations was the catalyst for the new G/L design. With that said, *flexibility* and *extensibility* of the new G/L specifically refer to the ability to perform financial reporting from a central source, with the ability to extend the totals table (table FAGLFLEXT) and produce financial statements by multiple dimensions. The new G/L also provides another set of tables (table FMGLFLEX*) for use in the public sector.

In the past, multiple totals tables were needed (e.g., tables GLT0, GLPCT). SAP has consolidated the multiple totals tables into a single totals table (table FAGLFLEXT) in the new GL. Having one summary table with multiple dimensions and the ability to add customer fields provides unprecedented flexibility in FI. In addition to the new totals table (table FAGLFLEXT), new G/L also has new line item tables: table FAGLFLEXA for actual line items and table FAGLFLEXP for planned line items.

With regards to the new G/L, the term *extensibility* more specifically refers to an extended data structure, which means you can activate additional fields, such as segments, or create your own fields.

Let's take a look at the activation of the new G/L.

A.2 Activation of the New General Ledger

To activate the new G/L, follow the IMG menu path, **Financial Accounting • Financial Accounting Global Settings • Activate New General Ledger Accounting**, as shown in Figure A.1.

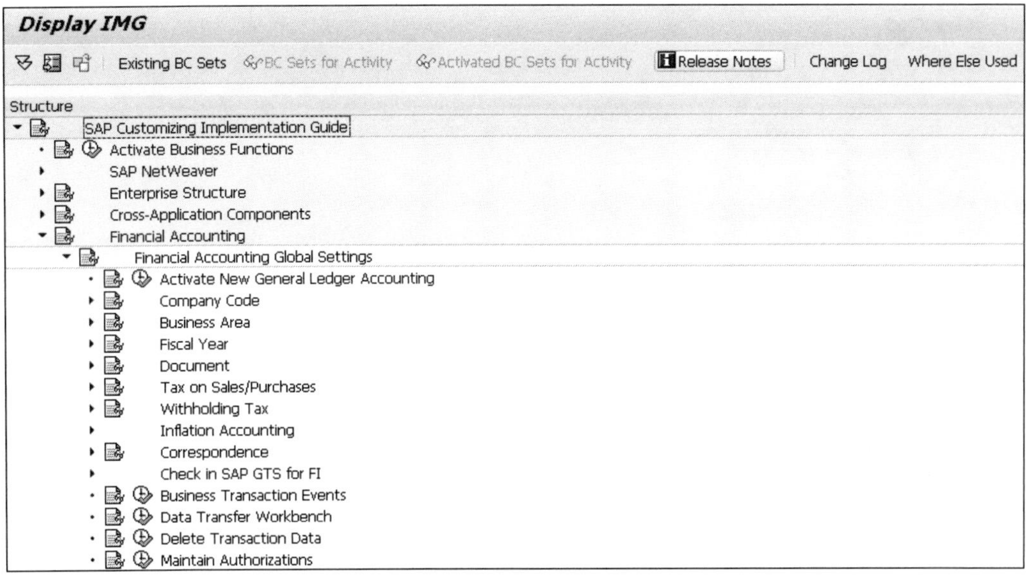

Figure A.1 Activate New G/L Menu Path in the IMG

Double-click on the **Activate New General Ledger Accounting** node. The **Change View "Activation of New General Ledger Accounting": Details** screen appears (Figure A.2).

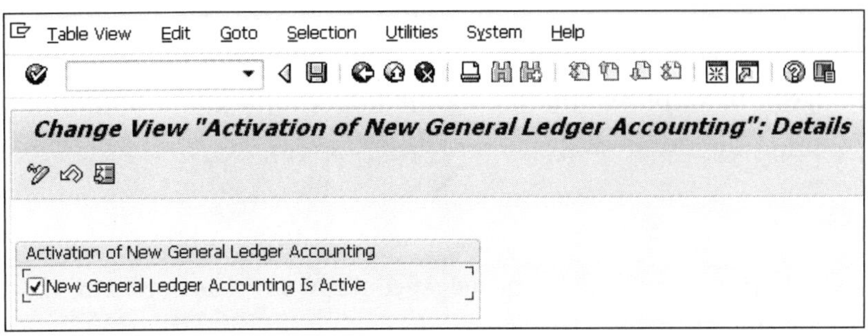

Figure A.2 Activate New G/L Screen

The **New General Ledger Accounting Is Active** checkbox is basically an on/off switch. By activating the new G/L, the functions for it become available, including the activation of the new G/L tables. In addition, in the IMG, the previous **Financial Accounting** menu is replaced by the **Financial Accounting (New)** menu (Figure A.3). This is where you configure the new G/L.

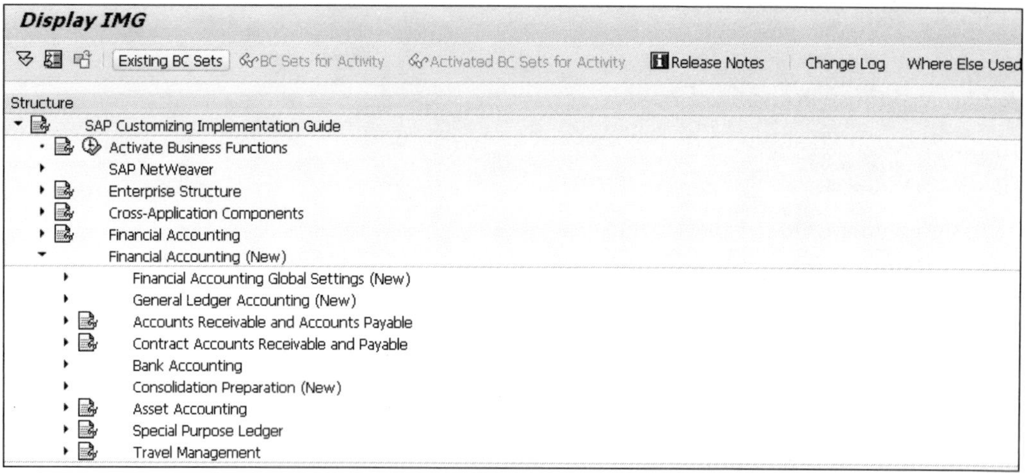

Figure A.3 Financial Accounting (New) Menu Path in the IMG

If you already use the classic G/L in your production system, the transition to the new G/L involves more than just flipping the switch. You need to perform the migration of your G/L data before you activate the new G/L. Migration is only possible as part of a project in collaboration with the SAP G/L migration service.

Now that you've learned about the flexibility, extensibility, and activation of the new G/L, let's discuss the concepts of ledgers and parallel ledgers. Note that SAP defines a *ledger* as a section of a database table that only contains dimensions of the totals table that the ledger is based on and that are required for reporting.

A.3 Ledgers

To begin, let's talk in more depth about the ledger concept. SAP was built with individual and separate ledgers that each served a different purpose and spanned across multiple modules. These ledgers include the classic G/L ledger for external and legal financial reporting, the CO-to-FI reconciliation ledger, a Cost of Goods Sold (COGS) or Cost of Sales ledger, a Profit Center Accounting ledger, and Special Purpose Ledgers. As you can imagine, this approach presented numerous challenges in reconciling the ledgers and pulling together pieces of data for financial reporting. In the new G/L, these ledgers can be combined.

Let's discuss in more detail the ledger concept in the new G/L.

A.3.1 Assigning Scenarios to Ledgers

In the new G/L, scenarios are assigned to ledgers, which in turn determine which fields are updated in the ledger when postings are made.

To assign scenarios to ledgers, follow the IMG menu path, **Financial Accounting (New) • Financial Accounting Global Settings (New) • Ledgers • Ledger • Assign Scenarios and Customer Fields to Ledgers**, as shown in Figure A.4.

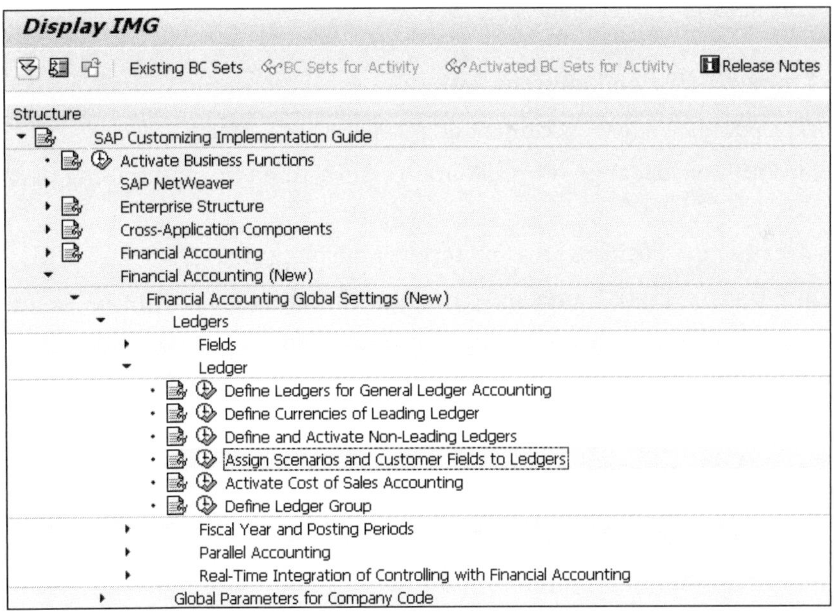

Figure A.4 Assign Scenarios to Ledgers Menu Path

Click on the **Assign Scenarios and Customer Fields to Ledgers** node, and the **New Entries: Overview of Added Entries** screen appears (Figure A.5). From this screen, you can use the **Dialog Structure** on the left of the screen to navigate to the specific scenarios assigned to a ledger.

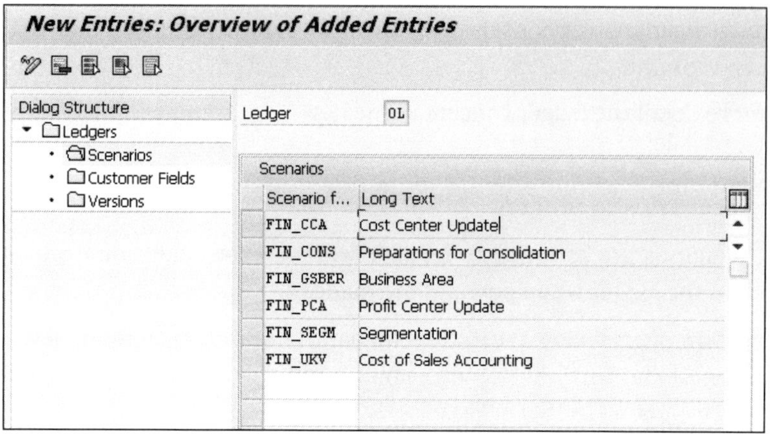

Figure A.5 Assigning Scenarios to Ledgers

The new G/L provides six standard scenarios:

- **Cost Center Update**: Sender cost center and receiver cost center
- **Preparations for Consolidation**: Consolidation transaction type and trading partner
- **Business Area**: Sender business area and receiver business area
- **Profit Center Update**: Profit center and partner profit center
- **Segmentation Scenario**: Segment, partner segment, and profit center
- **Cost of Sales Accounting**: Sender functional area and receiver functional area

Customer-specific scenarios can't be created, but custom fields can be required when assigning scenarios to a ledger. All six scenarios can be assigned to a ledger.

A.3.2 Parallel Ledgers

Companies need parallel accounting to reflect accounting valuations according to country-specific accounting principles and legal requirements. Global companies need the ability to meet International Accounting Standards (IAS) simultaneously in the global environment. The new G/L provides the capability of doing both with parallel ledgers.

Of course, the accounting principles followed in the country of incorporation dictates group reporting valuations, but local valuations and accounting principles still need to be reflected for each country in which you do business. This is the essence of parallel accounting: it enables you to provide accounting valuations and closing functions for each company code according to the accounting principles of the company as a whole, according to local accounting principles and regulatory requirements. Therefore, parallel accounting allows you to capture and report accounting principles globally and locally.

At this point, it's important to mention that a commonly accepted approach to implementing parallel accounting existed in the classic G/L. This approach involved creating additional G/L accounts in the same ledger. This is the old method of parallel accounting and no longer preferred. With this method, one joint account is needed for postings for both accounting principles. In addition, specific area accounts are used for each accounting principle. With the new G/L, you can post data to all ledgers, to a specified selection of ledgers, or to a single ledger.

In the new G/L, one leading ledger is created, and multiple local ledgers can be activated. It's important to understand the difference between the leading ledger and local ledgers. When the new G/L is configured, exactly one leading ledger is defined. This leading ledger contains the data required for consolidated financial statements. It's fully integrated with the subsidiary ledgers and updated in all company codes. In other words, the leading ledger is automatically assigned to all company codes. Nonleading ledgers, on the other hand, are specific to one accounting principle and must be assigned to company codes individually.

Each parallel ledger serves a different purpose in that it's used to account for different country-specific legal and accounting reporting requirements. For example, the leading ledger might manage the G/L according to International Financial Reporting Standards (IFRS), whereas a nonleading ledger may be designated for US Generally Accepted Accounting Principles (GAAP).

To make sure you thoroughly understand this concept, let's walk through an example of how ledgers in new G/L are set up. First, you must define your ledgers in the new G/L. To do so, follow IMG menu path, **Financial Accounting (New) • Financial Accounting Global Settings (New) • Ledgers • Ledger • Define Ledgers for General Ledger Accounting**, as shown in Figure A.6.

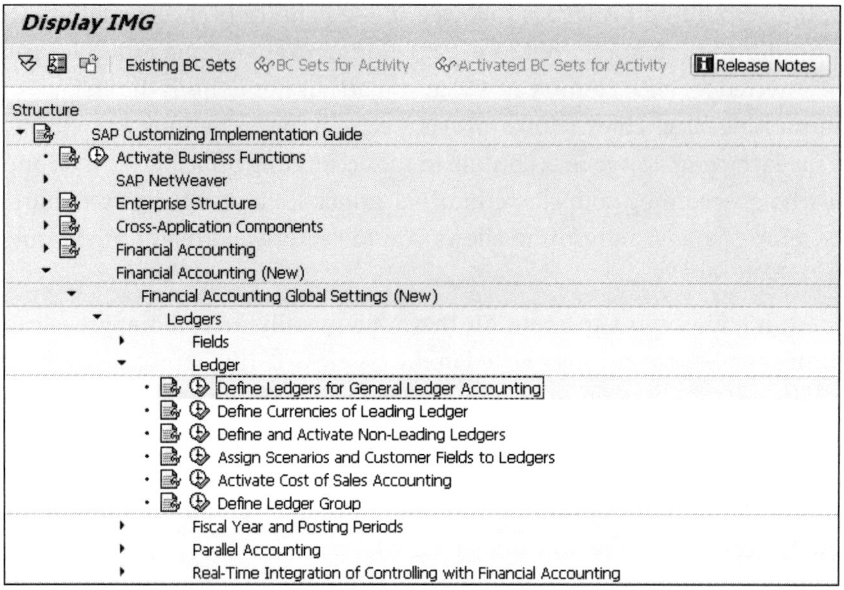

Figure A.6 Define Ledgers for General Ledger Accounting Menu Path

Click on the **Define Ledgers for General Ledger Accounting** node. The **Change View "Define Ledgers in General Ledger Accounting": Overview** screen appears (Figure A.7). Notice that a leading ledger and totals tables are specified.

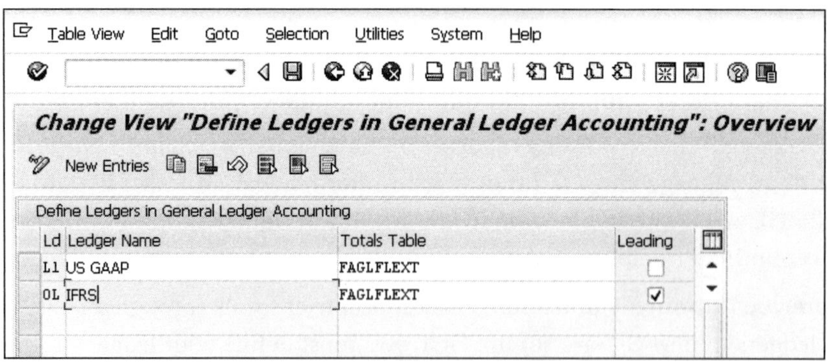

Figure A.7 Defining Ledgers in New G/L Accounting

After the ledgers are defined, accounting principles can be defined and assigned. To do so, follow IMG menu path, **Financial Accounting (New) • Financial Accounting Global Settings (New) • Ledgers • Parallel Accounting**, as shown in Figure A.8.

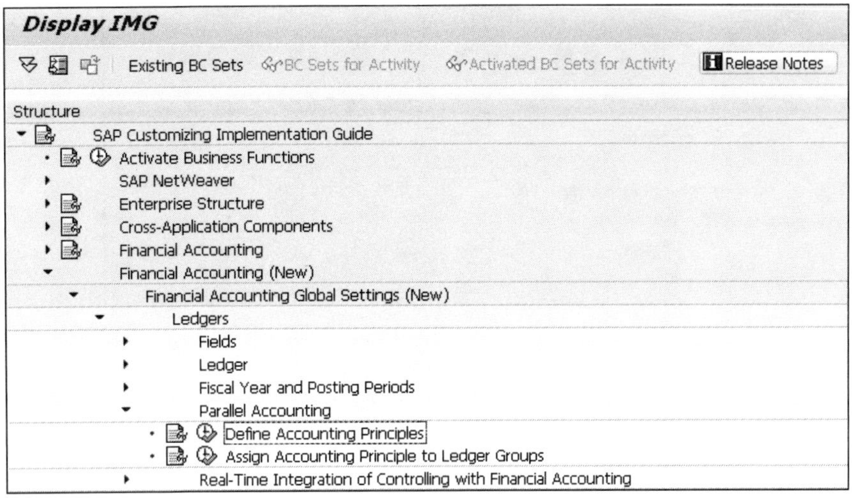

Figure A.8 Define Accounting Principles Menu Path

Click on the **Define Accounting Principles** node. The **Change View "Accounting Principles": Overview** screen appears (Figure A.9).

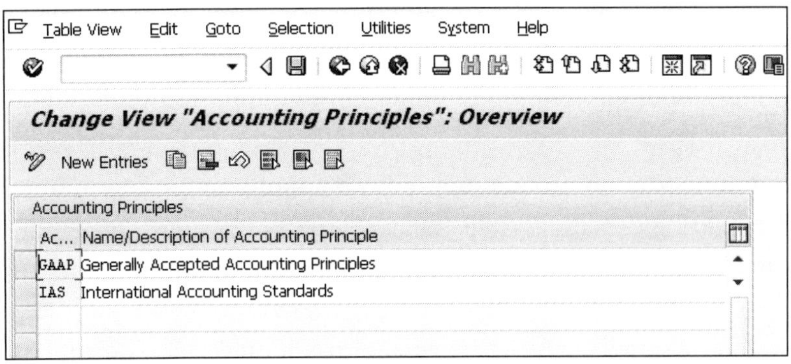

Figure A.9 Change View "Accounting Principles": Overview Screen

The last step is to assign an accounting principle to a target ledger. From Figure A.8, click the execute icon at IMG node **Assign Accounting Principle to Ledger Groups**. The **Change View "Assignment of Accounting Principle to Target Ledger Group** screen appears (Figure A.10).

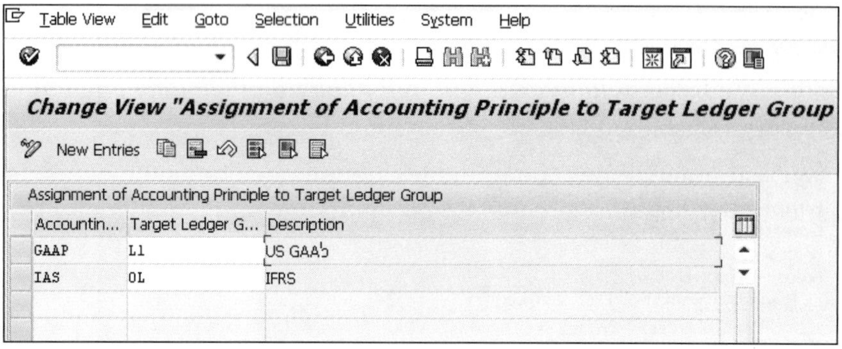

Figure A.10 Assigning Accounting Principle to Target Ledger

This concludes our discussion of parallel ledgers. In the next section, the topic of document splitting is presented.

A.4 Document Splitting

Document splitting is the ability to split document line items according to specified dimensions, such as segment, business area, or profit center. With real-time document splitting, balance sheets can be created for each dimension.

There are three types of document splitting:

- **Active splitting**
  The splitting of account assignments based on configuration settings. In essence, this method of splitting uses designated "sender" lines as the source of account assignments and "receiver" lines as the recipient for the account assignment.
- **Passive splitting**
  The automatic inheritance of splitting assignment based on clearing documents and invoice reference documents.
- **Zero balancing**
  The automatic generation of additional line item items to ensure that the specified dimension balances to zero in each transaction. An activation flag is set in configuration for each dimension for which to perform zero balancing.

Active document splitting is used to automatically split line items from sender line items to receiver lines for selected dimensions. For example, expense line items with the segment dimension can be sender lines with the payable line as a receiver. The net effect can be a zero balancing of line items in a financial document by the dimensions specified, and balance sheets can be created for these dimensions. In addition, document splitting enables the system to create additional clearing lines.

Now that you've learned the basics of document splitting, let's follow an example of active document splitting in which a vendor invoice is entered with the values listed in Table A.1.

Debit/Credit	Account	Segment	Amount
Credit	Vendor	Blank	1000
Debit	Expense	1001	200
Debit	Expense	1002	800

Table A.1 Example Vendor Invoice Data

Document splitting then creates the document in the G/L view (Table A.2), actively splitting the vendor lines according to the segment dimension specified in the expense line items.

Debit/Credit	Account	Segment	Amount
Credit	Vendor	1001	200
Credit	Vendor	1002	800
Debit	Expense	1001	200
Debit	Expense	1002	800

Table A.2 Example G/L View Document

The example in Table A.2 shows an active splitting controlled by configuration. Passive document splitting, on the other hand, isn't controlled by configuration. Passive splitting takes place for transactions that include clearing and transactions in which an invoice is referenced, such as an outgoing payment.

Building on the prior example of actively splitting a vendor invoice, Table A.3 shows the passive splitting of the segment dimension on cash when the outgoing payment is made.

Debit/Credit	Account	Segment	Amount
Debit	Vendor	1001	200
Debit	Vendor	1002	800
Credit	Cash/Bank	1001	200
Credit	Cash/Bank	1002	800

Table A.3 Passive Splitting Example

With the outgoing payment, the cash/bank document line items passively inherit the segment dimension according to the values in the vendor line items.

By using document splitting with zero balancing enabled per dimension, complete financial statements can be produced at any time for any of the following dimensions:

- Customer-defined fields
- Segments
- Profit centers
- Funds
- Business areas

Document splitting in the new G/L is a significant improvement over the classic G/L and provides additional reporting capabilities. Setting it up, however, can be time-consuming. To do so properly requires thorough analysis of your business processes and typically requires the introduction of several new FI document types.

Without getting into the configuration details, document splitting is based on the assignment of document types to business transactions and business transaction variants, as well as the assignment of G/L accounts to item categories. In turn, item categories are used to define document splitting rules, which determine the document line items to split and how. These document splitting rules are assigned to a document splitting method.

The logic of document splitting can be broken down into the following rules:

1. When posting, the system validates that the item categories (i.e., G/L accounts) are permitted. The link to item categories is made from the document type and the business transaction.

2. For clearing and reference transactions (e.g., outgoing payments), the system applies passive document splitting. With passive document splitting, the system transfers account assignments for the line items being created.
3. The system applies the document splitting rule for the document being posted. This is referred to as *active document splitting*.
4. Enhancement logic, if activated, provides account assignments for individual line items for which no account assignments could be determined (e.g., tax).
5. The system validates the document splitting characteristics to ensure that the document type logically matches the business transaction to be updated.
6. The system creates a zero balance setting for each document. In other words, if the document can't balance to zero according to the splitting dimensions specified, the system creates additional clearing items to make it balance to zero. This is necessary for creating balance sheets.

This concludes our discussion of document splitting. In the next section, we'll discuss segment dimension.

A.5 Segments

With the new G/L, SAP added the segment dimension. SAP defines a *segment* as a division of a company for which you can create financial statements for external reporting.

Why is this important? IFRS requires an entity to report financial data about its reportable segments, which are operating segments or aggregations of operating segments that meet certain criteria.

Note

For more information, reference IFRS statement 8 (and amendments) on operating segments at *www.IFRS.org*. You should also be familiar with GAAP or other local accounting rules for segment reporting. For GAAP, go to *www.FASB.org* for more information on financial segment reporting and FASB ASC 280.

Segments are defined in SAP configuration. **Segment** is a 10-character field with a 50-character **Description** field. It has no other fields, parameters, or control settings.

Document splitting is required to produce financial statements by segment. In addition, the zero balance setting needs to be made for the segment characteristic.

You've now learned what the **Segment** field is and why it's important, but the next important question is: How is it entered into a financial transaction? There are three different methods:

- Enter a segment in the master record of a profit center and therefore have the segment derived based on its association with the profit center master record.
- Manually enter the segment during posting (only possible for transactions in FI).
- Use a customer enhancement to set up your own rules for deriving the segment during posting.

As previously mentioned, segments are defined in the IMG. Let's look at an example of a segment that has been configured and assigned to a profit center.

To define the enterprise structure for FI, follow the IMG menu path, **Enterprise Structure • Definition • Financial Accounting • Define Segment**, as shown in Figure A.11.

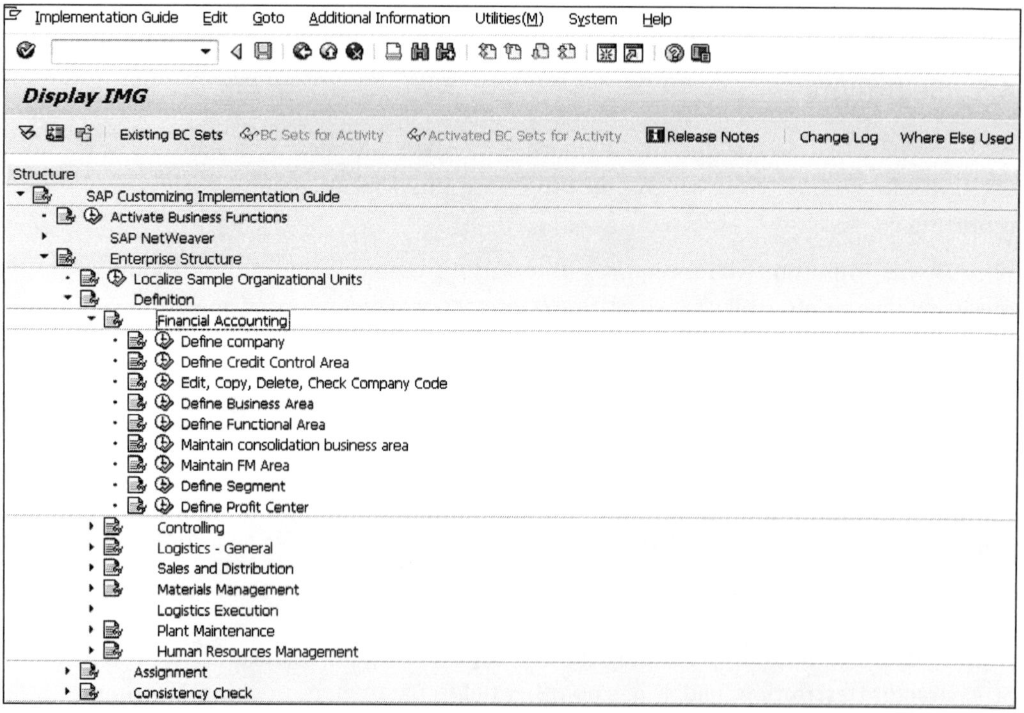

Figure A.11 Segment Menu Path

Click the **Execute** icon. The **Display View "Segments for Segment Reporting": Overview** screen opens (Figure A.12).

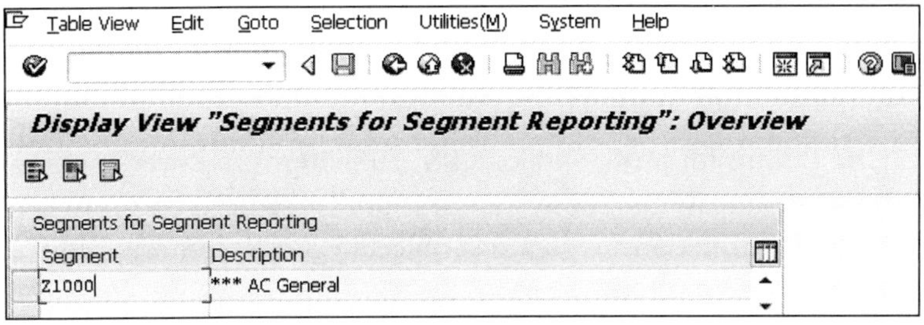

Figure A.12 Segments Display View

Once created, a segment can be assigned to a profit center, as shown in Figure A.13.

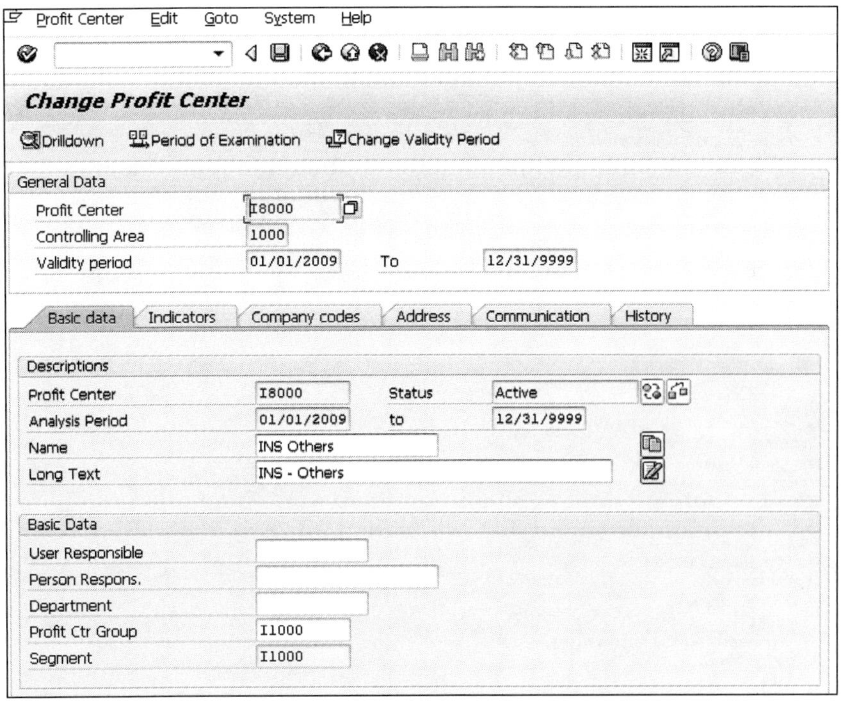

Figure A.13 Profit Center with Segment Assigned

This concludes our discussion of segments. In the next section, we'll discuss Profit Center Accounting (PCA).

A.6 Profit Center Accounting

One of the key features of the new G/L is the merging of PCA into the new G/L. In the classic PCA, a separate document is posted into PCA (ledger 8A). With the new G/L, there is no need for a separate document because the profit center is another dimension on the line item that can be reported from the new G/L.

The classic PCA had limitations for profit and loss (P&L) line items that were not cost elements and balance sheet line items. The system was unable to derive a profit center in real time because they aren't posted to a cost object (e.g., cost center).

In the new G/L, financial statements by profit center can be produced directly out of the G/L. New functionality exists to default a profit center into a financial line item when no cost element exists. To do so, a default profit center must be assigned for balance sheet account ranges using Transaction 3KEH.

To set up Transaction 3KEH, following the IMG menu path, **Controlling • Profit Center Accounting • Actual Postings • Choose Additional Balance Sheet and P&L Accounts • Choose Accounts**, as shown in Figure A.14.

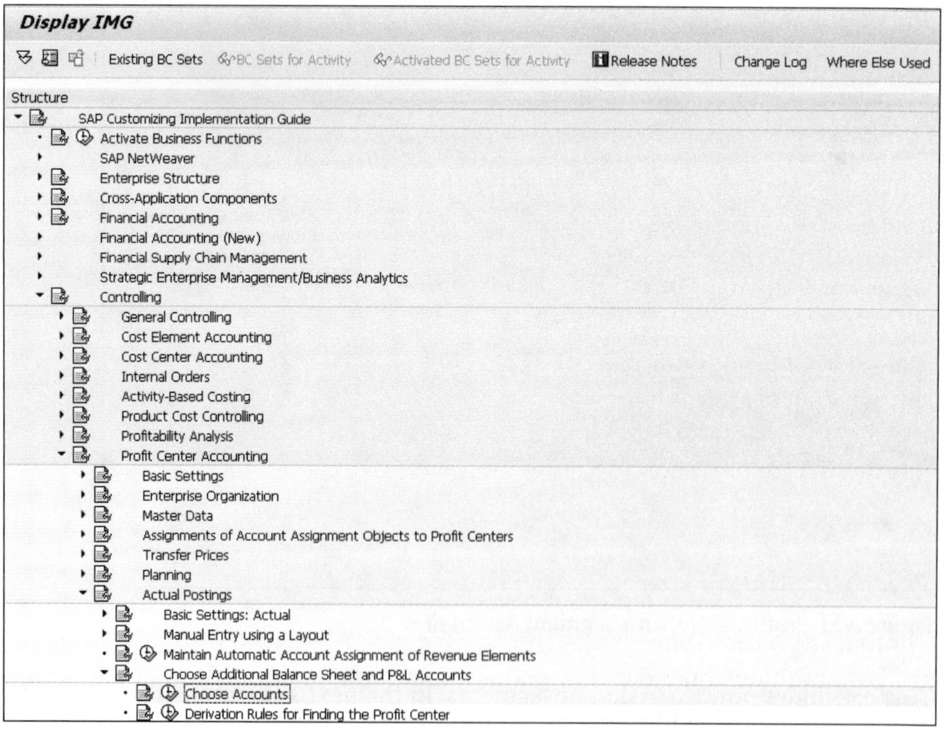

Figure A.14 Transaction 3KEH Menu Path

Click on the **Choose Accounts** node. The **Change View "EC-PCA: Additional Balance Sheet and Profit + Loss Accounts** screen appears (Figure A.15). In this example, a default profit center has been assigned to a range or balance sheet accounts.

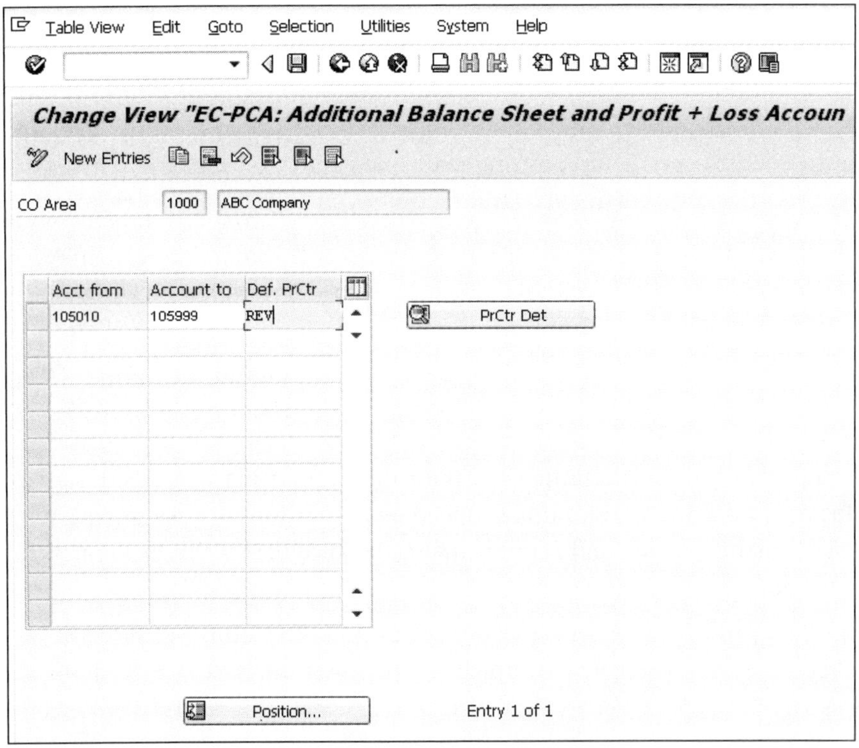

Figure A.15 Transation 3KEH Profit Center Assignment Screen

This concludes our discussion of PCA in the new G/L. Keep in mind that with the introduction of PCA into the new G/L, the old PCA tables are no longer used. These include the totals table (table GLPCT), the line item table (table GLPCA), and the planned line items table (table GLPCP).

A.7 Summary

The new G/L is described as enhanced G/L with greater flexibility and extensibility. In the past, multiple totals tables were needed, but with the new G/L, SAP has consolidated the multiple totals tables into a single totals table (table FAGLFLEXT). Having one summary table with multiple dimensions and the ability to add customer fields provides flexibility that didn't exist in the classic G/L. Along with that flexibility came enhanced reporting and the ability to produce a financial statement at a level lower than the company code.

The key features of the new G/L covered in this appendix include parallel ledgers, document splitting, segments, and PCA.

Parallel ledgers in the new G/L enable accounting valuations at a group level and according to country-specific accounting principles and legal requirements. With parallel ledgers, when posting financial transactions, you have the ability to post data to all ledgers, to a specified selection of ledgers, or to a single ledger.

When the new G/L is configured, a leading ledger is specified. This leading ledger contains the data required for consolidated financial statements. It's fully integrated with the subsidiary ledgers and updated in all company codes. Nonleading ledgers, on the other hand, are specific to one accounting principle and must be assigned to company codes individually.

Another concept introduced in the new G/L is document splitting, which is the ability to split document line items according to specified dimensions (e.g., segment). With real-time document splitting and zero balancing, balance sheets can be created for each dimension.

The twenty-first century has seen widespread adoption of accounting standards for segment reporting, and the new G/L added the segment dimension. SAP defines a segment as a division of a company for which you can create financial statements for external reporting.

The last topic we discussed in this appendix was PCA. The new G/L merges PCA into the new G/L. The classic PCA had several limitations, including the need to create a separate document in PCA and the inability to derive a profit center into P&L line items that were not cost elements and balance sheet line items. With the new G/L, these limitations are overcome, and financial statements using the profit center dimension can be produced directly out of the G/L. New functionality exists to default a profit center into a financial line item when no cost element or cost object exists.

Appendix B
Important Tables in Financial Accounting

In this appendix, you'll find a list of all the important tables in FI.

Table	Description
ANAR	Asset Types
ANAT	Asset Type Text
ANEK	Document Header Asset Posting
ANEKPV	Line Item View for AuC Settlement
ANEP	Asset Line Items
ANEV	Asset Downpymt Settlement
ANKA	Asset Classes: General Data
ANKB	Asset Class: Depreciation Area
ANKP	Asset Classes: Fld Cont Dpndnt on Chart of Depreciation
ANKT	Asset Classes: Description
ANKV	Asset Classes: Insurance Types
ANLA	Asset Master Record Segment
ANLB	Depreciation Terms
ANLBZA	Time-Dependent Depreciation Terms
ANLBZW	Asset-Specific Base Values
ANLC	Asset Value Fields
ANLH	Main Asset Number
ANLP	Asset Periodic Values

Table	Description
ANLT	Asset Texts
ANLV	Insurance Data
ANLX	Asset Master Record Segment
ANLZ	Time-Dependent Asset Allocations
BKPF	Accounting Document Header
BNKA	Bank Master Record
BSAD	Accounting: Secondary Index for Customers (Cleared Items)
BSAK	Accounting: Secondary Index for Vendors (Cleared Items)
BSAS	Accounting: Secondary Index for G/L Accounts (Cleared Items)
BSEC	One-Time Account Data Document Segment
BSEG	Accounting Document Segment
BSEGC	Document: Data on Payment Card Payments
BSET	Tax Data Document Segment
BSID	Accounting: Secondary Index for Customers
BSIK	Accounting: Secondary Index for Vendors
BSIM	Secondary Index, Documents for Material
BSIP	Index for Vendor Validation of Double Documents
BSIS	Accounting: Secondary Index for G/L Accounts (Cleared Items)
CEPC	Profit Center Master Data
CEPCT	Profit Center Master Data Text
FEBCL	Clearing Data for an Electronic Bank State
FEBEP	Electronic Bank Statement Line Items
FEBEXTTRN	External transaction code text definition
FEBKO	Electronic Bank Statement Header Records

Table	Description
GLFLEXA	Flexible General Ledger: Actual Line Items
GLFLEXP	Flexible G/L: Plan Line Items
GLFLEXT	Flexible G/L: Totals
GLS01	FI-SL Line Item Table with Objects for GLT01
GLS02	FI-SL Table with Objects, Structure Corresponds to GLS2
GLS03	FI-SL LI Table with Objects for GLTO3
GLT0	G/L Account Master Record Transaction Figures
GLT1	Local General Ledger Summary Table
GLT2	Consolidation Totals Table
GLT3	Summary Data Preparations for Consolidation
GLT01	FI-SL Table with Objects, Structure Corresponds to GLT1
GLT02	FI-SL Table with Objects, Structure Corresponds to GLT2
GLT03	FISL Table with Objects, Amounts and Quantities in Format P9
KNA1	General Data in Customer Master
KNAS	Customer master (VAT Registration Numbers General Section)
KNAT	Customer Master Record (Tax Groupings)
KNB1	Customer Master (Company Code)
KNB4	Customer Payment History
KNB5	Customer Master (Dunning Data)
KNBK	Customer Master (Bank Details)
KNBW	Customer Master Record (Withholding Tax Types)
KNC1	Customer Master (Transaction Figures)
KNC3	Customer Master (Special G/L Transaction Figures)
KNEA	Assign Bank Details and Payment Methods to Revenue Type

Table	Description
KNKA	Customer Master Credit Management: Central Data
KNKK	Customer Master Credit Management: Control Area Data
KNKKF1	Credit Management: FI Status Data
KNKKF2	Credit Management: Open Items by Days in Arrears
KNVI	Customer Master Tax Indicator
KNVK	Customer Master Contact Partner
KNVP	Customer Master Partner Functions
KNVV	Customer Master Sales Data
KNZA	Permitted Alternative Payer
LFA1	Vendor Master (General Section)
LFAS	Vendor master (VAT Registration Numbers General Section)
LFAT	Vendor Master Record (Tax Groupings)
LFB1	Vendor Master (Company Code)
LFB5	Vendor Master (dunning data)
LFBK	Vendor Master (Bank Details)
LFBW	Vendor Master Record (Withholding Tax Types)
LFC1	Vendor Master (Transaction Figures)
LFC3	Vendor Master (Special G/L Transaction Figures)
LFM1	Vendor Master Record Purchasing Organization
LFM2	Vendor Master Record: Purchasing Data
LFZA	Permitted Alternative Payee
PAYR	Payment Medium File
REGUH	Settlement Data from Payment Program
SKA1	G/L Account Master (Chart of Accounts)

Table	Description
SKAS	G/L Account Master (Chart Of Accounts: Key Word List)
SKAT	G/L Account Master Record (Chart of Accounts: Description)
SKB1	G/L Account Master (Company Code)
SKM1	Sample G/L Accounts
SKMT	Sample Account Names
T012	House Banks
T012K	House Bank Accounts
T012T	House Bank Names

Appendix C
The Author

David Burns has more than 25 years of experience in leadership positions as a principal solution architect, finance and budgeting consultant, author, and project manager. David regularly consults with leading public and private enterprises on the implementation and support of SAP and other enterprise applications. He advises on infrastructure and application selection, and provides expertise in finance, accounting, project and program management, and strategic planning.

David has been a contributing writer to SAP Experts, an ASUG presenter, and was featured in the 2015 Q1 edition of insiderPROFILES magazine.

Index

A

B

C

D

N

O

P

R

S

T

U

V

W

Y

Z